THE CONTEMPORARY READER

THE CONTEMPORARY READER

Canadian Edition

Gary Goshgarian
Northeastern University

Greg McSweeney
Dawson College

L. S. Young
Dawson College

PEARSON

Longman

Toronto

Library and Archives Canada Cataloguing in Publication

The contemporary reader / [edited by] Gary Goshgarian, Greg McSweeney, L. S. Young. — Canadian ed.

Includes index.
ISBN 0-321-25350-7

1. College readers. 2. English language — Rhetoric — Problems, exercises, etc.
3. Report writing — Problems, exercises, etc. I. Goshgarian, Gary II. McSweeney, Greg, 1956– III. Young, L. S. (Lee S.), 1961–

PE1417.C648 2006   808'.0427   C2005-905050-0

ISBN 0-321-25350-7

Vice President, Editorial Director: Michael J. Young
Acquisitions Editor: Patty Riediger
Signing Representative: Françoise Dykler
Marketing Manager: Cynthia Smith
Marketing Coordinator: Erica Willer
Developmental Editor: Patti Altridge
Production Editor: Richard di Santo
Copy Editor: Colleen Ste. Marie
Proofreader: Nancy Carroll, Wordreach
Production Coordinator: Peggy Brown
Manufacturing Coordinator: Susan Johnson
Permissions Research: Liviya Mendelsohn and Amanda McCormick
Composition: Debbie Kumpf
Cover and Interior Design: Julia Hall
Cover Image: Brand X Pictures

 2 3 4 5   10 09 08 07 06

Printed and bound in the United States of America.

PEARSON
Longman

Contents

Introduction: How to Read and Write Critically   1

1   The Canadian Experience: Culture and Identity   45

New Country, New Journalists   47

Adrienne Clarkson

"We have said as a country that we are going to bring over 200,000 immigrants a year to Canada. And what we have done in fact is invited these people to come and take part in our society and become citizens. It is incumbent upon us, therefore, to think about what we do to help them 'catch up' to other citizens who've been here for decades or even generations."

3 Advertising: Wanting It, Selling It 124

Advertising and the Invention of Postmodernity 125
Ken Sanes

"Commercials that convey a sense of life as celebration, full of enraptured people who can't help but sing out because they love their Skittles or who emerge from swimming pools, all luminescent, with magnificent hair and wonderful lives, surrounded by bright colors, upbeat music and dancing friends, in which everything is in motion convey a sense of what life can be if we buy the product."

The Rebel Sell 130
Joseph Heath and Andrew Potter

"In fact, the critique of mass society has been one of the most powerful forces driving consumerism for more than 40 years."

A Tough Sell On Campus 138
John Schofield

Quebec students protest corporate encroachment.

Excerpt from *No Logo* 141
Naomi Klein

"But there were those in the industry who understood that advertising wasn't just scientific; it was also spiritual."

Trademarks and Brand Logos 147

A Portfolio of Advertisements 148
GM

Vans

Ipod

Nokia

Hitachi

BP

M&Ms

Absolute

Honda

Phoenix

Parkinson's Disease

United Way

Rhetorical Contents

PROCESS ANALYSIS

Step-by-Step Explanation of How Something Operates

COMPARISON AND
CONTRAST

Explaining Similarities

HUMOUR AND SATIRE

Making Us Laugh While We Think

Preface

The Canadian edition of *The Contemporary Reader* provides a collection of well-written, thought-provoking readings that students can relate to—readings that stimulate classroom discussion, critical thinking, and writing. The nine chapters that comprise the first Canadian edition reflect the most popular topics from the seventh and eighth American edition, though with a significant increase in specifically Canadian material. Chapter 1 focuses on the Canadian experience, which will position the reader to start thinking about issues in popular culture within our country's unique political, demographic, and social contexts.

The Contemporary Reader, Canadian edition, is contemporary in more than just its selected readings. The introduction, first of all, includes strategies for critical writing. Continuing this theme throughout the book, the apparatus includes the latest and most effective rhetorical theory and practice. Preceding each reading is a **Critical Thinking** question that introduces the student to the topic and the reading. Directly following each reading is a **Freewriting Assignment**, designed to promote the flow of impressions and ideas about the article. Where appropriate, we have included a directional cue, such as "personal narrative" or "research and analysis," before certain writing questions to help students focus their critical writing. We have also retained the **Viewpoints** articles, a popular feature of the American editions, in which authors explore different aspects of the same issue.

A Closer Look at Chapter Themes

The nine thematic chapters are organized to resemble those in the American edition. We begin with a chapter on Canadian identity and popular culture. From there, we focus on the visual forces in our popular culture that help forge our behaviour—areas that influence us the most. Chapter 2, for instance, examines how we can be caught up in finding the "right look" to define ourselves and examines the effect that body image has on our social and personal consciousness. Chapter 3 explores how advertising so craftily capitalizes on our fantasies—including those previewed in chapter 2. Chapter 4 considers the positive and negative aspects of television, its role in our lives, and its influence on how we think.

The next four chapters focus on very disparate but timely issues. Chapter 5 examines the changing face of the family unit in Canada and the U.S., and takes a look at the role of marriage in contemporary society. Chapter 6 considers the ways new technology is forcing us to rethink what it means to be human, while chapter 7 takes a close look at the state of education today and some issues facing Canada's schools. Chapter 8 explores how we perceive gender in our society——from how men are portrayed on television to why women end up doing most of the house-work. Finally, chapter 9 focuses on juvenile crime and the vilification of youth in our society.

Variety of Readings

With the Canadian material, we include many types of readings. Expository com-munication comes in all shapes and models. This book includes newspaper stories, editorials, advertisements, academic essays, magazine articles, television inter-views, Internet articles from "e-zines" and a lot more. Students will read academic articles, personal narratives, objective essays, and political arguments.

Advertisements

The chapter on advertising, one of the most popular in previous American editions, has been updated with new advertisements. Each ad is accompanied by specific questions to help students closely analyze how advertising—and the particular ad at issue—affects us. The questions should spark lively class discussions about the art and craft of advertising. Beyond that, they should encourage students to increase their "visual literacy" and critical thinking powers by closely focusing on particular print ads and making new associations and discoveries.

Viewpoints

The **Viewpoints** articles try to focus the traditional pro/con debates by helping stu-dents explore the different sides of an issue, such as body stereotyping, human cloning, or a particular aspect of advertising. The questions following these readings aim to help students consider multiple sides of an issue and move toward a collabo-rative discussion rather than a heated debate.

Research Issues

Each Research Issue encourages students to explore new avenues of thinking or to pursue a topic in greater depth outside the text. The apparatus features critical think-ing questions designed to help students analyze the topic. Many include Web sites to help students begin their research on the issue online, and the book's Companion Website provides additional resources for students.

Rhetorical Features

Introduction to Critical Reading and Writing

The premise of *The Contemporary Reader* is that effective writing grows out of effective thinking, and effective thinking grows out of thoughtful reading. We intertwine these three concepts in the new introduction, featuring sections that discuss both critical reading and critical writing. The introductory chapter illustrates the process in a detailed sample analysis of John Leo's essay, "Now Cut That Out!" The sample analysis demonstrates systematic approaches to critical reading and then continues this exploration in the critical writing section.

Critical Thinking Considerations

Following the introduction of each essay is a **Critical Thinking** question that helps guide the student before and during the actual reading process. These questions also connect to the chapter's overall theme.

Freewriting Assignment

The **Freewriting Assignment** is designed to promote the free flow of thoughts, ideas, and impressions students may have immediately upon finishing the essay. Freewriting assignments may direct students to write about a particular issue or concept raised by the article or ask students to write about their impressions of it. These assignments can be part of a journal-keeping project throughout the course, or they can be a private exercise by the student.

Group Projects

Active communities work together—accepting multiple points of view and interacting with different identities, values, ideas, races, social outlooks, ethnicities, and educational backgrounds. In an effort to develop students' skills for working and learning together and to expose them to different points of view, **Group Projects** accompany each reading. These exercises emphasize collaborative research, topic exploration, group writing, and problem solving. They also may encourage students to incorporate resources outside the classroom—the Internet, pop-culture sources, interviews, observations—to explore further what they have read.

Supplements

Companion Website

The Companion Website, **www.pearsoned.ca/goshgarian**, adapted from the US website prepared by Kathryn Goodfellow, includes links to additional online readings for each chapter, thematic questions, a guide to researching popular culture issues, and much more.

Instructor's Manual

The Instructor's Manual includes suggested responses to the critical reading questions in the text and offers ideas for directing class discussion and eliciting student response. This supplement can be downloaded by instructors from a password-protected location on Pearson Education Canada's online catalogue (**vig.pearsoned.ca**). Simply search for the text, then click on Instructor under Resources in the left-hand menu. Contact your local sales representative for further information.

Acknowledgments

Our thanks go to the people of Pearson Education who worked so diligently in the preparation of this manuscript, especially Patti Altridge whose patience and expertise were greatly appreciated. We'd also like to thank Françoise Dykler for her assistance in initiating this project.

Introduction
How to Read and Write Critically

What Is Critical Thinking?

Whenever you read a magazine article, newspaper editorial, or a piece of advertising and find yourself questioning the author's claims, you are exercising the basics of critical reading. You are looking beneath the surface of words and thinking about their meaning and significance. And, subconsciously, you are asking the authors some of the following questions:

- What did you mean by that?
- Can you back up that statement?
- How do you define that term?
- How did you draw that conclusion?
- Do all the experts agree?
- Is this evidence dated?
- What is your point?
- Why do I need to know this?
- Where did you get your data?

You are also making some internal statements:

- That isn't true.
- You are contradicting yourself.
- I see your point, but I don't agree because . . .
- That's a poor choice of words.
- You are jumping to conclusions.
- Good point. I never thought of that.
- That was nicely stated.
- This is an extreme view.

Whether conscious or unconscious, such responses indicate that you are thinking critically about what you read. You are weighing claims, asking for definitions, evaluating information, looking for proof, questioning assumptions, and making judgments. In short, you are processing another person's words, rather than just accepting them at face value.

Why Read Critically?

When you read critically, you think critically. Instead of blindly accepting what is written on a page, you begin to separate yourself from the text and decide for yourself what is or is not important, logical, or right. And you do so because you bring to your reading your own perspective, experience, education, and personal values, as well as your powers of comprehension and analysis.

Critical reading is an active process of discovery. You discover an author's view on a subject, you enter into a dialogue with the author, you discover the strengths and weaknesses of the author's thesis or argument, and you decide if you agree or disagree with the author's views. The result is that you have a better understanding of the issue and the author. By questioning and analyzing what the author says with respect to other experiences or views of the issue—including your own—you actively enter into a dialogue or a debate and seek the truth on your own.

In reality, we understand truth and meaning through interplay. Experience teaches us that knowledge and truth are not static entities but the by-products of struggle and dialogue—of asking tough questions. We witness this phenomenon all the time, recreated in the media through dialogue and conflict. And we recognize it as a force of social change. Consider, for example, how, since the 1950s, our culture has changed its attitudes concerning race, and its concepts of success, kinship, social groups, and class. Perhaps the most obvious example regards gender: were it not for the fact that rigid old conventions have been questioned, most women would still be bound to the laundry and the kitchen stove.

The point is that critical reading is an active and reactive process that sharpens your focus on a subject and your ability to absorb information and ideas and at the same time encourages you to question accepted norms, views, and myths. And that is both healthy and laudable, for it is the basis of social evolution.

Critical reading also helps you become a better writer, because critical reading is the first step to critical writing. Good writers look at one another's writing the way architects look at a house: they study the fine details and how those details connect and create the whole. Likewise, they consider the particular slants and strategies of appeal. Good writers always have a clear sense of their audience—their reader's racial makeup, gender, and educational background; their political and/or religious persuasions; their values, prejudices, and assumptions about life; and so forth. Knowing your audience helps you to determine nearly every aspect of the writing process: the kind of language to use, the writing style (casual or formal, humorous or serious, technical or philosophical), the particular slant to take (appealing to the reader's reason, emotions, or ethics, or a combination of these), what emphasis to give the essay, the type of evidence to offer, and the kinds of authorities to cite.

The better you become at analyzing and reacting to another's written work, the better you will analyze and react to your own. You will ask yourself questions such as the following: Is it logical? Do my points come across clearly? Are my examples solid enough? Is this the best wording? Is my conclusion persuasive? Do I have a clear sense of my audience? What strategy did I take—an appeal to logic, emotions, or ethics? In short, critical reading will help you to evaluate your own writing, thereby making you both a better reader and a better writer. Although you may already use many strategies of critical reading, the following text presents some techniques to make you an even better critical reader.

How to Read Critically

To help you improve your critical reading, use these six proven basic steps:

- Keep a journal of what you read.
- Annotate what you read.
- Outline what you read.
- Summarize what you read.
- Question what you read.
- Analyze what you read.

To demonstrate just how these techniques work, we will apply each of them to a sample essay, "Now Cut That Out!" by John Leo, appearing in the June 30, 2003, issue of *U.S. News and World Report*. This piece works well because, like all of the pieces in this book, it addresses a contemporary issue and presents opportunities for debate.

Sample Essay for Analysis

Now Cut That Out!
John Leo

1   Which of the following stories would be too biased for schools to allow on tests? (1) Overcoming daunting obstacles, a blind man climbs Mount McKinley; (2) Dinosaurs roam the Earth in prehistoric times; (3) An Asian-American girl, whose mother is a professor, plays checkers with her grandfather and brings him pizza.

2   As you probably guessed, all three stories are deeply biased. (1) Emphasis on a "daunting" climb implies that blindness is some sort of disability, when it should be viewed as just another personal attribute, like hair color. Besides, mountain-climbing stories are examples of "regional bias," unfair to readers who live in deserts, cities, and rural areas. (2) Dinosaurs are a no-no—they imply acceptance of evolutionary theory. (3) Making the girl's mother a professor perpetuates the "model minority" myth that stereotypes Asian-Americans. Older people must not be shown playing checkers. They should be up on the roof fixing shingles or doing something vigorous. And pizza is a junk food. Kids may eat it—but not in a school story.

3   That's what's going on in schools these days. Diane Ravitch's new book, *The Language Police*, documents "an intricate set of rules" applied to test questions as well as textbooks. A historian of education who served as an assistant secretary of education for the first President Bush, Ravitch offers many eye-catching cases of subjects vetoed: peanuts as a good snack (some children are allergic), owls (taboo in Navajo culture), and the palaces of ancient Egypt (elitist).

4   Back in the 1980s and 1990s, lots of us chuckled at the spread of the "sensitivity" industry in schools. Words were removed from tests and books lest they hurt someone's feelings, harm the classroom effort, or impair morals. Most of us assumed that this was a fad that would soon disappear as grown-ups in education exerted the rule of reason.

5   But ridicule had little effect, and grown-ups either converted to the sensitivity ethic or looked the other way. Textbook publishers, with millions of dollars at stake, learned to insulate themselves from criticism by caving in to all objections and writing craven "guidelines" to make sure authors would cave, too.

6   No, no, no! Ravitch warns that these guidelines amount to a full-blown form of "censorship at the source" in schools and "something important and dangerous" that few people know about. She blames both the religious right and the multicultural-feminist left. The right objects to evolution, magic and witchcraft, gambling, nudity, suicide, drug use, and stories about disobedient children. The left objects to "sexist" fairy tales, Huckleberry Finn, religion, smoking, junk food, guns and knives, and what some guidelines call "activities stereotyping" (blacks as athletes, men playing sports or working with tools, women cooking or caring for children).

7   What started out as a sensible suggestion—don't always show women as homemakers or minorities in low-level jobs—developed into hard reverse stereotypes (women must not be shown in the home, maids can't be black). "In the ideal world of education-think," Ravitch writes, "women would be breadwinners, African-Americans would be academics, Asian-Americans would be athletes and no one would be a wife or a mother."

8   Whites are a group, perhaps the only group, not protected by smothering sensitivity. This follows multicultural dogma. One set of guidelines (McGraw-Hill) "express[es] barely concealed rage against people of European ancestry" as "uniquely responsible for bigotry and exploitation," Ravitch notes.

9   What can be done? Ravitch recommends eliminating the current system in which 22 states adopt textbooks for all their schools. She says it results in cartel-like behavior that allows extremists to manipulate textbook requirements, particularly in the two big states that matter most—California and Texas. Opening up the market, she thinks, would free teachers to choose biographies, histories, or anthologies, rather than sensitivity-laden textbooks.

10   Panels that analyze tests and texts should include teachers of the subjects, not just diversity specialists, Ravitch says. She insists we need better-educated teachers and an end to secrecy about sensitivity: State education officials must put bias and sensitivity reviews on the Internet, listing the reasons that passages and test items were rejected.

11   Unsurprisingly, *The Language Police* has gotten the cold shoulder from our education establishment, which usually limits discussion to three topics: promoting diversity, reducing classroom size, and increasing funding. Ravitch speaks for parents more concerned about something else: substituting censorship and propaganda for actual learning.

Keep a Journal on What You Read

Unlike writing an essay or a paper, journal writing is a personal exploration in which you develop your own ideas without set rules. It is a process of recording impressions and exploring feelings and ideas. Journal writing is a freewriting exercise in which you express yourself without restrictions and without judgment. You do not have to worry about breaking any rules—because in a journal, anything goes.

Reserve a special notebook just for your journal—not one you use for class notes or homework. Also, date your entries and include the titles of the articles to which you are responding. Eventually, by the end of the semester, you should have a substantial number of pages to review, enabling you to see how your ideas and writing style have developed over time.

What do you include in your journal? Although it may serve as a means to understanding an essay, you are not required to write only about the essay itself. Perhaps the article reminds you of a personal experience. Maybe it triggered an opinion you did not know you had. Or perhaps you wish to explore a particular phrase or idea presented by the author.

Some students may find keeping a journal difficult because it is so personal. They may feel as if they are exposing their feelings too much. Or they may feel uncomfortable thinking that someone else—a teacher or another student—may read their writing. Such apprehensions should not prevent you from exploring your impressions and feelings. If you must turn in your journal to your teacher, do not include anything you do not want others to read. Consider keeping a more private journal for your own benefit.

Reprinted below is one student's journal entry on our sample essay:

John Leo's essay on Diane Ravitch's book helps support his personal opinion that "language police" are controlling the content of texts and tests in American schools and hurting students.

Apparently, Ravitch feels that multicultural-feminists AND the religious right have distorted what material is presented in the classroom. The feminists and the religious right are demanding that the language used in textbooks and tests be "sensitive" and "unbiased."

Ravitch and Leo seem to think that the revisions made in the '80s and '90s have gone too far. At first, it seems as if Leo agrees that the original desire to be sensitive was a good idea, but he then agrees with Ravitch's opinion that the panels that decide what language to use on standardized tests have a cartel-like hold on our educational system. Leo often quotes Ravitch, and it is clear that he agrees with her. His fourth paragraph particularly reveals his position.

I think that both Ravitch and Leo are missing a very important point. Language can hurt. And it can influence how we think. They don't seem to acknowledge this. Maybe they have never experienced biased writing? I know from personal experience that it can affect students. I even remember stopping to think about how a question seemed biased on the SAT. I probably didn't need to waste my time thinking about that.

If language policing has gone to an extreme, like Leo says, there must be a happy middle, right?

Annotate What You Read

It's a good idea to underline (or highlight) key passages and make marginal notes when reading an essay. (If you do not own the publication in which the essay appears, or choose not to mark it up, make a photocopy of the piece and annotate that.) You should annotate on the second or third reading, once you have an understanding of the essay's general ideas.

There are no specific guidelines for annotation. Use whatever technique suits you best, but keep in mind that in annotating a piece of writing, you are engaging in a dialogue with the author. As in any meaningful dialogue, you hear things you may not have known—things that may be interesting and exciting to you, things with which you may agree or disagree, or things that give you cause to ponder. The other side of the dialogue, of course, is your response. In annotating a piece of writing, that response takes the form of underlining (or highlighting) key passages and jotting down comments in the margin. Such comments can take the form of full sentences or some shorthand codes. Sometimes "Why?" or "True" or "NO!" will be enough to help you respond to a writer's position or claim. If you come across a word or reference that is unfamiliar to you, underline or circle it. Once you have located the main thesis statement or claim, highlight or underline it and jot down "CLAIM" or "THESIS" in the margin.

On the following page is the Leo essay reproduced in its entirety with sample annotations.

Now Cut That Out!

John Leo

1   Which of the following stories would be too biased for schools to allow on tests? (1) Overcoming daunting obstacles, a blind man climbs Mount McKinley; (2) dinosaurs roam the Earth in prehistoric times; (3) an Asian-American girl, whose mother is a professor, plays checkers with her grandfather and brings him pizza.

Are these examples from a real test, or did Leo make them up?

2   As you probably guessed, all three stories are deeply biased. (1) Emphasis on a "daunting" climb implies that blindness is some sort of disability, when it should be viewed as just another personal attribute, like hair color. Besides, mountain-climbing stories are examples of "regional bias," unfair to readers who live in deserts, cities, and rural areas. (2) Dinosaurs are a no-no—they imply acceptance of evolutionary theory. (3) Making the girl's mother a professor perpetuates the "model minority" myth that stereotypes Asian-Americans. Older people must not be shown playing checkers. They should be up on the roof fixing shingles or doing something vigorous. And pizza is a junk food. Kids may eat it—but not in a school story.

Oh, come on!

Loose interpretation of evolutionary theory. Isn't evolutionary theory related to humans' connection to apes? Look up this issue.

3   That's what's going on in schools these days. Diane Ravitch's new book, *The Language Police*, documents "an intricate set of rules" applied to test questions as well as textbooks. A historian of education who served as an assistant secretary of education for the first President Bush, Ravitch offers many eye-catching cases of subjects vetoed: peanuts as a good snack (some children are allergic), owls (taboo in Navajo culture), and the palaces of ancient Egypt (elitist).

Check out this book in university library.

Whose rules?

Who "vetoed"?

Why is this word in quotes?

4   Back in the 1980s and 1990s, lots of us chuckled at the spread of the "sensitivity" industry in schools. Words were removed from tests and books lest they hurt someone's feelings, harm the classroom effort, or impair morals. Most of us assumed that this was a fad that would

Well, many words did hurt—especially ones that were racist or sexist.

soon disappear as grown-ups in education exerted the rule of reason.

5   But ridicule had little effect, and grown-ups either converted to the sensitivity ethic or looked the other way. Textbook publishers, with millions of dollars at stake, learned to insulate themselves from criticism by caving in to all objections and writing craven "guidelines" to make sure authors would cave, too.

This is a sweeping generalization as to motivation of teachers and publishers.

look up

6   No, no, no! Ravitch warns that these guidelines amount to a full-blown form of "censorship at the source" in schools and "something important and dangerous" that few people know about. She blames both the religious right and the multicultural-feminist left. The right objects to evolution, magic and witchcraft, gambling, nudity, suicide, drug use, and stories about disobedient children. The left objects to "sexist" fairy tales, Huckleberry Finn, religion, smoking, junk food, guns and knives, and what some guidelines call "activities stereotyping" (blacks as athletes, men playing sports or working with tools, women cooking or caring for children).

Check source for context.

look up

Says who?

7   What started out as a sensible suggestion—don't always show women as homemakers or minorities in low-level jobs—developed into hard reverse stereotypes (women must not be shown in the home, maids can't be black). "In the ideal world of education-think," Ravitch writes, "women would be breadwinners, African-Americans would be academics, Asian-Americans would be athletes and no one would be a wife or a mother."

So author approves that changes were made?

What about white women?

8   Whites are a group, perhaps the only group, not protected by smothering sensitivity. This follows multicultural dogma. One set of guidelines (McGraw-Hill) "express[es] barely concealed rage against people of European ancestry" as "uniquely responsible for bigotry and exploitation," Ravitch notes.

What exactly is "multicultural dogma"?

Ravitch's interpretation of the guideline's tone?

9   What can be done? Ravitch recommends eliminating the current system in which 22 states adopt textbooks for all their schools. She says it results in cartel-like behavior that allows extremists to manipulate textbook re-

She wants to overhaul the wa 22 states choose their textb Doesn't that go against wha seems to be an approved conse What about the other 28 st that don't use such guidelines

most—California and Texas. Opening up the market, she thinks, would free teachers to choose biographies, histories, or anthologies, rather than sensitivity-laden textbooks.

examples?

10   Panels that analyze tests and texts should include teachers of the subjects, not just diversity specialists, Ravitch says. She insists we need better-educated teachers and an end to secrecy about sensitivity: State education officials must put bias and sensitivity reviews on the Internet, listing the reasons that passages and test items were rejected.

They should be!
They aren't now?
Is this really true?

This is another issue entirely.

11   Unsurprisingly, *The Language Police* has gotten the cold shoulder from our education establishment, which usually limits discussion to three topics: promoting diversity, reducing classroom size, and increasing funding. Ravitch speaks for parents more concerned about something else: substituting censorship and propaganda for actual learning.

Censorship, maybe. But is Leo concerned that presenting blacks as academics or women Asians as athletes is actually propaganda?

Outline What You Read

Briefly outlining an essay is a good way to see how writers structure their ideas. When you physically diagram the thesis statement, claims, and supporting evidence, you can better assess the quality of the writing and decide how convincing it is. You may already be familiar with detailed, formal essay outlines in which structure is broken down into main ideas and subsections. However, for our purposes, a brief and concise breakdown of an essay's components will suffice. This is done by simply jotting down a one-sentence summary of each paragraph. Sometimes brief paragraphs elaborating the same point can be lumped together:

- Point 1
- Point 2
- Point 3
- Point 4
- Point 5
- Point 6, etc.

Such outlines may seem rather primitive, but they demonstrate how the various parts of an essay are connected—that is, the organization and sequence of ideas.

Below is a sentence outline of "Now Cut That Out." It identifies the point(s) of each paragraph in an unbiased way. The purpose of summarizing is to better understand the author's point and how this point is constructed.

POINT 1: The author provides three examples of stories that would not appear on a standardized test because they may use insensitive or biased language.

POINT 2: Diane Ravitch has written a book titled <u>The Language Police</u>, in which she discusses the language used in school textbooks and tests.

POINT 3: The author notes that some people may have viewed the language "sensitivity" movement in schools during the 1980s and 1990s as a passing "fad." He states that instead of passing, the movement became entrenched in schools, and publishers followed suit in order to please their buyers.

POINT 4: Ravitch feels that the guidelines developed to encourage language sensitivity in textbooks and tests is a form of censorship. She claims that people who hold extreme viewpoints are controlling the content of school materials.

POINT 5: The author concedes that language sensitivity was based on a good idea, but that it has reached extremes.

POINT 6: Ravitch advocates eliminating the current system used by 22 states to adopt textbooks in order to loosen the "cartel-like" hold extremists have on the educational system.

POINT 7: Ravitch also supports the idea that textbook selection panels include teachers who use the adopted texts and test, and that the panel should publicly explain its reasons for using certain questions on tests while rejecting others.

POINT 8: The author concludes that Ravitch's observation "speaks for parents," while the education establishment focuses on other issues, including diversity, class size, and educational funding.

At this point, you should have a fairly solid grasp of the points expressed in the essay, and the author's position on the issue. This exercise prepares you to critically evaluate the essay.

Summarize What You Read

Summarizing is perhaps the most important technique to develop for understanding and evaluating what you read. This means reducing the essay to its main points. In your journal or notebook try to write a brief (about 100 words) synopsis of the reading in your own words. Note the claim or thesis of the discussion (or argument) and the chief supporting points. It is important to write these points down (rather than passively highlighting them with a pen or pencil), because the act of jotting down a summary helps you absorb the argument.

Now let us return to the sample essay. In the following paragraph we offer a summary of Leo's essay, mindful of using our own words rather than those of the author to avoid plagiarism. Again, you should approach this aspect of critical reading impartially—summary is not your opinion, that will come later. At times, it may be impossible to avoid using the author's own words in a summary; but if you do, remember to use quotation marks.

> In this essay, John Leo discusses a book by Diane Ravitch, The Language Police, in which she asserts that language sensitivity in textbooks and tests is controlled by extreme groups such as the "religious right" and the "multicultural-feminist left." These groups have, in turn, influenced the language publishers use in order to better appeal to the panels that select the textbooks. Leo and Ravitch are in agreement that this control is a form of censorship and must stop. Panels that choose textbooks and test questions should include teachers and should also explain the reasons behind language choices.

Although this paragraph seems to do a fairly good job of summarizing Leo's essay, it took us a few tries to get it down to under 100 words. So, do not be too discouraged when trying to summarize a reading on your own.

Question What You Read

Although we break down critical reading into discrete steps, these steps will naturally overlap in the actual process of reading and writing critically. In reading this essay you were simultaneously summarizing and evaluating Leo's points, perhaps adding your own ideas or even arguing with him. If something strikes you as particularly interesting or insightful, make a mental note of it. Likewise, if something strikes you the wrong way, argue back. For beginning writers, a good strategy is to convert that automatic mental response into actual note taking.

In your journal (or, as suggested below, in the margins of the text), question and challenge the writer. Jot down any points in the essay that do not measure up to your expectations or personal views. Note anything about which you are skeptical. Write down any questions you have about the claims, views, or evidence. If some point or conclusion seems forced or unfounded, record it and briefly explain why. The more skeptical and questioning you are, the better reader you are. Likewise, note what features of the essay impressed you—outstanding points, interesting wording, clever or amusing phrases or allusions, particular references, the general structure of the piece. Record what you learn from the reading and the aspects of the issue you would like to explore.

Of course, you may not feel qualified to pass judgment on an author's views, particularly if the author is a professional writer or expert on a particular subject. Sometimes the issue discussed might be too technical, or you may not feel informed enough to make critical evaluations. Sometimes a personal narrative may focus on experiences completely alien to you. Nonetheless, you are an intelligent person with the instincts to determine if the writing impresses you or if an argument is sound, logical, and convincing. What you can do in such instances—and another good habit to get into—is to think of other views on the issue. If you have read or heard of experiences different from those of the author, or arguments with the opposing views, jot them down. Similarly, if you agree with the author's view, highlight the parts of the essay with which you particularly identify.

Let us return to Leo's essay, which is, technically, an argument. Although it is theoretically possible to question or comment on every sentence in the piece, let us select a few key points that may have struck you, made you question, or made you want to respond. Refer to your point-by-point outline to assist you in this exercise.

PARAGRAPHS 1 & 2: While I understand Leo's point here with these examples, are they real examples from actual tests or ones Leo just made up to support his argument? If they are real, it would greatly support his position. However, these examples probably represent extreme illustrations of test questions. Furthermore, I wonder why certain adjectives are used at all. The stories could stand up on their own without the story being about a blind man, or an Asian American professor. Couldn't the story just be about a girl whose mother is a professor and who also plays a <u>game</u> with her grandfather? Why is omitting the adjectives so controversial anyway?

PARAGRAPH 3: Leo states that there is "an intricate set of rules" that Ravitch cites in her book. His essay would be strengthened if he cited these rules and their source. That way, we would have more hard evidence, rather than what seems to be opinion.

PARAGRAPH 4: In this paragraph, Leo states his own position on language sensitivity by admitting he is one of "us" who "chuckled" at the "sensitivity industry" in schools during the '80s and '90s. As such, he admits that he thought that the movement was frivolous (he calls it a "fad"). However, he seems to admit in paragraph 7 that it wasn't entirely a bad idea.

PARAGRAPH 6: Leo takes quotations from Ravitch's book to support his assertion that the language police are out of control. While it is good to quote sources, Ravitch herself seems questionable as a reliable source.

PARAGRAPHS 7 & 8: It seems as if Leo admits that at one time unbiased language was a good idea—"a sensible suggestion." And he may have a point if things have really swung to an extreme. But why is he so against the idea that blacks not be portrayed as maids, etc.? Who does it hurt? Maybe more importantly, who does it help? Leo's comment on whites being the only group not "protected" by the language police is revealing. Elsewhere in his essay, he comments on the "rule" that women cannot be shown in the home or as mothers. Well, what about women who are white? What Leo really meant to say here was "white males." Another point about paragraph 8 relates to the last sentence. Is this Ravitch's interpretation? Can she really interpret "barely concealed rage" in a set of guidelines prepared by a textbook company? Quoting this material would help the readers decide for themselves.

PARAGRAPHS 9 & 10: Leo relays Ravitch's suggestions for change, and he clearly endorses these changes. This helps his essay because it isn't just a long complaint; the essay actually advocates something. Whether these solutions are possible, or even necessary, is up to his reader.

PARAGRAPH 11: Most of Leo's concluding paragraph could be read in a neutral way. Educators aren't really reacting to Ravitch's book. Rather, they are responding to more pressing issues. Leo's final sentence might make the reader pause—while influencing language may seem like a form of censorship, does he really feel that depicting women as professionals, blacks as academics, and Asians as athletes are equal to propaganda?

Analyze What You Read

To analyze something means breaking it down into its components, examining those components closely while evaluating their significance, and determining how they relate as a whole. In part, you already did this by briefly outlining the essay. However, there is more. Analyzing what you read involves interpreting and evaluating the points of a discussion or argument as well as its presentation—that is, its language and structure. Ultimately, analyzing an essay after establishing its key points will help you understand what may not be evident at first. A close examination of the author's words takes you beneath the surface and sharpens your understanding of the issues at hand.

Although there is no set procedure for analyzing a piece of prose, there are some specific questions you should raise when reading an essay, particularly one that is trying to sway you to its view.

- What kind of audience is the author addressing?
- What are the author's assumptions?
- What are the author's purpose and intentions?
- How well does the author accomplish those purposes?
- How convincing is the evidence presented? Is it sufficient and specific? Relevant? Reliable and not dated? Slanted?
- What types of sources were used—personal experience, outside authorities, factual references, or statistical data?
- Did the author address opposing views on the issue?
- Is the perspective of the author persuasive?

Using the essay by Leo once more, let us apply these questions to his article.

What Kind of Audience Is the Author Addressing?

Before the first word is written, a good writer considers his or her audience—that is, their age group, gender, ethnic and racial makeup, educational background, and socioeconomic status. Writers also take into account the values, prejudices, and assumptions of their readers, as well as their readers' political and religious persuasions. Some writers, including several in this book, write for a "target" audience—readers who share the same interests, opinions, and prejudices. Other authors write for a "general" audience. Although general audiences consist of very different people with diversified backgrounds, expectations, and standards, think of them as the people who read *Time, Newsweek,* and your local newspaper. You can assume general audiences are relatively well informed about what is going on in the country, that they have a good comprehension of language and a sense of humour, and that they are willing to listen to new ideas.

Because Leo's essay appeared in his column in *U.S. News and World Report,* he is clearly writing for a "general" audience—an audience with an average age of 35, possessing a high school education and some college, politically middle of the road, and comprised of a vast racial and ethnic makeup. A close look tells us more about Leo's audience:

1. The language level suggests at least a high school education.

2. The references to attitudes in the 1980s and the concerns of parents suggest an older audience—certainly at least 30 years old.

3. The references to politics, academic and political movements, and panel policies for textbook selection imply that the readers are culturally informed.

4. The slant of Leo's remarks assumes a more conservative view toward educational trends, perhaps one opposed to the "new" trend of multiculturalism.

5. The language level addresses an audience that will see the absurdity of the language situation, and that does not presumably belong to the groups criticized by Leo.

What Are the Author's Assumptions?

Having a sense of the audience leads writers to certain assumptions. If a writer is addressing a general audience as is Leo, then he or she can assume certain levels of awareness about language and current events, certain values about education and morality, and certain nuances of an argument. After going through Leo's essay, the following conclusions might be drawn about the author:

1. Leo assumes that his readers have a basic understanding of the concept of political "right" and "left."

2. He assumes that his audience is as exasperated as he is that extreme groups are controlling the content of textbooks and test questions in public schools.

3. He assumes that his readers believe that the claims of these groups (the religious right and the multicultural-feminist left) are questionable.

4. He assumes that his readers have a basic understanding of multiculturalism and suspect that these principles have gone too far.

5. He assumes his readers will agree that the issues the educational establishment are most concerned with—diversity, class size, and school funding—are not as important as stopping "censorship and propaganda" in schools.

What Are the Author's Purpose and Intentions?

A writer has a purpose in writing beyond wanting to show up in print. Sometimes it is simply the expression of how the writer feels about something; sometimes the intention is to convince others to see things in a different light; sometimes the purpose is to persuade readers to change their views or behaviour. We might infer the following about Leo's intentions:

1. To alert people that extreme interest groups are controlling the content of textbooks and tests in American schools.

2. To urge people to demand changes in their schools and in the way books and material are selected, especially in the 22 states that currently use this system.

3. To raise public awareness that apathy toward this trend is detrimental to education and harmful to students.

4. To urge people to stop "turning a blind eye" to the "language police" and say "enough is enough."

5. To encourage people to demand reform from the education establishment to focus on issues that matter most.

How Well Does the Author Accomplish Those Purposes?

Determining how well an author accomplishes such purposes may seem subjective, but in reality it comes down to how well the case is presented. Is the thesis clear? Is it organized and well presented? Are the examples sharp and convincing? Is the author's conclusion a logical result of what came before? Returning to Leo's essay, let us apply these questions:

1. Leo keeps to the point for most of his essay, although he sometimes blurs his opinion with that of Diane Ravitch's.

2. He offers many examples of the situation, presents his view clearly, and cites Ravitch's book.

3. Because Leo focuses on a book expressing the opinions of one person, the examples he uses to express his point need more support, perhaps from the original sources Ravitch uses.

4. Leo's essay is well constructed and entertaining. He holds his reader's attention through his strong writing style.

How Convincing Is the Evidence Presented? Is It Sufficient and Specific? Relevant? Reliable and Current? Slanted?

Convincing writing depends on convincing evidence—that is, sufficient and relevant facts along with proper interpretations of facts. Facts are pieces of information that can be verified—such as statistics, examples, personal experience, expert testimony, and historical details. Proper interpretations of such facts must be logical and supported by relevant data. For instance, it is a fact that SAT verbal scores went up in 2003, and that students from Massachusetts had the highest national scores. One reason might be that students are spending more time reading and less time watching TV than in the past. Or that Massachusetts has many colleges and universities available, prompting students to study harder for the test in that state. But without hard statistics documenting the viewing habits of a sample of students, such interpretations are shaky, the result of a writer jumping to conclusions.

Is the Evidence Sufficient and Specific? Writers routinely use evidence, but sometimes it may not be sufficient. Sometimes the conclusions reached have too little evidence to be justified. Sometimes writers make hasty generalizations based solely on personal experience as evidence. How much evidence is enough? It is hard to say, but the more specific the details, the more convincing the argument. Instead of generalizations, good writers cite figures, dates, and facts. Instead of paraphrasing information, they quote the experts verbatim.

Is the Evidence Relevant? Good writers select evidence based on how well it supports their thesis, not on how interesting, novel, or humorous it is. For instance, if you are claiming that Barry Bonds is the greatest living baseball player, you should not mention that he was born in California, had a father who played for the San Francisco Giants, or that his godfather is Willie Mays. Those are facts, and they are very interesting, but they have nothing to do with Bonds' athletic abilities. Irrelevant evidence distracts readers and weakens an argument.

Is the Evidence Reliable and Current? Evidence should not be so dated or vague that it fails to support your claim. For instance, it is not accurate to say that candidate Jones fails to support the American worker because 15 years ago she purchased a foreign car. Her current actions are more important. Readers expect the information writers provide to be current and to be specific enough to be verifiable. A writer supporting animal rights may cite cases of rabbits blinded in drug research, but such tests have been outlawed in the United States for many years. Another may point to medical research that appears to abuse human subjects, but not name the researchers, the place, or the year of such testing. Because readers may have no way of verifying the evidence, the claims become suspicious and will weaken your points.

Is the Evidence Slanted? Sometimes writers select evidence that supports their case and ignore evidence that does not. Often referred to as "stacking the deck," this practice is unfair and potentially self-defeating for a writer. Although some evidence presented may have merit, an argument will be dismissed if readers discover that evidence was slanted or suppressed. For example, suppose you heard a classmate state that he would never take a course with Professor Sanchez because she gives surprise quizzes, assigns 50 pages of reading a night, and does not grade on a curve. Even if these statements are true, that may not be the whole truth. You might discover that Professor Sanchez is a dynamic and talented teacher whose classes are stimulating. Withholding that information may make an argument suspect. A better strategy is to acknowledge counterevidence and to confront it—that is, to strive for a balanced presentation by raising views and evidence that may not be supportive of your own.

Let us take a look at the evidence in Leo's essay, applying some of the points we have just covered.

1. Leo quotes information from Ravitch's book without documenting her sources. This may make the reader wonder if the information is fact or opinion.

2. His use of quotes from Ravitch's book without verifying his own position may make it appear that he is hiding behind her words, rather than supporting his argument on his own.

3. He makes many assumptions about how the general public feels about the language sensitivity movement in schools.

4. Leo assumes that the reason the "fad" of language sensitivity didn't "go away" was because people looked the other way. He doesn't allow for alternative reasons, such as the possibility that people thought the idea was a good one.

5. His argument is emotional rather than logical. Likewise, his presentation of the facts is clearly one-sided.

6. He makes statements without qualifying them, such as "Ravitch speaks for parents more concerned about something else: substituting censorship and propaganda for actual learning." He does not prove that the language sensitivity movement has harmed education, or that parents are indeed concerned that it is hindering the learning process.

What Types of Sources Were Used—Personal Experience, Outside Authorities, Factual References, or Statistical Data?

Writers enlist four basic kinds of evidence to support their views or arguments: personal experience (theirs and others'), outside authorities, factual references and examples, and statistics. In your own writing, you should aim to use combinations of these.

Personal Testimony cannot be underestimated. Think of the books you have read or movies you have seen based on word-of-mouth recommendations. (Maybe you learned of the school you are attending through word of mouth!) Personal testimony—which provides eyewitness accounts not available to you or to other readers—is sometimes the most persuasive kind of evidence. Suppose you are writing about the rising abuse of alcohol on college campuses. In addition to statistics and hard facts, quoting the experience of a first-year student who nearly died one night from alcohol poisoning would add dramatic impact. Although personal observations are useful and valuable, writers must not draw hasty conclusions based only on such evidence. The fact that you and a few friends are in favour of replacing letter grades with a pass-fail system does not provide support for the claim that the student body at your school is in favour of the conversion.

Outside Authorities are people recognized as experts in a given field. Appealing to such authorities is a powerful tool in writing, particularly for writers wanting to persuade readers of their views. We hear it all the time: "Scientists have found . . ." "Scholars inform us that . . ." "According to his biographer, Abraham Lincoln . . ." Although experts try to be objective and fair-minded, their testimony may be biased. You would not expect scientists working for tobacco companies to provide unbiased opinions on lung cancer. And remember to cite who the authorities behind the statements are. It is not enough to simply state "scientists conducted a study"; you must say *who* they were and *where* the study was conducted.

Factual References and examples do as much to inform as to persuade. If somebody wants to sell you something, they will pour on the details. Think of the television commercials that show a sports utility vehicle climbing rocky mountain roads as a narrator lists all its great standard features—four-wheel drive, alloy wheels, second-generation airbags, power brakes, cruise control, etc. Or cereal infomercials in which manufacturers explain that new Yummy-Os have 15 percent more fibre to help prevent cancer. Although readers may not have the expertise to determine which data are useful, they are often convinced by the sheer weight of the evidence—like courtroom juries judging a case.

Statistics impress people. Saying that 77 percent of your school's student body approves of women in military combat roles is much more persuasive than saying "a lot of people" do. Why? Because statistics have a no-nonsense authority. Batting averages, polling results, economic indicators, medical and FBI statistics, and demographic percentages are all reported in numbers. If accurate, they are persuasive, although they can be used to mislead. The claim that 139 people on campus protested the appearance of a certain controversial speaker may be accurate; however, it would be a distortion of the truth not to mention that another 1500 people attended the talk and gave the speaker a standing ovation. Likewise, the manufacturer who claims that its potato chips are fried in 100 percent cholesterol-free vegetable oil misleads the public, because vegetable oil doesn't contain cholesterol—which is found only in animal fats. That is known as the "bandwagon" use of statistics—appealing to what people want to hear.

Now let us briefly examine Leo's sources of evidence:

1. Leo draws much of his support from one source, Diane Ravitch. Although her qualifications as a former assistant secretary of education may elevate her authority, she still represents only one opinion. His argument might be stronger if he had quoted some of the groups that held "extreme" views.

2. He provides examples of biased stories deemed unacceptable for tests without explaining whether these are real examples, and who rejected them.

3. Leo's citing of Ravitch's examples of vetoed subjects (peanuts, owls, and palaces in Egypt) may support his point to his target audience; but some readers may agree that these subjects were indeed unacceptable.

4. His statement that "women must not be shown in the home, maids can't be black" fails to support his premise that this "con-

trol" of language is harmful to students. He also fails to show the

other side of the issue, such as the idea that some students may

be hurt by certain stereotypes.

Did the Author Address Opposing Views on the Issue?

Many of the essays in this book will in varying degrees try to persuade you to agree with the author's position. But, of course, any slant on a topic can have multiple points of view. In developing their ideas, good writers will anticipate different and opposing views. They will cite alternative opinions, maybe even evidence that does not support their own position. By treating alternative points of view fairly, writers strengthen their own position. Failing to present or admit other views could leave their perspective open to scrutiny, as well as to claims of naïveté and ignorance. This is particularly damaging when discussing a controversial issue.

Let us see how Leo's essay addresses alternative points of view:

1. Leo does not introduce alternative points of view into his editor-

   ial. However, it is, after all, an editorial, and, thus, is based on

   his opinion as he can best support it.

2. Although it is an editorial, and therefore his own point of view,

   his discussion would have been made stronger if he had

   approached the issue more fairly. For example, if he had admit-

   ted the possibility that biased language can be harmful, or that

   some sensitivity is desirable, he may have reached a wider

   audience.

Is the Perspective of the Author Persuasive?

Style and content make for persuasive writing. Important points are how well a paper is composed—the organization, the logic, the quality of thought, the presentation of evidence, the use of language, the tone of discussion—and the details and evidence.

Turning to Leo's essay, we might make the following observations:

1. On the surface, Leo presents his argument well. A closer reading,

   however, raises more questions about the author's presentation of

   the material. He bases his argument primarily on generalizations

   and personal opinion.

2. He appears to be "pushing buttons" rather than presenting a well-

   formed, logical argument. He taps into his assumption of his audience's common view that the influence of multicultural feminists and the religious right on language is ridiculous and should be curtailed.

3. He makes many statements without qualifying them, and presents his own assumptions about the opinions of parents and teachers rather than providing proof of these assumptions.

By now, you should have a fairly clear idea of how critical reading can help your comprehension of a work and make you a better writer in the process. Make critical reading part of your daily life, not just something you do in the classroom or while studying. As you wait for the bus, look at some billboards and consider how they try to hook their audience. While watching TV, think about the techniques advertisers use to convince you to buy their products. And try to apply some of the elements of critical reading while perusing the articles and editorials in your favourite magazine or newspaper. The more you approach writing with a critical eye, the more natural it will become, and the better writer you will be.

What Is Critical Writing?

Critical writing is a systematic process. When following a recipe, you would not begin mixing ingredients together haphazardly. Instead, you would first gather your ingredients and equipment, and then combine the ingredients according to the recipe outlined. Similarly, in writing, you could not plan, write, edit, and proofread all at the same time. Rather, writing occurs one thoughtful step at a time.

Some writing assignments may require more steps than others. An in-class freewriting exercise may allow for only one or two steps—light planning and writing. An essay question on a midterm examination may permit enough time for only three steps—planning, writing, and proofreading. A simple plan for such an assignment need answer only two questions: "What am I going to say?" and "How am I going to develop my idea convincingly?" For example, you have to answer the following question: "Do you agree with Leo's assertion in 'Now Cut That Out!' that the 'language police' are controlling language in schools to the detriment of students?" You might decide to answer with the statement, "The words we use in textbooks and tests should reflect reality while also being sensitive to students' feelings." Or you could decide to answer, "Leo makes an interesting point in his essay that language sensitivity has gone too far. When textbooks no longer reflect reality because words are so controlled, education suffers." You would then develop your idea by comparing or contrasting your own experiences in school with the examples Leo gives in his essay, or presenting data or information that challenges or supports his argument.

A longer, out-of-class paper allows you to plan and organize your material, and to develop more than one draft. In this extended version of the writing process you will need to do the following to write a strong, critical paper:

- Develop your ideas into a focused thesis that is appropriate for your audience.
- Research pertinent sources.
- Organize your material and draft your paper.
- Proofread your paper thoroughly.

Those are the general steps that every writer goes through when writing a paper. In the following sections the use of these strategies will be discussed so that you can write most effectively.

Developing Ideas

Even the most experienced writers sometimes have trouble getting started. Common problems you may encounter include focusing your ideas, knowing where to begin, having too much or too little to say, and determining your position on an issue. There are developmental strategies that can help promote the free expression of your ideas and make you more comfortable with writing.

Although your finished product should be a tightly focused and well-written essay, you can begin the writing process by being free and sloppy. This approach allows your ideas to develop and flow unblocked onto your paper. Writing techniques such as brainstorming, freewriting, and ballooning can all help you through the process of development. As with all writing strategies, you should try all of them at first, to discover which ones work best for you.

Brainstorming

The goal of brainstorming is to generate and focus ideas. Brainstorming can be a personal exercise or a group project. You begin with a blank sheet of paper (or a blackboard) and, without paying attention to spelling, order, or grammar, simply list ideas about the topic as they come to you. You should spend at least 10 minutes brainstorming, building on the ideas you write down. There are no "dumb" ideas in brainstorming—the smallest detail may turn into a great essay.

Let us assume, for example, that you decide to write a paper supporting Leo's assertion in "Now Cut That Out!" Brainstorming for a few minutes may provide something like this:

language sensitivity may be getting out of hand when NO women are

allowed to be depicted as mothers and NO blacks may be presented

as athletes—it could imply that there is something wrong with

these choices

get a bunch of textbooks written after 1995 to see if such language

bias is prevalent, get real examples

read Ravitch's book—how does it connect to this essay? what

sources does she cite?

explore other multicultural issues

get other people's opinions (especially parents of school-age

kids) on this issue

try and locate the textbook adoption system in place in the 22

states that Leo/Ravitch cite

check out the McGraw-Hill guidelines (see Ravitch book?) Leo

cites in paragraph 8

You may notice that this brainstorming example has little structure, no apparent order, and even spelling errors. Its purpose is to elicit all the ideas you have about a subject so you can read your ideas and identify an interesting topic to develop.

Freewriting

Freewriting, just as brainstorming, is a free expression of ideas. It helps you jump-start the writing process and get things flowing on paper. Freewriting is unencumbered by rules—you can write about your impressions, ideas, and reactions to the article or essay. You should devote about 10 minutes to freewriting, keeping in mind that the goal is to write about the topic as ideas occur to you. If you are writing on a particular topic or idea you may wish to note it at the top of your paper as a visual reminder of your focus. Structure, grammar, and spelling are not important—just focus on the free flow of ideas. And above all, do not stop writing—even if you feel that what you are writing is silly or irrelevant. Any one, or a combination of the ideas expressed in a freewrite can be developed into a thoughtful essay.

Here is an example of a freewriting exercise:

In this essay Leo is presenting his opinion, and the opinion of

Diane Ravitch. In my opinion, I think Leo could actually make

a good point, if his information wasn't so skewed and his bias

so apparent. I guess it doesn't help matters much that he is a

white male, and so may be viewed as less likely to suffer from

language insensitivity. In one place in his essay, he begins to

admit that language sensitivity started out as a "sensible sug-

gestion," but he never elaborates, and that could be where his essay could be most helped, because it is at this point he could balance out his viewpoint. For example, he could have admitted that presenting women as mothers, maybe at the expense of presenting men as caregivers, was insensitive to women and girls, as well as to men and boys. He could have advocated for balance—sometimes women could be shown as both. The same could hold true for athletes and academics—when nationality has to be expressed at all. I sort of wonder about that—why do you need to say that someone is blind or that a girl's mother is Asian American and a professor at all? Just say a guy climbed a mountain or a girl's mother went to work (this actually allows the woman to be a mother AND a working woman . . .). I guess the other issue I wonder about is if this language policing is hurting anyone. Maybe it sort of upsets white guys like Leo, who are left out in the cold, but everyone else seems to be OK. I mean, it isn't as if there are no texts or tests anymore. Why all the fuss?

Ballooning

There are many names for ballooning, including "mind mapping," "clustering," or "grouping." These techniques all provide a more graphic presentation of ideas, allowing writers to visualize ideas and connections stemming from these ideas. Ballooning is particularly effective if you already have a fairly clear idea about your topic and wish to develop it more fully.

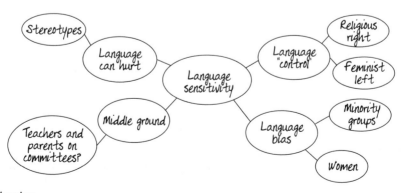

Ballooning

Write your main topic in the centre of a large sheet of paper or a blackboard and circle it. Using the circled idea as your focus, think of subtopics and place them in circles around the centre circle, connecting them to each other with lines (see figure). Remember to keep the subtopics short. Continue doing this until you feel you have developed all the subtopics more fully. When you have finished this exercise, you should be able to visualize the connections between your main topic and its subpoints, and have a starting point for your essay.

Narrowing the Topic

Although brainstorming, freewriting, and ballooning help list and develop general ideas, you still need to narrow one idea down to something more manageable. Narrowing a topic can be quite a challenge—you might like more than one idea, or you may be afraid of limiting yourself to only one concept. Nevertheless, you must identify one idea and focus on developing it into an essay. Choose an idea that will interest you and your audience. Remember that if you do not like the way one idea begins to develop, you can always go back and develop another one instead. Once you identify your topic, you are ready to develop the thesis statement for your essay.

Based on the freewriting exercise described earlier—and additional idea development using ballooning techniques—we will follow a student who has decided to write his paper on the idea that language sensitivity is a good idea, and it helps more students than it harms. The idea stems from a response to Leo's essay, but it will develop into a thesis that belongs uniquely to the student.

Identifying Your Audience

Identifying your audience is one of the most important steps in organizing your essay. Knowing what your audience needs and expects from your essay will help you compose a convincing, effective paper. The following questions can help you identify the expectations of your audience:

- Who is my audience?
- What do they already know about my topic?
- What questions do they have about my topic?
- What do they need to know to understand my point?
- What is the best order to present the information they need to know?
- How do they feel about this topic?
- Why would they want to read my essay?

Based on these questions, our student determined that her audience would be her teacher and her fellow expository writing classmates. All of them would be familiar with Leo's article and would have discussed it to some extent in class. As members of an academic institution, they should be familiar with the basics of multicultural theory, feminism, and politics, but may need some background on it. They may have different opinions on the issue, so supporting evidence (from both Leo's article and some outside research) would be necessary to effectively make her point. Because the essay would be about an issue directly concerning both teachers and students, it should generate some level of personal interest, and thus engage her readers.

Developing a Thesis

The **thesis** is a form of contract between the writer and reader. It makes a claim or declaration—telling your audience exactly what you are going to discuss. It should be stated in the opening paragraph, with the rest of the paper developing and supporting it.

As you write and develop your paper, your thesis should guide you as clearer and more precise thoughts evolve. Don't be constrained by your first thesis. If your paper is changing as you write, your thesis may change. Remember to go back and revise the thesis so that it matches the points made in your essay.

Although the thesis represents the last step in developing the topic for your essay, it is only the beginning of the actual writing process. For her paper, our student worked out the following sentence to help develop her thesis:

> The language sensitivity movement of the 1980s and 1990s grew out of a belief that stereotyping and racial or cultural bias could offend or negatively influence students' self-esteem. As a result, publishers and test panels began to carefully consider the language they used. While language sensitivity may sometimes seem extreme, it ultimately benefits students and the society of which they will later become a part.

Understanding Your Paper's Objective

Before determining how to research or organize your paper, consider what you are trying to achieve by writing it. Your objective may be to inform, to describe, or to persuade. To define your purpose, you should first determine your objective, and then identify what you need to do to accomplish this objective. This helps you determine what you need to put into the body of your paper.

Writing to inform involves anticipating the questions your audience may have regarding the topic, and how much background your audience will need to understand it. Once you have developed a list of questions, you can determine what order will best present the information that will answer these questions.

Writing to describe also involves answering some questions. First, you must identify what is important or relevant about the topic you intend to describe. Then you should determine what information is vital to conveying this importance. List these elements and order them in a way that presents a clear view of the experience to the reader.

Writing to persuade presents a perspective on an issue and attempts to convince readers to agree with it. You must provide reasons and supporting evidence to persuade your audience that your perspective makes sense. Although you might not sway all readers to your point of view, you should make enough of a case to allow them to understand your argument, even if they might not agree with it.

The first step in persuasive writing is to determine your position and to identify the objections others might have to it. Remember that there are many different reasons readers may not agree with you. By identifying the arguments against your position, you are better able to address them and thus support your own argument in the process. Three primary kinds of arguments are used in persuasive writing:

- *Arguments based on disputed facts or consequences,* such as the claim that the building of a gambling casino generated revenue for a bankrupt town, created jobs, and improved the quality of life there.
- *Arguments that advocate change,* such as arguing for a lower drinking age or changing the ways the penal system punishes juvenile offenders.
- *Arguments based on evaluative personal claims,* as right or wrong, ethical or immoral, or favouring one thing or idea over another—such as arguing that physician-assisted suicide is wrong or that supermodels contribute to the development of anorexia nervosa in young women.

The key to effective persuasive writing is to support your perspective with statistics, factual data, and examples. Although your opinions drive the essay, your supporting evidence is what convinces your audience of the validity of your main point.

Researching

Research can involve a few, or many, steps, depending on the type and length of the paper you are writing. In many cases, simply reviewing the article and applying the steps of critical reading will be the final step you take before organizing your paper. For longer research papers that require outside sources, you will probably need to tap into library resources or even find information online.

Researching may even involve taking surveys and conducting interviews. For her paper on language sensitivity in education, our student decided to speak to schoolchildren and teachers to determine their opinions on "language policing" and Leo and Ravitch's claims.

Selecting Sources for Your Paper

The best place to start is the library, either physically or online. Most libraries have their holdings archived on electronic cataloguing systems that let you look up books by author, title, and subject. Although books are a rich source of information, they can be dated, and are sometimes inappropriate for essays addressing contemporary issues. For such papers, journals and periodicals are better. With all the different ways of researching, gathering useful and appropriate information can be overwhelming. Do not be afraid to ask the librarian for help.

For many people, the Internet has become the first avenue of research on a topic, and it can be an extremely useful way to locate information on contemporary issues. In addition to Web sites, newsgroups and bulletin boards can aid your research process. Remember that the Internet is largely unregulated, so you should surf the Web with the careful eye of a critic. Simply because something is posted

Steel, Jon. *Truth, Lies and Advertis-ing*. New York: John Wiley & Sons, 1998. 150–178.

Kohner-Zuckerman, David. "Brokering Beauty." *BRNTWD Magazine* Jan/Feb 2000. http://www.brntwdmagazine .com/jan–feb/tech/tech–2.html.

online does not mean it is accurate or truthful. Whenever possible, take steps to verify your sources. When you do find a good source, write it down immediately. Many students lament the loss of a valuable resource because they forgot to write down the title of the book or Internet address. A good technique is to write down your sources on 3 × 5 cards. For example:

These cards allow you to add sources and arrange them alphabetically without having to rewrite as you would with a list. You can write down quotes for your paper on these cards for quick retrieval, and use them to help write your "Works Cited" section at the end of your essay.

Documenting Sources

Sources help support your ideas and emphasize your points. It is very important to cite these sources when you use them in your essay. Whether you quote, paraphrase, or use an idea from another source, you must identify the source from which your information came. Documenting sources gives credit to the person who did the work, and helps locate information on your topic. Even if you rewrite information in your own words, you must still document the source because it is borrowed information. Failure to document your sources is called plagiarism—presenting someone else's work as your own—and it is considered by most academic institutions a form of theft. The following checklist should help you determine when to document your sources:

- Using someone's exact words
- Presenting someone else's opinion
- Paraphrasing or summarizing someone else's ideas
- Using information gathered from a study
- Citing statistics or reporting the results of research not your own.

It is not necessary to cite dates, facts, or ideas considered common knowledge.

Organizing Your Paper

There are many ways to organize your paper. Some students prefer to use the standard outline technique, complete with roman numerals and indented subpoints. Other students prefer more flexible flow charts. The key to organizing is to define your focus and plan how to support your thesis statement from point to point in a logical order.

Drafting Your Essay

When writing your essay, think of your draft as a work in progress. Your objective should be to present your ideas in a logical order. You can address spelling, grammar, and sentence structure later. If you get stuck writing one paragraph or section, go on and work on another. Depending on how you write, you may choose to write your draft sequentially; or you may choose to move from your thesis to your body paragraphs, leaving your introduction and conclusion for last. Feel free to leave gaps or write notes to yourself in brackets to indicate areas to develop later when revising. Do not make the mistake of thinking that your first draft has to be your final draft. Remember that writing is a process of refinement—you can always go back and fix things later.

Writing Your Introduction

For many students, the hardest part of writing an essay is drafting the first paragraph. Humorist James Thurber once said, "Don't get it right, get it written." What Thurber means is just start writing, even if you do not think it sounds very good. Use your thesis statement as a starting point and build around it. Explain what your essay will do, or provide interesting background information that serves to frame your points for your audience. After you have written the first paragraph, take a break before you revise it. Return to it later with a fresh outlook. Likewise, review your first paragraph as you develop the other sections of your essay to make sure that you are meeting your objectives.

Turning back to our student paper, an introduction might look like this. Note that the introduction works with the thesis statement developed earlier, and builds in a few more ideas.

> The language sensitivity movement of the 1980s and 1990s grew out of a belief that stereotyping and racial or cultural bias could offend or negatively influence students' self-esteem. As a result, publishers and test panels began to carefully consider the language they used. Some people fear that language sensitivity has gone too far and no longer reflects reality. Others are concerned that panels are focusing too much on not offending anyone, at the expense of education. While language sensitivity may sometimes seem extreme, it ultimately benefits students, and the society of which they will later become a part.

Developing Paragraphs and Making Transitions

A paragraph is a group of sentences that supports and develops a central idea. The central idea serves as the core point of the paragraph, and the surrounding sentences support it.

There are three primary types of sentences that comprise a paragraph: the topic sentence, supporting sentences, and transitional sentences.

The core point, or the **topic sentence,** is usually the first or second sentence in the paragraph. It is the controlling idea of the paragraph. Placing the topic sentence first lets the reader immediately know what the paragraph is about. However, sometimes a transition sentence or some supporting material needs to precede the topic sentence, in which case the topic sentence may appear as the second or third sentence in the paragraph. Think of the topic sentence as a mini-thesis statement; it should connect logically to the topic sentences in the paragraphs before and after it.

Supporting sentences do just that, support the topic sentence. This support may be from outside sources in the form of quotes or paraphrased material, or it may be from your own ideas. Think of the support sentences as "proving" the validity of your topic sentence.

Transitional sentences link paragraphs together, making the paper a cohesive unit and promoting its "readability." Transitional sentences are usually the first and last sentences of the paragraph. When they appear at the end of the paragraph, they foreshadow the topic to come. Words such as *in addition, yet, moreover, furthermore, meanwhile, likewise, also, since, before, hence, on the other hand, as well,* and *thus* are often used in transitional sentences. These words can also be used within the body of the paragraph to clarify and smooth the progression from idea to idea. For example, the last sentence in our student's introductory paragraph sets up the reader's expectations that the paragraphs that follow will explain why language sensitivity in educational materials is a good idea. It forecasts what will come next.

Paragraphs have no required length. Remember, however, that an essay comprising long, detailed paragraphs might prove tiresome and confusing to the reader. Likewise, short, choppy paragraphs may sacrifice clarity and leave the reader with unanswered questions. Remember that a paragraph presents a single unified idea. It should be just long enough to effectively support its subject. Begin a new paragraph when your subject changes.

Use this list to help keep your paragraphs organized and coherent:

- Organize material logically—present your core idea early in the paragraph.
- Include a topic sentence that expresses the core point of the paragraph.
- Support and explain the core point.
- Use transitional sentences to indicate where you are going and where you have been.

Let us see how our student applies these ideas to the second paragraph of her essay.

To better approach this issue, we must first understand a little bit more about the "language sensitivity" movement. For much of the twentieth century, textbooks taught primarily from a white, Anglo-Saxon, Protestant-Christian, and male-centred perspective. Stereotyping was common, with girls playing with dolls, boys participating in sports, and mothers and fathers depicted in traditional roles as homemakers and wage earners, respectively. By the 1980s, however, publishers began to listen to the concerns expressed by academics and outside interest groups that educational material be more inclusive, more sensitive, and include the perspectives of women, racial, ethnic, and religious groups [**topic sentence**]. The goal was that through such language awareness, students would learn to avoid stereotyping, to be more tolerant of others, and to feel pride in their own social and cultural backgrounds [**supporting sentence**]. Considering the fact that America is often called the "great melting pot," it is surprising that it took so long to institute this inclusionary approach to language. Not everyone, however, has embraced this new academic approach [**transitional, "forecasting" sentence**].

Concluding Well

Your conclusion should bring together the points made in your paper and reiterate your final point. You may also use your conclusion as an opportunity to provoke a final thought you wish your audience to consider. Try to frame your conclusion to mirror your introduction—in other words, be consistent in your style. You may wish to repeat the point of the paper, revisit its key points, and then leave your reader with a final idea or thought on your topic.

Conclusions are your opportunity to explain to your reader how all your material adds up. In a short essay of about three to four pages, your conclusion should begin around the penultimate paragraph, "winding down" the discussion. Avoid the temptation to simply summarize your material; try to give your conclusions a little punch. However, it is equally important not to be overly dramatic, because you can undercut your essay. Rather, conclusions should sound confident and reflective.

Notice how our student concludes her essay, making references to her final point as well as to the paper against which she is arguing, the essay by John Leo. Based on her conclusion, we may infer that she has supported all of her final points within the actual body of her essay.

The key to language sensitivity is creating a balance between maintaining the principles of tolerance while maintaining reasonable expectations. Simply because the language sensitivity ethic is relatively new does not make it a "fad" or passing fancy. It means we are progressing as a culture. There is a saying "you can't please all of the people, all of the time," which holds particularly true for this issue. Understanding, and tolerating, alternative cultural, religious, and social points of view through language sensitivity does not mean that students are missing out on a good education. Moreover, language sensitivity ensures that children are not alienated by what they read. Rather than arguing that Asian American athletes are not a realistic norm, or questioning why panels avoid casting black women in the role of maids, we should instead consider how language sensitivity affords children more possibility, hope, and acceptance. It will help nurture future generations of children to be more tolerant and accepting of different viewpoints and ways of life.

Editing and Revising

Once you have drafted a paper and, if possible, spent several hours or even a day away from it, you should begin editing and revising it. To edit your paper, read it closely, marking the words, phrases, and sections you want to change. Have a grammar handbook nearby to quickly reference any grammatical questions that may arise. Look for things that seem out of place or sound awkward, passages that lack adequate support and detail, and sentences that seem wordy or unclear. Many students find that reading the essay aloud helps them to recognize awkward sentences and ambiguous wording. This technique may also reveal missing words.

As you read, you should always ask if what you have written refers back to your thesis:

- Does this paragraph support my thesis?
- What does my reader need to know?
- Do my paragraphs flow in a logical order?
- Have I deviated from my point?

As you revise your paper, think about the voice and style you are using to present your material. Is your style smooth and confident? How much of yourself is in the essay, and is this level appropriate for the type of paper you are writing? Some writers, for example, overuse the pronoun *I*. If you find that this is the case try to rework your sentences to decrease the use of this pronoun.

Using Active Voice

Although grammatically correct, the use of the passive voice can slow down the flow of a paper or distance the reader from your material. Many students are befuddled by the active versus the passive voice, confusing it with past, present, and future tense. The active voice can be used in any tense, and, in most situations, it is the better choice. In the active voice, you make your agent "actively" perform an action. Consider the following examples:

PASSIVE: In "Now Cut That Out!" in order to describe how extremist groups are controlling language, examples of rejected subjects are provided by John Leo.

ACTIVE: In his essay, "Now Cut That Out," John Leo provides examples of subjects language extremist groups have vetoed.

PASSIVE: The control of textbook content by the "language police" is feared by Ravitch.

ACTIVE: Ravitch fears that the "language police" are controlling textbook content.

In both of these examples, using the active voice makes the sentences clearer, stronger, and more engaging.

Grammar and Punctuation

You probably already have a grammar handbook; most first-year composition courses require students to purchase these invaluable little books. If you do not have a grammar handbook, get one. You will use it throughout your college—and probably your professional—career. Grammar handbooks can help you identify problems with phrases and clauses, parallel structure, verb tense agreement, commas, colons and semicolons, and punctuation. Most have useful sections on common usage mistakes, such as when to use "further" and "farther," and "effect" and "affect." Try not to rely on grammar checking software available on most word-processing programs. You are the best checker of grammar for your essay.

Proofreading Effectively

The final step in preparing a paper is proofreading, the process of reading your paper to correct errors. You will probably be more successful if you wait until you are fresh to do it: proofreading a paper at 3:00 A.M. immediately after finishing it is not a good idea. With the use of word-processing programs, proofreading usually involves three steps: spell-checking, reading, and correcting.

If you are writing your paper using a word-processing system, you probably have been using the spell checker throughout the composition process. Most word-processing systems highlight misspelled words as you type them into the computer. Remember to run the spell checker every time you change or revise your paper. Many students make last-minute changes to their papers and neglect to run the spell checker one last time before printing it, only to discover a misspelled word as they turn in their paper or when it is returned to them. Keep in mind that spell checkers can fix only words that are misspelled—not words that are mistyped but are still real words. Common typing errors in which letters are transposed such as *from* and *form*, and *won* and *own*, will not be caught by a spell checker because they all are real words. Other common errors not caught by spell checkers include words incompletely typed, such as leaving off the *t* in *the* or the *e* in *here*. Reading your paper carefully will catch these errors.

To proofread correctly, you must read slowly and critically. Try to distance yourself from the material. One careful, slow, attentive proofreading is better than six careless reads. Look for and mark the following: errors in spelling and usage, sentence fragments and comma splices, inconsistencies in number between nouns and pronouns and between subjects and verbs, faulty parallelism, other grammar errors, unintentional repetitions, and omissions.

After you have proofread and identified the errors, go back and correct them. When you have finished, proofread the paper again to make sure you caught everything. As you proofread for grammar and style, ask yourself the questions listed above and make corrections on your paper. Be prepared to read your essay through multiple times. Having only one or two small grammatical corrections is a good indication that you are done revising.

If your schedule permits, you might want to show your paper to a friend or instructor for review. Obtaining feedback from your audience is another way you can test the effectiveness of your paper. An outside reviewer will probably think of questions you have not thought of, and if you revise to answer those questions, you will make your paper stronger.

In the chapters that follow, you will discover over a hundred different selections, both written and visual, ranging widely across contemporary matters, that we hope you will find exciting and thought provoking. Arranged thematically into nine chapters, the writings represent widely diverse topics—from the ways we construct beauty, to what makes us want to buy something, to the way the Internet is changing our lives, to the ethical issues surrounding human reproduction and gene technology. Some of the topics will be familiar; others you may be encountering for the first time. Regardless of how these language issues touch your experience, critical thinking, critical reading, and critical writing will open you up to a deeper understanding of our culture as we begin the twenty-first century.

Approaching Visuals Critically

We have all heard the old saying, "a picture is worth a thousand words." Our daily lives are filled with the images of pop culture, influencing us about what to buy, how to look, even how to think. Symbols, images, gestures, and graphics all communicate instant information about our culture.

Now more than ever before, ours is a visual world. Everywhere we look there are images vying for our attention—magazine ads, T-shirt logos, movie billboards, artwork, traffic signs, political cartoons, statues, and storefront windows. Glanced at only briefly, visuals communicate information and ideas. They may project commonly held values, ideals, and fantasies. They can relay opinion, inspire reaction, and influence emotion. And because the competition for our attention today is so great, and the time for communication is so short, visuals compete to make an instant impression or risk being lost.

Consider the instant messages projected by brand names, company logos, or even a national flag. Or the emotional appeal of a photo of a lost kitten or dog attached to a reward notice on a telephone pole. Without the skills of visual literacy, we are at the mercy of a highly persuasive visual universe. Just as we approach writing with the tools of critical analysis, we should carefully consider the many ways visuals influence us.

Understanding the persuasive power of visuals requires a close examination and interpretation of the premise, claims, details, supporting evidence, and stylistic touches embedded in any visual piece. Just as when we examine written arguments, we should ask ourselves the following four questions when examining visual arguments:

- Who is the target *audience*?
- What are the *claims* made in the images?
- What shared history or cultural *assumptions*—or warrants—does the image make?
- What is the supporting *evidence*?

Like works of art, visuals employ colour, shape, line, texture, depth, and point of view to create their effect. Therefore, to understand how visuals work and to analyze the way visuals persuade, we must also ask questions about specific aspects of form and design. For example, some questions to ask about print images, such as those in newspaper and magazine ads, include:

- What in the frame catches your attention immediately?
- What is the central image? What is the background image? Foreground image? What are the surrounding images? What is significant in the placement of these images? Their relationship to one another?
- What verbal information is included? How is it made prominent? How does it relate to the other graphics or images?
- What specific details (people, objects, locale) are emphasized? Which are exaggerated or idealized?
- What is the effect of colour and lighting?
- What emotional effect is created by the images—pleasure? longing? anxiety? nostalgia?
- Do the graphics and images make you want to know more about the subject or product?
- What special significance might objects in the image have?
- Is there any symbolism imbedded in the images?

Because the goal of a calculated visual is to persuade, coax, intimidate, or otherwise subliminally influence its viewer, it is important that its audience can discern the strategies or technique it employs. To get you started, we will critically analyze two types of visuals—advertisements and editorial cartoons.

Images and Advertising

Images have clout, and none so obvious or so craftily designed as those that come from the world of advertising. Advertising images are everywhere—television, newspapers, the Internet, magazines, the sides of buses, and on highway billboards. Each year, companies collectively spend more than $150 billion on print ads and television commercials (more than the gross national product of many countries). Advertisements comprise at least a quarter of each television hour and form the bulk of most newspapers and magazines. Tapping into our most basic emotions, their appeal goes right to the quick of our fantasies: happiness, material wealth, eternal youth, social acceptance, sexual fulfillment, and power.

Yet, most of us are so accustomed to the onslaught of such images that we see them without looking and hear them without listening. But if we stopped to examine how the images work, we might be amazed at their powerful and complex psychological force. And we might be surprised at how much effort goes into the crafting of such images—an effort solely intended to separate us from our money.

Like a written argument, every print ad or commercial has an audience, claims, assumptions, and evidence. Sometimes these elements are obvious, sometimes understated, sometimes implied. They may boast testimonials by average folk or celebrities, or cite hard scientific evidence. And sometimes they simply manipulate our desire to be happy or socially accepted. But common to every ad and commercial, no matter what the medium, is the claim that you should buy this product.

Print ads are potentially complex mixtures of images, graphics, and text. So in analyzing an ad, you should be aware of the use of photography, the placement of the images, the use of text, company logos, and other graphics (such as illustrations, drawings, sidebar boxes, logos, etc.). And you should keep in mind that every aspect of the image has been thought about and designed carefully even in those ads where the guiding principle was minimalism. Let's take a look at a recent magazine ad for Altoids (see page 39).

Altoids Ad

When analyzing a print ad, we should try to determine what first catches our attention. In the accompanying Altoids ad, the image of the soldier, featured floating on a pale green solid background, pops from the page. This is a calculated move on the part of the ad's designers. The soldier fills the centre of the page, and the image is arresting—we stop and look. Ad images are staged and manipulated for maximum attention and effect. The uncluttered nature of this advertisement forces us to look at the soldier and the little tin he is holding in his hand.

The person featured in the ad is almost comic. He is wearing an ill-fitted uniform, he sports thick glasses, and he lacks the chiseled quality of many male models commonly used in advertising. This comic quality, coupled with the text under the ad, appeals to the viewer's sense of humour.

What Is the Claim? Because advertisers are fighting for our attention, they must project their claim as efficiently as possible in order to discourage us from turning the page. The Altoids ad states its "claim" simply and boldly in white letters against a pale green background below the central photograph. In large typeface, the slogan and "claim" come in two parts. The first two sentences presumably come from the soldier: "Thank you sir! May I have another!" The second statement tells us more specifically what the soldier wants: "The curiously strong mints." It is interesting to note that the actual name of the product, Altoids, only appears on the little tin held in the soldier's right hand.

But let's take a closer look at the intention of framing the claim in two sentences and at how the layout subtly directs us. The first statement is intended to tap into our shared cultural expectations of what we know about military service. Soldiers must shout responses to their superiors and thank them even for punish-

ments. For example, after being assigned 20 push-ups as disciplinary action, a soldier is expected to not only thank his sergeant for the punishment, but to actually ask for more. The ad twists this expectation by having Altoids be the "punishment." In this ad, the soldier is actually getting a treat.

The indirect claim is that the reader should also want these "curiously strong mints." The word *curiously* is designed to set the product apart from its competitors. *Curiously* is more commonly used in British English; and the parent company for

Altoids—Callard & Bowser-Suchard Inc.—has its roots in England. Viewers familiar with the mint will enjoy the ad for its comic appeal. Those readers who are unfamiliar with the product may wonder just what makes these mints "curiously strong." And curiosity is an effective hook.

Another possible claim could be connected to the scenario leading to the soldier's receiving the first mint. We know that soldiers are supposed to shout back responses to their commanding officer, often face to face. Perhaps his commanding officer was appalled at his recruit's bad breath and "punished" him with the directive to have a mint. The claim is that even at extremely close range, Altoids fixes bad breath.

What Is the Evidence? Altoid's tag line, "The curiously strong mints," implies that other mints are simply ordinary and unremarkable. Altoids are different—they are "curiously strong" and thus, presumably, superior to their bland competition. And referring back to the possible scenario that led to the soldier's first mint, viewers might presume that if a commanding officer would "treat" his company's bad breath with this mint, it must be good.

Around the language of advertising, we should tread cautiously. As William Lutz warns us about in his essay, "With These Words I Can Sell You Anything" (page 168), we hear promises that aren't really being made. The Altoids text does not say that it is, indeed, *better* than other mints, just that they are "curiously strong." What does the word *curiously* really mean? And stronger than what? According to Lutz, such words sound enticing, but are really telling readers nothing meaningful about the product.

What Are the Assumptions? The creators of this ad make several assumptions about the audience: (1) they are familiar with the phrase "Thank you sir, may I have another"; (2) they understand who is depicted in the ad—a soldier at boot camp; and (3) they want to have fresh breath.

Altoids Questions
1. What cultural conventions does this ad use to promote the product? What does it assume about the viewer? Would this be interpreted differently in Canada than in the United States? Explain.
2. This ad lists a Web site. Visit the Altoids Web site at **www.altoids.com**. How does the Web site complement the print ad? Who would visit this site? Evaluate the effectiveness of having companion Web sites in addition to printed advertisements.
3. Would you try Altoids based on this advertisement? Why or why not?
4. How does this photograph capture your attention? Can you tell at a glance what it is selling? Where is your eye directed?

Deciphering Editorial Cartoons

Editorial cartoons have been a part of life for over a century. They are a mainstay feature on the editorial pages in most newspapers—those pages reserved for columnists, contributing editors, and illustrators to present their views in words and pen and ink. As in the nineteenth century when they first started to appear, such editorial cartoons are political in nature, holding political and social issues up for public scrutiny and sometimes ridicule.

A stand-alone editorial cartoon—as opposed to a strip of multiple frames—is a powerful and terse form of communication that combines pen-and-ink drawings with dialogue balloons and captions. They're not just visual jokes, but visual humour that comments on social/political issues while drawing on viewers' experience and knowledge.

The editorial cartoon is the story of a moment in the flow of familiar current events. And the key words here are *moment* and *familiar*. Although a cartoon captures a split instant in time, it also infers what came before and, perhaps, what may happen next—either in the next moment or in some indefinite future. And usually the cartoon depicts a moment after which things will never be the same. One of the most famous cartoons of the last 40 years is the late Bill Mauldin's Pulitzer-Prize- winning drawing of the figure of Abraham Lincoln with his head in his hands. It appeared the morning after the assassination of American president John Kennedy in 1963. There was no caption nor was there a need for one. The image represented the profound grief of a nation that had lost its leader to an assassin's bullet. But to capture the enormity of the event, Mauldin brilliantly chose to represent a woeful America by using the figure of Abraham Lincoln as depicted in the sculpture of the Lincoln Memorial in Washington, D.C. In so doing, the message implied that so profound was the loss that it even reduced to tears the marble figure of a man considered to be the United States' greatest president, himself assassinated a century before.

For a cartoon to be effective, it must make the issue clear at a glance and it must establish where it stands on the argument. As in the Mauldin illustration, we instantly recognize Lincoln and identify with the emotions. We need not be told the circumstances, since by the time the cartoon appeared the next day, all the world knew the horrible news that the President had been assassinated. To convey less obvious issues and figures in a glance, cartoonists resort to images that are instantly recognizable, that we don't have to work at to grasp. Locales are determined by giveaway props: airports by an airplane out the window; the desert by a cactus and cattle skull; the standard living room by an overstuffed arm chair and TV. Likewise, human emotions are instantly conveyed: pleasure is a huge toothy grin; fury is steam blowing out of a figure's ears; love is two figures making goo-goo eyes with floating hearts. People themselves may have exaggerated features to emphasize a point or emotion.

In his essay "What Is a Cartoon?", Mort Gerberg (*The Arbor House Book of Cartooning*, HarperCollins, 1989) says that editorial cartoons rely on such visual clichés to instantly convey their messages. That is, they use stock figures for their representation—images instantly recognizable from cultural stereotypes. The fat-cat tycoon, the mobster thug, the sexy female movie star. And these come to us in familiar outfits and props that give away their identities and profession. The cartoon judge has a black robe and gavel; the prisoner wears striped overalls and a ball and chain; the physician dons a smock and forehead light; the doomsayer is a scrawny long-haired guy carrying a sign saying, "The end is near." These are visual clichés known by the culture at large, and we get them.

The visual cliché may be what catches our eye in the editorial cartoon, but the message lies in what the cartoonist does with it. As Gerberg observes, "the message is in twisting it, in turning the cliché around."

Cloning Cartoon

Consider the Jack Ohman cartoon that follows. The cliché is a woman shopping in a supermarket. We know that from the familiar props: the shopping cart, the meat display unit, the department banner, and the hint of shelving in the background. Even the shopper is a familiar figure, an elderly woman in her overcoat pushing her cart. The twist, of course, is that instead of a refrigeration unit displaying lamb, beef, and poultry, we see trays of neatly arranged embryo clones with their genetic specialties in stickup signs. The issue, of course, is the debate on human cloning. The cartoon was published on December 10, 2001, shortly after the announcement by the genetics firm Advanced Cell Technology in Worcester, Massachusetts, that they had cloned the first human embryo. (The embryos only -survived a few cell divisions

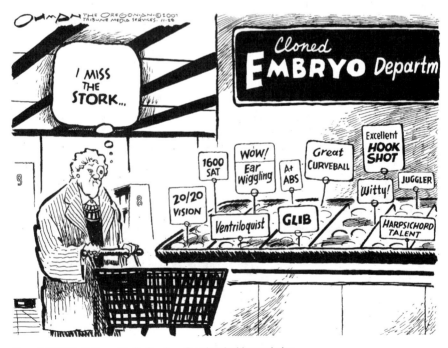

Copyright 2001, Tribune Media Services. Reprinted with permission.

before they ceased.) Although the lab claimed that the intention of cloning was not to create human beings but to treat particular human ailments, such as Parkinson's disease, cancer, and strokes, the publicity fanned the flames of debate over the ethics and morality of cloning. Some people view such breakthroughs as medically promising; others fear crossing the line of playing God.

The cartoon's joke is in the twist—the gap between the familiar and the unexpected. The familiar is the supermarket cliché; the unexpected is the casual display of embryo flagged for desirable traits in a Cloned Embryo Department. Of course the scene depicts some indefinite future time when cloning is permitted by law and widely practised.

What Is the Claim? The claim in this cartoon is that natural birth is better than genetic engineering. That is implicit in the satirical image of the human talents and traits quantified and commercialized in the meat section of the supermarket. And it is explicit in the woman's thoughts, "I miss the stork . . . "

What Are the Assumptions? This cartoon makes the assumptions that people see human beings as more complex and elusive than particular traits and talents, and that purchasing babies according to desired traits is perverse and unnatural.

What Is the Evidence? The evidence is in the darkly satirical notion that instead of natural procreation we would someday shop for scientifically perfected babies in a supermarket. Next to more "serious" preferences, such as embryos cloned from donors with "1600 SAT" scores and "20/20 vision," are the embryos cloned from people good at juggling and ear-wiggling. It is in these juxtapositions where the cartoonist gives away where he stands on the issue. He is mocking our society by reducing the aspiration of would-be parents to have kids with narrowly specific talents. To clinch Ohman's stand is the woman's thought bubble—"I miss the stork . . . " The message is that in the imagined new world where we can shop for our ideal babies, there are those who yearn for the good old days. Of course, "the stork" is a polite metaphorical reference to sexual reproduction—a term appropriate for the customer in the drawing—an elderly woman conservatively dressed. However, the term is another cliché, and in a curious twist it plays off the supermarket meat department display—as if *stork* were another kind of poultry option.

As you review the various visuals throughout the text, approach what you see with the critical eye of a skeptic. Many of the techniques used in reading critically can be applied to visuals. Consider the ways symbolism, brand recognition, stereotyping, and cultural expectations contribute to how such illustrations communicate their ideas. Try to think abstractly, taking into account the many different levels of consciousness that visuals use to communicate. Consider also the way shading, lighting, and subject placement in the photos all converge to make a point. "Read" them as you would any text.

1

THE **Canadian** Experience

Culture and Identity

Whether or not we deserve our reputation as a country preoccupied with articulating a nebulous national identity, Canadians have long taken comfort in declaring what we are not: the United States of America writ small. Of course, a negative definition rarely yields useful information. If resistance to the American influence is what coheres us from without, then what coheres us from within?

Less and less, it would seem. Immigration has steadily increased the influence of other cultures in Canada. We were probably never as homogeneous as we believed, but certainly we have never been more diverse than we are now. Regional interests clash; political parties are polarized, right and left. The divide between rich and poor remains alarming and intransigent. Farmers and ranchers are too busy trying to make a living to engage in a debate on national identity, and urban dwellers are discouraged from neighbourly relations by the very beehives that house them.

And yet there are people who continue to write about the Canadian identity—or experience, if identity is too definite. Adrienne Clarkson, in "New Country, New Journalists," reminds us that as the immigrant population grows, so does the responsibility of the media to accommodate their needs and to acknowledge that "the old idea" of Canada no longer holds true.

J.B. MacKinnon professes a dislike for this country in "I Am Anti-Canadian," but the Canada to which he objects is a very specific place, one that might not spring to mind when you think of this country.

In "Letter to America," Margaret Atwood wonders about the changing Canada/U.S. relationship, specifically addressing the ongoing American action in Iraq. Canada's position on the conflict was as philosophical as it was political; how does our idea of the United States change in light of the Iraqi action and the events that led up to it? Diana Coulter's "Canucks Are Full of Yuks at Yankee Blunders" (on page 61) looks at our differences in a less profound light. Americans don't know as much about us as we do about them, and for some reason we delight in seeing that perception confirmed.

In "Immigrants Isolated? Tell That to Their Children," Rosie DiManno reads between the lines of a Statistics Canada study that worries that immigrant families are not integrating at a satisfactory pace. DiManno thinks the government may be concerned unnecessarily, that the passing of a generation will solve the problem on its own. Raj Mazumdar found a different kind of isolation in Canada: unemployment and underemployment. Lured by the promise of a prosperous economy, he felt denied entry into it. In "Coming Here Was a Mistake," he recounts his experience, and asks us to think about some of the obstacles an educated immigrant to this country can face. If American Ken Victor faced obstacles adjusting to the Canadian experience, he doesn't mention them in "To Canada with Love." A paean to all things Canadian—from health care to moose—this article was written for the first Canada Day after Victor became a Canadian citizen.

In "Tough Rules Stand Guard Over Canadian Culture," Anthony DePalma reveals some of the foibles of the Canadian content regulations that have sprung up around the desire to nurture talent in this country, in the face of a massive American cultural presence in every form of media.

All of these writers talk about the problems and the promises of a country whose quest to define the national experience had better take into account the political, social, and demographic realities of the new Canada.

New Country, New Journalists

Adrienne Clarkson

Canada's demographic profile has changed over the past 20 years. Our traditionally European-based immigrant population has become more diverse, its origins, cultures, and ideologies more varied, stemming from national histories very different from that of the West. How has the Canadian media evolved to meet this new reality? Do journalists really know who their contemporary audience is, or are they writing for a generally mainstream Western readership with whom they share a social history and a set of cultural assumptions? If the Canadian media are not taking our "multiracial, multifaith" immigrant population into account, how can new Canadians be expected to see themselves as an integral part of the national identity?

Her Excellency the Right Honourable Adrienne Clarkson pursued a long and distinguished career as a journalist before being appointed Governor General of Canada. This article is based on an address presented at the Annual Conference of the McGill Institute for the Study of Canada, on February 14, 2003. It was first published in *Queen's Quarterly*.

CRITICAL THINKING

When someone is immigrating to this country, what does he or she need to know in order to become "Canadian"? Is it possible to retain the culture of one's country of origin and yet still be able to fully participate in the culture of a new country?

1   Every society has a discreet, almost unconscious coding of shared understanding—insider humour, insider cynicism, an unspoken attachment to values, and a sense of belonging. We feel pride in our society's achievements, even when these occurred long before we were born, just as we feel shame for injustices that took place before we came into the world and into this society. But like the rest of the world, Canada's people today are a much more connected, complicated community than we were only twenty years ago. And the country's journalists, even more than other citizens, must be better attuned than ever to the subtleties of our many shared messages.

2   Propaganda, ideology, and bias are extremely easy to promote in any kind of information medium, if you know how. And by "information" I mean not only newspapers, television, radio, and the Internet, but also advertising. People need diverse and quality sources of information in order to make sense not only of their own lives but also of their community. As a society, we have to worry, therefore, if

our citizens are not dealt a full deck of information. And this is the job of the journalists and editors, broadcasters, publishers, and media owners.

3   It has been said that journalists share a vocation of unhappiness and discontent. If that is so, I think that's precisely what makes them competent, and often superb, at what they do. Why on earth would you want a happy journalist? Kierkegaard said that people hardly ever make use of the freedom they already have; in place of freedom of thought, they settle for freedom of speech as compensation. Journalists, therefore, should examine themselves and think about whether or not they actually have the freedom of thought that gives them the privilege to communicate with others freely. That is a professional struggle. It is what we mean when we say that we expect them to aspire to the highest possible professional standards.

4   There is now a patchwork quilt of information out there that makes it very difficult for people to discern exactly what is really happening. I mentioned advertising as an aspect of information that is important for the public now. Remember that McLuhan told us thirty years ago that advertising creates a parallel world. But it may not be a parallel world for the majority of the population, who are struggling to piece together a patchwork quilt of information. Are we deliberately making it more difficult or less difficult for them to discern between what is really happening in the news and what has been carefully constructed to fit into part of the news and grab attention for commercial purposes?

5   A recent automobile ad features a little automotive object of desire gliding through a number of different situations in shots lasting about one second each. It ends up in a field with hundreds and hundreds of fighter airplanes going over it. What kind of message is actually being delivered by that car ad? It is designed to say that we will stop at nothing to have that new model. To those of us who have grown up in this country, long exposed to the subtle messages and inside jokes of popular culture and the advertising world, it may be an amusing juxtaposition between luxury on four wheels and the power and might of military force. But to others' minds, others not understanding either English or French very well, it could be an image of terror blandly accepted. Confusion and misunderstanding can be the order of the day, rather than factual information and the gathering of enough information to create thought.

6   And this is where the question of the makeup of the audience becomes extremely important. By this I do not mean gender, race, or demographic makeup; I mean that we must try to understand exactly how people in Canada have evolved. Where does the audience come from? From what parts of the public? How do they think? You can say, "Well we can't be saying all things to all people." But it is still very healthy to challenge yourself to try and think about who is actually reading, watching, listening to the media.

7   Why? Because I believe that much of the information we get—and how it is purveyed by the media—is based upon an old idea of Canada. It is based on an idea of a Canada of middle-class values, some historical memory, and a Canada seen as fully functioning in at least one of the official languages. It is a Canada where a stable democratic system is taken for granted. In other words, we basically see the audience in our own image of ourselves, more or less affluent, more or less committed to

a status quo. We see the audience as people who have some education in our kinds of schooling, as people curious to know about day-to-day events, though mainly interested in the outside world when it bursts into flame, floods, or loses electrical power.

8   Yes, that kind of "original" audience does exist. But even it is not getting all the information it needs. For instance, when we get news of an election in a foreign country, we are always told who won or lost. But we are rarely given hard information as to the number of seats gained by any particular party or what those parties really represent. As a result, our understanding of the world outside our own country is glib, frequently dismissive. And when we search for the information we need, we have to rely on foreign websites, articles in foreign publications, or on programs from abroad—information that often arrives a few days, a week, or even a month later in Canadian newspapers and magazines.

9   But that "original" audience—as ill-served as it is—was the audience of Canada twenty years ago. The audience you are looking for today is different—an audience that needs attention, that needs to be informed, needs to be given the absolute basics of our way of life, including our criticism of our way of life.

10   Today, we have a new kind of society in Canada. We live in the year 2003, and we are a multiracial, multifaith immigrant population on an aboriginal base. We have a society, a way of life, and a form of government that have served us well for the last several centuries and into which we have up to now successfully and rather efficiently integrated immigrants. We have many flaws in our system, but on the whole it has worked quite well. Can it continue to do so at that level?

11   Our original so-called multicultural society was built of immigrants from Europe, all of whom could be expected within a relatively short time—perhaps a generation around the beginning of the twentieth century and often half a generation in the postwar period—to achieve an economic and social status on a par with other Canadians. But, as Carol Goar of the Toronto Star recently pointed out in an article reporting on a conference on immigrants in Toronto, our new immigrants are different. The bulk of the 200,000 to 250,000 people we take in a year, expecting to become citizens, are different. They come from countries where war, strife, and destitution have been the norm. They come from different religious traditions. Many of them came here to escape horrific events in their homelands. These are the people who are urgently in need of information about how they can truly participate in their new society and become Canadian.

12   All information media must play a part in helping that process to happen—and not by relating only "good news" stories or somehow teaching citizenship lessons subliminally. Through good journalism, people learn things through a sort of osmosis. And, as people are watching hours and hours of television every day, that particular medium has a special obligation to these newcomers and their children.

13   Even such a small thing as the weather report can have a deep effect on newcomers. I have noticed a growing and regrettable tendency within the last 25 years to describe snow as "bad weather," when in fact it is normal weather for Canada. This may seem like a tiny detail, but why should we publicly deny our climate in this way? Why should we say to ourselves or to others that having snow constitutes

bad weather? Why should we pass on that kind of valuation of it to people who are coming here from countries where the average temperature is 40 degrees?

14   The "old immigration" from Europe had trades or could farm or had strong survival skills in Western culture. The people we now receive need different education, different acculturation, and certainly different approaches to information. Consider what that advertisement with the little car and the dozens of fighter planes would mean to somebody who has arrived here from a disputed border area in Southeast Asia or from bloody civil strife in Africa. An ad shown during a newscast is part of that newscast; the information is all knitted together. And of course the better the advertising is, the more likely that it will have an effect on the viewer. I like to remember what Stephen Leacock said about advertising—that it is the science of arresting the human intelligence long enough to get money from it.

15   We have said as a country that we are going to bring over 200,000 immigrants a year to Canada. And what we have done in fact is invited these people to come and take part in our society and become citizens. It is incumbent upon us, therefore, to think about what we do to help them "catch up" to other citizens who've been here for decades or even generations.

16   I believe that all the media are absolutely critical in this respect. They play a crucial role in building the new Canada and in the acculturation of those who have come here to make Canada their home. In fact, I believe that what you do as journalists is as important and critical as public education is in helping our new kind of immigrants to understand and become a really functioning part of our society. And remember, public education, important as it is, is a provincial responsibility—while many news outlets have a national audience. This means a greater responsibility, not just a greater market.

17   In order to be part of this country, you have to be a fully functioning citizen. Citizenship has its responsibilities as well as its rights. As an immigrant myself, I feel very strongly about this. And as Governor General, I am firmly convinced that it is the only way in which our nation can continue to live according to its beliefs, to its traditions, to its history, and to its often hard-won democratic processes. What I believe is that, by assuming citizenship, the new citizen of Canada takes on the entire history of the country.

18   So as a new Canadian you can be very proud of the sacrifices that Canada made in the First and Second World Wars. But you also have to acknowledge and accept the shame and tragedy of the residential schools for aboriginal children or the dislocation of Japanese-Canadians sixty years ago. We cannot continue to have a country if the huge numbers of people we involve in becoming citizens slough off any responsibility for what the country did before they got here.

19   Many of the immigrants we are now bringing to this country fully understand what it is to have a complex, tortured history. They have chosen to leave it and take up life in Canada. In remaking themselves as citizens of our country, they must learn to understand what we, as a country, have gone through in our evolution up to now. Citizenship is not a buffet table of rights, privileges, and perhaps some inconveniences—like the cranberry sauce you won't take with the turkey. If a country is to

have a continuous history, then it must have a history that all members of it comprehend and—most importantly—in which all members feel implicated.

20   I remember somebody once watching me singing the national anthem in French and asking me afterwards, in a polite and rather gingerly way, how I could sing the line "Land of our ancestors." And I replied that I really mean that line. Canada is the country of my ancestors, my adopted ancestors, the ones who struggled to create the kind of country to which I was able to come, of which I became a citizen, and of which I am now Governor General. My ancestors fought in 1837. They're the ancestors who created Confederation. All of that belongs to me and to each and every one of us when we are citizens of Canada.

21   For those of us who are immigrants, it doesn't mean an either/or situation. It's not that we forget where we came from, or what the food there tastes like, or when the festivals are. It means only that we have added another level of texture, a different kind of complexity, to our individual circumstances as citizens. But it is this kind of complex person that good journalism must reach, and indeed perhaps even shape. They may be new arrivals now, but their impact will be felt over generations. And you can bet that they will be actively involved in creating the Canadian society of the future.

22   It is these people to whom the world of media and information must be responsible—if we truly believe in freedom of thought. This is where freedom of the press should be operating. This is where freedom of the press can give people the keys to whole new worlds. And so if it is true that journalists share a "vocation of unhappiness and discontent" then this is where the journalist's unhappiness and discontent can create justice for others.

FREEWRITING ASSIGNMENT

How much of what you define as Canadian is based on your perceptions of the news media's portrayal of this country? Do you think that current Canadian journalism takes into account our large immigrant population?

CRITICAL READING

1. Clarkson claims that "propaganda, ideology, and bias are extremely easy to promote in any kind of information medium." What do these terms mean, and how do they differ from one another?
2. What is Clarkson's "old idea of Canada?"
3. Clarkson refers to Marshall McLuhan's statement that "advertising creates a parallel world." Describe this world. How does it differ from the world of your experience?
4. Clarkson refers to the idea that "journalists share a vocation of unhappiness and discontent." What does she mean by this?
5. Would you agree that our understanding of the world outside of Canada is "glib, frequently dismissive"? Would that include our understanding of the United States?

6. The author refers to Stephen Leacock's comment that advertising "is the science of arresting the human intelligence long enough to get money from it." In your own words, what does this statement mean?

7. In paragraph 11, Clarkson claims that the 200 000 to 250 000 people who immigrate to Canada each year are "different." What does she mean by this?

CRITICAL WRITING

8. *Research and Evaluation*: Interview several people who have immigrated to Canada, preferably of different generations and origins. Find out how they feel about the way that the news and current events of their home countries are represented in the Canadian media. How difficult is it for them to find news of their country of origin? Summarize your findings in an essay.

9. *Exploratory Writing*: Write a paper on the meaning of citizenship. What defines a citizen? What is the responsibility of the state to its citizens, and conversely, what are the rights and responsibilities of a citizen? Explain.

GROUP PROJECTS

10. Clarkson says that in the past 25 years we have come to describe snow as "bad weather," when in fact it is normal weather for Canada. Have each member of your group watch or listen to a different Canadian weather forecast over a period of a few days. Record how the meteorologists editorialize about their forecasts. Note which adjectives are used to describe the weather; what does this imply about our perception of our climate and even its role in our national identity? Present your findings to the class.

11. How does a country decide who would make a good citizen? Members of your group should take the Canadian Citizenship Practice Test at **www.yourlibrary.ca/citizenship/**. Score yourselves on the complete test. How do you perform as a group? Do you feel the questions are equally relevant? If not, which ones would you eliminate? What questions might you add?

I Am Anti-Canadian

J.B. MacKinnon

In this article, J.B. MacKinnon takes aim at Canadians' facile acceptance of our reputation for "tolerance, civility, and decency." Significant problems exist in this country, from child poverty to our treatment of Aboriginals, and Canada's political and military actions have not always shone with altruism. So the model of the "huggable Canadian" is inaccurate. In fact, warns

MacKinnon, the current identity model is "an ugly blend of neoconservative values coddled by a self-righteous 'caring and sharing' myth." It is this definition of Canadian that the author objects to, implying that the most authentic collective identity we may find could grow from smaller centres across the country, where residents are "reclaiming their sovereignty as their nation consigns itself to corporatist globalization."

J.B. MacKinnon is a freelance writer based in Vancouver. He is currently working on a book about the Dominican Republic, to be published in 2005.

CRITICAL THINKING   Would you describe Canada as a "caring and sharing" nation? Why or why not?

1   My first memory of fireworks is also my first memory of Canada Day, and neither is any big whoop. The small crowd on the upper field of Beattie Elementary in Kamloops, B.C., grew tired of waiting for nightfall; in the dusk, someone lit the roman candles and—*poomph!*—a yellowish ball doodled into the air, not even so high as the plume from the Weyerhaeuser pulp mill. I remember that first fireball only because it was the first, it was a dull show, put on by people who cared a little, not a lot. Like Canadians across the nation, they were saving themselves for Grey Cup.

2   I miss those elementary years, and not just because of little Laura Wong and Jennifer Mountfort. This year, Canada Day came on like a real holiday: three weeks early in an explosion of commercial come-ons. There was the wall-size maple leaf made of red and white cases of Coke at a Squamish grocery. In Vancouver, street vendors hawked flags that young drunks waved from sunroofs, and surf shops sold out of "Canada Kicks Ass" stickers. There was, of course, a sale at Roots. It all left me with a poignant longing for the freedom to feel unattachment to this country, to be a part of a place by chance rather than choice. As a legacy of that great Canadian project, the search for a national identity, I've settled into an isolated camp: I am anti-Canadian.

3   If this sounds like another clever game in which the writer bemoans Canada's foibles only to find true goodness at the heart of the nation, well, it's not. Contrary to popular belief, it is not difficult, let alone impossible, to distrust, dislike, and reject what Canada has come to represent. Great vistas, sure, but then there's the world's largest clearcut, in Northern B.C. There's Canada's top ranking from the UN—but also the lie we've forgotten we told ourselves, about solving child poverty by the turn of the millennium. At the heart of it all, there's the "new nationalism," an ugly blend of neoconservative values coddled by a self-righteous "caring and sharing" myth. Worse, this nationalism is rising just as it seemed that Canada would fade—and make a real contribution to the political necessities of the 21st century. The reasons have heaped on me like snowpack until, today, I recoil from every attempt to gather Canadians under any umbrella of national character. I see signs of many others like me, and I think we represent something important.

4   I suspect this makes me something of a bastard.

5   My position has taken decades to settle. Growing up as a "red-diaper baby," I was constantly reminded that I live among kindred spirits—ham-and-egger Canucks who, according to every vaguely pink voice from Maude Barlow to Farley Mowat, were simply bursting with social-democratic zeal. In his 1995 *Nationalism Without Walls*, Richard Gwyn sums up the attitude, declaring the debate about Canadianism a fool's game. "This isn't because people don't know what being Canadian is, he says, "it's that they're embarrassed to say it out loud. As everyone in fact knows full well, it means trying to live by the ideals of tolerance, civility, and decency."

6   This huggable Canadian is a powerful lodestone, one now crowded with politicians and Can-con artists. It has its own canon, defined by Margaret Atwood, who established Canadians as mutualistic survivors in the face of November gales and *The Partridge Family*. Its roots are in John Diefenbaker's late-1950s "One Canada" program, a nationalist appeal against American influence and the "hyphenated Canadian." As George Grant points out in his 1965 Red Tory bible, *Lament for a Nation*, the Chief's national vision struck a chord with the hoi polloi, but withered under an attack by both the capitalist and intellectual elites. Grant believed this marked the end of any hope for a distinct Canadian nation. But he sang the dirge too soon. As the socialist academic James Laxer wrote, "He was saying Canada is dead, and by saying it he was creating a country."

7   Canada came alive if not to Grant's words, then at least to his idea that if this nation became "a branch-plant society of American capitalism" then the issue of Canadian nationalism would be settled. In response, whole generations resisted the Americana machine and defined Canadianism as *something else*: a nation, strong, true, tolerant, caring and mildly anti-capitalist. Canadians were Hosers for Humanity.

8   If you were born too late, though, the whole myth-making machine reeks of the bogus.

9   It is 1986, and I am 15. These are shameful times, set to a soundtrack by Duran Duran; I have purchased and actually worn, twice, a pink acrylic sweater. The political scene is even uglier. In Ottawa, the reign of Brian Mulroney has begun; in England, it's Thatcher; in the U.S., Reagan. In my home province of British Columbia, the Social Credit government of real estate agents and hardware kingpins is in its 34th year, broken only by the NDP from 1972–75. My hometown has been nicknamed "the Newfoundland of B.C." in honour of its unemployment rate, and in Vancouver, they're evicting the poor to make way for Expo. It is springtime in the age of free-marketeers.

10   At least there's punk rock. Joe Shithead of DOA on a poster reading, "Destroy Canada." The Discords ripping the jodhpurs off the RCMP. All of it sounds queer and exciting as hell to small-town, teenage ears. *Destroy Canada?*

11   Before long, it began to make sense. From the punk years forward, without pause, the Canada I have lived in has been the nation of Social Credit, Mulroney conservatism, rising Reform, and the neoliberalism of Jean Chétien, Mike Harris, Ralph Klein and the "politics-of-the-possible" NDP. At age 30, a lifetime is still an imperfect measure, but it seems ridiculous to claim kinship with some caring Canadian in a textbook raising the flag against a leering Uncle Sam. If all I've known is a Chamber of Commerce nation, I can hardly heap the blame on Ronnie

Reagan, the New York Stock Exchange and Disney. At some point I have to bring it all home. This is Canada, and it sucks.

12   Today, the Hosers for Humanity myth is worse than dead. It's staggering with a kind of zombie life. In fact, there are sure signs that the idea of Canada—or rather, *an idea* of Canada—grows stronger every year. In 1995, University of Calgary political scientist Roger Gibbins pointed to a "new face of Canadian nationalism," rooted in the West and closely tuned to the fiscal conservatism and moral rectitude of Reform, and now the Canadian Alliance. This nationalism is populist but homogenizing, indifferent or hostile to multicultural concepts, focused on the future rather than the past, and rights-based, though hostile to group rights. It has firmly decided the Quebec question, Gibbins notes. "[T]he visions that are coming to dominate the political stage are directing our attention to a Canada without Quebec."

13   Five years later, the new nationalism is marching on. Today's Canadians learned nationalism under the "caring and sharing" regime, but they're finding it easy to slip into a darker cloak. In *The Globe and Mail* on July 13, historian Michael Bliss warned the Canadian Alliance not to stray from the New Politics: "fiscal conservatism plus political reform plus new nationalism." The new nationalism, Bliss bets, can bind Canadians' variable support for social and fiscal conservatism. As a historical example, he points again to the Diefenbaker years, when our prime minister told his people, from street to elite, "Get on board, or be left behind." The great capitalists didn't get on board for the Chief, prompting George Grant to write his most famous maxim: "No small country can depend for its existence on the loyalty of its capitalists." Today, though, the business class is dashing up the nationalist gangway. They've made a simple discovery: help Canadians find an "identity," and they'll finally feel secure enough to embrace a blandly universal consumer culture.

14   Our leading neocon voice, Conrad Black, appears to like the odds. At the turn of the millennium, Black used his mighty organ, the *National Post*, to argue the new nationalist end game: to "turn Canada into a greater enterprise state than the United States." All we need to do is cut taxes below the U.S. level, re-establish private medicine, "bury the putrid corpse of universality," curtail the right to strike, and encourage "easily assimilable immigration." I have few reasons to doubt that Canada and Canadianism will continue to drift, on the whole, toward Black's vision. Like him, I long ago lost faith in, as only he could put it, "self-serving fables about the pure snow-maiden of the North."

15   "If one cares about what Canada could become, it's difficult to restrain criticism of what it is. Which is a mess." So said author John Metcalf, a pioneering anti-Canadian who, unlike contrarians of Mordecai Richler's ilk, has taken aim at the powers that benefit from the Canadianism myth, and not only at the myth's more obvious interest-group dupes.

16   But what is this collective Canada that demands rejection? We are the global peacekeeper who used land mines against a small group of native sovereigntists at Gustafsen Lake in 1995, and force to limit freedom of expression during APEC 1997. We push nuclear reactors worldwide. As Naomi Klein made clear in an award-winning report last year, our policy of "trading our way to human rights" is transparent appeasement of dictators. We are softer on Burma than any other

Western nation, but quiet about the need to end sanctions on Iraq. Our prime minister, who promised to renegotiate NAFTA, was later nicknamed "the godfather of free trade" in Chile (and the "global village idiot" by a Vancouver cartoonist). We are monarchists, with a system of representative government that has been described as "five-year fascism." Our citizens consume the most energy per capita on Earth, and blocking a logging road in Canada is likely to earn you more jail time than assault or burglary. Our new federal opposition leader is the kind of Christian camp councillor not seen since the Scopes trial. We are a country that has come to depend for its identity on the marketing of its capitalists: Molson, Roots, Labatt. We took up vexillolatry late in our history, like a vegetarian who takes up smoking at age 65. We are Siamese twins in a Bay Street suit. We are, arguably, the sole remaining nation to consider neoconservative pundits a growth export.

17   Which is the right direction if you are, for example, Raymond Chrétien, ambassador to the U.S., and trying to market Canada as a deregulated tiger economy. "It is not an easy challenge because you almost have to start with a new definition of who is a Canadian," the ambassador told *Time* in July. Luckily for Chrétien, the new nationalism has finally developed enough street cred that Canadians have begun to proudly defend the faith.

18   My favourite recent example is a letter to sex-advice columnist Dan Savage, who had suggested a blue-collar man try Canada as a place where women might be more accepting of his working-class income. How dare an American lay out that musty old "tolerance" myth, wrote an incensed Canuck (also careful to dismiss, as usual, that lingering misperception that we all live in igloos). "Some Canadian women want more and won't settle for less than financial luxury," she declared. Savage sent along his thanks for the lesson in northern culture: "Someone had to tell the world that Canadian women can be money-grubbing whores, too, just like American women."

19   This "new Canadian" seems to shock people only upon re-entry from the outer space of nostalgia. Richard Gwyn returned to Canada after five years abroad to find the snowmaiden "had evaporated." Will Ferguson wrote *Why I Hate Canadians* after returning from Japan to find the "nice Canadian" drunk, picking fights, and endlessly bragging that the UN thinks he's pretty hot shit. I came home from a stay in Turkey to find that Canada had entered the war in Kosovo without a debate in parliament, just as we'd entered the more egregious Gulf War. In Turkey, and throughout Europe, politicians debated sending troops—or faced riots in the streets. Once we wake up, how do we react? The most common response is, at best, another call to renew the alleged Canadian commitment to caring and sharing. At the launch of the federal NDP's election platform this year, Alexa McDonough cracked the chestnut once again: "Canada is in danger of losing our unique way of life."

20   It's a doomed approach, because the old nationalism is complicit with the new. Within the new nationalism, the huggable Canadian identity is little more than a useful brand; it's a duster of what Will Ferguson calls "cultural tics," typified by the Canadian traveller's irritating claim to global innocence through that iconic flag on the backpack. The whole shtick softens and props up our obeisance to global

mercantilism. It's like a ponytail on a stockbroker: effective as long as you don't look beyond the surface.

21   Trying to rebuild a kinder, gentler nationalism, though, would be an error, because the nation-state is dying. Still, we continue to paint smiles on the carcass. On the Left, pundits have begun to applaud Canada as an oxymoron—a "postmodern nation." Again, Richard Gwyn sums it up most artfully: "We may finally arrive at the long-sought Holy Grail of our national identity by discovering that, uniquely in the world, we have an identity that is impermanent, mutable, plastic, fragile, and both opaque and transparent."

22   With nothing left to hang onto, we've decided that nothingness unites us. The Right, at least, offers flag-waving and beer, an "enterprise state" sponsored by the letter Zed. The alternative, I think, is to see Canada as a *location* rather than a place. Some fascinating things are happening in Canada, but there's nothing very Canadian about them. The polyglot cultures of Vancouver and Toronto, for example, are accidents that are finding surprising support. This isn't because of some benevolent Canadianism, but because Canadianism has been shallow enough to be overcome by, in the case of Vancouver, a large influx of people from the Asian Pacific Rim. Canada is still a location where political culture can be rapidly transformed in important ways—provided we don't keep demanding a nation as a result.

23   Anarchist writer and historian George Woodcock called this "creative anti-national disunity," recognizing that the movements most likely to rebuff global neo-conservative ideology are almost uniformly local and anti-national. In Canada, these include (without limiting the list) bioregionalist concepts such as Cascadia, classic confederation, Green politics, ideas of the modem "city-state," native sovereignty and social anarchism. Even Judy Rebick's "active citizenship" model, explored in her new book *Imagine Democracy*, is stronger as an anti-national idea than a national one. En route to the local, the Left in Canada can give up its faintly embarrassing association with nationalism, more correctly the domain of the coercive Right. In its proper place, nationalism can be a lightning rod for resistance. In Europe, the "no borders" movement attracts protesters willing to risk arrest in symbolic border-crossings that support the free movement of people over capital. America developed an internal anti-Americanism decades ago, an internal bullshit detector that has helped propel the civil-rights and peace movements, an enormous cultural underground, and now a growing list of small towns and cities that are reclaiming their sovereignty as their nation consigns itself to corporatist globalization.

24   One of the best expressions of anti-nationalism comes from a Canadian gentleman-of-letters, Douglas Fetherling. In *Travels By Night*, his memoir of the sixties, Fetherling describes why he felt an impulsive need to leave his nation of birth, America, and head for the Great White North. "I found it a constant struggle to keep out the terror and let the stimulation enter. It proved impossible, in fact." He was talking about the past and present; in Canada, the terror is the present and future. Our journey into exile, though, is necessarily more complex. We can't slip across some hopeful northern border. What we *can* do is slip out of an identity so thin that we'll feel naked for only a moment. ◆

FREEWRITING ASSIGNMENT

Can you define what it means to be Canadian? Do you consider yourself anti-Canadian? Pro-Canadian? Or are you indifferent to a national identity?

CRITICAL READING

1. In paragraph 3, the author claims that "Contrary to popular belief, it is not difficult, let alone impossible, to distrust, dislike, and reject what Canada has come to represent." In your own words, what does MacKinnon believe Canada has come to represent?
2. This essay begins with a personal memory of Canada Day. How is Canada Day celebrated in your community? Do you, like the author, feel that it has become "an explosion of commercial come-ons"?
3. The author refers to a DOA poster reading, "Destroy Canada." What was meant by the poster? How did it make the author feel?
4. In paragraph 22, MacKinnon claims that "nothingness unites us" and that one alternative is "to see Canada as a *location* rather than a *place*." What does he mean by these assertions? What is the difference between a place and a location?
5. What does the author mean by his statement, "Canadians were Hosers for Humanity" (paragraph 7)?
6. MacKinnon claims that Canadian "identity" only serves to allow Canadians to "finally feel secure enough to embrace a blandly universal consumer culture." What does he mean by this assertion?
7. What does the author mean by the notion of Canada being an "oxymoron" or a "postmodern nation"?

CRITICAL WRITING

8. *Personal Narrative*: Write an essay about what is important to your own sense of personal identity. Consider such aspects as race, gender, religious background, and education. What role, if any, does being Canadian play in your identity?
9. MacKinnon claims that "we are a country that has come to depend for its identity on the marketing of its capitalists: Molson, Roots, Labatt's." Visit the Web sites of these companies. How are they exploiting Canadian identity to sell their products? Do the presentation and content of these sites tend to support or refute MacKinnon's argument?

GROUP PROJECTS

10. With your group, research Canada's major political parties. Try to find their official policy statements on several of the issues that MacKinnon

mentions, such as land mines, logging practices, energy consumption, and universal health care. Based on your research, where does each party stand in relation to what MacKinnon calls "the new nationalism"?

Letter to America
Margaret Atwood

Historical friends as well as neighbours, Canada and the United States are used to enjoying a stable relationship based not only on proximity but also on shared self-interest and broadly similar cultural values. Because of America's large population and economic power, its cultural influence on Canada is greater than ours is on America, but we have lived more or less stoically with this fact, happily consuming American news and entertainment while implementing our own cultural safeguards.

With the post–9/11 American intervention in Iraq, however, our alignment with American foreign policy became suddenly more tentative, especially for Canadians situated on the left of the political spectrum. This article is part of a series commissioned by *The Nation*, an American news magazine in which "foreign commentators" were to share their reaction to current American foreign policy.

To contrast Atwood's view of the friendship between Canada and the U.S., we have included a short piece by Diana Coulter on the segment, "Talking to Americans" from the television program *This Hour Has 22 Minutes*. In this segment, Canadian comedian Rick Mercer exploits American ignorance about Canada and Canadian issues and demonstrates the unsurprising fact that we know more about them than they do about us. The article first appeared in *The Christian Science Monitor* in 2001.

Margaret Atwood, a Companion of the Order of Canada, is perhaps this country's best-known and most widely read author. Her novels, short stories, and poetry are among the most instantly recognizable in the Canadian literary canon. She has been the recipient of many literary awards, both here and abroad. This epistolary essay appeared in *The Nation* in 2003.

CRITICAL THINKING   How would you define Canada's relationship with the United States?

1   Dear America:

2   This is a difficult letter to write, because I'm no longer sure who you are. Some of you may be having the same trouble.

3   I thought I knew you: We'd become well acquainted over the past fifty-five years. You were the Mickey Mouse and Donald Duck comic books I read in the late 1940s. You were the radio shows—Jack Benny, Our Miss Brooks. You were the music I sang and danced to: the Andrews Sisters, Ella Fitzgerald, the Platters, Elvis. You were a ton of fun.

4   You wrote some of my favorite books. You created Huckleberry Finn, and Hawkeye, and Beth and Jo in Little Women, courageous in their different ways. Later, you were my beloved Thoreau, father of environmentalism, witness to individual conscience; and Walt Whitman, singer of the great Republic; and Emily Dickinson, keeper of the private soul. You were Hammett and Chandler, heroic walkers of mean streets; even later, you were the amazing trio, Hemingway, Fitzgerald and Faulkner, who traced the dark labyrinths of your hidden heart. You were Sinclair Lewis and Arthur Miller, who, with their own American idealism, went after the sham in you, because they thought you could do better.

5   You were Marlon Brando in On the Waterfront, you were Humphrey Bogart in Key Largo, you were Lillian Gish in Night of the Hunter. You stood up for freedom, honesty and justice; you protected the innocent. I believed most of that. I think you did, too. It seemed true at the time.

6   You put God on the money, though, even then. You had a way of thinking that the things of Caesar were the same as the things of God: That gave you self-confidence. You have always wanted to be a city upon a hill, a light to all nations, and for a while you were. Give me your tired, your poor, you sang, and for a while you meant it.

7   We've always been close, you and us. History, that old entangler, has twisted us together since the early seventeenth century. Some of us used to be you; some of us want to be you; some of you used to be us. You are not only our neighbors: In many cases—mine, for instance—you are also our blood relations, our colleagues and our personal friends. But although we've had a ringside seat, we've never understood you completely, up here north of the 49th parallel. We're like Romanized Gauls—look like Romans, dress like Romans, but aren't Romans—peering over the wall at the real Romans. What are they doing? Why? What are they doing now? Why is the haruspex eyeballing the sheep's liver? Why is the soothsayer wholesaling the Bewares?

8   Perhaps that's been my difficulty in writing you this letter: I'm not sure I know what's really going on. Anyway, you have a huge posse of experienced entrail-sifters who do nothing but analyze your every vein and lobe. What can I tell you about yourself that you don't already know?

9   This might be the reason for my hesitation: embarrassment, brought on by a becoming modesty. But it is more likely to be embarrassment of another sort. When my grandmother—from a New England background—was confronted with an unsavory topic, she would change the subject and gaze out the window. And that is my own inclination: Keep your mouth shut, mind your own business.

10   But I'll take the plunge, because your business is no longer merely your business. To paraphrase Marley's Ghost, who figured it out too late, mankind is your business. And vice versa: When the Jolly Green Giant goes on the rampage, many lesser plants and animals get trampled underfoot. As for us, you're our biggest trading partner: We know perfectly well that if you go down the plug-hole, we're going with you. We have every reason to wish you well.

11   I won't go into the reasons why I think your recent Iraqi adventures have been—taking the long view—an ill-advised tactical error. By the time you read this,

Baghdad may or may not be a pancake, and many more sheep entrails will have been examined. Let's talk, then, not about what you're doing to other people but about what you're doing to yourselves.

12   You're gutting the Constitution. Already your home can be entered without your knowledge or permission, you can be snatched away and incarcerated without cause, your mail can be spied on, your private records searched. Why isn't this a recipe for widespread business theft, political intimidation and fraud? I know you've been told that all this is for your own safety and protection, but think about it for a minute. Anyway, when did you get so scared? You didn't used to be easily frightened.

13   You're running up a record level of debt. Keep spending at this rate and pretty soon you won't be able to afford any big military adventures. Either that or you'll go the way of the USSR: lots of tanks, but no air conditioning. That will make folks very cross. They'll be even crosser when they can't take a shower because your shortsighted bulldozing of environmental protections has dirtied most of the water and dried up the rest. Then things will get hot and dirty indeed.

14   You're torching the American economy. How soon before the answer to that will be not to produce anything yourselves but to grab stuff other people produce, at gunboat-diplomacy prices? Is the world going to consist of a few mega-rich King Midases, with the rest being serfs, both inside and outside your country? Will the biggest business sector in the United States be the prison system? Let's hope not.

15   If you proceed much further down the slippery slope, people around the world will stop admiring the good things about you. They'll decide that your city upon the hill is a slum and your democracy is a sham, and therefore you have no business trying to impose your sullied vision on them. They'll think you've abandoned the rule of law. They'll think you've fouled your own nest.

16   The British used to have a myth about King Arthur. He wasn't dead, but sleeping in a cave, it was said; and in the country's hour of greatest peril, he would return. You too have great spirits of the past you may call upon: men and women of courage, of conscience, of prescience. Summon them now, to stand with you, to inspire you, to defend the best in you. You need them.

Canucks Are Full of Yuks at Yankee Blunders

Diana Coulter

1   The rhinoceros roams the Canadian hinterland, the hockey puck adorns Canada's flag, and this country is led by Prime Minister Jean Poutine. Or so many Americans, standing before Canadian TV crews, will swear.

2   Canucks have long suspected that Americans know little about their largest trading partner and cultural cousins to the north. Now, a comedy show

has apparently proved the point with a segment called "Talking to Americans," and the gag is gathering record-breaking audiences of shocked and delighted Canadians.

3   Part of a weekly show called *This Hour Has 22 Minutes*, the segment features comedian Rick Mercer as a newsman traveling the U.S. to conduct "man on the street" interviews on a range of bogus topics. The show is so popular that producers recently compiled them into an hour-long special. The show drew an audience of 2.7 million, making it the highest-rated TV comedy ever aired by the government-funded Canadian Broadcasting Corporation.

4   In the show, a Harvard University professor signs a petition to protest "the Canadian government's decision to resume the Saskatchewan seal hunt." (Everyone knows Saskatchewan is a land-locked prairie province . . . right?)

5   Enthusiastic Americans congratulate Canada for opening its first university recently, getting its first volunteer fire station, adding Grade 9 to schools, getting FM radio, permitting the Irish to vote, and allowing dogs as house pets.

6   A young man at New York University is outraged when told that 70 percent of Canadian Grade 7 students can't name their congressman or find their home states on a map (because Canada has neither states nor a Congress). "It's disgraceful that people are unaware of the world they live in," he says with disgust.

7   At New York City's Columbia University, students and a professor sign a petition demanding an end "to the Canadian tradition of placing senior citizens on northern ice flows, leaving them to perish."

8   Geoff D'Eon, the producer and director of "Talking to Americans," says the show works "because we exploit two things: the boundless ignorance of folks south of the border about Canada, and the great generosity of these people toward Canadians. Americans tend to be very friendly, open people who are, by and large, very opinionated."

9   Beneath the humor, "Talking to Americans" taps into an age-old inferiority complex often felt by the smaller partner in an economic relationship. "Let's face it. Why should the elephant know about the mouse?" he says. "All I know is that it somehow speaks very loudly to Canadians. It's not a consciousness-raising exercise or anything. It's just a joke, and we get paid to make Canadians laugh. It's as simple as that."

10   Whether it intends to have a real political impact or not, the show has made some bona fide news headlines. During the recent U.S. presidential campaigns, candidates George W. Bush and Al Gore were deftly skewered by Mercer gags.

11   Told his campaign was being endorsed by Canadian Prime Minister Jean Poutine, Mr. Bush said he was "honored" without realizing that the Canadian leader's name is Chretien, not "poutine," a French-Canadian dish of french fries, gravy, and cheese. Mr. Gore was caught when he didn't correct Mercer for suggesting that Canada's capital city is Toronto, not Ottawa.

12   A few US governors have also been duped. Arkansas Gov. Mike Huckabee congratulated Canada on preserving its "national igloo," which he

was told was a frozen copy of Washington's Capitol building. Iowa Gov. Tom Vilsack was pleased to hear Canada had finally switched from a 20- to 24-hour clock, so as not to confuse American tourists.

13   John Thompson, a Canadian studies professor at Duke University in North Carolina, says he's seen "Talking to Americans" and thinks it's "very funny, but not very fair. I think you could probably fool Canadians the same way, if you dressed someone up in a suit and gave them a microphone," he says. "Soon enough, you'd have Canadians congratulating Americans for executing their 5,000th inmate or some such thing."

14   Mr. Thompson, a Canadian who has lived in the US for 15 years, says "dissing Americans is a vital part of the Canadian identity. It's not a bad thing really, because most newer countries' identities are created by contrasting with others," he says.

15   While Canada is no newer than the US, the concept of "defining Canadian identity" is much more prevalent here. The American identity in the 19th century was equally oppositional, Thompson explains. "Back then, Americans were obsessed with comparing themselves to Europeans and standing up to the English, in particular."

16   Canadians know more about Americans than vice versa because they're constantly exposed to a multitude of US television shows, says Thompson, who is vaguely apologetic for recently becoming an American citizen. "I know how that will go over in Canada," he laughs.

17   Julie Commerford, still an American after living in Toronto for 15 years, says that when she first moved here, "Canadians were a little hostile to me. It's true that we're not taught a lot about Canada in American schools, but don't hold it against me just because I don't know how many provinces there are," says Ms. Commerford.

18   Still, she finds "Talking to Americans" extremely funny. "That bit about Jean Poutine—I just had to laugh out loud," she says. "But at the same time, I was a bit embarrassed that my countrymen don't know who Canada's leader is."

FREEWRITING ASSIGNMENT ─────────────────

Think about the American cultural icons you've grown up with, such as cartoon characters, musicians, or even product brands. How do you feel about these icons now? Have your feelings for these figures changed? Why?

CRITICAL READING

1. Margaret Atwood's "Letter to America" is an epistolary essay; that is, it's written in the form of a letter, in this case not to an individual recipient but rather to an entire country. How would Atwood's message change if she had chosen another form for this text? Would a different form be as effective?

2. What does Atwood say about the Canadian national "character" in this letter?

3. When Atwood compares the United States to the Jolly Green Giant in paragraph 10, what is her intent? Do you think this is an apt metaphor for her topic? Why or why not?
4. In Atwood's opinion, what is America's "sullied vision"?
5. Identify several of Atwood's rhetorical questions. How do they help to support her central claim?
6. In "Canucks Are Full of Yuks at Yankee Blunders," Canadian Studies Professor John Thompson claims that "dissing Americans is a vital part of the Canadian identity." Would you agree with this statement? How might it relate to Atwood's letter? Is she "dissing" America in her own way? How might an American reader answer that question?
7. How, according to John Thompson, is the formation of national identities an "oppositional" process?
8. Compare how much we know about America in "Letter to America" to how much Americans would appear to know about Canadians in "Canucks Are Full of Yucks at Yankee Blunders." Is the friendship Atwood writes about as close as she would have us believe?

CRITICAL WRITING

9. *Exploratory Writing*: The invasion of Iraq was the American policy decision that precipitated the writing of this text. As an American, write an open letter to Canada that corresponds to Atwood's letter. Make clear that your reason for writing is Canada's refusal to support the American decision to take military action in Iraq.
10. *Exploratory Writing*: What are the traditional American values that Atwood believes are eroding? What does she suggest has replaced these values? Write an essay that considers how this affects Canada and Canadians.

GROUP PROJECTS

11. In a group, compile a list of Canadian cultural icons. What image of Canada do these icons portray? How is this different from the way their American counterparts portray that country? Present your findings to the class.
12. Regarding "Talking to Americans," John Thompson suggests that "you could probably fool Canadians the same way. . . ." Do you agree? With your group, compose a list of false statements about the United States that you believe most Americans would be able to identify as such (e.g., the capital of California is Los Angeles; the vice-president is Condoleezza Rice; the average annual snowfall in Arkansas is 80 mm, etc.). You may have to research some statements to be sure you have the correct answer. Distribute your questionnaire to friends and family, or deliver it verbally in the form of a game show. If possible, videotape the results and present

them to the class. Do your victims fare better than the Americans on Mercer's show? What do the results suggest about Rick Mercer's formula in *Talking to Americans*?

Immigrants Isolated? Tell That to Their Children

Rosie DiManno

In March, 2004, Statistics Canada released a report warning about "the isolation of visible minority neighbourhoods in Canada's largest cities." Rosie DiManno suspects that what StatsCan sees as a problem is in fact a natural part of the process of cultural integration. When immigrants come to Canada they naturally look for communities whose language, history, and values coincide with their own. But the children of these immigrants seek no such security, as their upbringing combines both cultures. We should, therefore, think twice before judging the "isolation" of neighbourhoods of first-generation immigrants. There are social factors that work against the mingling and assimilation of immigrants in this country, but these are largely obviated by the second generation, who may carefully preserve aspects of their parents' culture, but who consider Canada their home.

Rosie DiManno is a columnist for *The Toronto Star*, from which this article was taken on March 15, 2004.

CRITICAL THINKING

Think about the immigrant experience in Canada. Do you feel it takes immigrants a long time to be accepted? Do they assimilate quickly, or does the process take generations to complete? Explain.

1 I liken the immigrant neighbourhood where I grew up to a jawbreaker, the orbicular candy that used to cost a penny from a bubblegum dispenser, changing hues and flavours the longer you sucked on it.

2 A more gifted writer would probably come up with a better metaphor, a more elegant way to describe the generational metamorphosis of a community that was sequentially transformed by every ethnic wave that settled within its ragged boundaries. The urban neighbourhood as a recycled oil canvas, perhaps; a painting that, when scratched, reveals an earlier piece of work beneath the surface patina.

3 At the centre of the jawbreaker was English Canada, which in my west-end enclave of Toronto meant blue-collar Irish and Scots, although not so dominant as they were elsewhere in the city. Then, in succeeding layers, came the Jews and the Italians, the Germans, the Greeks, the more ambiguous—to me—Eastern Europeans, the blacks, and then later the Chinese, the East Indians, the Koreans, and so on. A rubric of what would become multicultural Canada, although none of us

thought of it then in those terms, this being the era before Multiculturalism became capitalized and politicized and hyphenated in its ethnic subdivisions.

4   We may have lived within our ethnic pockets—Little Italy or Little Greece and the like—because that is the natural tendency for immigrants venturing into a new world, seeking the sheltering embrace of the known in an unknown environment, a niche where people speak your language and eat your food, share your beliefs and understand your cultural otherness. This companionship of like to like took the edge off our strangeness, allowed us to feel less alien.

5   It was, and remains, the normal coalescing of newcomers who huddle in cultural clans—for at least one generation, or a part of a generation, before the native-born offspring of immigrants begin to assert their own imperatives on the dichotomy of the family, on their transplanted parents. This is the normal rhythm of the immigrant experience, although apparently a concept poorly understood by the authors of a Statistics Canada report released last week that warned about the isolation of visible minority neighbourhoods in Canada's largest cities where segregation, it claims, has become entrenched.

6   I suspect the problem, if one exists (and I'm not broadly convinced of this), is largely about time—not giving these uprooted and transplanted constituencies enough of it before expecting that they become something else entirely, particularly if they come from non-European, non-white countries with their own millennia of traditions, where attitudes have been shaped by vastly different experiences, where the liberal virtues we cherish in Canada do not have the same traction, indeed where they are viewed with suspicion and alarm.

7   What's also problematic, I think, is that Canada has devalued the concept of assimilation, promoting instead a mosaic of ethnic identification that is inherently splintering and isolationist, emphasizing as it does the details that make us different rather than the aspirations that make us so much the same.

8   The ethnic neighbourhood—the cultural ghetto, as clearly disapproved by the StatsCan report—was like the warmth of a womb for post-war immigrants only a decade removed from a global conflagration, and surely no less so for more recent arrivals fleeing other tyrannies, other unpromising futures. Those of us born here as first-generation offspring, as gestated Canadians, sprang from this same amniotic sac of cultural nourishment but grew up rapidly absorbing the dominant ethos, pining to assimilate, glad to shed old country peculiarities. I see little evidence that a new generation of made-in-Canada Canadians feels greatly different.

9   It was harder for our parents, and no wonder, but they tried, they did try. We were a polyglot of peoples, fusing gradually, by osmosis, by a generosity of spirit that found its expression in church, at christenings and weddings where neighbours of different backgrounds were welcome, in the exchange of ethnic food—have some homemade wine, try this strudel—in the early and quite scandalous phenomenon of intermarriage and, most critically, in the public schools attended by that first generation of immigrant children. We were Canadian tadpoles, swimming into the mainstream, even within the ethnic patchwork of our neighbourhoods.

10   The street where I lived was primarily Italian in the '60s, a post-war influx that steadily displaced the Jewish families that had converged there previously. I remember

my mother using a knife to remove the mezuzahs that former owners had affixed on the doorframes in our house on Grace St. But when my parents arrived in the neighbourhood, the Jewish presence was still strong and our existences overlapped. Remarkably, there was very little clash of culture. My father worked for a Jewish-owned construction company; my mother worked in a Jewish-owned industrial laundry on Shaw St. For two decades, that Jewish family spent Christmas with our extended Italian family. I don't recall any resentment, on my parents' part, toward this earlier wave of immigrants who had preceded them up the economic ladder. We wanted more to emulate their success than grumble about it.

11   Our separate cultures, confident within their own essence, were not averse to engaging with each other. It was the overlapping, I think, that encouraged this engagement and made us less alien to each other, certainly less threatening.

12   Maybe that, in its clumsy and unsophisticated fashion, is what the StatsCan report was trying to get at. But the isolation indexes applied in this overview put too much emphasis on where people live and too little on how they live, where their lives intersect, socially and economically. It is entirely normal for a Jamaican family, say, to patronize a Jamaican grocers or for an Indian family to buy from an Indian retailer. It's natural to hire one another, to support one another's business ventures, even to gather in social clubs and puzzle over this weird thing called Canadian society.

13   Perhaps it was indeed easier, in another time, to mingle with different cultures, when most families lived in tidy houses and couples strolled along the street at night, neighbours stopping to chat in variously accented English on one another's front stoop. Those high-rise suburban clusters are not conducive to neighbourliness. But the children of newer immigrants still, overwhelmingly, go to school with one another, watch the same TV shows, listen to the same pop music, have the same rebellious conflicts with their parents. It is the segregation of religious-based schools and the imposition of ethnocentric exclusivity on young social groups that should be discouraged.

14   But, you know what? The children of immigrants, straddling two cultures, inevitably turn away from their parents' experience and assert their own commingled identity. The ethnicity becomes diluted. They will keep the bits that they value and discard the rest. It has always been thus, one generation to the next.

15   Just give it time.

FREEWRITING ASSIGNMENT

Describe the neighbourhood in which you grew up or in which you currently live. How has it changed? How have your feelings about it changed?

CRITICAL READING

1. Rosie DiManno opens with a metaphor, comparing the immigrant neighbourhood where she grew up to a jawbreaker. What is this metaphor meant to suggest? How do these images foreshadow her thesis? Is this an effective opening for her essay?

2. In paragraph 3, the author suggests that multiculturalism in Canada has become "capitalized and politicized and hyphenated in its ethnic subdivisions." What does this mean?

3. DiManno refers disapprovingly to "the imposition of ethnocentric exclusivity on young social groups" in paragraph 13. What does she mean by this? Who is doing the imposing? What harm is done through this imposition?

4. What is implied by the last line of this essay?

5. In paragraph 4, DiManno says that in her youth, new immigrants to Canada "lived within [their] ethnic pockets. . . ." What reasons does she give for this tendency? In your experience, has the concentration of immigrant populations changed over the years? What does this imply?

6. What does the author identify as the problem with the Statistics Canada report in paragraph 12?

CRITICAL WRITING

7. *Research and Exploratory Writing*: Research the history of a neighbourhood in your community that has been traditionally associated with an immigrant population. Write a brief essay about how this neighbourhood has evolved over the last century. If possible, find photographs that reflect this evolution.

8. *Research and Exploratory Writing*: Online and in the library, research autobiographical material by immigrant writers now based in Canada. What is their experience of assimilation into Canadian society? Was this a goal, or was it important to maintain a strong identification with the culture of origin? Do these writers discuss the previous or subsequent generations? How do their attitudes differ from one another?

GROUP PROJECTS

9. It is generally accepted that regarding immigration, the United States is a "melting pot"; that is, immigrants to that country are expected to assimilate into the mainstream of American society. (The motto *e pluribus unum*, "out of many, one," dates from 1776, and though its specific reference is to the original 13 colonies that combined to form the nation, it has also come to be associated with the idea of a single, strong country composed of individuals and communities of many national and ethnic backgrounds, united in the desire to live in the kind of society espoused by the American political system.) Canada, on the other hand, is known for its "cultural mosaic," encouraging immigrants to retain their cultural identities rather than blending in with a more or less European-descended mainstream. This attitude would presumably result in the mainstream being influenced and modified over generations by many different cultures, resulting in a national profile that would accurately reflect its population.

Divide your group into two countries, the United States and Canada. In a debate, defend your country's attitude toward cultural assimilation.

10. Read the text of Emma Lazarus's "The New Colossus":

> Not like the brazen giant of Greek fame
> With conquering limbs astride from land to land;
> Here at our sea-washed, sunset gates shall stand
> A mighty woman with a torch, whose flame
> Is the imprisoned lightning, and her name
> Mother of Exiles. From her beacon-hand
> Glows world-wide welcome; her mild eyes command
> The air-bridged harbor that twin cities frame,
> "Keep, ancient lands, your storied pomp!" cries she
> With silent lips. "Give me your tired, your poor,
> Your huddled masses yearning to breathe free,
> The wretched refuse of your teeming shore,
> Send these, the homeless, tempest-tossed to me,
> I lift my lamp beside the golden door!"

You may recognize this sonnet, written in 1883, as the inscription on the base of the Statue of Liberty in New York Harbor, meant as a symbolic welcome to immigrants to the United States. What attitude is evidenced in this poem? Do you believe that in the intervening years that attitude has changed? If so, how?

Could this sonnet serve as a welcome to Canadian immigrants? What changes might be necessary? With your group, write a poem that could be inscribed on a statue in the harbours of Halifax, Montreal, or Vancouver, welcoming immigrants to Canada. Share it with the other groups in the class.

VIEWPOINTS

▶ **To Canada With Love**
Ken Victor

▶ **Coming Here Was a Mistake**
Raj Mazumdar

In Canada, Ken Victor has found the familiar geographical and social markers of his native United States—but improved in their Canadian incarnation. So impressed is Victor with his adopted country that he abandons the usual essay format for an embellished list of Canada's wonders as seen through an outsider's eyes.

Canada enjoys the reputation internationally of being one of the best places in the world to live. For this reason, we tend to believe that any immigrant narrative that ends in Canada must therefore end happily. This is not always the case, as Raj Mazumdar shows in his article.

While Canada's immigration policy appears to welcome newcomers to share in the advantages of living in this country, there are laws and rules still in place that can make getting a start here both difficult and disheartening. As surprising as it may seem, there is a segment of the immigrant population who simply decides to turn around and go home, or to seek another country whose education and employment regulations are less hostile to new residents.

Ken Victor, who became a Canadian in 2003, is a management consultant in Chelsea. His article is from *The Montreal Gazette*, June 27, 2004. Raj Mazumdar works for an employment agency that supplies contract workers to Calgary companies. His piece appeared in *The Calgary Herald* in May 2004.

 ## To Canada with Love

Ken Victor

1   When I first moved up here 12 years ago, I was surprised to learn that Canada Day happens just before July 4th. I thought you wanted simply to beat us Americans to the punch. Canada Day might be a few days earlier, I thought, but, hey, we'll always do a celebration bigger and better than you. (Thinking like a true American, I was.)

2   Well, after 12 years, I've decided it's time to fess up—I love this place. And this year, I'm finally going to focus on Canada Day, my first one as a Canadian. July 4th, I'll call up the family in the States to say hello, but the party will be on Canada Day. Here are 12 reasons why.

3   Your Electoral Process. At this time last year, the campaign for the U.S. presidency was already under way. We Americans might be efficient at some things but election campaigns aren't one of them. Canada, your warp-speed campaigns are a thing of beauty. It's so short that candidates can practically make a new promise every day, pollsters can go hog-wild, newspapers can add special campaign sections and then—boom!—it's all over. We can get back to our regular lives. You might or might not like tomorrow's results, but you gotta love the speed. Just like a good hockey game.

4   Your health-care system. My third child was born prematurely weighing 1 lb., 4 oz. I was so scared and confused that I went on-line to find communities of parents experiencing the same thing. The only topic parents from the U.S. could focus on was what their insurance covered and didn't cover. Not Canadians. They wanted to talk about what mattered: prognosis, treatments, risks. Canada, I don't know how much those three months of intensive care in the hospital and four years of follow-up cost, but believe me, I am forever grateful. You can tax me as much as you want. I'll never complain. I know I'll never pay off how selflessly your medical system was there for us when we needed it. And I have a healthy 6-year-old daughter to prove it.

5   Your lakes and rivers. If you haven't been in them or on them, can you be Canadian? Your water is what brought me up here in the first place. You've got big untamed rivers swimming with hungry fish and vast empty lakes waiting for the wind to turn them into a froth of waves. Canada, your fresh water has spoiled me— how many times I've been able to paddle alone on a sky-blue lake without a cottage in sight. And, heck, I was on a river trip where we didn't see another soul for 23 days. That is the big lonesome. It's beautiful, it's empty and it's calling you.

6   The gun registry, decriminalizing marijuana, approving gay marriages. First, let me come clean here and state my biases: I think it's idiocy to lock people up for toking on a joint, a greater idiocy for allowing everybody who doesn't toke to arm themselves to the hilt and more than a bit foolish to legalize only those committed relationships that have certain approved combinations of genitalia. That said, I'm not celebrating these because I think they're particularly wise, effective or moral. Nope, I name these because—to paraphrase Dorothy—they let me know I'm not living in Kansas anymore. Could you imagine any of these taking root in Kansas? Not on your life, Bubba. So Canada, go for it. It makes you you.

7   Your government ads. Let me get this straight: Federal departments actually run ads on TV about their services and benefits? You must be joking! The first time I saw one I was so baffled I had to ask friends what I'd just seen. Clearly, these departments believe they're part of the solution. They actually invite you to use their services. I'm for any country that believes government has a positive contribution to make.

8   Your bureaucrats. Living in the Ottawa area, I've come to know some of these people. Not what I expected. Some of these folks work awfully hard. Too hard, in fact. If truth be known, they're workaholics. They're a dedicated and conscientious lot. And why? I guess they think they have to live up to the billing in those ads. These folks put in the honest 9 to 5 and then some. Any country would be only too happy to replace their public servants with Canada's. OK, I'll admit they're not perfect; after all, money has disappeared. But hey, wasn't it one of the bureaucrats who blew the whistle on the lack of perfection in the first place?

9   Your political parties. "What," you might ask in shock. "Are you crazed?" Probably, but that's beside the point. It is simply because you have them. I grew up in an either-or world. Either Republicans or Democrats. Here, you've got either-or-or-or-or-or (if I can include the Green Party). Now and then, a third candidate shows up on the American stage, but everyone knows they're going to be yanked off before too long. The truth is following political parties in the States is like living with nothing but 100 years of Bruins-Rangers games. Up here, you've simply got more teams to watch. Keeps it interesting.

10   The Rockies. Maybe the summer traffic slows down in some of the parks a bit too much, but when the cause is people craning their necks to look at what the word "grandeur" was invented for, who can complain? And having to stop because an elk with antlers as wide as your rivers (See reason No. 4) has ambled onto the road is nothing less than a moment of grace. Notice I'm not even talking about what you can see if you get out of your car and head into that immensity! A gift of beauty for all of us to enjoy.

11   Curling. I don't have a clue when it comes to curling. Never saw *Men with Brooms*, the movie or the reality. I figure that any country that buries NBA news inside the sports section so it can lead with a curling story has to be in on some important secret. What finally won me over, however, was when you made a national hero out of a woman curler who won an Olympic gold medal. Something in the way you then mourned her too-early death was heartbreaking even for me. Hockey might be your national sport, but something tells me your relationship with curling is about your national soul.

12   Quebec. It's a place apart, isn't it, in the very best sense of that phrase. Is it a distinct culture? You bet. I'm glad I've been a bit around it, married one of its daughters and am having my kids educated in French. Let's face it: English Canada's more button-down decorum is nicely balanced by Quebec's joie de vivre—good wine, good humour, and you can even light up a cigarette without being banished to the nether regions of Pluto. What has me most appreciative isn't just Quebec, but rather it's the number of Canadians I've met in outposts far from "the French fact" who want their children to be bilingual, who want to have an immersion program of some sort in their school system. It's a kind of cultural appreciation that's particularly touching when one comes from a land where Texans and New Yorkers live in separate, parallel universes.

13   Your introspection. Ah Canada, what would you be without the questions you constantly ask yourself? Questions like "what exactly does it mean to be Canadian?" and, of course, "what exactly does it mean to be Canadian?" You ask that a lot, and loudly. I think you even know you're never going to come up with the answer, mainly because the truth of the matter is that the question is the answer. And I love you for it.

14   Canada, I hope you'll join me in celebrating you. I could, of course, continue with more reasons, but instead I'm going to mosey on down to one of your rivers with my wife and kids, pop open one of your beers (reason No. 12) and give thanks I'm up here.

15   Happy birthday!

 # Coming Here Was A Mistake
Raj Mazumdar

1 There is a myth about the Canadian Experience—that this country has virtually unlimited opportunity. But for new immigrants like me, the term Canadian Experience has taken on a whole new meaning.

2   When I was still living in India, I met an accountant who had emigrated to Canada. He bitterly complained that he had blisters on his hands from washing piles of dishes in a fast-food joint. I dismissed that as a one-off case. My visa interview with the Canadian High Commission went quite well—they indicated I could get a job as soon as I arrived—and my wife, Arpita, and I were elated when we were

approved. It was time for us to give our career an international touch. Calgary was our preferred destination, because we have some acquaintances here and we were well aware of the booming economy.

3   We arrived in Calgary in June 2001, full of optimism. Within the first month of arriving, we got our first big jolt. Many job applications I submitted didn't get me to the interview stage, apparently because employment agencies did not believe I would be able to speak English well. Perhaps discrimination has taken shape as the underestimation of an individual's capabilities.

4   Someone suggested I shorten my name to make it more trendy here to avoid that, but it is my only inheritance from my proud parents and it took me quite a while to come to terms with such an idea.

5   My chosen profession is human resources, which I trained for by earning a bachelor's degree in psychology from the University of Calcutta, a state school, and an internationally accredited post-graduate diploma in human resources management from India. But employment agencies made me feel as if I were applying for a job with NASA. After the optimistic employment view given by the Canadian High Commission, I began to feel like a child who has been abandoned by its adoptive parents. Two-and-a-half years later, I have a low-paying job in an unrelated field. Arpita found work in the customer service field, and her steady income has enabled us to stay.

6   Here's what my experience has taught me: It is a logical goal for the Canadian government to seek foreign workers to plug prospective labour shortages in a projected profession. But, the incoming labour is not being used for the profession intended. Instead, quite a number of the immigrants use Canada as a stepping-stone to migrate to greener pastures—the U.S.—where they are convinced they will get better jobs. The majority of immigrants who stay in Canada will either end up as office cleaners or cab drivers, and will be frustrated in their desire to practise their own profession. I would surely like to know how much the government is paying for stress-related disorders experienced by new immigrants.

7   To improve my chances at employment, I enrolled in a human resources management program at the University of Calgary. I was not surprised to learn the same human resources techniques are being taught here as are taught in India. Of course, every organization has its own customs and it goes without saying that one has to adapt to them quickly. It is quite understandable that one has to be open in one's learning habits whenever there is a switch—be it in a position, job, organization, province or even a wider scenario, like moving to a new country.

8   But, underpaid and not working in my field of expertise, I now consider my move the mistake of a lifetime. After saving up a fortune just to come here, we have some jaw-dropping additions to our expense accounts with a high home mortgage, car insurance and, now, golfing lessons—because apparently that skill is necessary to get ahead.

9   Quite recently, I happened to come across a recruitment advertisement that read: "New Immigrants are welcome—will train." That's the spirit that we expected out of employers here. I am sure every one of the immigrants would support me when I say that all we need are employers willing to give us a fair chance and not go by their mental blocks, setting a resume aside because the name of a visible minority is on it.

10   I wish the Canadian High Commission had advised us to change our names to "Barry" or "Tom" before we set foot here. If the government is going to encourage people to move to this country, it must have a program in place to rectify employers' attitude[s] towards new immigrants. Having a mandatory intake and a paid training program for new immigrants in organizations of 100 employees or more would definitely help the cause.

11   I sincerely hope that Human Resources Development Canada acknowledges the problem and has some strategy in place to counter it. We have already started to gauge the consequences in the impending scarcity of doctors in the province and this is just the beginning. I hope that with some positive thinking and some sincere and honest endeavours, we can get over this issue.

CRITICAL THINKING   What do you think an immigrant to Canada might expect of this country upon arriving here? Do you believe that Canada is meeting these expectations in terms of employment, social integration, and standard of living?

FREEWRITING ASSIGNMENT

Compare Ken Victor's feelings about the Canadian experience in "To Canada with Love" to those of Raj Mazumdar in "Coming Here Was a Mistake." How do you think Mazumdar would respond to Victor's glowing evaluation of Canada? How might being an immigrant from the United States be different from being one from another part of the world, such as India?

CRITICAL READING

1. Analyze the tone of both essays. How does the tone influence the message that each author is trying to convey? Explain, using examples from the texts.
2. In his opening, Mazumdar claims that one myth about the Canadian experience is that it suggests that Canada has virtually unlimited opportunities. Do you feel that unlimited opportunity is a part of the Canadian experience? If, like Mazumdar, you feel that it's a fallacy, who created it and for what purpose?
3. How do both authors use personal experience to make their points? Is this technique effective? Explain.
4. Mazumdar mentions taking golf lessons "because apparently that skill is necessary to get ahead." How would this skill help his job search?
5. What suggestion does Mazumdar make regarding the mandatory hiring of new immigrants? Do you find this a reasonable recommendation? Why or why not?

6. List some examples of how Ken Victor uses humour to communicate his message. Does this use of humour weaken or enhance his argument?

CRITICAL WRITING

7. *Persuasive Writing*: Choose one of Victor's points and write a response in which you disagree with his assertion.
8. *Research and Persuasive Writing*: Raj Mazumdar would qualify for Canadian immigration as a skilled worker due to such factors as his command of the English language, his work experience, and his education. Go to the Canadian Immigration and Citizenship Web site at **www.cic.gc.ca/ english/skilled/index.html** to see how the rules of admission for skilled workers have changed. In an essay, argue whether you think these new rules are fair.
9. *Research and Exploratory Writing*: Speak with someone you know who has immigrated to Canada. How did their expectations—especially regarding employment—differ from the reality of living here? If he or she has a university degree in the country of origin, was appropriate work available here for that person? Does your respondent have any regrets about coming to this county? If so, what are they?

GROUP PROJECTS

10. Ken Victor asserts that one of the things that he admires about Canada is the questions that we constantly ask ourselves as a nation, particularly, "What exactly does it mean to be a Canadian?" As a group, discuss possible answers to this question and develop a definition. If you were to answer this question for a foreign visitor, what would you say? How do you think J.B. MacKinnon, author of "I Am Anti-Canadian," might answer the question?
11. Assign a country to each group member, and find out how easy or difficult it would be for a Canadian to emigrate to that country. You may contact the country's consulate or embassy, and research personal narratives online. Does the country have a generally open immigration policy, or is it restricted? Is there a quota system? A point system? If so, give details. Are there age, ethnic, or education requirements? Does the country require financial guarantees? A personal or work sponsor? Is there a refugee program? How difficult or disruptive to your life would emigration to that country be? What changes in your quality of life could you expect in return? Present your findings to the class and compare your information with other groups. Which countries appear to be most welcoming to immigrants, and which are the most restrictive? Investigate the specifics of Canada's immigration policy. How do we stack up in the international community in terms of our willingness to accept immigrants?

RESEARCH ISSUE

Canadian Content Regulations
Tough Rules Stand Guard over Canadian Culture
Anthony DePalma

In Canada, many believe that our unique position in relation to the United States and our rav-enous appetite for American popular culture represent a dangerous challenge to the develop-ment of Canadian talent and even to the survival of Canadian popular culture as a whole. For this reason, Canada has cultural content regulations. These rules and measures attempt to limit the domination of American culture while encouraging Canadian culture to flourish. In this article, Anthony DePalma writes about the problems Canada encounters in trying to legis-late cultural content.

Anthony DePalma was the first foreign correspondent of *The New York Times* to serve as bureau chief in both Mexico and Canada. His book, *Here: A Biography of the New American Continent* (2001), was published in the United States and Canada in 2001. This article appeared in *The New York Times* on July 14, 1999.

1 Lenny Kravitz's raunchy remake of the '70s classic "American Woman" had been thoroughly dissected, and the music director of Toronto's CHUM-FM radio station was satisfied that it was, indeed, Canadian. Surprising, since neither the singer nor the subject of the song has a direct connection to the Great White North. But the music and anti-American lyrics—reflecting common Canadian views—were writ-ten by members of the Guess Who, a popular Canadian band of the 1970s. That gives "American Woman" the two points it needs under Canada's intricate system of rankings to help meet CHUM-FM's government-imposed requirement that 35 percent of its daytime playlist be devoted to Canadian content.

2 Determining what to do with "Baby Feel My . . ." by Patria, a young Filipino artist, was not so easy. "She came to Canada at age 2, but I think she's a landed immigrant now," said Barry Stewart, CHUM-FM's music director, as the weekly music meeting dragged on. "That makes her Canadian, right?"

3 Welcome to the bizarre world of Canadian cultural regulation, a sometimes arbitrary, often contradictory system of rules and measures cobbled together over several decades to protect Canadian culture—not just music but film, television, magazines and literature—from what some Canadians consider the menace of American cultural imperialism. Canada is not alone in trying to draw a Maginot line against Mickey, Rambo and Homer Simpson. France requires theaters to reserve 20 weeks of screen time a year for French feature films. Australia demands that 55 per-cent of a television broadcaster's schedule be filled with domestic programs. And while Mexico allows foreign films to be shown, with subtitles in Spanish, it does not

allow them to be dubbed because that would increase the mass appeal of new Hollywood films in a country where literacy rates are low.

4   By most counts Canada is the Death Star of cultural fortifications, bristling with regulatory armaments to preserve what little is left of its own cultural territory. But at a glance it might appear the battle is already lost. Eighty percent of what Canadians watch on television, outside of news, comes from the United States. So do up to 80 percent of English-language magazines on Canadian newsstands; 65 percent of the songs heard on the radio, 60 percent of English books and 95 percent of feature films. No other country is so vulnerable to invasion by the American colossus. Except for the French-speaking province of Quebec, Canada shares the same language with the United States and is separated from its loud neighbor to the south by a peaceful, 3,000-mile border that is largely invisible. Where cultural differences exist, they tend to be subtle.

5   At the same time, few people in the world match Canadians' appetite for American cultural goods, everything from Walt Disney to "Fresh Prince of Bel Air." And Canadians enjoy being a part of a cultural scene much larger than their own population of 30 million people, spread over a vast and wild continent, could ever support. Thus, as barriers are thrown up to keep Hollywood from dominating the Canadian scene, both Vancouver and Toronto welcome film production crews with incentives and a cheap Canadian dollar to dress up Canadian streets to look like New York and Chicago. The efforts have been so successful that the Screen Actors Guild in the United States estimates that Canada lured away the equivalent of almost 19,000 full-time film production jobs last year. It has vowed to get them back.

6   Critics say the maze of cultural restrictions really is intended to protect the 700,000 Canadians who depend on culture for their jobs. But those like Norman Jewison, the director of "Moonstruck" and "Fiddler on the Roof," argue that much more is at stake. "This isn't just cars or refrigerators for sale; this is ideas," Jewison said. "And when you start exporting ideas, philosophies, behavior, products, ways of living, it becomes an assault on the culture. Americans have to understand that."

7   It isn't always clear that Americans do, especially since entertainment is now one of the most important United States exports. For Washington, every question involving culture and trade has assumed enormous importance because of the impact it might have on business. For example, the office of the U.S. trade representative threatened to start a trade war over a proposed Canadian law intended to protect Canadian magazines. The law would have made it a criminal offense for Canadian companies to take out advertisements in the Canadian edition of American magazines like *Sports Illustrated*. Canada's position is that domestic magazines are important conveyors of Canadian voices and will be undercut if Americans can simply place a maple leaf on a magazine cover, call it a Canadian edition and sell cut-rate advertising that would otherwise go to Canadian magazines. The Americans respond that if magazines are so important, Canada can subsidize outright; otherwise, free trade laws mean that the market is open to all comers. After months of argument, Canada's cultural minister, Sheila Copps, agreed to allow Canadians to provide up to 18 percent of the advertising in an American magazine. The percentage could increase only if more than half the content of the magazine is Canadian.

8   Ms. Copps was pilloried from coast to coast for selling out Canadian culture, although the compromise represented a crack in Washington's defense against cultural restrictions. "This decision gives France and other countries the opportunity to argue that the precedent of taking cultural considerations into account has already been set," said William S. Merkin, a former U.S. deputy chief trade negotiator.

9   In defending itself against brashly aggressive American culture, Canada sometimes seems like a fastidious gardener who fumes and fusses over the riot of dandelions on his neighbor's lawn while realizing that ultimately there is little he can do to keep them from encroaching on his property. But that doesn't keep him from trying. Elaborate systems have developed to preserve a portion of the culture market for Canadian products, and they are largely considered here to have been successful in helping the nation break out of its colonial dependence—first on Britain, then on the United States—and develop its own creative universe.

10   Celine Dion, Shania Twain, Alanis Morissette, Sarah McLachlan, Bryan Adams, the Tragically Hip and the Barenaked Ladies are all Canadian stars in the music field. In film, Mike Myers, Jim Carrey, David Cronenberg, Atom Egoyan, James Cameron and Norman Jewison share Canadian roots. Television programs like "The Outer Limits" and, until recently, "The X-Files," have been filmed in Canada. In literature, Margaret Atwood and Alice Munro have been joined by a stable of accomplished writers including Michael Ondaatje, Rohinton Mistry and Guy Vanderhaeghe. What is less clear is the degree to which the system of percentages and regulation is responsible for such cultural blossoming. Many Canadian pop stars signed contracts with major labels after leaving Canada, suggesting that the Canadian content regulations cannot be credited with their success.

11   In fact, stars like Ms. Dion are penalized by the regulations. The point system for determining Canadian content goes by the acronym MAPL—music, artist, production, lyrics—and assigns one point for each category where a Canadian is predominantly involved. At least two points are required for a record to be treated as Canadian. So while Rod Stewart's "Rhythm of My Heart" is accorded the two points because the music and lyrics were written by Mark Jordan, a Canadian, Celine Dion's hit "My Heart Will Go On" from the movie "Titanic" cannot be counted in a radio station's quota for Canadian content because it gets only one point, for the artist.

12   The Canadian content rule also creates a kind of musical ghetto in which songs that are not popular enough to make it on their own are replayed endlessly just to meet requirements. Stewart, the CHUM-FM music director, said that because there are not enough hits meeting the criteria that identifies them as Canadian, a song by an artist like Shania Twain has to be kept on a playlist for more than five months—an eternity in radio. Listeners tire of it, he said, and are tempted to tune in to radio stations from the United States that can play whatever they wish.

13   The radio regulation is intended to support up-and-coming Canadian artists. But some argue that it can foster mediocrity or generate an artificial popularity that comes back to haunt Canadian groups. "If an artist has success in Canada, international markets often see that as 'rigged' because they believe that artist 'has to be

played by law,'" Steven Page, lead singer for the Barenaked Ladies, said in an e-mail interview conducted while he was backstage at a concert in England.

14   At times, Page said, Canadian artists don't know where to turn. The impression that Canadian songs are played only because they must be played "can make taking your success elsewhere a more difficult endeavor," he said. And the government's protectionist attitude sometimes trickles down to fans who "turn their backs on artists they feel are not Canadian enough," he said. With its overwhelming impact, television is the fiercest battleground for Canada's protectionist policies—and the most controversial, because broadcasters often find themselves opposing government regulations.

15   Canadians watch Canadian television channels, but they see very little that is produced in Canada by Canadians. Regulations allow commercial stations to broadcast popular American programs at the same time they are broadcast on American channels—which most Canadians can receive. But the law allows Canadian broadcasters to substitute their own commercials. So while Canadians saw the Super Bowl at the same time as Americans did, they were treated to dated Canadian beer ads instead of flashy new American commercials.

16   Regulations now require 60 percent of a television station's schedule to be Canadian. But with unceasing opposition from broadcasters, regulators are constantly redefining what Canadian content is, and even what prime time is. "Top Cops," a CBS program that tells American police stories, fulfills Canadian content regulations because it is produced in Canada. But the Disney company's "Never Cry Wolf," a 1983 film version of the Canadian author Farley Mowat's book about the Arctic, is not Canadian enough because it was produced in the United States. Broadcast executives like Ivan Fecan, president of CTV, one of Canada's largest commercial television networks, argue that while Canada's cultural regulations may be necessary, their effect is limited because they can never overcome a fundamental premise: popular culture must be popular.

17   "You can't force people to read Canadian magazines or watch Canadian dramas, but you should provide them with the choice," he said. "I don't think anyone would confuse this with being anti-American. It's not. Canada is not another state, and we don't want to be one."

CRITICAL THINKING

1. How important is Canadian culture to you? What percentage of the entertainment you experience—films, music, books—is in fact American? In your mind, is "American Cultural Imperialism" a real threat? What, if any, are the dangers in Canadians enjoying too much American entertainment?

2. DePalma claims that the effect of cultural regulations is limited because ultimately "popular culture must be popular." What makes American culture so much more popular than Canadian culture?

3. DePalma points out some of the apparent absurdities of the point system for determining Canadian content in the music industry. What makes a

work of art Canadian? Does it depend solely on the nationality of the artist, the content of the work, or where it was produced? Explain.

RESEARCH PROJECTS

4. Compare the Web sites of an American magazine that puts out a Canadian edition of a magazine such as *Time*, at **www.timecanada.com/** and **www.time.com/time/**. In your mind, is the Canadian edition of your chosen magazine a fair purveyor of Canadian voices, or is it simply an example of how "Americans can simply place a maple leaf on a magazine cover, call it a Canadian edition and sell cut-rate advertising that would otherwise go to Canadian magazines"? Support your position with evidence from the sites.

5. Identify the Canadian TV shows, if any, that you watch regularly. Compile a list of attributes that differentiate these shows from their American counterparts. Try to determine what makes a Canadian show Canadian. Summarize your ideas in an essay.

6. DePalma mentions Canadian film and television director Norman Jewison. Visit the CBC Web site dedicated to Jewison at **archives.cbc.ca/IDD-1-68-733/arts_entertainment/norman_jewison/**, listen to a number of the clips, and summarize his views on the Canadian film and television industry.

Additional essay topics, writing assignments, research guidelines, and readings for this chapter can be found online at **www.pearsoned.ca/goshgarian**.

Fashion
and Flesh
The Images We Project

2

Pick up a magazine. Turn on the television. View a film. Every day we are bombarded with images and messages telling us that slim is sexy and beauty means happiness. The right labels mean success and respect. The right look means acceptance. And overwhelmingly, our culture buys into these messages.

We live in a society caught up in images of itself—a society seemingly more driven by the cultivation of the body and how we clothe it than in personal achievement. In fact, so powerful is the influence of image that other terms of self-definition are difficult to identify. In this chapter, several writers grapple with questions raised by our cultural preoccupation with flesh and fashion. Are we our bodies? Can our inner selves transcend the flesh? Do the clothes we wear express the self we want to be? From where does all the body-consciousness pressure come? Some essays in this chapter recount people at war with their bodies due to cultural pressure. Other essays are accounts of people rising above the din of fashion's dictates to create a sense of self that is authentic and rooted in personal happiness. And some explore the cultural trends that help direct contemporary fashion.

Many women feel that men are free from the social pressures associated with body image. It may come as a surprise to some people that many men, like women, are concerned with body image. The first selection, "Never Too Buff" by John Cloud, reports the disturbing trend that many men, and even young boys, are struggling with the cultural pressure to achieve physical perfection with which women often must deal. In "What I Think about the Fashion World," former fashion editor Liz Jones questions the influence of the fashion industry on women's feelings about their bodies. Why does the fashion industry continue to promote tall, emaciated models on runways and magazine covers when the average woman is 1.6 m tall and about 72.6 kg?

The next essay deals with how we, as individuals, feel about our bodies. In a society in which beauty seems to be precisely defined, there is little room for variations from the prescribed parameters of beauty. Sandra Hurtes discusses how watching the perfect bodies of actresses on the Academy Awards made her go off her diet in frustration.

Although many people equate social acceptability with standard definitions of beauty, others strive to exhibit their individuality and assert their independence by setting their own styles. "Making Peace with the Pierced," Karen Romell's examination of the culture of body modification, explores this unconventional aspect of fashion.

From there, we take a look at Canada as a whole and its place in the fashion world. Serena French argues that when it comes to high fashion, Canada isn't even on the map. In "Canada Falls Out of Fashion," she shows that Canada just doesn't get it and doesn't even seem to care.

Finally, the Viewpoints section ends the chapter with a bit of humour, and, at the same time, raises some poignant questions. First, *Ottawa Citizen* reporter Scott McKeen provides a list of ways for men to hide a pot belly in "A Man's Guide to Slimming Couture." Following this light and witty advice, Catherine Lawson, the fashion editor for the *Ottawa Citizen*, raises the question, "Why Do We Get to Laugh at Fat Guys?" Her article zeroes in on some of the inequities in our society concerning obesity, which, considering current trends in how our culture connects body image and body size, are unlikely to change.

The final reading, and this chapter's Research Issue, addresses the concept of beauty. Elizabeth Snead's report, "The Beauty of Symmetry," explains that we instinctually prefer symmetrical faces, and why. Is beauty really skin deep?

Never Too Buff
John Cloud

While men with lean and muscular bodies have always been admired, the idea that men obsess about their body image as much as women may seem ludicrous to some people. We tend to assume that most men simply do not care about their appearance the way women do. Not so, according to psychiatrists Harrison Pope, Katharine Phillips, and psychologist Roberto Olivardia. Their research reveals a disturbing trend: just as many young women aspire to be supermodel thin, an increasing number of young men yearn for the steroid-boosted and buff bodies typical of today's action heroes and weightlifters. In the following article, John Cloud reports on this groundbreaking research, and what it might mean for boys and men in the years ahead.

Harrison Pope, a professor of psychiatry at Harvard Medical School, and Katharine Phillips, a professor of psychiatry at Brown University, in conjunction with Roberto Olivardia, a clinical psychologist at McLean Hospital in Massachusetts, have researched male body image for the past 15 years. Their book, *The Adonis Complex*, published in 2000, concludes that "something awful has happened to American men over the past few decades"—they have become obsessed with their bodies. Journalist John Cloud discusses some of the key highlights of their research in this article, which first appeared in *Time* magazine on April 24, 2000, one week before their book was published.

CRITICAL THINKING
Try to imagine the "perfect" male body. What does it look like? Is your image influenced by outside forces, such as the media, your gender, or your age? How do real men you know compare to the image in your mind?

---

1   Pop quiz. Who is more likely to be dissatisfied with the appearance of their chests, men or women? Who is more likely to be concerned about acne, your teenage son or his sister? And who is more likely to binge eat, your nephew or your niece?

2   If you chose the women and girls in your life, you are right only for the last question—and even then, not by the margin you might expect. About 40 percent of Americans who go on compulsive-eating sprees are men. Thirty-eight percent of men want bigger pecs, while only 34 percent of women want bigger breasts. And more boys have fretted about zits than girls, going all the way back to a 1972 study.

3   A groundbreaking new book declares that these numbers, along with hundreds of other statistics and interviews the authors have compiled, mean something awful has happened to American men over the past few decades. They have become obsessed with their bodies. Authors Harrison Pope and Katharine Phillips, professors of psychiatry at Harvard and Brown, respectively, and Roberto Olivardia, a clinical psychologist at McLean Hospital in Belmont, Mass., have a catchy name to describe this obsession—a term that will soon be doing many reps on chat shows: the Adonis Complex.

4   The name, which refers to the gorgeous half man, half god of mythology, may be a little too ready for Oprah, but the theory behind it will start a wonderful debate. Based on original research involving more than 1,000 men over the past 15 years, the book argues that many men desperately want to look like Adonis because they constantly see the "ideal," steroid-boosted bodies of actors and models and because their muscles are all they have over women today. In an age when women fly combat missions, the authors ask, "What can a modern boy or man do to distinguish himself as being 'masculine'?"

5   For years, of course, some men—ice skaters, body builders, George Hamilton —have fretted over aspects of their appearance. But the numbers suggest that body-image concerns have gone mainstream: nearly half of men don't like their overall appearance, in contrast to just 1 in 6 in 1972. True, men typically are fatter now, but another study found that 46 percent of men of normal weight think about their appearance "all the time" or "frequently." And some men—probably hundreds of thousands, if you extrapolate from small surveys—say they have passed up job and even romantic opportunities because they refuse to disrupt workouts or dine on restaurant food. In other words, an increasing number of men would rather look brawny for their girlfriends than have sex with them.

6   Consider what they're spending. Last year American men forked over $2 billion for gym memberships—and another $2 billion for home exercise equipment. *Men's Health* ("Rock-hard abs in six weeks!" it screams every other issue) had 250,000 subscribers in 1990; now it has 1.6 million. In 1996 alone, men underwent some 700,000 cosmetic procedures.

7   At least those profits are legal. Anabolic steroids—the common name for synthetic testosterone—have led to the most dramatic changes in the male form in modern history, and more and more average men want those changes for themselves. Since steroids became widely available on the black market in the 1960s, perhaps 3 million American men have swallowed or injected them—mostly in the past 15 years. A 1993 survey found that 1 Georgia high school boy in every 15 admitted having used steroids without a prescription. And the Drug Enforcement Administration reports that the percentage of all high school students who have used steroids has increased 50 percent in the past four years, from 1.8 percent to 2.8 percent. The abuse of steroids has so alarmed the National Institute on Drug Abuse that on Friday it launched a campaign in gyms, malls, bookstores, clubs and on the Internet to warn teenagers about the dangers. Meanwhile, teenagers in even larger numbers are buying legal but lightly regulated food supplements, some with dangerous side effects, that purport to make you bigger or leaner or stronger.

8   As they infiltrated the body-building world in the '70s and Hollywood a decade later, steroids created bodies for mass consumption that the world had literally never seen before. Pope likes to chart the changes by looking at Mr. America winners, which he called up on the Internet in his office last week. "Look at this guy," Pope exclaims when he clicks on the 1943 winner, Jules Bacon. "He couldn't even win a county body-building contest today." Indeed, there are 16-year-olds working out at your gym who are as big as Bacon. Does that necessarily mean that today's body builders—including those 16-year-olds—are 'roided? Pope is careful. "The possibility exists that rare or exceptional people, those with an unusual genetic makeup or a hormonal imbalance," could achieve the muscularity and leanness of today's big body builders, he says.

9   But it's not likely. And Pope isn't lobbing dumbbells from an ivory tower: the professor lifts weights six days a week, from 11 A.M. to 1 P.M. (He can even mark historical occasions by his workouts: "I remember when the Challenger went down; I was doing a set of squats.") "We are being assaulted by images virtually impossible to attain without the use of drugs," says Pope. "So what happens when you change a million-year-old equilibrium of nature?"

10   A historical loop forms: steroids beget pro wrestlers—Hulk Hogan, for one, has admitted taking steroids—who inspire boys to be just like them. Steroids have changed even boys' toys. Feminists have long derided Barbie for her tiny waist and big bosom. The authors of *The Adonis Complex* see a similar problem for boys in the growth of G.I. Joe. The grunt of 1982 looks scrawny compared with G.I. Joe Extreme, introduced in the mid-'90s. The latter would have a 55-in. chest and 27-in. biceps if he were real, which simply can't be replicated in nature. Pope also points out a stunning little feature of the three-year-old video game Duke Nukem: Total Meltdown, developed by GT Interactive Software. When Duke gets tired, he can find a bottle of steroids to get him going. "Steroids give Duke a super adrenaline rush," the game manual notes.

11   To bolster their argument, the Adonis authors developed a computerized test that allows subjects to "add" muscle to a typical male body. They estimate their own size and then pick the size they would like to be and the size they think women want. Pope and his colleagues gave the test to college students and found that on average, the men wanted 28 lbs. more muscle—and thought women wanted them to have 30 lbs. more. In fact, the women who took the test picked an ideal man only slightly more muscular than average. Which goes a long way toward explaining why Leonardo DiCaprio can be a megastar in a nation that also idealizes "Stone Cold" Steve Austin.

12   But when younger boys took Pope's test, they revealed an even deeper sense of inadequacy about their bodies. More than half of boys ages 11 to 17 chose as their physical ideal an image possible to attain only by using steroids. So they do. Boys are a big part of the clientele at Muscle Mania (not its real name), a weight-lifting store that *Time* visited last week at a strip mall in a Boston suburb. A couple of teenagers came in to ask about tribulus, one of the many over-the-counter drugs and body-building supplements the store sells, all legally.

13   "A friend of mine," one boy begins, fooling no one, "just came off a cycle of juice, and he heard that tribulus can help you produce testosterone naturally." Patrick, 28, who runs the store and who stopped using steroids four years ago because of chest pain, tells the kid, "The s__ shuts off your nuts," meaning steroids can reduce sperm production, shrink the testicles and cause impotence. Tribulus, Patrick says, can help restart natural testosterone production. The teen hands over $12 for 100 Tribulus Fuel pills. (Every day, Muscle Mania does $4,000 in sales of such products, with protein supplements and so-called fat burners leading the pack.)

14   Patrick says many of his teen customers, because they're short on cash, won't pay for a gym membership "until they've saved up for a cycle [of steroids]. They don't see the point without them." The saddest customers, he says, are the little boys, 12 and 13, brought in by young fathers. "The dad will say, 'How do we put some weight on this kid?' with the boy just staring at the floor. Dad is going to turn him into Hulk Hogan, even if it's against his will."

15   What would motivate someone to take steroids? Pope, Phillips and Olivardia say the Adonis Complex works in different ways for different men. "Michael," 32, one of their research subjects, told *Time* he had always been a short kid who got picked on. He started working out at about 14, and he bought muscle magazines for advice. The pictures taunted him: he sweated, but he wasn't getting as big as the men in the pictures. Other men in his gym also made him feel bad. When he found out they were on steroids, he did two cycles himself, even though he knew they could be dangerous.

16   But not all men with body-image problems take steroids. Jim Davis, 29, a human-services manager, told *Time* he never took them, even when training for body-building competitions. But Davis says he developed a form of obsessive-compulsive disorder around his workouts. He lifted weights six days a week for at least six years. He worked out even when injured. He adhered to a rigid regimen for every session, and if he changed it, he felt anxious all day. He began to be worried about clothes, and eventually could wear only three shirts, ones that make him look big. He still felt small. "I would sit in class at college with a coat on," he says. You may have heard this condition called bigorexia—thinking your muscles are puny when they aren't. Pope and his colleagues call it muscle dysmorphia and estimate that hundreds of thousands of men suffer from it.

17   Even though most boys and men never approach the compulsion of Davis or Michael (both eventually conquered it), they undoubtedly face more pressure now than in the past to conform to an impossible ideal. Ripped male bodies are used today to advertise everything that shapely female bodies advertise: not just fitness products but also dessert liqueurs, microwave ovens and luxury hotels. The authors of *The Adonis Complex* want guys to rebel against those images, or at least see them for what they are: a goal unattainable without drug use.

18   Feminists raised these issues for women years ago, and more recent books such as *The Beauty Myth* were part of a backlash against the hourglass ideal. Now, says Phillips, "I actually think it may be harder for men than women to talk about these problems because it's not considered masculine to worry about such things." But

maybe there is a masculine alternative: Next time WWE comes on, guys, throw the TV out the window. And order a large pizza. ◆

FREEWRITING ASSIGNMENT ————————————————

Pope, Phillips, and Olivardia report that, in general, men would like to add 28 pounds more muscle to their frames but believe women would prefer even more—at least 30 pounds more muscle. What, in your opinion, accounts for this perception? Does it seem reasonable?

CRITICAL READING

1. Evaluate the comment made by Pope, Phillips, and Olivardia that young men are increasingly obsessed with body image because they feel that muscle is all men have "over women today." Do you agree or disagree with this statement? Explain.
2. Analyze the author's use of statistics to support his points. Do their conclusions seem reasonable based on the data they cite? Why or why not?
3. Visit the Muscle Memory Web site and look at the photographs of some of the Mr. America winners over the past 50 years at **www.musclememory .com/articles/MrAmerica.html**. How do they compare to today's body builders? Explain.
4. According to the author, what cultural messages tell children that steroid use is okay? Describe some of the ways children receive these messages.

CRITICAL WRITING

5. *Analytical Writing*: Write a detailed description of your ideal male image (what you desire in a male or what you would most want to look like as a male). How does your description compare with the conclusions drawn by the psychiatrists and psychologist in the article? Did outside cultural influences direct your description? Explain.
6. *Personal Narrative:* Looking back at your experience in high school, write a narrative about the males who were considered the most "buff." What qualities made these particular males more desirable and more enviable than their peers? How much of their appeal was based on their physical appearance? How much on something else?
7. *Persuasive Writing*: Pope, Phillips, and Olivardia comment that media pressure is connected to the emergence of men's new obsession with body image. Write an essay discussing whether this is true or not true. Support your perspective using examples from Cloud's article and your own experience.

GROUP PROJECTS

8. Create and administer your own survey regarding the ideal male appearance. As a group, come up with a list of qualities—such as intelligence, body build, facial features, sense of humour, and physical strength—that can be ranked in order of importance. Try to come up with 8–12 qualities or characteristics. Distribute your poll among men and women on your campus (indicate whether the poll is given to a man or a woman). Tabulate the results and present your findings to the class. (For an interesting comparison, groups may also want to distribute a similar list of female characteristics and qualities.)

9. Have everyone in the group bring a copy of a men's magazine (*Details*, *GQ*, *Esquire*). Different group members may want to focus on different aspects of the magazines—such as advertising, articles, fashion, or advice columns. Do the models in the magazine fit the description in Cloud's article? What do the articles suggest men should aspire to look like? How many articles on improving appearance are featured? After reviewing the magazines, discuss your findings and collaborate on an essay about how men's fashion magazines help define the "ideal" male.

10. Working in small groups, arrange to visit your campus gym or local health club. Split up and take notes about what kinds of men you see working out there. What patterns of behaviour do you see—for example, are there more men working with weights than doing aerobics? Write brief descriptions of the men's workout attire. Do they seem concerned with how they look? Why or why not? After your visit, get together and compare notes. Write a report on your findings and present your conclusions to the class.

What I Think about the Fashion World
Liz Jones

For many young women, perfect beauty is defined by the supermodels. Tall, thin, long limbed, and with sculpted features, supermodels and popular actresses embody what it means to be beautiful in our society. Images in magazines further promote this often unattainable ideal. In a culture in which women are often measured by how they look, the pressure to be thin can be great. But such women represent a very small minority of body type. In this article, Liz Jones gives her perspective on the way women are treated by the fashion industry. Are thin models part of a fashion conspiracy, or are they merely reflective of what the public wants to see?

Liz Jones is the former editor of the British edition of *Marie Claire*, a women's fashion magazine. In June 2000, while still editor of *Marie Claire*, she shocked the fashion world by featuring two covers, one featuring Pamela Anderson and one with voluptuous Sophie Dahl, then a size 12. The Dahl cover prevailed, but many critics spoke out against Jones for using the magazine as a forum to "forward her own agenda." Jones, a recovering anorexic, admitted she used her position as editor to highlight the issue, claiming it was an issue that needed to be addressed. Jones is now editor of the Life and Style section of the *London Evening Standard*. This article was first published in *You* magazine, a supplement of the *Mail on Sunday*, in the April 15, 2001 edition of the *London Daily Mail*.

CRITICAL THINKING Try to picture your version of the perfect female body. What does it look like? Is your image influenced by outside forces, such as the media, your gender, or your age? How do real women you know compare to the image in your mind?

1 For four weeks last month I sat in the front row of catwalk shows in London, Milan, Paris and New York watching painfully thin models walking up and down inches from my nose.

2 Kate Moss, the original 'superwaif', was looking positively curvaceous compared to the current bunch of underweight teenagers.

3 For those used to the fashion industry there was nothing unusual about the shows at all. But for me it was the end; it was then that I decided to resign as editor of *Marie Claire* magazine.

4 I had reached the point where I had simply had enough of working in an industry that pretends to support women while it bombards them with impossible images of perfection day after day, undermining their self-confidence, their health and hard-earned cash.

5 My decision to quit was partly precipitated by the failure of a campaign I started a year ago to encourage magazines, designers and advertisers to use models with more realistic, representative body images. Then I could not have anticipated the extraordinarily hostile reaction to my fairly innocuous suggestions from fellow editors and designers. A year later I have come to realize the sheer terrorism of the fashion industry and accept that, alone, I cannot change things.

6 But in the spring last year I was full of optimism that we could change. I believed wholeheartedly that we could stop magazines and advertisers using underweight girls as fashion icons. I had already banned diets and slimming advice from our pages but after meeting Gisele, the Brazilian supermodel credited with bringing 'curves to the catwalk', and discovering that she is a tiny size 8, I decided to challenge the status quo.

7 We decided to publish two covers for the same edition—one featuring Sophie Dahl, a size 12; the other, Pamela Anderson, a minute size 6—and we asked readers to choose between the skinny, cosmetically enhanced 'perfection', or a more attainable, but still very beautiful curvy woman. Sophie Dahl won by an overwhelming majority.

8 But you would think that we had declared war. The reaction was staggering. Newspapers, radio and TV stations were largely behind us. They welcomed the opportunity to demystify the closed and cliquey world of fashion. Our covers were

in the national press for weeks—even making headlines in the *New York Post*. I had requests from universities here and abroad wanting to include our experiment in their college courses. Documentaries were made in the US and Germany. The response from readers was unprecedented. We received 4,000 letters in two weeks.

9   However, the very people from whom I had expected the most support—my fellow female editors—were unanimous in their disapproval.

10   I was invited to speak at the Body Image Summit set up by Tessa Jowell, Minister for Women, in June 2000 to debate the influence of media images on rising problems of anorexia and bulimia among women. One suggestion was that a group—consisting of editors, designers, young women readers and professionals who treat women with eating disorders—should get together on a regular basis to monitor the industry, bring in guidelines on using girls under a certain body size and weight and discuss ways the industry could evolve. My job was to gather these people: not one single other editor agreed to take part.

11   Instead most of them were hostile and aggressive. Jo Elvin, then editor of *New Woman*, accused *Marie Claire* of 'discriminating against thin women'. (As if there aren't enough role models in the media for thinness, from Jennifer Aniston to Gwyneth Paltrow to American supermodel Maggie Rizer.) Another fashion editor made the point that there had always been skinny women—look at Twiggy, for example. Jasper Conran absurdly suggested we should be looking at obesity as a serious health problem instead of anorexia and bulimia. I didn't bother to point out that people with obesity were not usually put on magazine covers as fashion icons.

12   The next day, after the summit, I received a fax, signed by nearly all the other editors of women's magazines and some model agencies, stating that they would not be following any initiative to expand the types of women featured in their magazines—one of the topics up for discussion at the summit was how to introduce more black and Asian women onto the pages of Britain's glossies.

13   When I read the list of names, I felt like giving up the fight there and then. I was isolated, sickened to my stomach that something so positive had been turned into a petty catfight by women I respected and admired. They were my peers, friends and colleagues I sat next to in the front row of the fashion shows. They were also the most important, influential group of women in the business, the only people who could change the fashion and beauty industry. Why were they so reluctant to even think about change?

14   Like me, they had sat at the summit while a group of teenage girls, black, Asian and white, some fat, some thin, had berated us all for what we were doing to their lives. I had found it moving to listen to these young women, brave enough to come and talk in front of all these scary high profile people. Anyway, to me, it made good business sense to listen to them and address their concerns: why alienate your readers? I could see those teenagers turning away from magazines because we seemed hopelessly outmoded, old fashioned, unattainable. But I was clearly alone.

15   The other editors seemed to revel in the chance to counter attack. Alexandra Shulman, editor of *Vogue*, denounced the whole campaign as a promotional tool for *Marie Claire* and said that suggestions of an agreement to set up a self-regulatory body within the industry was 'totally out of order'. Debbie Bee, then editor of

Nova—a supposedly cutting edge fashion magazine for young women—asserted in her editorial the following month that magazines didn't cause anorexia as readers were intelligent enough to differentiate between an idealized model and real life.

16   Fiona McIntosh, editor of *Elle*, published a cover picture of Calista Flockhart with the caption, 'I'm thin, so what?' She accused me of 'betraying the editors' code'. Frankly, I didn't even know there was a code; only one, surely, to put your readers first.

17   Some model agencies blacklisted the magazine. Storm, who represents Sophie Dahl and who you would have thought would have been happy that one of their models was being held up as an example of healthy gorgeousness, told us that we could no longer book any of their girls. Several publicists from Hollywood, reacting both to the cover and a feature called 'Lollipop ladies' about women in Hollywood whose heads are too big for their tiny bodies, wrote to me saying their stars would not be gracing our covers—ever.

18   I had clearly put my head too far above the parapet. I realized that far from being the influential trendsetters I had thought, magazine editors are more often ruled by fear—and advertisers. No one feels that they can afford to be different. They are happy to settle, instead, for free handbags and relentless glamour.

19   To be honest, it would have been very easy to give up then. Every time the contacts of a fashion shoot landed on my desk with a model whose ribs showed, whose bony shoulders and collar bone could have cut glass, whose legs were like sticks, we could have published them anyway and said, 'oh well, we tried'. But we didn't. We threw them out, set up a reshoot, and eventually, slowly, agencies started to take us seriously and would only send girls with curves in all the right places.

20   I cannot deny the campaign got the magazine talked and written about. The choice of covers got the readers involved and made them have a little bit of power for a change; they got to choose who they wanted on the cover. The Sophie Dahl cover started to sell out, and readers would phone me, frantic, saying, 'I could only buy the Pamela Anderson cover, but I want you to register my vote for Sophie.' It could never have been a scientific exercise—subscribers to the magazine had to take pot luck; but still they would phone up saying, 'No, I wanted Sophie!'

21   But I was dismayed by accusations that this was just another way to boost sales. I suffered from anorexia from the age of 11 until my late twenties and understand first hand the damaging effect of a daily diet of unrealistically tiny role models gracing the pages of the magazines that I was addicted to. Although it did not cause my illness, the images definitely perpetuated the hatred I had for my own body.

22   I agree with Debbie Bee of *Nova* that young women are intelligent enough to be able to tell the difference between a model and real life but the effects are often subliminal. One piece of research we did at *Marie Claire* was to ask a group of intelligent professional women about their bodies then let them browse a selection of magazines for an hour, before asking them again. Their self-esteem had plummeted.

23   Never before have we been bombarded with so many images of perfection: more and more glossies on the shelves, web sites, digital satellite channels, more and more channels showing music videos 24 hours a day. New technology is also removing the images we see of women even further from reality. Just try finding a cover on the

shelves this month where the star has not had her spots removed, the dark circles under her eyes eradicated, the wrinkles smoothed and her waist trimmed.

24   It is common practice nowadays to 'stretch' women whose legs aren't long enough. One men's magazine currently on the shelves, so the industry gossip has it, has put one star's head on another woman's body—apparently, her original breasts weren't 'spherical enough'.

25   So women have been conditioned to go to the gym and diet, or if they don't, to feel guilty about it, but that still won't achieve 'cover girl' perfection because you can't be airbrushed in real life. I've seen the models close up: believe me, lots of them have varicose veins, spots, appendectomy scars and, yes, cellulite. Only the 16 year olds don't have fine lines.

26   The pressure on actresses in Hollywood to be a certain size is enormous. You would think we would have been on pretty safe ground shooting Renee Zellweger, the star of *Bridget Jones*, for our April cover. I had seen the movie; she was, well, Bridget: curvy, busty, with cellulite and a healthy appetite. On the shoot? She was an American size two (UK six). All the outfits, which were samples—clothes made for the catwalk and fitted on size 8 models—swamped her.

27   She turned down the Bridget sequel because it would mean piling on the pounds all over again. Jennifer Aniston admits in the current issue of *Vanity Fair* that she lost 30 pounds to get the role of Rachel in *Friends*. On the rare occasion a star is a 'normal' size, it is very hard getting hold of clothes that will be big enough. None of the samples will fit, so fashion editors have to trawl the stores borrowing off the rails. One of the most beautiful women in the world, Liv Tyler, is a healthy size 12; none of the designers are able to dress her directly from clothes that are on the catwalk.

28   So did I achieve anything with my campaign? I believe so. One newspaper conducted a survey of high street and designer shops and proved how women over size 12 were not being catered to. Stores are now providing a broader range of sizes.

29   In the May issue, we published naked pictures of eight ordinary women, and asked readers to fill in a questionnaire telling us honestly how they feel about the women in the photographs, and about their own bodies. Interestingly, of the respondents so far, all the women say their boyfriends find the size 16 woman the most attractive. The results will be made into a Channel 4 documentary in the autumn.

30   In the next issue, my final edition as editor, we have on our cover three young women, all a size 12, curvy, imperfect, but very beautiful all the same. On the shoot, it was apparent that Suzanne, Myleene and Kym from Hear'Say were all happy in their own skin. For now. On the Popstars program, Nasty Nigel had told the girls they should go on a diet. 'Christmas is over,' he said to Kym, 'but the goose is still fat.' How long before the girls start feeling paranoid about their bodies, under the constant pressure of fame, is anybody's guess.

31   In Britain an estimated 60,000 people, most of them young women, suffer from eating disorders while far greater numbers have an unhealthy relationship with food. Many of them take up smoking or eat diet pills to keep their weight below a certain level. Of all psychiatric disorders, anorexia has the most fatalities—it is very hard to recover from. I refuse to conform to an industry that could, literally, kill.

32   It's time for the industry—the photographers, the editors, the casting directors, designers and the advertisers—to wake up and allow women to just be themselves. From the phone calls and letters I received at *Marie Claire*, I know that women are fed up with feeling needlessly bad about their wobbly bits.

33   I only hope that my successor listens to them. ◆

FREEWRITING ASSIGNMENT

Is the fashion industry exerting pressure on women to be thin? Consider the women featured on the covers of popular magazines for men and women, including *Marie Claire, Cosmopolitan, Vogue, Maxim,* and *Vibe.* Do you think such magazine covers influence how we define beauty and desirability?

CRITICAL READING

1. In your opinion, is the fashion industry's use of extremely thin models harmful? In your opinion, has mass media created unrealistic expectations of beauty? Explain.

2. By running the two covers, Jones sought to discover whether women wanted perfection and aspiration or something more realistic and attainable. What did sales of the June 2000 cover reveal? Based on your own observations, how do you think North American women would have reacted to the same experiment?

3. How did other fashion magazine editors react to Jones's *Marie Claire* covers? What do you think their reaction reveals about the fashion industry?

4. Debbie Bee of *Nova,* another British fashion magazine, argues that young women are "intelligent enough to be able to tell the difference between a model and real life." How does Jones test this theory? What does she discover?

5. Evaluate how well Jones supports her viewpoint in this essay. Does she provide supporting evidence? Is she biased? Does she provide a balanced perspective, or does she slant her data? Explain.

6. Jones is a former editor for a major fashion magazine. Does the fact that she held this position and was willing to risk her career for this issue influence your opinion of her essay or her points? Why or why not?

CRITICAL WRITING

7. *Exploratory Writing*: Do you know someone who seems obsessed with his or her weight or who suffers from an eating disorder? Discuss what you feel are the causes of the problem. Do you agree with Jones that many eating disorders are influenced by the cult of thinness perpetuated by the fashion industry? Why or why not?

8. *Exploratory Writing*: Write an essay exploring the connections among the fashion industry, body image, and self-esteem. Does the fashion industry have a direct role in our feelings of self-worth and acceptance? Support your viewpoint with examples from the text and your own personal experience.

9. *Personal Narrative*: Write an essay in which you analyze your own feelings about your self-image. What factors do you think shaped your feelings? What elements of our culture, if any, influenced your development of body consciousness? Explain.

GROUP PROJECTS

10. With your group, gather magazine photographs of several models and analyze their body types. What common elements do you notice? How are they similar or different? How do they compare to "real" people? Based on the photographs, can you reach any conclusions about fashion models in today's culture?

11. Discuss in your group the following question: If you could be either very beautiful or very wealthy, which would you choose? Explain the motivation behind your choice. Based on your group's multiple responses, can you reach any conclusions about the influence of beauty on men and women in today's society?

I'm So Fat (NEDA advertisement)

Most people—often young women—who suffer from eating disorders such as anorexia nervosa or bulimia also experience distorted self-perception. The person they see in the mirror differs drastically from their physical reality. In 2004, the National Eating Disorders Association (NEDA) launched the "Get Real" awareness campaign to portray how distorted the self-image of someone suffering from an eating disorder can be. The campaign ran ads in several magazines including *People* and *In Style* and also aired television spots on major stations. The goal of the campaign was to increase awareness while encouraging people with eating disorders to seek assistance through its free hotline. This print ad was created for NEDA by Porter Novelli, a public relations firm known for health promotion campaigns.

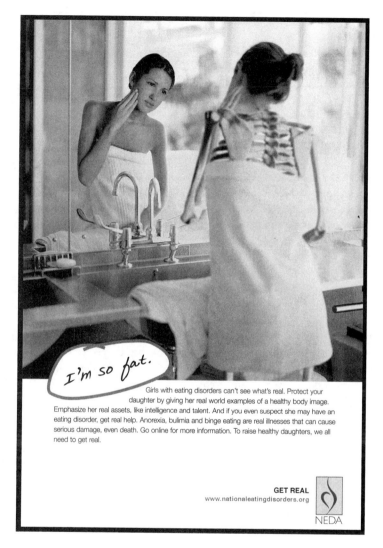

1. If you were leafing through a magazine and saw this ad, would you stop to read it? Why or why not? What catches your eye? How long would you spend looking at the ad? Explain.
2. Visit the NEDA Web site at **www.nationaleatingdisorders.org** and read about eating disorders in men and women (look at the "eating disorder info" pages). Who is at risk for an eating disorder? What role does social and cultural pressure play in exacerbating eating disorders? Explain.
3. What is happening in the photo? What is the woman thinking? What does she see? What do we see? What message does the photo convey?
4. Who is the target audience for this ad? Do you think someone with an eating disorder will be persuaded to follow the advice in the ad? If not, who is likely to respond to it? Explain.

Weighing In
Sandra Hurtes

Popular culture is strongly influenced by the images projected by Hollywood. In the next essay, Sandra Hurtes describes how watching actresses on the Academy Awards made her want to go off of her diet. How much of our own personal identity becomes blurred by media images of beauty? Is Hollywood promoting an unrealistic, and even unhealthy, ideal?

Sandra Hurtes teaches creative nonfiction at Hunter College in New York. Her essays and articles have appeared in many publications, including *The New York Times*, *New Age*, *The Washington Post*, and *The Forward*. She has been nominated for the Jackauer Award for excellence in Jewish Journalism for her essay on 9/11. She is currently working on a family memoir about the Holocaust. This essay was first posted on *Feminist.com*.

CRITICAL THINKING

Does the size of your clothing influence how you feel about your body? Do you think women think more about clothing size than men do?

1   After watching the Academy Awards I decided to go off my diet. Looking at actresses who earn enough money to feed entire nations, yet appear emaciated and in desperate need of a good meal, sent me charging to the fridge. That's not to say I wouldn't like to be a size two and wear a clingy dress like Uma or Hilary. I have been as thin as they are, and the truth is, once the novelty wore off, I wasn't any happier than I am right now.

2   I've spent over one-half of my life concerned about my weight. The eternal ten pounds that I mull over in my mind, for a minute here, a minute there, add up to a nice chunk of time that I could be thinking about far meatier issues—raising money for AIDS research, housing the homeless, even my next article. But with the self-centeredness of the body-obsessed, the scale in my mind never sleeps. While waiting for a train, attending a business meeting, or sitting at my computer, a voice inside my head comes out of nowhere, and tells me, "I'm so fat."

3   In the movie "Sex, Lies and Videotape," Andie MacDowell's character tells her therapist that women would be fat and happy if there were no men in the world. Although all the women in the audience laughed in acknowledgment, I don't believe it's as simple as a female/male issue. I've never been with a man who thought I needed to lose ten pounds. Still, I wage a daily war with myself, equating sexuality with being thin and I dole out self acceptance with how closely I weigh in.

4   When the television program "Melrose Place" was on the air, I wanted to send the show's female stars a care package. They were scarily skinny. Was I jealous? Yes. But I was angry too. Although I knew better than to let the media define me, the messages fed into what I've been taught ever since I began to care about how I look. If Heather Locklear, a size 2, had a different man every week begging her for sex, somewhere inside me I believed that if I was ever to have sex again, I had to

look, at least from the back, like a pubescent girl. So during commercials, instead of writing a letter to producer Aaron Spelling, I was on the floor doing sit ups.

5   Don't get me wrong. I'm not opposed to healthful living. It's just that often the true meaning of the terms get blurred. Especially by me. Several years ago I went to a health spa for a vacation. Comfortable with my weight, I didn't go there for the dieting but to relax and spend a week of healthy living.

6   After three days I got caught up in the low calorie meals and strenuous exercise and the effect they were having on my body. I loved it, believing I was only in it for the week. But when I got home, something strange happened to me. I couldn't start my day without a bowl of shredded wheat, couldn't even look at 'fattening' food, and the early morning hikes I enjoyed so much, translated in city terms to walking everywhere, forget about subways or buses. After a month of continuous diet and exercise the pounds began to fall off. I was in awe of the process and loved getting skinny. Three months later I was two sizes smaller, and my hip bones stuck out prominently enough that I could see them through my clothes. What a rush.

7   I looked good, although some friends thought I was too thin. I felt fit and was eating healthfully. Sounds great. The problem was that all I thought about was food. What I would eat for my next meal. What I wasn't eating. What other people were eating that they shouldn't be. How many miles I would walk the next day to work off the extra bites of something I wished I hadn't eaten. I wasn't aware of the tread-mill I was on until I ran into a friend I hadn't seen in a long time, and she asked me how my summer was. I realized that the only pleasure I had during those leisurely months was showing off my new body in skimpy clothes. A day at the beach was less about fun and more about saying no to food and comparing myself to other women. It felt a little crazy and dangerously close to anorexia.

8   I loosened my grip on myself, and my weight went up a bit. I've gained a few pounds, an indicator that I love to eat and get great pleasure from food. I'm not skinny anymore, but I'm not overweight. Can I leave myself alone?

9   I'm trying. I went shopping for clothes the other day. Browsing through the store I caught a glimpse of myself in the mirror, and what I saw upset me. It wasn't my body, but the way I was dressed. Long flannel shirt, baggy pants—a woman in hiding. I rummaged through the racks and found something black, sexy, with a little cling. I bought it.

10   Still, this body acceptance thing is going to take time, and I can't do it alone. You see, when I was shopping I noticed an interesting phenomenon. Women's clothes now start at size zero. How low can we possibly go? Before starving into non-existence, it's time to stop and think about something. Is this the change that we've been fighting for—to be heard but not seen? ◆

FREEWRITING ASSIGNMENT ─────────────────────────

Is body size a part of who you are? Do we try to pretend body size doesn't matter, while feeling that it really does? Explain.

CRITICAL READING

1. Why does watching thin women featured on the Academy Awards actually make Hurtes go off of her diet? Why is this ironic?
2. Sandra Hurtes notes that she has been very thin before, but it didn't make her any happier. What is the connection between thinness and happiness? Explain.
3. Analyze Hurtes's tone. How does her tone influence the message of her article? Explain.
4. Who is Hurtes's audience and what assumptions does she make about this audience?
5. Although Hurtes says that she no longer obsesses about her weight, she notes, in her first paragraph, that she is dieting. How does this information influence the rest of her essay? Explain.

CRITICAL WRITING

6. *Exploratory Writing*: Vanity and obsessive preoccupation with self-image have historically been connected to women more than men. In your opinion, do men and women approach the issue of fashion and body image differently? If so, in what ways?
7. *Exploratory Writing*: Social scientists conjecture that physical appearance may indeed affect our chances of securing higher paying jobs and achieving greater social acceptance. In this essay, Sandra Hurtes discusses that her thinness was a source of pride to her, but soon became an obsession. She enjoyed comparing herself to others. Write an essay in which you address how we strive to look a certain way to conform to social expectations that imply success and confidence. Drawing from this article and others in the chapter, write an essay in which you explore the connection between our personal sense of success and our physical appearance.
8. *Exploratory Writing*: In paragraph 3, Hurtes quotes Andie MacDowell's character in *Sex, Lies and Videotape*, in which she tells her therapist that women would be fat and happy if there were no men in the world. Write an essay responding to this idea. On what social and cultural assumptions is it based? Does it have a kernel of truth? Explain.

GROUP PROJECT

9. Make a list of the most popular prime-time shows on television. After compiling the list, identify the body size of the characters on each program. How many male and female characters could be considered overweight? What is the male-to-female ratio of these characters? Discuss your findings with the rest of the class in a discussion about how actors on television promote (or do not promote) certain body types as more desirable than others.

Making Peace with the Pierced
Karen Romell

Perhaps no other fashion statement separates the generations as much as the practice of body modification. Today's youth hardly consider it unusual to have a belly button or an eyebrow pierced. Many of them would argue that it is, in fact, a form of self-expression with deep personal significance, though much of mainstream society still shudders at the thought and judges piercing and tattooing as a disturbing, dangerous, and even threatening trend. Many schools have written piercing out of their dress codes and have instated serious consequences for those who choose to express themselves in this manner. At the same time, other forms of body modification, such as liposuction, facelifts, or breast enhancements, are seen as more and more acceptable, even commonplace. In this article from the *Edmonton Journal*, Karen Romell examines how our culture draws the line between the acceptable and the outrageous concerning body modification.

Karen Romell is a Vancouver journalist. This article first appeared in the *Edmonton Journal* on September 21, 2003.

CRITICAL THINKING   What is your personal opinion about body modification? If you have had parts of your own body tattooed or pierced, including earlobes, what motivated you to do so?

1 Just before my 18th birthday, I almost got a tattoo. I wanted that tattoo for the same reason that Tracy, the vulnerable, central character of *Thirteen*, a hair-raising new coming-of-age flick, wants a tongue piercing: to declare uniqueness, individuality and autonomy over oneself.

2 Thinking about that close call today induces one of those brow-mopping moments when you realize how close you came to altering your destiny in potentially regrettable ways. Had I followed through on that impulse, right now I'd be just another fortysomething gal with a rose on her shoulder. Not unique, and certainly not fashionable.

3 Still, if I were turning 18 today—or a precocious 13—I'd probably go through with that rite of passage. I'd get the tattoo, the piercing or the branding; I'd book it with a group of my friends, and we'd slum it down to the closest epicentre of body-modification.

4 The irony (and beacon of hope for concerned parents) is that tattooing and piercing have become so commonplace in our culture that they've essentially lost their status as a mark of cool and slightly unwholesome otherness and become a badge of group identification as endemic as pukka shells and mood rings were to a previous generation.

5 Blame Baywatch's Pamela Anderson and other Celtic-armband flashing celebs for pushing body modification to the brink of becoming unhip.

6   The practice of cutting, piercing, colouring, splitting and otherwise altering one's body has had a major function in rites of passage, religious practices and transformative rituals in groups and tribes, ranging from Australian aboriginals, who self-induced severe nosebleeds, to certain Roman Catholic communities who today practise self-flagellation and crucifixion.

7   But, in our society, almost no other human activity, with the exception of those related to sexuality, seems so fraught with cultural baggage.

8   This is probably because, in the western world, body modification is considered to be largely a practice of the young; as such, it's prone to the us-versus-them mind-set that characterizes other adolescent behaviours that provoke parents. And now that a growing number of suburban moms are prancing around the poolside with a navel ring, young adults are falling over themselves to up the ante on their declarations of independence and distinction.

9   Enter tongue-splitting. Tongue-splitting entails separating the extension muscle of the tongue into two serpent-like sections by sawing into it, usually over a period of days, with a material like dental floss or fishing wire.

10   Ick.

11   To most of us, the very thought is repugnant. But the visceral torsion we experience at tongue-splitting has little to do with the validity of the exercise and much more to do with an arbitrary, but permeable, line that our culture is constantly re-drawing between accepted and disallowed behaviour (breast implants are OK, having horns implanted on your head is not).

Lawmakers in some U.S. States Drawing the Line at Tongue-Splitting

12   Though exceedingly rare, tongue-splitting is where the hand-wringers are now focusing their energies; like every other divisive youth-generated cultural force that's come before it, from zoot suits to free love, it generates tumultuous questions for our society.

13   In the United States, debate over the issue has reached such a pitch that Illinois recently enacted legislation banning it, and similar legislation is being considered in Tennessee. Tongue-splitting stirs such innate revulsion that it may never be incorporated into the mainstream. On the other hand, the speed with which our culture adopts fringe social trends just might make tongue-splitting one more popular alternative to the standard "let's piss off our parents" teen lexicon.

14   Why do they do it? (When I told people I was writing this article, the response of many wasn't even mild curiosity—it was "Well, they do it because they're sick freaks.")

15   Attempts to engage in any kind of dialogue with the more extreme body modifiers are, to say the least, challenging. In one of my forays into a downtown Vancouver storefront in search of an elusive individual named "Six," (I was told he could help me), a young woman with a variety of facial piercings and a stretched ear-lobe politely but firmly said, "We're not talking to the media."

16   I never did find Six; instead I got Fogg. Fogg wasn't the Jim Rose Circus main-stage attraction I was expecting: Fogg is a middle-aged man with a few visible mod-

ifications (piercings, ear-lobe divots) that aren't much more out-there than your average teenager's—and his latest tattoo is a heart over his heart to commemorate a recent angioplasty.

17   We met downtown on a blindingly bright summer day. Fogg squinted a lot in the light; he looks like a guy who doesn't get a lot of UV. As we walked down the street in search of his suggested venue, a goulash house, he was greeted by a few people along the way. The Granville Mall downtown is Fogg's world—or one of them.

18   We sat down across the street from his piercing and tattooing studio called Next. He used to do the work himself; now he trains and hires his own staff. It's a walk-in turnkey operation with a $250,000 annual cash flow.

19   Body modification has become so commonplace Fogg was able to effectively "retire" four years ago. "I just sit at home and collect the cheques," he said only half-jokingly.

20   Fogg is positioned right in the heart of the paradox inherent in the body-modification culture today: the seamless mainstreaming of a once-edgy form of self-expression. He started the business 10 years ago after training with San Francisco bod-mod guru Fakir Musafar, who is to the BM culture what Carlos Castaneda was to peyote.

21   When I asked Fogg about the new extremes in the movement—the tongue-splitting, the sub-dermal implants, Fogg responds with, "Well, extreme to whom?" It's an answer that has something of a teenager's disingenuousness about it: When I pressed him, even he admitted there are some procedures (such as splitting) that he would not do—"They're too messy."

22   Maybe it's an age thing, but Fogg seems to have lost (if he ever had it) the kind of prickly up-yours attitude that characterizes some of the younger members of the BM community. He's also frankly cynical: He's seen body modification go from an arcane practice embraced by a maverick few, to a banal birthday-party activity for bored teenagers.

23   "In the '90s, it seemed like every college-level girl had to shave off her hair, get a tattoo or some piercings and try an alternative sexuality for three months," he says. "Piercings and tattoos have become a rite of passage in kids' lives now.

24   "Traditionally, it was boy to warrior and girl to woman; you knew someone in your tribe was going to be hurting you. Now the rite of passage is convincing your parents that it's OK."

25   Next's primary clientele is a steady stream of sweet young things in Hello Kitty tuques and Justin Timberlake crop-top T's.

26   The use of BM as fashion accessory wasn't what its first practitioners had in mind. Though BM has occurred throughout all human societies in all periods of history, it really got its toehold in the contemporary western world through the efforts of Fakir Musafar. Musafar happened upon body modification in (where else?) California in (when else?) 1967. He certainly didn't invent BM, but through his book Modern Primitives, he enlarged it in the popular Western consciousness.

27   Western response to body modification was set decades earlier through circuses and carnivals. These fixtures of the North American small-town landscape capi-

talised largely on what could be termed a theatre of the grotesque, presenting, for the eyeball-popping gratification of the viewing public, individuals with so-called "primitive" tribal affiliations: pygmies from New Guinea; women from certain African tribes with what were considered freakishly oversized genitals; people with huge lip-saucers.

28   Purloined from the reaches of colonialism, they were presented along with such exotic tribal specimens as tattooed men and shrunken heads. The ceremonial and cultural implications of their differences were completely ignored. Arrayed alongside the bearded ladies, the two-headed babies, the dwarfs and giants, these human exhibits simply represented a freakish and fascinating otherness that titillated and enthralled millions. And, as Musafar pointed out: "Physical difference frightens people in our culture more than anything else."

'Net Surfing Plumbs the Dark Side of Body Modification

29   Certain groups co-opted body modification practices as signifiers for their own use: tattooed sailors and organized crime members with amputated pinkies come to mind. The link between body modification and the shady, unsavoury and unhealthy was established in Western consciousness very early on.

30   Despite the navel-pierced yummy mummies at your local playgroup, there seems a certain unwillingness among elements of the BM community to let those associations go. Googling the subterranean diaspora of this world is like descending into your teenage nephew's basement bedroom: eerie horror-movie-style music; pictures of feral human faces with lips pulled back over teeth. And, for some reason, a preponderance of creepy clowns—clowns, of course, being figures of such primal malevolence that a good half of the attendees at any kiddie birthday party are pathologically terrified of them.

31   Looking at this stuff—penile sub-incision; urethra re-tooling; pocketing (inserting implements under flaps of skin); suspension (hanging in the air via hooks inserted in various parts of your body)—is mindnumbing, kind of like watching a dozen or so porn movies back to back.

32   Extreme body modification has generated much discussion in psychological and psychiatric literature. A survey of recent diagnostic literature measures the extreme variants of BM on a sort of Richter scale of self-injurious behaviour, along with cutting (another behaviour the rebellious teen exhibits in the movie *Thirteen*) and biting or chewing oneself.

33   A number of these theories suggest that the actual physical act of being altered in some way is "positively reinforcing" for these people; in other words, they get off on the pain.

34   The neurochemical response to physical trauma is a subject of much current medical interest; what's certain is that the brain responds to pain with its own exquisite arsenal of self-created pharmaceuticals, potent chemicals that mimic the effects of opiates.

35   Body-modification practitioners insist that saying you're into it for the pain is like saying women have babies because they love childbirth. But in many of the tra-

ditional tribal rituals with which body modification is associated, pain serves [as] a powerful catalyst for transformation and transcendence.

36 In our culture, where even going to the dentist scares a lot of people, the inclination of most is to be averse to pain. Of more probable relevance is the link between pain and so-called "self- medication."

37 The theory of self-medication is prevalent right now, referencing examples from all kinds of human behaviour, from alcoholism to drug addiction to compulsive shopping. It posits that certain human beings, under stress or with innate neurochemical deficiencies, learn to manipulate their own inner pharmaceuticals by engaging in behaviours that create the release of positively reinforcing brain chemicals. According to this view, BM may be one of many human activities we intuitively undertake to self-correct brain dysfunction.

38 Other psychological theories explore the link between self-image and BM. A number of academic studies (including one recently conducted by psychologist Del Paulhus and associates at the University of B.C.) have linked BM practices with low self-esteem in their subjects. Mark Schaeller, a psychologist at UBC, cites pain studies that suggest some people use pain as a way of escaping from what's called "objective self-awareness." In other words, I'm looking at myself the way I think others are looking at me, making me hyper-aware of my perceived flaws and faults.

39 "This may be useful when we are attempting to make a transformation from the person we've been for the last few years . . . into a brand-new person," Schaeller said.

40 Dr. Armando Favazza, a University of Missouri psychiatry professor who is one of the few academics to have studied the phenomenon extensively, has written a book, *Bodies Under Siege*, on the subject. Though the title makes it sound like a Moral Majority pamphlet against perversion, Favazza is in fact a careful, cautious and analytic observer of present BM practices.

41 "First of all, you have to remember that we're talking about a very small number of people," he said when I interviewed him by phone.

42 Most individuals engage in BM for aesthetic reasons, whether it's a pair of pierced ears or a full-body tattoo. The remaining minority can be divided into even smaller groups whose motivations range from the age-old adolescent avenue of "shock value," to those with mental or emotional illness.

43 "A few individuals get involved for therapeutic reasons, as a way to try to establish some control over their own bodies," Favazza said. "Some of these people who do this heavy-duty stuff, it's a type of morbid self-help; without realising it, they're trying to establish some sort of order and a spiritual sense in their lives."

Intrusive Procedures Bring to Some a Sense of Vindication, Even Joy

44 This is certainly true from the testimonies I read of some of the BM practitioners; one "Pierre," for example, whose online story about an attempt at suspension, "It Just Didn't Feel Right. This Time," is a heart-breaker ("I had been drained for awhile of a lot of feelings . . . sure I could still put on a happy face, but finding happiness seemed like a hopeless cause") enmeshed with lamentations about his excess weight and disastrous personal relationships.

45   Still, it's abundantly clear reading through the posted literature and the exultant testimonies from individuals who've had (or claim to have had) extraordinarily intrusive procedures done to them (suspensions, tongue-splitting) that it often serves as a catharsis, a clearing-out of negativity and doubt that's replaced by a profound sense of vindication, ebullience, the restoration of balance and harmony—and even joy.

46   Other studies have noted a link between BM practices, particularly of the more extreme variety (tongue-splitting and suspensions) as being linked with higher anxiety levels, increased openness to experience, and perhaps most interestingly, a link between BM and psychopathy—one of the most exquisitely troubling and clinically unsolvable personality disorders.

47   That link, however, is related to, not a cause of, psychopathy. In other words, don't worry too much if your kid comes home with multiple piercings; do worry, however, if he comes home with multiple piercings and starts torturing the cat.

48   BM practitioners understandably distrust the gamut of explanations offered for their behaviour. This was brought home to me when I engaged in a brief e-mail dialogue with Shannon Larratt, arguably the king of Canada's BM movement. Larratt edits an E-zine called BMEzine. Our e-mail correspondence started cordially but turned icy almost instantly.

49   When I asked him the obvious question: why do you do it?, he replied, "I think it's very sad that people who make decisions outside of the mainstream—that is, for themselves, not just because they were in effect forced to 'fit in'—are somehow expected to go to great lengths to validate their behaviour through complex explanations."

50   How about, how are you positioned vis-à-vis mainstream society? I assume you're not working at Starbucks.

51   "Well," Larratt responded testily, "Starbucks won't hire people with piercings, so instead I formed my own IVR (Interactive Voice Response) corporation. As a result, I've got a net worth in the millions and two Porsches sitting in my driveway—those people at Starbucks who refuse to hire 'people like me' can kiss my a—."

52   He finished by making a very good point about how no one ever bothers to grill a woman about her breast implants.

53   In this respect Larratt is right; it's inherently absurd to demand a thoughtfully constructed justification of behaviour from one population and not another. But it's also counter-intuitive to declare that most people aren't into body modification as a way of positioning themselves outside conventional culture, no matter how widespread some BM practices are becoming.

54   Body modification is, at its core, a form of overt social communication; and this holds true whether you do it because you want to look cool, or because it expresses your neo-primitive spirituality, or because it's personally totemic, or because the rest of the girls in your Grade 9 class are doing it, or because you're a deeply disturbed person whose body modification practice has a significance that is known only to yourself.

55 It's not much of a stretch to see BM as a marker of disengagement from mainstream society, and/or as a self-created rite-of-passage—"Look, I'm not afraid of clowns/pain/death any more!"

56 But it has also become a mark of engagement, as with Tracy in *Thirteen*, "Look, I'm not a loser anymore." In truth, body modification—even more than the clothes you wear—is the most obvious thing you can do to represent your internal state/tribe/ community/esthetic.

57 Schaeller observed: "Even though most of the bod-mod people I talked to said, 'There is no tribe,' everything they do and the way they construct their lifestyle seems to contradict this."

58 If it is a tribe, however, it's one that still claims to be special by virtue of being outside the mainstream. Every Web site I hit had, as its overt message, an ecstatic endorsement of the joys of belonging to a unique and astonishing gathering of wonderful "individuals."

59 This shouldn't be truly surprising; you can find that same mind-set in everything from a Mary Kay convention to a gathering of Freemasons. Moreover, BM is perfect for someone with a chip on his/ her shoulder: nothing vindicates alienation like the pure objectification that results from, say, having horns implanted in your forehead.

60 This may also be why body modification is so heartily embraced (along with Marilyn Manson, Satanism/witchcraft, gory video games and devil metal) by a small though highly visible segment of youth. In other times and cultures, these kids might have become perfectly functional shamans or honoured warriors.

61 Today, suburban blandness and cultural sameness have rendered entire groups of youth without a ring to hang on to—unless it's dangling from their nipple. Kids love theatre, after all; it normalizes their own over-developed and intense emotionality.

62 Legislating against something like tongue-splitting because it's unappealing to most people is treading dangerous ground in terms of social policy, says Bethra Szumski, the president of the U.S.-based Association of Professional Piercers. Besides, she says, it makes no sense.

63 "I'm very middle of the road, but our government is now saying that there's no reason we can find that this (tongue-splitting) would be okay." Szumski adds that Illinois's anti-splitting legislation is "a form of legislative bigotry."

64 "The separation they're making is that if you wanted a doctor to cut your chest open and stick some bags of water in there because you want big breasts, then that's okay, but if you want something that's not a popular esthetic then they can say that that's not right. . . . I think that legislating it out of existence is incredibly dangerous."

Canadian Legislators Unlikely to Copy U.S. Crackdown

65 It's highly unlikely that Canadian legislators will tackle the issue the way some of their U.S. colleagues have, given our often more vigorous and liberal stand on personal rights. And the fact is, it's an issue that impacts very few.

66 The odd teenager in Windsor or Edmonton may be sawing his tongue with fishing wire as we go to press, but the recovery down-time, invasiveness of the proce-

dure and general ramifications on a social and even financial basis (you drastically limit your employability if your tongue is divided in two) likely mean that it will never become hugely popular.

67   What's more certain is that 'soft' body modification will continue, for a while at least, to have some kind of significance and appeal to a wide range of otherwise mainstream North Americans.

68   How that particular cultural skew will fare in the next 20 years is open to debate.

69   Szumski sees body modification becoming a more commonplace and accepted part of popular culture, and it's difficult to argue with her.

70   "My mom was a hippie, was in Berkeley for the Summer of Love, and when I showed up with a pierced navel 14 years ago she suggested that I seek professional help," Szumski laughs. "I don't think that it flip-flops; I think the layer just moves up a rung.

71   "In the '60s it was a big deal, and now in another 10 years it's not going to be a big deal to have our ears stretched; it's just going to be part of the mainstream."

72   On the other hand, this generation of pierced and tattooed "fashionistas," as Fogg disparagingly calls them, may, in 50 years time, all be as hopelessly branded by virtue of their various piercings and tattoos as they are by names like Brittany, Jason and Madison, or indeed as I would have been had I had that rose tattooed on my shoulder.

73   Given the way our culture works—a kind of warp-drive factory of ideas and trends that seems to speed up faster than the cream-puff conveyer belt on that classic *I Love Lucy* episode—BM may lose its cool as quickly as platform shoes did.

74   As Shannon Larratt puts it: "Death to BM; long live BM!" ◆

FREEWRITING ASSIGNMENT

Did you try to distinguish yourself physically at some point in your life? If so, what did you do and what motivated this form of expression?

CRITICAL READING

1. Do you agree with the author's claim that BM (body modification) is "a form of social communication"? What is being communicated?
2. Why does Bethra Szumski feel that legislating tongue-splitting out of existence would be "extremely dangerous"?
3. What is meant by Shannon Larrett's concluding statement, "Death to BM; long live BM"? To what historical expression does this refer?
4. What is the author's position on BM? Does she believe that this practice will endure?
5. How might BM be considered a rite of passage today?

CRITICAL WRITING

6. *Exploratory Writing*: Discuss the distinction between forms of body modification that are socially acceptable and those that are not. Why are breast implants and plastic surgery acceptable by the majority of North American society, whereas tongue-splitting and horn implants are unacceptable?

7. *Persuasive Writing*: Do you feel there should be legal limits to the degree of body modification that a member of our society is allowed? Why or why not? Take a position and argue your point in an essay.

8. *Personal Narrative*: Write an essay describing a time when you discovered a deeper sense of self-awareness by changing something about yourself. Perhaps you wore different clothes or makeup, dyed or cut your hair, or got a tattoo or piercing. Did people react or treat you differently because of your new look? Did you act differently? Did you find the experience empowering? Explain.

9. In her article, Karen Romell quotes Shannon Larratt, editor of BMEzine. Explore Larratt's site, and particularly his response to this article, at **www.bmezine.com/news/pubring/20030904.html**. In it, he criticizes Romell's bias. After viewing the site and reading some of Larratt's columns, do you agree with his assertions about Romell's objectivity? Why or why not?

GROUP PROJECTS

10. With your group, explore the ways in which youth culture attempts to distinguish itself. Make a list of the cultural expressions that separate each generation and discuss the motivation behind these expressions. With your group and later with the class, discuss emerging trends and conjecture what trends might come next.

11. Do a class survey. How many students have some form of BM? What kinds? What were their motivations? Have the modifications had the desired effect? Are there any regrets or reversals?

12. In a group, explore a number of body modification Internet sites. How do these sites differ from one another? Is there a common underlying message? Summarize your findings and share them with the class.

Canada Falls Out of Fashion

Serena French

Serena French gives some surprising statistics that support what you may already have suspected: Canada is in a state of sartorial decline. It wasn't always that way, but over the past several decades many disparate factors have conspired to reduce us from star to bit player on the international fashion scene. French uses examples to illustrate her point that demographics, monetary policy, weak retailing, and diversified discretionary spending may have as much to do with Canada's fall from fashion grace as does our reputation as discount shoppers.

Serena French is the executive director of *Suede Magazine*. This article appeared in the *National Post* on December16, 2000.

CRITICAL THINKING	How do you think Canada compares with other countries in our appreciation of designer fashion?

1   A fashion-conscious friend of mine recently took a trip to New York City and, brimming with incredulity, had a revelation to share upon her return.

2   "Women—down—there—shop—in-stilettos!"

3   It was not as though she'd never seen a pair of unsensible shoes in action before: What was remarkable was that it reinforced how one could never expect the same sighting—of a heel that is the height of fashion in places where this sort of thing matters—on Canadian pavement.

4   Imagine: A stiletto, on Bloor Street or Robson, in broad daylight? It's not just a dearth of sexy footwear on our streets. Ever seen one of those Christian Dior saddle bags, the logoed purse in those ads with the sweaty models? In a store here? Ever heard of Earl? They've been the hot jeans brand from L.A. for two years. Michel Perry boots? Cameron Diaz steps on a villain's neck in a pair in Charlie's Angels.

5   Did you know that miniskirts and tapered pant legs—that is, bigger at the thigh, tighter at the ankle—are just coming back into style, and should not have been in your closet, let alone on your person, for the last four years? The iron curtain of fashion has silently fallen, and no one even noticed.

6   Sure, Gucci just opened on Bloor Street. There are also Chanel, Prada and Louis Vuitton boutiques. McDonald's went to Moscow, too. "Too provincial for Tom," said a guest referring to designer Tom Ford's absence at Gucci's recent store opening in Toronto.

7   Balenciaga? Anyone?

8   The name of the hot Paris house, whose clothes were snapped up by fashion people during show week, does not exactly trip off the tongue here. In fact, Canadians are spending less on fashion. In 1992, the amount of income spent on apparel was 4.9%; by 1996, it had dropped to 3.6%. According to retail consultant J.C. Williams Group's national retail report, the number of respondents who agree

with the statement "I try to keep abreast of changes in style and fashions" dropped from 36% in 1990 to 27% in 1999.

9   This in spite of the fact that 600,000 copies of fashion magazines are consumed in this country every month. Which doesn't even begin to touch the fashion education contained in *In Style*, the magazine of celebrity fashion picks, with a circulation of more than 100,000 in Canada, or fashion coverage in newspapers, magalogues and myriad other birdcage liners.

10   Is it that Canadians think they're fashionable, the same way the French think they're funny? *Vogue* may think so. Readers of the fashion bible would have stopped dead on some damning evidence in last month's issue. The article advocated cross-border shopping: "Head north—to the great sample sale in the sky."

11   The tragic truth was what a Seattle makeup artist breathlessly told the writer: "And stuff that sells out here doesn't sell out there. Like if you wanted to buy one of those Hermes dog-collar cuffs . . ." Items such as Roberto Cavalli gilded jeans, sold out across the United States thanks to an appearance on *Sex and the City*, hung "naively" on a rack at a store in Montreal, according to the *Vogue* feature. Naively.

12   Sadly, it's not just *Vogue*. There are accounts of celebrities shopping for that last pistol-hot Cartier watch model with a waiting list of hundreds who find it at . . . a store in Toronto, where they don't want, God forbid, such pistol-hot things. Like, the peasants don't understand what gold lies in their own backyards.

13   How did this happen?

14   In decades past, Canadians seemed to be more in the vanguard of things fashion. There was the Festival of Canadian Fashion. Alfred Sung was on the cover of *Maclean's*. Canada gave birth to M.A.C., the cosmetics of choice of celebrities and the fashion world. Club Monaco. A plethora of top models. Linda Evangelista. Fashion Television was invented here, for God's sake. In *Flare* magazine's 20th anniversary, John MacKay, founding editor of *Toronto Life Fashion*, put the bygone era down to the Baby Boomer bulge. "In the last year of the '70s and the first six years of the '80s . . . the world embraced clothing and shopping in a way it never had before. You had the largest group of the population . . . all reaching 30, all with some money, all looking, in their narcissism, to clothing."

15   Sound familiar?

16   Fortunes have risen again, but even in this bull market, Canadians seem not to have joined the fashion frenzy. Our fashion-loser reputation is partly reflected in the difficulty Canadian journalists have in getting into the top runway shows. "We didn't let in anyone from Africa either," as one veteran was told at a recent round in Paris. Canada is not merely small, but small and unimportant.

17   The only hamlet of exception may be Montreal. The myth that la belle province is more steeped in fashion may have support: More Montrealers than the national average agreed in the Williams Group survey that they try to

keep abreast of style and fashion, and really enjoy shopping for clothes. They also enjoy extravagance more than the average Canadian and Torontonian. Their reward? Quebec's very own edition of *Elle* (for French-speaking fashionistas). English-speaking Canadians will receive their belated *Elle* this spring.

18   But two Canadian fashion magazines have risen and thrived over the last two decades, with the third arriving, not because we have more fashion chromosomes per capita but because they function as local catalogues: Much of the merchandise featured in American magazines is not available in Canada. We don't get a lot of the stuff everyone else considers must-haves of the moment, and what we do get, we don't buy.

19   Is it weak retailing or weak demand?

20   In Canada, high-end designer fashion is such a small percentage of the market it's not even counted. "You're talking about what the one percent wear," says David Howell, of NPD Group, a market-research firm that tracks apparel sales.

21   Only retailers know, and they don't like to say who, how many or how much. Andrew Jennings, president of Holt Renfrew, reveals in *Toronto Life* this month that regular customers buying designer sportswear spend $20,000 to $30,000 a season. In boutiques such as Calvin Klein, Giorgio Armani and Yves Saint Laurent, a top customer spends $100,000 per season. But an upscale American department store, a Holt's competitor, looked into coming to Canada many years ago and discovered in focus groups that target Canadian shoppers were less interested in labels. It was a taste of declines to come.

22   Anecdotal retail evidence stands up: Many Canadian stores that sold high fashion have closed or haven't kept up with the buying boom elsewhere. Toronto is a case in point. Simpson's had the powerhouse of The Room. Eaton's had three tiers. At the top end, higher than The Room, was The French Room, then the Townhouse, and several designer boutiques, all gone. A long list of independents that sold fashion with credibility has not been replaced. The Polo/Ralph Lauren store closed and the Versace boutique is closing. Uptown, Ira Berg, after 65 years serving the carriage trade, became, briefly, a fast-food chicken restaurant and is now a New Balance sneaker store.

23   "There's a clear trend toward casual clothing," says Ed Hayes, a retail analyst at Canadian Imperial Bank of Commerce. "People don't get dressed up for occasions the way they used to." After the first pair of chinos, it's a slippery slope. Canadians have become badly dressed.

24   John Williams, a Toronto-based retail consultant, says the trend cuts across North America. "People are less hooked on fashion, but think they're more sophisticated," he says, "so I think they're expressing it through wine cellars, where they eat, smoking cigars, driving BMWs, they're sinking fortunes into homes. What's on your back is far less important."

25   Particularly when the back has developed unsightly bulges. The big-spending Boomer cohort is ageing. "The fashion has to cover the body, rather than show it off," Mr. Williams points out. "You spend less, I think, statistically, on clothing as you get older. So there's a demographic shift behind this, too."

26   Weak demand for swank clothes is understandable in some Fargo backwater, but we're Canadian! We're better educated. We're cosmopolitan. We have musical theatre, Starbucks, an appreciation for scented candles. We have a robust economy, too. But in Vancouver, Toronto and elsewhere, we're not dressing the part of the world-class city, as we so often like to call ourselves.

27   Alas, Mr. Hayes says, "It's also true that, on average, incomes are lower in Canada [than in the United States]." John, a Toronto man who says he spends $175,000 a year on fashion, does all his shopping one-stop at Holt Renfrew. "People have the money," he says. "But a lot of people are afraid to spend the money. They conform. They're not very daring. I interview people who make maybe $40,000 a year who look incredible. And then I'll interview someone who makes a quarter mil', who looks like she just came out of Cactus."

28   Canadians have not been sold on "investment" fashion purchases, be it an Hermes belt, Prada bag or Burberry coat. Instead they have been seduced by "value" retailers. "There are lots of stores now that knock off," says John, "so people don't have to buy a $4,000 coat when they can get a perfectly good one for $600. I don't think people here are worldly enough to care and to appreciate the quality and what goes into making major designer goods. That's something you get or you don't."

29   Fashion has become democratized to the point where it is no longer fashion. It is uniform. Bitching that everyone has the same pants as you? If they cost $50, most people have $50 to spend. Pay more, get exclusivity. Lower disposable incomes and a weak dollar have contributed to a discount culture. Canadians have a reputation for being cheap. Why else would Old Navy and American Eagle come to Canada, bargain-priced jeans flapping from the flagpole, staking a claim with dozens of stores? We like good value.

30   Hence the Guccis and Pradas and Louis Vuittons are here to cater to migrators with foreign currencies, like the Vogue writers coming up to pillage Marc Jacobs jeans and Chloe tops and cackling about it all the way to the border: "And it's cheap, because of the strength of the dollar." So even though you don't see much luxe on Canadian streets, one executive of a French luxury goods house says sales have steadily risen in Canada, coinciding with the luxury goods boom worldwide. The owner of Fritz Lang in Calgary and the new Bruce boutique in Vancouver told *Saturday Night* that more than half of his clientele at Bruce is tourist, and 70% is Asian. Campbell McDougall says the few Canadians "who are into [fashion] so often shop abroad, or in New York."

31   Canadians who shop when they travel have discovered something: Those Europeans and New Yorkers are so well dressed for two reasons. First, it's cheaper there. A pair of Balenciaga pants that cost 2,000 French francs in Paris, $400 at the current exchange rate, cost $895 plus tax at a boutique in Toronto. If you remember to take advantage of the tax refund at the airport (about 13%), the savings of shopping abroad are significant.

32   Are Canadian retailers being gougey with imports? Call it the cost of doing business. One retailer who shops in Paris uses a rule of thumb: If something costs the store 100 francs to buy from a designer, it will end up costing $100 on the store floor.

33   But there's a consequence to shopping abroad or at the same cheap places: Shopping at home will start to hurt. Stores will close for lack of business; none will take their place, and before you know it, shopping at home starts to feel about as exciting as choosing between a tube of toothpaste and a potato at the GUM.

34   Canadians shop abroad and in the United States in spite of the exchange rate, for reasons as old as cross-border shopping itself: the groaning board of selection. "When I go to the U.S., I power shop," says Jill, a woman who will spend $1,600 on a bag and $800 on a pair of boots and $3,000 on a dress. "I can be happy on the third floor of Bergdorf's. Sales are phenomenal down there. And even with the exchange, it's worth it."

35   Most of the reason the selection is better in the United States is demographic: It's a bigger market. But it's also the toughest. "Canadian [retailers] going to the U.S. tend not to do very well, whereas U.S. retailers coming to Canada tend to do relatively well," notes Mr. Hayes. "And one of the explanations is that they just are stronger retailers . . . They will have an offering that will attract the customer more—I suppose, even in some way, stimulate consumer demand."

36   Oh yeah, merchandising. A novel assortment. Could it be weak retailing leaving us style-starved?

37   "I just think a lot of buyers here aren't really tuned in to what people want," says John. "A lot of them are afraid to order a ton of stuff and get stuck with it. I don't think they have the confidence in what people are going to buy. And it comes to price. I don't think men especially are prepared to spend on clothes. You see someone getting out of a Benz in an ugly ski jacket and a pair of Roots boots."

38   Risk has left the building in Canada. Simpson's was bought by The Bay; The Bay has kept alive The Room, its enclave of designer fashion, by adding safer fit designers such as Moschino, Balmain and Nina Ricci, not rocking out with collections such as Chloe because the customers don't have "It Girl" figures. Sales and numbers of customers have increased over the years, but that might be due to consolidation of the market.

39   Eaton's tried to go deep into fashion and high end against Holt Renfrew all at once, failed, was bought by Sears and, with its grand reopening a couple of weeks ago, has settled somewhere mid-market again—this time with a "boutique" level of service. One Saturday a woman riding the escalator at Toronto's flagship Eaton Centre had to ask her friend: "Does it look any different to you?" More to the point: Does it look any different from anywhere else? What is surprising is how few of the lines are new to the Canadian market. The top end of the fashion offering includes what are known as designer "bridge" lines, that is, lower-priced spinoffs, all previously available in Canada at other stores. So far the kudos from observers have been reserved for the home floors. "Mundane" is the descriptor for the fashion floors.

40   If fashion retailing in Canada persists in being dictated by focus groups, it will quickly lead to consumer boredom. It's the same trap retailers in some American cities have fallen into, according to the J.C. Williams Group. "On a recent trip to malls in Nashville, Chicago, and Toronto," said its October report, "we were shocked by the sameness of store format, design, levels of staffing, and actual

merchandise. If you didn't know the store name, you wouldn't know which [one] you were in."

41 "I don't know what's happened here," says Jill. "Maybe it's the end of the boutiques, where you'd go and find all these interesting designers. There was much more variety when I was younger. It's either completely matronly or it's too young and faddy."

42 While there are few independent boutiques left in Toronto, other cities have seen the rebirth of more creative environments, lifestyle stores, like Colette, in Paris, that offer a discerning selection of home decor, personal gadgets, clothes and accessories. Mr. McDougall, with his Bruce boutique in Vancouver, is the only one in Canada so far to attempt that mix.

43 Holt Renfrew, after having unveiled plans internally to lower the overall "price position" of its merchandise almost two years ago, is now poised to unveil a "lab"— a separately merchandised area that will offer a medley of new designers. In this month's *Toronto* Holt's president Andrew Jennings says he hopes to raise sales of private labels from 28% to 38%, and keep his jet-set clientele in Canada "by offering her a greater selection than she can find on one of her international weekend jaunts." Some customers feel he, and others, are failing.

44 "Holt Renfrew should be ashamed of themselves," says Jill. "It's convenient, it's a great-looking store, they've got great sales staff, but they just don't have the merchandise. What happened to private label? I used to live in it, and now it's just bad. I had a black tie to go to eight months ago. Couldn't find a damn thing. Bloor Street I find has very little to offer, other than if you want a pair of black pants."

45 While some members of the press also blame the insipid retail landscape for Canada's poor reputation in the international fashion scene, some retailers scoff at the notion that a more adventurous, Colette-type store could fly in Canada because the market is too conservative.

46 The next time you find yourself complaining about big brands taking over your shopping experience, blame your choices. And then blame retailers for listening to you. ◆

FREEWRITING ASSIGNMENT

Calculate what percentage of your disposable income you spend on fashion in a year. Do you think this figure is too high, too low, or just right? Does the amount you spend on clothing reflect your interest in fashion, the limitations of your income, or some other influence?

CRITICAL READING

1. French asserts that Canada is not a "fashionable" country. In your own words, what does she mean by fashionable? Is it important to you that Canada is fashionable? Explain.

2. French claims that Canadians are less interested in fashion now than we were even a decade ago. What evidence does she give to support this statement?

3. While fashion retail has declined in Canada, fashion magazines are "thriving" here; what accounts for this apparent discrepancy?

4. The author mentions Montreal as an exception to the general decline of interest in fashion in Canada, but offers no explanations for this anomaly. Can you think of any?

5. What does the *Vogue* article referred to mean when it says that a pair of Roberto Cavalli jeans were hung "naively" on a rack in a Montreal store?

6. Is it true that "[p]eople are less hooked on fashion, but think they're more sophisticated"? That is, are we now diverting our spending to expensive cars and luxury items for the home, rather than devoting our discretionary income to high-end clothing? What would account for this shift in consuming patterns?

7. What assumptions does French make about her audience in this piece? What is their probable social, political, and economic background? Refer to examples from the article to support your response.

8. French implies that the lack of availability of designer fashion in Canada is due in large part to the unwillingness of Canadian shoppers to support this segment of the industry. Do you agree with her conclusion, based on her evidence? Why or why not?

CRITICAL WRITING

9. *Exploratory Writing:* In your mind, what are some of the reasons Canada may lag behind in terms of the fashion world? How, for instance, could factors such as our weather contribute to our hesitation to "shop in stilettos"?

10. Read an American magazine such as *Vogue* or one of the other glossies. Take note of the sources in the ads. How much of the advertised merchandise is available in Canada?

11. Explore the **www.style.ca** Web site. How do you think the creators of this site might respond to this article?

GROUP PROJECTS

12. In your group, create a mock inventory of Canadian fashion. Compile a list of items of clothing that other cultures might recognize as definitively Canadian—winter boots or toques, for example. Share your list with the rest of the class. As a class, discuss what these items of clothing suggest about Canadians and fashion.

13. Visit the Web sites of some Canadian designers and those of European designers. How do they differ? Do the European designers appear to have characteristics in common that the Canadians don't have, and vice versa?

If so, what are they? Is there something about the Canadian designs that make them uniquely Canadian?

14. Have each member of your group conduct several interviews with members of your parents' generation and with your own peers. How do their attitudes about fashion differ? Summarize your findings.

VIEWPOINTS

► **A Man's Guide to Slimming Couture**
Scott McKeen

► **Why Do We Get to Laugh at Fat Guys?**
Catherine Lawson

The next two readings explore different views of the same issue. Although obesity is a sensitive issue for many people, it is also a common theme in humour. And culturally, we seem to like fat guys. They play funny sidekicks in movies, goofy fathers and husbands in sitcoms, and everybody's pal at the bar. In "A Man's Guide to Slimming Couture," Scott McKeen treats the issue of a pot-belly with humour and cunning as he details eight ways to hide one's middle region.

Although popular media seem to welcome the comedic outlet provided by fat men, the same does not seem to hold true for women. Socially, we simply do not find fat women as funny, or as acceptable, as fat men. Catherine Lawson, responding to McKeen's article, asks "Why Do We Get to Laugh at Fat Guys?" After laughing at McKeen's list, Lawson suddenly realizes that she would not be laughing if the article gave advice to fat women. Is this lack of sensitivity to male obesity fair to men? And why is it more acceptable for men to be fat than for women? But why do we feel it is permissible to lampoon fat people in general?

Scott McKeen and Catherine Lawson are both reporters for the *Ottawa Citizen*, in which their articles appeared on December 9, 1999.

CRITICAL THINKING

Think of the number of popular movies and television programs featuring fat men as the focal point for humour. Now think of the number of programs that feature fat women. How do the two compare?

A Man's Guide to Slimming Couture
Scott McKeen

1 Trick No. 1: Never, ever wear horizontal stripes. Vertical stripes, in shirts and in suits, are good because they lengthen one's silhouette, which is slimming, don't you know?

2 Trick No. 2: Always wear a jacket or suit, unless you work near dangerous industrial machinery. Jackets are good because they hide that stuff spilling over your belt.

3 Trick No. 2A: A double-breasted jacket, with its large lapels, can create a slimming V-shape and is always buttoned, putting a curtain between your gut and the world.

4 Trick No. 2B: Warning: if a double-breasted jacket is too long it will shorten your legs, visually, and you'll be a fat troll in a blazer. On some men, blazers look tent-like. Ask your wife or girlfriend: "Do I look fat in this?"

5 Trick No. 2C: A three-button single-breasted jacket is often better than a two-button because the lapels are shorter, making the body of the suit—and you—appear longer and slimmer.

6 Trick No. 3: Never, ever, tie your necktie too short. It will sit over your belly like a neon motel sign, pointing directly to your straining waistline, screaming "NO VACANCY."

7 Trick No. 4: The fat man's paradox: a big man squeezed into small clothes will look bigger, what with all the tell-tale strains, wrinkles, rolls, button gaps and—yeesh—underwear lines.

8 Trick No. 4A: Buy one size too big and you'll look relaxed; your collar won't create an unsightly skin turtleneck and your clothes will drape properly, hiding those rolls or bulges.

9 Trick No. 4B: When shopping, don't even look at the suit or waist size. If it fits, it fits. Just because you're now wearing a 42 waist doesn't mean you're not still a great big loveable guy. Honest.

10 Trick No. 4C: If you scrutinize waist size, pride will take over. You'll walk out with a size 34 waist and in those pants, you'll look stressed, fat, and your vitals will go numb. Hence the stress.

11 Trick No. 5: Stick with dark, classic, and solid colors—black, blue and grey. Anything else, especially on a shirt, will draw the eye to your stomach. You don't want eyes on your stomach.

12 Trick No. 5A: Be mostly monochromatic in your entire ensemble. A dark shirt and trousers create one, long, slimming silhouette. A light shirt with dark trousers draws the eye to the border between the two, your belt line, which, to the observer, looks like the equator.

13 Trick No. 5B: The same rules apply to a jacket and shirt. Wear an unbuttoned dark jacket with a white shirt and it will be like opening the curtain on an off-Broadway production of Porky's.

14 Trick No. 5C: Same goes for dark suspenders over a white shirt. The suspenders will frame the bulk like a photo of fat. A dark vest with dark trousers is good, though.

15 Trick No. 6: Damn the fashions, pleats on pants are good for pot bellies. Straight, slim-profile pants contrast with a larger upper half, creating "chicken legs," as one well-known local sartor put it.

16 Trick No. 7: To tuck or not to tuck? Unless you're in the cast of *Friends*, skinny, or under 25, tuck your shirt into your pants. Anything else screams: FAT GUY HIDING HIS FAT.

17 Trick No. 8: Don't fret over The Big Question About Pot Bellies, which is: where should my belt ride—below the gut, on the gut, or above the gut? Let comfort decide. . . .

18 Trick No. 8A: But be warned: a belt riding below the gut can cause an unsightly case of cascading corpulence. On the other hand, chest-high pants makes it appear as if your shoulders are riding directly atop your butt.

19 Trick No. 8B: Suspenders can work, especially on bigger pots. They allow for large pants to cross just below the navel—and stay there. No problems then with butt crack, shirt-tail escape or that cinched look you get with a too-tight belt across the stomach.

20 Trick No. 8C: Owners of difficult-to-fit potbellies might want to try a pair of tailored slacks, especially if the proper waist size creates other problems, like an unwieldy crotch. (Don't even go there.) Handmade slacks will cost you so much money, though, that you might actually prefer numb vitals. Ask your wife. ◆

Why Do We Get to Laugh at Fat Guys?

Catherine Lawson

1 The first time I read Scott McKeen's article on eight tricks to hide a pot belly [above], I laughed all the way through it. I loved its hectoring tone, and the way he didn't mince words on the best way to disguise fat wrinkles, rolls, button gaps and underwear lines.

2 Then it hit me. Would I be laughing if these were fashion tips for women? I thought of all the fashion advice for overweight women that I have ever read. The tone is usually deadly serious, and there are terms like "empowerment," "self-acceptance" and "body image" sprinkled liberally throughout.

3 Mr. McKeen, on the other hand, although he dispenses some excellent advice, is playing it for laughs.

4 So why is it still OK to make jokes about fat men, but completely taboo to laugh at fat women? (Heck, I'm not even comfortable putting the words "fat" and "women" together.)

5 Would I have accepted a story for publication that described portly women in double-breasted blazers as looking like fat trolls? Definitely not. Would I have chosen to illustrate a story on fashion for plus-size women with a close-up photo of a stomach encased in a too-tight top? Unthinkable.

6 It's conventional wisdom that men and women have vastly different body images. Kellogg's Special K has spun an entire ad campaign on this. Remember the TV commercial with the men sitting around a bar, whining about their figures? We laughed because it was ludicrous to think of men obsessing that way. The current ad shows a very flabby, but very happy, man at a beach. "You accept his imperfections. Why not your own?" the ad asks.

7 The subtext is that overweight women should lighten up, so to speak, and be more like those jolly, chubby men, who can still enjoy a day at the beach, despite the fact their flesh has all the pretense, but none of the cuteness, of a baby beluga.

8 There is truth in the Special K campaign, or it would not resonate as it does. However, it would be a simplification to say that overweight men are happy and overweight women are not. It's been reported that aspiring comic Flip Schultz, the star of the Special K commercial, has lost 20 pounds since he saw himself in that Speedo. The late John Candy was known to be extremely sensitive about his weight, and never wanted his comedy to be focused on it.

9 And we all know women who are comfortable in their own skins. Remember actress Camryn Manheim when she accepted her Emmy award exclaiming, "This is for all the fat girls!"

10 But there's only one funny fat girl on TV these days—Mimi on The Drew Carey Show. And the writers and producers have gone out of their way to stress that Mimi is not funny because she is fat. It's because she wears neon blue eyeshadow, her clothes look like they came from a circus, and she has the personality of a piranha.

11 Drew Carey has to put up with jokes about his weight, but he is also held to be loveable. He's part of a long tradition of loveable fat guys. In *Only the Lonely,* John Candy's cuddly character didn't have to lose an ounce to win the heart of a young, slim woman. Neither did John Belushi in *Continental Divide.* Even Mr. Special K guy has someone to call honey. But no one has cast Ms. Manheim as a romantic lead.

12 Women pick up on that kind of inequity.

13 And it leads us to the stark truth that, in our society, a woman's appearance is still far more important than a man's. We can laugh at fat guys because they are also inherently loveable, well-dressed or not. A woman who fails to dress in a way that disguises those extra pounds is out of the game. If you make a joke about a man's gut, all you've done is make fun of his stomach. Insult a woman's body, and you wound her soul.

14 I called Scott McKeen to ask if there had been any complaints about his article when it ran in the *Edmonton Journal.*

15 "Not a one," he said.

16 Many people did ask if the pot belly in the photo is his. He stresses that it definitely is not.

17 You see, fat guys may be funny, but no one aspires to be one. ◆

FREEWRITING ASSIGNMENT

Answer Lawson's question in your own words: "Why do we get to laugh at fat guys?"

CRITICAL READING

1. Analyze McKeen's tone. How does his tone influence the message of his article? Explain.
2. Who is McKeen's audience, and what assumptions does he make about this audience? Refer to examples from his article to support your response.
3. Did you find McKeen's article funny? Why or why not?
4. Why is Lawson uncomfortable even "putting the words 'fat' and 'women' together"? What is the source of her discomfort?
5. According to Lawson, what are some of the disparities between fat men and fat women? Do you agree or disagree with her assessment? Explain.
6. Evaluate Lawson's conclusion. How does her conclusion support the points she makes in her essay?
7. How do people learn prejudice against fat people in the first place? Why do we think it is okay to make fun of obese people? How do you think Lawson and McKeen would respond to this question? Explain.

CRITICAL WRITING

8. *Research and Analysis*: Write an essay in which you trace the development of the "fat funny guy" in cinema and/or television. Try to identify several overweight male comedians from previous decades and discuss whether their size was part of their comedy, or merely incidental. Can you draw any conclusions from your research?
9. *Exploratory Writing*: Lawson comments that if you joke about a man's gut, all you have done is made fun of his stomach. But if you "insult a woman's body, you wound her soul." Write an essay in which you explore this idea.
10. *Persuasive Writing*: Lawson notes that overall, it is more socially acceptable for us to laugh at fat men than at fat women. Write a response to Lawson in which you agree or disagree with her conclusion.

GROUP PROJECTS

11. Make a list of the prime-time comedy shows on television. After compiling the list, identify the overweight characters on each program. What is the male-to-female ratio of these characters? Compare your findings with

some of the points made in Lawson's essay, and formulate a response in which you support or question her conclusions.

12. With your group, consider the parts of the body we consider funny and why. Adopting McKeen's format, compile a list of tricks to hide a physical flaw. Share your list with the rest of the class. As a class, discuss whether gender is an important part of the comedy. Is it easier to make fun of men's body parts? Why or why not?

RESEARCH ISSUE **The Beauty of Symmetry**
Elizabeth Snead

Can your looks be measured by a mathematical ratio? Studies show that "beautiful" people actually are just "more proportional" people. *USA Today* reporter Elizabeth Snead explains that beauty may simply be a numbers game.

1 Everyone knows the adage "Don't judge a book by its cover." But we can't help it; we do just that, day in and day out, consciously and subconsciously. We rate others on the basis of their appearance and compare our own looks with the enhanced images of beautiful women and handsome men in movies and magazines and on TV and billboards.

2 Beauty not only sells—it pays off. Beautiful babies get more attention from parents and teachers. Good-looking guys get more dates than average ones. Pretty women get out of traffic tickets and into exclusive clubs. The list of pluses for being one of the "beautiful people" goes on and on.

3 So what makes a person attractive? Don't bother looking in the mirror; just get out a measuring tape. Widespread studies, such as those conducted by Randy Thornhill (University of New Mexico) and Karl Grammer (University of Vienna), confirm that beauty is simply balance: The more symmetrical a face, the more appealing it appears. The concept applies to bodies, too. Physical symmetry is subconsciously perceived as a reflection of a person's youth, fertility, health and strength. And although bilateral (left-right) symmetry might not be a bona fide health certificate these days, it has been a marker of good health and genes throughout human evolution.

4 "Our sensitivity to beauty is hard-wired—that is, governed by circuits in the brain shaped by natural selection," says Nancy Etcoff, author of *Survival of the Prettiest: The Science of Beauty.* "We love to look at smooth skin, shiny hair, curved waists and symmetrical bodies because, over the course of evolution, people who noticed these signals and desired their possessors had more reproductive success. We're their descendants."

5 Symmetry also is sexy. In a study by biology professor Thornhill and University of New Mexico psychology professor Steven Gangestad, hundreds of college-age women and men were measured (including their ears, feet, ankles,

hands and elbows). Questionnaires revealed that men who were more symmetrical started having sex three to four years earlier and had more sex partners than their asymmetrical counterparts.

6   Symmetrical people smell better, too. Thornhill and Gangestad found that women prefer the scent of symmetrical men, and vice versa. So much for Old Spice and Chanel No. 5.

7   If you weren't born symmetrical, don't despair. Plastic surgeons are skilled at creating and restoring symmetry through popular procedures such as face-lifts, nasal refinements, eyelid lifts, collagen injections, liposuction and cheek and breast implants. Once reserved for the wealthy, plastic surgery now is fairly common for middle-class folks seeking to gain confidence and improve their career and romance prospects.

8   Stephen Marquardt, a retired California plastic surgeon who researches attractiveness, has moved from beauty's medical side to its mathematical side. He notes that a certain ratio has been found to recur in beautiful things both natural (flowers, pine cones, seashells) and man-made (the Parthenon, Mozart's music, da Vinci's paintings). This "golden ratio" is 1:1.618, with the number rounded to 1.618 known as "phi."

9   Using phi as his guide, Marquardt designed a mask that applies the golden ratio to the face. For example, the ideal ratio between the width of the nose and the width of the mouth is—you guessed it—1:1.618. The closer a face fits the mask, he finds, the more attractive the face is perceived to be. "Even average-looking people fit the mask, just not as closely as really attractive people," he says. "A lot of this is biology. It's necessary for us to recognize our species. Humans are visually oriented, and the mask screams, 'Human!'"

10   Marquardt's Web site shows the mask on timeless beauties from Queen Nefertiti to Marilyn Monroe (it works on all ethnicities, with slight variations). There's also a mask for men—a close fit on Pierce Brosnan, but not quite right on Tom Cruise.

11   Not everyone seeking symmetry goes under the knife. Although makeup artists don't slap Marquardt's mask on their clients, they do emulate its template, making eyes appear larger, cheeks higher, noses narrower and lips fuller using the magic of light-reflective foundations, powders and lip glosses. (Sorry, guys: Women have a slight edge on achieving symmetry.) Anyone can create the illusion of a symmetrical face, says Hollywood makeup artist Jeanine Lobell, founder of Stila cosmetics. "Creating symmetry is all about using light, dark and reflection," says Lobell, whose clients include actresses Heather Graham, Liv Tyler, Michelle Pfeiffer, Kate Hudson and Mena Suvari.

12   Sure, when you look good, you feel better. But don't get carried away in search of symmetry. Nobody's perfect, and that's just fine, Lobell says. "When you look at a beautiful face, embrace the unique qualities, including the unevenness." Individuality—now that's beautiful. ◆

CRITICAL THINKING

1. Snead reports that the "golden ratio" of phi fits closely on faces that are considered the most beautiful because these faces are also the most symmetrical. Think about the actors and models you consider the most beautiful. What accounts for their appeal? Is it, indeed, simply the symmetry of their parts?

2. In paragraph 3, Snead asks, "So what makes a person attractive?" Answer this question from your own personal perspective. In your response, consider the information Snead provides in her article, and explain why you agree or disagree, in whole or in part, with them.

RESEARCH PROJECTS

3. Plastic surgeon Stephen Marquardt created a mask that applied the "golden ratio" of 1:1.618 (1.618) known as "phi." Learn more about phi and the mask Marquardt developed at **www.beautyanalysis.com**. Apply the mask to some faces you consider beautiful, and see how they measure up. (You can even apply the mask to your own face by uploading a digital photo.) Discuss your experiments, as well as Marquardt's explanation of phi, in a short essay.

4. In paragraph 7, Snead tells readers that if they wish for more symmetrical faces, plastic surgery could be a solution. Visit the Web site of the American Society of Plastic Surgeons (ASPS) at **www.plasticsurgery.org** and the Canadian Society of Plastic Surgeons (CSPS) at **www.plasticsurgery.ca**. Read about some of the procedures and review the statistics on plastic surgery (you can directly access the statistics by typing in **www.plasticsurgery.org/public_education/Statistical-Trends.cfm** into the Web address line). Who is having plastic surgery and why? What procedures are the most common? What conclusions might you infer from the statistics? Is plastic surgery becoming more or less common? Based on your research, write an essay about the role of plastic surgery in North American life. If you wish, you may include personal perspectives on this topic, including whether you were likely to consider plastic surgery yourself after reading about it on the ASPS and CSPS Web sites.

Additional essay topics, writing assignments, research guidelines, and readings for this chapter can be found online at **www.pearsoned.ca/goshgarian**.

Advertising

Wanting It, Selling It

3

Advertising is everywhere—television, newspapers, magazines, the Internet, the sides of buses and trains, highway billboards, T-shirts, sports arenas, and even license plates. It is the driving force of our consumptive economy, accounting for US$150 billion worth of commercials and print ads each year (more than the gross national product of many countries in the world), and filling a quarter of each television hour and the bulk of most newspapers and magazines. It is everywhere people are, and its appeal goes to the quick of our fantasies: happiness, material wealth, eternal youth, social acceptance, sexual fulfillment, and power. Through carefully selected images and words, it is the most pervasive form of persuasion in North America, and, perhaps, the single most significant manufacturer of meaning in our consumer society. And many of us are not aware of its astounding influence on our lives.

Most of us are so accustomed to advertising that we hear it without listening and see it without looking. However, if we stop to examine how it works on our subconscious, we would be amazed at how powerful and complex a psychological force it is. This chapter examines how words compel us to buy, how images feed our fantasies, and how the advertising industry tempts us to part with our money.

To begin, Ken Sanes takes a close look at how television commercials create a simulated life—a life better than we could possibly hope to attain, because it isn't real. This construction of "postmodernity," says Sanes, inspires in the consumer a desire to achieve the utopian world depicted on the television set.

In "The Rebel Sell," Joseph Heath and Andrew Potter examine our complex relationship with the culture of consumerism, and the pitfalls of adopting an anti-consumerist stance.

Advertising in academic institutions is the subject of John Schofield's "A Tough Sell on Campus." Should schools be neutral spaces that refuse to endorse any specific product? Or should they make up for the lack of funding by giving selected companies exclusive campus contracts? We hear from both sides here. In an excerpt from *No Logo* (2000), Naomi Klein discusses the birth of branding, a process that isn't quite the same as advertising. In the transition from handmade to machine-produced manufacturing, connotative proper names became linked with particular products that otherwise would be indistinguishable from other similar products. Sometimes, as in the case of Kraft, the name—and the customer loyalty it inspires—becomes even more valuable than the company itself.

Countering all this criticism of advertising and the consumer market, James Twitchell, in "A (Mild) Defense of Luxury," argues that while academics like to wring their hands over the materialistic excesses of society, the truth is, humans have always loved nice things. He contends that even academics would have to admit that the things they think are essential are considered luxuries to another segment of society. It is all in how you look at it.

"A Portfolio of Advertisements," featuring 12 magazine ads, is followed by a set of questions to help you analyze how ads work their appeal. Apply a critical eye to all the advertisements, and consider the universal and individual ways they appeal to us.

This chapter's Viewpoints focuses on advertising language. By its nature, the language of advertising is a very special one, combining words cleverly and methodically to get us to spend our money. In "With These Words, I Can Sell You Anything," "word-watcher" William Lutz explores how advertisers twist simple words so that these words appear to promise what the consumer wants to hear. In the second piece, "The Language of Advertising," advertising executive Charles A. O'Neill concedes that the language of ads can be very appealing, but that's the point. However, unless consumers are willing, no ad can force them to part with their money.

The chapter ends with a piece by Damien Cave, "On Sale at Old Navy: Cool Clothes for Identical Zombies!" in which he questions the trend of mass-market stores that essentially sell the same bland things. This chapter's Research Issue explores how such stores encourage conformity in the name of convenience.

Advertising and the Invention of Postmodernity

Ken Sanes

Advertising is based on implied promises. Whether products follow through with their promises is beside the point—the goal is to get us to first want, and then buy the merchandise. In the next essay, Ken Sanes explores the simulated world of television commercials, in which everyone and everything is better than the mundane world that we inhabit. The message is if we want to be like the beautiful, blissfully happy people in the ad, we must buy the product. The problem is that products don't come with soundtracks, and utopia can't be found in a bottle of shampoo, an allergy medication, or a fruity candy.

Ken Sanes is a former newspaper writer and columnist. His articles have been published in the *Boston Globe*, the *San Diego Union-Tribune*, the *Nation,* and *Newsday*. He is the creator of the acclaimed media literacy Web site *Transparency,* from which this essay was taken.

CRITICAL THINKING How does the world depicted in television commercials compare to the "real" world in which we live? How do the people look? What landscapes do they inhabit? How do they interact with their environment? Consider how commercials create a simulated reality to sell a product.

1   When we examine television advertising we once again find art and technology being used to create simulations that tell stories in an effort to evoke desired reactions from audiences. But in advertising we see a strange new cultural creation: the 30-second "cinematic" production full of dancing, singing and joke-telling characters playing physicians, housewives, and used car salesmen, with ultra-abbreviated

plots and quick resolutions of conflict in which the characters overcome obstacles and fulfill their desires in record time with the help of the product. Unlike movies, which will evoke the wrath of the audience if the unfolding of the story is interrupted, in commercials there is virtually no story to interrupt. The entire commercial is a dynamic, graphic field composed of images, music, theatrical performances, superimposed illustrations, narration, and other elements, which reinforce each other to achieve their effect.

2   Like other complex simulations, these inventions of sound-bite television are typically made up of a great many individual forms of fakery and illusion. For example, they display products that are cosmetically altered to seem more appealing to viewers. Raw turkeys are made to look baked and delicious with food coloring, while the sizzle of cooking food turns out to be a sound effect that has been added to the scene. These sensory deceptions are supplemented by exaggerated claims, to create a false identity for the product.

3   Commercials also include another kind of simulation in the form of digitally manipulated images, which are used to portray another realm of fantasy in which the limits imposed by the physical world no longer seem to be in effect. As a result, they are full of talking dogs, children who grow to giant size, products that zoom into space, dancing credit cards and scenes that suddenly become two-dimensional screens, which spin out of existence, creating a virtual world that surpasses anything produced by Imax or Nintendo.

4   Commercials take these elements—visual fantasy, deceptive images of the products, and false claims—and weave them into their various approaches. There are, perhaps, a half dozen kinds of approaches that they rely on and put together in different ways, just as the theme parks, video games, television and news fall into a few basic categories. Some present trivial product information as if it is of momentous importance. Others use glamour or sex, or they try to evoke a sense of empathy and sincerity in an effort to melt viewers emotionally into buying the product. A great many use humor to win over viewers and reduce the pretentiousness of the message, since pretending to be absurd is the best camouflage for something that really is absurd.

5   But what may be most common, are commercials that convey a sense of life as celebration, full of enraptured people who can't help but sing out because they love their Skittles, or who emerge from swimming pools, all luminescent, with magnificent hair and wonderful lives, surrounded by bright colors, upbeat music and dancing friends, in which everything is in motion to convey a sense of what life can be if we buy the product. These kaleidoscope-like images of endlessly festive situations, which are the same as we saw in Disney, are a constant presence, conveying the ultimate image that consumer culture can offer of the good life as an endless party.

6   Whatever form they take, commercials are, ultimately, about what the product will allow consumers to achieve. If politics is about the transformation of the nation to an ideal state, then commercial advertising is about the transformation of you, the viewer, offering the promise of prestige and self-esteem, control over your life, luxury and good times, and a work-free existence. In effect, commercials try to inspire

in viewers a sense that they can escape from the flawed and mundane state of everyday existence. They appeal to the same desires for freedom and perfection that Disney appeals to, turning the yearning for a better life into a tool of manipulation.

7   Many television commercials thus give us another variation on Umberto Eco's absolute fakes; they are false promises that make everything seem better than it is. Like theme parks, they make mundane realities look like transcendent utopias. One might say that if Disney is a permanent world's fair that creates fictions intended to reveal the way technology will one day free us from the constraints of life, then television advertising is a virtual world's fair that creates fictions about how the products of technology can free us now.

8   Like Disney, all of these 30-second spots end up inventing a postmodern world for us. It isn't that we live in anything that deserves to be called postmodern; it is just that the fictionalizers of American culture keep pretending we do, and inviting us to pretend along. A truly postmodern society (although I doubt it would call itself that) would be one that is able to use technology to significantly transcend the limits imposed by the physical world. We aren't a postmodern society. We merely play one on television.

* * *

9   Some commercials create invented "worlds" based on fantasy and desire. To achieve their effects, they engage in the new production process of high-tech capitalism, which is to turn everything into an image.

10   This process is very evident in what happens to the actors—they are turned into simplified human images. Their role is to become characters in false utopias so they can act as living sales pitches for products.

11   Like Charlie Chaplin in *Modern Times*, and the workers in the movie *Metropolis*, they become cogs in the machine of technology. But now that machine is about etherealizing—using the appearance of actual people, objects, places and situations to create images and stories that can be sold and/or used to sell other things that are, themselves, increasingly made up of images or simulations.

12   I don't mean to make all that much of this—I'd rather be an actor than a factory worker; and I'd rather live in a society that has the luxury of devoting many of its resources to creating images, than one stuck trying to figure out how to get coal out of the ground. And many kinds of work are repetitive and alienating. Even being an actor in a Shakespearean drama involves repetition and can involve a feeling of being lost in one's character.

13   But most of today's human images aren't doing Shakespeare. They are doing sales-entertainment, of which commercials are an extreme version that casts light on the rest.

14   Audiences suffer forms of alienation, as well, as they feel increasingly trapped in a culture of con artistry in which they are surrounded by sensory images, stories, rhetoric and presentations that are intended to get them to buy something or buy into something. This culture fakes the appearance of places and people and situations, as

the window dressing for fake promises and false claims. It offers sales pitches disguised to look like a new and better "postmodern" reality.

15   All cultures place people inside invented worlds; so that, in itself, isn't what is new about all this. The human world is by nature full of fictionalization and metaphor and drenched in stories and metaphysical assumptions, much of it contrived by conscious and unconscious design to support the claims of those in power. But never before has a culture been scientifically invented in this way, using the tools of rationalization—including marketing studies and computers—to sell products and a way of life. These tools of rationality extract the essence of our own irrationality—our fantasies, imbued with fears and desires—and give them back to us in the form of their invented worlds.

16   Most viewers know it is all a manipulation, even if they don't always reflect on what they know. But many still respond by buying the product, voting for the candidate and admiring the celebrity, as if they have been taken in by the message. It is as if the radio audience in 1938 had realized it was listening to a performance by Orson Welles but decided to panic anyway because the play was so convincing and so much fun to believe. ◆

FREEWRITING ASSIGNMENT

How much attention do you give to television commercials? What makes you stop and watch a commercial? Beauty? Humour? Spectacle? What holds your attention?

CRITICAL READING

1. Sanes notes that commercials employ multiple tools to create tightly woven mini "cinematic" productions to promote their product. How does he feel about this approach to advertising? Explain.

2. How does the simulated world of television commercials influence our general perceptions of the real world? Do we create unrealistic expectations based upon these commercials, or do we see through the spectacle? Explain.

3. Sanes notes that many products are cosmetically altered to make them more appealing to viewers (paragraph 2). Do advertisers have a right to do this? Is such modification unethical? Is it lying? Or do viewers simply expect advertisers to skew the truth?

4. What elements does Sanes identify as used by commercials to weave their productions of simulated reality? How do these elements work together? Can you think of any others?

5. Sanes notes that the most popular tactic used by commercials today is "life as a celebration." Why is this form of commercial so popular? Identify a few commercials that follow this format.

6. What assumptions does Sanes make concerning his audience? What do his language choices and his cultural references tell you about this audience? Explain.

7. What does Sanes mean when he says "We aren't a postmodern society? We merely play one on television"? What is the connection between the invented worlds presented in television commercials and our "postmodern" society?

CRITICAL WRITING

8. Sanes's essay addresses the way images manipulate viewers of television commercials in much the same way language can sway consumers to buy a product. How do you think William Lutz or Charles O'Neill would respond to Sanes's observations? Write a response to Sanes's essay from the perspective of either Lutz or O'Neill.

9. *Exploratory Writing*: Sanes postulates that the utopian world created by television commercials creates unrealistic social expectations of our real world. Write an essay exploring the psychological aspects of desire. Why are we so vulnerable to the implicit promises made by commercials?

10. Sanes makes references to the movies *Modern Times* and *Metropolis*. Watch one of these movies and write a summary of it, connecting its theme to points expressed by Sanes in his essay. What parallels can you make between the movie and the world of television commercials?

11. Write an essay evaluating advertising techniques in the twenty-first century. Have ads changed over the past 20 years or so? What accounts for similarities or differences? Has advertising become more or less ethical? Creative? Focused? Be sure to explain your position and support it with examples from real advertisements.

GROUP PROJECTS

12. As a group, watch several commercials (you may wish to record them to reference later) and analyze them, applying some of the points made by Sanes in his essay. How do they use colour, music, graphics, narration, and celebrity to promote the product? What cultural assumptions do they make? What promises do they imply? Finally, how do they contribute to the simulated utopia Sanes discusses?

13. **Adbusters.org** is committed to exposing the unethical ways advertisers manipulate consumers to "need" products. However, if we consider ads long enough we can determine for ourselves the ways we may be manipulated. Visit their Web site and select a campaign to discuss as a group. Summarize the points made by Adbusters against the campaign you selected and add some observations of your own. Share your summary with the class.

The Rebel Sell

Joseph Heath and Andrew Potter

As consumers, how do we reconcile our acquisitive behaviour with our self-proclaimed horror of mass marketing and mass consumption? We may choose to see ourselves as "anti-consumers," but as Joseph Heath and Andrew Potter point out in this article, the true anti-consumer is a rare animal indeed. Through their discussion of the films *American Beauty* and *Fight Club*, along with their introduction of the idea of "positional goods," the authors invite us to ask ourselves whether *anti-consumer* is really just another term for *discriminating consumer*.

Joseph Heath is associate professor of philosophy at the University of Toronto. He is the author of two books, *The Efficient Society* (2002) and *Communicative Action and Rational Choice* (2001). Andrew Potter is a research fellow at the Centre de Recherche en Éthique at l'Université de Montréal, and he is on the editorial board of *This Magazine*. He and Joseph Heath are co-authors of the book *The Rebel Sell* (2004). The following article was originally published in *This Magazine*, November/December 2002.

| CRITICAL THINKING | What is an "anti-consumer"? How does an anti-consumer cope with living in a consumer culture? |

1   Do you hate consumer culture? Angry about all that packaging? Irritated by all those commercials? Worried about the quality of the "mental environment"? Well, join the club. Anti-consumerism has become one of the most important cultural forces in millennial North American life, across every social class and demographic.

2   This might seem at odds with the economic facts of the 1990s—a decade that gave us the "extreme shopping" channel, the dot-com bubble, and an absurd orgy of indulgence in ever more luxurious consumer goods. But look at the non-fiction best-seller lists. For years they've been dominated by books that are deeply critical of consumerism: *No Logo, Culture Jam, Luxury Fever* and *Fast Food Nation*. You can now buy *Adbusters* at your neighbourhood music or clothing store. Two of the most popular and critically successful films in recent memory were *Fight Club* and *American Beauty*, which offer almost identical indictments of modern consumer society.

3   What can we conclude from all this? For one thing, the market obviously does an extremely good job at responding to consumer demand for anti-consumerist products and literature. But isn't that a contradiction? Doesn't it suggest that we are in the grip of some massive, society-wide, bipolar disorder? How can we all denounce consumerism, and yet still find ourselves living in a consumer society?

4   The answer is simple. What we see in films like *American Beauty* and *Fight Club* is not actually a critique of consumerism; it's merely a restatement of the "critique of mass society" that has been around since the 1950s. The two are not the

same. In fact, the critique of mass society has been one of the most powerful forces driving consumerism for more than 40 years.

5   That last sentence is worth reading again. The idea is so foreign, so completely the opposite of what we are used to being told, that many people simply can't get their head around it. It is a position that Thomas Frank, editor of *The Baffler*, has been trying to communicate for years. Strangely, all the authors of anti-consumerism books have read Frank—most even cite him approvingly—and yet not one of them seems to get the point. So here is Frank's claim, simply put: books like *No Logo*, magazines like *Adbusters*, and movies like *American Beauty* do not undermine consumerism; they reinforce it. This isn't because the authors, directors or editors are hypocrites. It's because they've failed to understand the true nature of consumer society.

6   One of the most talked-about cinematic set-pieces in recent memory is the scene in *Fight Club* where the nameless narrator (Ed Norton) pans his empty apartment, furnishing it piece by piece with Ikea furniture. The scene shimmers and pulses with prices, model numbers and product names, as if Norton's gaze was drag-and-dropping straight out of a virtual catalogue. It is a great scene, driving the point home: the furniture of his world is mass-produced, branded, sterile. If we are what we buy, then the narrator is an Allen-key-wielding corporate-conformist drone.

7   In many ways, this scene is just a CGI-driven update of the opening pages of John Updike's *Rabbit, Run*. After yet another numbing day selling the MagiPeel Kitchen Peeler, Harry Angstrom comes home to his pregnant and half-drunk wife whom he no longer loves. Harry takes off in his car, driving aimlessly south. As he tries to sort out his life, the music on the radio, the sports reports, the ads, the billboards, all merge in his consciousness into one monotonous, monolithic brandscape.

8   It may give us pause to consider that while *Fight Club* was hailed as "edgy" and "subversive" when it appeared in 1999, *Rabbit, Run* enjoyed enormous commercial success when it was first published—in 1960. If social criticism came with a "sell by" date, this one would have been removed from the shelf a long time ago. The fact that it is still around, and still provokes awe and acclaim, makes one wonder if it is really a criticism or, rather, a piece of modern mythology.

9   What *Fight Club* and *Rabbit, Run* present, in a user-friendly fashion, is the critique of mass society, which was developed in the late 1950s in classic works like William Whyte's *The Organization Man* (1956), Vance Packard's *The Status Seekers* (1959) and Paul Goodman's *Growing up Absurd* (1960). The central idea is quite simple. Capitalism requires conformity to function correctly. As a result, the system is based upon a generalized system of repression. Individuals who resist the pressure to conform therefore subvert the system, and aid in its overthrow.

10   This theory acquired such a powerful grip on the imagination of the left during the 1960s that many people still have difficulty seeing it for what it is—a theory. Here are a few of its central postulates:

11   1. Capitalism requires conformity in the workers. Capitalism is one big machine; the workers are just parts. These parts need to be as simple, predictable, and interchangeable as possible. One need only look at an assembly line to see

why. Like bees or ants, capitalist workers need to be organized into a limited number of homogeneous castes.

12   2. Capitalism requires conformity of education. Training these corporate drones begins in the schools, where their independence and creativity is beaten out of them—literally and figuratively. Call this the Pink Floyd theory of education.

13   3. Capitalism requires sexual repression. In its drive to stamp out individuality, capitalism denies the full range of human expression, which includes sexual freedom. Because sexuality is erratic and unpredictable, it is a threat to the established order. This is why some people thought the sexual revolution would undermine capitalism.

14   4. Capitalism requires conformity of consumption. The overriding goal of capitalism is to achieve ever-increasing profits through economies of scale. These are best achieved by having everyone consume the same limited range of standardized goods. Enter advertising, which tries to inculcate false or inauthentic desires. Consumerism is what emerges when we are duped into having desires that we would not normally have.

15   Both *Fight Club* and *American Beauty* are thoroughly soaked in the critique of mass society. Let's look at *Fight Club*.

16   Here's the narrator's alter ego, Tyler Durden (Brad Pitt), explaining the third thesis: "We're designed to be hunters and we're in a society of shopping. There's nothing to kill anymore, there's nothing to fight, nothing to overcome, nothing to explore. In that social emasculation this everyman is created." And the fourth: "Advertising has us chasing cars and clothes, working jobs we hate, so we can buy shit we don't need." And here he is giving the narrator a scatological summary of the whole critique: "You're not your job. You're not how much money you have in the bank. You're not the car you drive. You're not the contents of your wallet. You're not your fucking khakis. You're the all-singing, all-dancing crap of the world."

17   *Fight Club* is entirely orthodox in its Rousseauian rejection of the modern order. Less orthodox is its proffered solution, which in the middle and final acts moves swiftly from Iron John to the Trenchcoat Mafia.

18   A more conventional narrative arc, combined with a more didactic presentation of the critique, can be found in *American Beauty*, the Oscar-winning companion piece to *Fight Club*. The two films offer identical takes on the homogenizing and emasculating effects of mass society, though the heroes differ in their strategies of resistance. *Fight Club* suggests that the only solution is to blow up the whole machine; in *American Beauty*, Lester (Kevin Spacey) decides to subvert it from within.

19   When Lester first starts to rebel against his grey-scale, cookie-cutter life, he begins by mocking his wife's (Annette Bening) Martha Stewart materialism. Here's Lester in a voice-over: "That's my wife, Carolyn. See the way the handle on her pruning shears matches her gardening clogs? That's not an accident."

20   Later, Carolyn halts Lester's sexual advances in order to prevent him from spilling beer on the couch. They fight. "It's just a couch," Lester says. Carolyn:

"This is a $4,000 sofa upholstered in Italian silk. It is not just a couch." Lester: "It's just a couch!" Capitalism offers us consumer goods as a substitute for sexual gratification. Lester strains at the bit.

21   The relationship between sexual frustration and mass society is a general theme of the movie. Here is Lester giving his family theses one and three over dinner:

22   Carolyn: Your father and I were just discussing his day at work. Why don't you tell our daughter about it, honey?

23   Lester: Janie, today I quit my job. And then I told my boss to go fuck himself, and then I blackmailed him for almost $60,000. Pass the asparagus.

24   Carolyn: Your father seems to think this type of behaviour is something to be proud of.

25   Lester: And your mother seems to prefer I go through life like a fucking prisoner while she keeps my dick in a mason jar under the sink.

26   So what does Lester do to reassert his individuality, his masculinity? He takes a new job. He starts working out. He lusts after, then seduces, his daughter's friend. He starts smoking pot in the afternoon. In short, he rejects all of the demands that society makes on a man of his age. But does he stop consuming? Of course not. Consider the scene in which he buys a new car. Carolyn comes home and asks Lester whose car that is in the driveway. Lester: "Mine. 1970 Pontiac Firebird. The car I've always wanted and now I have it. I rule!"

27   Lester has thrown off the shackles of conformist culture. He's grown a dick, become a man again. All because he bought a car. Carolyn's couch may be "just a couch," but his car is much more than "just a car." Lester has become the ultimate consumer. Like a teenager, he consumes without guilt, without foresight, and without responsibility. Meanwhile, Carolyn's questions about how he intends to make the mortgage payments are dismissed as merely one more symptom of her alienated existence. Lester is beyond all that. He is now what Thomas Frank calls "the rebel consumer."

28   What *American Beauty* illustrates, with extraordinary clarity, is that rebelling against mass society is not the same thing as rebelling against consumer society. Through his rebellion, Lester goes from being right-angle square to dead cool. This is reflected in his consumption choices. Apart from the new car, he develops a taste for very expensive marijuana—$2,000 an ounce, we are told, and very good. "This is all I ever smoke," his teenaged dealer assures him. Welcome to the club, where admission is restricted to clients with the most discriminating taste. How is this any different from Frasier and Niles at their wine club?

29   What we need to see is that consumption is not about conformity, it's about distinction. People consume in order to set themselves apart from others. To show that they are cooler (Nike shoes), better connected (the latest nightclub), better informed (single-malt Scotch), morally superior (Guatemalan handcrafts), or just plain richer (BMWs).

30   The problem is that all of these comparative preferences generate competitive consumption. "Keeping up with the Joneses," in today's world, does not always mean buying a tract home in the suburbs. It means buying a loft downtown, eating at

the right restaurants, listening to obscure bands, having a pile of Mountain Equipment Co-op gear and vacationing in Thailand. It doesn't matter how much people spend on these things, what matters is the competitive structure of the consumption. Once too many people get on the bandwagon, it forces the early adopters to get off, in order to preserve their distinction. This is what generates the cycles of obsolescence and waste that we condemn as "consumerism."

31   Many people who are, in their own minds, opposed to consumerism nevertheless actively participate in the sort of behaviour that drives it. Consider Naomi Klein. She starts out *No Logo* by decrying the recent conversion of factory buildings in her Toronto neighbourhood into "loft living" condominiums. She makes it absolutely clear to the reader that her place is the real deal, a genuine factory loft, steeped in working-class authenticity, yet throbbing with urban street culture and a "rock-video aesthetic."

32   Now of course anyone who has a feel for how social class in this country works knows that, at the time Klein was writing, a genuine factory loft in the King-Spadina area was possibly the single most exclusive and desirable piece of real estate in Canada. Unlike merely expensive neighbourhoods in Toronto, like Rosedale and Forest Hill, where it is possible to buy your way in, genuine lofts could only be acquired by people with superior social connections. This is because they contravened zoning regulations and could not be bought on the open market. Only the most exclusive segment of the cultural elite could get access to them.

33   Unfortunately for Klein, zoning changes in Toronto (changes that were part of a very enlightened and successful strategy to slow urban sprawl) allowed yuppies to buy their way into her neighbourhood. This led to an erosion of her social status. Her complaints about commercialization are nothing but an expression of this loss of distinction. What she fails to observe is that this distinction is precisely what drives the real estate market, what creates the value in these dwellings. People buy these lofts because they want a piece of Klein's social status. Naturally, she is not amused. They are, after all, her inferiors—an inferiority that they demonstrate through their willingness to accept mass-produced, commercialized facsimiles of the "genuine" article.

34   Klein claims these newcomers bring "a painful new self-consciousness" to the neighbourhood. But as the rest of her introduction demonstrates, she is also conscious—painfully so—of her surroundings. Her neighbourhood is one where "in the twenties and thirties Russian and Polish immigrants darted back and forth on these streets, ducking into delis to argue about Trotsky and the leadership of the international ladies' garment workers' union." Emma Goldman, we are told, "the famed anarchist and labour organizer," lived on her street! How exciting for Klein! What a tremendous source of distinction that must be.

35   Klein suggests that she may be forced to move out of her loft when the landlord decides to convert the building to condominiums. But wait a minute. If that happens, why doesn't she just buy her loft? The problem, of course, is that a loft-living condominium doesn't have quite the cachet of a "genuine" loft. It becomes, as Klein puts it, merely an apartment with "exceptionally high ceilings." It is not her land-

lord, but her fear of losing social status that threatens to drive Klein from her neighbourhood.

36   Here we can see the forces driving competitive consumption in their purest and most unadulterated form.

37   Once we acknowledge the role that distinction plays in structuring consumption, it's easy to see why people care about brands so much. Brands don't bring us together, they set us apart. Of course, most sophisticated people claim that they don't care about brands—a transparent falsehood. Most people who consider themselves "anti-consumerist" are extremely brand-conscious. They are able to fool themselves into believing that they don't care because their preferences are primarily negative. They would never be caught dead driving a Chrysler or listening to Celine Dion. It is precisely by not buying these uncool items that they establish their social superiority. (It is also why, when they do consume "mass society" products, they must do so "ironically"—so as to preserve their distinction.)

38   As Pierre Bourdieu reminds us, taste is first and foremost distaste—disgust and "visceral intolerance" of the taste of others. This makes it easy to see how the critique of mass society could help drive consumerism. Take, for example, Volkswagen and Volvo advertising from the early 1960s. Both automakers used the critique of "planned obsolescence" quite prominently in their advertising campaigns. The message was clear: buy from the big Detroit automakers and show everyone that you're a dupe, a victim of consumerism; buy our car and show people that you're too smart to be duped by advertising, that you're wise to the game.

39   This sort of "anti-advertising" was enormously successful in the 1960s, transforming the VW bug from a Nazi car into the symbol of the hippie counterculture and making the Volvo the car of choice for an entire generation of leftist academics. Similar advertising strategies are just as successful today, and are used to sell everything from breakfast cereal to clothing. Thus the kind of ad parodies that we find in *Adbusters*, far from being subversive, are indistinguishable from many genuine ad campaigns. Flipping through the magazine, one cannot avoid thinking back to Frank's observation that "business is amassing great sums by charging admission to the ritual simulation of its own lynching."

40   We find ourselves in an untenable situation. On the one hand, we criticize conformity and encourage individuality and rebellion. On the other hand, we lament the fact that our ever-increasing standard of material consumption is failing to generate any lasting increase in happiness. This is because it is rebellion, not conformity, that generates the competitive structure that drives the wedge between consumption and happiness. As long as we continue to prize individuality, and as long as we express that individuality through what we own and where we live, we can expect to live in a consumerist society.

41   It is tempting to think that we could just drop out of the race, become what Harvard professor Juliet Schor calls "downshifters." That way we could avoid competitive consumption entirely. Unfortunately, this is wishful thinking. We can walk away from some competitions, take steps to mitigate the effects of others, but many more simply cannot be avoided.

42   In many cases, competition is an intrinsic feature of the goods that we consume. Economists call these "positional goods"—goods that one person can have only if many others do not. Examples include not only penthouse apartments, but also wilderness hikes and underground music. It is often claimed that a growing economy is like the rising tide that lifts all boats. But a growing economy does not create more antiques, more rare art, or more downtown real estate, it just makes them more expensive. Many of us fail to recognize how much of our consumption is devoted to these positional goods.

43   Furthermore, we are often forced into competitive consumption, just to defend ourselves against the nuisances generated by other people's consumption. It is unreasonable, for example, for anyone living in a Canadian city to own anything other than a small, fuel-efficient car. At the same time, in many parts of North America, the number of big SUVs on the road has reached the point where people are forced to think twice before buying a small car. The SUVs make the roads so dangerous for other drivers that everyone has to consider buying a larger car just to protect themselves.

44   This is why expecting people to opt out is often unrealistic; the cost to the individual is just too high. It's all well and good to say that SUVs are a danger and shouldn't be on the road. But saying so doesn't change anything. The fact is that SUVs are on the road, and they're not about to disappear anytime soon. So are you willing to endanger your children's lives by buying a subcompact?

45   Because so much of our competitive consumption is defensive in nature, people feel justified in their choices. Unfortunately, everyone who participates contributes just as much to the problem, regardless of his or her intentions. It doesn't matter that you bought the SUV to protect yourself and your children, you still bought it, and you still made it harder for other drivers to opt out of the automotive arms race. When it comes to consumerism, intentions are irrelevant. It is only consequences that count.

46   This is why a society-wide solution to the problem of consumerism is not going to occur through personal or cultural politics. At this stage of late consumerism, our best bet is legislative action. If we were really worried about advertising, for example, it would be easy to strike a devastating blow against the "brand bullies" with a simple change in the tax code. The government could stop treating advertising expenditures as a fully tax-deductible business expense (much as it did with entertainment expenses several years ago). Advertising is already a separately itemized expense category, so the change wouldn't even generate any additional paperwork. But this little tweak to the tax code would have a greater impact than all of the culture jamming in the world.

47   Of course, tweaking the tax code is not quite as exciting as dropping a "meme bomb" into the world of advertising or heading off to the latest riot in all that cool mec gear. It may, however, prove to be a lot more useful. What we need to realize is that consumerism is not an ideology. It is not something that people get tricked into. Consumerism is something that we actively do to one another, and that we will continue to do as long as we have no incentive to stop. Rather than just posturing, we should start thinking a bit more carefully about how we're going to provide those incentives.

FREEWRITING ASSIGNMENT

Do you consider yourself a consumer or an anti-consumer? Do you spend as freely as your income allows, or do you resist the impulse to buy? Do you consider advertising merely an annoyance, or is it a service that informs you as to what products and services are available to you as a consumer?

CRITICAL READING

1. Heath and Potter begin their article by pointing out a long-standing confusion between the critique of consumerism and the critique of mass society. What do they claim is the difference between these two terms?
2. The authors make the surprising claim that "the critique of mass society has been one of the most powerful forces driving consumerism for more than 40 years." How do they support this assertion? Do you agree with their reasoning in this claim?
3. It has been theorized that a capitalist system requires conformity in both the amount and the variety of the goods and services we consume. Heath and Potter refute that theory, insisting instead that "consumption is not about conformity, it's about distinction." What examples are used to illustrate this claim? Are you convinced by the authors' argument on this point? Why or why not?
4. Heath and Potter mention "positional goods" in relation to the discriminating consumer; what are positional goods, and how does their consumption differ from that of other goods or services that are available in a capitalist economy?
5. The authors claim that the current theory of capitalism includes the requirement for "sexual repression" (paragraph 13). What is their explanation for this requirement?
6. Who are the "rebel consumers"? What sets them apart from the mass of consumers in the capitalist system? Which kind of consumer are you?
7. What, according to the authors, is the concept of "anti-advertising"? How does it work?
8. How is the title of this essay appropriate for its purpose?

CRITICAL WRITING

9. *Research and Exploratory Writing:* What was the sexual revolution mentioned by the authors in their third tenet of the theory of capitalism (paragraph 13)? Who were some of the leading figures in this social movement? What did they have to say on the connection between sexuality and capitalism?
10. *Exploratory Writing:* View *Fight Club* and *American Beauty*. How do these movies depict the current capitalist reality, and what are their solutions to

the problems it poses? Does either of these films offer a viable alternative to the status quo, or are they meant to show the impracticality of certain courses of action? Are there ways in which both films actually defend or support the current form of capitalism?

11. *Persuasive Writing:* The authors suggest that people who consider themselves anti-consumerist are in fact "extremely brand-conscious." Make a list of the products or services you would "never be caught dead" buying or consuming because of their brand. What makes these brands so distasteful? In a brief essay, explain why a certain brand should be avoided while another may be freely embraced. What makes your brand preferable to another brand? Is this a permanent status, or can it change?

GROUP PROJECTS

12. The authors talk about the impossibility of complete "downshifting," of walking away from the practice of competitive consumption. With your group, discuss ways in which downshifting might be achieved, either for an individual or for a family or even an entire community. Create a report with recommendations that could be realistically undertaken. Share your report with the class.

13. With your group, make a list of all the positional goods you can think of. Are you a consumer of any of these goods? Try to determine who is the most positional consumer in your group. Discuss how in a capitalist system, one's behaviour as a consumer can be affected by factors other than the price and desirability of a product. Is this a basic feature of capitalism, or is it a "loophole" in the system?

A Tough Sell on Campus
John Schofield

While advertising is ubiquitous in the media and on street corners, we still don't expect to see ads in the classroom. Or do we? Faced with government cutbacks and increasing costs, many Canadian schools and universities are now viewing corporate advertising as a possible injection of much-needed cash. Many students and faculty members fear and abhor this new trend, and numerous protests have arisen against what many see as the "branding" of schools. John Schofield explores the corporate encroachment on campuses in this next article.

John Schofield is an independent journalist and the former education editor of *Maclean's* magazine, in which this article appeared on April 10, 2000.

CRITICAL THINKING   Are there ads in the washrooms at your college? How do you feel about them?

1   It was the beginning of Thomas Ingersoll's own revolutionary war. Three years ago, the American history professor at l'Université de Montréal was surprised to see several garish ads plastered outside the main library. Dismayed, he lodged an informal complaint with his faculty union. Today, hundreds of ads dot the university's washrooms and public hallways. In February, Ingersoll took the bold step of resigning over the issue, effective this summer. "I'm a representative of this institution," says the tenured professor, "and inevitably I'm associated with these ads."

2   For some time, academics and students have been growing increasingly incensed about the corporate presence on Canadian campuses. But in recent months, that fury has been especially evident in Quebec. Last week, students at Concordia University in Montreal voted in favour of eliminating virtually all of the 374 ads in washrooms and on walls across campus. The advertising is sold by Montreal-based Zoom Media Inc., the same company that provides ads at Université de Montréal and about 70 other colleges and universities across Canada. And last month, students at McGill narrowly rejected a proposed agreement with Coca-Cola that would have made the soft-drink giant the exclusive cold-beverage supplier on the campus. In recent months, similar contracts have been defeated at Université du Québec à Montréal and Université Laval, and the fight has now spread to Dawson College, a Montreal CEGEP. Says Zach Dubinsky, a third-year student at McGill: "We don't want to be marketing toys, and we don't want to be part of this corporatization trend."

3   To date, more than 20 universities across Canada have inked exclusive deals with Pepsi, while an estimated seven have similar arrangements with Coke. Soft-drink makers are paying top dollar for access to the coveted youth market. The McGill agreement was reportedly worth an estimated $10 million over 11 years, with money earmarked for a $1.5-million upgrade to the University Student Centre and to hire new faculty. Students were represented at the bargaining table, but a confidentiality agreement prevented the disclosure of any details before, during and after the campaign that led up to the vote. While the vote was not binding, McGill has agreed to kill the deal. "Everyone would have benefited," says Morty Yalovsky, McGill's vice-principal for administration and finance. "And the way we negotiated the agreement, I believe it was harmless."

4   Those on the Yes side argue that the soft-drink companies already enjoy virtual monopolies on most campuses, and that universities might as well capitalize on the fact. Based on the volume of advertising, Zoom ads generated $92,000 for the Université de Montréal last year, and about $25,000 for Concordia. But critics counter that there is a principle at stake: schools should be neutral spaces for learning. For most of last year, students entering Ingersoll's class had to pass a large poster of a scantily clad woman flogging perfume. Says Ingersoll: "It's the abandonment of an ideal for a small piece of change."

5   Many applaud the tough stance being taken in Quebec. Faculty at the University of Saskatchewan are especially disappointed with the outcome of their school's 10-year contract with Coke, signed two years ago and worth a rumored $2 million. The Arts Building snack bar alone is plastered with about 45 Coke logos, estimates history professor Michael Hayden. Last November, the company built an

electronic message board at the university entrance that periodically flashes Coke ads. "We're being buried in propaganda," says Hayden. "Everywhere you look, you'd swear this is Coke U."

6   Some observers say the surge of campus protest signals a new cynicism among youth towards global corporations. Last year's protests during the World Trade Organization talks in Seattle have come to symbolize that stance. Last month, students at the University of Toronto occupied president Robert Prichard's office for 10 days. Their aim: to accelerate the passage of a policy to prevent the use of sweatshop labour in producing university merchandise. "There's a feeling of being overbranded, and they're fighting back," says Naomi Klein, author of *No Logo: Taking Aim at the Brand Bullies* [2000]. "This is the politics that is galvanizing university campuses today." And increasingly, that voice of protest is being heard. ◆

FREEWRITING ASSIGNMENT ────────────────────

Given the current difficulty of funding colleges and universities in Canada, do you feel that advertising on campus is wrong? How much is it worth to you? For example, if advertising on campus were to lower your tuition fees, would you be willing to allow it?

CRITICAL READING

1. Thomas Ingersoll, formerly of l'Université de Montréal, says that advertising on campus constitutes "the abandonment of an ideal for a small piece of change." What is the ideal to which he is referring? Do you agree that advertising compromises that ideal?

2. In paragraph 1, Ingersoll justifies resigning over the issue of campus ads by saying, "I'm a representative of this institution . . . and inevitably I'm associated with these ads." Would you agree with this statement? Is every member of an institution necessarily associated with the ads that its administration chooses to allow?

3. What is the position of those critical of campus advertising? What do they perceive as the danger?

4. What does Naomi Klein mean by her assertion that students are feeling "overbranded"? As a student yourself, would you agree with her? Explain.

CRITICAL WRITING

5. *Persuasive Writing:* In a brief essay, take one of the two sides in this debate and defend it. Your position should be either that advertising has no place in an academic setting because students should not be subjected to commercials in an ostensibly neutral environment, or that advertising on campus is harmless, because students are aware enough to resist commercial messages and because the school can put the revenue to good use.

6. *Research and Exploratory Writing:* Do you feel you are being "over-branded"? Research the concept of branding, and decide whether or not you are subjected to an excess of advertising that seeks to win your loyalty to a certain brand of product, especially because of your age, gender, social status, or other factors.

GROUP PROJECTS

7. Find out if your educational institution has an advertising contract with an outside corporation. If not, has the administration been approached by such a corporation? Why did administrators refuse to host advertising in your school? If your institution does have an advertising contract, how visible are the ads in your school? Do they enhance or detract from the physical environment? Interview several students outside of your class to discover how they feel about the ads. How effective are they? Do your interviewees like the ads? Resent them? Feel indifferent?

8. Visit the Zoom Media Web site at **www.zoom-media.com** and read about their approach to identifying marketing "niches" for whom they tailor their advertising. In your group, discuss this company's attitude toward advertising in an academic setting. Based on this site, do you think their approach is effective? Why or why not?

9. *Research and Analysis:* Schofield mentions how a group of University of Toronto students protested their institution's use of sweatshop labour in producing university merchandise. Find out whether your own institution has its merchandise, such as hats and T-shirts, ethically produced. Present your findings to the class.

Excerpt from *No Logo*
Naomi Klein

Think of the number of ads you encounter every day on television, on the Internet, or on the way to class. If you're like most consumers, chances are you hardly notice the vast majority of them. As the advertising industry expands exponentially, the public is becoming indifferent or immune to the messages it sends out. To counter this, marketers are forced to dream up newer, more elaborate and intrusive techniques. In this excerpt from her international best-seller, *No Logo: Taking Aim at the Brand Bullies* (2000), Naomi Klein briefly reviews the history of "branding" and discusses some of the marketing world's strategies to reach consumers hardened by a greater and greater onslaught of daily advertising.

Naomi Klein is an award-winning journalist who has been at the forefront of the global justice movement. Her internationally syndicated column appears in *The Nation*, *The Guardian*, and *The Globe and Mail*. In 2004, she released *The Take*, a film about Argentina's occupied factories, co-produced with director Avi Lewis.

Have consumers become immune to advertising? If so, how are corporations responding to this?

The Beginning of the Brand

1 It's helpful to go back briefly and look at where the idea of branding first began. Though the words are often used interchangeably, branding and advertising are not the same process. Advertising any given product is only one part of branding's grand plan, as are sponsorship and logo licensing. Think of the brand as the core meaning of the modern corporation, and of the advertisement as one vehicle used to convey that meaning to the world.

2 The first mass-marketing campaigns, starting in the second half of the nineteenth century, had more to do with advertising than with branding as we understand it today. Faced with a range of recently invented products—the radio, phonograph, car, light bulb and so on—advertisers had more pressing tasks than creating a brand identity for any given corporation; first, they had to change the way people lived their lives. Ads had to inform consumers about the existence of some new invention, then convince them that their lives would be better if they used, for example, cars instead of wagons, telephones instead of mail and electric light instead of oil lamps. Many of these new products bore brand names—some of which are still around today—but these were almost incidental. These products were themselves news; that was almost advertisement enough.

3 The first brand-based products appeared at around the same time as the invention-based ads, largely because of another relatively recent innovation: the factory. When goods began to be produced in factories, not only were entirely new products being introduced but old products—even basic staples—were appearing in strikingly new forms. What made early branding efforts different from more straightforward salesmanship was that the market was now being flooded with uniform mass-produced products that were virtually indistinguishable from one another. Competitive branding became a necessity of the machine age—within a context of manufactured sameness, image-based difference had to be manufactured along with the product.

4 So the role of advertising changed from delivering product news bulletins to building an image around a particular brand-name version of a product. The first task of branding was to bestow proper names on generic goods such as sugar, flour, soap and cereal, which had previously been scooped out of barrels by local shopkeepers. In the 1880s, corporate logos were introduced to mass-produced products like Campbell's Soup, H.J. Heinz pickles and Quaker Oats cereal. As design historians and theorists Ellen Lupton and J. Abbott Miller note, logos were tailored to evoke familiarity and folksiness . . . in an effort to counteract the new and unsettling anonymity of packaged goods. "Familiar personalities such as Dr. Brown, Uncle Ben, Aunt Jemima, and Old Grand-Dad came to replace the shopkeeper, who was traditionally responsible for measuring bulk foods for customers and acting as an

advocate for products . . . a nationwide vocabulary of brand names replaced the small local shopkeeper as the interface between consumer and product." [1] After the product names and characters had been established, advertising gave them a venue to speak directly to would-be consumers. The corporate "personality," uniquely named, packaged and advertised, had arrived.

5   For the most part, the ad campaigns at the end of the nineteenth century and the start of the twentieth used a set of rigid, pseudoscientific formulas: rivals were never mentioned, ad copy used declarative statements only and headlines had to be large, with lots of white space—according to one turn-of-the-century adman, "an advertisement should be big enough to make an impression but not any bigger than the thing advertised."

6   But there were those in the industry who understood that advertising wasn't just scientific; it was also spiritual. Brands could conjure a feeling—think of Aunt Jemima's comforting presence—but not only that, entire corporations could themselves embody a meaning of their own. In the early twenties, legendary adman Bruce Barton turned General Motors into a metaphor for the American family, "something personal, warm and human," while GE was not so much the name of the faceless General Electric Company as, in Barton's words, "the initials of a friend." In 1923 Barton said that the role of advertising was to help corporations find their soul. The son of a preacher, he drew on his religious upbringing for uplifting messages: "I like to think of advertising as something big, something splendid, something which goes deep down into an institution and gets hold of the soul of it. . . . Institutions have souls, just as men and nations have souls," he told GM president Pierre du Pont. [2] General Motors ads began to tell stories about the people who drove its cars—the preacher, the pharmacist or the country doctor who, thanks to his trusty GM, arrived "at the bedside of a dying child" just in time "to bring it back to life."

7   By the end of the 1940s, there was a burgeoning awareness that a brand wasn't just a mascot or a catchphrase or a picture printed on the label of a company's product; the company as a whole could have a brand identity or a "corporate consciousness," as this ephemeral quality was termed at the time. As this idea evolved, the adman ceased to see himself as a pitchman and instead saw himself as "the philosopher-king of commercial culture," [3] in the words of ad critic Randall Rothberg. The search for the true meaning of brands—or the "brand essence," as it is often called—gradually took the agencies away from individual products and their attributes and toward a psychological/anthropological examination of what brands mean to the culture and to people's lives. This was seen to be of crucial importance, since corporations may manufacture products, but what consumers buy are brands.

8   It took several decades for the manufacturing world to adjust to this shift. It clung to the idea that its core business was still production and that branding was an important add-on. Then came the brand equity mania of the eighties, the defining moment of which arrived in 1988 when Philip Morris purchased Kraft for $12.6 billion—six times what the company was worth on paper. The price difference, apparently, was the cost of the word "Kraft." Of course Wall Street was aware that decades of marketing and brand bolstering added value to a company over and above its assets and total annual sales. But with the Kraft purchase, a huge dollar

value had been assigned to something that had previously been abstract and unquan-
tifiable—a brand name. This was spectacular news for the ad world, which was now
able to make the claim that advertising spending was more than just a sales strategy:
it was an investment in cold hard equity. The more you spend, the more your company is worth. Not surprisingly, this led to a considerable increase in spending on
advertising. More important, it sparked a renewed interest in puffing up brand identities, a project that involved far more than a few billboards and TV spots. It was
about pushing the envelope in sponsorship deals, dreaming up new areas in which to
"extend" the brand, as well as perpetually probing the zeitgeist to ensure that the
"essence" selected for one's brand would resonate karmically with its target market.
For reasons that will be explored in the rest of this chapter, this radical shift in corporate philosophy has sent manufacturers on a cultural feeding frenzy as they seize
upon every corner of unmarketed landscape in search of the oxygen needed to
inflate their brands. In the process, virtually nothing has been left unbranded. That's
quite an impressive feat, considering that as recently as 1993 Wall Street had pro-
nounced the brand dead, or as good as dead. . . .

9   The marketing world is always reaching a new zenith, breaking through last
year's world record and planning to do it again next year with increasing numbers of
ads and aggressive new formulae for reaching consumers. The advertising industry's astronomical rate of growth is neatly reflected in year-to-year figures measuring total ad spending in the U.S. . . . , which have gone up so steadily that by 1998
the figure was set to reach $196.5 billion, while global ad spending is estimated at
$435 billion.[4] According to the 1998 United Nations Human Development Report,
the growth in global ad spending "now outpaces the growth of the world economy
by one-third."

10   This pattern is a by-product of the firmly held belief that brands need continuous and constantly increasing advertising in order to stay in the same place.
According to this law of diminishing returns, the more advertising there is out there
(and there always is more, because of this law), the more aggressively brands must
market to stand out. And of course, no one is more keenly aware of advertising's
ubiquity than the advertisers themselves, who view commercial inundation as a
clear and persuasive call for more—and more intrusive—advertising. With so much
competition, the agencies argue, clients must spend more than ever to make sure
their pitch screeches so loud it can be heard over all the others. David Lubars, a
senior ad executive in the Omnicom Group, explains the industry's guiding principle with more candor than most. Consumers, he says, "are like roaches—you spray
them and spray them and they get immune after a while."[5]

11   So, if consumers are like roaches, then marketers must forever be dreaming up
new concoctions for industrial-strength Raid. And nineties marketers, being on a
more advanced rung of the sponsorship spiral, have dutifully come up with clever
and intrusive new selling techniques to do just that. Recent highlights include these
innovations: Gordon's gin experimented with filling British movie theaters with the
scent of juniper berries; Calvin Klein stuck "CK Be" perfume strips on the backs of
Ticketmaster concert envelopes; and in some Scandinavian countries you can get
"free" long-distance calls with ads cutting into your telephone conversations. And

there's plenty more, stretching across ever more expansive surfaces and cramming into the smallest of crevices: sticker ads on pieces of fruit promoting ABC sitcoms, Levi's ads in public washrooms, corporate logos on boxes of Girl Guide cookies, ads for pop albums on takeout food containers, and ads for Batman movies projected on sidewalks or into the night sky. There are already ads on benches in national parks as well as on library cards in public libraries, and in December 1998 NASA announced plans to solicit ads on its space stations. Pepsi's ongoing threat to project its logo onto the moon's surface hasn't yet materialized, but Mattel did paint an entire street in Salford, England, "a shriekingly bright bubblegum hue" of pink— houses, porches, trees, road, sidewalk, dogs and cars were all accessories in the televised celebrations of Barbie Pink Month.[6] Barbie is but one small part of the ballooning $30 billion "experiential communication" industry, the phrase now used to encompass the staging of such branded pieces of corporate performance art and other "happenings."

12   That we live a sponsored life is now a truism and it's a pretty safe bet that as spending on advertising continues to rise, we roaches will be treated to even more of these ingenious gimmicks, making it ever more difficult and more seemingly pointless to muster even an ounce of outrage. ◆

Notes

1. Ellen Lupton and J. Abbott Miller, *Design Writing Research: Writing on Graphic Design* (New York: Kiosk, 1996), p. 177.
2. Roland Marchand, "The Corporation Nobody Knew: Bruce Barton, Alfred Sloan, and the Founding of the General Motors' Family," *Business History Review*, December 22, 1991, p. 825.
3. Randall Rothberg, *Where the Suckers Moon* (New York: Vintage, 1995), p. 137.
4. Stats are from McCann-Erikson's ad spending forecast appearing in Advertising Age and the United Nations Human Development Report, 1998. Most industry watchers estimate that U.S. spending from global brands represents 40 percent of the total ad spending in the rest of the world. Canadian ad spending, which is less rigorously tracked by the industry, follows the same growth, but with smaller figures. Between 1978 and 1994, for instance, it grew from a $2.7 billion industry to a $9.2 billion industry (source: "A Report Card on Advertising Revenues in Canada," 1995).
5. Yumiko Ono, "Markerters Seek the 'Naked' Truth in Consumer Psyches," *Wall Street Journal*, May 30, 1997, B1.
6. *Daily Mail* (London), November 17, 1997.

FREEWRITING ASSIGNMENT

Klein comments that the new ways that advertisers are exploiting our public and private space makes it "even more difficult and more seemingly pointless to muster even an ounce of outrage." Do you find the new gimmicks she mentions in her second to last paragraph disturbing? Other critics argue that we should not be concerned by these developments. React to that viewpoint.

CRITICAL READING

1. In paragraph 2, Klein refers to the first mass-marketing campaigns of the nineteenth century and makes a distinction between advertising and branding. What is the difference between these two terms?
2. What does Klein mean by her claim that we are living a "sponsored life"?
3. Klein quotes advertising executive, David Lubars (paragraph 10), who says that consumers are like "roaches" in that they become immune to advertising after a while. Is this an effective quote for Klein's message? Why?
4. According to this piece, the estimate for global ad spending for 1998 was $435 billion and the growth of global spending on advertising "now outpaces the growth of the world economy by one-third." What is so disturbing about this trend? How else could this money be spent?
5. Evaluate Klein's tone in this piece. What phrases or words reveal her tone? Who is her intended audience? How does this tone connect to her intended audience?
6. What is the "experiential communication" industry? How does it differ from traditional advertising methods of the past?

CRITICAL WRITING

7. *Exploratory Writing:* Are you comfortable with the examples of intrusive advertising that Klein mentions in paragraph 11? Should a company, for example, be allowed to project a logo onto the moon as Pepsi has threatened to do? Explain.
8. *Research and Exploratory Writing:* Think about a recent advertising campaign that uses particularly ingenious or particularly irritating gimmicks to get the consumer's attention. Write down the details of this campaign and explain whether you think it is intrusive, effective, or both. Explain why.
9. *Research and Exploratory Writing:* In the preceding article, "The Rebel Sell," Heath and Potter refer to the introduction of *No Logo* and claim that Klein considers herself an anti-consumer, when in fact, she is really a discriminating consumer. Attain a copy of *No Logo* and read the introduction. How do you think Klein might respond to this claim?

GROUP PROJECTS

10. With your group, explore the *No Logo* Web site at **www.nologo.org**. What is the tone of this site? What is its message and how does it get that message across? Who is the audience for such a site? How is the Internet advantageous for groups such as this?
11. You and the members of your group are part of an advertising agency developing a campaign for a new brand, such as a cologne, a line of clothing, or a soft drink. Create an advertising strategy for this brand along the lines of the "experiential communication" examples cited in this excerpt. Explain the rationale of your campaign to the class.

Trademarks and Brand Logos

Logos are graphic designs that represent and help market a particular brand or company. Some logos are instantly recognizable, needing no words to explain what they represent. A good example of a logo with international recognition is the image of the Olympic rings. Other logos may be more obscure—specific to particular countries or demographic groups. Chances are most senior citizens wouldn't recognize the Lugz logo, or know what product was associated with it. Sometimes a logo can simply be the initial or name of the brand. Chanel is famous for its interlocking C design, and Kate Spade's name serves as her logo. Spade's logo is distinctive because of the font face used to spell her name, written in lower-case letters.

Most logos have meaning behind their design. For example, the Olympic ring logo was designed by Pierre de Coubertain for the 1914 Paris Congress of the Olympic Movement, celebrating its twentieth anniversary. The Olympic ring logo itself was probably designed by him, despite some references to using a stone unearthed in Delphi, Greece, as his inspiration. A Frenchman, de Coubertain was president of the USFSA French sports federation (Union des Sociétés Françaises des Sports Athlétiques), which used an emblem consisting of two interlocking rings. The symbol of the USFSA probably served as his model. For the colours, de Coubertain decided to use the colours from the flags of all countries that were part of the Olympic Movement; white for the cloth and red, yellow, green, blue, and black for the rings. The Olympic Charter identifies the five rings as representing the union of the five continents and the convergence of athletes from throughout the world at the Olympic Games. No continent is represented by any specific ring. The choice of a circle is also deliberate: circles represent wholeness, and interlocking them "joins" the continents they represent.

As you look at these logos, consider the brands they represent and what they say about the people who use or purchase that brand.

1. Identify the brands represented by the logos above. What do the logos stand for? Who buys the products they represent? What does the logo tell you about the person who uses that brand?
2. What brands do you tend to purchase, and why? Are there particular logos that are associated with the brands you prefer? Explain.
3. Are you more likely to purchase a product with a prominent or prestigious logo than a "no name" brand? Why or why not?
4. Examine the clothing you are wearing and the personal items within ten feet of you right now. How many items bear a logo? What are they?
5. What is your college or university's "logo"? Is it a shield? A phrase? A mascot? How does the symbol chosen by your school reflect its values and identity? Explain.

A Portfolio of Advertisements

The following section features 12 magazine advertisements. Diverse in content and style, some ads use words to promote the product, while others depend on emotion, name recognition, visual appeal, or association. They present a variety of sales pitches and marketing techniques.

Following the ads are a list of questions to help you analyze how the ads work their appeal to promote their products. When studying them, consider how they target our social perceptions of and basic desires for happiness, beauty, and success. Approach each as a consumer, an artist, a social scientist, and a critic with an eye for detail.

GM Certified Vehicles

1. What is happening in this ad? How long does it take you to figure out the point? Does this work in the ad's favour? Explain.
2. How are humour and surprise used to promote the product in this advertisement? Is humour important to the product? The success of the ad? Explain.
3. After viewing this ad, are you more likely to follow its "advice"? Why or why not?
4. What catches your attention in this ad? What do you read first? Do you look at the car, the woman, or the cart? Would the ad be as effective if it featured a man eating? A different setting such as a beach or shopping mall? Is setting important? Explain.

Vans

1. Analyze the different images featured in the ad. What do they depict? How do the different photos contribute to the tone the ad wishes to set?
2. Do you know who the woman is in the ad? What sort of person do you imagine her to be? What is she wearing? Is her clothing important in promoting the product—sneakers? How does her location promote the product's image?
3. What is this woman known for? Why do you think she is pictured without the equipment she uses as part of her profession?
4. Who would you say is the target audience for this ad? Why? Consider age, gender, lifestyle, etc. in your response.
5. Consider the different angles at which photographs included in this ad were taken. How would its impact be different if it were shot from above? What if the woman in the photo was looking away from the camera? Explain.

Apple iPod Mini

1. If you did not know what an iPod was, could you determine anything about it from this ad? Explain.
2. How important is brand/name recognition to the success of this ad? Who would know what this brand was, and what it was selling?
3. Who is the target audience for this brand? How does this ad appeal to that audience?
4. How does this ad use colour and graphics to catch your eye? If you were looking through a magazine and saw this ad, would you stop and look at it? Why or why not?

Nokia

1. What is this ad selling? Can you tell? If you had never heard of the company, Nokia, what might you guess this ad was selling? Explain.
2. How does the woman next to the guitar visually contribute to the advertisement? Would the image work as well with a man? Why or why not?
3. Who is the target audience for this ad? How does the ad appeal to this target audience?

Hitachi

1. What makes you stop and look at this ad? After looking at the picture, are you motivated to read the ad copy? Why or why not?
2. What is this ad selling? After viewing this ad, are you likely to remember the brand? Explain.
3. Apply the Fog Index described in Charles O'Neill's essay "The Language of Advertising" to the blurb at the bottom of the page. What is the grade level of the language? What does the language level reveal about the target audience for the ad?
4. In what type of magazines would you expect to see this ad?
5. Would this ad be as effective if the cat were farther away from the camera? If another animal were featured? Explain.

BP/Beyond Petroleum

1. At first glance, who do you look at first in the ad? Why?
2. Who are the people in the ad? What do they do? Why do you think BP mentions their profession in the ad? Explain.
3. What is the woman in the ad doing? Why do you think she is there? Would the ad be any different if it were just the man featured in the ad? Explain.
4. What do you think is happening in this ad? What situation does it aim to convey? Where are the subjects located?
5. After reading this ad, have you learned something that you did not know about foreign and domestic energy sources? Did it serve to educate you? Do you think that is the purpose of the ad?

Buying a GM Certified Used Vehicle is always a good decision. They're from the GM brands you trust. Plus each one gets a 100+ Point Inspection, a 3-Month/3,000-Mile Comprehensive Limited Warranty, 24-Hour GM Roadside Assistance and a 3-Day/150-Mile Satisfaction Guarantee. Check out over 70,000 Certified vehicles at gmcertified.com.

Low **3.9%** APR Financing for Qualified Buyers† CHEVROLET PONTIAC OLDSMOBILE BUICK GMC **THE RIGHT WAY. THE RIGHT CAR.®**

where the beach >>>>>>>>> meets the street >>
where the beach >>>>>>>>> meets the street >>>>>>>>>

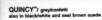

QUINCY™/ grey/confetti
also in black/white and seal brown suede

available at Vans / vans.com

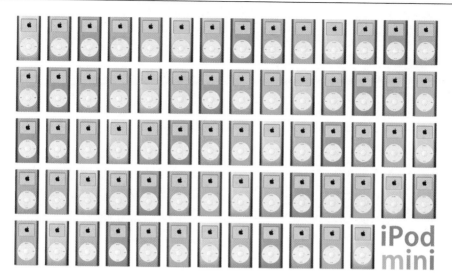

The new sound system

NOKIA
MUSIC STAND

"There's not much we can do about our dependence on foreign oil. We only have so many reserves."

▲ Laron Johnson and Rima Koka/Medical Professionals

Though we do have some options. As we continue to invest in alternative energy sources like solar, the immediate need for oil and gas still remains. Over the next 10 years, we're investing $15 billion in the Gulf of Mexico to find and produce new energy supplies. Today, nearly 70% of the oil we use to make fuels in the U.S. comes from North America.

It's a start.

bp

beyond petroleum™

bp.com

SITTING PRETTY

This spokescandy for "M&M's"® Chocolate Candies, photographed in the factory, surrounds himself with thousands of the little chocolate guys that made him famous.

"I know people undress me in their minds. Chocolate... peanut...that's what they see."

www.m-ms.com

©Mars, Incorporated 2000

ABSOLUTE ON ICE.

M&M's

1. Evaluate this advertisement's use of colour and texture. How does it promote the product? Would the effectiveness of this ad be the same if it were printed in black and white, such as in a newspaper? Explain.
2. What is this ad mimicking? Explain.
3. None of the text in this advertisement is "serious"; that is, the advertisers do not "speak" to the audience about the product. Evaluate the use of text in this ad. How does it complement the picture? Is anything lost by not telling the audience about the product? Why or why not?
4. Would you stop and look at this ad? Why or why not?
5. Evaluate the personification of the candy in this ad. Does this seem like an effective vehicle to promote the product? Explain.

Absolute on Ice

1. What is the purpose of this ad? What is it "selling?"
2. How does this ad rely on our previously established expectations regarding the product it satirizes, and how it has been marketed?
3. Visit the Absolut Vodka Web site at **www.absolutvodka.com** to see real ads produced by this company. How does the spoof ad incorporate elements of the real ads? Explain.
4. What are your gut reactions to this ad? Do you find it disturbing? Offensive? Effective? Enlightening? Explain.
5. Evaluate the effectiveness of photographic decisions in this ad. Would it be as effective if the ad featured an entire body? A face? Explain.

honda.com 1-800-33-Honda EX model shown. ©2003 American Honda Motor Co., Inc.
*NHTSA NCAP frontal crash test: October 2000; side crash test: November 2000.

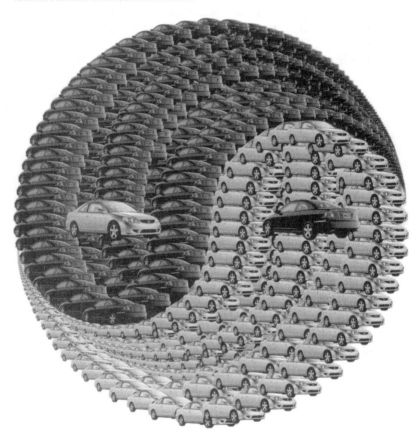

YOUR RIGHT BRAIN AND YOUR LEFT BRAIN WILL FINALLY BE OF THE SAME MIND.   A car that

can quench your emotional side and satiate your rational side. The stylish and 5-star-crash-test-rated* Civic Coupe

Honda

1. How does this photograph capture your attention? Can you tell at a glance what this ad is selling? How long does it take to figure out what the product is? Is this a positive or negative aspect of the ad?

2. What visual conventions does this ad employ? What symbolism does it use? How much does this ad rely on symbol recognition? What are the implications of this symbolism toward the product? If you didn't know what the symbolism was in this ad, would it fail to effectively sell the product? Explain.

3. Consider the text at the bottom of the ad. What does it say about the product? About the person who buys the product?

4. Rate this advertisement on a scale of 1–10 in terms of appeal, with 10 being a perfect score. What score would you give it, and why does it deserve such a ranking?

Phoenix Wealth Management

1. Who is depicted in this picture? What do their clothing, hairstyle, and demeanor imply about them? Why is how they look important to the product and its message? Would it be different if the same women were photographed in sweatshirts and jeans? Jogging suits? Explain.

2. What is the setting for this ad? How does the setting contribute to the mood? Explain.

3. What do the statements next to each woman tell the viewer about her? About the product?

4. How does the slogan "Money. It's just not what it used to be" connect to the people in the ad? To the product the ad is promoting? Explain.

5. If you were perusing a magazine and saw this ad, would you stop to read it? Why or why not? In what types of magazines would you expect to see this ad, and why?

Maybe I was supposed to get Parkinson's.

Maybe the last 20 years were just a warm-up for this moment. After all, my career has given me a certain stature (even for a short guy). And people seem to pay attention when I speak. So listen to this: Of all the brain disorders, Parkinson's is the one that scientists truly believe may be closest to a cure. Yet it remains severely underfunded. In fact, with enough funding, they feel they can crack it within 10 years. And if they can cure Parkinson's, then similar diseases like Alzheimer's, Huntington's, and ALS (Lou Gehrig's Disease) may not be far behind. You can help make that happen. Go to my Web site. Or call to make a donation. You have the power to wipe out this disease. To affect millions of lives. Okay, okay. I'll get off my soapbox now.

Make a donation today. Visit www.michaeljfox.org or call 1-800-708-7644.

Parkinson's Foundation

1. Do you find this ad particularly compelling? Why or why not? What kind of an impact does the spokesman's statement have on his audience? Explain.

2. What is the man standing on? Why?

3. Who is the man in the advertisement? What is his connection to the "product"? How is he dressed and posed? Do these photographic elements make the ad more effective? If so, why?

4. How does the text featured at the bottom of the ad work to complement the overall ad, including the quote at the top. What tense and voice does it use? To whom is it addressed?

Courtesy of United Way.

United Way Ad

1. Is it immediately obvious that this ad is for a charity rather than for a product? If so, how?
2. What is the effect of the jarring juxtaposition of scale and the contrast between foreground and background in the photograph?
3. Which elements of the ad are dynamic (showing movement) and which are static? What is the effect on the mood of the photograph?
4. What is the purpose of the hand in this picture? What are the connotations of the word *hand* in the context of charity and charitable organizations?
5. Who is the audience for this ad? In which publications(s) might you expect to find it? Why?
6. How does the composition of the photograph draw the eye across or down the page? Where does your eye start, and where does it end up? How does this enhance the message of the ad?

A (Mild) Defense of Luxury
James Twitchell

While media and academic critics question the methods of advertising agencies and lament the sacrifice of values in the name of consumerism, professor James Twitchell openly embraces the media-driven world of advertising. In the next piece, Twitchell explores the joys of luxury and challenges the academic criticism that condemns our material instincts as shallow and self-centred. He realizes that his viewpoint may not be popular, but it is honest. Because the truth is, we love nice stuff. Is that so wrong?

James Twitchell is a professor of English and advertising at the University of Florida. He switched from teaching poetry to the study of mass culture and advertising after discovering that his students could recite more ad jingles than they could lines of poetry. Since then, he has written many books on the subject, including *Twenty Ads that Shook the World* (1998) and *Lead Us into Temptation: The Triumph of American Materialism* (1999). This essay is an excerpt from his 2002 book, *Living It Up: America's Love Affair with Luxury.*

CRITICAL THINKING   Why is materialism so criticized, yet obviously so wholeheartedly embraced by North American society? If we are basically lovers of luxury, why are we so quick to condemn advertising and consumerism?

---

1 Who but fools, toadies, and hacks have ever come to the defense of modern American luxury? No one, not even bulk consumers of the stuff, will ever really defend it. And why should they? The very idea that what we have defines who we are is repulsive to many of us. The irrationality of overvaluing certain rocks, fabrics, logos, textures, wines, bottles, appliances, nameplates, tassels, zip codes, T-shirts, monograms, hotel rooms, purses, and the like is insulting to our intellect. At one level this kind of luxury is indefensible. The "good life" seems so blatantly unnecessary, even evil, especially when millions of people around the globe are living without the bare necessities. Plus, after all, it's just cake, a sugar high. Empty calories.

2 And few of us truly admire those who have amassed vast quantities of this stuff. If Donald Trump has his defenders, it is primarily those who are entertained, not edified, by his obstreperousness. Imelda Marcos is a pathetic character. Ditto Leona Helmsley. It's hard to be on Rodeo Drive and see a man wearing a pinkie ring, a flashy Rolex, decked out like Regis Philbin, getting into a Lincoln Navigator, and not feel a kind of smug self-satisfaction with one's own life. And let's face it, the Vegas Strip is an exciting place to visit, but most of us wouldn't want to live there.

3 Generations ago the market for luxury goods consisted of a few people who lived in majestic houses with a full complement of servants, in some time-honored enclave of the privileged. As Holly Brubach (1998) has wittily observed, they ordered their trunks from Louis Vuitton, their trousseaus from Christian Dior, their

Dom Perignon by the case, and spent lots of time looking out over water. Their taste, like their politics, was determined largely by considerations of safeguarding wealth and perpetuating the social conventions that affirmed their sense of superiority. They stayed put. We watched them from afar. We stayed put. Maybe they had money to burn. We had to buy coal.

3   The very unassailability of old luxe made it safe, like old name, old blood, old land, old pew, old coat of arms, or old service to the crown. Primogeniture, the cautious passage and consolidation of wealth to the first-born male, made the anxiety of exclusion somehow bearable. After all, you knew your place from the moment of birth and had plenty of time to make your peace. If you drew a short straw, not to worry. A comfortable life as a vicar would await you. Or the officer corps. For females marriage became the defining act of social place.

5   The application of steam, and then electricity, to the engines of production brought a new market of status, an industrial market, one made up of people who essentially bought their way into having a blood line. From them this new generation of consumer has descended. First the industrial rich, then the inherited rich, and now the incidentally rich, the accidentally rich. Call them yuppies, yippies, bobos, nobrows, or whatever; although they can't afford a house in Paris's Sixteenth Arrondissement or an apartment on Park Avenue, they have enough disposable income to buy a Vuitton handbag (if not a trunk), a bottle of Dior perfume (if not a flagon), a Bombay martini (if not quite a few), and a timeshare vacation on the water (if not a second home). The consumers of the new luxury have a sense of entitlement that transcends social class, a conviction that the finer things are their birthright—never mind that they were born into a family whose ancestral home is a tract house in the suburbs, near the mall, not paid for, and the family crest comes downloaded from the Internet.

6   These new *customers* for luxury are younger than *clients* of the old luxe used to be, they are far more numerous, they make their money far sooner, and they are far more flexible in financing and fickle in choice. They do not stay put. They now have money to burn. The competition for their attention is intense, and their consumption patterns—if you haven't noticed—is changing life for the rest of us. How concerned should we be? I say, not very. Let them eat cake.

The Economic Defense of Opuluxe

7   While making status distinctions on the basis of luxury consumption seems silly, even incompatible with common sense, contemporary economists and sociologists aren't so sure. Economists like Martin Feldstein at Harvard and Paul David at Stanford have been arguing that certain acts of consumption mimic a kind of equitable savings, a kind of universal investment in a mythic bank of communal value (Lewis 1998:B7). After all, it may be more efficient—not to mention, more fun—to spend your money buying a badge good like a fancy car or an Armani wardrobe to announce your social place than to do it the old-fashioned way and join the country club. Plus, you don't have to play golf.

8   Although it is not pictured this way in popular culture, the consumption of high-end goods is rarely impulsive, emotional, or extravagant. Instead it may more often be thoughtful, clever, and sensible. *Pretty Woman* makes a point worth considering. In a sense modern luxury is insurance against misunderstanding, a momentary stay against panic and confusion. If you can't tell where you are in life by consulting the Social Register; then check your car nameplate, your zip code, the amount of stainless steel wrapped around your barbecue.

9   That such "peace of mind" can be bought may seem shallow until you realize that the transformation is dependent only on money, and the color of money is always the same. This is a far more equitable currency than the capriciousness of ancestry and the whimsy of gender and birth order. Well into the nineteenth century the placement of your family pew was a marker of status. The higher your birth and the larger your bank account, the closer you were to the front—the closer, by implication, to God. Given a choice between a lucky-sperm culture in which birth decides social place or a lucky-stock-option culture in which market whimsy decides social place, I think I prefer the latter.

Why Academics Criticize the New Luxury

10   Remember in *King Lear* when the two nasty daughters want to strip Lear of his last remaining trappings of majesty? He has moved in with them, and they don't think he needs so many expensive guards. They convince themselves by saying that their dad, who is used to having everything he has ever wanted, doesn't need a hundred or even a dozen soldiers around him. They whittle away at his retinue until only one is left. "What needs one?" they say. Rather like governments attempting to redistribute wealth or like academics criticizing the consumption habits of others, they include that his needs are excessive. They are false needs: sumptuous, wasteful, luxurious. Lear, however, knows otherwise. Terrified and suddenly bereft of purpose, he bellows from his innermost soul, "Reason not the need."

11   True, Lear doesn't need these soldiers any more than Scrooge needed silver, Midas needed gold, the characters on *Friends* need stuff from Crate & Barrel, those shoppers on Rodeo/Worth/Madison Avenues need handbags, or I need to spend the night at the Luxor. But not needing doesn't stop the desiring. Lear knows that possessions are definitions—superficial meanings, perhaps, but meanings nonetheless. Without soldiers he is no king. Without a BMW there can be no yuppie, without tattoos no adolescent rebel, without big hair no southwestern glamourpuss, without Volvos no academic intellectuals, without cake no Marie Antoinette.

12   Professor Robert Frank tells a revealing story in his *Luxury Fever: Why Money Fails to Satisfy in an Era of Excess*. It seems a relative of his bought a red Porsche in France. When the relative returned to California, he found that the German car couldn't be retrofitted to meet the state's rigorous pollution regulations. He offered it to the professor at a fraction of its market value. Now, in Professor Frank's words,

I was sorely tempted. Yet my small upstate college town has a strong, if usually unstated, social norm against conspicuous consumption. People here are far more likely to drive Volvos than Jaguars, and although ours is a cold climate, we almost never see anyone wearing a fur coat. At that time, a red Porsche convertible really would have been seen, as an in-your-face car in a community like ours. Although I have never thought of myself as someone unusually sensitive to social pressure, I realized that unless I could put a sign on the car that explained how I happened to acquire it, I would never really feel comfortable driving it. (168)

Professor Frank knows exactly what goods to buy and exactly what goods *not* to buy. He doesn't want to keep up with the Joneses or ditch the Joneses. He wants to fit in with the Joneses. He knows who the Joneses are. It's pretty much bow ties, Volvos, and horn-rimmed glasses, thank you very much.

13   My point is simple: This is a social decision, not a moral one or even an economic one. He has decided not to define himself in terms of a red Porsche convertible. He wants what his consumption community wants. But this opens up such an interesting question, at least to me. Why have academics proved such myopic observers of the consumerist world? Why so universally dour and critical? And why can't they see that their own buying habits are more a matter of taste than degree?

14   Here, for instance, is Frank talking in *Luxury Fever* not about consumption per se but about the anxieties of relative position. He is using his sons' behavior to illustrate the childish nature of competitive consumption. Read just a bit between the lines:

Having been raised as an only child, I have always observed the sibling rivalries among my own children with great interest. On returning from a friend's house, my 8-year-old son immediately asks, "Where's Chris?" if his 11-year-old brother is not in sight. When Chris is at his violin lesson, or at the orthodontist's office, we have no problem. But let him be at a movie, or just visiting a friend, the next thing we'll hear is Hayden's angry shout of "That's not fair!"—the inevitable prelude to an anguished outburst about the injustice of life. (1999:109–10)

Now, I don't know either Professor Frank or his sons, but I'll make a prediction. Here's what the boys can look forward to: straight teeth, plenty of soccer (not football) equipment, music lessons galore (preferably piano and violin), summer camp at Duke, magnet school or maybe a year or two at Deerfield, trips to Europe, four years at a private college or university or at one of the public Ivys (celebrated on the rear windscreen of the professor's BMW—not Volvo; remember he's in the B-school, not arts and sciences), and then postgraduate polishing. Nothing extraordinary about this expenditure of—what?—about $400,000 a kid.

15   What's extraordinary is that rarely, if ever, will Frank roll over at night and think he is spending foolishly. Never will he see himself as a luxury consumer, deeply embedded in a consumption community. No, to bobos like the professor (and me, I hasten to add), these choices have nothing to do with taste. They are needs, goddammit! Educational affiliations for academic offspring have nothing to do with

the lawyer next door who drives an S-class Mercedes or the software designer I play tennis with who sports a Patek Philippe wristwatch. Nothing! We're talking education here, not tail fins!

16   I think one reason we academics have been so unappreciative of the material world, often so downright snotty about it, is that we don't need it. Academics say they don't need it because they have the life of the mind, they have art, they contemplate the best that has been thought and said. (Plus, not a whole lot of disposable income.) But that's not the entire story. I think that another reason most academics don't need store-bought affiliation is because the school world, like the church world it mimics, is a cosseted world, a world in which rank and order are well-known and trusted and stable. In fact, buying stuff is more likely to confuse status than illuminate it.

17   Let me tell you who I am in this context. I am a professor in the English department at the University of Florida; I teach romanticism. Here's what that sentence looks like when I explode it to show how each part marks me on the academic totem pole.

	named professor		philosophy
I am a	*professor*		mathematics
	associate professor	in the	*English* department
	assistant professor		history
	instructor		sociology
	teaching assistant		
			medieval lit
	Ivy League		Renaissance lit
	public Ivy		postmodern litcrit
	good big school		eighteenth-century lit
at the	*University of Florida*	I teach	*romanticism*
	not so good big school		modern lit
	community college		American lit
			film
			popcrit

18   Now of course, if you are an academic, you will immediately disagree with how I have arranged the hierarchies. But you can't disagree with the depth of the description, nor, when you think about it, how deep the academic system is relative to others. If you are an academic, I instantly know about you from just a few words. Just say something like "I am a visiting assistant professor of sociology at Podunk U" and I can pretty accurately spin a description of what your life has been like. Give me a bit more, like a publication cite (not the subject, but where it appears), and you are flying right into my radar. This system of social place is so stable that you wear it like a pair of Gucci sunglasses or an old school tie. Little wonder acade-

mics are so perplexed by an outside world that seems preoccupied with social place via consumption. Little wonder we misunderstand it. I can't imagine what it would be like to tell someone I was a DFO of a pre-IPO dot-com. I'd much rather just have them check out my nifty chunky loafers from Prada and my Coach edition of Lexus out in the driveway.

Was It Worth It?

19   The question then becomes: Are we better off for living in a culture in which luxuries are turned into necessities, in which mild addictions are made into expected tastes, in which elegancies are made niceties, expectancies are made into entitlements, in which opulence is made into populence?

20   And the answer, from the point of view of those historically excluded, is yes. Absolutely, yes. Ironically, just as the very stuff that I often find unaesthetic and others may find contemptible has ameliorated the condition of life for many, many millions of people, the very act of getting to this stuff promises a better life for others. I don't mean to belittle the value of religion, politics, law, education, and all the other patterns of meaning making in the modern world but only to state the obvious. Forget happiness; if decreasing pain and discomfort is a goal, consumption of the "finer things" has indeed done what governments, churches, schools, and even laws have promised. Far more than these other systems, betterment through consumption has delivered the goods. Paul Krugman is certainly correct when he writes, "On sheer material grounds one would almost surely prefer to be poor today than upper middle class a century ago" (2000:A15).

21   But is it fair? Do some of us suffer inordinately for the excesses of others? What are we going to do when all this stuff we have shopped for becomes junk? What about the environment? How close is the connection between the accumulation of the new luxury and the fact that the United States also leads the industrialized world in rates of murder, violent crime, juvenile violent crime, imprisonment, divorce, abortion, single-parent households, obesity, teen suicide, cocaine consumption, per-capita consumption of all drugs, pornography production, and pornography consumption? What are we going to do about the lower sixth of our population that seems mired in transgenerational poverty?

22   These are important questions I will leave to others. Entire academic, governmental, and commercial industries are dedicated to each of them. One of the most redemptive aspects of cultures that produce the concept of luxury is that they also produce the real luxury of having time and energy to discuss it. Who knows? Perhaps the luxury of reflection will help resolve at least some of the shortcomings of consumption. ◆

Write about how you feel about luxury. What is luxury to you? Is there a point when it seems excessive? If so, what is your luxury threshold, and why?

CRITICAL READING

1. In his opening paragraph, Twitchell comments, "who but fools, toddies, and hacks have ever come to the defense of modern American luxury," right before he proceeds to do precisely that. How does this approach set the tone for his essay? What can you surmise from his tone and use of language? Does it make him more or less credible? Explain.
2. How does Twitchell's opinion expressed in this essay differ from others in this section in his attitude toward advertising? Are they likely to be swayed by his argument? Why or why not?
3. What, according to Twitchell, is the general attitude of academia toward consumerism? How does Twitchell feel about this attitude? Why does he say this viewpoint is fundamentally flawed?
4. According to Twitchell, why is luxury so important to us? What is the connection between desire and social status? Self-image? Explain.
5. How well does Twitchell support his argument? Evaluate his use of supporting evidence. How well does he convince his readers that his position is reasonable and correct? Explain.
6. Evaluate Twitchell's analysis of excerpts from Professor Frank's book. What does he determine about Frank? Do you think he is probably right? Explain.
7. In his conclusion, Twitchell asserts that while consuming luxury goods may seem wasteful, it really isn't all that bad when you consider how much better off society is as a whole. Do you agree with this conclusion? Why or why not?

CRITICAL WRITING

8. *Exploratory Writing*: Twitchell wonders in his conclusion whether luxury consumption is fair. "Is it fair? Do some of us suffer inordinately for the excesses of others?" Respond to his question, addressing one or more of the issues he raises (crime, environment, etc.).
9. *Personal Narrative*: Write a brief narrative about a time you experienced a decadent spending situation—either for yourself or with someone else. What motivated your spending? How did you feel after it? Can you relate your experience to any of the motivations Twitchell describes in his essay?
10. *Exploratory Writing*: Twitchell outlines his personal "context" as an academic at the University of Florida. Our context, he explains, influences our

consumer habits. Prepare a similar outline for yourself. What does your "explosion" tell you about yourself? If someone constructed a sentence based on your diagram, what might they assume about your consumer habits?

GROUP PROJECTS

11. With your group, make a list of standard appliances, equipment, and possessions that people have in their homes—refrigerators, microwave ovens, pocketbooks, personal planners, fans, coffeemakers, DVD players, computers, VCRs, televisions, stereos (include components), ipods, blowdryers, scooters, etc. Make a list of at least 25–30 items. After the group has created a list, separately rank each item as a necessary, a desirable, or a luxury item. For example, you may decide a refrigerator is a necessary item, but list an air conditioner as a luxury item. Do not look at how other members of your group rank the items until you are all finished. Compare your list with others in your group. Do the lists match, or are there some surprising discrepancies? Discuss the similarities and differences between your lists.

12. Examine the collection of ads on the preceding pages. Select one of the ads and identify the consumer group it targets. Develop a profile of a typical consumer of the product it promotes; and, like Twitchell does with Professor Frank in his essay, try to create a likely summary of their lives or the lives of their children.

VIEWPOINTS

▶ **With These Words, I Can Sell You Anything**
William Lutz

▶ **The Language of Advertising**
Charles A. O'Neill

Words such as "help" and "virtually" and phrases such as "new and improved" and "acts fast" seem like innocuous weaponry in the arsenal of advertising. But not to William Lutz, who analyzes how such words are used in ads—how they misrepresent, mislead, and deceive consumers. In this essay, he alerts us to the special power of "weasel words"—those familiar and sneaky little critters that "appear to say one thing when in fact they say the opposite, or nothing at all." The real danger, Lutz argues, is how such language debases reality and the values of the consumer. Marketing executive Charles A. O'Neill, however, disputes Lutz's criticism of advertising doublespeak. Although admitting to some of the craftiness of his profession, O'Neill defends the huckster's language—both verbal and visual—against claims that it distorts reality. Examining some familiar television commercials and magazine ads, he explains why the language may be charming and seductive, but it is far from brain-washing.

William Lutz teaches English at Rutgers University and is the author of several books, including *The New Doublespeak: Why No One Knows What Anyone's Saying Anymore* (1997) and *Doublespeak Defined* (1999). The following essay is an excerpt from Lutz's book, *Doublespeak* (1990). Charles O'Neill is senior vice president of marketing for Colonial Investment Services in Boston. His essay first appeared in the textbook *Exploring Language* (2004).

CRITICAL THINKING   Consider the phrases used in advertising such as "new and improved" and "cleans like a dream." Do we think about such advertising phrases? How much do such phrases influence you as a consumer? Explain.

With These Words, I Can Sell You Anything
William Lutz

1   One problem advertisers have when they try to convince you that the product they are pushing is really different from other, similar products is that their claims are subject to some laws. Not a lot of laws, but there are some designed to prevent fraudulent or untruthful claims in advertising. Even during the happy years of non-regulation under President Ronald Reagan, the FTC did crack down on the more blatant abuses in advertising claims. Generally speaking, advertisers have to be careful in what they say in their ads, in the claims they make for the products they advertise. Parity claims are safe because they are legal and supported by a number of court decisions. But beyond parity claims there are weasel words.

2   Advertisers use weasel words to appear to be making a claim for a product when in fact they are making no claim at all. Weasel words get their name from the way weasels eat the eggs they find in the nests of other animals. A weasel will make a small hole in the egg, suck out the insides, then place the egg back in the nest. Only when the egg is examined closely is it found to be hollow. That's the way it is with weasel words in advertising: Examine weasel words closely and you'll find that they're as hollow as any egg sucked by a weasel. Weasel words appear to say one thing when in fact they say the opposite, or nothing at all.

"Help"—The Number One Weasel Word

3   The biggest weasel word used in advertising doublespeak is "help." Now "help" only means to aid or assist, nothing more. It does not mean to conquer, stop, eliminate, end, solve, heal, cure, or anything else. But once the ad says "help," it can say

just about anything after that because "help" qualifies everything coming after it. The trick is that the claim that comes after the weasel word is usually so strong and so dramatic that you forget the word "help" and concentrate only on the dramatic claim. You read into the ad a message that the ad does not contain. More importantly, the advertiser is not responsible for the claim that you read into the ad, even though the advertiser wrote the ad so you would read that claim into it.

4   The next time you see an ad for a cold medicine that promises that it "helps relieve cold symptoms fast," don't rush out to buy it. Ask yourself what this claim is really saying. Remember, "helps" means only that the medicine will aid or assist. What will it aid or assist in doing? Why, "relieve" your cold "symptoms." "Relieve" only means to ease, alleviate, or mitigate, not to stop, end, or cure. Nor does the claim say how much relieving this medicine will do. Nowhere does this ad claim it will cure anything. In fact, the ad doesn't even claim it will *do* anything at all. The ad only claims that it will aid in relieving (not curing) your cold symptoms, which are probably a runny nose, watery eyes, and a headache. In other words, this medicine probably contains a standard decongestant and some aspirin. By the way, what does "fast" mean? Ten minutes, one hour, one day? What is fast to one person can be very slow to another. Fast is another weasel word.

5   Ad claims using "help" are among the most popular ads. One says, "Helps keep you young looking," but then a lot of things will help keep you young looking, including exercise, rest, good nutrition, and a facelift. More importantly, this ad doesn't say the product will keep you young, only "young *looking*." Someone may look young to one person and old to another.

6   A toothpaste ad says, "Helps prevent cavities," but it doesn't say it will actually prevent cavities. Brushing your teeth regularly, avoiding sugars in foods, and flossing daily will also help prevent cavities. A liquid cleaner ad says, "Helps keep your home germ free," but it doesn't say it actually kills germs, nor does it even specify which germs it might kill.

7   "Help" is such a useful weasel word that it is often combined with other action-verb weasel words such as "fight" and "control." Consider the claim, "Helps control dandruff symptoms with regular use." What does it really say? It will assist in controlling (not eliminating, stopping, ending, or curing) the *symptoms* of dandruff, not the cause of dandruff nor the dandruff itself. What are the symptoms of dandruff? The ad deliberately leaves that undefined, but assume that the symptoms referred to in the ad are the flaking and itching commonly associated with dandruff. But just shampooing with *any* shampoo will temporarily eliminate these symptoms, so this shampoo isn't any different from any other. Finally, in order to benefit from this product, you must use it regularly. What is "regular use"—daily, weekly, hourly? Using another shampoo "regularly" will have the same effect. Nowhere does this advertising claim say this particular shampoo stops, eliminates, or cures dandruff. In fact, this claim says nothing at all, thanks to all the weasel words.

8   Look at ads in magazines and newspapers, listen to ads on radio and television, and you'll find the word "help" in ads for all kinds of products. How often do you read or hear such phrases as "helps stop . . . ," "helps overcome . . . ," "helps eliminate . . . ," "helps you feel . . . ," or "helps you look . . ."? If you start looking for this weasel word

in advertising, you'll be amazed at how often it occurs. Analyze the claims in the ads using "help," and you will discover that these ads are really saying nothing.

9   There are plenty of other weasel words used in advertising. In fact, there are so many that to list them all would fill the rest of this book. But, in order to identify the doublespeak of advertising and understand the real meaning of an ad, you have to be aware of the most popular weasel words in advertising today.

Virtually Spotless

10   One of the most powerful weasel words is "virtually," a word so innocent that most people don't pay any attention to it when it is used in an advertising claim. But watch out. "Virtually" is used in advertising claims that appear to make specific, definite promises when there is no promise. After all, what does "virtually" mean? It means "in essence of effect, although not in fact." Look at that definition again. "Virtually" means *not in fact*. It does *not* mean "almost" or "just about the same as," or anything else. And before you dismiss all this concern over such a small word, remember that small words can have big consequences.

11   In 1971 a federal court rendered its decision on a case brought by a woman who became pregnant while taking birth control pills. She sued the manufacturer, Eli Lilly and Company, for breach of warranty. The woman lost her case. Basing its ruling on a statement in the pamphlet accompanying the pills, which stated that, "When taken as directed, the tablets offer virtually 100% protection," the court ruled that there was no warranty, expressed or implied, that the pills were absolutely effective. In its ruling, the court pointed out that, according to *Webster's Third New International Dictionary*, "virtually" means "almost entirely" and clearly does not mean "absolute" (*Whittington* v. *Eli Lilly and Company*, 333 F. Supp. 98). In other words, the Eli Lilly company was really saying that its birth control pill, even when taken as directed, *did not in fact* provide 100 percent protection against pregnancy. But Eli Lilly didn't want to put it that way because then many women might not have bought Lilly's birth control pills.

12   The next time you see the ad that says that this dishwasher detergent "leaves dishes virtually spotless," just remember how advertisers twist the meaning of the weasel word "virtually." You can have lots of spots on your dishes after using this detergent and the ad claim will still be true, because what this claim really means is that this detergent does not *in fact* leave your dishes spotless. Whenever you see or hear an ad claim that uses the word "virtually," just translate that claim into its real meaning. So the television set that is "virtually trouble free" becomes the television set that is not in fact trouble free, the "virtually foolproof operation" of any appliance becomes an operation that is in fact not foolproof, and the product that "virtually never needs service" becomes the product that is not in fact service free.

New and Improved

13   If "new" is the most frequently used word on a product package, "improved" is the second most frequent. In fact, the two words are almost always used together. It

seems just about everything sold these days is "new and improved." The next time you're in the supermarket, try counting the number of times you see these words on products. But you'd better do it while you're walking down just one aisle, otherwise you'll need a calculator to keep track of your counting.

14   Just what do these words mean? The use of the word "new" is restricted by regulations, so an advertiser can't just use the word on a product or in an ad without meeting certain requirements. For example, a product is considered new for about six months during a national advertising campaign. If the product is being advertised only in a limited test market area, the word can be used longer, and in some instances has been used for as long as two years.

15   What makes a product "new"? Some products have been around for a long time, yet every once in a while you discover that they are being advertised as "new." Well, an advertiser can call a product new if there has been "a material functional change" in the product. What is "a material functional change," you ask? Good question. In fact it's such a good question it's being asked all the time. It's up to the manufacturer to prove that the product has undergone such a change. And if the manufacturer isn't challenged on the claim, then there's no one to stop it. Moreover, the change does not have to be an improvement in the product. One manufacturer added an artificial lemon scent to a cleaning product and called it "new and improved," even though the product did not clean any better than without the lemon scent. The manufacturer defended the use of the word "new" on the grounds that the artificial scent changed the chemical formula of the product and therefore constituted "a material functional change."

16   Which brings up the word "improved." When used in advertising, "improved" does not mean "made better." It only means "changed" or "different from before." So, if the detergent maker puts a plastic pour spout on the box of detergent, the product has been "improved," and away we go with a whole new advertising campaign. Or, if the cereal maker adds more fruit or a different kind of fruit to the cereal, there's an improved product. Now you know why manufacturers are constantly making little changes in their products. Whole new advertising campaigns, designed to convince you that the product has been changed for the better, are based on small changes in superficial aspects of a product. The next time you see an ad for an "improved" product, ask yourself what was wrong with the old one. Ask yourself just how "improved" the product is. Finally, you might check to see whether the "improved" version costs more than the unimproved one. After all, someone has to pay for the millions of dollars spent advertising the improved product.

17   Of course, advertisers really like to run ads that claim a product is "new and improved." While what constitutes a "new" product may be subject to some regulation, "improved" is a subjective judgment. A manufacturer changes the shape of its stick deodorant, but the shape doesn't improve the function of the deodorant. That is, changing the shape doesn't affect the deodorizing ability of the deodorant, so the manufacturer calls it "improved." Another manufacturer adds ammonia to its liquid cleaner and calls it "new and improved." Since adding ammonia does affect the cleaning ability of the product, there has been a "material functional change" in the product, and the manufacturer can now call its cleaner "new," and

"improved" as well. Now the weasel words "new and improved" are plastered all over the package and are the basis for a multimillion-dollar ad campaign. But after six months the word "new" will have to go, until someone can dream up another change in the product. Perhaps it will be adding color to the liquid, or changing the shape of the package, or maybe adding a new dripless pour spout, or perhaps a _____. The "improvements" are endless, and so are the new advertising claims and campaigns.

18   "New" is just too useful and powerful a word in advertising for advertisers to pass it up easily. So they use weasel words that say "new" without really saying it. One of their favorites is "introducing," as in, "Introducing improved Tide," or "Introducing the stain remover." The first is simply saying, here's our improved soap; the second, here's our new advertising campaign for our detergent. Another favorite is "now," as in, "Now there's Sinex," which simply means that Sinex is available. Then there are phrases like "Today's Chevrolet," "Presenting Dristan," and "A fresh way to start the day." The list is really endless because advertisers are always finding new ways to say "new" without really saying it. If there is a second edition of this book, I'll just call it the "new and improved" edition. Wouldn't you really rather have a "new and improved" edition of this book rather than a "second" edition?

Acts Fast

19   "Acts" and "works" are two popular weasel words in advertising because they bring action to the product and to the advertising claim. When you see the ad for the cough syrup that "Acts on the cough control center," ask yourself what this cough syrup is claiming to do. Well, it's just claiming to "act," to do something, to perform an action. What is it that the cough syrup does? The ad doesn't say. It only claims to perform an action or do something on your "cough control center." By the way, what and where is your "cough control center"? I don't remember learning about that part of the body in human biology class.

20   Ads that use such phrases as "acts fast," "acts against," "acts to prevent," and the like, are saying essentially nothing, because "act" is a word empty of any specific meaning. The ads are always careful not to specify exactly what "act" the product performs. Just because a brand of aspirin claims to "act fast" for headache relief doesn't mean this aspirin is any better than any other aspirin. What is the "act" that this aspirin performs? You're never told. Maybe it just dissolves quickly. Since aspirin is a parity product, all aspirin is the same and therefore functions the same.

Works Like Anything Else

21   If you don't find the word "acts" in an ad, you will probably find the weasel word "works." In fact, the two words are almost interchangeable in advertising. Watch out for ads that say a product "works against," "works like," "works for," or "works longer." As with "acts," "works" is the same meaningless verb used to make you

think that this product really does something, and maybe even something special or unique. But "works," like "acts," is basically a word empty of any specific meaning.

Like Magic

22 Whenever advertisers want you to stop thinking about the product and to start thinking about something bigger, better, or more attractive than the product, they use that very popular weasel word, "like." The word "like" is the advertiser's equivalent of a magician's use of misdirection. "Like" gets you to ignore the product and concentrate on the claim the advertiser is making about it. "For skin like peaches and cream" claims the ad for a skin cream. What is this ad really claiming? It doesn't say this cream will give you peaches-and-cream skin. There is no verb in this claim, so it doesn't even mention using the product. How is skin ever like "peaches and cream"? Remember, ads must be read literally and exactly, according to the dictionary definition of words. (Remember "virtually" in the Eli Lilly case.) The ad is making absolutely no promise or claim whatsoever for this skin cream. If you think this cream will give you soft, smooth, youthful-looking skin, you are the one who has read that meaning into the ad.

23 The wine that claims "It's like taking a trip to France" wants you to think about a romantic evening in Paris as you walk along the boulevard after a wonderful meal in an intimate little bistro. Of course, you don't really believe that a wine can take you to France, but the goal of the ad is to get you to think pleasant, romantic thoughts about France and not about how the wine tastes or how expensive it may be. That little word "like" has taken you away from crushed grapes into a world of your own imaginative making. Who knows, maybe the next time you buy wine, you'll think those pleasant thoughts when you see this brand of wine, and you'll buy it. Or, maybe you weren't even thinking about buying wine at all, but now you just might pick up a bottle the next time you're shopping. Ah, the power of "like" in advertising.

24 How about the most famous "like" claim of all, "Winston tastes good like a cigarette should"? Ignoring the grammatical error here, you might want to know what this claim is saying. Whether a cigarette tastes good or bad is a subjective judgment because what tastes good to one person may well taste horrible to another. Not everyone likes fried snails, even if they are called escargot. (*De gustibus non est disputandum,* which was probably the Roman rule for advertising as well as for defending the games in the Colosseum.) There are many people who say all cigarettes taste terrible, other people who say only some cigarettes taste all right, and still others who say all cigarettes taste good. Who's right? Everyone, because taste is a matter of personal judgment.

25 Moreover, note the use of the conditional, "should." The complete claim is, "Winston tastes good like a cigarette should taste." But should cigarettes taste good? Again, this is a matter of personal judgment and probably depends most on one's experiences with smoking. So, the Winston ad is simply saying that Winston cigarettes are just like any other cigarette: Some people like them and some people don't. On that statement, R. J. Reynolds conducted a very successful multimillion-

dollar advertising campaign that helped keep Winston the number-two-selling cigarette in the United States, close behind number one, Marlboro.

Can't It Be Up to the Claim?

26 Analyzing ads for doublespeak requires that you pay attention to every word in the ad and determine what each word really means. Advertisers try to wrap their claims in language that sounds concrete, specific, and objective, when in fact the language of advertising is anything but. Your job is to read carefully and listen critically so that when the announcer says that "Crest can be of significant value . . ." you know immediately that this claim says absolutely nothing. Where is the doublespeak in this ad? Start with the second word.

27 Once again, you have to look at what words really mean, not what you think they mean or what the advertiser wants you to think they mean. The ad for Crest only says that using Crest "can be" of "significant value." What really throws you off in this ad is the brilliant use of "significant." It draws your attention to the word "value" and makes you forget that the ad only claims that Crest "can be." The ad doesn't say that Crest *is* of value, only that it is "able" or "possible" to be of value, because that's all that "can" means.

28 It's so easy to miss the importance of those little words, "can be." Almost as easy as missing the importance of the words "up to" in an ad. These words are very popular in sale ads. You know, the ones that say, "Up to 50 percent Off!" Now, what does that claim mean? Not much, because the store or manufacturer has to reduce the price of only a few items by 50 percent. Everything else can be reduced a lot less, or not even reduced. Moreover, don't you want to know 50 percent off of what? Is it 50 percent off the "manufacturer's suggested list price," which is the highest possible price? Was the price artificially inflated and then reduced? In other ads, "up to" expresses an ideal situation. The medicine that works "up to ten times faster," the battery that lasts "up to twice as long," and the soap that gets you "up to twice as clean"—all are based on ideal situations for using those products, situations in which you can be sure you will never find yourself.

Unfinished Words

29 Unfinished words are a kind of "up to" claim in advertising. The claim that a battery lasts "up to twice as long" usually doesn't finish the comparison—twice as long as what? A birthday candle? A tank of gas? A cheap battery made in a country not noted for its technological achievements? The implication is that the battery lasts twice as long as batteries made by other battery makers, or twice as long as earlier model batteries made by the advertiser, but the ad doesn't really make these claims. You read these claims into the ad, aided by the visual images the advertiser so carefully provides.

30 Unfinished words depend on you to finish them, to provide the words the advertisers so thoughtfully left out of the ad. Pall Mall cigarettes were once advertised as "A longer finer and milder smoke." The question is, longer, finer, and

milder than what? The aspirin that claims it contains "Twice as much of the pain reliever doctors recommend most" doesn't tell you what pain reliever it contains twice as much of. (By the way, it's aspirin. That's right; it just contains twice the amount of aspirin. And how much is twice the amount? Twice of what amount?) Panadol boasts that "nobody reduces fever faster," but, since Panadol is a parity product, this claim simply means that Panadol isn't any better than any other product in its parity class. "You can be sure if it's Westinghouse," you're told, but just exactly what it is you can be sure of is never mentioned. "Magnavox gives you more" doesn't tell you what you get more of. More value? More television? More than they gave you before? It sounds nice, but it means nothing, until you fill in the claim with your own words, the words the advertisers didn't use. Since each of us fills in the claim differently, the ad and the product can become all things to all people, and not promise a single thing.

31 Unfinished words abound in advertising because they appear to promise so much. More importantly, they can be joined with powerful visual images on television to appear to be making significant promises about a product's effectiveness without really making any promises. In a television ad, the aspirin product that claims fast relief can show a person with a headache taking the product and then, in what appears to be a matter of minutes, claiming complete relief. This visual image is far more powerful than any claim made in unfinished words. Indeed, the visual image completes the unfinished words for you, filling in with pictures what the words leave out. And you thought that ads didn't affect you. What brand of aspirin do you use?

32 Some years ago, Ford's advertisements proclaimed "Ford LTD—700 percent quieter." Now, what do you think Ford was claiming with these unfinished words? What was the Ford LTD quieter than? A Cadillac? A Mercedes Benz? A BMW? Well, when the FTC asked Ford to substantiate this unfinished claim, Ford replied that it meant that the inside of the LTD was 700 percent quieter than the outside. How did you finish those unfinished words when you first read them? Did you even come close to Ford's meaning?

Combining Weasel Words

33 A lot of ads don't fall neatly into one category or another because they use a variety of different devices and words. Different weasel words are often combined to make an ad claim. The claim, "Coffee-Mate gives coffee more body, more flavor," uses Unfinished Words ("more" than what?) and also uses words that have no specific meaning ("body" and "flavor"). Along with "taste" (remember the Winston ad and its claim to taste good), "body" and "flavor" mean nothing because their meaning is entirely subjective. To you, "body" in coffee might mean thick, black, almost bitter coffee, while I might take it to mean a light brown, delicate coffee. Now, if you think you understood that last sentence, read it again, because it said nothing of objective value; it was filled with weasel words of no specific meaning: "thick," "black," "bitter," "light brown," and "delicate." Each of those words has no specific, objective meaning, because each of us can interpret them differently.

34   Try this slogan: "Looks, smells, tastes like ground-roast coffee." So, are you now going to buy Taster's Choice instant coffee because of this ad? "Looks," "smells," and "tastes" are all words with no specific meaning and depend on your interpretation of them for any meaning. Then there's that great weasel word "like," which simply suggests a comparison but does not make the actual connection between the product and the quality. Besides, do you know what "ground-roast" coffee is? I don't, but it sure sounds good. So, out of seven words in this ad, four are definite weasel words, two are quite meaningless, and only one has any clear meaning.

35   Remember the Anacin ad—"Twice as much of the pain reliever doctors recommend most"? There's a whole lot of weaseling going on in this ad. First, what's the pain reliever they're talking about in this ad? Aspirin, of course. In fact, any time you see or hear an ad using those words "pain reliever," you can automatically substitute the word "aspirin" for them. (Makers of acetaminophen and ibuprofen pain relievers are careful in their advertising to identify their products as nonaspirin products.) So, now we know that Anacin has aspirin in it. Moreover, we know that Anacin has twice as much aspirin in it, but we don't know twice as much as what. Does it have twice as much aspirin as an ordinary aspirin tablet? If so, what is an ordinary aspirin tablet, and how much aspirin does it contain? Twice as much as Excedrin or Bufferin? Twice as much as a chocolate chip cookie? Remember those Unfinished Words and how they lead you on without saying anything.

36   Finally, what about those doctors who are doing all that recommending? Who are they? How many of them are there? What kind of doctors are they? What are their qualifications? Who asked them about recommending pain relievers? What other pain relievers did they recommend? And there are a whole lot more questions about this "poll" of doctors to which I'd like to know the answers, but you get the point. Sometimes, when I call my doctor, she tells me to take two aspirin and call her office in the morning. Is that where Anacin got this ad?

Read the Label, or the Brochure

37 Weasel words aren't just found on television, on the radio, or in newspaper and magazine ads. Just about any language associated with a product will contain the doublespeak of advertising. Remember the Eli Lilly case and the doublespeak on the information sheet that came with the birth control pills. Here's another example.

38   In 1983, the Estée Lauder cosmetics company announced a new product called "Night Repair." A small brochure distributed with the product stated that "Night Repair was scientifically formulated in Estée Lauder's U.S. laboratories as part of the Swiss Age-Controlling Skincare Program. Although only nature controls the aging process, this program helps control the signs of aging and encourages skin to look and feel younger." You might want to read these two sentences again, because they sound great but say nothing.

39   First, note that the product was "scientifically formulated" in the company's laboratories. What does that mean? What constitutes a scientific formulation? You wouldn't expect the company to say that the product was casually, mechanically, or

carelessly formulated, or just thrown together one day when the people in the white coats didn't have anything better to do. But the word "scientifically" lends an air of precision and promise that just isn't there.

40   It is the second sentence, however, that's really weasely, both syntactically and semantically. The only factual part of this sentence is the introductory dependent clause—"only nature controls the aging process." Thus, the only fact in the ad is relegated to a dependent clause, a clause dependent on the main clause, which contains no factual or definite information at all and indeed purports to contradict the independent clause. The new "skincare program" (notice it's not a skin cream but a "program") does not claim to stop or even retard the aging process. What, then, does Night Repair, at a price of over $35 (in 1983 dollars) for a .87-ounce bottle do? According to this brochure, nothing. It only "helps," and the brochure does not say how much it helps. Moreover, it only "helps control," and then it only helps control the "*signs* of aging," not the aging itself. Also, it "encourages" skin not to *be* younger but only to "look and feel" younger. The brochure does not say younger than what. Of the sixteen words in the main clause of this second sentence, nine are weasel words. So, before you spend all that money for Night Repair, or any other cosmetic product, read the words carefully, and then decide if you're getting what you think you're paying for.

Other Tricks of the Trade

41   Advertisers' use of doublespeak is endless. The best way advertisers can make something out of nothing is through words. Although there are a lot of visual images used on television and in magazines and newspapers, every advertiser wants to create that memorable line that will stick in the public consciousness. I am sure pure joy reigned in one advertising agency when a study found that children who were asked to spell the word "relief" promptly and proudly responded "r-o-l-a-i-d-s."

42   The variations, combinations, and permutations of doublespeak used in advertising go on and on, running from the use of rhetorical questions ("Wouldn't you really rather have a Buick?" "If you can't trust Prestone, who can you trust?") to flattering you with compliments ("The lady has taste." "We think a cigar smoker is someone special." "You've come a long way baby."). You know, of course, how you're *supposed* to answer those questions, and you know that those compliments are just leading up to the sales pitches for the products. Before you dismiss such tricks of the trade as obvious, however, just remember that all of these statements and questions were part of very successful advertising campaigns.

43   A more subtle approach is the ad that proclaims a supposedly unique quality for a product, a quality that really isn't unique. "If it doesn't say Goodyear, it can't be polyglas." Sounds good, doesn't it? Polyglas is available only from Goodyear because Goodyear copyrighted that trade name. Any other tire manufacturer could make exactly the same tire but could not call it "polyglas," because that would be copyright infringement. "Polyglas" is simply Goodyear's name for its fiberglass-reinforced tire.

44   Since we like to think of ourselves as living in a technologically advanced country, science and technology have a great appeal in selling products. Advertisers are quick to use scientific doublespeak to push their products. There are all kinds of elixirs, additives, scientific potions, and mysterious mixtures added to all kinds of products. Gasoline contains "HTA," "F–130," "Platformate," and other chemical-sounding additives, but nowhere does an advertisement give any real information about the additive.

45   Shampoo, deodorant, mouthwash, cold medicine, sleeping pills, and any number of other products all seem to contain some special chemical ingredient that allows them to work wonders. "Certs contains a sparkling drop of Retsyn." So what? What's "Retsyn"? What's it do? What's so special about it? When they don't have a secret ingredient in their product, advertisers still find a way to claim scientific validity. There's "Sinarest. Created by a research scientist who actually gets sinus headaches." Sounds nice, but what kind of research does this scientist do? How do you know if she is any kind of expert on sinus medicine? Besides, this ad doesn't tell you a thing about the medicine itself and what it does.

Advertising Doublespeak Quick Quiz

46   Now it's time to test your awareness of advertising doublespeak. (You didn't think I would just let you read this and forget it, did you?) The following is a list of statements from some recent ads. Your job is to figure out what each of these ads really says:

DOMINO'S PIZZA: "Because nobody delivers better."
SINUTAB: "It can stop the pain."
TUMS: "The stronger acid neutralizer."
MAXIMUM STRENGTH DRISTAN: "Strong medicine for tough sinus colds."
LISTERMINT: "Making your mouth a cleaner place."
CASCADE: "For virtually spotless dishes nothing beats Cascade."
NUPRIN: "Little. Yellow. Different. Better."
ANACIN: "Better relief."
SUDAFED: "Fast sinus relief that won't put you fast asleep."
ADVIL: "Advanced medicine for pain."
PONDS COLD CREAM: "Ponds cleans like no soap can."
MILLER LITE BEER: "Tastes great. Less filling."
PHILIPS MILK OF MAGNESIA: "Nobody treats you better than MOM (Philips Milk of Magnesia)."
BAYER: "The wonder drug that works wonders."
CRACKER BARREL: "Judged to be the best."
KNORR: "Where taste is everything."
ANUSOL: "Anusol is the word to remember for relief."
DIMETAPP: "It relieves kids as well as colds."
LIQUID DRANO: "The liquid strong enough to be called Drano."
JOHNSON & JOHNSON BABY POWDER: "Like magic for your skin."

PURITAN: "Make it your oil for life."

PAM: "Pam, because how you cook is as important as what you cook."

IVORY SHAMPOO AND CONDITIONER: "Leave your hair feeling Ivory clean."

TYLENOL GEL-CAPS: "It's not a capsule. It's better."

ALKA-SELTZER PLUS: "Fast, effective relief for winter colds."

The World of Advertising

47   In the world of advertising, people wear "dentures," not false teeth; they suffer from "occasional irregularity," not constipation; they need deodorants for their "nervous wetness," not for sweat; they use "bathroom tissue," not toilet paper; and they don't dye their hair, they "tint" or "rinse" it. Advertisements offer "real counterfeit diamonds" without the slightest hint of embarrassment, or boast of goods made out of "genuine imitation leather" or "virgin vinyl."

48   In the world of advertising, the girdle becomes a "body shaper," "form persuader," "control garment," "controller," "outerwear enhancer," "body garment," or "anti-gravity panties," and is sold with such trade names as "The Instead," "The Free Spirit," and "The Body Briefer."

49   A study some years ago found the following words to be among the most popular used in U.S. television advertisements: "new," "improved," "better," "extra," "fresh," "clean," "beautiful," "free," "good," "great," and "light." At the same time, the following words were found to be among the most frequent on British television: "new," "good-better-best," "free," "fresh," "delicious," "full," "sure," "clean," "wonderful," and "special." While these words may occur most frequently in ads, and while ads may be filled with weasel words, you have to watch out for all the words used in advertising, not just the words mentioned here.

50   Every word in an ad is there for a reason; no word is wasted. Your job is to figure out exactly what each word is doing in an ad—what each word really means, not what the advertiser wants you to think it means. Remember, the ad is trying to get you to buy a product, so it will put the product in the best possible light, using any device, trick, or means legally allowed. Your only defense against advertising (besides taking up permanent residence on the moon) is to develop and use a strong critical reading, listening, and looking ability. Always ask yourself what the ad is *really* saying. When you see ads on television, don't be misled by the pictures, the visual images. What does the ad say about the product? What does the ad *not* say? What information is missing from the ad? Only by becoming an active, critical consumer of the doublespeak of advertising will you ever be able to cut through the doublespeak and discover what the ad is really saying. ◆

The Language of Advertising

Charles A. O'Neill

1   His name is Joe. But he's not just your ordinary Joe. You've probably seen him; he's Joe Camel. On the billboards and in the magazine ads, he looked vaguely like a cartoonist's composite sketch of the Rolling Stones, lounging around in a celebrity waiting area at MTV headquarters in New York. He was poised, confident, leaning against a railing or playing pool with his friends. His personal geometry was always just right. He often wore a white suit, dark shirt, sunglasses. Cigarette in hand, wry smile on his lips, his attitude was distinctly confident, urbane.

2   Joe was very cool and very powerful. So cool and powerful that more than 90% of six-year-olds matched Joe Camel with a picture of a cigarette, making him as well-known as Mickey Mouse.[1]

3   Good advertising, but bad public relations.

4   Finally, in 1997, after extended sparring with the tobacco company about whether in fact Joe promoted smoking, and whether cartoons were most likely to be noticed by children or adults, the FTC brought the ads to an end. President Clinton spoke for the regulators when he said, "Let's stop pretending that a cartoon camel in a funny costume is trying to sell to adults, not children."

5   Joe's 23-year-old advertising campaign was stopped because it was obvious that his mission was to turn kids into lung cancer patients. That's bad enough. But beneath the surface, the debate about Joe typifies something more interesting and broad based: the rather uncomfortable, tentative acceptance of advertising in our society. We recognize the legitimacy—even the value—of advertising but on some level we can't quite fully embrace it as a "normal" part of our experience.

6   At best, we view advertising as distracting. At worst, we view it as dangerous to our health and a pernicious threat to our social values. One notable report acknowledged the positive contribution of advertising (e.g., provides information, supports worthy causes, and encourages competition and innovation), then added, "In the competition to attract even larger audiences . . . communicators can find themselves pressured . . . to set aside high artistic and moral standards and lapse into superficiality, tawdriness and moral squalor."[2]

7   How does advertising work? Why is it so powerful? Why does it raise such concern? What case can be made for and against the advertising business?

8   In order to understand advertising, you must accept that it is not about truth, virtue, love, or positive societal values. It is about money. It is about moving customers through the sales process. Sometimes the words and images are concrete; sometimes they are merely suggestive. Sometimes ads provide useful information; sometimes they convince us that we need to spend money to solve a problem we never knew we had. Ads are designed to be intrusive. We're not always pleased about the way they clutter our environment and violate our sense of private space. We're not always happy with the tactics they use to impose themselves upon us.

9   Whatever the product or creative strategy, advertisements derive their power from a purposeful, directed combination of images. These can take the form of words, sounds, or visuals, used individually or together. The combination of images is the language of advertising, a language unlike any other.

10   Everyone who grows up in the civilized world soon learns that advertising language is different from other languages. Read this aloud: "With Nice 'n Easy, it's color so natural, the closer he gets the better you look." Many children would be unable to explain how this classic ad for Clairol's Nice 'n Easy hair coloring differs from "ordinary language," but they would say, "It sounds like an ad." Whether printed on a page, blended with music on the radio, or whispered on the sound track of a television commercial, advertising language is *different*.

11   The language of advertising changes with the times. Styles and creative concepts come and go. But there are at least four distinct, general characteristics of the language of advertising that make it different from other languages. They lend advertising its persuasive power:

1. The language of advertising is edited and purposeful.
2. The language of advertising is rich and arresting; it is specifically intended to attract and hold our attention.
3. The language of advertising involves us; in effect, *we* complete the message.
4. The language of advertising is simple and direct. It holds no secrets from us.

Edited and Purposeful

12   In his book, *Future Shock*, Alvin Toffler described various types of messages we receive from the world around us each day. He observed that there is a difference between normal "coded" messages and "engineered" messages. Much of normal, human experience is "uncoded." When a man walks down a street, for example, he sees where he is going and hears random sounds. These are mental images, but they are not messages "designed by anyone to communicate anything and the man's understanding of it does not depend directly on a social code—a set of agreed-upon signs and definitions." [3] In contrast, Toffler describes a talk show conversation as "coded"; the speaker's ability to exchange information with the host depends upon societal conventions.

13   The language of advertising is coded. It exists in the context of our society. It is also carefully engineered, and ruthlessly purposeful. When he wrote in the 1960s, he estimated that the average adult was exposed to 560 advertising messages each day. That was back in the 1960s. Now, our homes are equipped with 400-channel, direct-broadcast satellite television, the Internet, video streaming mobile devices, video games and other new forms of mass media. We're literally swimming in a sea of information. We're totally wired and wireless. We're overwhelmed by countless billboards in subway stations, stickers on light poles, 15-second spots on television, and an endless stream of spam and pop up messages online.

Demanding Attention

14 Among the hundreds of advertising messages in stores for us each day, very few will actually command our conscious attention. The rest are screened out. The people who design and write ads know about this screening process; they anticipate and accept it as a premise of their business.

15 The classic, all-time favorite device used to breach the barrier is sex. There was a time, many years ago, when advertisers used some measure of subtlety and discretion in their application of sexual themes to their mass media work. No more. Sensuality has been replaced by in-your-face, unrestrained sexuality. One is about romance and connection; the other, physical connection and emotional distance.

16 A poster promotes clothing sold by the apparel company, French Connection group, United Kingdom: (FCUK). Large type tells us, "Apparently there are more important things in life than fashion. Yeah, right." This text is accompanied by a photo of two young people in what has become a standard set up: A boy. A girl. She is pretty, in a detached, offhand sort of way. He has not shaved for 48 hours. Behind them there is a vague impression of a waterfront. They are sharing physical space, but there is no sense of human contact or emotion. The company name appears on the lower right hand side of the poster. The headline is intended to be ironic: "Of course there are things that are more important than fashion, but right now, who cares?" The company maintains that they are "not trying to shock people." As absurd as it may seem, this is actually the truth. This company is not in the business of selling shock. They are selling clothes. They are making a lot of money selling clothes because they know what motivates their teenaged customers—a desire to separate from their parents and declare their membership in the tribe of their peers.

17 Fortunately, advertisers use many other techniques to attract and hold the attention of the targeted consumer audience. The strategy may include strong creative execution or a plain, straightforward presentation of product features and customer benefits. Consider this random cross-section of advertisements from popular media.

- An ad for SalesForce.com used a photo of the Dalai Lama beneath the headline, "There is no software on the path to enlightenment." (What does this mean? "SalesForce.com provides computer services, so I won't have to buy software myself.")
- An ad for two products—the Volkswagen Beetle, and the Apple iPod—used only one word: "Duh." Above it, moving from left to right, we see a photo of the car, a plus sign and to the right, the iPod. (What makes this work? Fast Company (10/03) described this as "a marriage of two classic 'underdog' brands . . . a psychographic match made in heaven. VW and Apple both appeal to young, high-income, adventure-seeking customers. . . .")
- "Can a security blanket be made of sheet metal?" (GM) In the background, there is a photo of a tot asleep in a car seat. (Who doesn't like cute little kids? What parent doesn't think about safety these days?)
- Some ads entertain us and are effective, even though they don't really focus on the product. They work because we remember them. Geico is an automobile insurance company, but they use a cute little lizard as a character in their ads.

(What does a lizard have to do with an insurance company? More than meets the eye. A *gecko* is a type of lizard.)

- Some ads tell us we have problems—real or imagined—that we'd better solve right away. Do you have dry skin or "unsightly eyebrow hairs?" ("I never really noticed, but now that you mention it. . . .")

"Give your car the pink slip." (A short term car rental company lets us know that we don't need to own a car—we can pick one up whenever and wherever we need it.)

18   Soft drink companies are in an advertising category of their own. In the archetypical version of a soft drink TV spot, babies frolic with puppies in the sunlit foreground while their youthful parents play touch football. On the porch, Grandma and Pops quietly smile as they wait for all of this affection to transform the world into a place of warmth, harmony, and joy.

19   Dr. Pepper ads say "Be you!" and feature dancers prancing around singing songs about "Individuality." In Coke's ads, the singer Maya tells us this can of syrupy fizz is "Real." And Pepsi has Britney Spears singing "Pepsi: for those who think young!" The message: If you are among the millions of people who see the commercial and buy the product, you will become 'different'. You will find yourself transformed into a unique ("Be you", "Individuality", "Real"), hip ("young") person. [4]

20   These "slice of life" ads seduce us into feeling—somewhere in the back of our heads—that if we drink the right combination of sugar, preservatives, caramel coloring, and a few secret ingredients, we'll fulfill our yearning for a world where folks from all nations, creeds and sexual orientations live together in a state of perfect bliss. At least for the five minutes it takes us to pour the stuff down our parched, fast-food-filled throats.

21   If you don't buy this version of the American Dream, look around. You are sure to find a product that promises to help you gain prestige in whatever posse you do happen to run with.

22   When the connection is made, the results can be very powerful. Even a commodity product like coffee can be artfully changed from a mere beverage into an emotional experience. *The Wall Street Journal* (7/14/03) summarized the challenge the marketers at Starbucks faced in promoting their stores in China: "Selling an upscale, Western lifestyle that is both in demand in China yet meets resistance among those unfamiliar with the taste of coffee." The article goes on to describe a customer in Shanghai, who drinks tea at home but coffee in public. He said he prefers the taste of tea, but he likes the image that drinking Starbucks coffee conjures up: relaxed affluence. "It's an attitude." A medium size latte costs the equivalent of $2.65. In Shanghai, the monthly disposable income of an average three-person household is $143.00. One cup of coffee costs nearly 2% of the average household's monthly income.

23   What Starbucks has accomplished is not far short of astonishing. They have been successful in taking a purely commodity product that their prospective customers do not particularly enjoy and turning it into not just another drink, but a hip, groovy and chic "attitude"; and they've done this in a Communist country, where

the rules according to Mao would have us believe that there are no class distinctions. What's more, they have created primary demand for a product category; a difficult, if not nearly impossible, feat.

24   Ad campaigns and branding strategies do not often emerge like Botticelli's Venus from the sea, flawless and fully grown. Most often, the creative strategy is developed only after extensive research. "Who will be interested in our product? How old are they? Where do they live? How much money do they earn? What problem will our product solve?" The people at Starbucks did not decide to go to China on a whim. The people at French Connection did not create their brand name just to offend everyone who is old-fashioned enough to think that some words don't belong on billboards, T-shirts and store fronts.

Involving

25   We have seen that the language of advertising is carefully engineered; we have discovered a few of the devices it uses to get our attention. Coke and Pepsi have entranced us with visions of peace and love. An actress offers a winsome smile. Now that they have our attention, advertisers present information intended to show us that their product fills a need and differs from the competition. Advertisers exploit and intensify product differences when they find them, and invent them when they do not.

26   As soon as we see or hear an advertisement, our imagination is set in motion, and our individual fears, aspirations, quirks and insecurities come out to play.

27   It was common not long ago for advertisers in the fashion industry to make use of gaunt, languid models. To some observers, these ads promoted "heroin chic." Perhaps they were not substance abusers, but something was most certainly unusual about the models appearing in ads for Prada and Calvin Klein Products. A young woman in a Prada ad projects no emotion whatsoever. Her posture suggests that she is in a trance or drug-induced stupor. In a Calvin Klein ad, a young man, like the woman from Prada, is gaunt beyond reason. He is shirtless. As if to draw more attention to his peculiar posture and "zero body fat" status, he is shown pinching the skin next to his navel. To some, this also suggests that he is preparing to insert a needle.

28   The fashion industry backed away from the heroin theme. Now the models look generally better fed. But they are, nonetheless, still lost in a world of ennui and isolation. In an ad by Andrew Mark NY, we see a young woman wearing little leather shorts. Her boyfriend's arm is wrapped around her, his thumb pushing ever-so-slightly below the waistband of her pants. What does he look like? He appears to be dazed. He is wearing jeans, an unzipped leather jacket. He hasn't shaved for a couple of days. We are left with the impression that either something has just happened here, or is about to. It probably has something to do with sex.

29   Do these depictions of a decadent lifestyle exploit certain elements of our society—the young, insecure or clueless? Or did these ads, and others of their ilk, simply reflect profound bad taste? Most advertising is about exploitation—the systematic, deliberate identification of our needs and wants, followed by the delivery of a carefully constructed promise that the product will satisfy them.

30 Advertisers make use of a great variety of techniques and devices to engage us in the delivery of their messages. Some are subtle, making use of warm, entertaining or comforting images or symbols. Others, as we've seen, are about as subtle as an action sequence from Quentin Tarantino's latest movie. Although it may seem hard to believe, advertising writers did not invent sex. They did not invent our tendency to admire and seek to identify ourselves with famous people. Once we have seen a famous person in an ad, we associate the product with the person. When we buy Coke, we're becoming a member of the Friends of Maya Club. The logic is faulty, but we fall for it just the same. Advertising works, not because Maya and Britney have discriminating taste, or the nameless waif in the clothing ad is a fashion diva, but because we participate in it.

Keeping It Simple

31 Advertising language differs from other types of language in another important respect, it is a simple language. To measure the simplicity of an ad, calculate its Fog Index. Robert Gunning[5] developed this formula to determine the comparative ease with which any given piece of written communication can be read.

- Calculate the number of words in an average sentence.
- Count the number of words of three or more syllables in a typical 100-word passage, omitting words that are capitalized, combinations of two simple words, or verb forms made into three-syllable words by the addition of -ed or -es.
- Add the two figures (the average number of words per sentence and the number of three-syllable words per 100 words), then multiply the result by 4.

32 In an advertisement for Harry Potter books, the visual is a photo of a slightly menacing fellow standing next to his bike in an alley. Here is the text:

> Flying cars. Fire Whiskey. Death Eaters.

There's some pretty tough stuff in Harry Potter—bad guys so bad they're called Death Eaters. That's only one of the wicked reasons even bikers think Harry Potter is cool enough to ride with them.

33 *Reader's Digest* has a Fog Index of 8. *US News & World Report* and *Time Magazine* are about 9. There are 8.5 words—none three syllables—in the average "sentence."

1. Words per sentence: 8.5
2. Three syllable words/100:   0
3. Subtotal: 8.5
4. Multiply by .4:   3.4

34 According to Gunning's scale, you should be able to comprehend this ad if you are about half way through the third grade. Comic books weigh in at 6; *Reader's Digest* at 9; *Atlantic Monthly* is 12.

35 Why do advertisers generally favor simple language? The answer lies with the consumer. As a practical matter, we would not notice many of these messages if

length or eloquence was counted among their virtues. Today's consumer cannot take the time to focus on anything for long, much less blatant advertising messages. Every aspect of modern life runs at an accelerated pace. Voice mail, pagers, cellular phones, e-mail, the Internet—the world is always awake, always switched on, and hungry for information. Time generally, and TV-commercial time in particular, is dissected into increasingly smaller segments.

36   Toffler views the evolution toward shorter language as a natural progression: three-syllable words are simply harder to read than one- or two-syllable words. Simple ideas are more readily transferred from one person to another than complex ideas. Therefore, advertising copy uses increasingly simple language, as does society at large. In *Future Shock,* Toffler speculates:

> If the [English] language had the same number of words in Shakespeare's time as it does today, at least 200,000 words—perhaps several times that many—have dropped out and been replaced in the intervening four centuries. The high turnover rate reflects changes in things, processes, and qualities in the environment from the world of consumer products and technology.

37   It is no accident that the first terms Toffler uses to illustrate his point ("fast-back," "wash-and-wear," and "flashcube") were invented not by engineers, or journalists, but by advertising copywriters.

38   Advertising language is simple language; difficult words are deleted and replaced by simple words or images not open to misinterpretation.

Who Is Responsible?

39   Some critics view the advertising industry as a cranky, unwelcomed child of the free enterprise system—a noisy, whining, brash kid who must somehow be kept in line, but can't just yet be thrown out of the house. In reality, advertising mirrors the fears, quirks, and aspirations of the society that creates it (and is, in turn, sold by it). This alone exposes advertising to parody and ridicule. The overall level of acceptance and respect for advertising is also influenced by the varied quality of the ads themselves. Some ads, including a few of the examples cited here, are deliberately designed to provoke controversy. Critics have declared Advertising guilty of other failings as well:

1. Advertising encourages unhealthy habits.
2. Advertising feeds on human weaknesses and exaggerates the importance of material things, encouraging "impure" emotions and vanities.
3. Advertising sells daydreams—distracting, purposeless visions of lifestyles beyond the reach of the majority of the people who are most exposed to advertising.
4. Advertising warps our vision of reality, implanting in us groundless fears and insecurities.
5. Advertising downgrades the intelligence of the public.
6. Advertising debases English.
7. Advertising perpetuates racial and sexual stereotypes.

40   What can be said in advertising's defense? Does it encourage free-market competition and product innovation? Sure. But the real answer is simply this: Advertising is, at heart, only a reflection of society.

41   What can we say about the charge that advertising debases the intelligence of the public? Exactly how intelligent is "the public?" Sadly, evidence abounds that the public at large is not particularly intelligent, after all. Americans now get 31 percent of their calories from junk food and alcoholic beverages.[6] Michael can't read. Jessica can't write. And the entire family spends the night in front of the television, watching idiots eat living insects in the latest installment for a 'reality' show.

42   Ads are effective because they sell products. They would not succeed if they did not reflect the values and motivations of the real world. Advertising both reflects and shapes our perception of reality. Ivory Snow is pure. Federal Express won't let you down. Absolut is cool. Sasson is sexy. Mercedes represents quality. Our sense of what these brand names stand for may have as much to do with advertising as with the objective "truth."

43   Good, responsible advertising can serve as a positive influence for change, while fueling commerce. But the obverse is also true: Advertising, like any form of mass communication, can be a force for both "good" and "bad." It can just as readily reinforce or encourage irresponsible behavior, ageism, sexism, ethnocentrism, racism, homophobia, heterophobia—you name it—as it can encourage support for diversity and social progress.

44   As Pogo once famously said, "We have met the enemy, and he is us."[7] ◆

Notes

1. Internet: **www.joechemo.org**.
2. Pontifical Council for Social Communications, "Ethics in Advertising," published 2/22/97.
3. Alvin Toffler, *Future Shock* (New York: Random House, 1970), p. 146.
4. Shannon O'Neill, a student at the University of New Hampshire, contributed this example and others cited here.
5. Curtis D. MacDougall, *Interpretive Reporting* (New York: Macmillan, 1968), p. 94.
6. 2000 study by the American Society for Clinical Nutrition (Boston Globe, 7/29/93).
7. Walt Kelly, "Pogo" cartoon (1960s); referring to the Vietnam War.

 FREEWRITING ASSIGNMENT ———————————————

Describe an experience in which you purchased a product because you were influenced by its advertising language. For example, did you buy a hair, beauty, or electronic product because of the promises made by its ad? Explain.

CRITICAL READING

1. Consider Lutz's argument that advertisers are trying to "trick" consumers with their false promises and claims. How much are our expectations of

product performance influenced by the claims and slogans of advertising? How do you think O'Neill would respond to Lutz's accusation?

2. Does the fact that O'Neill is a professional advertiser influence your reception of his essay? Does it make his argument more or less persuasive?

3. Review the rules and regulations concerning the words "new" and "improved." How do advertisers address the problem of product regulations? Do such rules really protect consumers? Explain.

4. O'Neill is an advertising professional. Does his writing style reflect the advertising techniques he describes? Cite examples to support your answer.

5. How does O'Neill address any objections his audience may have to his argument? Are the objections he anticipates indeed the ones you had as a reader? Does his "answer" make his essay stronger? Explain.

6. O'Neill notes that symbols have become important elements in the language of advertising. Can you think of some specific symbols from advertising that you associate with your lifestyle? How important are these symbols to you? How do they work as wordless advertising? Explain.

7. A "weasel word" is a word so hollow it has no meaning. Consider your own reaction to weasel words when you hear them. Try to identify as many weasel words as you can. What are the words and what do consumers think they mean?

8. Do you think it is ethical for advertisers to create a sense of product difference when there really isn't any? Consider advertisements for products such as gasoline, beer, or coffee.

CRITICAL WRITING

9. *Exploratory Writing*: O'Neill, in his essay, makes several generalizations that characterize the language of advertising. Think about ads that you have recently seen or read and make a list of your own generalizations about the language of advertising. Refer to some specific advertisements in your response.

10. *Persuasive Writing*: O'Neill believes that advertising language mirrors the fears, quirks, and aspirations of the society that creates it. Do you agree or disagree with this statement? Explain your perspective in a brief essay supporting your response with examples.

11. *Analytical Writing*: Choose a brand-name product that you use regularly or to which you have particular loyalty, and identify one or more of its competitors. Examine some advertisements for each brand. Write a short paper explaining what makes you prefer your brand to the others.

GROUP PROJECTS

12. Review Lutz's "Doublespeak Quick Quiz." Choose five items and analyze them, using dictionary meanings to explain what the ads are really saying.

13. With your group, think of some recent advertising campaigns that created controversy (Abercrombie and Fitch, Calvin Klein, Benetton, etc.). What made them controversial? How did this impact sales?

14. O'Neill (paragraph 30) notes that sometimes advertisers use symbols to engage their audience. With your group, create a list of brand symbols or logos, their corresponding products, and what lifestyle we associate with the logo or symbol. Are some logos more popular or prestigious? Explain.

15. Working in a group, develop a slogan and advertising campaign for one of the following products: sneakers, soda, a candy bar, or jeans. How would you apply the principles of advertising language to market your product? After completing your marketing plan, "sell" your product to the class. If time permits, explain the reasoning behind your selling technique.

RESEARCH ISSUE **On Sale at Old Navy: Cool Clothes for Identical Zombies!**

Damien Cave

Mass-market retail stores like Old Navy, Gap, Pottery Barn, and Ikea have enjoyed enormous popularity in recent years. Part of their appeal is that they market the concept of "cool." But are these stores just marketing conformity under the guise of "cool"? Are they crushing our individuality? Are we moving rapidly to the day where we will all dress the same way, own the same furniture, and want the same things? Writer and Phillips Foundation fellow Damien Cave thinks so. This article first appeared in the November 22, 2000, issue of the e-zine *Salon*.

1 Thomas Frank walks by the candy-cane-adorned displays of Old Navy, passing the sign exclaiming "priced so low, you can't say no," and into the chain's San Francisco flagship store. The all-devouring Christmas rush hasn't started yet, but it's clear from the frown on Frank's face that he's not being seduced by the cheap but stylish clothes, the swirling neon and the bass-heavy hip-hop pounding in his ears.

2 "Oh God, this is disgusting," Frank says. This reaction isn't surprising. The bespectacled Midwesterner is a pioneering social critic—one of the first writers to document how, starting in the '60s, American businesses have co-opted cool anti-corporate culture and used it to seduce the masses. His arguments in the *Baffler*, a pugnacious review Frank founded in 1988, and in 1997's "The Conquest of Cool" read like sermons, angry wake-up calls for consumers who hungrily ingest hipper-than-thou ("Think Different") marketing campaigns without ever questioning their intent.

3   Old Navy and other cheap but tasteful retailers provide perfect fodder for Frank's critique. Their low prices and hip-but-wholesome branding strategy are supposed to present a healthy alternative to the conspicuous consumption of a Calvin Klein. But critics like Frank and Naomi Klein, author of "No Logo," argue that the formula is really nothing more than the wolf of materialism wrapped in cheaper sheep's clothing.

4   Consumers are being scammed, says Klein, arguing that stores like Old Navy and Ikea are duping millions, inspiring mass conformity while pretending to deliver high culture to the masses. "It's this whole idea of creating a carnival for the most homogeneous fashions and furniture," says Klein. "It's mass cloning that's being masked in a carnival of diversity. You don't notice that you're conforming because everything is so colorful."

5   Klein and Frank say that few consumers recognize just how conformist their consumption habits have become. And certainly, it's hard to argue that Ikea's and Old Navy's items haven't become icons of urbanite and suburbanite imagination. Watch MTV, or rent "Fight Club," to see Ikea's candy-colored décor, then truck down to your local Old Navy flagship store. When you arrive, what you'll find is that hordes of people have beaten you there. At virtually every opening of Old Navy's and Ikea's stores—in the New York, Chicago and San Francisco areas, for example—tens of thousands of people appeared in the first few days. Even now, long after the stores first opened, lines remain long.

6   What's wrong with these people? Nothing, say defenders of the companies. The popularity of brands like Ikea and Old Navy, they argue, derives from the retailers' ability to offer good stuff cheap. "They provide remarkable value," says Joel Reichart, a professor at the Fordham School of Business who has written case studies on Ikea. "They're truly satisfying people's needs."

7   Despite his irritation with the way companies like Old Navy market themselves, Frank acknowledges that businesses have always sought to offer cheap, relatively high-quality merchandise and concedes that there is some value in their attempts. He even admits that consumerism is good for the economy.

8   But he and other critics argue that in the end we're only being conned into thinking that our needs are being satisfied. What's really happening, they argue, is that clever marketers are turning us into automatons who equate being cool with buying cheap stuff that everyone else has. Under the stores' guise of delivering good taste to the general public, any chance we have at experiencing or creating authenticity is being undermined. Ultimately, our brave new shopping world is one in which we are spending more time in the checkout line than reading books, watching movies or otherwise challenging ourselves with real culture.

9   "Shopping is a way of putting together your identity," laments "Nobrow" author John Seabrook. And the "homogenized taste" of today's Old Navy and Ikea shoppers proves, he says, that Americans either are consciously choosing to look and live alike or are determined not to notice that that is what they're doing.

10   According to Christine Rosen, a professor in the Haas School of Business at UC-Berkeley, people who fill their closets, homes and lives with Old Navy and Ikea—or Pottery Barn or a host of other slick stores—are simply new examples of

the trend toward conformity that started when the first "brands" appeared in the 1910s and '20s. "We're Pavlovianly trained to respond to this," she says.

11   And we're also just too damn lazy. That's the theory floated by Packard Jennings, an anti-consumerism activist who says that stores like Old Navy are designed to numb the brain and remove all semblance of creativity from the purchasing process. "Ikea pre-arranges sets of furniture in its stores, thereby lessening individual thought," he says. Once people are in the store, they can't resist. "Entire households are purchased at Ikea," he says.

12   Indeed, Janice Simonsen, an Ikea spokeswoman, confirmed that a large part of the chain's demographic consists of "people who come in and say, 'I need everything.'" Meanwhile, those who don't want everything usually end up with more than they need, says Fordham's Reichart. "The way they design their stores"—with an up escalator to the showroom and no exit until the checkout—"you end up going through the entire store," he says.

13   Old Navy plays by the same sneaky rules. When Frank and I entered the San Francisco store, clerks offered us giant mesh bags. Ostensibly, this is just good service, but since the bags are capable of holding at least half a dozen pairs of jeans and a few shirts, it's obvious that they're also meant to encourage overconsumption.

14   Frank called the bags "gross" but not out of line with other state-of-the-art retailing practices. But according to Klein, the sacks, in conjunction with Old Navy's penchant for displaying T-shirts in mock-1950s supermarket coolers, prove that the company is aiming to do something more. The idea behind this "theater for the brand" architecture is to commodify the products, to make them "as easy to buy as a gallon of milk," Klein says. "The idea is to create a Mecca where people make pilgrimages to their brand," Klein says. "You experience the identity of the brand and not the product."

15   Disney, which opened its first store in 1987, was the first to employ this strategy. And since then others have appeared. Niketown, the Body Shop, the Discovery Store—they all aim to sell products by selling a destination.

16   Old Navy and Ikea, however, are far more popular than those predecessors—and, if you believe the more pessimistic of their critics, more dangerous. Not only are the two chains remaking many closets and homes into one designer showcase, says Klein, but they are also lulling consumers to sleep and encouraging them to overlook some important issues.

17   Such as quality. People think they're getting "authenticity on the cheap," says David Lewis, author of "The Soul of the New Consumer." But the truth may be that they're simply purchasing the perception of quality and authenticity. "Because [Ikea and Old Navy] create these self-enclosed lifestyles," Klein explains, "you overlook the fact that the products are pretty crappy and fall apart." Adds Jennings, "Things may be cheaper, but you keep going back to replace the faulty merchandise."

18   Then there is the trap of materialism. Survey after survey suggests that people who place a high value on material goods are less happy than those who do not, says Eric Rindfleisch, a marketing professor at the University of Arizona. The focus on bargains, incremental purchases and commodification plays to a uniquely American blind spot.

19   "We operate with a duality," explains Rindfleisch, who has conducted studies linking materialism with depression. "Americans know that money doesn't buy happiness, but most people somehow believe that increments in pay or goods will improve our lives. It's a human weakness—particularly in America."

20   The most insidious danger may be more abstract. The anti-consumerism critics argue that by elevating shopping to cultural status, we are losing our grip on real culture. We live in a time where college kids think nothing of decorating their rooms with Absolut vodka ads and fail to realize that they're essentially turning their rooms into billboards. Meanwhile, museum stores keep getting larger, Starbucks sells branded CDs to go with your coffee and because Ikea and other stores now look like movie theaters or theme parks, we don't just shop, "we make a day of it," as Klein puts it.

21   This only helps steer us away from other endeavors. When people spend so much time buying, thinking and talking about products, they don't have time for anything else, for real conversations about politics or culture or for real interaction with people.

22   Ultimately, the popularity of Old Navy, Ikea and their ilk proves that we're stuck in what Harvard professor Juliet Schor calls "the cycle of work and spend." Breaking that cycle may not be easy, but if one believes critics like Frank, it's essential if we are to control our own culture, instead of allowing it to be defined by corporations.

23   The cycle may not be possible to break. Frank, for one, is extremely pessimistic about our chances for turning back the tide of conformity and co-opted cool. Maybe that's one reason why he wanted to get out of Old Navy as fast as he could.

24   But I'm not so sure. When "Ikea boy," Edward Norton's character in "Fight Club," watched his apartment and his Swedish furniture explode in a blaze of glory, I wasn't the only one in the theater who cheered. ◆

CRITICAL THINKING

1. In paragraph 2, Cave notes that American businesses have "co-opted cool anti-corporate culture." What does he mean? What is "anti-corporate" culture, and why is it "cool"? What started it, and how are businesses using it to their advantage? In what ways is this ironic? Before responding, read "The Rebel Sell" [p. 130]. Are Cave's assertions supported by the theoretical framework provded by Heath and Potter?

2. In paragraph 20, Cave observes that "college kids think nothing of decorating their rooms with Absolut vodka ads and fail to realize that they're essentially turning their rooms into billboards." What decorating choices have you made to your personal space? In what ways has your decorating style been influenced by outside forms of advertising? Explain.

3. What techniques do mass-market stores employ to squeeze the maximum profit from consumers who enter them? Were you aware of these techniques? Have you fallen victim to them yourself? Explain.

RESEARCH PROJECTS

4. In paragraph 9, author John Seabrook comments, "Shopping is a way of putting together your identity." Consider the ways your shopping habits put together your identity. Arrange to go shopping with a few friends at several popular stores. As you shop, consider whether you or your companions seem to be influenced by some of the techniques described in this essay. Consider not just what you buy, but where you shop, why you shop, and with whom. Note whether your companions criticize certain products, and why. How do your shopping companions influence each other's choices? Finally, how does branding appeal to their desire to buy particular things as part of presenting a personal identity? Write an essay describing the experience, and what you learned about marketing culture from your observations.

5. Visit the Web sites of the stores that Cave cites in his essay (**www.pottery barn.com**, **www.ikea.com**, **www.oldnavy.com**, etc.) and review their merchandise from the perspective of a cultural analyst. Acting like a social anthropologist, write an essay describing what North American consumers are like—for example, what they buy, their personal style preferences, and what they desire based on what you see on the websites you analyzed. Can you determine any common themes? Does anything seem surprising? What might a person from another country, such as China or El Salvador determine about North American consumers based on the offerings at these stores? Explain.

Additional essay topics, writing assignments, research guidelines, and readings for this chapter can be found online at **www.pearsoned.ca/goshgarian**.

Television

For Better or for Worse?

4

Television is the prime mover of modern culture. In five decades, it has become the country's foremost source of entertainment and news. More than any other medium, television regulates commerce, lifestyles, and social values. But the medium is also the object of considerable scorn. For years, television has been blamed for nearly all of our social ills—the rise in crime, increased divorce rates, lower voter turnouts, racism, increased sexual promiscuity, drug addiction, and the collapse of the family. In short, it has been cited as the cause of the decline of Western civilization.

Certainly, television can be blamed for piping into our homes hours of brain-numbing, excessively violent, exploitative trash. And given the fact that the average 20-year-old viewer will have spent nearly three years of his or her life in front of the television set, it plays a significant and influential role in our daily lives. But to categorically condemn the medium is to be blind to some of the quality programs television is capable of producing—and not just those produced by PBS and educational channels such as TLC, Discovery, and the History Channel. The essays in this chapter will explore some of the ways television is a part of our lives—for better or worse—and will examine the areas in which television appears to have failed, and where it shines.

The chapter opens with an essay exploring the powerful influence television exerts on our culture. Despite the criticism, says writer Jane Rosenzweig, television's influence is not always a bad one—television can serve as an effective vehicle to promote social awareness and moral values. In "Can TV Improve Us?" Rosenzweig describes some of the positive ways television serves society.

Not everyone, however, agrees with Rosenzweig that television can improve us. Just as television can promote positive values, it may advance stereotypes and violence. Teaching children how to critically evaluate what they see on television may be more important than ever in this era of media violence. According to George Gerbner of the Cultural Indicators project, the average American child will have witnessed 8000 murders on television by the age of 12. In "The Man Who Counts the Killings," Scott Stossel reports some of the findings resulting from Gerbner's 30 years of research into media violence and its effects on society.

In a sidebar, "How to Erase Conscience," the Canadian Pediatric Society warns about the dangers of desensitizing young people to violence through television and video games, comparing some of these entertainments to the "killing simulators" on which soldiers train.

While television programming can be quite violent, television talk shows seem to follow similar patterns, reaching audiences through conflict and aggression. In "TV's War of Words," linguist Deborah Tannen explains how "Scream TV" reduces all discussions to oversimplified, polarized arguments. Shades of grey are scorned as weak and distracting, because the goal is not to understand an issue, but to win an argument. And, sometimes, winning does not mean that your argument was the best, but that your argument was the *loudest*.

Many of us rely on the evening news to inform us of local, national, and international events. Television's unique ability to combine print, voice, and televised images makes its news programming distinctly different from newspapers or radio journalism. Neil Postman and Steve Powers argue that television's primary function as an entertainment medium conflicts with its role as an objective source of information. In "TV News: All the World in Pictures," they explain that television news is essentially entertainment disguised as objective journalism.

The chapter's three Viewpoints discuss television programming, parental responsibilities, and young children. First, we present a press release by the American Academy of Pediatrics warning against television viewing for very young children. "AAP Discourages Television for Very Young Children" explains that children need personal interaction that television cannot provide, and are, because of their age, unable to be "media educated persons." In "TV Can Be a Good Parent," Ariel Gore disagrees with the AAP policy, arguing that there is a time and place for television for young viewers. She questions the timing of the AAP policy and the logic behind its decision.

For a Canadian perspective on this issue, we turn to Carmen Wittmeier's "Tune In, Turn On and Buy, Buy, Buy." Given young children's difficulty in differentiating reality from fantasy, how much influence does children's programming have on their assimilation of materialistic ideals? How can parents mitigate this influence? Or is it true that "materialism is inevitable in a market-driven, capitalist society"? If so, then television may be showing children a world of fantasy while simultaneously giving them some hard truths about the realities of advertising and acquisition.

Our research issue is Elaine Showalter's discussion of the merits of reality programs, "Windows on Reality: American Idol and the Search for Identity."

Can TV Improve Us?
Jane Rosenzweig

Although television is often cited as the source of many social ills—from teen violence to the decline of the family—many people point out that it also teaches, informs, and entertains us. The next article takes the debate one step further by postulating that TV can actually improve us. Jane Rosenzweig describes some of the ways in which television has forced us to think about social issues and has promoted moral values. And although television may not be the ideal vehicle to advocate values, it may be the best one we have.

A former staff editor for the *Atlantic Monthly*, Jane Rosenzweig now teaches writing at Yale University. This article was first published in the July/August 1999 issue of the *American Prospect*.

CRITICAL THINKING   Think about how television can increase awareness about a particular issue or promote certain values in audiences. What social or moral themes can you recall that were recently featured in popular television programs?

1   It's eight o'clock Wednesday evening and a rumor is circulating at a small-town high school in Massachusetts that a student named Jack is gay. Jack's friends—one of whom is a 15-year-old girl who has been sexually active since she was 13, and another of whom has a mother who has recently committed adultery—assure him it would be okay with them if he were, but admit their relief when he says he isn't. An hour later, in San Francisco, a woman named Julia is being beaten by her boyfriend. Meanwhile, in Los Angeles, a young stripper who has given birth out of wedlock learns that her own mother locked her in a basement when she was three years old, an experience that she thinks may explain her inability to love her own child.

2   A typical evening in America? If a visitor from another planet had turned on the television (specifically the WB and Fox networks) on the evening of Wednesday, February 10, 1999, with the aim of learning about our society, he would likely have concluded that it is made up pretty exclusively of photogenic young people with disintegrating nuclear families and liberal attitudes about sex. It's obviously not an accurate picture, but what might our visitor have learned from the programs he watched? Would all the sex, violence, and pathology he saw teach him antisocial behavior? Or might he glean from prime-time dramas and sitcoms the behavior and attitudes that he would do well to adopt if he intended to go native in America?

3   This is not an idle question—not because aliens might be watching American television, but because people are, particularly impressionable children and teenagers. In a time when 98 percent of U.S. households own at least one television set—a set which is turned on for an average of nearly seven hours a day—the degree to which people learn from and emulate the behavior of the characters they see on TV is an academic cottage industry. Some evidence does support the widespread belief that children and teenagers are affected by violence and other antisocial behavior in the media. When Dan Quayle made his infamous comments in 1992 about Murphy Brown having a baby out of wedlock, he was merely doing what numerous concerned parents, ethnic groups, religious organizations, gun-control advocates, and others were already doing—blaming television for encouraging certain types of behavior.

4   But if television contributes to poor behavior, might it also be a vehicle for encouraging good behavior? In 1988, Jay Winsten, a professor at the Harvard School of Public Health and the director of the school's Center for Health Communication, conceived a plan to use television to introduce a new social concept—the "designated driver"—to North America. Shows were already dealing with the topic of drinking, Winsten reasoned, so why not add a line of dialogue here and there about not driving drunk? With the assistance of then-NBC chairman Grant Tinker, Winsten met with more than 250 writers, producers, and executives over six months, trying to sell them on his designated driver idea.

5   Winsten's idea worked; the "designated driver" is now common parlance across all segments of American society and in 1991 won entry into a Webster's dictionary for the first time. An evaluation of the campaign in 1994 revealed that the designated driver "message" had aired on 160 prime-time shows in four seasons and had been the main topic of twenty-five 30-minute or 60-minute episodes. More important, these airings appear to have generated tangible results. In 1989, the year

after the "designated driver" was invented, a Gallup poll found that 67 percent of adults had noted its appearance on network television. What's more, the campaign seems to have influenced adult behavior: polls conducted by the Roper Organization in 1989 and 1991 found significantly increasing awareness and use of designated drivers. By 1991, 37 percent of all U.S. adults claimed to have refrained from drinking at least once in order to serve as a designated driver, up from 29 percent in 1989. In 1991, 52 percent of adults younger than 30 had served as designated drivers, suggesting that the campaign was having greatest success with its target audience.

6   In 1988 there were 23,626 drunk driving fatalities. By 1997 the number was 16,189. While the Harvard Alcohol Project acknowledges that some of this decline is due to new laws, stricter anti-drunk driving enforcement, and other factors, it claims that many of the 50,000 lives saved by the end of 1998 were saved because of the designated driver campaign. (The television campaign was only a part of the overall campaign; there were strong community-level and public service components as well.) As evidence, the project cites statistics showing the rapid decline in traffic fatalities per 100 million vehicle miles traveled in the years during and immediately following the most intensive period of the designated driver campaign. Officials at the National Highway Traffic and Safety Administration have stated that the only way to explain the size of the decline in drinking-related traffic fatalities is the designated driver campaign.

7   Following the success of the Harvard Alcohol Project's campaign, various other advocacy groups—the majority of them with progressive leanings—have begun to work within the existing structures of the television industry in a similar fashion, attempting to influence programming in a positive direction. In truth, there are limits to the effect any public interest group can have on what gets broadcast. Commercial television's ultimate concerns are Nielsen ratings and advertisers. Thus there will always be a hefty quantity of sex and violence on network television. As Alfred Schneider, the former vice president of policy and standards for ABC, asserts in his contribution to the forthcoming anthology *Advocacy Groups and the Television Industry,* "While [television] can raise the consciousness of the nation, it should not be considered as the major vehicle for social relief or altering behavior." But why not?

8   Other groups remain optimistic, emulating Winsten's method of treating television as a potential ally rather than an adversary and approaching writers and producers likely to be receptive to particular ideas. When writers and producers for the WB network's critically acclaimed new drama *Felicity* were working on the script for a two-part story about date rape, they wanted to make sure they got the details right. They sought the advice of experts from the Kaiser Family Foundation, a nonprofit that focuses on education about health issues; its Program on Entertainment Media and Public Health offers briefings, research services, and a hotline for script writers with health-related questions. "We were really aware of the message we were sending out," the show's executive producer Ed Redlich told me recently. "Given that our audience is teenage girls, we wanted to be correct. At the same time we didn't want it to be an extended public service announcement." As the scripts went through revisions, the show's writers sat down to discuss date rape with representatives from

Kaiser, who had previously offered their services to the WB. In whom might a young woman confide after being raped? What kind of advice might a rape counselor provide? What physical tests would the woman undergo? What kind of message would the show be sending if the rapist didn't use a condom?

9   Meanwhile, WB network executive Susanne Daniels sought input on the *Felicity* scripts from Marisa Nightingale at the National Campaign to Prevent Teen Pregnancy, an advocacy group formed in 1995 with the goal of reducing teen pregnancies by one-third by the year 2005. Nightingale, the manager of media programs, spends her days meeting with writers and producers to offer statistics, information on birth control methods, and suggestions for how to incorporate pregnancy prevention into storylines. "I can't knock on every door in the country and discuss safe sex with teenagers," she says, "but if Bailey and Sarah on [the Fox network's] *Party of Five* discuss it, that's the next best thing."

10   According to a recent Kaiser Foundation survey, 23 percent of teens say they learn about pregnancy and birth control from television and movies. Clearly, we should be mindful of what exactly teenagers are watching. On a recent episode of *Dawson's Creek* two 16-year-olds contemplating sex ran into each other at a drugstore only to discover they were standing in front of a condom display, which led to a frank discussion about safe sex. An episode of *Felicity* featured the title character researching birth control methods and learning the proper way of putting on a condom. Once prepared, Felicity then decided in the heat of the moment she wasn't quite ready to have sex. A young woman's decision to put off having sex is rarely portrayed in prime time, but Felicity is a strong character and her reasoning is probably convincing to a teenage audience. She may well have more influence on teenage girls than a public service announcement.

11   Of course, making television an explicit vehicle for manipulating behavior has its dangers. My idea of the good may not be yours; if my ideas have access to the airwaves but yours don't, what I'm doing will seem to you like unwanted social engineering. We can all agree that minimizing drunk driving is a good thing—but not everyone agrees on the messages we want to be sending to, say, teenage girls about abstinence versus condoms, about having an abortion, or about whether interfaith marriages are okay. Television's power to mold viewers' understanding of the world is strong enough that we need to be aware that embedding messages about moral values or social behavior can have potent effects—for good or for ill.

12   For the moment, Hollywood's liberal tilt (yes, it really has one) makes it likely that the messages and values it chooses to incorporate into its television programs will be agreeable to progressives. But how active a role do we want television to play in the socialization of our youth? If advocacy groups can gain access to Hollywood with messages that seem like positive additions to existing fare, then they may someday be able to do the opposite—to instill, say, values of a particular religion or an intolerant political group through television.

13   Consider the popularity of CBS's *Touched by an Angel*, which has just completed its fifth season and has secured a regular place among the top ten Nielsen-rated programs. The show, which features angels—not winged creatures, but messengers of God who arrive to help mortals in times of crisis—has sparked a mini-trend in prime

time. Along with its spin-off *Promised Land* and the WB's *7th Heaven, Touched by an Angel* has carved out a new niche in family hour entertainment: fare that's endorsed by many groups on the religious right (as well as, to be fair, by people not of the Christian right who are seeking wholesome television entertainment).

14 *7th Heaven*'s producer Brenda Hampton, who created the show for Aaron Spelling's production company (the creative force behind such racier fare as *Beverly Hills 90210* and *Melrose Place*), emphasizes in interviews that she is not influenced by religious groups and that her goal is simply to create entertaining television. But Martha Williamson, the producer of *Touched by an Angel,* is very outspoken about her Christianity. While Williamson, too, emphasizes that she aims primarily to entertain, the program's religious message is unmistakably in the foreground. Williamson says she is regularly contacted by viewers who say the show helped them make a decision—to get in touch with a long-estranged relative or to stop smoking.

15 On its face there's nothing objectionable about this; in fact, it's probably good. And there's no evidence that *Touched by an Angel* is actively converting people, or making unwilling Jews or atheists into Christians. Still, the show does proselytize for a set of values that some viewers might find alienating or offensive. A more extreme version could become Big Brotherish propaganda, beamed into the homes and receptive minds of the seven-hour-a-day TV watchers. At this point, the most offensive thing about *Touched by an Angel* is its saccharine writing (even some religious groups have criticized it on these grounds). But it is perhaps telling that a Republican Congress has awarded Williamson a "Freedom Works Award" for "individuals and groups who seek the personal reward of accepting and promoting responsibility without reliance on or funding from the federal government."

16 Given that writers have to create 22 episodes each season, it's not surprising that they are receptive to outside groups pitching socially redeeming story ideas. *Dawson's Creek* producer Paul Stupin estimates he sits down with three to five advocacy groups at the beginning of each season and always finds the meetings useful. The fact that large numbers of writers and producers attend briefings sponsored by Kaiser, the National Campaign to Prevent Teen Pregnancy, or Population Communications International (which recently sponsored a "Soap Summit") suggests that others feel the same way.

17 The strongest evidence that advocates can effect change through partnerships with the television industry comes from the success of the designated driver campaign. While there are as of yet no large-scale studies exploring the effects of public health advocacy through television, a survey conducted by the Kaiser Foundation is enlightening. On April 10, 1997, NBC aired an episode of *ER* focusing on morning-after contraception, put together with the help of Kaiser Foundation research. Before the show aired, independent researchers interviewed 400 of the show's regular viewers about their knowledge of options for preventing unwanted pregnancy even after unprotected sex. In the week after the show aired, 305 more viewers were interviewed. The number of *ER* viewers who said they knew about morning-after contraception went up by 17 percent after the episode aired. The study concluded that up to six million of the episode's 34 million viewers learned about emergency

contraception for the first time from the show (and 53 percent of *ER* viewers say they learn important health care information from the show).

18   Even the limited evidence provided by the *ER* study suggests the scope of television's power to educate and influence. And additional Kaiser studies suggest that the lobbying of public health groups advocating safe sex and birth control is not yet having nearly enough of a beneficial effect. While 25 percent of teenagers say they have learned "a lot" about pregnancy and birth control from TV shows and movies, and 40 percent say they have gotten ideas about how to talk to their boyfriend or girlfriend about sex from TV and movies, 76 percent say that one reason teens feel comfortable having sex at young ages is that TV shows and movies "make it seem normal" to do so.

19   Another problem: According to Kaiser, while 67 percent of *ER* viewers knew about morning-after contraception when questioned immediately following the show, only 50 percent knew about it when questioned two-and-a-half months later. This suggests that the 17 percent who gained new information about contraception from the episode may not have retained it. Jay Winsten says that because new information fades without repetition, for a single message to take hold the way the designated driver campaign did will require a barrage of appearances on a wide range of TV shows, over an extended period of time.

20   The role of advocacy groups as a resource for Hollywood writers and producers is growing, and it's worth taking seriously. Their approach—presenting ideas to a creative community that is constantly in need of ideas—is proving effective. Yes, the messages are diluted to fit sitcom or drama formats. Yes, for every "good value" that makes its way onto the small screen, a flurry of gunshots on another network will partly counteract it. And yes, when *Time* cites Ally McBeal as a factor in the demise of feminism, it is placing absurdly disproportionate responsibility on a television character, and on the creative community that invented her. Yet if the college women on *Felicity* practice safe sex, or if a prime-time parent talks about drugs—or adoption, or eating disorders, or the Holocaust—with a child, the message is likely to resonate with an audience comprised of people who relate to their favorite television characters as if they knew them.

21   Is television the ideal forum for a culture to define its values? No. As long as television remains a profit-driven industry, the best we can hope to do—especially those of us who have views in common with those who create television content (and fortunately for liberals, we tend to)—is to work within the existing system to make it better. We do need to be realistic about the limits of television in packaging messages to fit this format. To turn *Friends* into a show about capital punishment would be ineffective as well as dramatically unconvincing; but to encourage the producers of *Dawson's Creek* to portray young people facing the realistic consequences of adult decisions just might work. ◆

FREEWRITING ASSIGNMENT

In paragraph 11, Rosenzweig states that "manipulating behavior has its dangers." In what ways can using television as a vehicle for public service announcements be dangerous?

CRITICAL READING

1. Assess Rosenzweig's question in paragraph 4, "if television contributes to poor behavior, might it also be a vehicle for encouraging good behavior?" What assumptions does Rosenzweig make about her audience by phrasing the question this way?
2. Based on your overall impression of Rosenzweig's article, what conclusions can you make about the author's social and political leanings? Cite some examples from the text to support your answer.
3. Evaluate the author's use of supporting evidence and examples in this article. Is her evidence fair and balanced? Does it seem credible? Is it accessible to her audience? Explain.
4. Rosenzweig notes that although it was easy for Hollywood to incorporate the issue of drunk driving into its programming, other issues have met with less success. What makes a social issue interesting, and why?
5. Rosenzweig states in a side comment that Hollywood "really has" a liberal tilt (paragraph 12). On what evidence does she base this statement? Do you agree or disagree with her view?

CRITICAL WRITING

6. *Creative Analysis*: In her introduction, Rosenzweig questions what visitors from another planet would think about our society based on what they learned from watching television on one specific evening. Pretend you are such a visitor, and you know nothing about North American culture or social values. Based on an evening's television viewing (you may hop between several programs), what conclusions would you make about our culture? Cite specific examples in your analysis.
7. *Personal Narrative*: Has a television program ever made you think about a social or moral issue that you would not otherwise have thought about had you not watched the program? Write a personal narrative about a television program that influenced, or even changed, how you felt about a social or moral issue.
8. *Exploratory Writing*: Rosenzweig comments that television programs may attempt to promote social agendas with which some viewers may not agree. Watch one, or several, of the programs she cites in her article to which people may object. What concerns may some audiences have with these programs? What social agendas do they promote? Write an essay in

which you support or argue against the use of television to promote social, political, or religious perspectives.

GROUP PROJECTS

9. Rosenzweig notes that although the issue of drunk driving was easy for Hollywood to incorporate into its programming, other issues have met with less success. With your group, make a list of the issues that television programming has addressed in your viewing experience. After reviewing the list, expand it to include other important, but less "exciting" issues, such as the hole in the ozone layer or recycling. Develop a story line together for a popular program dealing with one of these less stimulating issues and present it to the class.

10. Using a television weekly programming guide for reference, try to identify the political "tilt" of prime-time programs with the members of your group. In your analysis, include television dramas, news programs, and sitcoms. Based on your results, personal experience, and the information provided by Rosenzweig, participate in a class discussion on the social and political influences of television programming.

The Man Who Counts the Killings
Scott Stossel

In 1968, as a result of American President Lyndon Johnson's National Commission on the Causes and Prevention of Violence, George Gerbner, the former dean of the Annenberg School of Communication at the University of Pennsylvania, founded the Cultural Indicators project. For over 30 years, Gerbner and his team of researchers have studied the role of media violence in American society. One of the most disturbing estimates made by the Cultural Indicators project is that the average American child will have watched over 8000 murders on television by the time he or she reaches 12 years of age. The next article discusses some of Gerbner's findings, how television violence influences the social perception of violence, and what this might mean to American culture in the future.

A former staff editor at the *Atlantic*, Scott Stossel is now the associate editor of the *American Prospect*. This article first appeared in the May 1997 issue of the *Atlantic*.

CRITICAL THINKING   Think about the level of violence in the programs you watch on television. Is violence a common theme? Does it make an impression on you? Why or why not?

1   In 1977 Ronny Zamora, a fifteen-year-old, shot and killed the eighty-two-year-old woman who lived next door to him in Florida. Not guilty, pleaded his lawyer, Ellis Rubin, by reason of the boy's having watched too much television. From watching television Ronny had become dangerously inured to violence. Suffering from what Rubin called "television intoxication," he could no longer tell right from wrong. "If you judge Ronny Zamora guilty," Rubin argued, "television will be an accessory." The jury demurred: Ronny was convicted of first-degree murder.

2   Although few anti-television activists would agree that excessive television viewing can exculpate a murderer, a huge body of evidence—including 3,000 studies before 1971 alone—suggests a strong connection between television watching and aggression. "There is no longer any serious debate about whether violence in the media is a legitimate problem," Reed Hundt, the chairman of the Federal Communications Commission, said in a speech in 1996. "Science and common-sense judgments of parents agree. As stated in a year-long effort, funded by the cable-TV industry . . . 'there are substantial risks of harmful effects from viewing violence throughout the television environment.'"

3   The study cited by Hundt reveals nothing new. Researchers have been churning out studies indicating links between television violence and real-life violence for as long as television has been a prominent feature of American culture. Just a few examples demonstrate the range of the investigations.

4   In 1960 Leonard Eron, a professor of psychology at the University of Michigan's Institute for Social Research, studied third-graders in Columbia County in semi-rural New York. He observed that the more violent television these eight-year-olds watched at home, the more aggressive they were in school. Eron returned to Columbia County in 1971, when the children from his sample were nineteen. He found that the boys who had watched a lot of violent television when they were eight were more likely to get in trouble with the law when older. Eron returned to Columbia County a third time in 1982, when his subjects were thirty. He discovered that those who had watched the most television violence at age eight inflicted more violent punishments on their children, were convicted of more serious crimes, and were reported more aggressive by their spouses than those who had watched less violent television. In 1993, at a conference of the National Council for Families & Television, Eron estimated that 10 percent of the violence in the United States can be attributed to television.

5   Although Eron's study did not make a special effort to control for other potentially violence-inducing variables, other longitudinal studies have done so. For example, in 1971 Monroe Lefkowitz published "Television Violence and Child Aggression: A Follow-up Study," which confirmed that the more violence an eight-year-old boy watched, the more aggressive his behavior would be at age eighteen. Lefkowitz controlled for other possible variables, directly implicating media violence as an instigator of violent behavior.

6   Shouldn't the weight of thousands of such studies be sufficient to persuade broadcasters, required by law since the 1930s to serve the public interest, to change the content of television programming? Especially when polls—such as one conducted by *U.S. News & World Report*—indicate that 90 percent of Americans think

that violent television shows hurt the country? We don't want to become a nation of Ronny Zamoras, do we?

7   In 1968 President Johnson's National Commission on the Causes and Prevention of Violence appointed George Gerbner, who had already been studying violence in the media at the Annenberg School, to analyze the content of television shows. Thus began the Cultural Indicators project, the longest-running continuous media-research undertaking in the world. Gerbner and his team presented findings about both the quantity of violence on prime-time television—that is, how many violent acts are committed each night—and the quality. In analyzing these acts Gerbner's team asked questions like: Was it serious or funny? Was it the only method of conflict resolution offered? Were realistic repercussions of violence shown? Who committed most of it? Who suffered the most because of it? The quantity of violence on television was stunning; no less significant to Gerbner, though, were the ways in which this violence was portrayed. But in the first instance of what has since become a frustrating pattern for him, the mainstream media seized on the quantity and ignored his findings about the quality of television violence.

8   The media continue to be fixated on the amount of violence the Cultural Indicators project finds, because the numbers are staggering. Today someone settling down to watch television is likely to witness a veritable carnival of violent behavior. On average there are more than five violent scenes in an hour of prime time, and five murders a night. There are twenty-five violent acts an hour in Saturday-morning cartoons—the programs most watched by children, usually without any supervision. And that's only network television. A survey by the Center for Media and Public Affairs that looked at all programming—including cable—in Washington, D.C., on April 7, 1994, tallied 2,605 acts of violence that day, the majority occurring in the early morning, when kids were most likely to be watching. By the reckoning of the Cultural Indicators project, the average American child will have witnessed more than 8,000 murders and 100,000 other violent acts on television by the time he or she leaves elementary school. Another study, published in the *Journal of the American Medical Association* in 1992, found that the typical American child spends twenty-seven hours a week watching television and will witness 40,000 murders and 200,000 other violent acts by the age of eighteen. Ellis Rubin's defense of Ronny Zamora begins to sound plausible.

9   "Never was a culture so filled with full-color images of violence as ours is now," Gerbner wrote recently. This is an assertion he makes often, in his writings and speeches and interviews.

10   Of course, there is blood in fairy tales, gore in mythology, murder in Shakespeare, lurid crimes in tabloids, and battles and wars in textbooks. Such representations of violence are legitimate cultural expressions, even necessary to balance tragic consequences against deadly compulsions. But the historically defined, individually crafted, and selectively used symbolic violence of heroism, cruelty, or authentic tragedy has been replaced by the violence with happy endings produced on the dramatic assembly line.

11   The Cultural Indicators project has since 1968 amassed a database of reports on the recurring features of television programming. Today its archive contains obser-

vations on more than 3,000 programs and 35,000 characters. In looking at characters, coders record, among other characteristics, sex, race, height, level of aggressiveness, and drug, alcohol, or tobacco use. For every conflict the coder records how the character acts: Did he get angry? How did he resolve the conflict? If a character is part of a violent act, the coder records whether he suffered or committed it, and whether it was committed in self-defense. The results are then analyzed statistically to try to account for differences in the behavioral trends of the characters. Are there statistically significant differences in the percentage of, say, victimhood or alcohol abuse by sex? By level of education? By race? By social status?

12   In addition to this "message system analysis," Gerbner's researchers do "cultivation analysis," which tries to measure how much television contributes to viewers' conceptions of reality. Cultivation analysis asks, in other words, to what extent television "cultivates" our understanding of the world. Gerbner believes this to be the most important aspect of his research. It is also the part routinely ignored by the mainstream press and attacked by the broadcasting industry.

13   One of the basic premises of Gerbner's cultivation analysis is that television violence is not simple acts but rather "a complex social scenario of power and victimization." What matters is not so much the raw fact that a violent act is committed but who does what to whom. Gerbner is as insistent about this as he is about anything, repeating it in all his writings and speeches. "What is the message of violence?" he asks me rhetorically over tea in his office at the University of Pennsylvania, a cozy, windowless rectangle filled with books, pictures, and objets d'art. "Who can get away with what against whom?" He leans forward intently, as though confiding something, although he has already said this to me several other times, during several other conversations. His eagerness to make me understand is palpable. "The media keep focusing on the amount of violence. But concentrating on that reinforces the message of violence. It concentrates on the law-and-order aspect of violence. Harping on this all the time makes people more fearful—which is the purpose of violence to begin with."

14   So what, exactly, has nearly thirty years of cultivation analysis shown? Among other things, the following:

15   Americans spend fully a third of their free time with television. This is more than the next ten highest-ranked leisure-time activities put together.

16   Women make up a third or less of the characters in all samples except daytime serials.

17   The "lower classes" are almost invisible on television. According to the U.S. Census, at least 13 percent of the population is "poor," with a significant additional percentage being classified as "low-income wage-earners." Yet the lower classes make up only 1.3 percent of prime-time characters.

18   For every white male victim of violence there are seventeen white female victims.

19   For every white male victim there are twenty-two minority female victims.

20   For every ten female aggressors there are sixteen female victims.

21   Minority women are twice as likely to be victims as they are to be aggressors.

22   Villains are disproportionately male, lower-class, young, and Latino or foreign.

23   What is the significance of all this? First, the sheer quantity of violence on television encourages the idea that aggressive behavior is normal. Viewers become desensitized. The mind, as Gerbner puts it, becomes "militarized." This leads to what Gerbner calls "the Mean World Syndrome." Because television depicts the world as worse than it is (at least for white suburbanites), we become fearful and anxious—and more willing to depend on authorities, strong measures, gated communities, and other proto-police-state accouterments. Discounting the dramatic increase in violent crime in the real world, Gerbner believes, for example, that the Mean World Syndrome is an important reason that the majority of Americans now support capital punishment, whereas they did not thirty years ago. "Growing up in a violence-laden culture breeds aggressiveness in some and desensitization, insecurity, mistrust, and anger in most," he writes. "Punitive and vindictive action against dark forces in a mean world is made to look appealing, especially when presented as quick, decisive, and enhancing our sense of control and security."

24   The more violence one sees on television, the more one feels threatened by violence. Studies have shown direct correlations between the quantity of television watched and general fearfulness about the world: heavy viewers believe the world to be much more dangerous than do light viewers. Thus heavy viewers tend to favor more law-and-order measures: capital punishment, three-strikes prison sentencing, the building of new prisons, and so forth. And the fact that most of the heavy viewers are in low-income, low-education families means that the most disenfranchised in our society—and, it should be said, the people most exposed to real violence—are making themselves even more so by placing their fate in the hands of an increasingly martial state. Politicians exploit this violence-cultivated sensibility by couching their favored policies in militaristic terms: the War on Crime, for example, or the War on Drugs. "We are headed in the direction of an upsurge in neofascism in a very entertaining and very amusing disguise," Gerbner told a lecture audience in Toronto two years ago.

25   The first time I talked to Gerbner after reading his writings, I asked him if this wasn't all a bit Big Brotherish. "TV images are complex," he told me. "The disempowering effects of television lead to neofascism. That kind of thing is waiting in the wings. Nazi Germany came on the heels of a basic sense of insecurity and powerlessness like we have here now. I don't want to oversimplify, but that is the direction we might be heading."

26   Violence, Gerbner says, is all about power. The violence on television serves as a lesson of power that puts people in their place. Members of minority groups grow up feeling that they're more vulnerable than others. Television cultivates this view. But, I counter, minorities *are* more vulnerable. They are victims more often than middle-class white Americans are. Improving the depiction of minorities on television will not change this social fact. Gerbner strives to clarify:

27   Television doesn't 'cause' anything. We're wary of saying television 'causes' this or that. Instead we say television 'contributes' to this or that. The extent of contribution varies. But it's there.

28   Elsewhere Gerbner is less circumspect. "The violence we see on the screen and read about in our press bears little relationship either in volume or in type, especially in its consequences, to violence in real life," he has written. "This sleight of hand robs us of the tragic sense of life necessary for compassion." No doubt a victim of the Mean World Syndrome myself, I was surprised to learn that Gerbner is absolutely right, at least about the volume of violence. Scary and crime-ridden though the world is these days (violent crime has more than doubled over the past thirty years; an American is six times as likely to be the victim of assault with a weapon as he or she would have been in 1960), prime-time television presents a world in which crime rates are a hundred times worse. ◆

How to Erase Conscience
Carmen Wittmeier

1   Every year, the average Canadian child witnesses 12 000 violent acts— including rape and murder—on television. The Canadian Pediatric Society (CPS) warns that more than 1000 studies confirm that exposure to heavy doses of media violence increases aggressive behaviour in children.

2   This is old news to David Grossman, an American psychology professor and founder of a new scientific field called "killology," who believes that violent television and video games can turn children into killers. On August 24, the retired U.S. army lieutenant-colonel told a meeting of Canadian police chiefs that games have the same desensitizing effect as military killing simulators which ingrain soldiers with a homicidal reflex. "These kids go on autopilot," he argued. "They're drilled to kill every living target."

3   Killing, Prof. Grossman has emphasized, does not come naturally. In his 1995 book, *On Killing*, he says that in wars prior to 1950, only 10% of soldiers in combat used their weapons with intent to kill. Numbers, however, rose to 55% during the Korean War, and as high as 95% in Vietnam, after new training techniques relying on desensitization, propaganda and diffusion of responsibility were developed.

3   "If manipulation of the minds of impressionable teenagers is a necessary evil that we accept only reluctantly and with reservations for combat soldiers," Prof. Grossman writes, "how should we feel about its indiscriminate application to the civilian teenagers of this nation?"

4   In response to this disconcerting question, the CPS urges parents to help children differentiate between fantasy and reality, criticizing and analyzing media violence, and to simply spend more time with them, instead [of] abdicating to television. ◆

FREEWRITING ASSIGNMENT

What types of television programs do you prefer to watch and why? Do you prefer action, drama, comedy? Do you view television as a chance to escape reality, or connect to a larger community?

CRITICAL READING

1. Evaluate Stossel's use of examples to support his essay's points. How effective are his examples? Do they seem credible and/or appropriate? Are they balanced and fair? Explain.
2. Since 1930, broadcasters have been "required by law" to serve the public interest (paragraph 6). Do you think that they have successfully lived up to this expectation? As you form your response, refer to information from the essay as well as from your personal experience.
3. What is the happy violence that Stossel describes (paragraph 10)? Can you think of any examples from your own television viewing experience?
4. Stossel explains that according to Gerbner, "What matters is not so much the raw fact that a violent act is committed, but who does what to whom" (paragraph 13). What does Gerbner mean? Explain.
5. Review the list of some of the results of Gerbner's cultivation analysis (paragraphs 15–22). Can you develop a "violence profile" based on his results? Is this profile an accurate or predominantly fabricated reflection of real social violence? Explain.
6. Stossel states that "the more violence one sees on television, the more one feels threatened by violence" (paragraph 24). What evidence does Stossel use to support this statement? Do you agree or disagree with him?
7. Why might Gerbner's studies seem "Big Brotherish" (paragraph 25)? How does he stand on this aspect of his research? What is your opinion of his research and results? Explain.

CRITICAL WRITING

8. *Exploratory Writing*: Stossel cites a report conducted by *U.S. News & World Report* that indicates that 90 percent of Americans think that violent television programs hurt the country (paragraph 6). Does this figure seem accurate? Where do you stand on this issue? Write an essay in which you describe your position on television violence and its overall impact on North American society.
9. *Research and Analysis*: Read the interview between George Gerbner and media author/critic Todd Gitlin at **www.hotwired.com/synapse/ braintennis/97/27/index2a.html**. Evaluate how each expert defends his views on media violence. Which authority do you agree with more, and why? Write an essay explaining your view using examples from the interview.

10. *Critical Analysis*: Stossel states that "blood in fairy tales" is a legitimate cultural expression necessary to "balance tragic consequences against deadly compulsions" (paragraph 10). Read some traditional fairy tales in their original (not "Disneyfied") versions from authors such as the Brothers Grimm or Perrault. Select one or two of the tales and analyze the violence in them. Does the violence seem to be a justifiable "cultural expression"?

GROUP PROJECTS

11. *Class Project*: Stossel begins his essay with the story of 15-year-old Ronny Zamora, who claimed that television violence had caused the "media intoxication" that incited him to kill his next-door neighbor. Stage your own trial in the spirit of the Zamora case, and put on trial a fictitious teenager tried for a violent act using the "media intoxication" defense. If you wish, you may use another high-profile case, such as the case of William and Joshua Buckner, who told police they were emulating the video game *Grand Theft Auto* on the night of June 25, 2003, when they opened fire on vehicles driving on Interstate 40 in Tennessee. The class should be split into two or four groups to help prepare one side of the case. From these groups, your teacher will select students to serve as defense and prosecuting attorneys, defendant, judge, and, if desired, experts. The rest of the class will act as jury to decide the case based on the arguments of the lawyers, experts, and defendant. Discuss as a group the verdict after it has been reached.

12. Stossel states that "today someone settling down to watch television is likely to witness a veritable carnival of violent behavior" (paragraph 8). With your group engage in a media study of your own. Track the number of violent acts in a specific period of time, such as prime time or during Saturday morning cartoons. Each member of the group should be responsible for counting and describing violent acts on a single network during the specified time period. Compare your findings with the statistics cited in Stossel's article, and discuss the implications of your results with the group.

13. The Cultural Indicators project tracks not only the number of violent acts, but their specific characteristics, such as race, sex, height, level of aggressiveness, substance abuse, and the reason for conflict of the people involved in the act. With your group, conduct a similar study of a few nights of programming and compare your results. Address some of Gerbner's questions. Are there statistically significant differences in the percentage of victimhood or alcohol abuse by sex, race, age, level of education, or social status? Share your results with the rest of the class.

TV's War of Words
Deborah Tannen

Since the 1980s, television talk shows have become part of almost every network's program offerings. More recently, however, some of these "talk shows" have changed into screaming matches between the program's participants, especially programs that profess to "debate" a particular issue. Instead of understanding the nuances of an issue or point of view, these programs promote conflict and argument. Although ratings may be part of the appeal of "scream TV," Deborah Tannen explains in this essay that it is simply another characteristic of our argument culture. Television is both promoting and supporting a growing attitude in the viewing public: watching people fight is fun.

Deborah Tannen is a professor of linguistics at Georgetown University. She is the author of many best-selling books on linguistics, including *I Only Say This Because I Love You* (2001), *The Argument Culture* (1999), and *You Just Don't Understand* (1997). She has been a guest on *20/20*, *48 Hours*, *CNN*, and *The NewsHour with Jim Lehrer*. This article first appeared in the September 1999 issue of *Brill's Content*.

CRITICAL THINKING Think about some popular television debate programs. How many of them aim to resolve conflicts or promote understanding and how many of them thrive on dissent and discord? What programs enjoy higher ratings?

1   When my book *The Argument Culture* was published, I appeared on *Charles Grodin*. Returning home after the show, I found a message on my answering machine. "I tuned in at the time you told me," a friend's voice said, "but there were two men shouting over each other, and it set my teeth on edge. I switched it off."

2   I laughed at the irony. In introducing me, Grodin confessed that he had at times been guilty of the kind of interview I wrote about. He had an illustration for the viewers to see: himself and then Senator Alan Simpson shouting at each other. This is what drove my friend from her screen—proving a point I made in the book and on the show.

3   Why are more news and public-affairs shows turning into shouting matches between left and right, liberal and conservative, Democrat and Republican? For one thing, with round-the-clock news, the airwaves have to be filled, and these shows are easy and economical to assemble: Find a conservative and a liberal and you've got your show. Also, with the advent of cable has come increased competition, so producers need to make shows entertaining. But where do they get the idea that watching fights is fun? The answer is the argument culture.

4   The argument culture is a pervasive war-like atmosphere that makes us approach public dialogue, and just about anything else we need to accomplish, as if it were a fight. It rests on the assumption that opposition is the best way to get anything done: The best way to discuss an idea is to set up a debate; the best way to set-

tle a dispute is litigation that pits one party against the other; the best way to begin an essay is to attack someone; the best way to show you're really thinking is to criticize; and—as we see in the scream TV shows—the best way to cover news is to find spokespeople who express the most extreme views and present them as "both sides." Conflict and opposition are as necessary as cooperation and agreement, but the scale is off balance, with conflict and opposition overweighted.

5   By turning everything into a left-right fight, the argument culture gives us trumped-up, showcase "debates" between two oversimplified sides, leaving no room for the real arguments. What's wrong with lively debate? Nothing, when debate is a synonym for open discussion. But in most televised debates, the goal is not to understand but to win. You can't explore nuances or complexities; that would weaken your position. And few issues fall neatly into just two sides. Most are a crystal of many sides—and some have just one. Perhaps most destructive, if the goal is a lively fight, the most polarized views are best, so the extremes get the most airtime and are allowed to define the issues. Viewers conclude that if the two sides are so far apart, the problem can't be solved, so why try?

6   If everything has to be squeezed into the procrustean bed of left and right, moderate views are drowned out. *The Boston Globe* columnist Ellen Goodman (perceived as "the left") notes that if she's invited to appear on a show that she'd just as soon not do, all she needs to say is, "I can see both sides; it's complicated." Ann Coulter (a commentator on "the right") also finds that when she takes a position that doesn't fit producers' ideas of conservative, they don't want her.

7   The time crunch is a major factor in scream TV. A half-hour show (only 22 minutes of programming), is broken into three or four segments, each treating a different issue in progressively shorter chunks of time that are shared among four, five, even six, commentators. As if even these short segments aren't fast enough, each show presents instant pronouncements, such as McLaughlin's end-of-show round-the-table predictions, the mid-show highlights on *Hardball With Chris Matthews*, or *The Capital Gang*'s viewer-submitted "Outrage of the Week." (It's telling that it's the outrage of the week: in this format, provocative typically means "provoking to anger.")

8   The battle imagery starts with the names: *Crossfire* (hinting war), *Hardball* (hinting super-competitive sports), *The Capital Gang* (a whiff of brash street fighters). The very structure of these shows is based on underlying metaphors of war and sports: Two sides duke it out; one wins, the other loses. But it's all a game: See the warring parties jocularly sparring at the end of the show, as the camera pulls away? Those who take part in these pseudo-debates know that there is a display aspect to it.

9   The shout-down shows distort public discussion of vital issues. Their pacing corrupts the information viewers get. Eleanor Clift (as I quoted her in *The Argument Culture*) explains, "The nature of these shows is you're forced to speak more provocatively to make a point in the short time you have before you get interrupted. People know there's an entertainment factor, but the danger is, it turns us all into stereotypes, because you don't have time to express the ifs, ands, or buts."

10   When I talk about the argument culture, I am often asked about *Jerry Springer*. Springer's show is also scream TV. Phil Donahue, who pioneered the format, used it

to convey information provided by experts with the audience interaction added. Oprah Winfrey saw the potential of the format to create a sense of connection among her guests, the studio audience, viewers, and herself by focusing less on the expert guests and more on the average people who come on to talk about their lives. Springer dispenses with experts entirely and exploits only one kind of drama: getting average people to come on his show to fight. But I worry less about Springer because no one is watching his show to form opinions about current events, as they are with news and information shows.

11   The argument culture also encompasses an ethic of aggression—praising those in power would be boring, rolling over. Those who take positions against the president, for example, don't just criticize—they sneer, ridicule, and heap scorn. By setting that tone, scream TV encourages viewers to approach others in an adversarial spirit, creating an atmosphere of animosity that spreads like a fever. As the Egyptian author Leila Ahmed wrote, describing the effect of the terms and tone in which Gamal Abdel Nasser habitually denounced his enemies, "once you make hatred and derision . . . normal and acceptable in one area, they become generalized to everything else."

12   [. . .] *Larry King Live* is also a talking-heads cable show that airs weeknights, but one that gives viewers an extended conversation with one guest at a time. Though King is often ridiculed by his peers for asking only "softball" questions of his guests, far more viewers prefer his approach, giving him, according to Nielsen, 0.5 percent (or 538,000) of households. That's far larger than the audience of *Crossfire* and *Hardball* [0.3 percent].

13   What do audiences like about these shows? Part of their appeal, I think, lies in their hosts. John McLaughlin's booming voice sounds like an old newsreel voice-over. Introducing a topic, he uses strategic pauses and sudden loudness to add drama: "The AMA," he tells viewers, "has voted to allow doctors [pause] TO UNIONIZE!!" American bombing of the Chinese Embassy in Belgrade "was . . . CRIMINAL NEGLIGENCE!!" (though he adds, sotto voce, "many believe"). McLaughlin's manner comes across as good-natured bluster.

14   Chris Matthews of *Hardball* does not shout or pronounce in dramatic highs and lows, stops and starts. He charms with his blond, boyish good looks and ready smile. The drama comes from the fast pace at which the words roll off his tongue, like a sportscaster rushing to keep up with the plays—in keeping with the metaphor of the show's name and his nightly call to arms: "Let's play hardball."

15   Why has talk on radio and TV become more a matter of having arguments than of making arguments? As I explain in *The Argument Culture*, part of the cause is the medium itself. Television (like radio) returns, in some ways, to the past. It was the advent of print that made Western society less disputatious, according to cultural linguist Walter Ong: In the absence of audiences before which to stage debates, attention gradually focused on the internal argumentation of published tracts rather than debaters' performance. The rise of contentiousness today is fueled in part by the return of oral argument on TV and radio, where once again the ability to dispute publicly is valued—and judged—as a performance. ◆

FREEWRITING ASSIGNMENT

In this essay, Tannen ascribes the emergence of "scream TV" to our "argument culture." In your own words, what is "argument culture" and what is its current role in modern society?

CRITICAL READING

1. Why was the fact that Tannen's friend shut off the TV while watching *Charles Grodin* ironic? How does this gesture help frame the points Tannen makes in her essay?
2. According to Tannen, what is the "argument culture"? What is your opinion on her theory? Explain.
3. Define *debate*. Is argument the same as debate?
4. What happens when guests invited to "debate" on scream TV shows express that they "can see both sides" of an issue? Why do producers often turn these individuals down?
5. How can "shout downs" on debate programs distort public discussion of vital issues? Do you think, as Tannen does, that they can actually work against public discussion of important issues? Explain.
6. What accounts, according to Tannen, for the appeal of television debate programs—especially ones that feature the attributes of "scream TV"? Do the ratings really reflect that this debate technique is popular?

CRITICAL WRITING

7. *Research and Analysis*: Watch a few of the programs Tannen mentions in her essay *(Crossfire, Hardball, Larry King Live, The Capital Gang,* etc.). Look up the definition of *debate* and *argument* in the dictionary. Based on your observation of the programs, write an essay on whether these programs are debate, argument, both, or neither. Support your points with examples from your viewing experience, Tannen's essay, and your personal perspective.
8. *Exploratory Writing*: Tannen comments that defenders of "scream TV" claim that "audiences love it. Ratings . . . are the pudding-proof." Is scream TV delivering what audiences want to see and hear? In a carefully considered essay, discuss and describe your own television viewing desires. What do you watch on television? What do you like to see, and what causes you to change the channel or turn off the set? How do your own viewing likes and dislikes compare to the points Tannen makes in her essay?

9. Make a list of TV debate programs (use the programs Tannen cites as a starting point) and select four programs from the list. Group members should watch all four of the programs (try to synchronize so you are all watching the same debates on the same nights) and analyze each program for its effectiveness as a debate program. Note the topic discussed, the opinions of each guest, their backgrounds, and their debate styles. Rate each program on a 1–5 scale, with 5 indicating a highly effective and engaging debate. Compare your ratings with other members of the group. How are your impressions similar and how are they different?

10. Stage your own debate program. The teacher should propose a social or political question to the class and have students briefly write about where they stand on the issue. Based on student responses, the teacher should select four to five students to debate the issue in front of the class and select one student to serve as moderator. (Debate "guests" should all agree to "obey" the moderator.) The rest of the class will serve as the audience. After the debate, the audience can discuss the effectiveness of the debate and the "performance" of each of the participants. Here are some sample topics: We should reintroduce prayer in public schools; television promotes eating disorders; we need more strict gun laws; it should be harder for people to divorce; college athletes should be held accountable for their academic performances; and/or affirmative action laws are no longer necessary.

TV News: All the World in Pictures
Neil Postman and Steve Powers

It's 6 P.M. and you turn on the local evening news. You depend on it to keep you informed of the day's events in your area, your nation, and worldwide. But how much do you really learn from that nightly news broadcast? According to Neil Postman and Steve Powers, the answer is not very much. The nightly news, they argue, is really visual entertainment that only creates the illusion of keeping the public informed.

A professor at New York University, the late Neil Postman founded the Steinhardt School of Education's program in media ecology at NYU in 1971. He was chair of the Department of Culture and Communication until 2002. During his career, he wrote 20 books on a wide variety of subjects ranging from education to television to technology's influence on modern life. His most recent books include *The End of Education: Redefining the Value of School* (1995) and *Building a Bridge to the 18th Century: How the Past Can Improve Our Future* (1999).

Steve Powers is an award-winning journalist with more than 30 years of experience in broadcast news. Postman and Powers are co-authors of *How to Watch TV News* (2000) from which this essay was taken.

CRITICAL THINKING   Think about your local television news broadcast. How much does it rely on video clips to tell the story? How are events narrated? How much information do you learn from each clip?

1   When a television news show distorts the truth by altering or manufacturing facts (through re-creations), a television viewer is defenseless even if a re-creation is properly labeled. Viewers are still vulnerable to misinformation since they will not know (at least in the case of docudramas) what parts are fiction and what parts are not. But the problems of verisimilitude posed by re-creations pale to insignificance when compared to the problems viewers face when encountering a straight (no-monkey-business) show. All news shows, in a sense, are re-creations in that what we hear and see on them are attempts to represent actual events, and are not the events themselves. Perhaps, to avoid ambiguity, we might call all news shows "re-presenta-tions" instead of "re-creations." These re-presentations come to us in two forms: language and pictures. The question then arises: what do viewers have to know about language and pictures in order to be properly armed to defend themselves against the seductions of eloquence (to use Bertrand Russell's apt phrase)? . . .

2   [Let us look at] the problem of pictures. It is often said that a picture is worth a thousand words. Maybe so. But it is probably equally true that one word is worth a thousand pictures, at least sometimes—for example, when it comes to understanding the world we live in. Indeed, the whole problem with news on television comes down to this: all the words uttered in an hour of news coverage could be printed on one page of a newspaper. And the world cannot be understood in one page. Of course, there is a compensation: television offers pictures, and the pictures move. Moving pictures are a kind of language in themselves, but the language of pictures differs radically from oral and written language, and the differences are crucial for understanding television news.

3   To begin with, pictures, especially single pictures, speak only in particularities. Their vocabulary is limited to concrete representation. Unlike words and sentences, a picture does not present to us an idea or concept about the world, except as we use language itself to convert the image to idea. By itself, a picture cannot deal with the unseen, the remote, the internal, the abstract. It does not speak of "man," only of a man; not of "tree," only of a tree. You cannot produce an image of "nature," any more than an image of "the sea." You can only show a particular fragment of the here-and-now—a cliff of a certain terrain, in a certain condition of light; a wave at a moment in time, from a particular point of view. And just as "nature" and "the sea" cannot be photographed, such larger abstractions as truth, honor, love, and false-hood cannot be talked about in the lexicon of individual pictures. For "showing of" and "talking about" are two very different kinds of processes: individual pictures give us the world as object; language, the world as idea.

4   There is no such thing in nature as "man" or "tree." The universe offers no such categories or simplifications; only flux and infinite variety. The picture documents and celebrates the particularities of the universe's infinite variety. Language makes them comprehensible.

5   Of course, moving pictures, video with sound, may bridge the gap by juxtaposing images, symbols, sound, and music. Such images can present emotions and rudimentary ideas. They can suggest the panorama of nature and the joys and miseries of humankind.

6   Picture—smoke pouring from the window, cut to people coughing, an ambulance racing to a hospital, a tombstone in a cemetery.

7   Picture—jet planes firing rockets, explosions, lines of foreign soldiers surrendering, the American flag waving in the wind.

8   Nonetheless, keep in mind that when terrorists want to prove to the world that their kidnap victims are still alive, they photograph them holding a copy of a recent newspaper. The dateline on the newspaper provides the proof that the photograph was taken on or after that date. Without the help of the written word, film and videotape cannot portray temporal dimensions with any precision. Consider a film clip showing an aircraft carrier at sea. One might be able to identify the ship as Soviet or American, but there would be no way of telling where in the world the carrier was, where it was headed, or when the pictures were taken. It is only through language—words spoken over the pictures or reproduced in them—that the image of the aircraft carrier takes on specific meaning.

9   Still, it is possible to enjoy the image of the carrier for its own sake. One might find the hugeness of the vessel interesting; it signifies military power on the move. There is a certain drama in watching the planes come in at high speeds and skid to a stop on the deck. Suppose the ship were burning: that would be even more interesting. This leads to an important point about the language of pictures. Moving pictures favor images that change. That is why violence and dynamic destruction find their way onto television so often. When something is destroyed violently it is altered in a highly visible way; hence the entrancing power of fire. Fire gives visual form to the ideas of consumption, disappearance, death—the thing that burned is actually taken away by fire. It is at this very basic level that fires make a good subject for television news. Something was here, now it's gone, and the change is recorded on film.

10   Earthquakes and typhoons have the same power. Before the viewer's eyes the world is taken apart. If a television viewer has relatives in Mexico City and an earthquake occurs there, then he or she may take a special interest in the images of destruction as a report from a specific place and time; that is, one may look at television pictures for information about an important event. But film of an earthquake can be interesting even if the viewer cares nothing about the event itself. Which is only to say, as we noted earlier, that there is another way of participating in the news—as a spectator who desires to be entertained. Actually to see buildings topple is exciting, no matter where the buildings are. The world turns to dust before our eyes.

11   Those who produce television news in America know that their medium favors images that move. That is why they are wary of "talking heads," people who simply appear in front of a camera and speak. When talking heads appear on television, there is nothing to record or document, no change in process. In the cinema the situation is somewhat different. On a movie screen, closeups of a good actor speaking dramatically can sometimes be interesting to watch. When Clint Eastwood narrows his eyes and challenges his rival to shoot first, the spectator sees the cool rage of the Eastwood

character take visual form, and the narrowing of the eyes is dramatic. But much of the effect of this small movement depends on the size of the movie screen and the darkness of the theater, which make Eastwood and his every action "larger than life."

12   The television screen is smaller than life. It occupies about 15 percent of the viewer's visual field (compared to about 70 percent for the movie screen). It is not set in a darkened theater closed off from the world but in the viewer's ordinary living space. This means that visual changes must be more extreme and more dramatic to be interesting on television. A narrowing of the eyes will not do. A car crash, an earthquake, a burning factory are much better.

13   With these principles in mind, let us examine more closely the structure of a typical newscast, and here we will include in the discussion not only the pictures but all the nonlinguistic symbols that make up a television news show. For example, in America, almost all news shows begin with music, the tone of which suggests important events about to unfold. The music is very important, for it equates the news with various forms of drama and ritual—the opera, for example, or a wedding procession—in which musical themes underscore the meaning of the event. Music takes us immediately into the realm of the symbolic, a world that is not to be taken literally. After all, when events unfold in the real world, they do so without musical accompaniment. More symbolism follows.

14   The sound of teletype machines can be heard in the studio, not because it is impossible to screen this noise out, but because the sound is a kind of music in itself. It tells us that data are pouring in from all corners of the globe, a sensation reinforced by the world map in the background (or clocks noting the time on different continents). The fact is that teletype machines are rarely used in TV news rooms, having been replaced by silent computer terminals. When seen, they have only a symbolic function.

15   Already, then, before a single news item is introduced, a great deal has been communicated. We know that we are in the presence of a symbolic event, a form of theater in which the day's events are to be dramatized. This theater takes the entire globe as its subject, although it may look at the world from the perspective of a single nation. A certain tension is present, like the atmosphere in a theater just before the curtain goes up. The tension is represented by the music, the staccato beat of the teletype machines, and often the sight of news workers scurrying around typing reports and answering phones. As a technical matter, it would be no problem to build a set in which the newsroom staff remained off camera, invisible to the viewer, but an important theatrical effect would be lost. By being busy on camera, the workers help communicate urgency about the events at hand, which suggests that situations are changing so rapidly that constant revision of the news is necessary.

16   The staff in the background also helps signal the importance of the person in the center, the anchor, "in command" of both the staff and the news. The anchor plays the role of host. He or she welcomes us to the newscast and welcomes us back from the different locations we visit during the filmed reports.

17   Many features of the newscast help the anchor to establish the impression of control. These are usually equated with production values in broadcasting. They include such things as graphics that tell the viewer what is being shown, or maps

and charts that suddenly appear on the screen and disappear on cue, or the orderly progression from story to story. They also include the absence of gaps, or "dead time," during the broadcast, even the simple fact that the news starts and ends at a certain hour. These common features are thought of as pure technical matters, which a professional crew handles as a matter of course. But they are also symbols of a dominant theme of television news: the imposition of an orderly world—called "the news"—upon the disorderly flow of events.

18   While the form of a news broadcast emphasizes tidiness and control, its content can best be described as fragmented. Because time is so precious on television, because the nature of the medium favors dynamic visual images, and because the pressures of a commercial structure require the news to hold its audience above all else, there is rarely any attempt to explain issues in depth or place events in their proper context. The news moves nervously from a warehouse fire to a court decision, from a guerrilla war to a World Cup match, the quality of the film most often determining the length of the story. Certain stories show up only because they offer dramatic pictures. Bleachers collapse in South America: hundreds of people are crushed—a perfect television news story, for the cameras can record the face of disaster in all its anguish. Back in Washington, a new budget is approved by Congress. Here there is nothing to photograph because a budget is not a physical event; it is a document full of language and numbers. So the producers of the news will show a photo of the document itself, focusing on the cover where it says "Budget of the United States of America." Or sometimes they will send a camera crew to the government printing plant where copies of the budget are produced. That evening, while the contents of the budget are summarized by a voice-over, the viewer sees stacks of documents being loaded into boxes at the government printing plant. Then a few of the budget's more important provisions will be flashed on the screen in written form, but this is such a time-consuming process—using television as a printed page—that the producers keep it to a minimum. In short, the budget is not televisable, and for that reason its time on the news must be brief. The bleacher collapse will get more time that evening.

19   While appearing somewhat chaotic, these disparate stories are not just dropped in the news program helter-skelter. The appearance of a scattershot story order is really orchestrated to draw the audience from one story to the next—through the commercial breaks to the end of the show. The story order is constructed to hold and build the viewership rather than place events in context or explain issues in depth.

20   Of course, it is a tendency of journalism in general to concentrate on the surface of events rather than underlying conditions; this is as true for the newspaper as it is for the newscast. But several features of television undermine whatever efforts journalists may make to give sense to the world. One is that a television broadcast is a series of events that occur in sequence, and the sequence is the same for all viewers. This is not true for a newspaper page, which displays many items simultaneously, allowing readers to choose the order in which they read them. If newspaper readers want only a summary of the latest tax bill, they can read the headline and the first paragraph of an article, and if they want more, they can keep reading. In a sense, then, everyone reads a different newspaper, for no two readers will read (or ignore) the same items.

21   But all television viewers see the same broadcast. They have no choices. A report is either in the broadcast or out, which means that anything which is of narrow

interest is unlikely to be included. As NBC News executive Reuven Frank once explained:

> A newspaper, for example, can easily afford to print an item of conceivable interest to only a fraction of its readers. A television news program must be put together with the assumption that each item will be of some interest to everyone that watches. Every time a newspaper includes a feature which will attract a specialized group it can assume it is adding at least a little bit to its circulation. To the degree a television news program includes an item of this sort . . . it must assume that its audience will diminish.

22   The need to "include everyone," an identifying feature of commercial television in all its forms, prevents journalists from offering lengthy or complex explanations, or from tracing the sequence of events leading up to today's headlines. One of the ironies of political life in modern democracies is that many problems which concern the "general welfare" are of interest only to specialized groups. Arms control, for example, is an issue that literally concerns everyone in the world, and yet the language of arms control and the complexity of the subject are so daunting that only a minority of people can actually follow the issue from week to week and month to month. If it wants to act responsibly, a newspaper can at least make available more information about arms control than most people want. Commercial television cannot afford to do so.

23   But even if commercial television could afford to do so, it wouldn't. The fact that television news is principally made up of moving pictures prevents it from offering lengthy, coherent explanations of events. A television news show reveals the world as a series of unrelated, fragmentary moments. It does not—and cannot be expected to—offer a sense of coherence or meaning. What does this suggest to a TV viewer? That the viewer must come with a prepared mind—information, opinions, a sense of proportion, an articulate value system. To the TV viewer lacking such mental equipment, a news program is only a kind of rousing light show. Here a falling building, there a five-alarm fire, everywhere the world as an object, much without meaning, connections, or continuity. ◆

FREEWRITING ASSIGNMENT

Consider the phrase "a picture is worth a thousand words." Do you think it is true? How does it apply to television journalism?

CRITICAL READING

1. According to Postman and Powers, what is wrong with news programs recreating actual events? How does re-creation affect the viewer? How does it affect the story?
2. Consider the "pictures" in paragraphs 6 and 7. Imagine you are seeing each of these pictures without any explanation accompanying them. How many different ways could these pictures be interpreted? How important are words to the contexts of these pictures?

3. What is the authors' position on news broadcasts? How can you tell?
4. How do you think a broadcast journalist from your local television network would respond to this essay? How argumentative is this essay? Explain.
5. What is the price viewers pay for fragmented video clips? Evaluate the pros and cons of this style of journalism.
6. How does the order in which news stories are presented during the news broadcast "control" the audience? Does the knowledge that you are being manipulated change your opinion of the nightly news? Explain.
7. Analyze the authors' last paragraph that television programs cannot offer a sense of coherence and meaning. Do you agree with this? Why might this be ironic when you consider the reasons why people watch the news?

CRITICAL WRITING

8. What is news? Many of us think we know the answer, but what might be newsworthy to one person may seem superfluous to another. Write a short essay on what you expect (or want) from a news program and what you actually get. How much does the tradition of news broadcasts influence your expectations?
9. You are a television news producer who must develop a new local television news program to compete against others in the early evening time slot. Conduct a survey on what people want to watch on local television news. After gathering your information, design your newscast and explain in detail the reasons for your design. How much does your new program resemble others already on the air? What assumptions do you make about your overall audience? Predict the success of your broadcast, based on your program's rationale.

GROUP PROJECTS

10. Evaluate television newscasts. Each member of your group should watch several television newscasts from major networks. What differences, if any, are notable between networks? Are there differences between local and national news broadcasts? What assumptions seem to be made about the audiences of the various newscasts? Consider the stories reported, their order, how newscasters are dressed, the set, and the advertisements appearing on each program. Write a group-informed essay in which you describe your discoveries and analyze their relevance.
11. Prepare a survey questionnaire that seeks to find out just what it is that people want to watch on television news. Do they watch it to be entertained, informed, or both? What expectations do they bring to the programs? Do they feel newscasts are reliable sources of information? Each member of the group should survey at least 10 people and be prepared to discuss the responses with the group. Based on the responses, do viewers think the purpose of television news programs is to inform or to entertain?

VIEWPOINTS

► **AAP Discourages Television for Very Young Children**
American Academy of Pediatrics

► **TV Can Be a Good Parent**
Ariel Gore

► **Tune In, Turn On, and Buy, Buy, Buy**
Carmen Wittmeier

In August 1999, the American Academy of Pediatrics (AAP) issued a new policy statement urging parents to avoid exposing their children under the age of two years to television of any kind, and to carefully monitor viewing in children over that age. It further recommended that pediatricians incorporate questions about media exposure into routine child health visits. Although the policy seems to make some sense, some parents question the sweeping judgments it makes about the use of television in American homes. One such parent, Ariel Gore, argues that television can be a good co-parent, giving parents, especially working or single ones, needed relief from the demands of parenting. Although she agrees with the AAP's claim that young children need direct interaction with adults to grow mentally and socially, she questions how this assessment translates into a policy advocating no television exposure at all.

For a Canadian perspective on this issue, we've included "Tune In, Turn On and Buy, Buy, Buy." In this 1999 article, Carmen Wittmeier writes about how the Canadian Pediatric Society is also recommending limiting the hours of television for both preschoolers and school-age children. The concern is that TV is creating a generation of hypermaterialists— that is, children who measure their self-worth by the number of advertised products they and their family possess.

The American Academy of Pediatrics is a national organization of physicians specializing in children's health. The press release that follows was released on August 2, 1999. It summarizes some of the points made in AAP's new policy that appeared in the August 1999 issue of *Pediatrics*, the scientific journal of the AAP. Ariel Gore is the author of two books on parenting, *The Hip Mama's Survival Guide* (1998) and *The Mother Trip: Hip Mama's Guide to Staying Sane in the Chaos of Motherhood* (2000). Her most recent book is *Atlas of the Human Heart: A Memoir* (2003). This article appeared in the August 16, 1999, publication of *Salon*. Carmen Wittmeier is a writer, editor, and educator, and a reporter for Edmonton's *The Report Newsmagazine*, where this article first appeared in September 1999.

CRITICAL THINKING   Think about some of the children's television programs popular today. Who is responsible for developing and distributing these programs?

AAP Discourages Television for Very Young Children
American Academy of Pediatrics

1   A new policy from the American Academy of Pediatrics (AAP) urges parents to avoid television for children under 2 years old.

2   "While certain television programs may be promoted to this age group, research on early brain development shows that babies and toddlers have a critical need for direct interactions with parents and other significant care givers for healthy brain growth and the development of appropriate social, emotional, and cognitive skills," the policy says. The new AAP statement on media education also suggests parents create an "electronic media-free" environment in children's rooms, and avoid using media as an electronic babysitter. In addition, it recommends pediatricians incorporate questions about media into routine child health visits, as education can reduce harmful media effects.

3   "With an educated understanding of media images and messages, users can recognize media's potential effects and make good choices about their and their children's media exposure," states the new policy.

4   According to the AAP, a media educated person understands that:

- all media messages are constructed;
- media messages shape our understanding of the world;
- individuals interpret media messages uniquely; and
- mass media has powerful economic implications.

5   Research strongly suggests that media education may result in young people becoming less vulnerable to negative aspects of media exposure, the AAP says. In some studies, heavy viewers of violent programming were less accepting of violence or showed decreased aggressive behavior after a media education intervention. Another study found a change in attitudes about wanting to drink alcohol after a media education program. Canada, Great Britain, Australia and some Latin American countries have successfully incorporated media education into school curricula, the statement says. "Common sense would suggest that increased media education in the United States could represent a simple, potentially effective approach to combating the myriad of harmful media messages seen or heard by children and adolescents."

6   In addition, the AAP emphasized that media education should not be used as a substitute for careful scrutiny of the media industry's responsibility for its programming. ◆

TV Can Be a Good Parent
Ariel Gore

1 Let me get this straight.

2 The corporations have shipped all the living-wage jobs off to the developing world, the federal government has "ended welfare" and sent poor women into sub-minimum wage "training programs" while offering virtually no child-care assistance, the rent on my one-bedroom apartment just went up to $850 a month, the newspapers have convinced us that our kids can't play outside by themselves until they're 21, and now the American Academy of Pediatrics wants my television?

3 I don't think so.

4 Earlier this month, the AAP released new guidelines for parents recommending that kids under the age of 2 not watch TV. They say the box is bad for babies' brains and not much better for older kids. Well, no duh.

5 When I was a young mom on welfare, sometimes I needed a break. I needed time to myself. I needed to mellow out to avoid killing my daughter for pouring bleach on the Salvation Army couch. And when I was at my wits' end, Barney the Dinosaur and Big Bird were better parents than I was. My daughter knows that I went to college when she was a baby and preschooler. She knows that I work. And, truth be told, our television set has been a helpful co-parent on rainy days when I've been on deadline. Because I'm the mother of a fourth-grader, Nickelodeon is my trusted friend.

6 There was no TV in our house when I was a kid. My mother called them "boob tubes." But that was in the 1970s. My mother and all of her friends were poor—they were artists—but the rent she paid for our house on the Monterey (Calif.) Peninsula was $175 a month and my mother and her friends helped each other with the kids. The child care was communal. So they could afford to be poor, to stay home, to kill their televisions. I, on the other hand, cannot.

7 Now the AAP is saying I'm doing my daughter an injustice every time I let her watch TV. The official policy states that "Although certain television programs may be promoted to [young children], research on early brain development shows that babies and toddlers have a critical need for direct interactions with parents and other significant caregivers for healthy brain growth and the development of appropriate social, emotional, and cognitive skills. Therefore, exposing such young children to television programs should be discouraged."

8 Maybe my brain has been warped by all my post-childhood TV watching, but I'm having a little trouble getting from point A to point B here. Babies and toddlers have a critical need for direct interactions with actual people. I'm with them on this. "Therefore, exposing such young children to television programs should be discouraged." This is where they lose me. I can see "Therefore, sticking them in front of the TV all day and all night should be discouraged." But the assumption that TV-watching kids don't interact with their parents or caregivers is silly. Watching TV and having one-on-one interactions with our kids aren't mutually exclusive.

9   I've been careful to teach my daughter critical thinking in my one-woman "mind over media" campaign. It started with fairytales: "What's make-believe?" and "How would you like to stay home and cook for all those dwarves?" Later we moved on to the news: "Why was it presented in this way?" and "What's a stereotype?" But if you think I was reading "Winnie the Pooh" to my toddler when I thought up these questions, think again. I was relaxing with a cup of coffee and a book on feminist theory while Maia was riveted to PBS.

10   I read to my daughter when she was little. We still read together. But even a thoughtful mama needs an electronic baby sitter every now and again. Maybe especially a thoughtful mama.

11   Not surprisingly, the television executives feel there's plenty of innocuous programming on television to entertain young kids without frying their brains. "It's a bunch of malarkey," said Kenn Viselman, president of the itsy bitsy Entertainment Co., about the new policy. Itsy bitsy distributes the British show *Teletubbies*, which is broadcast on PBS. While I prefer Big Bird to Tinky Winky, I have to agree with him when he says, "Instead of attacking shows that try to help children, the pediatricians should warn parents that they shouldn't watch the Jerry Springer show when kids are in the room."

12   The AAP's policy refers to all television, of course, but it's hard not to feel like they're picking on PBS. *Teletubbies* is the only program currently shown on noncable television marketed toward babies and toddlers. Just two weeks ago, the station announced a $40 million investment to develop six animated programs for preschoolers. The timing of the AAP's report is unfortunate.

13   Cable stations offer a wider variety of kid programming. Take for example Nick Jr., an offshoot of the popular Nickelodeon channel. On weekdays from 9 a.m. to 2 p.m., the programming is geared specifically toward the preschool set. "Our slogan for Nick Jr. is 'Play to Learn'," Nickelodeon's New York publicity manager, Karen Reynolds, told me. "A child is using cognitive skills in a fun setting. It's interactive. With something like *Blues Clues*, kids are talking back to the TV. They are not just sitting there."

14   Still, the station has no beef with the new AAP policy on toddlers. "Nick Jr. programs to preschool children ages 2 to 5, but we are aware that children younger than 2 may be watching television," said Brown Johnson, senior vice president of Nick Jr. "We welcome a study of this kind because it encourages parents to spend more time bonding and playing with their children."

15   In addition to telling parents that young children shouldn't watch television at all and that older kids shouldn't have sets in their bedrooms, the AAP is recommending that pediatricians ask questions about media consumption at annual checkups. The difference between recommending less TV-watching and actually mandating that it be monitored by the medical community is where this could become a game of hardball with parents. What would this "media file" compiled by our doctors be used for? Maybe television placement in the home will become grounds for deciding child custody. ("I'm sorry, your honor, I'll move the set into the bathroom immediately.") Or maybe two decades from now Harvard will add TV abstention to their ideal candidate profile. ("*Teletubbies* viewers need not apply.")

Better yet, Kaiser could just imprint "Poor White Trash" directly onto my family's medical ID cards. Not that those cards work at the moment. I'm a little behind on my bill.

16   I called around, but I was hard-pressed to find a pediatrician who disagreed with the academy's new policy. Instead, doctors seemed to want their kids to watch less TV, and they're glad to have the AAP's perhaps over-the-top guidelines behind them. "If all your kids did was an hour of *Barney* and *Sesame Street* a day, I don't think that the academy would have come out with that statement," said a pediatrician at La Clinica de la Raza in Oakland, Calif., who asked not to be named. "It's not the best learning tool." And he scoffs at the notion of "interactive" TV. "It's not a real human interaction. When you're dealing with babies and toddlers, this screen is an integral part of their reality. You want kids to be able to understand interaction as an interaction. It's like the Internet. We're getting to a place where all of your relationships are virtual relationships."

17   Fair enough.

18   I'm not going to say that TV is the greatest thing in the world for little kids—or for anyone. I'm not especially proud of the hours I spend watching *Xena: Warrior Princess*, *The Awful Truth* and *Ally McBeal*. Mostly I think American television is a string of insipid shows aired for the sole purpose of rounding up an audience to buy tennis shoes made in Indonesian sweatshops.

19   But it seems that there is a heavy middle-class assumption at work in the AAP's new policy—that all of us can be stay-at-home moms, or at least that we all have partners or other supportive people who will come in and nurture our kids when we can't.

20   I say that before we need a policy like this one, we need more—and better— educational programming on TV. We need to end the culture of war and the media's glorification of violence. We need living-wage jobs. We need government salaries for stay-at-home moms so that all women have a real career choice. We do not need "media files" in our pediatricians' offices or more guilt about being bad parents. Give me a $175 a month house on the Monterey Peninsula and a commune of artists to share parenting responsibilities, and I'll kill my TV without any provocation from the AAP at all. Until then, long live Big Bird, *The Brady Bunch* and all their very special friends! ◆

Tune In, Turn On and Buy, Buy, Buy
Carmen Wittmeier

1   Despite their tender age, Calgary mother Wendy Holden fears her two children are budding materialists. An enthusiastic fan of popular Japanese television cartoons Pokemon and Sailor Moon, six-year-old Kaitlyn recently threw a temper-tantrum at Deerfoot Mall when denied a Pokemon poster. Along with her 10-year-old brother, she convinced a sympathetic aunt to drive to Chinatown to purchase highly-coveted

plastic Pokemon figurines. And both children regularly extol the virtues of McDonald's. "They don't care about what they eat," Ms. Holden notes. "They just want to collect Inspector Gadget pieces. We're going to have to go back at least eight times to build the entire character!"

2   Fed up with greasy food and incessant whining, Ms. Holden now limits her children's daily television consumption to one hour, an amount that more than matches the latest recommendations of the Canadian Pediatric Society. In a report released August 26, the CPS urged Canadians to limit school-age children's television viewing to two hours daily, and preschoolers to one. "The influence of the media on the psychosocial development of children is profound," the report warns. Physicians should provide parents with "guidance on age-appropriate use of all media, including television, radio, music, video games and the Internet."

3   The average Canadian child watches 23 hours of television weekly and sees more than 20,000 commercials a year, according to Peter Nieman, a Calgary pediatrician who heads the CPS's psychosocial committee. Dr. Nieman says the report and its recommendations are based on a five-year study which involved analysis of numerous studies examining the medium's impact on childhood obesity, violent behaviour, inappropriate sexuality and academic performance.

4   Children, the report says, are unable to understand the concept of a sales pitch, and therefore believe what they are told, and will consider themselves deprived if not given an advertised product. Children under the age of eight have difficulty differentiating between regular programming and commercials, 60% of which promote sugared cereal, candy, fatty foods and toys. "Fast food places like McDonald's wouldn't be advertising if it didn't pay off," Dr. Nieman says, pointing out that up to 20% of Canadian children are obese.

5   Dr. Nieman notes that materialism is the driving ethos of the electronic media. It teaches children to measure their self-worth by the things they and their family own, increases peer pressures and encourages conformity. Furthermore, he says, advertising condones smoking, drinking and sexual promiscuity. A group of pediatricians were astonished by the embedded sexual innuendo they saw when a Budweiser commercial was played in slow motion, he says. "It was quite impressive."

6   Dr. Nieman encourages parents to discuss the messages conveyed by television with their children, tape programs in advance to avoid commercials, and establish ground rules for viewing within the first year of a child's life. "The television should not be used as an electronic nanny," he emphasizes.

7   But Peter Moss, vice-president of programming and production for YTV and Treehouse TV, says that materialism is inevitable in a market-driven, capitalist society. Pointing fingers at television, Mr. Moss declares, is unfair. "I was upset by the CPS's report," he says. "It focused on the harm television can do, rather than examining the damage caused when parents don't spend 'X' amount of hours with their children."

8   Last week, YTV's Internet site was promoting a six-hour "Toon Typhoon," described as an "all-animation-no-education-must-see-celebration" of Japanese animation, including Pokemon, Monster Rancher and Dragonball Z. Mr. Moss makes no apologies for YTV's role in drawing kids away from sports and outdoor activi-

ties, into stores and in front of television screens. "Just because something is available doesn't mean it's negative," he argues, claiming that children are indoors and inactive mainly in rainy weather. "Some kids will watch all six hours, but others won't. It always comes back to parental supervision."

9   Dan Blake, a teacher and past-president of the Vancouver-based Canadian Association for Media Education, does not buy these arguments. Mr. Blake says children are generally more eager to be amused than instructed, do not voluntarily tune in to positive children's programming, and are seldom lured away from television screens by warm weather. Commercials and advertising within regular programming, Mr. Blake says, convey the message that pleasure is primarily derived from the consumption of material goods. Children who cannot compete with their wealthier peers, he says, end up frustrated, disillusioned and unmotivated. "This philosophy is very limiting," Mr. Blake warns. "Children fail to recognize that pleasure can be found in other sources, such as sports, art, music and literature." ◆

 FREEWRITING ASSIGNMENT ───────────────────

Do you think that television is harmful to babies and toddlers? Why or why not?

CRITICAL READING

1. In "Tune In, Turn On and Buy, Buy, Buy," what are the specifics of the study on which the Canadian Pediatric Society bases its recommendations on children's television viewing? On what does the American Academy of Pediatrics base its new policy? Do these recommendations seem logical and sound? What is their basic point?

2. Ariel Gore explains that when she called to pediatricians for their viewpoint on the new AAP policy, she was "hard-pressed" to find a pediatrician who disagreed with it. How does she respond to this reaction?

3. Carmen Wittmeier presents opposing viewpoints from authorities in the field of children's television viewing. Dan Blake implicates children's programming in children's assimilation of materialist ideas, while Peter Moss argues that it is the parents' responsibility to spend more time with their children in order to instill proper values. With which of these arguments would Gore agree? Which do you find more compelling? Why?

4. According to Dr. Peter Nieman in "Tune In, Turn On and Buy, Buy, Buy," what are some of the inappropriate practices condoned by the television advertising to which children are exposed?

5. In Wittmeier's article, Dr. Nieman appears to draw a causal link between McDonald's advertising and the fact that 20 percent of Canadian children are obese (paragraph 4). Is this a fair conclusion? Are there other television-related factors that may figure in the problem of obesity among these children? Explain.

6. Does Gore's response to the AAP's sweeping ban on television for toddlers seem reasonable and well considered? Does it change or influence your view of the AAP's policy decision?

7. Do you find that young children today are more materialistic than you were at their age? What do you base your opinion on?

CRITICAL WRITING

8. *Persuasive Writing:* Carmen Wittmeier quotes Peter Moss, vice-president of programming and production for YTV and Treehouse TV, as saying that "materialism is inevitable in a market-driven, capitalist society." Do you agree? If not, how can it be avoided? If so, should young children learn this lesson through programming directed at them or through other, real-world experiences? Write a brief essay supporting your position.

9. *Research and Exploratory Writing:* To what famous (or notorious) text does the title "Tune In, Turn On and Buy, Buy, Buy" allude? Find out, and discuss in a brief essay what clues the connotations of that text give us to Wittmeier's approach to her topic. How is it an especially appropriate title for this text?

10. Wittmeier refers to recommendations by the Canadian Pediatric Society. Examine their Web site at **www.cps.ca/english/media/NewsReleases/ TVTurnoffWeek.htm**, and compare it to the American Academy of Pediatrics' recommendations at **www.aap.org/family/tv1.htm**. Do you agree with these recommendations? Imagine that you are a representative of the AAP or CPS. Write a thoughtful response to Gore's argument in which you carefully critique her logic and argue against her claims. Be sure to refer to specific statements from both her article and either the AAP policy or the CPS recommendations.

11. *Research and Analysis:* Wittmeier mentions YTV (**www.ytv.com**) and Treehouse TV (**www.treehousetv.com/**). Compare these sites with other television sites for young people, such as CBC's at **www.cbc.ca/kids/** or PBS's at **www.pbskids.org**. Review some of the available programming for children. What are the differences between the offerings of these different networks? What conclusions can you draw from this?

GROUP PROJECTS

12. Each group member should analyze the viewing habits of a young child of his or her acquaintance. How many hours per day does the child watch? What sort of content is the child most interested in? Do the child's parents have any concerns regarding his or her television viewing? Does the child seem excessively affected by advertising? Compare your findings with those of other group members.

13. Watch several hours of children's programming one Saturday morning. What values do you see endorsed? What products are advertised? Do you

find this alarming, or fairly innocuous? Evaluate the programs for content, style, interactivity, and audience age. With your group, discuss the following question: "If I had a toddler, would I let him or her watch these programs?" Explain your stance to the group, allowing for rebuttal or agreement.

 RESEARCH ISSUE

Window on Reality: *American Idol* and the Search for Identity
Elaine Showalter

While reality television programs are fodder for critics, there is no denying their popularity. Far from a passing fad, there are more reality television programs than ever before. Several programs have emerged as constant hits, including *Survivor*, *The Bachelor*, and *American Idol*. In this essay, sociologist Elaine Showalter explains how *American Idol* isn't just entertainment— it is a fascinating and engaging look at teen popular culture. And critics aside, it presents a positive social message—that in America, you can be a star, regardless of your race or religion, as long as you have the talent and personality to make it to the top.

Elaine Showalter is a professor of English at Princeton University. She is the author of several books, including *The Female Malady: Women, Madness, and English Culture, 1830–1980* (1986), and *Hystories* (1997). She is a frequent contributor to the *Times Literary Supplement,* the *London Review of Books*, and many other journals. This article first appeared in the July 3, 2003, issue of the *American Prospect.*

CRITICAL THINKING   Do you watch reality TV programs? If so, which ones? What inspires you to watch these programs?

---

1   "Reality" television is generally scorned as mindless, vulgar, exploitative and contrived. So is it ever sociology, is it ever real? Yes, if it's *American Idol*, the FOX show that recently wrapped up its blockbuster second season. The program, for the uninitiated, pitted 12 young performers against one another for a chance at a $1 million recording contract. True, *American Idol* was adapted from a British series, *Pop Idol*, which had attracted a record 14 million voters and made an instant celebrity of a colorless boy singer. True, the program's producers were motivated by only the slickest of intentions: to manufacture a lucrative audience for a recording star before even one CD had been released. True, the twice-weekly programs, with their drawn-out commercial breaks and clumsily staged group numbers, were not the material of art.

2   And yet, in its shape and timing, *American Idol* has provided a fascinating snapshot of American youth culture in the 21st century. At once a competition, a talent show, a soap opera, a makeover fest, a patriotic celebration and an election,

American Idol showed how the postmillennial United States is changing with regard to race, class, national identity and politics. As its affiliate FOX News was cheering on the Iraq War, the FOX network's *American Idol*—one of the top-rated TV shows of the period leading up to, during and after the Iraq invasion—offered both a mirror image and a contradictory view of the nation's mind-set. Appealing simultaneously to Marines, Mormons, gays, blacks and Latinos, and to every region of the country, *American Idol* has a legitimate claim to its label of reality TV.

Playing the Race Chord

3 *American Idol* promoted multiculturalism with an ease missing from most network television, and quite distinct from its precursor. Although the British show began with a wide range of candidates, black and Indian aspirants were quickly eliminated; despite the influence of Asian styles from Bollywood and Bhangra, and black styles from the Caribbean, Africa and American hip-hop, the British pop scene is still white. In contrast, *American Idol* showed a youth culture and a young generation past the tipping point of racial harmony. Sociologically the program has been what one critic called "the Ellis Island of talent shows." In order to achieve this particular American dream of fame, 70,000 aspirants dressed in everything from yellow pimp suits to preppy khakis, then flew, drove and hitchhiked to grueling auditions in seven iconic American cities—New York, Detroit, Miami, Atlanta, Nashville, Austin and Los Angeles—for the second season.

4 Vying for only a dozen finalists' slots, an astonishing mix of blond Asians, yodeling twins, inner-city rappers, hopeful ex-convicts and desperate single mothers slept on the sidewalks and endured the blunt dismissals of multicultural judges Randy Jackson (a black music-company executive), Paula Abdul (a Brazilian/French-Canadian recording star and choreographer), and Simon Cowell (a white British music producer whose merciless insults and fearless observations as a *Pop Idol* judge had delighted U.K. audiences). The *American Idol* finalists included several black candidates plus two from biracial families. Despite the fears of some critics that no black candidate could win, Ruben Studdard, the soulful "velvet teddy bear" from Birmingham, Ala., who proudly displayed his 205 area code on his size XXXL T-shirt, took home the prize. Imagine a black singer as a Birmingham booster in the '60s! Ruben's distance from the racist history of the city where Martin Luther King, Jr., began the civil rights movement is a statement of how far this country has come.

5 In a vote so close that it recalled the 2000 presidential election, Clay Aiken, a white college student from North Carolina who worked with autistic teens and had become Ruben's best friend, came in second. At his audition, one reviewer recalled, Clay looked "like Alfred E. Neuman and Howdy Doody crashed head-on." Twenty weeks later, tanned, ironed and styled to rock-star perfection, Clay still retained his down-home charm and modesty. Guest judges alternated between Motown gods (Lamont Dozier, Gladys Knight) and white songwriters (Diane Warren, Billy Joel). Jackson's slang epithets ("dawg," as a term of affectionate greeting, was a favorite) domesticated the outlaw rapper idiom of hip-hop culture and repackaged it for middle America.

6   But there was a subtext to this surface of racial harmony and equality. Three black or biracial finalists and semifinalists were disqualified for concealing criminal records or for behavior unfitting to American Idols, suggesting disparities of opportunity and continuing cultural differences. One ex-finalist, Corey Clark, accused the producers of exploiting him for ratings when a web site revealed that he was facing trial on assault charges, and he had to tape an on-air defense interview for *American Idol* that he claimed was misleadingly edited.

U.K. and U.S.A.: The Pop Coalition

7 The change of venue from England to the United States not only shifted racial meanings but highlighted national differences. To the British, "Pop Idol" means something specific: a mainstream, TV-packaged, youth-oriented, music-biz phenomenon. There was no conscious sense of national identity in the choice of *Pop Idol* winners Will Young and Gareth Gates. But *American Idol* had a different agenda, especially the second series, which coincided with the buildup to and climax of the Iraq War. For their charity single benefiting the American Red Cross, 10 of the finalists recorded a hokey Reaganesque anthem, "God Bless the USA," which zoomed to the top of the charts. Part of the patriotic message was the presence among the finalists of husky Marine Josh Gracin, whose commanding officers hinted that he could be sent to Iraq at any moment. (He wasn't.)

8   Yet in the midst of all this flag waving, the edgy presence of Cowell shocked the American judges into taking a tougher line, just as the critical, even whining, war coverage of the BBC balanced and challenged the excessive optimism of American news correspondents. Cowell's refusal to be kind, tactful, warm and fuzzy, or euphemistically upbeat, made him a bracing presence on the show. Unintimidated by the politically correct, he told biracial Kimberley Locke that her performance improved as soon as she had her bushy curls straightened and highlighted. "Now," he said approvingly, "you look cute." Unmoved by the tears of losers, he was also the only judge unsoftened by the shrill audition of a 5-year-old black child. "I didn't think it was any good," he said forthrightly. The studio audience regularly booed Cowell, but his candor and insistence on high standards made the pop coalition of *American Idol* work.

The Democratic Process: Elections and Parodies

9 In the show's finale on May 21, more than 24 million votes came in to *American Idol*. We can't compare the percentage of response to a real election because *Idol* participants were allowed to vote more than once. But the electoral structure of the program reflected American attitudes about the political process, and perhaps even served as a mass-culture referendum on the mood of the nation. Both professional reviewers and fans chatting on the Web speculated on voting blocs, on campaigns and on whether the voting was rigged; Cowell told *People* magazine that some of the finalists "play the role like presidential candidates. If there was a baby in the

audience, they'd be running over to kiss it." Local newspapers ran opinion polls on behalf of hometown candidates. In the end, some reviewers even wondered about having the votes audited, bringing back memories of counting chads.

10 With *American Idol* providing its own parody of elections, it's no wonder that satirists were also attracted to the format. The *Onion* proposed a new FOX reality show called *Appointed by America*, in which contestants would vie in "a democracy quiz, a talent competition, and nation-building activities" to lead postwar Iraq. Who would it be: Ahmed Chalabi, leader of the exiled Iraqi National Congress? A pesh-murga fighter from Kurdistan? Or Kymbyrley Lake, a cashier from Garland, Texas, who has always dreamed of "doing something to help bring about a more peaceful world"?

11 A third series of *American Idol* is promised for next year, with Paul McCartney rumored to be a guest judge. I'd bet the Bush twins and some Democratic candidates will be in the audience, too. This reality show could be a better political photo-op than the USS Abraham Lincoln. ◆

FREEWRITING ASSIGNMENT

If you could be a contestant on a reality television program, which one would you go on, and why?

CRITICAL READING

1. In her introductory comments, Showalter asks of reality programming, "is it ever real?" *American Idol*, she explains, is indeed a *reality* program. Why does she feel this program, as opposed to many others of its genre, is more real than others? Explain.

2. Showalter comments that *American Idol* promotes multiculturalism and that Americans have positively responded to it. Explain the ways in which Americans have supported the multicultural aspects of the program?

3. In what ways is *American Idol* a "fascinating snapshot of American youth culture" in the twenty-first century? Explain.

4. Showalter is a renowned sociologist. What elements in her essay reveal her professional interests? Does the fact that she is a serious academic make her points seem more valid? Why or why not?

5. What made *American Idol* different from its British inspiration, *Pop Idol*?

6. Showalter notes that there is a "subtext to [the] surface of racial harmony and equality" on *American Idol* (paragraph 6). Explain what she means?

7. What strikes Showalter as particularly remarkable about Ruben Studdard's victory in the second season of *American Idol*? What are the sociological and cultural messages suggested by his victory? Explain.

CRITICAL WRITING

8. When Showalter wrote this essay in August 2003, *American Idol* had just completed its second season. By the end of August, the search for contestants for the third season, scheduled to air in January 2004, had already begun. Visit the *American Idol* Web site and view the contestants, including the top runners-up at **www.idolonfox.com**. View their profiles and respond to Showalter's observation that *American Idol* presents a truly multicultural America. If you do not feel this is true, explain why, referring to her essay and from your research on the FOX Web site.

9. *Research and Analysis*: Compare and contrast *American Idol* (at **www.idolonfox.com**) with its British progenitor, *Pop Idol* (**www.itv.com/popidol/index.stm**). In what ways are they similar? Based on Showalter's essay, do you notice any fundamental differences between the two programs? If so, would you have noticed these differences before you read her essay? Explain.

10. Visit the *NewsHour* Web site on the popularity of reality programming featuring Robert Thompson, head of the Center for the Study of Popular Television at Syracuse University, and Frank Farley, a past president of the American Psychological Association, and professor at Temple University at **www.pbs.org/newshour/forum/july00/reality.html**. Read the questions and responses posted at the Web site, and respond to them with your own viewpoint. Note that the Web site was first posted in 2000. How has reality television changed since then?

GROUP PROJECTS

11. With your group, compile a list of reality programs and their contestant profiles. (You may have to look up these programs online to see the most recent contestant roster.) What programs were the most successful? Did they appeal to a broad, multicultural audience? Discuss your list and observations in class as part of a wider discussion on diversity and reality television programs.

12. Develop your own reality television program. Include the show's premise, its object and goal, why people would want to watch it, and who would be a typical contestant. Outline the program and present it to the class. The class should vote on which program it finds the most engaging.

CRITICAL THINKING

1. In what ways is *American Idol* a "fascinating snapshot of American youth culture" in the twenty-first century?

2. Do you watch reality TV programs? If so, which ones? What inspires you to watch these programs? If you could be a contestant on one of them, which one would you go on and why?

3. Develop your own reality television program. Include the show's premise its objective, why people would want to watch it, and who would be a typical contestant. Outline the program and present it to the class. The class should vote on which program it finds the most engaging.

RESEARCH PROJECTS

4. When Elaine Showalter wrote this essay in August 2003, *American Idol* had just completed its second season. Visit the *American Idol* Web site at **www.idolonfox.com** and view the current contestants, including the top runners-up. View their profiles and respond to Showalter's observation that *American Idol* presents a truly multicultural America. If you do not think this is true, explain why, referring to her essay and to your research on the FOX Web site.

5. Compare and contrast American Idol with its Canadian equivalent, *Canadian Idol*, at **www.ctv.ca/idol/gen/Home.html**. In what ways are they similar? Based on Showalter's essay, do you notice any fundamental differences between the two programs? Write an essay on your findings.

The Family
in Flux
Love and Marriage

5

The notion of family is always in a state of change. How we perceive the very concept of family is based largely on where we come from and what values we share. We have a tendency to base our views on traditional constructs—models that are generations old and perpetuated by media archetypes. As a result, sociologists tell us, our vision of family is usually not based on realistic examples but on political ideals and media images. Yet the traditional family is obviously changing. Stepfamilies, same-sex relationships, single-parent households, and extended families with several generations living in one home all force us to redefine, or at least re-examine, our traditional definitions of family.

This chapter examines love and marriage in modern families. From traditional "nuclear family" models of husband, wife, children, to same-sex unions, this chapter takes a look at how our concept of marriage has changed. Divorce, for example, is a widely accepted reality of life, and is no longer viewed as a deviation from the norm. Single motherhood is no longer ascribed the social stigma it had 30 or 40 years ago. Canada is taking steps to legalize same-sex unions. Our perspective of marriage is shifting, and so have our attitudes. And as attitudes change, so do our expectations and social collective consciousness.

We open the chapter with one writer's view of what we can do to counter the international aging trend that many feel is a threat to our very well being. As the size of nuclear families shrinks, there will be fewer and fewer younger people to support an increasingly aging population. The results could prove catastrophic for the world economy. In "Be Fruitful or Else: How Having More Babies Can Solve All Our Problems," Peter Shawn Taylor suggests a remedy—having more children—and examines reasons why this suggestion is not taken seriously.

The next essay further examines our desire for nostalgia and how we often base our vision of the perfect marriage and family on a media-influenced ideal. In "The New Nostalgia," Rosalind C. Barnett and Caryl Rivers explain that old television models of marriage and family such as *Ozzie and Harriet* and *Leave It to Beaver* create complicated messages for modern couples. Politicians who lament the loss of the traditional family and people who long for "the way things used to be" are recalling an illusion rather than reality. Such nostalgia is not only misplaced, but it can also be dangerous, setting an unachievable standard.

The next essay, by college student Lowell Putnam, argues that children of divorce are not as scarred by the experience as politicians and the media seem to think. Having lived most of his life as a "child of divorce" he wonders, "Did I Miss Something?"

In "What's Love Got to Do with It?" Anjula Razdan provides a different look at marriage—that of a young woman raised by traditional Indian parents who support the practice of arranged marriages. While her parents believe that arranged marriages are the most practical and logical way to unify young couples—and Razdan wonders if they are on to something—she would still prefer to hold out for love.

This chapter's Viewpoints section addresses the issue of same-sex marriage. The issue has been hotly debated for the past few years, as some provinces legalize same-sex unions and others hold back. As of this writing, a debate in Parliament is imminent. We have included a senate speech delivered by historian and retired senator, Laurier LaPierre. He claims that to deny same sex couples the right to marry is to treat them as inferior citizens. Countering this, in "A Blow to Canada's Families," David Frum argues that gay and lesbian marriages will threaten the institution of marriage as a whole. Finally, we include "Dodging the Altar," a thoughtful piece by Matthew Hays, who believes that most gays and lesbians will never take advantage of the right to marry anyway since marriage as we conceive of it today is primarily a heterosexual construct developed to meet heterosexual needs.

The final reading, entitled "Cohabiting Is Not the Same as Commitment" by Karen S. Peterson, presents the Research Issue of cohabitation before marriage. Peterson reports that men who cohabit with women are less bound to marry at all. The big question is, "Why?"

Be Fruitful or Else: How Having More Babies Can Solve All Our Problems

Peter Shawn Taylor

One of the more alarming predictions for upcoming generations is what is becoming known as the aging trend in developed countries around the world. This trend refers to problems associated with a declining birth rate, which many predict will put unprecedented strain on social programs, such as health care and pensions, and on national economies as a whole. In this article, Peter Shawn Taylor argues that one overlooked solution to this problem is for families to produce more children, a solution that few people are willing to take seriously.

Peter Shawn Taylor is a freelance writer specializing in economic issues. He is a contributing editor to *National Post Business Magazine* and was a member of the *National Post* editorial board from 1998 to 2002. This article appeared in *Saturday Night* on July 7, 2001

1   The crisis in health-care funding. Collapsing public pension plans. A looming economic slowdown. What if I told you all these problems could be easily solved but that the solution might offend some people? Would you still want to hear it?

2   Canada, along with most other developed countries, is in a demographic straitjacket, and the consequences are dire. Canadians are living longer than ever and, thus, expecting more from public health care, pensions, and welfare systems. At the same time, Statistics Canada forecasts that between 2000 and 2040, the ratio of seniors to members of the working population will double from the current two per ten workers to four per ten. And by 2040, the overall population of Canada will begin to shrink due to a declining birth rate. The strain these twin phenomena— more seniors and fewer young workers to support them—place on Canadian social programs such as medicare and the Canada Pension Plan is plain to see. In more mature countries such as Japan, Germany, and Italy, where the birth rate is even

lower, these problems are far more advanced. In his 1999 book Gray Dawn, Peter Peterson argued that an ageing population is a "global hazard" on par with nuclear weapons and super viruses. The United Nations last year declared that only massive international migration on a scale never before seen could keep the ageing trend at bay and economies in rich nations functioning. The future, however, is more flexible than most people seem to think.

3   All these grim discussions are strangely incomplete. While no one would wish to reverse the many improvements in life expectancies, nearly every demographic jeremiad leaves out the equally important front end of the population equation—the birth rate. The number of children an average Canadian woman bears over her lifetime has fallen to 1.48 from 1.65 twenty years ago. The rate required for a population to maintain itself without immigration is 2.1 per woman (one each to replace the parents and a fraction to cover the possibility that a child might die before procreating). If we were to make a concerted effort to push the birth rate above 2.1, it would create a growing supply of young workers to support ageing pensioners and their health problems. More young workers would keep the economy staffed-up and remove the need for massive tax increases to sustain our imperilled social programs. Despite the views of the United Nations, increased fertility is the only permanent solution to the future work-force shortage since immigrants tend to be adults and are already that much closer to retirement age. Encouraging greater fertility is not an argument against immigration, mind you. Immigrants would still be a necessary part of the equation since it takes eighteen years for a rising birth rate to produce more workers.

4   Given the simplicity of the prescription, it is puzzling that so few people are willing to seriously discuss the fact that having more babies would be a good thing. In Germany, when conservative politicians promote richer baby bonuses, this argument is dismissed as anti-immigrant rhetoric. And when Bjorn Borg, the Swedish tennis icon, sponsored a full-page ad in a newspaper earlier this year urging his countryfolk to procreate because "there aren't enough babies being born," his concerns rated only a twitter—just another libidinous Swede advocating more nookie. Back home, the only province to make it an explicit objective has been Quebec. Between 1988 and 1997 the province offered a sliding scale of baby bonuses that peaked with an $8,000 payment on the birth of a third child. That system was then replaced with a range of programs aimed at making parents' lives easier, such as five-dollars-a-day universal daycare and a generous parental-leave system. While the baby bonuses did have a positive impact on the birth rate, the results seemed to diminish over time. All other jurisdictions in Canada appear to accept insufficient fertility as part of the landscape.

5   Some might say that this is a good thing, that governments have no business sticking their noses into what is a very private and complex decision. True enough; but Ottawa has not exactly been shy in lecturing us on such delicate matters as smoking, drinking, exercise, and safe sex when it has been deemed to be in the national interest. And the need for more babies is surely that. Even still, many women will doubtless take the suggestion that they should have more children to be a personal insult and a step backwards for feminism, and oppose it on those grounds.

Certainly no one wants to press parenthood onto people who are unwilling to accept the burdens. And the responsibility for the birth dearth should be properly shouldered by males as well as females who have put off or decided against having progeny for careers or other reasons. Thus the goal of any pro-natalist policy must be to convince people of the greater good in having offspring. It will not be an easy task. But consider that in the 1970s, wild predictions of massive global overpopulation spurred governments and international agencies around the world to focus on lowering birth rates through public campaigns as well as direct action such as birth-control distribution and education with obvious, and now regrettable, success. Surely a similar level of urgency and purpose could be mustered to promote the opposite notion.

6   Whether changing several generations of attitudes on parenthood and family size is best accomplished by a hard sell, as with Quebec's cash payments and universal daycare, or a softer approach that merely promotes fecundity as a virtue, is open for debate. Perhaps the best chance for success comes from a recent high-court ruling in Germany that held that childless adults constitute a greater burden on society and thus should be expected to pay more in taxes to support future social programs. From this perspective, making babies is not only patriotic, productive, and a lot of fun; it is also cheaper than the alternative. ◆

CRITICAL THINKING

Given the declining birth rate in Canada, should the government offer financial incentives for families to have more children? Why or why not? What is your viewpoint on this issue?

FREEWRITING ASSIGNMENT

Why do people decide to have or not have children? What factors might influence this decision? Should government policy ever have a role?

CRITICAL READING

1. How is Canada in a "demographic straitjacket"?
2. Taylor opens with a provocative question. Do you feel this is an effective way to introduce his message?
3. What are some of the ways that governments could encourage families to produce more children? How do you feel about these ideas?
4. Examine the Statistics Canada figure that compares the size of Canadian families in 1931 to the size of those in 1996. What reasons do you think people had for having larger families in 1931?
5. According to Taylor, why is the discussion of a pro-natalist policy not taken seriously?

CRITICAL WRITING

6. *Research and Persuasive Writing:* Taylor refers to Peter Peterson's *Gray Dawn*, a book that speculates about a future with a burgeoning older population and refers to this as a "global hazard." Many critics disagree with this view. Research both sides of the argument on the Internet. Which side do you feel is more valid? Why? Express your point of view in a well-reasoned essay.

7. *Exploratory Writing:* In his conclusion, Taylor suggests that the best solution might be to expect childless adults to pay more in taxes in order to support future social programs. Do you see this as a fair or viable proposal? Explain.

GROUP PROJECTS

8. Survey the members of your group about how many children they have or would like to have one day. Would the final number meet the 2.1 per woman rate needed to maintain a constant population without immigration? Based on the result, decide whether we need to make increasing the birth rate more of a political priority.

9. In your group, brainstorm about all the ways an aging population could impact Canadian society. Consider such aspects as health care, education, pensions, and some of the other issues mentioned in Taylor's article. Which issues do you see as the most threatening? Present your findings to the class.

The New Nostalgia
Rosalind C. Barnett and Caryl Rivers

Many people today feel the family is in a state of decline. Underlying this feeling is the social sense that the decay of the family is linked to the loss of "traditional family" values held in the 1950s. However, in this article, Rosalind C. Barnett and Caryl Rivers tell us that we're actually in much better shape than we think we are. Rather than apologizing for the state of our families, Barnett and Rivers say we should start appreciating our amazing adaptability. In fact, the very "problems" that critics of new family structures want to fix may actually be creating more stable families and healthier relationships.

Rosalind C. Barnett is a clinical psychologist and expert on dual-earner issues, job-related stress, the American family, and work/family relations. She is a senior research scientist in the women's studies program at Brandeis University. Caryl Rivers is a professor of journalism at Boston University and the author of several books, including *Slick Spins and Fractured Facts: How Cultural Myths Distort the News* (1996). This piece is excerpted from the authors' book, *He Works/She Works* (1996).

CRITICAL
THINKING

Are you familiar with the television programs *Leave It to Beaver, Father Knows Best, Ozzie and Harriet,* and *The Donna Reed Show?* If so, what kinds of families were portrayed in each? What was the established family structure, and how was this structure conveyed in these programs?

1   As he drops his daughter off at a very good day-care center staffed with well-trained, caring professionals, a father worries whether he's doing the right thing. Should he or his wife stay home with their daughter, even though they can't afford to? Will day care cause some problems for his child that he can't foresee? Is he doing something dreadfully wrong because his life is so different from that of his parents back in the 1960s?

2   Guilt is the universal malady of working parents today, and one to which parents in past generations were seemingly immune. Did the woman setting out in the covered wagon for a prairie homestead worry about whether her children would be well-adjusted out there on the plains? Did the women in colonial times, whose days were filled with manufacturing the clothing and food that would keep the family alive, brood about whether she and her children were "relating" well enough? Did Victorian men worry that their children were spending too much time with nannies?

3   It's safe to say that no modern working parent has completely escaped those sudden, painful stabs of guilt. It might help to understand its roots, and we will examine them in this essay. But first, it's important to realize how this guilt feeds into the mistaken conviction that today's parents can't quite measure up to those of the past.

4   It is imperative, we believe, to understand that those of us in the two-earner lifestyle have been as good or better parents—not worse ones—than the Ozzie and Harriet model. The two-earner lifestyle that has emerged in the past two decades of American life has been a positive development, fitting well with current economic realities. While it has not been easy, men and women have connected to the world of work and its demands while expending considerable energies on nurturing their children. If this meant that at times they felt they had to juggle too much, that there were times they wondered if they were going to be able to do it all, they lived with that problem—and, most often, survived it in good health and good humor.

5   We are already raising a generation of children in two-earner families; if we really want them to be stressed, let's tell them that what we are doing is all wrong, that what we should be doing was what their grandparents did in the 1950s, and that that's the ideal they, too, should aspire to.

6   In fact, we must prepare our children for the world they will really be facing—not some rosy image of a past that never was all that wonderful, and which is not going to return. With a global economy on the horizon and with the United States continually having to compete with the Pacific Rim and Europe, we will probably continue to see a pattern of downsizing of U.S. companies as high productivity becomes the watchword of industry. Men's real wages have been declining since 1960: The median income of employed white men in 1967 was about $19,800; by

1987 it was $19,008, adjusted for changes in earning power—roughly $750 less than it had been twenty years before.[1]

7   More and more, women's wages will become essential to a family's economic survival—as they are today in so many families. The days when women worked for "extras" are long gone and are not likely to return. More and more, in such an unstable work world, men will turn to their families as a way of finding self-esteem. And women, like men, will prepare early for careers or jobs in which they will be involved for most of their lives. Economists who predict the shape of the early twenty-first century say that no longer will people remain in one job for a lifetime; the successful worker of the future will be one who is flexible, learns quickly, and can transfer skills from one work setting to another. Women may have to retool as the economy twists and turns, but few will have the chance to be full-time, lifelong homemakers.

8   Not until we accept the working woman as the norm can we adequately prepare our sons and daughters for the lives they will really be leading. Our study conclusively proves that holding up the rigid and outdated lifestyle of the 1950s as a sacred icon will only add stress to their busy and often difficult lives. Perhaps the most important finding of the study on which the book is based is the fact that for working couples, a gap in gender-role ideology is a major and consistent source of stress. It is not merely annoying when your image of the ideal family does not jibe with that of your spouse; it can be an important source of stress in your life.

9   On the whole, we do not help young women prepare for the flexible jobs that will protect their economic futures and that of their families if we plant in their heads the idea that what they really ought to be doing is staying home. We don't prepare young men for the deep involvement they are going to have with their families if we create in them the idea that the real man doesn't change a diaper or drive the kids to nursery school.

10   But the actual facts about what is good for real American couples and their families today may well be drowned out by the clamor of what we call the "new nostalgia," a combination of longing for the past and a fear of change. It not only feeds the guilt that can tie individuals in knots, but can be a major stumbling block to the creation of corporate and government policies that will help, not hinder, working families. The new nostalgia has already calcified in politics, in the media, in a spate of books that tell us we must retreat to the past to find solutions for the future. The messages of a reinvigorated right wing in politics pushes a brand of family values with which Ozzie and Harriet would have felt quite at home.

11   One steady, unblinking beacon of a message has been flashed to men and women over the past few years: Change is dangerous, change is abnormal, change is unhealthy. This message permeates our mass media, the books we read, the newscasts to which we listen, the advice from pop psychologists, the covers of news magazines. Men and women must stay in their traditional places, or there will be hell to pay.

12   The message comes in many guises. It comes from warnings that women are working themselves into sickness on the so-called second shift—the housework women do after they come home from work—doing so much that their health is in

peril. It may be national magazines trumpeting the mommy track, concluding that women must seek achievement on a lower and slower track than men. It nests in headlines that claim women are simply unable to juggle the demands of work and home and are going to start having heart attacks just like men. It may be warnings that day care interferes with the mother-child bond—despite solid evidence to the contrary. It can be found in publications concluding that if people would just stay married or kids would stop having sex, all our social problems would disappear. It may be Robert Bly warning in *Iron John* that men have become weak, thanks to women, and they must find their warrior within.[2]

13   It is more than a backlash against the women's movement. Indeed, many of the warnings insist that men had better stay in the straitjacket of traditional masculinity. These warnings are implicit in the spate of action-adventure movies aimed at young men, in which manhood is defined as domination and mayhem, with no ongoing relationships with women or children. They are implicit also in the ease with which the word "wimp" is hurled at any political candidate who does not employ slash-and-burn macho tactics.

14   The flashing message is only intensified by widely held but outdated ideas from the behavioral sciences proclaiming that a man's emotional health is primarily based on his life at work, while a woman can only find her identity through being a wife and mother. So intense has this bias been that, until recently, social scientists rarely examined men's lives at home or women's at work.

15   The new nostalgia fuels the guilt that many working parents feel. The flames are fanned by forces that many working parents don't understand—and the media play a large role in keeping the bonfire going.

16   Never in the past were parents confronted with constant and ongoing images of how their grandparents raised children. Old folk remedies may have been passed down, mothers and grandmothers gave advice, but times changed and people changed with them. It was the natural order of things. But parents today see Ozzie and Harriet and Donna Reed and all their ilk as wonderful, ideal parents night after night on the tube. (Even the President and the First Lady, whose lives resemble most working families' more than those of the old sitcoms, admitted that one of their favorite TV shows was reruns of *The Donna Reed Show.*)

17   The power those TV parents still exercise has more to do with the durability of images than it does with today's reality. As Newsweek magazine points out, "The television programs of the fifties and sixties validated a family style during a period in which today's leaders—congressmen, corporate executives, university professors, magazine editors—were growing up or beginning to establish their own families. (The impact of the idealized family was magnified by the very size of the postwar generation.)"[3]

18   It can be somewhat frightening to think that the legislators who are voting on family leave plans, the aides who create policies for presidential candidates, the chairs of university departments who decide what courses should be staffed—all have inside their heads the very same model of the way our families ought to be.

19   Yale historian John Demos points out that "the traditional model reaches back as far as personal memory goes for most of us who currently teach and write and

philosophize."[4] And in a time when parents seem to feel a great deal of change, "that image is comfortingly solid and secure, counterpoint to what we think is threatening to the future." In other words, an unreal past seems so much more soothing than a bumpy present.

20   In the manufacture of guilt, add another potent factor: the nature of the news media. The news media don't hold a mirror up to the world, despite what news executives like to say. The media not only select which facts and images will be churned out as news, but they determine the frame in which those images will be presented. This frame is most often one of conflict, tension, and bad news. It's no wonder everyone assumes that the American family is falling apart. That's all we read or hear about.

21   Of course, what the TV news anchor doesn't tell you is that in the past, "family" issues were rarely part of the news. Domestic violence and child abuse were shameful secrets, rarely written about. Dramatic images of violent crime were less a part of daily life. In Washington, D.C., where Caryl Rivers grew up in the 1950s, some 90 percent of crimes by young men were committed by juveniles who were graduates of one city reform school. But you never saw their victims on the evening news—because there were no minicams to capture the mayhem on video and the kids didn't spray the streets with automatic weapons fire. Americans now consume many hours of television each day—and research shows that people who watch a lot of TV see the world as a much more frightening place than it really is.

22   One of the bad-news frames of which the media is most fond today is the decline of the family. A Nexis search of the past five years reveals 15,164 references in the press to either the breakup or the decline of the American Family, a chorus that is relentless. Do you believe that the decline of the family is absolute fact? Many Americans do. However, most media coverage of the alleged decline of the family does not answer a key question: What position of lofty perfection is the family declining from? There must have been a golden age of family, since the words *decline* and *breakdown* imply that very notion. But when was it? And do we really want to go back there? . . . Many Americans believe that past family life was always—and should always be—like *Leave It to Beaver, Father Knows Best,* and *Ozzie and Harriet.*

23   In fact, the 1950s were a golden age—economically. Never before had Americans enjoyed a period of such affluence. Women reversed a long-standing trend of moving into the workforce, and went home. One would have thought that with women in such a traditional role, social critics would have approved. Mom was by the hearth with her kiddies nestled about her. But what happened? In perhaps no decade were women savaged as thoroughly as they were in the 1950s. Sweet Mom, baking cookies and smiling, was destroying her kids—the boys, anyway. While nostalgic articles in today's media hark back to the happy 1950s, the critics of the time had no such beatific vision.

24   Social critic Philip Wylie, in his best-seller *Generation of Vipers,* coined the term "Momism." Momism, Wylie decreed, had turned modern men into flaccid and weak creatures and was destroying the moral fiber of America.[5] When American soldiers sometimes failed to resist "brainwashing" when they were captured by the

Communist Chinese in Korea, it was said that their overprotective mothers had made them weak and traitorous. Children often got too much Mom and not enough Dad. The memoirs of men who grew up in the 1950s reveal that their fathers were often distant and overly involved in work.

25   It's not surprising that depression was the malady that most affected women in those years. What Betty Friedan termed "the feminine mystique" came smack up against the lengthening life span. At a time when society was telling women that home and children must be their whole lives, technology and medicine were making those lives last longer than ever before in history. Women would outlive, by many years, the childhood of their last-born, and the notion that they could spend all their time in mothering was absurd. The cultural messages and the reality of the modern world were at odds. Kept out of the world of work in the suburban cocoons, physically healthier and longer-lived than their sisters in the past, women were far more prone than men to depression, and in fact the mental health of married women had reached crisis proportions by the end of the 1960s. Statistics rolling in from all across the developed world were so grim that the noted sociologist Jessie Bernard called marriage a "health hazard" for women.[6] . . .

26   One reason we hear so much today about how wonderful the 1950s were is that the voices of male cultural critics are those most often heard. Men and women, it seems, remember that era differently. In many ways, the 1950s were good for men. It was the first era in history in which the average middle-class man could, on his salary alone, support a lifestyle that was available only to the upper classes in the past. The mental health of men was vastly superior to that of women. The daughters of 1950s homemakers rejected en masse a lifestyle that created so much depression and anxiety, and few women today would trade their lives for that of their mothers. But many men today would gladly opt for the financial security and economic opportunities their fathers had.

27   Because the 1950s live on endlessly in rerun land, it is hard for us to accept that the decade was such an atypical time. Stephanie Coontz warns that "the first thing to understand about the Fifties family is that it was a fluke, it was a seven-year aberration in contradiction to a hundred years of other trends."[7] And Arlene Skolnick notes that "far from being the last era of family normality from which current trends are a deviation, it is the family patterns of the 1950s that are deviant."

28   Deviant? Ozzie and Harriet? Indeed they were, from the point of view of history. Theirs was an atypical era, in which trends that had been firmly established since early in the century briefly reversed themselves in the aftermath of World War II. For years, women had been moving into the workforce in increasing numbers. The high point was epitomized by Rosie the Riveter, the symbol of the women who went to work in the factories to produce the tanks and the guns and the planes needed to win the war. After the war, during the brief period of unprecedented affluence when America's economic engine was unchallenged throughout the world, women went home, and the American birthrate suddenly jumped to approach that of India. A huge baby-boom generation grew up in middle-class affluence that no other generation had known. . . .

29   By the late 1970s, the 1950s were only a distant echo. The women's movement unleashed women's untapped brainpower and economic potential, and millions of women flooded into the marketplace. This movement of women into the workforce in the late twentieth century is one of the great mass migrations of history, comparable to the push westward and the move from the farms to the cities. And just as those mass movements changed not only the face of American society but the lives of individual citizens, so too did this new movement rearrange our social geography.

30   Despite the media drumbeat about the decline of the family, despite those thousands of references to its decay in the media, the American family is a thriving institution. We are both more centered on the family and more frantic about its problems than our European counterparts. Arlene Skolnick writes, "Paradoxically, Americans have a stronger sense of both familistic values and family crisis than do other advanced countries. We have higher marriages rates, a more home-centered way of life, and greater public devotion to family values."[8]

31   The notion that we can return to some mythic past for solutions to today's problems is tempting, but it is a will-o'-the-wisp that should not engage our attention. The idea that we can find in Ozzie and Harriet and their lives workable solutions for today's rapidly changing economic and social patterns is a dream. Unfortunately, when we combine the new nostalgia with the old images, it's like taking a trip with only a 1955 road map to guide us. The old landmarks are gone, little backroads have become interstates, and the rules of the road have changed beyond recognition. Absurd as this image is, it is often precisely what we do when we think about the American family. Women who hurry out to work every morning can be trapped into thinking that this isn't what they are supposed to be doing; men with their hands in soapsuds after dinner can remember their fathers sitting and reading the newspaper while mom did the dishes. It's easy to feel resentful.

32   But the new nostalgia is more than harmless basking in the trivia of the past—it is, in fact, a major toxin affecting the health of today's men and women.

33   The "family values" crusade of the right wing, to the degree that it succeeds in invading people's thoughts, will only add to the stress of working couples by insisting on a model from the past that is increasingly impossible to achieve in the present. One newspaper poll showed that the proportion of adults who agreed with the statement "A preschool child is likely to suffer if his or her mother works" went up between 1989 and 1991.

34   As science, that statement is nonsense. There is plenty of evidence that no child is "likely to suffer" if his or her mother goes to work. But those adults agreeing with that statement—who are likely to be working parents—will get a huge dose of unnecessary stress. The family values crusade, to the extent that it glorifies homemakers and demonizes working mothers, will succeed only in making the lives of twenty-first-century Americans harder. The clock will not be turned back to the 1950s; that's as impossible as holding back the tide. If Americans feel guilty because they can't live up to some impossible, vanished ideal, their health will suffer.

35   The era of the two-earner couple may in fact create more closeness in families, not less. As the fast track becomes less available, men and women alike will turn to family for a strong sense of self-esteem and happiness. Divorces may decline as

marriages become once again economic partnerships more like the ones they were before the industrial revolution. Today, of course, marriages will be overlaid with the demands for intimacy and closeness that have become a permanent part of modern marriage, but fewer people will be able to waltz easily out of marriage, as they might have in the days when a thriving economy made good jobs easy to come by. Middle-class couples are marrying later and many women are getting established in a career before having children. This pattern may promote more responsibility and happier marriages than those in the 1950s, when many young people felt they had to get married to have sex and discovered their emotional incompatibility only after they had children.

36   Negotiation and juggling, not the established gender roles of yesterday's marriages, are the features of modern coupledom. Who will stay home when a child is sick? Who will take over what jobs when one partner has to travel for an important meeting? Whose career will take first place? Who has to sacrifice what—and when? Such issues, ones that June and Ward and Ozzie and Harriet never had to confront, are the day-to-day problems that today's partners have to wrestle with.

37   Today's couples are facing the demands of very busy lives at home and at work. If you listen to the media tell their story, they are constantly stressed, the women are disenchanted with trying to have it all, and the men are bitter about having to do work their fathers never had to do. Some of this is true—no lifestyle offers nirvana. On the other hand, today's couples have a better chance at achieving full, rich lives than did the men and women of the sitcom generation. While it may be no picnic to juggle the demands of work and family, research shows that working women are less depressed, less anxious, and more zestful about their lives than are homemakers. Today's man may have the stress of caring for children, but his relationship with his children may be warmer and more satisfying than was his own with his father. Most men who grew up in the 1950s don't tell stories about the warm, available dads we see in the sitcoms. More often, they speak of fathers who were distant, preoccupied, and unable to communicate with their sons on more than a superficial level. Many modern fathers, in fact, set out purposely to design lives that will be the exact opposite of their distant fathers'.

38   In their lifestyle, the men and women in our study are at the opposite end of the spectrum from Ozzie and Harriet. Both are breadwinners; and if they have children, both share the nitty-gritty everyday chores of parenting. They are true partners in supporting and nurturing their children and each other. They represent the new face of the American family, and the world they live in is not very much like the America of the 1950s.

39   Despite the ersatz glow of the new nostalgia, not much would be gained by a trip back in time—even if it were possible. How many women would want to return to the widespread depression and mental health problems of the 1950s? Catherine E. Ross, an Illinois University sociologist, says, "Any plea to return to the 'traditional' family of the 1950s is a plea to return wives and mothers to a psychologically disadvantaged position, in which husbands have much better health than wives."[9] And since research shows that the emotional health of the mother has a strong impact on her children, that's one bit of time travel we don't especially want to take. ◆

Notes

1. Janet Riblett Wilkie, "The Decline in Men's Labor Force Participation and Income and the Changing Structure of Family Economic Support," *Journal of Marriage and the Family* 53 (February 1991).
2. Robert Bly, *Iron John* (New York: Holiday House, 1994).
3. "What Happened to the Family?" *Newsweek* Special Issue (Winter 1990/Spring 1991).
4. "What Happened to the Family?" (Winter 1990/Spring 1991).
5. Philip Wylie, *Generation of Vipers* (New York: Holt, Rinehart & Winston, 1955).
6. Jessie Bernard, *The Future of Marriage* (New York: World-Times, 1972).
7. Stephanie Coontz, *The Way We Never Were: American Families and the Nostalgia Trap* (New York: Basic Books, 1992).
8. Cited in Arlene Skolnick, *Embattled Paradise: The American Family in an Age of Uncertainty* (New York: Basic Books, 1991).
9. Quoted in Betsy A. Lehman, "Parenting Pain—But Also Joy," *Boston Globe* (February 15, 1993).

FREEWRITING ASSIGNMENT

Why do parents in two-earner families feel guilty? What is the cause of their guilt and how is it perpetuated? How founded are their fears?

CRITICAL READING

1. What is "gender-role ideology" as described in paragraph 8? In paragraphs 8–14, how are traditional roles described as harmful to men? How do the authors feel about the current men's movement urging men to "find their warrior within"? How can you tell their opinions on this movement?

2. What are the authors' attitudes toward change—specifically toward changes in family roles and responsibilities? What phrases, images, and metaphors help you identify their attitudes in paragraphs 11–22?

3. The authors describe what the 1950s were really like for families in paragraphs 23–28. What were some of the problems these families had? What were some of the problems people faced fitting into these families? Why have we adopted this family model as the ideal?

4. What improvements do the authors see in today's families? Why do they believe such families are becoming stronger, rather than falling apart? Do you agree with their conclusions? Explain.

5. What are the authors' attitudes toward the media? (See paragraphs 13, 20, and 21.) How important to their argument is the media's role in shaping American perceptions about the state of the family?

CRITICAL WRITING

6. *Exploratory Writing*: If you are a parent, or if you are thinking about marriage and children in your future, do you (or would you) feel the kind of guilt that Barnett and Rivers describe in this article? If so, what do you think would help you feel less guilty—support from family and friends? Different government policies? Media messages? More and better child-care facilities? Other factors? Explore your perspective in a well-considered essay.

7. *Personal Narrative*: Write a personal narrative in which you describe the structure of your family during your childhood. How does your family compare to the family situations described in this article? Did your family strive for the 1950s "ideal"? Explain.

GROUP PROJECTS

8. Working in small groups, discuss and compare the structures of families within your own experiences. Think about the families you grew up in, the families you know well, and the families you may have started. Evaluate the kinds of families you find. These may include two-earner families, traditional families, families with no children, blended families with stepparents and children, children raised by other relatives, and other groupings. Compare notes with your group. How well do your results match the description offered by Barnett and Rivers?

9. Working in small groups, research criticism and scholarly discussion of the four television shows the authors mention in this article, and try to watch a few episodes of each show. How do these shows reflect our expectations for family roles and values? Select four current programs that use a family unit as their central theme. How do the current programs compare to these 1950s prototypes?

Did I Miss Something?
Lowell Putnam

Divorce has become a way of life. Nearly half of all children will see their parents' marriage terminate by the time they turn 18. And although society may shake its collective head at such a statistic, lamenting the loss of the traditional family, not all children of divorce see it as a problem. In this piece, student Lowell Putnam wonders why divorce is still such a taboo topic. Having known no other way of life, children of divorced parents, explains Putnam, simply take such a lifestyle for granted.

Lowell Putnam is a junior majoring in English at Harvard University. When he is not living on campus in Cambridge, he splits his time between his mother's home in New York and his father's home in Massachusetts.

CRITICAL THINKING

In this essay, Lowell Putnam notes that people speak of divorce in hushed tones. If half of all marriages end in divorce, why does society still treat it as a taboo topic?

1   The subject of divorce turns heads in our society. It is responsible for bitten tongues, lowered voices, and an almost pious reverence saved only for life threatening illness or uncontrolled catastrophe. Growing up in a "broken home," I am always shocked to be treated as a victim of some social disease. When a class assignment required that I write an essay concerning my feelings about or my personal experiences with divorce, my first reaction was complete surprise. My second was a hope for large margins. An essay on aspects of my life affected by divorce seems completely superfluous, because I cannot differentiate between the "normal" part of my youth and the supposed angst and confusion that apparently comes with all divorces. The divorce of my parents over fifteen years ago (when I was three years old) has either saturated every last pore of my developmental epidermis to a point where I cannot sense it or has not affected me at all. Eugene Ehrlich's *Highly Selective Dictionary for the Extraordinarily Literate* defines divorce as a "breach"; however, I cannot sense any schism in my life resulting from the event to which other people seem to attribute so much importance. My parents' divorce is a true part of who I am, and the only "breach" that could arrive from my present familial arrangement would be to tear me away from what I consider my normal living conditions.

2   Though there is no doubt in my mind that many unfortunate people have had their lives torn apart by the divorce of their parents, I do not feel any real sense of regret for my situation. In my opinion, the paramount role of a parent is to love his or her child. Providing food, shelter, education, and video games are of course other necessary elements of successful child rearing, but these secondary concerns branch out from the most fundamental ideal of parenting, which is love. A loving parent will be a successful one even if he or she cannot afford to furnish his or her child with the best clothes or the most sophisticated gourmet delicacies. With love as the driving force in a parent's mind, he or she will almost invariably make the correct decision. When my mother and father found that they were no longer in love with each other after nine years of a solid marriage, their love for me forced them to take the precipitous step to separate. The safest environment for me was to be with one happy parent at a time, instead of two miserable ones all the time. The sacrifice that they both made to relinquish control over me for half the year was at least as painful for them as it was for me (and I would bet even more so), but in the end I was not deprived of a parent's love, but merely of one parent's presence for a few short weeks at a time. My father and mother's love for me has not dwindled even slightly over the past fifteen years, and I can hardly imagine a more well-adjusted and contented family.

3   As I reread the first section of this essay, I realize that it is perhaps too optimistic and cheerful regarding my life as a child of divorced parents. In all truthfulness, there have been some decidedly negative ramifications stemming from our family separation. My first memory is actually of a fight between my mother and

father. I vaguely remember standing in the end of the upstairs hallway of our Philadelphia house when I was about three years old, and seeing shadows moving back and forth in the light coming from under the door of my father's study, accompanied by raised voices. It would be naïve of me to say that I have not been at all affected by divorce since it has permeated my most primal and basic memories.

4   However, I am grateful that I can only recall one such incident, instead of having parental conflicts become so quotidian that they leave no mark whatsoever on my mind. Also, I find that having to divide my time equally between both parents leads to alienation from both sides of my family. Invariably, at every holiday occasion, there is one half of my family (either my mother's side or my father's) that has to explain that "Lowell is with his [mother/father] this year," while aunts, cousins, and grandparents collectively arch eyebrows or avert eyes. Again, though, I should not be hasty to lament my distance from loved ones, since there are many families with "normal" marriages where the children never even meet their cousins, let alone get to spend every other Thanksgiving with them. Though divorce has certainly thrown some proverbial monkey wrenches into some proverbial gears, in general my otherwise strong familial ties have overshadowed any minor snafus.

5   Perhaps one of the most important reasons for my absence of "trauma" (for lack of a better word) stemming from my parents' divorce is that I am by no means alone in my trials and tribulations. The foreboding statistic that sixty percent of marriages end in divorce is no myth to me, indeed many of my friends come from similar situations. The argument could be made that "birds of a feather flock together" and that my friends and I form a tight support network for each other, but I strongly doubt that any of us need or look for that kind of buttress. The fact of the matter is that divorce happens a lot in today's society, and as a result our culture has evolved to accommodate these new family arrangements, making the overall conditions more hospitable for me and my broken brothers and shattered sisters.

6   I am well aware that divorce can often lead to issues of abandonment and familial proximity among children of separated parents, but in my case I see very little evidence to support the claim that my parents should have stayed married "for the sake of the child." In many ways, my life is enriched by the division of my time with my father and my time with my mother. I get to live in New York City for half of the year, and in a small suburb of Boston for the other half. I have friends who envy me, since I get "the best of both worlds." I never get double-teamed by parents during arguments, and I cherish my time with each one more since it only lasts half the year.

7   In my opinion, there is no such thing as a perfect life or a "normal" life, and any small blips on our karmic radar screen have to be dealt with appropriately but without any trepidation or self-pity. Do I miss my father when I live with my mother (and vice-versa)? Of course I do. However, I know young boys and girls who have lost parents to illness or accidental injury, so my pitiable position is relative. As I leave for college in a few short months, I can safely say that my childhood has not been at all marred by having two different houses to call home. ◆

FREEWRITING ASSIGNMENT ─────────────

Is divorce detrimental to children or simply a way of life? Explain your point of view.

CRITICAL READING

1. Evaluate Putnam's description of the way people discuss divorce in "lowered voices, and an almost pious reverence saved only for life-threatening illness." What accounts for this attitude? Do you agree with his assessment? Explain.
2. At the end of his first paragraph, Putnam comments that "my parents' divorce is a true part of who I am." Why does Putnam associate his personal identity with his parents' marital status? Discuss how parent relationships influence how children view themselves and their world.
3. Analyze Putnam's definition of what makes a good parent. Do you agree or disagree with this viewpoint?
4. Critics of divorce say it is a selfish act of the parents, who put their wants before their children's needs. Putnam contends that his parents divorced out of love for him, and their divorce was a kind of sacrifice. Evaluate these two perspectives. Can divorce be a positive event for children?
5. Putnam comments that his parents' love for him has not dwindled as a result of their divorce, and that he "can hardly imagine a more well-adjusted and contented family." Why do you think he uses the singular "family"? Explain. How would his meaning change if he had used the plural form "families"?

CRITICAL WRITING

6. *Research and Analysis*: Using newspapers and newsmagazines, research a topic related to children and divorce. You might examine the issue of "deadbeat dads," the psychological aspects of divorce on children, or social perspectives of broken families. Write an essay analyzing the results of your research.
7. Draft a letter to a pair of married friends with children who are considering divorce. Assume that both parents are working and they are considering an amicable divorce in which they intend to continue a close relationship with their children.
8. *Personal Narrative*: Putnam's essay is a personal narrative describing his view of how his parents' divorce influenced his life. Write a personal narrative describing how your parents' marriage or divorce has influenced your own life. Can you relate to anything Putnam says in his essay? Explain.

GROUP PROJECTS

9. As a group, design and administer a poll for your classmates to answer anonymously, asking questions about family status (divorce, remarriage, single parenthood, absentee fathers or mothers, etc.). Then administer the same poll to a group of people a generation or two older than you (perhaps your professors or college staff members). How do the results compare? Are divorced families more "normal" than nondivorced families? Explain. What structures are more common among the different age groups? Discuss your results with the class.

10. In your group, discuss the effects of divorce on children. Further develop Putnam's idea that it is just another way of life. Compare notes with classmates to assemble a complete list. Based on this list, develop your own response about the effects of divorce on children.

What's Love Got to Do with It?

Anjula Razdan

For thousands of years, marriage was traditionally an arrangement based on economic and social considerations. It is only over the last century or so that marriage was the capstone of a loving relationship. But with over half of all marriages ending in divorce, are we going about this the wrong way? Many countries still view marriage as a political, social, and economic arrangement. The Western view of marriage is considered odd by many cultures that consider arranged marriages far more fruitful and intelligent than ones based on something as fickle as love. Are arranged marriages healthier than romantic attraction?

Anjula Razdan is associate editor of *Utne* magazine, in which this article was first published in the May/June 2003 issue.

CRITICAL THINKING   Is love the most important element in a marriage? What other factors are important for a successful marriage?

1 One of the greatest pleasures of my teen years was sitting down with a bag of cinnamon Red Hots and a new LaVyrle Spencer romance, immersing myself in another tale of star-crossed lovers drawn together by the heart's mysterious alchemy. My mother didn't get it. "Why are you reading that?" she would ask, her voice tinged with both amusement and horror. Everything in her background told her that romance was a waste of time.

2 Born and raised in Illinois by parents who emigrated from India 35 years ago, I am the product of an arranged marriage, and yet I grew up under the spell of

Western romantic love—first comes love, then comes marriage—which both puzzled and dismayed my parents. Their relationship was set up over tea and samosas by their grandfathers, and they were already engaged when they went on their first date, a chaperoned trip to the movies. My mom and dad still barely knew each other on their wedding day—and they certainly hadn't fallen in love. Yet both were confident that their shared values, beliefs, and family background would form a strong bond that, over time, would develop into love.

3   "But, what could they possibly know of real love?" I would ask myself petulantly after each standoff with my parents over whether or not I could date in high school (I couldn't) and whether I would allow them to arrange my marriage (I wouldn't). The very idea of an arranged marriage offended my ideas of both love and liberty—to me, the act of choosing whom to love represented the very essence of freedom. To take away that choice seemed like an attack not just on my autonomy as a person, but on democracy itself.

4   And, yet, even in the supposedly liberated West, the notion of choosing your mate is a relatively recent one. Until the 19th century, writes historian E.J. Graff in *What Is Marriage For?: The Strange Social History of Our Most Intimate Institution*, arranged marriages were quite common in Europe as a way of forging alliances, ensuring inheritances, and stitching together the social, political, and religious needs of a community. Love had nothing to do with it.

5   Fast forward a couple hundred years to 21st-century America, and you see a modern, progressive society where people are free to choose their mates, for the most part, based on love instead of social or economic gain. But for many people, a quiet voice from within wonders: Are we really better off? Who hasn't at some point in their life—at the end of an ill-fated relationship or midway through dinner with the third "date-from-hell" this month—longed for a matchmaker to find the right partner? No hassles. No effort. No personal ads or blind dates.

6   The point of the Western romantic ideal is to live "happily ever after," yet nearly half of all marriages in this country end in divorce, and the number of never-married adults grows each year. Boundless choice notwithstanding, what does it mean when the marital success rate is the statistical equivalent of a coin toss?

7   "People don't really know how to choose a long-term partner," offers Dr. Alvin Cooper, the director of the San Jose Marital Services and Sexuality Centre and a staff psychologist at Stanford University. "The major reasons that people find and get involved with somebody else are proximity and physical attraction. And both of these factors are terrible predictors of long-term happiness in a relationship."

8   At the moment we pick a mate, Cooper says, we are often blinded by passion and therefore virtually incapable of making a sound decision.

9   *Psychology Today* editor Robert Epstein agrees. "[It's] like getting drunk and marrying someone in Las Vegas," he quips. A former director of the Cambridge Center for Behavioral Studies, Epstein holds a decidedly unromantic view of courtship and love. Indeed, he argues it is our myths of "love at first sight" and "a knight in a shining Porsche" that get so many of us into trouble. When the heat of passion wears off—and it always does, he says—you can be left with virtually nothing "except lawyer's bills."

10   Epstein points out that many arranged marriages result in an enduring love because they promote compatibility and rational deliberation ahead of passionate impulse. Epstein himself is undertaking a bold step to prove his theory that love can be learned. He wrote an editorial in *Psychology Today* last year seeking women to participate in the experiment with him. He proposed to choose one of the "applicants," and together they would attempt to fall in love—consciously and deliberately. After receiving more than 1,000 responses, none of which seemed right, Epstein yielded just a little to impulse, asking Gabriela, an intriguing Venezuelan woman he met on a plane, to join him in the project. After an understandable bout of cold feet, she eventually agreed.

11   In a "love contract" the two signed on Valentine's Day this year to seal the deal, Epstein stipulates that he and Gabriela must undergo intensive counseling to learn how to communicate effectively and participate in a variety of exercises designed to foster mutual love. To help oversee and guide the project, Epstein has even formed an advisory board made up of high-profile relationship experts, most notably Dr. John Gray, who wrote the best-selling *Men Are From Mars, Women Are From Venus*. If the experiment pans out, the two will have learned to love each other within a year's time.

12   It may strike some as anathema to be so premeditated about the process of falling in love, but to hear Epstein tell it, most unions fail exactly because they aren't intentional enough; they're based on a roll of the dice and a determination to stake everything on love. What this means, Epstein says, is that most people lack basic relationship skills, and, as a result, most relationships lack emotional and psychological intimacy.

13   A divorced father of four, Epstein himself married for passion—"just like I was told to do by the fairy tales and by the movies"—but eventually came to regret it. "I had the experience that so many people have now," he says, "which is basically looking at your partner and going, 'Who are you?'" Although Epstein acknowledges the non-Western tradition of arranged marriage is a complex, somewhat flawed institution, he thinks we can "distill key elements of [it] to help us learn how to create a new, more stable institution in the West."

14   Judging from the phenomenon of reality-TV shows like *Married By America* and *Meet My Folks* and the recent increase in the number of professional matchmakers, the idea of arranging marriages (even if in nontraditional ways) seems to be taking hold in this country—perhaps nowhere more powerfully than in cyberspace. Online dating services attracted some 20 million people last year (roughly one-fifth of all singles—and growing), who used sites like Match.com and Yahoo Personals to hook up with potentially compatible partners. Web sites' search engines play the role of patriarchal grandfathers, searching for good matches based on any number of criteria that you select.

15   Cooper, the Stanford psychologist and author of *Sex and the Internet: A Guidebook for Clinicians*, and an expert in the field of online sexuality, says that because online interaction tends to downplay proximity, physical attraction, and face-to-face interaction, people are more likely to take risks and disclose significant things about themselves. The result is that they attain a higher level of psychological

and emotional intimacy than if they dated right away or hopped in the sack. Indeed, online dating represents a return to what University of Chicago Humanities Professor Amy Kass calls the "distanced nearness" of old-style courtship, an intimate and protected (cyber)space that encourages self-revelation while maintaining personal boundaries.

16   And whether looking for a fellow scientist, someone else who's HIV-positive, or a B-movie film buff, an online dater has a much higher likelihood of finding "the one" due to the computer's capacity to sort through thousands of potential mates. "That's what computers are all about—efficiency and sorting," says Cooper, who believes that online dating has the potential to lower the nation's 50 percent divorce rate. There is no magic or "chemistry" involved in love, Cooper insists. "It's specific, operationalizable factors."

17   Love's mystery solved by "operationalizable factors"! Why does that sound a little less than inspiring? Sure, for many people the Internet can efficiently facilitate love and help to nudge fate along. But, for the diehard romantic who trusts in surprise, coincidence, and fate, the cyber-solution to love lacks heart. "To the romantic," observes English writer Blake Morrison in *The Guardian*, "every marriage is an arranged marriage—arranged by fate, that is, which gives us no choice."

18   More than a century ago, Emily Dickinson mocked those who would dissect birds to find the mechanics of song:

Split the Lark – and you'll find the Music –
Bulb after Bulb, in Silver rolled –
Scantily dealt to the Summer Morning
Saved for your Ear when Lutes be old.

Loose the Flood – you shall find it patent –
Gush after Gush, reserved for you –
Scarlet Experiment! Skeptic Thomas!
Now, do you doubt that your Bird was true?

19   In other words, writes Deborah Blum in her book, *Sex on the Brain*, "kill the bird and [you] silence the melody." For some, nurturing the ideal of romantic love may be more important than the goal of love itself. Making a more conscious choice in mating may help partners handle the complex personal ties and obligations of marriage; but romantic love, infused as it is with myth and projection and doomed passion, is a way to live outside of life's obligations, outside of time itself—if only for a brief, bright moment. Choosing love by rational means might not be worth it for those souls who'd rather roll the dice and risk the possibility of ending up with nothing but tragic nobility and the bittersweet tang of regret.

20   In the end, who really wants to examine love too closely? I'd rather curl up with a LaVyrle Spencer novel or dream up the French movie version of my life than live in a world where the mechanics of love—and its giddy, mysterious buzz—are laid bare. After all, to actually unravel love's mystery is, perhaps, to miss the point of it all. ◆

In this essay, Razdan notes that she wouldn't let her parents arrange a marriage for her because to take away that choice "seemed like an attack not just on my autonomy . . . but on democracy itself." Expand on this idea. Is the right to choose one's mate a democratic ideal? Explain.

CRITICAL READING

1. Why is Razdan's mother both amused and horrified at her daughter's delight in romance novels? How does her concern mirror the difference between their generations and social experience?
2. Despite the fact that Razdan's parents no longer live in India, they clearly still want their daughter to follow in their marital footsteps. Furthermore, their arranged marriage seems to be working out well. The idea of arranged marriages seems to be outrageous to most North Americans. In your opinion, could arranged marriages ever have a place in the North American social system? Why or why not?
3. Robert Epstein, editor of *Psychology Today*, argues that marrying for love alone is "like getting drunk and marrying someone in Las Vegas." Does he have a point? Consider the reasons you have ended romantic relationships. Would they have been more successful if they had been based on things other than love first?
4. Razdan makes several references to reality programs designed to help people make successful matches. Do these programs serve as modern "matchmakers"? Why or why not?
5. How is the Internet becoming a major conduit for matchmaking? Explain.
6. How does the author feel about romantic love? Identify passages from the essay that reveal her viewpoint.
7. What is the meaning of the Dickinson poem? How does it connect to the point Razdan is trying to make?

CRITICAL WRITING

8. Arranged marriages differ from culture to culture. Some involve a matchmaker, who asks the participants to describe themselves and what they are looking for in a mate (much like a Western dating service). Prepare an information package about yourself, to give to a matchmaker. What does your description tell you about yourself? About what you hope for in a partner? Based on your description, answer the question Razdan raises in her title, "What's Love Got to Do with It?"
9. *Research and Analysis*: Razdan states that her parents' marriage was arranged by their grandfathers. Research arranged marriages online. Why

are they promoted and encouraged? Are they longer lasting? Happier? Prepare a report based on your research.

GROUP PROJECT

10. Razdan notes that in the West, marriage is driven by love, often with unsuccessful long-term results. As a group, discuss whether you feel arranged marriages could work in the United States. Outline your reasons why you feel they could or could not work. Be sure to consider the pros and cons of the issue.

VIEWPOINTS

▶ **A Blow to Canada's Families**
David Frum

▶ **Under the Stars Without Fear**
Laurier LaPierre

▶ **Dodging the Altar**
Matthew Hays

It is a debate that rarely stays on a theoretical level. Those who seek to prevent the legalization of same-sex marriage risk appearing homophobic, reactionary, intolerant, and desirous of imposing fundamentalist religious values on a society whose laws and courts are meant to be secular. Those who support same-sex marriage can be viewed with equal negativity as shrill, reckless liberals, special-interest groups, and social engineers who'd like to tinker with one of the oldest and most revered institutions in our culture. Both sides frequently fall into the traps of identity politics and ad hominem arguments.

In "A Blow to Canada's Families," David Frum asks if the entire debate has been merely "a destructive diversion." Same-sex marriage, in Frum's view, is yet another in the proliferation of relationship options increasingly available to Canadians, options that he believes undermine the social directive to sustain the traditional model of marriage—which, he implies, will undermine the traditional structure and stability of society.

Laurier LaPierre's "Under the Stars, Without Fear" takes a historical look at both traditional marriage and same-sex unions. He shows that heterosexual marriage, far from being the stable, enduring institution we tend to think of it as, has in fact undergone significant evolution. Same-sex unions, on the other hand, are not a new and untried notion, as their centuries of documented existence shows. LaPierre also indicts "the hegemony of a fragile orthodoxy" for its historical persecution of gays, and invokes the Charter of Rights and Freedoms in his discussion of discrimination against sexual minorities.

In "Dodging the Altar," Matthew Hays claims that the right to marry is largely symbolic for the gay community, and that far fewer gay couples than expected have actually taken this step. One reason for this may be that marriage as an institution was created for heterosexual

relationships in a heterosexual society, while same-sex relationships are not always structured in the same way. Hays alludes to the Stonewall Riots of 1969, a watershed in gay history that galvanized the "gay liberation" movement. Should gay men and women therefore
trade the oppression and erasure of a pre-Stonewall society for the new pressure to inhabit
a social model that was not designed for them?

David Frum is a political commentator and author of several books, including *The
Right Man: the Surprise Presidency of George W. Bush* (2003) and *How We Got Here*
(1999), a history of the 1970s. His article was originally published in the *National Post* on
December 14, 2004. Laurier LaPierre is an Officer of the Order of Canada, a retired senator, a journalist and broadcaster, and author. He is a leading authority on Canadian history
and public affairs. His speech was printed in *Xtra!* on April 4, 2002. Matthew Hays is associate editor of *The Montreal Mirror* and has written for *The New York Times*. "Dodging the
Altar" appeared in *The Advocate* in 2004.

**CRITICAL
THINKING**   In your opinion, should gay men and women be permitted to legally marry?
Explain your perspective with a reasonable argument.

A Blow to Canada's Families
David Frum

1   'We've had gay and lesbian marriages in six provinces for almost a year and society
hasn't collapsed." So said NDP MP Bill Siksay in the House of Commons last week.
You have to wonder: Isn't that setting the policy bar a little low? Normally, we
expect a new government idea to pass a higher threshold than, "It didn't cause an
utter catastrophe during its first few months in operation."

2   Same-sex marriage has now been grafted into the Canadian constitution; very
shortly it will be legislated into Canadian law. But before Canadians accept Mr.
Siksay's "What, me worry?" point of view, they might want to wait for the answers
to some urgent questions:

3   • **Did homosexuals ever really want to marry in the first place?**

4   There are about 24 million Canadians between the ages of 18 and 65. It's a reasonable guess that about 750,000 of them are gay.

5   In June and July 2003, the two largest English-speaking provinces, Ontario and
British Columbia, began issuing marriage licences to same-sex couples. Within the
first six months, some 300 Canadian same-sex couples had been married in B.C.
Within the first year, about 4,000 Canadian couples had been married in Ontario.

6   Since then, the number of same-sex marriages seems to have dropped off.
National statistics are hard to come by, but it's a good guess that 18 months after
same-sex marriage arrived in Canada, some 98% of adult Canadian gays have chosen to ignore their new legal right.

7 • **Will same-sex marriage damage the institution of marriage generally?**

8 Forty years ago, Canadian men and women faced one choice: Get married or stay single. Unsurprisingly, most of them chose to get married. Today, Canadians can choose from a proliferating menu of lifestyle options. Next year, there will be one more: a new form of marriage recognized by the government but condemned by every major religion in Canada.

9 As alternatives to traditional marriage multiply, the proportion of Canadians choosing marriage has declined. The Vanier Institute of the Family reports that 65% of Canadians could expect to be married by age 50 in 1981. Today, only 51% of women and 48% of men can expect as much. (Why the gap? Men are more likely to remarry after a divorce than women—so some of the male 48% are marrying twice.)

10 It is not fashionable to say so, but this decline presents a very serious social problem. Single people and people in nontraditional relationships are more likely to be poor, to get sick, and to need help from the government than married people. Cohabiting women are more likely to be victims of domestic violence than married women; single men are more likely to abuse drugs and alcohol than married men.

11 If Mr. Siksay is right, the move to a redefinition of marriage should not make these problems significantly worse. Well—we'll see, won't we?

12 • **Will the weakening of marriage harm Canadian children—and Canadian society?**

13 When marriage declines, children lose. Children who grow up with their biological mother and biological father are dramatically—that is by margins from 50% to 300%—less likely to break the law, drop out of school, get pregnant in their teens and end up as single parents themselves than children raised by single parents or in stepfamilies. Today, after three decades of anti-family policy, a Canadian child's odds of reaching age 18 in the same home as his or her father and mother are less than 50-50.

14 As if recognizing that Canada is becoming an inhospitable place for children, Canadian women are giving birth to fewer and fewer of them. Historically, Canadian and American birthrates have tracked each other pretty closely. And even today, Canadian and American women express a desire for about the same number of children: an average of 2.2, according to surveys. Yet while the U.S. fertility rate has been rising, to almost 2.1, Canada's has plunged to 1.5—not nearly enough to replace the existing population.

15 Canada has spent the past decade reinventing marriage in ways that do not address any of its family problems—and will very likely aggravate them. The harm done to Canadian family policy might just possibly have been justifiable if it were necessary to protect some endangered minority. But it turns out that the same-sex marriage was of only very theoretical concern to gay Canadians: Canada will soon have same-sex marriage, but it is likely to see very few same-sex marriages.

16 Is it too early to conclude that this whole debate has been a very destructive diversion? Since 1980, Canada has made policy choices that have brought about a plunging birthrate, deteriorating home conditions for children and instability in domestic partnerships among adults, with all the attendant problems of poverty,

illness, dependency and violence. Open discussion of these choices is made impossible by a climate of denial.

17   Mr. Siksay is right to say that Canadian society has not collapsed, not yet anyway. But the ability of Canada's governing elite to think rationally and talk honestly about priorities sure has. ◆

Under the Stars without Fear
Laurier LaPierre

1   Honourable senators, first, I must admit to my own sexual orientation. I am a gay man, living in harmony—harmony conditioned by human nature—with a kind and gentle man and whose silver ring I wear with comfort on the ring finger of my right hand.

2   Having admitted that, I must also tell you that my opposition to this bill has nothing to do with my sexual happiness, nor do I want to be married to my ring bearer, nor do I need my union with him to be recognized by the government and society, for I need only the recognition of my children and grandchildren, my immediate and extended family and my friends. I have that. Why then do I oppose this bill? I oppose it, first of all, because it is not necessary. It is a bill, according to its framer and sponsor, that makes evident what has been the rule of law since at least the beginning of Confederation and confirmed ever since on numerous occasions. I also oppose it because it defies reality.

3   Here is what the Law Commission of Canada stated in its December 2001 report: It appears that a significant minority of Canadian households consists of same-sex couples.

4   So we have these unions. They are part and parcel of the fabric of our national life. The reality is that gay people form unions and perform the responsibilities imposed by that union just like married couples do and just like common-law couples do. That is the reality.

5   Above all, I oppose [the bill] because it is discriminatory.

6   By arguing that marriage as a civil right and conferring a civil status is the exclusive right and status of heterosexuals denies that right and status to those who are homosexuals. Thus, it is an affront to the Charter of Rights and Freedoms. We are told that marriage has been ordained since time immemorial for the union of a man and a woman. Well, it is not so. It became so. However, it is well to remember or to know that antiquity was full of same-union marriages; also, it was so in the early times of Christianity and Orthodoxy. This practice of same-sex union endured for centuries.

7   Honourable senators, if one looks at the historical evidence, one cannot escape the fact that marriage became a same-couple extravaganza, blessed by all sorts of deities, in order to assure the legitimacy of the children, the safe passage of the inheritance and the status of royals, feudal lords and families. They feared that

illegitimacy, the fruits of which they came to enjoy through adultery, would cause havoc with the social status of the family and the tribal order.

8   The church went along with it, no doubt because men of the cloth have always feared the power of women, particularly in sexual matters. Marriage made a woman the property of her husband and subject to him, thus controlling her to the largest possible degree. They forced her to hide her femininity under yards of cloth and contrived with the men of her family and with her husband to keep her ignorant and chained to the stove—a state that has been the fate of women in every conceivable church and religion we believe in and which have all been established by men wearing skirts.

9   In the long and cruel campaign against homosexuals of either sex, but particularly gay men, many have been discriminated against in the name of the gods and their lives ruined to maintain the hegemony of a fragile orthodoxy. They died in the dungeons of the princes of the churches and of the states or burned at the stake by order of the churches or stoned in the public square of Imams. They died as well in the concentration camps of the Nazis. They died abandoned; they were denied comfort; they were reviled in the pulpits during the first days of AIDS, a moment in our history that I know much about; and they still die in the dark streets and parks of our cities.

10   Moreover, while they lived and live, they were and are discriminated against— an abuse of human rights too often blessed by the silence or the conspiracy of the churches.

11   But we have survived. Even though our denials of rights and status and recognition continue, the gay women and men of today living in my country are better off than I was in my youth, in my early manhood, in my middle age and even 10 years ago at the beginning of my old age.

12   Why am I telling honourable senators all this? It has nothing to do with bitterness for the atrocities of the past. I am telling you all of this because I do not want any more exclusion for any citizen of my beloved country. Exclusion always leads to betrayal and persecution. This is the lesson of history. ◆

Dodging the Altar
Matthew Hays

1   Gay men and lesbians aren't exactly rushing to marry in Canada. Why marriage equality isn't such a big deal up north.

2   In June 2003 same-sex marriages were legalized in the Canadian province of Ontario. Other provinces quickly followed suit: British Columbia in August and Quebec in March. Yet for all the fuss that's been made over Canada's pioneering foray into gay matrimony, an *Advocate* analysis shows that far fewer couples are taking the plunge than expected.

3   In fact, twice as many gay and lesbian couples were married in San Francisco during the three-day Valentine's Day weekend (2,340) than were married in an entire nine-month period in Toronto from June to February (1,143). In British Columbia—which includes Vancouver, with about 546,000 residents—a mere 214 same-sex marriages occurred in August. That number nose-dived to 85 in November and 70 in December.

4   Canada's same-sex wedding party appears to have fizzled. "I sense that there are simply a lot of other priorities for Canadian gays and lesbians," says Jude Tate, coordinator of the office for queer issues at the University of Toronto. "Many just don't see same-sex marriage as something to chase after. In Canada, over the past 20 years we've had more rights for gays and lesbians than Americans have. That makes it less of a burning issue here.

5   "It's an accomplishment, the legalization of same-sex marriage. But I think the desire for it in the community simply doesn't match that accomplishment."

6   Canadian residents enjoy universal health care coverage, so marriage doesn't necessarily mean access to better care. And in nine Canadian provinces, after one year of living together, a couple—straight or same-sex—are considered common-law spouses. This allows spouses to claim pension benefits and be recognized in insurance claims. In Quebec such recognition takes hold after three years of living together. In 2000, Canada passed a far-reaching law that granted same-sex common-law relationships the same legal footing as straight unions.

7   "We need to be careful what we wish for," says Montreal writer Eleanor Brown, who is known for her antimarriage op-eds that have appeared in some of Canada's largest newspapers. "Marriage and divorce rules are created with a very specific kind of relationship in mind, the traditional hetero-support paradigm, but our relationships aren't often structured like that."

8   Canada's influential gay press has also refused to endorse same-sex marriage. Toronto's *Xtra* and sister magazines in Vancouver and Ottawa have covered same-sex marriage with indifference or hostility. Ken Popert, executive director of the Pink Triangle Press (publisher of the *Xtra* papers), says that figuring out how to cover the marriage issue was a huge problem for his editorial team. "We're still fighting about it now," he says, adding that he has "no interest" in same-sex marriage himself despite being in a relationship with another man for decades. "I would argue that we should be fighting to have the state out of our rights entirely. I don't think the government should have any place in regulating relations between adults, straight or gay."

9   Popert adds, "I'm completely unconvinced that once we've won the right to marry, that means our struggle for freedom is over."

10   Toronto's *Fab*, a competitor to *Xtra*, has also raised questions about same-sex marriage's effect on gay culture. In a Valentine's Day story, one writer ruminated on being single in a brave new gay world in which marriage seems to be the only option: "Is there room for me in a post-Stonewall era where the push to partner with a man has replaced the pressure to marry a woman?"

11   Even in the Canadian mainstream press, the issue seemed to be of greater concern to U.S. residents than Canadians. When the national weekly news affairs magazine

Maclean's (the Canadian equivalent of *Time* or *Newsweek*) put the issue of same-sex marriage on its March 29 cover, the gay couple featured were not Canadians but two gay men from Nebraska who'd crossed the border to wed on the Canadian side of Niagara Falls.

12   Even gay rights organizations display an antimarriage bent. "The state has no right in the marriages of the nation," reads a statement by the Coalition for Lesbian and Gay Rights in Ontario. "Marriage should be a purely religious ceremony with no legal implications." Tom Warner, a spokesman for the group, says he does not want to see married couples given more rights than single people, gay or straight. "This issue doesn't inspire a lot of interest among gays and lesbians, because they recognize that their relationships aren't necessarily in that model," he says. "We're also deeply concerned about other issues, like homophobia in schools or censorship."

13   However, Canadian same-sex marriage activists—who've spent millions of their own dollars on lengthy court battles—say the nuptial naysayers are wrong. "No one is advocating that all gays and lesbians get married," says Kevin Bourassa, who along with husband Joe Varnell authored the book *Just Married: Gay Marriage and the Expansion of Human Rights.* They are among the most prominent same-sex marriage activists in Canada.

14   Most of the support for gay marriage has come from mainstream media. *The Globe and Mail* of Toronto, Canada's oldest newspaper, has carried editorials in favor of the recognition of same-sex marriages. "When we go to rural areas in Canada we're met with a groundswell of support," Bourassa says. "Not everyone lives in downtown Toronto, Montreal, or Vancouver, where it's inevitably going to be easier to be out and gay. I would argue this is a case of bigotry within our community. Perhaps we need a George W. Bush here in Canada, and then people would realize how easily our rights could be taken away." ◆

FREEWRITING ASSIGNMENT

What are the "virtues" of marriage? Why do people marry? What do they hope to gain by marriage? How might those hopes and expectations be different for a same-sex couple?

CRITICAL READING

1. "Under the Stars without Fear" is taken from a speech addressed to the Canadian Senate. How does the fact that it is a speech make it rhetorically different from an article or an essay?

2. LaPierre closes his speech with the line, "This is the lesson of history." Consider his use of *history*. Is it an effective device in this speech?

3. LaPierre opens his speech by declaring, "I am a gay man," but he then claims that his opposition to the bill is not connected to his sexual orientation. How do his comments about his own sexual orientation affect your impression of his argument? How effective would his speech be if he were not gay?

4. How does LaPierre use irony to deliver his message? How does his tone influence the way you accept (or do not accept) his points? Explain by referring to specific examples from the text.

5. Who is the audience for Frum's essay? What tells you this? What is he hoping to achieve by addressing this audience?

6. Examine Frum's Web site in detail at **www.davidfrum.com/**. What does the Web site tell you about him? What is his position on other issues?

7. According to Laurier LaPierre, why should gay and lesbian couples be allowed to marry? How do you think that David Frum would respond to his argument?

8. Both Frum and Hays have serious reservations about the prospect of same-sex marriage, though they have clearly arrived at this agreement through very different paths. Review their articles. Are there other cases of "accidental" agreement in their positions?

9. LaPierre and Hays are both gay writers, yet they appear to have no desire to avail themselves of the opportunity to marry a same-sex partner. How does this affect the impact of their respective arguments?

CRITICAL WRITING

10. *Persuasive Writing:* Write a letter to a minister, rabbi, or other religious leader. Explain why you think he or she should agree to perform a marriage ceremony celebrating the commitment of two of your best friends—a gay couple. Assume that this leader has not given much thought to gay marriage. Alternatively, you may write a letter arguing against such a marriage. Assume that you care about your friends and know that your opinions can cause them pain, but that you still must advise against such a union.

11. *Exploratory Writing:* It has been suggested that as an alternative to marriage, same-sex couples should be offered the option of a civil union, an arrangement that would entail the same legal rights and obligations afforded a married couple, and that would reserve the term marriage exclusively for opposite-sex couples. Do you consider this a reasonable compromise? Why or why not?

12. *Exploratory Writing:* Gay couples have been more prominent in the media over the past few years. What images of gay relationships has television presented to its viewers? Are they depicted in "the traditional hetero-support paradigm" that Eleanor Brown mentions in "Dodging the Altar," or are they depicted as something entirely different? Write an essay in which you explore the portrayal of gay life in the media, and how this portrayal may or may not influence public opinion on the issue of gay marriage.

GROUP PROJECTS

13. Working as a team using Internet resources, see what information you can find about the issue of same-sex marriage in Canada. Examine the Canadian same-sex marriage site at **www.samesexmarriage.ca/** for one view and The Canada Family Coalition at **www.familyaction.org/** for another view. Assemble a list of resources and compare it with that of other groups. Then select a narrower topic for each group to research online. Prepare a brief description of what Internet users might find at each site. What cultural and social conclusions about gay marriage can you make based on your research?

14. Should marriage be a public or a political institution? Alternatively, should it be a religious, private, and moral institution? Or should it have features of both? List the qualities that a marriage draws from each of these realms. After you have compiled your list, discuss with your group what marriage should be and for whom.

15. Design a survey that you will administer anonymously to other members of your class or students in the student union asking for their opinions on gay marriage. Design your survey to allow people to formulate opinions and express their views while incorporating some of the ideas presented in this Viewpoints section. Collect the surveys and discuss the results. How do the responses connect to the arguments presented in this section? Explain.

RESEARCH ISSUE # Cohabiting Is *Not* the Same as Commitment

Karen S. Peterson

Are couples who live together less likely to marry? Some experts believe that rather than serving as a test run for marriage, cohabitation deters many men from tying the knot. This article, by reporter Karen S. Peterson, appeared in the July 8, 2002, edition of *USA Today*.

1   Women living unmarried with guys and expecting a lasting, committed marriage down the line had better review their options [says] researcher Scott Stanley. His research finds that men who cohabit with the women they eventually marry are less committed to the union than men who never lived with their spouses ahead of time. Stanley presented his findings at a 2002 conference sponsored by the Coalition for Marriage, Family and Couples Education in Washington, D.C.

2   But rather than settle anything for the more than 5 million unmarried American couples who live together, the research will likely spark the ongoing dispute over living together vs. marriage, and true commitment vs. a spirit of "maybe I do," in

Stanley's words. And it will also raise fresh questions about who's more of a slacker in the commitment department: men or women.

3   Stanley, co-director of the Center for Marital and Family Studies at the University of Denver, says the evidence from his research is so strong that cohabiting women "should be very careful about how aligned they are with a particular man if he does not show any strong sense of marriage and a future together."

4   Men who either drift into marriage "through inertia" following a cohabiting arrangement or who are "dragged down the aisle" by women who finally put their feet down are not good marriage risks, he says.

5   Many researchers agree with Stanley: It is young men, not women, who move toward marriage with the speed of a wounded sloth. Their findings will reinforce stereotypes and infuriate many of both sexes who want to look before they leap. But still it is men, these researchers say, who drag their feet—big time.

Testing the Relationship

6   Stanley says his results do not mean there are not "a lot of super men out there," who have cohabited and are dedicated to their women both before and after heading down the aisle. But his findings do hold up on average, he says, and are reinforced by another of his current research projects.

7   The cohabiting women in Stanley's small but pioneering study did not show differences in commitment to their unions before or after marriage. He speculates that men who want "to test marriage out first" are less committed to the institution in general and their partners specifically than men who move directly to marriage without cohabiting. And he speculates that women are still socialized to put relationships first and tend to be as committed to both the union and the partner, after marriage as they were before it.

8   His findings will interest those who monitor marriage trends. Setting up shop together—before marriage or without any plans to marry—has become commonplace. Between 50% and 60% of new marriages now involve couples who have lived together first.

9   Many who live together feel it is a vaccination against divorce. "I've been dating the same girl for three years, and it just seemed the natural progression for our relationship, the next step to take," says Scott Tolchinsky, 23, of Bethesda, Md., who has just set up housekeeping with his girlfriend. "You see so many get divorced that you want to try things out."

10   Divorce is "just a huge issue for my generation," says Rosanne Garfield, 28, of Arlington, Va. "My family has not had good success with marriage. I was living with my boyfriend for the last year. I told him to make a decision (about marriage), and that ended it. But it would never cross my mind not to live together with someone before marrying him." Ironically, the divorce rate among those who once lived together is higher than among those who have not. Experts say that is often because those who choose to cohabit are not great believers in marriage in the first place.

11   Stanley sees other factors at play. In his study on live-ins who married, less religious men were particularly apt to be less committed. It may be that higher divorce

rates among onetime cohabitors are a result of "the presence of males who are less dedicated, less religious and more negative" than males who didn't cohabit, he says.

12 The co-author of *Fighting for Your Marriage*, Stanley helped develop a communication skills course for couples based on 20 years of the center's research. Much of its work is funded by the National Institute of Mental Health. His current study is based on a sub-sample of 207 men and women married 10 years or less and culled from ongoing marital research on 950 adults nationwide. Standard assessments of commitment were employed during telephone interviews.

13 Stanley says his results dovetail with those from a controversial Rutgers University study released June 25. That research by sociologist David Popenoe has become a hot topic. Popenoe will elaborate further on his findings at the "Smart Marriages" conference.

14 The Rutgers study found that young men are reluctant to marry because just living with a woman is easier. They fear the cost of a divorce. They are not excited about sharing the everyday chores of parenting with their future wives. And they'd like to be financially stable first.

15 Both he and Popenoe agree, Stanley says, that "it is a bigger switch for men than women to go from being non-married to married. And men are more reluctant to throw that switch."

16 Women, Stanley says, are more willing to sacrifice for others, more willing to undergo the burdens that babies bring. And women's fertile years are limited. They hear their biological clocks ticking while men hear only the sounds of silence.

Seekers of Commitment

17 Many experts agree men are the foot-draggers. Atlanta psychiatrist Frank Pittman, author of *Grow Up!*, says men still have not been raised to be good candidates for today's egalitarian marriages. "Marriage is by its nature, total, permanent and equal. In that way it is different from any other relationship or activity." Men are still reluctant to move toward such a binding relationship, he says.

18 But the Rutgers study is causing a fuss elsewhere. The Alternatives to Marriage Project (AtMP) debunks the concept that men would rather have a live-in lover than a wife. Marshall Miller and Dorian Solot, live-ins themselves and co-founders of the non-profit group supporting non-marrieds, say that "men actually tend to be more interested in marriage than women." Among the polls and surveys they cite:

- A 1996 Gallup poll found 39% of unmarried men would prefer to be married; 29% of unmarried women would.
- A government-funded survey of high-schoolers, from 1996–2000, found 38% of senior boys believe marriage leads to a fuller and happier life; 29% of senior girls said so.
- A 1994 government-funded survey found 59% of unmarried men ages 18–35 want to get married; 48% of women agreed.

19 Men are committed to women, Miller says. "Their only hesitation is whether to commit to the institution of marriage."

20   Steve Penner of Brighton, Mass., called *USA Today* to object to the Rutgers survey. Over the last 20 years, he says, he has talked to more than 21,000 singles as head of LunchDates, an upscale dating service in the Boston area. Both the men and women of today seek commitment, he says. "I really think we are picking on men. Men and women are equally looking for relationships."

21   Whether or not anyone wants to commit depends on age, financial situation and life experiences, not gender, many others say. "People are always saying all men are dogs," Tolchinsky says. "But there are lots of nice men out there who are looking to settle down. Maybe women are looking in the wrong places."

Days of Delayed Unions

22   Both sexes are delaying marriage today for financial reasons, Penner says. "They both want to buy a house first. They both want to pursue a career. These are the children of the baby boom generation, and the men and women are very similar." Indeed, both sexes are tending to marry later. The median age for first marriage for men is now about 27; for women, it is 25.

23   Her generation is waiting, says Garfield. "We have had experiences with functional and dysfunctional families all around us." A lasting commitment really depends on "trial and error," she says. And living together first is a good option.

24   Maybe, says researcher Scott Stanley. But still, there are his findings on men who cohabit first vs. those who don't, the men who live with a woman but 10 years after marriage don't feel a solid commitment to them. He says to women: "If you want someone to marry, choose someone who won't live with you."

CRITICAL THINKING

1. Stanley's study reveals that men and women who live together before marriage are in fact less likely to have successful marriages in the future. What reasons does he attribute to this statistic? Can you think of any other reasons that might bear on the outcome of marriages between people who have lived together first? Explain.

2. What reasons do people give for living together before marriage? What cultural factors influence this decision? Explain.

RESEARCH PROJECTS

3. Visit the Coalition for Marriage, Family, and Couples Education Web site at **www.smartmarriages.com/articles.html** and review some of the statistical and research information posted there. Pick a topic related to marriage and divorce on the coalition's Web site that interests you and research it using the information on the Web site and additional web resources. Write a short research report on your topic, connecting it to the subject of trends in marriage in the twenty-first century.

4. Stanley's study indicates that men are less likely to marry the women they cohabitate with, and when they do marry, more likely to later divorce. Prepare a survey and interview at least 20 men and 20 women between the ages of 18 to 24 for their opinions about cohabitation versus marriage. Would they live together with someone before marrying them? Would they live together regardless of future marriage plans? Do they view cohabitation as the natural precursor to marriage? Should the possibility of a future marriage even be a factor when deciding to live together? Compare your data to Stanley's and write an essay based on your research. Like Stanley, try to draw some conclusions from your data, and what it might mean for the future of marriage for your generation.

Additional essay topics, writing assignments, research guidelines, and readings for this chapter can be found online at **www.pearsoned.ca/goshgarian**.

Humans Inc.   6

Our Genetic Future

That discussion every parent dreads—the talk about the birds and the bees—may get even harder for parents. Reproductive technology has moved beyond test-tube babies into what seems to many people the realm of science fiction. It is now possible for us to clone animals and, presumably, ourselves. With the mapping of the human genome, there is the selective possibility of creating "perfect" children. In light of these dramatic scientific breakthroughs, parents might need more than a biology textbook to answer Junior's question, "Where did I come from?"

In June 2000, scientists announced that they had completed a working draft of the human genome. Now that they had isolated and identified every gene within the 23 pairs of human chromosomes, they could begin research on the connection between these genes and human disease.

The first piece, "Baby, It's You and You and You," by Nancy Gibbs, presents an overview of human cloning and genetic engineering. The mapping of the human genome means we are opening the door to understanding how these genes work, and will soon be able to manipulate DNA to achieve certain predictable outcomes. Such genetic manipulation may also mean cloning the first human could be only months away, if it hasn't already happened since this book entered production. Gibbs warns that the ethical issues around abortion and euthanasia will seem "tame" compared to the issues genetic manipulation raises.

Bill McKibben, in "Enough," doesn't agree that genetic manipulation will make humans better. Sure, they may be smarter, stronger, and live longer than their creators, but what happens to the people who aren't genetically modified? Genetic manipulation could create a power shift in which the regular guys simply can't compete. This idea is further explored by Ruth Hubbard and Stuart Newman in "Yuppie Eugenics," in which they wonder, "are we creating a world of genetic haves and have-nots?"

In "Biotech Hope and Hype," environmental journalist Stephen Leahy questions the so-called achievements of the biotechnology industry as a whole. The industry has made some optimistic promises for the future, but how many of those promises have borne fruit, and who's really reaping the benefits?

This section's Viewpoints presents an argument over the ethics of human cloning. When people say that they are against cloning, they usually mean human cloning in a lab. Human clones have always existed—identical twins and triplets are technically clones, each containing exact matching sets of DNA. But identical twins still start out the same way everyone else does—DNA from a sperm cell joins with DNA from an egg cell. However, in 1997, scientists at Roslin Institute in Scotland announced that they had successfully cloned an adult sheep, named Dolly. Soon after, they cloned Cedric, Cecil, Cyril, and Tuppence from cultured embryo cells—four Dorset rams that are genetically identical to one another. And everything we thought we knew about reproduction was turned upside down.

After Roslin Institute made the announcement, researchers, religious leaders, politicians, legal experts, and journalists responded to the news with strong opinions—especially as this new technology could someday relate to humans. What dangers does human cloning pose for cloned children, and for society? What measures must we take to prevent the abuse of this technology? Could cloned children become shunned by society as scientific freaks? In "Should Human Cloning Be Permitted?" Patricia A. Baird presents reasons why it should not—spanning from unknown genetic alterations generations from now, to concern for the social status of the clones themselves.

But not everyone is concerned. It is unlikely that a cloned human would be a perfect replica of its DNA parent—the conditions in the uterus, the health of the mother, and environmental factors can all influence fetal development. After birth, external factors help create who we are. Supporters of human cloning, such as Chris MacDonald in "Yes, Human Cloning Should Be Permitted," argue that scientific horror stories, such as cloning for body parts, are just that—horror stories that will never happen in the real world.

The final piece proposes a "Genetic Bill of Rights" drafted by the Council for Responsible Genetics. The Council believes that we must take steps now to ensure that our genetic future is not compromised. Do we have a right to our own genetic integrity? Could our genetic rights be at risk? This Research Issue explores the concept of genetic rights in greater depth.

Baby, It's You and You and You
Nancy Gibbs

When researchers at Roslin Institute in Scotland announced that they had cloned a sheep in 1997, no one could have prepared them for the calls and letters from people eager to clone their loved ones. Said Ian Wilmut, one of the scientists who created Dolly, the first cloned sheep, "Such pleas are based on a misconception that cloning of the kind that produced Dolly confers instant, exact replication—a virtual resurrection." As anyone who has taken college biology knows, we are more than our DNA—we are products of our environment, beginning with the first divisions of fetal cells. Nevertheless, many people are indeed interested in human cloning; and one sect, the Raelians, has even claimed to have done just that. In this article, Nancy Gibbs discusses the various reasons why people wish to pursue human cloning and some of the arguments against it.

Nancy Gibbs is a senior editor at *Time* magazine, where she divides her time between writing major stories on national affairs and domestic policy issues and editing various sections of the magazine. She has taught a seminar, "Politics and the Press," at Princeton University. In addition to publication in *Time* and other magazines and journals, Gibbs's work is included in the *Princeton Anthology of Writing* (2001). This article was first printed in the February 19, 2001, issue of *Time*.

CRITICAL THINKING   What do you know about human cloning? Do you think it should be banned? After reading the articles in this section, re-evaluate your position and see if your position remains the same.

1   Before we assume that the market for human clones consists mainly of narcissists who think the world deserves more of them or neo-Nazis who dream of cloning Hitler or crackpots and mavericks and mischief makers of all kinds, it is worth taking a tour of the marketplace. We might just meet ourselves there.

2   Imagine for a moment that your daughter needs a bone-marrow transplant and no one can provide a match; that your wife's early menopause has made her infertile; or that your five-year-old has drowned in a lake and your grief has made it impossible to get your mind around the fact that he is gone forever. Would the news then really be so easy to dismiss that around the world, there are scientists in labs pressing ahead with plans to duplicate a human being, deploying the same technology that allowed Scottish scientists to clone Dolly the sheep four years ago?

3   All it took was that first headline about the astonishing ewe, and fertility experts began to hear the questions every day. Our two-year-old daughter died in a car crash; we saved a lock of her hair in a baby book. Can you clone her? Why does the law allow people more freedom to destroy fetuses than to create them? My husband had cancer and is sterile. Can you help us?

4   The inquiries are pouring in because some scientists are ever more willing to say yes; perhaps we can. Last month a well-known infertility specialist, Panayiotis Zavos of the University of Kentucky, announced that he and Italian researcher Severino Antinori, the man who almost seven years ago helped a 62-year-old woman give birth using donor eggs, were forming a consortium to produce the first human clone. Researchers in South Korea claim they have already created a cloned human embryo, though they destroyed it rather than implanting it in a surrogate mother to develop. Recent cover stories in *Wired* and the *New York Times* Magazine tracked the efforts of the Raelians, a religious group committed to, among other things, welcoming the first extraterrestrials when they appear. They intend to clone the cells of a dead 10-month-old boy whose devastated parents hope, in effect, to bring him back to life as a newborn. The Raelians say they have the lab and the scientists, and—most important, considering the amount of trial and error involved—they say they have 50 women lined up to act as surrogates to carry a cloned baby to term.

5   Given what researchers have learned since Dolly, no one thinks the mechanics of cloning are very hard: take a donor egg, suck out the nucleus, and hence the DNA, and fuse it with, say, a skin cell from the human being copied. Then, with the help of an electrical current, the reconstituted cell should begin growing into a genetic duplicate. "It's inevitable that someone will try and someone will succeed," predicts Delores Lamb, an infertility expert at Baylor University. The consensus among biotechnology specialists is that within a few years—some scientists believe a few months—the news will break of the birth of the first human clone.

6   At that moment, at least two things will happen—one private, one public. The meaning of what it is to be human—which until now has involved, at the very least, the mysterious melding of two different people's DNA—will shift forever, along with our understanding of the relationship between parents and children, means and ends, ends and beginnings. And as a result, the conversation that has occupied scientists and ethicists for years, about how much man should mess with nature when it

comes to reproduction, will drop onto every kitchen table, every pulpit, every politician's desk. Our fierce national debate over issues like abortion and euthanasia will seem tame and transparent compared with the questions that human cloning raises.

7   That has many scientists scared to death. Because even if all these headlines are hype and we are actually far away from seeing the first human clone, the very fact that at this moment, the research is proceeding underground, unaccountable, poses a real threat. The risk lies not just with potential babies born deformed, as many animal clones are; not just with desperate couples and cancer patients and other potential "clients" whose hopes may be raised and hearts broken and life savings wiped out. The immediate risk is that a backlash against renegade science might strike at responsible science as well.

8   The more scared people are of some of this research, scientists worry, the less likely they are to tolerate any of it. Yet variations on cloning technology are already used in biotechnology labs all across the country. It is these techniques that will allow, among other things, the creation of cloned herds of sheep and cows that produce medicines in their milk. Researchers also hope that one day, the ability to clone adult human cells will make it possible to "grow" new hearts and livers and nerve cells.

9   But some of the same techniques could also be used to grow a baby. Trying to block one line of research could impede another and so reduce the chances of finding cures for ailments such as Alzheimer's and Parkinson's, cancer and heart disease. Were some shocking breakthrough in human cloning to cause "an overcompensatory response by legislators," says Rockefeller University cloning expert Tony Perry, "that could be disastrous. At some point, it will potentially cost lives." So we are left with choices and trade-offs and a need to think through whether it is this technology that alarms us or just certain ways of using it.

10   By day, Randolfe Wicker, 63, runs a lighting shop in New York City. But in his spare time, as spokesman for the Human Cloning Foundation, he is the face of cloning fervor in the U.S. "I took one step in this adventure, and it took over me like quicksand," says Wicker. He is planning to have some of his skin cells stored for future cloning. "If I'm not cloned before I die, my estate will be set up so that I can be cloned after," he says, admitting, however, that he hasn't found a lawyer willing to help. "It's hard to write a will with all these uncertainties," he concedes. "A lot of lawyers will look at me crazy."

11   As a gay man, Wicker has long been frustrated that he cannot readily have children of his own; as he gets older, his desire to reproduce grows stronger. He knows that a clone would not be a photocopy of him but talks about the traits the boy might possess: "He will like the color blue, Middle Eastern food and romantic Spanish music that's out of fashion." And then he hints at the heart of his motive. "I can thumb my nose at Mr. Death and say, 'You might get me, but you're not going to get all of me,'" he says. "The special formula that is me will live on into another lifetime. It's a partial triumph over death. I would leave my imprint not in sand but in cement."

12   This kind of talk makes ethicists conclude that even people who think they know about cloning—let alone the rest of us—don't fully understand its implica-

tions. Cloning, notes ethicist Arthur Caplan of the University of Pennsylvania, "can't make you immortal because clearly the clone is a different person. If I take twins and shoot one of them, it will be faint consolation to the dead one that the other one is still running around, even though they are genetically identical. So the road to immortality is not through cloning."

13   Still, cloning is the kind of issue so confounding that you envy the purists at either end of the argument. For the Roman Catholic Church, the entire question is one of world view: whether life is a gift of love or just one more industrial product, a little more valuable than most. Those who believe that the soul enters the body at the moment of conception think it is fine for God to make clones; he does it about 4,000 times a day, when a fertilized egg splits into identical twins. But when it comes to massaging a human life, for the scientist to do mechanically what God does naturally, is to interfere with his work; and no possible benefit can justify that presumption.

14   On the other end of the argument are the libertarians who don't like politicians or clerics or ethics boards interfering with what they believe should be purely individual decisions. Reproduction is a most fateful lottery; in their view, cloning allows you to hedge your bet. While grieving parents may be confused about the technology—cloning, even if it works, is not resurrection—their motives are their own business. As for infertile couples, "we are interested in giving people the gift of life," Zavos, the aspiring cloner, told *Time* this week. "Ethics is a wonderful word, but we need to look beyond the ethical issues here. It's not an ethical issue. It's a medical issue. We have a duty here. Some people need this to complete the life cycle, to reproduce."

15   In the messy middle are the vast majority of people who view the prospect with a vague alarm, an uneasy sense that science is dragging us into dark woods with no paths and no easy way to turn back. Ian Wilmut, the scientist who cloned Dolly but has come out publicly against human cloning, was not trying to help sheep have genetically related children. "He was trying to help farmers produce genetically improved sheep," notes Hastings Center ethicist Erik Parens. "And surely that's how the technology will go with us too." Cloning, Parens says, "is not simply this isolated technique out there that a few deluded folks are going to avail themselves of, whether they think it is a key to immortality or a way to bring someone back from the dead. It's part of a much bigger project. Essentially the big-picture question is: To what extent do we want to go down the path of using reproductive technologies to genetically shape our children?"

16   At the moment, the American public is plainly not ready to move quickly on cloning. In a *Time*/CNN poll, 90% of respondents thought it was a bad idea to clone human beings. "Cloning right now looks like it's coming to us on a magic carpet, piloted by a cult leader, sold to whoever can afford it," says ethicist Caplan. "That makes people nervous."

17   And it helps explain why so much of the research is being done secretly. We may learn of the first human clone only months, even years, after he or she is born—if the event hasn't happened already, as some scientists speculate. The team that cloned Dolly waited until she was seven months old to announce her existence. Creating her took 277 tries, and right up until her birth, scientists around the world

were saying that cloning a mammal from an adult cell was impossible. "There's a significant gap between what scientists are willing to talk about in public and their private aspirations," says British futurist Patrick Dixon. "The law of genetics is that the work is always significantly further ahead than the news. In the digital world, everything is hyped because there are no moral issues—there is just media excitement. Gene technology creates so many ethical issues that scientists are scared stiff of a public reaction if the end results of their research are known."

18   Of course, attitudes often change over time. In-vitro fertilization was effectively illegal in many states 20 years ago, and the idea of transplanting a heart was once considered horrifying. Public opinion on cloning will evolve just as it did on these issues, advocates predict. But in the meantime, the crusaders are mostly driven underground. Princeton biologist Lee Silver says fertility specialists have told him that they have no problem with cloning and would be happy to provide it as a service to their clients who could afford it. But these same specialists would never tell inquiring reporters that, Silver says—it's too hot a topic right now. "I think what's happened is that all the mainstream doctors have taken a hands-off approach because of this huge public outcry. But I think what they are hoping is that some fringe group will pioneer it and that it will slowly come into the mainstream and then they will be able to provide it to their patients."

19   All it will take, some predict, is that first snapshot. "Once you have a picture of a normal baby with 10 fingers and 10 toes, that changes everything," says San Mateo, Calif., attorney and cloning advocate Mark Eibert, who gets inquiries from infertile couples every day. "Once they put a child in front of the cameras, they've won." On the other hand, notes Gregory Pence, a professor of philosophy at the University of Alabama at Birmingham and author of *Who's Afraid of Human Cloning?*, "if the first baby is defective, cloning will be banned for the next 100 years."

20   "I wouldn't mind being the first person cloned if it were free. I don't mind being a guinea pig," says Doug Dorner, 35. He and his wife Nancy both work in health care. "We're not afraid of technology," he says. Dorner has known since he was 16 that he would never be able to have children the old-fashioned way. A battle with lymphoma left him sterile, so when he and Nancy started thinking of having children, he began following the scientific developments in cloning more closely. The more he read, the more excited he got. "Technology saved my life when I was 16," he says, but at the cost of his fertility. "I think technology should help me have a kid. That's a fair trade."

21   Talk to the Dorners, and you get a glimpse of choices that most parents can scarcely imagine having to make. Which parent, for instance, would they want to clone? Nancy feels she would be bonded to the child just from carrying him, so why not let the child have Doug's genetic material? Does it bother her to know she would, in effect, be raising her husband as a little boy? "It wouldn't be that different. He already acts like a five-year-old sometimes," she says with a laugh.

22   How do they imagine raising a cloned child, given the knowledge they would have going in? "I'd know exactly what his basic drives were," says Doug. The boy's dreams and aspirations, however, would be his own, Doug insists. "I used to dream

of being a fighter pilot," he recalls, a dream lost when he got cancer. While they are at it, why not clone Doug twice? "Hmm. Two of the same kid," Doug ponders. "We'll cross that bridge when we come to it. But I know we'd never clone our clone to have a second child. Once you start copying something, who knows what the next copies will be like?"

23   In fact the risks involved with cloning mammals are so great that Wilmut, the premier cloner, calls it "criminally irresponsible" for scientists to be experimenting on humans today. Even after four years of practice with animal cloning, the failure rate is still overwhelming: 98% of embryos never implant or die off during gestation or soon after birth. Animals that survive can be nearly twice as big at birth as is normal, or have extra-large organs or heart trouble or poor immune systems. Dolly's "mother" was six years old when she was cloned. That may explain why Dolly's cells show signs of being older than they actually are—scientists joked that she was really a sheep in lamb's clothing. This deviation raises the possibility that beings created by cloning adults will age abnormally fast.

24   "We had a cloned sheep born just before Christmas that was clearly not normal," says Wilmut. "We hoped for a few days it would improve and then, out of kindness, we euthanized it, because it obviously would never be healthy." Wilmut believes "it is almost a certainty" that cloned human children would be born with similar maladies. Of course, we don't euthanize babies. But these kids would probably die very prematurely anyway. Wilmut pauses to consider the genie he has released with Dolly and the hopes he has raised. "It seems such a profound irony," he says, "that in trying to make a copy of a child who has died tragically, one of the most likely outcomes is another dead child."

25   That does not seem to deter the scientists who work on the Clonaid project run by the Raelian sect. They say they are willing to try to clone a dead child. Though their outfit is easy to mock, they may be even further along than the competition, in part because they have an advantage over other teams. A formidable obstacle to human cloning is that donor eggs are a rare commodity, as are potential surrogate mothers, and the Raelians claim to have a supply of both.

26   Earlier this month, according to Brigitte Boisselier, Clonaid's scientific director, somewhere in North America, a young woman walked into a Clonaid laboratory whose location is kept secret. Then, in a procedure that has been done thousands of times, a doctor inserted a probe, removed 15 eggs from the woman's ovaries and placed them in a chemical soup. Last week two other Clonaid scientists, according to the group, practiced the delicate art of removing the genetic material from each of the woman's eggs. Within the next few weeks, the Raelian scientific team plans to place another cell next to the enucleated egg.

27   This second cell, they say, comes from a 10-month-old boy who died during surgery. The two cells will be hit with an electrical charge, according to the scenario, and will fuse, forming a new hybrid cell that no longer has the genes of the young woman but now has the genes of the dead child. Once the single cell has developed into six to eight cells, the next step is to follow the existing, standard technology of assisted reproduction: gingerly insert the embryo into a woman's

womb and hope it implants. Clonaid scientists expect to have implanted the first cloned human embryo in a surrogate mother by next month.

28 Even if the technology is basic, and even if it appeals to some infertile couples, should grieving parents really be pursuing this route? "It's a sign of our growing despotism over the next generation," argues University of Chicago bioethicist Leon Kass. Cloning introduces the possibility of parents' making choices for their children far more fundamental than whether to give them piano lessons or straighten their teeth. "It's not just that parents will have particular hopes for these children," says Kass. "They will have expectations based on a life that has already been lived. What a thing to do—to carry on the life of a person who has died."

29 The libertarians are ready with their answers. "I think we're hypercritical about people's reasons for having children," says Pence. "If they want to re-create their dead children, so what?" People have always had self-serving reasons for having children, he argues, whether to ensure there's someone to care for them in their old age or to relive their youth vicariously. Cloning is just another reproductive tool; the fact that it is not a perfect tool, in Pence's view, should not mean it should be outlawed altogether. "We know there are millions of girls who smoke and drink during pregnancy, and we know what the risks to the fetus are, but we don't do anything about it," he notes. "If we're going to regulate cloning, maybe we should regulate that too."

30 Olga Tomusyak was two weeks shy of her seventh birthday when she fell out of the window of her family's apartment. Her parents could barely speak for a week after she died. "Life is empty without her," says her mother Tanya, a computer programmer in Sydney, Australia. "Other parents we have talked to who have lost children say it will never go away." Olga's parents cremated the child before thinking of the cloning option. All that remains are their memories, some strands of hair and three baby teeth, so they have begun investigating whether the teeth could yield the nuclei to clone her one day. While it is theoretically possible to extract DNA from the teeth, scientists say it is extremely unlikely.

31 "You can't expect the new baby will be exactly like her. We know that is not possible," says Tanya. "We think of the clone as her twin or at least a baby who will look like her." The parents would consider the new little girl as much Olga's baby as their own. "Anything that grows from her will remind us of her," says Tanya. Though she and her husband are young enough to have other children, for now, this is the child they want.

32 Once parents begin to entertain the option of holding on to some part of a child, why would the reverse not be true? "Bill" is a guidance counselor in Southern California, a fortysomething expectant father who has been learning everything he can about the process of cloning. But it is not a lost child he is looking to replicate. He is interested in cloning his mother, who is dying of pancreatic cancer. He has talked to her husband, his siblings, everyone except her doctor—and her, for fear that it will make her think they have given up hope on her. He confides, "We might end up making a decision without telling her."

33 His goal is to extract a tissue specimen from his mother while it's still possible and store it, to await the day when—if—cloning becomes technically safe and

socially acceptable. Late last week, as his mother's health weakened, the family began considering bringing up the subject with her because they need her cooperation to take the sample. Meanwhile, Bill has already contacted two labs about tissue storage, one as a backup. "I'm in touch with a couple of different people who might be doing that," he says, adding that both are in the U.S. "It seems like a little bit of an underground movement, you know—people are a little reluctant that if they announce it, they might be targeted, like the abortion clinics."

34   If Bill's hopes were to materialize and the clone were born, who would that person be? "It wouldn't be my mother but a person who would be very similar to my mother, with certain traits. She has a lot of great traits: compassion and intelligence and looks," he says. And yet, perhaps inevitably, he talks as though this is a way to rewind and replay the life of someone he loves. "She really didn't have the opportunities we had in the baby-boom generation, because her parents experienced the Depression and the war," he says. "So the feeling is that maybe we could give her some opportunities that she didn't have. It would be sort of like we're taking care of her now. You know how when your parents age and everything shifts, you start taking care of them? Well, this would be an extension of that."

35   A world in which cloning is commonplace confounds every human relationship, often in ways most potential clients haven't considered. For instance, if a woman gives birth to her own clone, is the child her daughter or her sister? Or, says bioethicist Kass, "let's say the child grows up to be the spitting image of its mother. What impact will that have on the relationship between the father and his child if that child looks exactly like the woman he fell in love with?" Or, he continues, "let's say the parents have a cloned son and then get divorced. How will the mother feel about seeing a copy of the person she hates most in the world every day? Everyone thinks about cloning from the point of view of the parents. No one looks at it from the point of view of the clone."

36   If infertile couples avoid the complications of choosing which of them to clone and instead look elsewhere for their DNA, what sorts of values govern that choice? Do they pick an uncle because he's musical, a willing neighbor because she's brilliant? Through that door lies the whole unsettling debate about designer babies, fueled already by the commercial sperm banks that promise genius DNA to prospective parents. Sperm banks give you a shot at passing along certain traits; cloning all but assures it.

37   Whatever the moral quandaries, the one-stop-shopping aspect of cloning is a plus to many gay couples. Lesbians would have the chance to give birth with no male involved at all; one woman could contribute the ovum, the other the DNA. Christine DeShazo and her partner Michele Thomas of Miramar, Fla., have been in touch with Zavos about producing a baby this way. Because they have already been ostracized as homosexuals, they aren't worried about the added social sting that would come with cloning. "Now [people] would say, 'Not only are you a lesbian, you are a cloning lesbian,'" says Thomas. As for potential health problems, "I would love our baby if its hand was attached to its head," she says. DeShazo adds, "If it came out green, I would love it. Our little alien . . ."

38 Just as women have long been able to have children without a male sexual partner, through artificial insemination, men could potentially become dads alone: replace the DNA from a donor egg with one's own and then recruit a surrogate mother to carry the child. Some gay-rights advocates even argue that should sexual preference prove to have a biological basis, and should genetic screening lead to terminations of gay embryos, homosexuals would have an obligation to produce gay children through cloning.

39 All sorts of people might be attracted to the idea of the ultimate experiment in single parenthood. Jack Barker, a marketing specialist for a corporate-relocation company in Minneapolis, is 36 and happily unmarried. "I've come to the conclusion that I don't need a partner but can still have a child," he says. "And a clone would be the perfect child to have because I know exactly what I'm getting." He understands that the child would not be a copy of him. "We'd be genetically identical," says Barker. "But he wouldn't be raised by my parents—he'd be raised by me." Cloning, he hopes, might even let him improve on the original: "I have bad allergies and asthma. It would be nice to have a kid like you but with those improvements."

40 Cloning advocates view the possibilities as a kind of liberation from travails assumed to be part of life: the danger that your baby will be born with a disease that will kill him or her, the risk that you may one day need a replacement organ and die waiting for it, the helplessness you feel when confronted with unbearable loss. The challenge facing cloning pioneers is to make the case convincingly that the technology itself is not immoral, however immorally it could be used.

41 One obvious way is to point to the broader benefits. Thus cloning proponents like to attach themselves to the whole arena of stem-cell research, the brave new world of inquiry into how the wonderfully pliable cells of seven-day-old embryos behave. Embryonic stem cells eventually turn into every kind of tissue, including brain, muscle, nerve and blood. If scientists could harness their powers, these cells could serve as the body's self-repair kit, providing cures for Parkinson's, diabetes, Alzheimer's and paralysis. Actors Christopher Reeve, paralyzed by a fall from a horse, and Michael J. Fox, who suffers from Parkinson's, are among those who have pushed Congress to overturn the government's restrictions on federal funding of embryonic-stem-cell research.

42 But if the cloners want to climb on this train in hopes of riding it to a public relations victory, the mainstream scientists want to push them off. Because researchers see the potential benefits of understanding embryonic stem cells as immense, they are intent on avoiding controversy over their use. Being linked with the human-cloning activists is their nightmare. Says Michael West, president of Massachusetts-based Advanced Cell Technology, a biotech company that uses cloning technology to develop human medicines: "We're really concerned that if someone goes off and clones a Raelian, there could be an overreaction to this craziness—especially by regulators and Congress. We're desperately concerned—and it's a bad metaphor—about throwing the baby out with the bath water."

43 Scientists at ACT are leery of revealing too much about their animal-cloning research, much less their work on human embryos. "What we're doing is the first step toward cloning a human being, but we're not cloning a human being," says

West. "The miracle of cloning isn't what people think it is. Cloning allows you to make a genetically identical copy of an animal, yes; but in the eyes of a biologist, the real miracle is seeing a skin cell being put back into the egg cell, taking it back in time to when it was an undifferentiated cell, which then can turn into any cell in the body." Which means that new, pristine tissue could be grown in labs to replace damaged or diseased parts of the body. And since these replacement parts would be produced using skin or other cells from the suffering patient, there would be no risk of rejection. "That means you've solved the age-old problem of transplantation," says West. "It's huge."

44   So far, the main source of embryonic stem cells is "leftover" embryos from IVF clinics; cloning embryos could provide an almost unlimited source. Progress could come even faster if Congress were to lift the restrictions on federal funding—which might have the added safety benefit of the federal oversight that comes with federal dollars. "We're concerned about George W.'s position and whether he'll let existing guidelines stay in place," says West. "People are begging to work on those cells."

45   That impulse is enough to put the Roman Catholic Church in full revolt; the Vatican has long condemned any research that involves creating and experimenting with human embryos, the vast majority of which inevitably perish. The church believes that the soul is created at the moment of conception, and that the embryo is worthy of protection. It reportedly took 104 attempts before the first IVF baby, Louise Brown, was born; cloning Dolly took more than twice that. Imagine, say opponents, how many embryos would be lost in the effort to clone a human. This loss is mass murder, says David Byers, director of the National Conference of Catholic Bishops' commission on science and human values. "Each of the embryos is a human being simply by dint of its genetic makeup."

46   Last week 160 bishops and five Cardinals met for three days behind closed doors in Irving, Texas, to wrestle with the issues biotechnology presents. But the cloning debate does not break cleanly even along religious lines. "Rebecca," a thirty-something San Francisco Bay Area resident, spent seven years trying to conceive a child with her husband. Having "been to hell and back" with IVF treatment, Rebecca is now as thoroughly committed to cloning as she is to Christianity. "It's in the Bible—be fruitful and multiply," she says. "People say, 'You're playing God.' But we're not. We're using the raw materials the good Lord gave us. What does the doctor do when the heart has stopped? They have to do direct massage of the heart. You could say the doctor is playing God. But we save a life. With human cloning, we're not so much saving a life as creating a new being by manipulation of the raw materials, DNA, the blueprint for life. You're simply using it in a more creative manner."

47   A field where emotions run so strong and hope runs so deep is fertile ground for profiteers and charlatans. In her effort to clone her daughter Olga, Tanya Tomusyak contacted an Australian firm, Southern Cross Genetics, which was founded three years ago by entrepreneur Graeme Sloan to preserve DNA for future cloning. In an e-mail, Sloan told the parents that Olga's teeth would provide more than enough DNA—even though that possibility is remote. "All DNA samples are placed into computer-controlled liquid-nitrogen tanks for long-term storage," he wrote. "The

cost of doing a DNA fingerprint and genetic profile and placing the sample into storage would be $2,500. Please note that all of our fees are in U.S. dollars."

48   When contacted by *Time,* Sloan admitted, "I don't have a scientific background. I'm pure business. I'd be lying if I said I wasn't here to make a dollar out of it. But I would like to see organ cloning become a reality." He was inspired to launch the business, he says, after a young cousin died of leukemia. "There's megadollars involved, and everyone is racing to be the first," he says. As for his own slice of the pie, Sloan says he just sold his firm to a French company, which he refuses to name, and he was heading for Hawaii last week. The Southern Cross factory address turns out to be his mother's house, and his "office" phone is answered by a man claiming to be his brother David—although his mother says she has no son by that name.

49   The more such peddlers proliferate, the more politicians will be tempted to invoke prohibitions. Four states—California, Louisiana, Michigan and Rhode Island—have already banned human cloning, and this spring Texas may become the fifth. Republican state senator Jane Nelson has introduced a bill in Austin that would impose a fine of as much as $1 million for researchers who use cloning technology to initiate pregnancy in humans. The proposed Texas law would permit embryonic-stem-cell research, but bills proposed in other states were so broadly written that they could have stopped those activities too.

50   "The short answer to the cloning question," says ethicist Caplan, "is that anybody who clones somebody today should be arrested. It would be barbaric human experimentation. It would be killing fetuses and embryos for no purpose, none, except for curiosity. But if you can't agree that that's wrong to do, and if the media can't agree to condemn rather than gawk, that's a condemnation of us all." ◆

FREEWRITING ASSIGNMENT

Would you clone yourself or a loved one for any reason—such as to save a living child, or even yourself?

CRITICAL READING

1. What reasons does Gibbs list for why people are interested in human cloning? Are these the same reasons cited by researchers? How are the expectations of the general population different from the expectations of the scientific world?
2. What "backlash" do "responsible" scientists fear will happen as a result of human cloning research? Are their fears well founded? Explain.
3. What are some of the misconceptions people seem to have about cloning themselves? Explain.
4. Gibbs notes that the issue of human cloning is "so confounding that you envy the purists at either end of the argument." What are the opinions of

the "purists"? Do you find one side of the argument more compelling than another? Explain.

5. Ian Wilmut observes that there is a tragic twist to parents' desire to clone their dead children—that the success rate is so miniscule that they are more likely to end up with another dead child. Should parents be able to pursue this option? Is any chance—no matter how remote—worthy of the risk? Why or why not?

6. In paragraph 20, Doug Dorner states that he "wouldn't mind being a guinea pig." Would the donor of the cells used to create a human clone be the "guinea pig"? Or is the clone the "guinea pig"?

7. In paragraph 29, Pence comments that cloning is "merely another reproductive tool" now available to us. Respond to his statement expressing your own viewpoint.

8. Gibbs observes that many people who support human cloning seem to do so without considering the point of view of the clone. How do the examples in her article of people who support cloning support this viewpoint?

CRITICAL WRITING

9. *Research and Analysis*: In 1997, the National Bioethics Advisory Council recommended against human cloning because of the dangers it presented to the child born of such reproductive technology. In 2000, researchers reported that Dolly's cells appeared to age faster than normal. Through online and library research, track Dolly's development. If Dolly were human, what biological problems would she face? Based on your research, can you make a recommendation for or against human cloning at this time?

10. Research the cloning claims of the Raelians and their efforts to clone a human being. After the announcement of the cloning of Dolly, Rael, the founder of the Raelian movement, founded Clonaid, a company offering human cloning services (**www.clonaid.com**). Visit the Clonaid Web site. Are their efforts dangerous? Noble? Write a short newspaper report on the most recent activities of Clonaid.

GROUP PROJECTS

11. One of the arguments against human cloning is that the technology could be abused to create clones of exceptional people, such as athletes, geniuses, and supermodels. With your group, discuss the likelihood of such an application of cloning technology. Who are possible candidates for cloning and why? In your discussion, also address the idea of "the right to genetic identity." Should such a right exist? How could it be violated?

Enough
Bill McKibben

In the next piece, Bill McKibben shares his grim perspective on the issue of genetic engineering. He warns that we are approaching the transformation of our species as if we were "sleepwalking." Unless we open our eyes and take a good hard look at what genetic technology means for the future of the human race, we will soon reach a point of no return. We must consider the implications before it is too late.

Bill McKibben is a scholar in residence at Middlebury College. He is a regular contributor to many publications, including the *New York Review of Books*, *The New York Times*, and *The Atlantic*. He is the author of many books, most recently *Maybe One* (1998), *Long Distance: A Year of Living Strenuously* (2000), and *Enough* (2003), from which this essay was excerpted.

CRITICAL THINKING   Twenty years ago, we were raising serious questions about the ethics of in vitro fertilization and "test-tube" babies—a practice that most people now find acceptable. Do you think it's likely that we will feel the same way about human genetic engineering? Will it become acceptable as time passes? Why or why not?

1   For the first few miles of the marathon, I was still fresh enough to look around, to pay attention. I remember mostly the muffled thump of several thousand pairs of expensive sneakers padding the Ottawa pavement—an elemental sound, like surf, or wind. But as the race wore on, the herd stretched into a dozen flocks and then into a long string of solitary runners. Pretty soon each of us was off in a singular race, pitting one body against one will. By the halfway point, when all the adrenaline had worn off, the only sound left was my breath rattling in my chest. I was deep in my own private universe, completely absorbed in my own drama.

2   Now, this run was entirely inconsequential. For months I'd trained with the arbitrary goal of 3 hours and 20 minutes in my mind. Which is not a fast time: it's an hour and a quarter off the world record. But it would let a forty-one-year-old into the Boston Marathon. And given how fast I'd gone in training, I knew it lay at the outer edge of possible. So it was a worthwhile target, a number to live with through one early-morning run after another, a number to multiply and divide against the readouts on the treadmill display when downpours kept me in the gym. It's rare enough in my life to have a goal so concrete and unambiguous.

3   By about, say, mile 23, two things were becoming clear. One, my training had worked. I'd reeled off one 7:30 mile after another. Two, my training wouldn't get me to the finish by itself. My legs were starting to slow and wobble, my knees and calves were hard pressed to lift and push at the same pace as an hour earlier. I could feel my goal slipping away, my pace dropping. With every hundred yards the race became less a physical test and more a mental one, game spirit trying to rally sag-

ging flesh before sagging flesh could sap game spirit and convince it the time had come to walk. Someone stronger passed me, and I slipped onto her heels for a few hundred crucial yards, picking up the pace. The finish line swam into my squinted view, and I stagger-sprinted across. With 14 seconds to spare.

4   A photographer clicked a picture, as he would of everyone who finished. I was a cipher to him—a grimacing cipher, the 324th person to cross, an unimportant finisher in an unimportant time in an unimportant race. In the picture you can see the crowd at the finish, looking right past me toward the middle distance, waiting for their mom or dad, son or daughter to move into sight. It mattered not at all what I had done.

5   But it mattered to me. When it was done, I had a clearer sense of myself, of my power and my frailty. For a period of hours, and especially those last gritty miles, I had been absolutely, utterly *present*, the moments desperately, magnificently clarified. As meaningless as it was to the world, that's how meaning*ful* it was to me. I met parts of myself I'd never been introduced to before, glimpsed more clearly strengths and flaws I'd half suspected. A marathon peels you down toward your core for a little while, gets past the defenses we erect even against ourselves. That's the high that draws you back for the next race, a centering elation shared by people who finished an hour ahead and two hours behind me. And it must echo in some small way what runners have always felt—the Tarahumara Indians on their impossible week-long runs through the canyons of Mexico, the Masai on their game trails. Few things are more basic than running.

6   And yet it is entirely possible that we will be among the last generations to feel that power and that frailty. Genetic science may soon offer human beings, among many other things, the power to bless their offspring with a vastly improved engine. For instance, scientists may find ways to dramatically increase the amount of oxygen that blood can carry. When that happens, we will, though not quite as Isaiah envisioned, be able to run and not grow weary.

7   This is one small item on the long list of "improvements" that the proponents of human genetic engineering envision, and one of the least significant corners of human life they propose to alter. But it serves as a decent template for starting to think about all the changes they have in mind, and indeed the changes that may result from a suite of other new engineering marvels like advanced robotics and nanotechnology.

8   Consider sports. Attempts to alter the human body are nothing new in sports, of course. It's been more than a century since Charles-Edouard Brown-Sequard, the French physiologist called "the father of steroids," injected himself with an extract derived from the testicle of a guinea pig and a dog.[1] Athletes have been irradiated and surgically implanted with monkey glands; they have weight-trained with special regimens designed to increase mitochondria in muscle cells and have lived in special trailers pressurized to simulate high altitudes.[2] For endurance athletes, the drug of choice has for the last decade been erythropoietin, or EPO, a man-made version of a hormone released by the kidneys that stimulates the production of red blood cells, so that the blood can carry extra oxygen. With EPO, the red blood cells can get so thick that the blood curdles, turns into a syrupy ooze—in the early days of the

drug, elite cyclists started dropping dead across their handlebars, their hearts unable to pump the sludge running through their veins.

9   In 1995, researchers asked two hundred Olympic hopefuls if they'd take a drug that would guarantee them a five-year winning streak and then kill them. Almost half said yes.[3] The Tour de France has been interrupted by police raids time and again; in 2001, Italian officials found what they described as a "mobile hospital" trailing the Giro d'Italia bike race, well-stocked with testosterone, human growth hormone, uro-fillitophin, salbutamol, and a synthetic blood product called HemAssist.[4] The British sports commentator Simon Eassom said recently that the only people likely to be caught for steroid abuse were from Third World countries: everyone else could afford new-generation drugs that didn't yet show up on tests.[5] Some sports, like power lifting, have had to give in and set up "drug-free" or "natural" divisions.[6]

10   In other words, you could almost say that it makes no difference whether athletes of the future are genetically engineered—that the damage is already done with conventional drugs, the line already crossed. You could almost say that, but not quite. Because in fact, in the last couple of years, the testing has gotten better. The new World Anti-Doping Agency has caught enough offenders to throw a scare into dirty athletes, and some heart into clean ones. Some distance athletes who had decided to retire because they felt they couldn't compete have gone back into train-ing; a new group of poststeroids shotputters and discus hurlers have proved their point by winning meets with shorter throws than the records of a decade ago.[7] And both athlete and fan remain able to draw the line in their minds: no one thought Ben Johnson's 1988 dash record meant anything once the Olympic lab found steroids in his system. It was erased from the record books, and he was banned from competi-tion. Against the odds, sports just manages to stay "real."

11   But what if, instead of crudely cheating with hypodermics, we began to literally program children before they were born to become great athletes? "Picture this," writes one British journalist. "It is 2016. A young couple are sitting in a doctor's waiting room. They know that what they are about to do is illegal, but they are deter-mined. They have come to make their child a world-beating athlete," by injecting their embryo with the patented genes of a champion.[8] Muscle size, oxygen uptake, respiration—much of an athlete's inherent capacity derives from her genes. What she makes of it depends on her heart and mind, of course, as well as on the accidents of where she's born, and what kind of diet she gets, and whether the local rulers believe that girls should be out running.

12   And her genes aren't entirely random: perhaps her parents were attracted to each other in the first place because both were athletes, or because they were not. But all those variables fit within our idea of fate. Flipping through the clinic cata-logue for athletic genes does not; it's a door into another world.

13   If it happens—and when that girl grows up to compete—it won't be as if she is "cheating." "What if you're born with something having been done to you?" asks the Olympic dash champion Maurice Greene. "You didn't have anything to do with it."[9] But if that happens, what will be the point of running? "Just what human excel-lences are we supposed to be celebrating?" asks the medical ethicist Eric Juengst. "Who's got the better biotech sponsor?"[10]

14   Soon, says Simon Eassom, most sport may become Evel Knievelish pageantry: "'Roll up, roll up, let's see somebody who'll break six seconds for the hundred meters.'" Spectacle will survive, and for many fans that may be enough. But the emptiness will be real.

15   To get a small sense of what it will feel like, consider the 2002 Winter Olympics in Salt Lake City. While the North American media obsessed over figure skating disputes, the highest drama may have come on the Nordic skiing trails. Erling Jevne of Norway, a grand old man of the sport, was readying himself for one last race, the 50-kilometer, the marathon of winter. He was the sentimental favorite, in part because he had one of those sad stories that, were he an American, would have earned him hours of maudlin airtime. Raking hay on his fifth-generation family farm one day, he'd watched helplessly as his four-year-old son climbed a fence, stumbled onto a road, and was killed by a car. "I don't have a single workout where I don't think about Erich Iver," he said before the Games. "Yes, I would go far enough to say that he is an inner inspiration for my training now"—which makes Jevne not so different from all the thousands of people who run marathons in honor of their mothers, their fathers, their sons, their daughters, their friends who have died before their time or live amidst tragedy.[11] Half the people running next to me in Ottawa seemed to be wearing T-shirts with the image of some dead or dying relative.

16   Once before Jevne had won Olympic silver, losing to a Finn who, years later, was caught doping. This was his final stand—and he was crushed. Not long after the start, the Spaniard Johann Muehlegg caught up with him and cruised past. "His pace was simply too fast for me. He skied faster than I've ever done in my life," said Jevne.[12] As one commentator put it, Muehlegg "looked like he was skiing on another planet."[13] As indeed he was—the Planet NESP, a new EPO derivative discovered in his urine right after the race. He was stripped of his medal, although he's still appealing.

17   Before he heard the news—when he thought he'd simply been passed by a stronger man, or one who'd trained harder—Jevne said, "I'll recover from the disappointment. It's after all just a skiing race."[14] Which is, I suppose, the right way to think about it; for those of us who will never win a race, it should be easy to nod. But as we move into this new world of genetic engineering, we won't simply lose races, we'll lose racing: we'll lose the possibility of the test, the challenge, the celebration that athletics represents. Forget elite athletes—they drip one drop of sweat for every thousand that roll off the brows of weekend warriors. It's the average human, once "improved," who will have no more reason for running marathons. Say you've reached Mile 23, and you're feeling strong. Is it because of your hard training and your character, or because the gene pack inside you is pumping out more red blood cells than your body knows what to do with? Will anyone be impressed with your dedication? More to the point, will you be impressed with your dedication? Will you know what part of it is you, and what part is your upgrade? Right now we think of our bodies (and our minds) as givens; we think of them as us, and we work to make of them what we can. But if they become equipment—if your heart and lungs (and eventually your character) are a product of engineering—then running becomes like driving. Driving can be fun, and goodness knows there are people who care passionately about their cars, who will come to blows on the question Ford vs.

Chevy. But the skill, the engagement, the meaning reside mostly in those who design the machines. No one goes out and drives in honor of a dying sister.

18   Sport is the canary in a miner's cage. It's possible the canary will die; there are those who think, with good reason, that genetic engineering of the human organism may be crude and dangerous, especially at first. But the even greater danger is that the canary will be souped up into an ever perkier, ever tougher, ever "better" specimen. Not a canary anymore, but a parrot, or a golden eagle, or some grand thing we can only guess at. A canary so big and strong that it . . . won't be a canary anymore. It will be something else entirely, unable to carry the sweet tune it grew up singing.

19   No one needs to run in the twenty-first century. Running is an outlet for spirit, for finding out who you are, no more mandatory than art or music. It is a voluntary beauty, a grace. And it turns out to be a fragile beauty. Its significance depends on the limitations and wonders of our bodies as we have known them. Why would you sign up for a marathon if it was a test of the alterations some embryologist had made in you, and in a million others? If 3 hours and 20 minutes was your design spec? We'll still be able to run hard; doubtless we'll even hurt. It's not the personal challenge that will disappear. It's the personal. ◆

Notes

1. John M. Hoberman, Mortal Engines: *The Science of Performance and the Dehumanization of Sport* (New York: 1992), p. 72.
2. Ibid., pp. 136, 102; Sharon Begley, "Good Medal Workouts," *Newsweek*, Dec. 17, 2001.
3. Mark Compton, "Enhancement Genetics: Let the Games Begin," *DNA Dispatch*, July 2001.
4. "More Giro Shocks Still to Come," *Pro Cycling*, March 5, 2002.
5. Amanda Swift, "The Sports Factor," ABC radio [Australia], July 12, 2001.
6. Ira Berkow, "This Lifter Is Fueled by Natural Power," *New York Times*, Feb. 6, 1994.
7. Rod Osher, "Hot Performances," *Time.com*, Sept. 6,1999.
8. Michael Butcher, "Next: The Genetically Modified Athlete," *The Guardian*, Dec. 15, 1999.
9. Jere Longman, "Getting the Athletic Edge May Mean Altering Genes," *New York Times*, May 11, 2001.
10. Compton, "Enhancement Genetics."
11. "Erling Jevne: Down to Earth," *Skisport* magazine, translated and archived at *www.xcskiworld.com*.
12. "Jevne's Last Campaign," *www.langrenn.com*, Feb. 25, 2002.
13. J. D. Downing, "GoldenJustice," *www.xcskiworld.com*, Feb. 25, 2002.
14. "Jevne's Last Campaign."

FREEWRITING ASSIGNMENT ─────────────────────

Would knowing you were genetically enhanced to perform better at sports or mathematics reduce your pride when you excelled in these areas? Why or why not?

CRITICAL READING

1. Why does McKibben choose to open his argument with a story of his first marathon? How does this story frame the points that follow? Is it an effective way to draw in his readers? How does it relate to his thesis? Explain.

2. McKibben comments, "you could almost say that it makes no difference whether athletes of the future are genetically engineered—the damage is already done with conventional drugs, the line already crossed." On what grounds does he disprove this statement?

3. Several authors in this section have brought up the issue of biological enhancement as it relates to athletics. If genetic engineering were used to create better athletes, how would it change sports in general? Would people still be impressed by excellence? Would athletes have to undergo genetic screenings before they could compete? Would it create a different "race"—a race of athletes bred for muscle? Discuss.

4. McKibben wonders if we were genetically engineered to be stronger runners, would the inherent challenge in running a race disappear. "It's not the personal challenge that will disappear. It's the personal." What does he mean?

CRITICAL WRITING

5. McKibben warns that genetic engineering will change what it means to be human—for the worse. But are people likely to heed his concerns and those of others like him? Imagine that we could go back in time 150 years and warn government leaders that weapons of war soon to be invented—such as automatic weapons, missiles, gases, mines, and grenades—would result in millions of deaths in a 30-year time period between 1915 and 1945. Would they have banned such technology? Would this have been good for humanity? (Remember that many forms of technology used in modern weaponry are also used in modern medicine.) Explore this idea from your own viewpoint.

6. A deeper issue connected to genetic alteration that McKibben raises is that it could irrevocably alter how we feel about ourselves as individuals and how we relate to others. Imagine a world in which there are genetically enhanced individuals who have been made smarter, stronger, or more beautiful than conventionally conceived children. What issues are likely to arise? How would the nonenhanced people function in a world in which there was no hope to ever compete on the same level as the enhanced?

7. *Personal Narrative*: McKibben describes how a marathon made him realize things about himself he never knew. "For a period of hours, and especially those last gritty miles, I had been absolutely, utterly *present*, the moments desperately, magnificently clarified. As meaningless as it was to the world, that's how mean*ingful* it was to me." Write a personal narrative describing a time when you pushed yourself beyond your expectations. What did you learn about yourself, and why?

GROUP PROJECT

8. McKibben wonders what a world of genetically modified superathletes would be like. With your group, outline the reasons we compete in sports, or watch them. If you knew that other players had been enhanced, would that change your opinion of athletic competition? Discuss this issue with your group, writing down important points. Share your points as part of a larger class discussion.

Yuppie Eugenics
Ruth Hubbard and Stuart Newman

The concept of eugenics is nothing new. In *The Republic*, the ancient philosopher Plato proposed that, in an effort to create a more perfect state, the government should control the procreation of children. Tall people would reproduce with short ones, fat with thin, comely with ugly, and, in so doing, create a more uniformly perfect population. Of course, we know that such techniques wouldn't work, but we are approaching a time when we could manipulate the genetic code in order to create taller, stronger, or more healthy children. In the next piece, Ruth Hubbard and Stuart Newman claim that a form of eugenics is being practised right now among those who can afford it. Genetic testing allows parents to terminate "disappointing" pregnancies, and select embryos known to be free of certain genetic diseases such as cystic fibrosis. But such technology isn't available to everyone, and Hubbard and Newman fear that we may create a world of genetic haves and have-nots.

Ruth Hubbard is professor emerita of biology at Harvard University and author of *The Politics of Women's Biology* (1990) and co-author of *Exploding the Gene Myth* (1999). Stuart Newman is professor of cell biology and anatomy at New York Medical College. They are founding members of the Council for Responsible Genetics in Cambridge, Massachusetts. This article first appeared in *Z Magazine*, in March 2002.

CRITICAL THINKING   What is eugenics? What connotations does the word have?

1   We have entered the era of Yuppie Eugenics. A contemporary, ostensibly voluntary form of older ideas and practices, Yuppie Eugenics is based in modern molecular genetics and concepts of "choice," and has begun to raise the high-tech prospect of employing prenatal genetic engineering. What it shares with the earlier doctrines is the goal of improving and perfecting human bloodlines and the human species as a whole.

2   The eugenics movement arose in the late 19th century in the wake of new scientific thinking about animal and plant breeding that culminated in evolutionary biology and genetics. While thus part of the scientifically-influenced "progressive"

thinking of the time, it was based on the fallacious argument that since nature had yielded "fit" species by "natural selection" and humans had "improved" domesticated animal breeds by "artificial selection," there was now a scientific warrant to use social and political means to discourage propagation of biologically "inferior" sorts of people. It soon gave rise to a set of State-directed programs in the United States and Europe.

3   The legal assault against people of "bad heredity" began in the United States with compulsory sterilization bills. The first of these was introduced into the Michigan legislature in 1897, but was defeated. A second bill, aimed at "idiots and imbecile children," passed the Pennsylvania legislature in 1905, but was vetoed by the governor. Indiana was the first state to actually enact a compulsory sterilization law in 1907 and it was followed by some 30 others. California did not repeal its law until 1979 and, in 1985, around 20 states still had laws on their books that permitted the involuntary sterilization of "mentally retarded" persons. The United States was by no means alone. In that liberal paragon Sweden, compulsory sterilizations of "unfit" persons were performed into the 1970s. All these laws were meant to improve the genetic make-up of the population, and especially of poor people, by preventing those judged to be "defective" from passing on their "defects" to future generations.

4   State Eugenics reached an abhorrent extreme in the Nazi extermination programs of the 1930s and 1940s. Initially directed at people with similar health or social problems as were targeted by the U.S. and Swedish sterilization laws, these were eventually expanded to cover entire populations—Jews, Gypsies, Poles— judged by the Nazi regime to represent "worthless lives" ("lebensunwerte Leben"). While certain overt State policies such as the use of gas chambers are now avoided, "ethnic cleansing," practiced on three continents in recent times, shows that eugenic cruelties have far from disappeared.

5   Technologies developed in the past three decades, however, have permitted a change in focus in the implementation of eugenics, at least in more affluent countries, from the State to the individual. Increasing numbers of diagnostic tests have been developed that enable physicians to assess some aspects of a fetus's future health status early enough to permit termination of a pregnancy during the second or even the first trimester. Though all such predictions have pitfalls and problems, they have made it possible for prospective parents not to bear a child they expect to be too ill or disabled to knowingly make part of their family. Though the intent of these methods is to widen choice in matters of procreation, they are eugenic in that they are meant to prevent the birth of people who are expected to perpetuate certain types of inborn conditions, such as cystic fibrosis, Huntington's disease, sickle cell disease, or phenylketonuria (PKU). Some scientists and physicians, indeed, have explicitly argued that it is wrong to permit ill or disabled people to procreate unless society is prepared to provide them with the "choice" to abort any fetus likely to manifest a condition like their own.

6   The new profession of genetic counseling has arisen to meet the need for information about the availability and significance of appropriate preconceptive and prenatal tests and about the decisions with which such tests confront prospective

parents. Now a central factor in the shift of "scientific" selection from coercive state programs to socially-sanctioned personal initiatives, advice about Choice Eugenics has become a routine part of prenatal care. In fact, practitioners have been sued by parents of children born disabled for not offering such information. Meanwhile, other prospective parents complain that their obstetrician or genetic counselor was excessively insistent that they accept a prenatal test and terminate a pregnancy that was predicted to produce a disabled child. So, though Choice Eugenics is not comparable to the earlier, compulsory state practices, some people experience it as coercive. Indeed, anxiety about social disapproval can sometimes be a more compelling dictator of choice than the law.

7   Extending the range of such "choices" since the 1970s and increasingly in the 1990s, hospital-based, non-profit fertility clinics, as well as a growing for-profit fertility industry, have been devising new technologies and social practices and expanding the use of the traditional ones, such as artificial insemination. The basis for most of the newer reproductive practices is in vitro fertilization (IVF). Initially, IVF was intended to help women whose ovaries and uterus were intact, so that they could produce eggs and gestate an embryo, but whose fallopian tubes were missing or blocked. It involves hyper-stimulation of the ovaries to induce several ova to mature simultaneously and then extracting a few of these and incubating them with fertile sperm outside the body ("in vitro"). Once an egg and sperm have fused and the first few cell divisions have occurred, several embryos are inserted into the woman's uterus in the hope that at least one of them will become implanted and develop into a baby.

8   Since the first successful attempt, in 1977, resulted in the birth of Louise Brown, IVF has become a widely offered and virtually routine part of reproductive medicine. It is covered by some state and private insurance programs in the United States and by the national health insurance programs of other countries. In addition to its procreative potential, it also enables prospective parents to have predictive tests performed on the embryos before they are implanted. It has therefore become an option for Choice Eugenics, especially for couples who strongly object to aborting an initiated pregnancy.

9   The access to human embryos offered by IVF has also made the technology a point of departure for a range of previously unavailable manipulations that raise complex questions not just for the individuals they affect directly, but for society at large. The technically least challenging of these involves the participation of two women, instead of just one, in producing a child—one who produces the egg, the other who gestates the embryo. This arrangement raises the novel question of which of them is the child's biological mother. In cases of disagreement, judges have often come down on the side of genes—hence of the egg donor—but that simply acts out our current genomania, because it ignores the biological major role of the woman who gestates and gives birth.

10   The explosive proliferation of preconceptive and prenatal tests has provided more and more reasons to terminate pregnancies in the hope of a better roll of the dice. Given certain features of modern prosperous societies, there is an increasing tendency to exercise such options on the basis of notions of biological perfectibility.

This tendency is transforming Choice Eugenics into Yuppie Eugenics. What was once a preventative choice has become a pro-active entitlement, exacerbated by the sense prevailing among current elites that one has the right to control all aspects of one's life and shape them by buying and periodically upgrading the best that technology has to offer, be it a computer, a car, or a child. Because this trend enjoys broadly based, mainstream sanction in the United States, what may begin as elite yuppie-ism is poised to become more widely disseminated as the technologies become cheaper and their use becomes more routine.

11   Fair-minded people differ on the point at which Choice Eugenics grades into Yuppie Eugenics. For some people with congenital disabilities, much Choice Eugenics, directed to preventing the birth of people like themselves, is going too far. People with congenital disabilities typically feel whole, and consider themselves victimized not by their genes, but by disaccomodating social arrangements. At the same time, a lack of extended family and health support systems can, for many, shift the balance against "preventable diversity." All eugenics defines some people as biologically unacceptable. Each turn of the screw en route to Yuppie Eugenics potentially excludes more and more people.

12   The false hope that scientists can alter an embryo genetically so as to "enhance" its potential and to make it conform to the future parents' image of a desirable child is also part of Yuppie Eugenics. Such unrealistic expectations, built on intrinsically unreliable genetic foreknowledge as well as on unscientific notions of the correspondence of specific genes to complex traits, can tempt prospective parents to agree to novel biological manipulations that are at least as likely to introduce problems as to remedy them. Also called germ-line genetic engineering or germ-line "gene therapy," this possibility has aroused widespread opposition. There are religious, but also secular, philosophical reasons for resisting a technology that plays into the idea of the developing human as a perfectible item. The goal of perfection encourages a view of existing life as imperfect. It transforms life into an ahistorical object, without context and eventually artifactual.

13   Objections also center on the fact that a genetic alteration introduced into an embryo is likely to become a permanent part of the genetic endowment of the person into whom that embryo develops and thus also of all of her or his progeny. Considering that the procedures themselves are experimental and the results are unpredictable (laboratory mice on which such procedures are performed often produce progeny with malformations, behavioral abnormalities, or increased cancer rates), germ-line genetic engineering poses unacceptable risks for "persons" who have just barely been conceived. There is no justification for undertaking such manipulations. If the prospective parents of the child into whom the embryo would develop are concerned that it may not meet their expectations, they need not gestate it.

14   Unfortunately this insidious prospect of germline engineering has found advocates among scientists such as James D. Watson, the Nobel Prize winning co-discoverer of the structure of DNA and the first director of the Human Genome Project, and Princeton University biologist Lee Silver. In his book *Remaking Eden* and in numerous appearances on television and the college speaking circuit, Silver

has been trying to persuade the public to get used to the prospect of a world with genetic haves and have-nots that would eventually lead to separate, and intentionally unequal, human species.

15 Fortunately, other more responsible scientists, writers, and activists have warned about the ominous safety and social implications of following this path, and have called for a ban on producing genetically-engineered humans. Indeed many European countries already prohibit such procedures.

16 This makes it particularly discreditable that the American Association for the Advancement of Science (AAAS), the largest professional organization of scientists in the United States, has gone on record with a statement that dances around the hazards of germline modification without even raising the possibility of a ban. Although the panel that prepared the AAAS report considers that the time is not yet ripe for implementing inheritable genetic modifications (IGM), it leaves the door open for future uses: "Although there are major technical obstacles to developing human IGM in the responsible ways that we have recommended," they write, "it is possible that at some time in the future scientific advances will make it feasible to undertake IGM." The AAAS panel failed to explain that only an unethical line of research, in contravention of the internationally endorsed Nuremburg Code on human experimentation, would have to be undertaken before any assurances can be made as to the risks of these procedures.

17 Cloning, another experimental genetic technology touted as a new "reproductive option," is being advocated by maverick physicians and scientists despite wide evidence of pathology in animals produced in this fashion. Some of these proponents, including a representative of the Raelians, a Canadian religious cult that claims to have received an extraterrestrial directive to clone its adherents, were given a respectful hearing at a forum at the prestigious National Academy of Sciences in August 2001.

18 Yuppie Eugenics also has its boosters among journalists and professional bioethicists. Michael Kinsley, writing in *Slate* (April 2000), suggested that genetic tests should eventually be used as qualifications for employment. He was seconded by Andrew Sullivan in the *New York Times Magazine* (July 2000), where he argued that genetic testing for future capacities is less objectionable than using SAT scores or letters of recommendation, since genetic tests are "more reliable." Arthur Caplan, Glenn McGee, and David Magnus of the University of Pennsylvania Institute of Bioethics follow the Kinsley-Sullivan thesis to its logical conclusion when they state, in a 1999 *British Medical Journal* article, "it is not clear that it is any less ethical to allow parents to pick the eye color of their child or to try to create a fetus with a propensity for mathematics than it is to permit them to teach their children the values of a particular religion or require them to play the piano." Here the intersubjective nature of the parent-child relationship is conflated with the one-way imposition of a chancy, irreversible genetic alteration during the earliest stages of embryonic development.

19 What is generally ignored in such prescriptions is that each gene contributes to numerous traits, and that any trait of significance depends on the functions of many

different genes. Genes and other features involved in growth and development constitute integral wholes that genetic alterations are more likely to disturb than enhance.

20   Yuppie Eugenics builds on the mirage that applications of genetics and biotechnology will be able to make us more perfect as well as to counter all forms of pain, illness, and death. The best way to restore us to sanity is to remember that genetics will never tell us what it takes to make a worthy human being and that the major causes of human illness and death continue to be not enough healthful food and too much unhealthful work. Eugenic and other gene dreams will not cure what ails us. ◆

FREEWRITING ASSIGNMENT

Is genetic testing of embryos for certain diseases technically ethical? Why or why not?

CRITICAL READING

1. Why do the authors call genetic selection, including genetic testing, "Yuppie Eugenics"? What does this term tell you about their position on this issue?
2. Are the extermination programs conducted by the Nazis during the 1930s and 1940s parallel to the types of genetic practices used now? How are they similar, and how are they different?
3. In paragraph 6, the authors state that the "anxiety about social disapproval" couples may face when deciding what to do about a pregnancy predicted to produce a disabled child might compel them to terminate a pregnancy against their deeper wishes. Is such pressure a form of forced eugenics? Could Canadian health care administrators one day make couples terminate a pregnancy if genetic tests reveal the fetus to have abnormalities?
4. Why do the authors put quotation marks around the words, "reproductive option" in paragraph 17?
5. The authors observe that genetic testing is being used to weed out unhealthy pregnancies. Do they approve or disapprove of this practice? Explain.
6. In paragraph 13, the authors state that there "is no justification for undertaking [genetic] manipulations." What do they suggest be done to embryos that do not "meet [parental] expectations" instead of genetic manipulation? How does their solution correspond to other positions they have taken on genetic technology in the essay? Explain.

CRITICAL WRITING

7. In paragraph 18, the authors quote several well-known journalists and bioethicists. Look up the articles to which they refer and evaluate the arguments presented by these prominent names: Michael Kingsley, *Baby*

Needs a New Set of Genes, **slate.msn.com/id/80604/**; Andrew Sullivan, *Promotion of the Fittest* (see Lexis/Nexis); and Caplan, McGee, and Magnus, *What is Immoral about Eugenics?*, **cmgm.stanford.edu/ biochem118/Papers/Genome%20Papers/Eugenics.pdf**. Are these writers really encouraging eugenics, or engaging in intellectual argument? Did the authors correctly convey the position of these individuals? Explain.

8. Many politicians are calling for a ban on human cloning. Research the issue online at Web sites such as **bioethics.gov**, **www.ornl.gov**, **www.nsplus.com/nsplus/insight/clone/clone.html**, and others you locate through search engines using key words such as "human cloning," "ethics," and "cloning debate." How has the cloning debate changed since the creation of Dolly was announced? Is a moratorium on human cloning likely to be lifted within the next few years? Write an essay in which you advocate either for, or against, a ban on human cloning.

GROUP PROJECTS

9. If genetic manipulation could be performed with accuracy and was made available to the general population, what rules should govern its use to prevent a gap between the haves and the have-nots? Develop a set of recommendations with your group, considering points raised by the authors.

10. One of the arguments against human cloning is that the technology could be abused to create clones of exceptional people, such as athletes, geniuses, and supermodels. With your group, discuss the likelihood of such an application of cloning technology. Who are possible candidates for cloning and why? In your discussion, also address the idea of "the right to genetic identity." Should such a right exist? How could it be violated?

Biotech Hope and Hype
Stephen Leahy

The biotechnology industry has made many promises in the past few decades. The study of genetics has been optimistically undertaken to cure a host of incurable diseases, feed the world's hungry, and clean up the environment. But, in reality, how many of these promises have panned out, and who's really reaping the benefits? According to environmental journalist Stephen Leahy, the golden age of biotechnology has yet to materialize. In this article, which appeared in the September 30, 2002 issue of *Maclean's* magazine, Leahy reviews the achievements of the biotech business since the early '80s and wonders what the hidden costs might ultimately be to the environment and to our pocketbooks.

Stephen Leahy is a freelance journalist from Brooklin, Ontario, who covers biotechnology, science, and environmental issues. He is a regular contributor to *Wired* and *Maclean's*.

CRITICAL
THINKING
What do you see as the benefits of biotechnology now and in the future? What are some of the claims that the biotechnology business has promised? Have expectations been met?

1   Come to Canada. We have lovely scenery, low crime, industry-friendly regulators and low corporate taxes. That, in essence, was the sales pitch Industry Minister Allan Rock gave the 15,565 biotechnonauts from 52 countries attending the world's largest biotechnology industry convention in Toronto this summer. And if that wasn't enticement enough, Rock announced $200 million in new funding for biotech start-ups to go with Ontario's $51 million in new funding initiatives.

2   Federal and provincial governments have long had a love affair with genetics, pumping billions into the biotech biz since the early 1980s. And who wouldn't love a new technology that promises to feed the hungry, cure intractable diseases, clean up the environment and, thanks to patent rights, usher in the Golden and Profitable Age of Biotechnology?

3   So, 20 years later and how many breakthrough products has biotech produced? Gene therapy may actually have harmed more people than it's helped. Genetically engineered (GE) crops haven't aided hard-pressed farmers, improved the quality of our food or fed the hungry. The few drugs derived from GE such as insulin simply replace existing products while creating new risks. And Canadians remain nervous about the technology.

4   With good reason. The industry consistently overhypes the benefits and downplays the potential risks of a revolutionary new technology. Genetic engineering is revolutionary because its products incorporate genes from unrelated species. The process of evolution and traditional plant and animal breeding is an incestuous, only-with-close-relatives affair—a vertical gene exchange. The between-species aspect of biotechnology, a horizontal gene exchange, is a whole new ball game.

5   Only through GE can a gene from a soil bacterium that makes a toxin become part of a corn plant's DNA. Now this exchange is not easily done. First a DNA package has to be built that contains the toxin-producing bacterial gene as well as elements known as promoters and vectors of bacterial viruses, antibiotic-resistance marker genes and other assorted bits of DNA. These packages are "glued" onto thousands of tiny metal pellets and blasted into corn plant cells with a device called a gene gun. A few will hit the right place, and the bacterial virus promoters and vectors will stitch the foreign gene into the corn's DNA. The process will produce many freakish, non-functional plants. The odd corn plant will produce the bacterial toxin in every cell. Known as Bt corn, it kills any moth or butterfly larvae that nibble on it.

6   One major reason to proceed with caution on bioteck innovation: the pedal-to-the-metal attitude in an industry where even the biggest players concede that many vital questions remain unanswered. "My view of biology is, we don't know shit," the U.S. geneticist Craig Venter told a magazine writer. Yet the company he founded heralded its successful decoding of the human genome (the total DNA package) two years ago as a key step in ushering in the Biotech Age. It discovered—

surprise!—that the human genome contains just 35,000 genes instead of the expected 100,000. So, rather than performing single duties, genes appear to multi-task and work in combination with other genes. In other words, pluck a gene from an organism because it performs one desired function, place it in another organism—and who knows what unanticipated business it will get up to. Besides, genes are just a small part of DNA.

7   Biotech critics like geneticist David Suzuki say it's much too soon to have planted GE crops and used them in food and drugs. "Scientists just don't know enough about the technology right now," argues Suzuki. Not surprisingly, the biotech business says it's high time to move forward. "People don't realize that biotechnology is starting to transform the world," says Janet Lambert, president of the industry trade association, BIOTECanada. "Is it too soon to feed the starving in Africa?"

8   Canada's first GE crops were planted in 1996. Three patented versions—canola, corn and soy—are now found in 60 to 70 per cent of our food. Yet they don't improve food quality or boost yields appreciably—in fact, critics argue both quality and yield are poorer. The main reason farmers plant something like Monsanto's Round-Up Ready canola is that it offers them the convenience of using a single herbicide—made by Monsanto, natch—to control weeds, rather than a whole bunch. But the jury is still out as to whether GE farmers actually spray less.

9   The economics are also iffy. Although GE seeds cost more than the seeds they replace, some farmers, mainly those with large operations, make a couple more dollars per acre using them. Others, however, are being badly hurt. First it was the loss of export markets for formerly GE-free crops in GE-shy Europe. Now, because GE plants are living creatures that reproduce, disperse and evolve, there's genetic pollution and contamination. Thanks to winds and insects, engineered genes are travelling long distances in pollen and seeds, turning up in non-GE crops across the Prairies.

10   Given those concerns, it's not surprising there was an uproar in Prairie farm communities last year when Agriculture Canada announced that Monsanto's GE wheat will be submitted to regulators for approval this fall. While the company stands to make as much as $7 billion from that crop, a University of Saskatchewan study showed Canadian farmers would end up losing $185 million a year through lost sales. Monsanto says it is sensitive to the contamination concerns. "We are not going to sell it," says company spokesperson Trish Jordan, "until a segregation system is in place to keep it separate from non-GE wheat."

11   Meanwhile, hundreds of millions of North Americans are eating foods made from GE crops without any documented ill effects. But then, how could we document any harm without data on who is eating those foods and in what quantities? That would require food labelling and a tracking system for GE crops. But while the vast majority of Canadians want foods with GE ingredients to be labelled, that's not going to happen. The reason: it would spell the end of agricultural biotech. Food processors admit they'd insist on GE-free crops from farmers because if people could easily identify GE foods, some, perhaps many, wouldn't buy them.

12   As for global hunger, no one can deny it's a major economic and social problem. But the GE crops that the large multinationals have brought to developing countries so far are cotton, corn and soy—all engineered to resist herbicides, and all affordable only by large commercial farmers. If biotechnologists really want to feed the poor, notes Sakiko Fukuda-Parr of the United Nations Development Program, they need to create virus-resistant, drought-tolerant, nutrient-enhanced versions of such staple crops as millet, sorghum and cassava. "Of course," she adds, "farmers living on less than a dollar a day don't represent much of a market."

13   Perhaps that's why fewer companies are now involved in "green" (agricultural) biotech and many more in "red" (medical/health) biotech. With one blockbuster health product capable of bringing in billions in revenue, the big drug companies are quickly transmogrifying into biopharmaceutical corporations. Today, something like 100 medical products are derived from genetic engineering. Thousands more are being tested.

14   The first, and likely the most profitable, GE product is "human- derived" insulin. Approved for use in Canada in 1983, it rapidly replaced the more expensive insulin traditionally made from the pancreas of cows and pigs. It also produced biotech's first human casualties.

15   Hundreds of Canadian diabetics have reported reactions to GE insulin, says Vancouver health policy expert Colleen Fuller, spokesperson for Society for Diabetic Rights. Using access-to-information law, that new group has associated the deaths of eight Canadians with use of synthetic insulin as of January, 2001. Fuller, a diabetic who has reacted badly to GE insulin, has also heard from more than 400 people complaining of bad responses to the medication. Hundreds of deaths and thousands of unwanted side effects have also been noted in the U.S., Britain and elsewhere. Problems clear up quickly when diabetics return to animal insulin, says Fuller. What really makes her angry, she says, is that she and thousands like her have paid a high price so insulin manufacturers could make more money.

16   The financial successes of GE insulin and another multi-billion dollar product, GE erythropoietin (EPO), an anti-anemia drug made by placing a human gene in the ovarian cells of a Chinese hamster, jump-started the production of "biofactories." The term refers to bacteria, plants and animals engineered to produce human proteins of all kinds. Wisconsin dairy cows produce a blood-clotting agent called fibrinogen in their milk. Sheep, rabbits, goats and even mice make human proteins in their milk. While the mammary gland is the biofactory of choice, TGN Biotech of Quebec City produces complex proteins in pig semen.

17   Plants are the bargain-basement biofactories with the potential for manufacturing material at just a fraction of the traditional costs. Molecular farmers at Medicago Inc. of Sainte-Foy, Que., have genetically engineered alfalfa to produce human hemoglobin proteins for blood transfusions. Tobacco fields outside London, Ont., produce Interleukin-10, a human immune system modulator, for treating Crohn's disease. In the U.S. there are experimental fields

of corn containing anti-sperm and anti-herpes antibodies, an HIV protein for a future vaccine, and an enzyme that may help cystic fibrosis patients digest food.

18   While none of these products are in general use yet, some are in human trials. Critics worry about the possibility of contamination of other crops or the altered items getting into food. Joe Cummins, a retired University of Western Ontario geneticist, is concerned about the effects human proteins may have on bugs and micro-organisms in the soil and water. There is a danger, he says, that by incorporating a human protein, a common soil virus could become a health threat.

19   Gene therapy is a more direct route to solving medical problems—introducing engineered genes straight into human cells. While billions of dollars have been invested and some 3,500 clinical trials conducted worldwide since 1990, there have been few claims of cures. But there are substantial risks. In 1999, 18-year-old Jesse Gelsinger died while undergoing gene therapy at the University of Pennsylvania. Researchers have since reported hundreds of adverse reactions among patients in gene therapy trials, 691 in the U.S. alone. In Canada, where more than 30 human trials have been approved, one man, James Dent, died while undergoing gene therapy for a brain tumour. Human trials continue.

20   The heart of the problem with gene therapy and genomic medicine in general is the complexity of the human body. Single-gene diseases, the kind most likely to be treatable by gene therapy, are very rare. And nearly all ailments, including cancer, diabetes and cardiovascular disease, are the result of many factors: lifestyle, diet, exposure to toxins, stress, hygiene and, yes, genes. The current focus and fascination with genes produces a fix-it mentality toward disease and health, rather than a better examination of the conditions that create illness.

21   Currently 99 per cent of genomic research is about making money, not curing people, says Dr. Nancy Olivieri, head of the thalassemia and sickle cell anemia research programs at Toronto's Hospital for Sick Children. Moreover, Olivieri questions huge investments in biotech research that may never yield results when that money could be put to good use improving conventional treatments or the distribution of existing medicines, particularly in emerging countries.

22   The current passion for all things genetic has blinded many to biotech's faults and limitations. The hard-hearts of Canadian business continue to pump billions into an industry where only a small number of companies has ever made a profit. Last year, the publicly traded firms netted a collective loss of $784 million. Perhaps, in the end, genetics is a numbers game. Canadian biotechs have 17,000 new products in the pipeline. Undoubtedly some will earn substantial profits and benefit some people. But at what cost, and at what risk to the public and the planet?

FREEWRITING ASSIGNMENT ————————————————

In this article, Stephen Leahy claims that Canadians are "nervous" about biotechnology. What are your feelings about some of the technologies mentioned here, such as genetically modified crops or gene therapy?

CRITICAL READING

1. What is Leahy's thesis in this article? Does he believe that the biotech industry is good for Canada? Why or why not?
2. Why does the author believe that genetic research should proceed with caution? What are some of the dangers he mentions here?
3. Why are genetically engineered crops not being used to fight global hunger? Who benefits from Canada's production of genetically engineered crops?
4. What does Leahy mean by the "fix-it mentality" produced by the current focus on genes (paragraph 20)? What might be a better focus to combat disease?
5. Why is there no available data on the possible results of eating genetically modified food?

CRITICAL WRITING

6. *Research and Analysis:* Stephen Leahy refers to Canadian scientist and environmental activist David Suzuki in this article. Read Suzuki's views on genetic engineering at **www.davidsuzuki.org/files/General/ DTSbiotech.pdf**. Summarize his arguments in an essay.
7. *Persuasive Writing:* Compose a letter to a Canadian government official stating why you feel that the labelling, or even the banning altogether, of GE foods is necessary. Alternatively, compose a letter to the same government official urging him or her to invest more into Canada's expanding biotech industry. Use points from Leahy's article or other research to support your argument.
8. *Interview:* Leahy mentions how Canadians are wary about the biotech industry as a whole. Interview several people of varying ages about their knowledge of biotechnology. What are their general ideas, fears, hopes, and beliefs on the subject? How do they feel about specific technologies, such as cloning, genetically modified food, or gene therapy? How do they feel about the government subsidizing such industries? Evaluate the results in a short essay on how Canadians view the biotech business in general.

GROUP PROJECTS

9. In this article, the author mentions the industry trade association, BIOTECanada. Go to their Web site at **www.biotech.ca/EN/biotech.html** and read the material they distribute to teachers as a teaching resource. How does the material deal with many of the questions in this article? Does this change your opinion of some of Leahy's points? With your group, discuss how you would teach a class of elementary schoolchildren about the subjects mentioned on the BIOTECanada Web site.

VIEWPOINTS

▸ **Should Human Cloning Be Permitted?**
Patricia A. Baird, M.D.

▸ **Yes, Human Cloning Should Be Permitted**
Chris MacDonald, Ph.D.

Many of the authors in this chapter focus on how human cloning can benefit, or harm, individuals. In the next piece, Dr. Patricia A. Baird explains why such a perspective is "dangerously" incomplete. The implications of human cloning must be viewed in its entire *social* context. How will human cloning affect our society, not just in the present, but for generations down the line? How would a cloned child be viewed by society, and how might he or she feel about being a cloned person? If we pursue human cloning, will future generations look back on our actions as reckless and irresponsible? And why endanger the future if there is no true need to create human clones in the first place?

Responding directly to her argument, ethicist Chris MacDonald explains why he disagrees with Baird's argument. He feels that Baird is too severe in her condemnation of human cloning, and fails to provide sufficient evidence that human cloning should be banned. Moreover, he disagrees with her point that if a majority of society wishes to ban something, we should heed the voice of the people. In principle, he explains, a majority shouldn't impose its viewpoint on a minority, and this applies to human cloning as well.

Patricia A. Baird is a geneticist and head of the Department of Medical Genetics at the University of British Columbia. She frequently writes on the social, ethical, and health consequences connected to human reproductive biology and genetics, and the resulting implications for public policy. Baird presented this paper to an ethics committee created by the California state legislature, addressing the issue of human cloning. The committee invited individuals to present their recommendations on what position should be taken on human cloning, and the reasons for their position. This abridged version of her presentation was published in the June 2000 *Annals of the RCPSC.*

Chris MacDonald teaches ethics, philosophy, and moral theory at Dalhousie University in Halifax, Nova Scotia. His research spans health care ethics, professional ethics, business ethics, and moral theory. This response to Patricia Baird's paper was published in the October 2000 issue of the *Annals of the RCPSC.*

CRITICAL THINKING

Baird raises some questions about the well-being of the cloned person, and how cloned people would feel about themselves, their identity, and how they fit into a society where most people were not cloned. She also wonders how society would treat cloned people. How do you think a cloned person would fit into our society today? Would he or she be an object of curiosity? A celebrity? A freak? Would he or she ever be able to lead a normal life? Explain.

Should Human Cloning Be Permitted?

Patricia A. Baird, M.D.

A Qualitatively Different Type of Reproduction

1   Producing humans by somatic-cell nuclear-transfer cloning differs from sexual reproduction—it separates reproduction from recombination. Normally, in an out-bred species such as humans, we cannot predict what the overall characteristics of an embryo will be. In sexual reproduction, it is unpredictable which combination of the parents' thousands of genes will occur. To date, in creating the next generation, we have had to give ourselves over to chance. But if nuclear transfer is used, the nucleus can be taken from an adult whose characteristics are known—and the process reproduces the biology of the former individual. It becomes possible to select by known characteristics which humans will be copied. The new technology allows the asexual replication of a human being, the ability to predetermine the full complement of a child's nuclear genes, and the easier alteration of the genes of prospective individuals. Cloning is a change in the integrity of our species, and we must think about the long-term consequences.

Public Reaction to Human Cloning

2   Cloning used to produce a human is rejected by the overwhelming majority of people. Polls on new scientific developments have limitations, but the *Economist* reported that over 90 percent of Americans were opposed to human cloning.[1] Other polls have shown similar results.[2,3] Polls, however, are affected by how the questions are asked, so an in-depth approach is needed. Many experts believe that lay people cannot understand complicated scientific topics, but there are data showing that they can assimilate and make judgments about complex issues. The Wellcome Trust did a qualitative focus-group study, and reported that opposition to human cloning was "nearly universal" among participants.[4] Most were against the idea of using cloning for reproductive purposes, stemming from concerns for the children and society, as much as from fears about interfering with nature. When over 90 percent of citizens in a democracy oppose human cloning, it is difficult for a government to justify a policy that permits it. There are a few people, however, who would pursue cloning because they see potential advantages for themselves.

Foreseeable Requests for Cloning

3   There are foreseeable situations where individuals may want to pursue cloning—for example, for couples where both are infertile and have neither eggs nor sperm, or where the male produces no sperm. Given that there are new treatment techniques using cells from testicular biopsy, such problems are rare. A second example is

where a lesbian couple might wish to use one partner's body cell and the enucleated egg of the other to produce a child together. In these scenarios, there are other options available to form a family—such as sperm donation, egg and embryo donation, or adoption. Other situations where cloning may be pursued is when a couple's child is dying or is killed, and they want to replace him or her by using one of his or her cells in nuclear-transfer cloning; or when a clone could provide a genetically compatible organ for transplantation. There will be instances where people wish to pursue cloning for particular reasons.[5-7]

4   The arguments about physical and psychological harm to clones have also been well-delineated.[8,9] For example, with regard to possible physical harms, congenital malformations, handicap, early death, increased risk of cancer, premature aging, and death have all been raised. Possible psychological harms to cloned individuals (replicands) have also been outlined, including diminished individuality, a sense of foreclosed future, or a disturbed sense of identity. An important part of human identity is the sense of arising from a maternal and a paternal line while at the same time being a unique individual. Many children who are adopted, or conceived from donor insemination, show a deep need to learn about their biological origins. Making children by cloning means that they do not have this dual genetic origin; they are not connected to others in the same biological way as the rest of humanity. The first person born this way would have to cope with being the first not to come from the union of egg and sperm. Social, family, and kinship relationships that support human flourishing have evolved over millennia—but there is no way to place replicands. Is the DNA source the twin? The mother? The father?

Widening the Frame

5 Most debate on human cloning focuses on a weighing of harms and benefits to individuals. This is a dangerously incomplete framing. Looking at the issue as a matter of reproductive technology choice, although it focuses on individual autonomy, reproductive freedom, and protection of children, means that other issues are omitted.[10] We need to shift from the framing as individual choice, to a framing that reveals how permitting cloning affects future generations and society. I am reminded of one of the consultations of the Royal Commission on New Reproductive Technologies with an aboriginal group in Canada. They told the commission about their seventh-generation rule. They said that when they had to make a big decision in their community, they always considered what the consequences were likely to be in the seventh generation. This is a useful perspective to have, because viewing cloning as a personal matter inappropriately minimizes potentially serious social consequences. Individual choices in reproduction are not isolated acts—they affect the child, other people, and future generations. The wider consequences must be considered because we all have a stake in the type of community that we live in. We do not want it to be one where the use of cloning commodifies children, commercializes family formation, or increases social injustice. Cloning raises issues about the future of our species. We have not yet found the wisdom to

deal with hunger, poverty, and environmental degradation—we are unlikely to have the wisdom to direct our own evolution.

6   Nuclear-transfer cloning allows third parties to choose the genotypes of people who will be cloned. Before, when two people mated, no one could control which genes the child received out of a myriad of possibilities. This lottery of reproduction has been a protection against people being predetermined, chosen, or designed by others—including parents.

7   Cloning directs the production of human beings in an unprecedented way. When a child of a particular genetic constitution is "made," it is easier to look on him or her as a product, rather than a gift of providence. If we can, and some people do, make children "to order," it is likely to change the way we view children.

8   An impetus to developing nuclear-transfer cloning for producing animals has been that it could then be combined with genetic enhancement—genes could be added to give the animals desired traits. Genes are inserted into cells in culture, then the cells screened to pick the ones that have incorporated the desired genes. These altered cells are used as the donors of nuclei for cloned animals. It is then possible to create transgenic cloned animals with commercially desirable genetic traits (for example, heavier meat yield or production of insulin in the milk).[11]

9   Reproduction by nuclear-transfer cloning makes it possible to think about genetically enhancing humans. A person's cells could be cultured, genes inserted, and those cells taking up the desired genes used to produce a cloned "improved" individual. We could insert genes for viral-disease resistance, or to protect against baldness or degenerative diseases, or insert genes related to height or intelligence. If nuclear-transfer cloning is permitted, what will stop genetic enhancement being used eventually? There would be strong individual motivation to have a taller or disease-resistant child. We would then be taking human evolution into our own hands. Are we wise enough to manage it or the social consequences? Most people will want their child to be brighter, taller, disease-resistant—so this technology could make people more standard, based on individual choices and market forces. If it works, it is likely to become used more often than just occasionally.

10   Who would have access to cloning or genetic improvements? Everyone? It is likely that those with financial resources would have access, but not other people, because cloning or enhancement would have to be provided as a socially underwritten "good" if it were to be available to everyone. And it is unlikely that most countries would provide publicly supported cloning, given that there are few social benefits and many potential harms.

11   If cloning or enhancement technology were provided as a public good to ensure equality of access, the government would have to decide in what circumstances people may clone themselves, and what traits were desirable. Docility? Height? Ability to provide a tissue transplant? Unless the market is to decide, criteria as to who may clone themselves, and a regulatory body will be needed.

12   If cloning is used, will we undermine the unconditional parental acceptance of offspring that is central to nurturing human beings? Parental acceptance is likely to become conditional when we are able to program for certain characteristics. If cloning technology or genetic enhancement is permitted, people with disabilities, or

members of racial or ethnic minorities, will be affected differently, and in a way unlikely to lead to greater equality and respect.

13   There are forces favoring the use of cloning—particular individuals will pursue it, and it will benefit financially those who provide it, so it is likely to be marketed to the public.

14   Many issues arising from cloning cannot be resolved in the framework of individual autonomy and reproductive choice. The focus on autonomy leads us to overlook the collective and transgenerational consequences of leaving the use of reproductive technologies to individual choices.[12] The use of scientific technology focused on individual wishes may result in social harms because individual interests differ from the public good at times. It is analogous to the tragedy of the commons,[13] which is exemplified by ranchers sharing grazing land, or fishers sharing a fishing ground. There is an incentive for individuals to overgraze or overfish because the benefits of doing so accrue to the individual, whereas the costs and harms occur to the community. The aggregate effect of individually beneficial choices may harm the long-term common good, and the cumulative impact of individual choices can result in an unethical system. Public policy-making differs from individual-based decision-making—because the moral unit of a physician is the patient, while the moral unit of public policy is all citizens.[14] If there is a conflict between the total social good and the good of an individual, public policy must uphold the public interest.

15   All members of the public have a stake in whether cloning is permitted, because if cloned people exist, the changes affect everyone. Even though a majority do not want to allow it, if it is permitted, we would all live in a world where people are cloned. Even though initially, individuals on whom cloning technology had a direct impact would be a minority, their collective experiences would influence social values. In public policy-making, it is inappropriate to subordinate every consideration to the question of whether it helps a couple to have a family. Society has a legitimate role in deciding whether cloning will be used. The far-reaching nature of this choice means more voices must be involved in making decisions. The decisions should not be taken preemptively by a clinical facility or a group of scientists who ignore the wishes of the rest of the community. We need the perspectives not just of those who are knowledgeable in biology or science; we also need the perspectives of sociologists, humanists, and citizens from a variety of life experiences. On something that affects our species' future, it would be valuable to have the perspectives of people from many countries.

Conclusions Regarding Policy

16   There is no compelling case to make people by asexual means; human reproductive cloning is without potential benefits to almost all citizens, and other options are available in most situations. Many institutions have come to this conclusion; the prospects of making human beings by cloning have elicited concern in many countries, and there have been calls for a worldwide ban on cloning used to produce humans by many political and religious leaders, and by organizations such as the World Health Organization, the World Medical Organization, the American

Medical Association, and UNESCO. Nineteen countries in the Council of Europe have signed an agreement that bans human cloning. Medicine, science, and technology are worldwide endeavors, so this is an issue facing humans as a species. For this reason, WHO is making an international effort to cooperate on guidelines for cloning in humans.

17   History shows that where there is a demand for a new service and the ability of a few to pay for it, unless there is legislation, there will be professionals willing to provide it. There is licensing of fertility clinics in several European countries, but in some other countries, reproductive technologies are highly commercialized and little regulated. If human cloning were permitted in the United States, it would likely proceed in the billion-dollar private reproductive-medicine sector. In this market-driven context, its use is unlikely to be controlled. It is now possible to peruse catalogues if you wish to buy eggs or surrogate pregnancies; so it seems likely that if human cloning is permitted in the United States, it is only a matter of time before pressure from individuals with specific interests would open up the field. Legislation is needed to ban the implantation into a woman of an egg cell that has had its nucleus transferred from a body cell. When such legislation is written, its wording should not inadvertently ban nonreproductive cloning research, or animal cloning research that may be of benefit, and that many people see as acceptable.

18   How we use cloning is not an individual or medical matter. It is a matter of social policy that cannot be viewed in a narrow framework of reproductive technology and individual choice. How we choose to use this technological capacity will shape society for our children, their children, and after. How it is used is likely to entrench existing inequalities, and create new ones.

19   In conclusion, using nuclear-transfer cloning to allow people to have a child introduces a different way of reproduction for our species. Once we breach this barrier, it leaves us with no place to stop. Given all the problems outlined, the reasons for permitting cloning to produce a person are insufficiently compelling. Even in the few circumstances where the case for human cloning seems justified, there are alternative solutions. We are at an appropriate stopping place on a slippery slope. Not all reasons why a person might wish to copy his or her cells are unethical, but given there are other options open to people wishing to form a family, concerns about individual and social harms from cloning are strong enough that it is not justified to permit it. These issues affecting the creation of the next generation are important for the future of our species; we must deal with them wisely. I hope we can. ◆

References

1. "Whatever next?" *The Economist*, 1997, March 1;79–81.
2. *Time*/CNN poll. 1997 March.
3. International Food Information Council. Wirthlin group quorum survey, 1997 March 21–24.
4. Public perspectives on human cloning, Medicine in society program. The Wellcome Trust, 1999 June (http://www.wellcome.ac.uk/en/1/awtpubrepcln.html).
5. McGee G. *The Human Cloning Debate*. Berkeley: Berkeley Hills Books, 1998.
6. Hummer J, Almeder R. *Human Cloning. Biomedical Ethics Reviews*. Totowa: 1998.

7. Andrews L. *The Clone Age: 20 Years at the Forefront of Reproductive Technology*. New York: Henry Holt, 1999.
8. Wilson JQ, Kass L. *The Ethics of Human Cloning*. Washington: American Enterprise Press, 1999:10(2).
9. "Cloning Human Beings." Report of the national bioethics advisory commission. Hastings Centre Report 1997:27(5).
10. Baylis F. *Human Cloning: Three Mistakes and a Solution*. Unpublished manuscript.
11. Pennis E. "After Dolly, a Pharming Frenzy." *Science* 1998:279;646–8.
12. Baird PA. "Individual Interests, Societal Interests, and Reproductive Technologies." *Perspectives Biology Medicine* 1997;40(3):440-51.
13. Hardin G. "The Tragedy of the Commons." *Science* 1968;162:1243–8.
14. Lamm RD. "Redrawing the Ethics Map." Hastings Centre Report 1999;29(2):28–9

 # Yes, Human Cloning Should Be Permitted
Chris MacDonald, Ph.D.

1   Patricia Baird's discussion of human cloning challenges the prospect of nuclear-transfer cloning for the purposes of human reproduction. Baird reviews a long list of familiar worries about human cloning, but the most striking feature of her discussion is its frankness in placing the onus of justification on the shoulders of those who would permit human cloning. The reasons for permitting cloning, she argues, are "insufficiently compelling," so cloning should be prohibited. The implication is that any new technology should be forbidden unless and until enough justification can be found for allowing its use.

2   Baird is to be commended for her frankness. But the onus is misplaced, or at least too severe. One need not be a single-minded defender of liberty to think that, contrary to Baird's implication, we need good reasons to limit the actions of others, particularly when those actions do no clear and specific harm. The fact that a portion of society—even a majority—finds an activity distasteful is insufficient grounds for passing a law forbidding it. For example, it is presumably true that at one point, roughly 90 percent of the public (the same proportion that Baird says is against human cloning) was opposed to homosexuality. Does (or did) this justify action on the part of government to ban homosexual lifestyles? Surely not.

3   There may be a flaw in my analogy. Human cloning, according to critics, has harmful effects (or at least risks). Indeed, Baird suggests that the arguments regarding potential physical and psychological harm to clones have been "well-delineated." In fact, a convincing case has yet to be made for the claim that the physical and psychological risks to clones are more severe than, or different in kind from, those faced by children produced in more traditional ways. Identical twins live with the psychological "burden" of not being genetically unique. Children born to women over 35 are at an increased risk of genetic illness. Children resulting from in vitro fertilization or other reproductive technologies live with the knowledge that their origins were unusual. They may even live with the knowledge that their genetic pro-

file has been manipulated (for example, through pre-implantation selection of embryos). Human cloning for reproductive purposes is another novel—and as yet untested—medical technology. As such, it should be approached with caution. Thorough animal trials should be completed before attempts on humans are contemplated. But this is true of any new medical technology.

4   Baird worries about the shift that human cloning might provoke in the way that we view children. This in turn would change the type of community that we are. The central worry is that human cloning "commodifies" children (i.e., that cloning may make us think of children as a commodity or product to be bought and sold). Why would cloning have this effect? Is it simply because it is likely to be expensive, so that it costs money to have children? Surely this is insufficient to worry us. Raising children already costs money—the statistics show us how many hundreds of thousands of dollars it costs to raise a child through to adulthood. Yet no one has suggested that we see our children as products, or love them any less. (In the mid 1940s—before publicly funded health care—my grandparents sold their car to pay the hospital bill related to my father's birth, so "purchasing" the birth of a child is nothing new!)

5   Baird argues that an "important part of human identity is the sense of arising from a maternal and a paternal line while at the same time being a unique individual." Yet without supporting evidence, this sounds like pop psychology. And we can reply in kind: most people I know do not identify with both their maternal and paternal lineages. One of my friends, who was raised by a single mother, identifies with her maternal Eastern European heritage, and not with the French paternal heritage implied by her surname. Another friend identifies with his father's black heritage, rather than with his maternal Chinese lineage, despite his Asian physical features. Such patterns are not unusual. Dual heritage may be normal, but it hardly seems central to our conception of ourselves as humans. And identical twins seem none the worse for the knowledge that they are not genetically unique individuals. Claims about challenges to what makes us "human" may be powerful rhetorical devices, but they must be substantiated if they are to be convincing.

6   Baird is correct to exhort us to look beyond harms to identifiable individuals, to the social implications that human cloning might have. As a comparison, think of fetal sex selection. Most of us think that sex selection is a bad thing—not because of any purported harm to the child, but because we worry about the social implications of valuing children of one sex over those of another. So Baird rightly reminds us that focusing on potential harms to individuals constitutes a "dangerously incomplete framing" of the problem. Furthermore, cloning (and genetic technology in general) is sufficiently new—and its implications sufficiently poorly understood—to warrant a healthy respect, and even the allowance of a margin of safety. But this does not suggest the need for the ban that Baird (with others) proposes. What these worries suggest is a need for caution, for discussion, and for regulation. For instance, laws limiting the number of clones that might be created from one individual, restricting the combination of cloning with genetic modification, and defining lines of parental obligation, would alleviate many of the concerns associated with

human cloning. (Françoise Baylis argues that cloning is so likely to be used in combination with gene transfer that we should think of cloning as an enhancement technology rather than as a reproductive technology, in her article "Human cloning: three mistakes and a solution," which has been accepted for publication in the *Journal of Medicine and Philosophy.*)

7   What I have said here should not be taken as an absolute defense of human cloning in all circumstances. (Indeed, there may be only a few circumstances in which cloning is appropriate.) Nor have I suggested that public monies should be spent on cloning research. All I have suggested is that a ban on research leading toward human cloning is unwarranted by the arguments raised thus far. Caution and discretion are warranted; a ban is not.

8   Finally, I worry that Baird's point of view exemplifies the way in which human reproductive cloning is being singled out, among cloning-related techniques, as a bogeyman. Almost in chorus, scientists are pleading with regulators not to place restrictions on cloning experimentation per se. At the same time, most scientists seem to be more than willing to swear off reproductive cloning, and indeed to wring their hands over the moral implications of its use. Yet this has the air of a too-hasty concession. The scientific community seems to be too willing to condemn one unpopular application of cloning technology, on the basis of too little convincing argumentation, to appease those who oppose cloning technology in general. But human cloning for reproductive purposes has legitimate, morally acceptable applications—for example, for infertile couples, and for gay couples. And none of the criticisms have been convincingly made. We should not let reproductive human cloning be abandoned as the moral sacrificial lamb of the cloning debate. ◆

FREEWRITING ASSIGNMENT

Because no one has actually cloned a human being (that has been proven), much of the debate on this issue is theoretical. Are hypothetical arguments sufficient grounds to create laws against something like human cloning? Why or why not?

CRITICAL READING

1. What does Baird mean when she says that human cloning will create a change in the "integrity" of reproduction? What does this word mean? What does it imply when used this way? Explain.
2. MacDonald presents an analogy between the acceptance, or nonacceptance, of homosexuality and the controversy over human cloning. Are these two subjects similar? Does it support his point? Why or why not?
3. In paragraph 3, MacDonald argues that no convincing case has been made that human clones would suffer more physical and psychological risks than children "produced in more traditional ways." How do you

think Baird would respond to this claim? Other authors in this section? Explain.

4. What is the "seventh generation rule"? How does Baird apply it to the issue of human cloning? Do you think her use of this rule is an effective way to support her argument? Explain.

5. Baird comments that "we have not yet found the wisdom to deal with hunger, poverty, and environmental degradation—we are unlikely to have the wisdom to direct our own evolution." Are these examples parallel? Why or why not? Does she make a good point? Explain.

6. How does MacDonald argue against Baird's essay? Identify the points he selects to argue against, how he addresses these points. Does he address all of the points in Baird's piece? Explain.

7. In paragraphs 9–11, Baird raises questions connected to creating "improved" babies that possess the genetic traits we prefer, such as creating children to be taller, brighter, or more disease resistant. Why does she feel such an application of this nuclear-transfer cloning would be harmful? Explain.

8. Analyze Baird's conclusion. How does she end her argument? What ideas and points does she leave with her audience?

9. Consider the perspective from which MacDonald writes. Baird is a medical professional, MacDonald is an ethicist. Does he convince his audience that he has the credentials to debate this issue? Is it important to Baird's argument that she is herself a geneticist? Does the fact that MacDonald is not a physician undercut his argument? Why or why not?

10. MacDonald argues that just because most people (90%) want to ban human cloning, we should not bend to majority rule because such concessions can be dangerous. Do you agree? Why or why not?

CRITICAL WRITING

11. Is human cloning likely to "change the way we view children"? Why or why not? Frame your answer in terms of how society may view cloned children.

12. Baird raises the question, if there is no real need to clone, why try it at all? Respond to her statements by expressing your own opinion on this aspect of the cloning debate.

13. *Personal Narrative:* Write a personal narrative from the point of view of a teenager who has just found out that he or she was a clone of a dead sibling. Until this point, you had grown up thinking you were just like any other person. Now, you discover you are actually a clone. How do you feel? Would you be angry? Accepting? Explain.

14. Scientists warn that once DNA is altered in a human being, there is no going back. An alteration may continue with each new generation. Moreover, such DNA alteration may become undesirable, with some people discriminating against genetically altered people out of a desire to

produce "pure" genetic lines. (Consider the controversy concerning genetically enhanced foods.) Write an essay in which you explore some of the future issues genetic engineering in humans may cause. Support your predictions with information provided in the chapter.

GROUP PROJECTS

15. Baird states, "Cloning raises issues about the future of our species. . . . Before, when two people mated, no one could control which genes the child received out of a myriad of possibilities. This lottery of reproduction has been a protection against people being predetermined, chosen, or designed by others—including parents." With your group, discuss this idea. Would human cloning remove the "lottery" aspect of human reproduction? Would this be a bad thing? Debate the issue, and, later, summarize the discussion in a short essay.

16. With your group, develop a policy statement in which you ban, allow, or partially allow certain aspects of human cloning. Under what conditions is it acceptable, if ever, and why? Share your policy statement with the class as part of a larger group discussion.

17. Baird conjectures that human cloning technology could lead to the creation of "genetically enhanced" humans—a possibility to which she objects. However, if such technology was successfully applied, could it be considered parental irresponsibility not to genetically alter offspring? For example, if a woman has the gene for breast cancer, and bears children without genetic engineering to prevent the transmission or activation of this gene, could she potentially face a charge of manslaughter if her daughter developed the disease? With your group, develop a short list of possible ethical scenarios of this nature for a broader class discussion.

RESEARCH ISSUE **The Genetic Bill of Rights**

The Board of Directors of the Council for Responsible Genetics

The Council for Responsible Genetics (CRG) drafted the Genetic Bill of Rights in order to introduce "a global dialogue on the fundamental values that have been put at risk by new applications of genetics." The council explains that the Genetic Bill of Rights is a basic set of common principles that are "essential for creating a framework for understanding the ethical, legal, social, and environmental implications of biotechnology." Although this document has not been adopted by any official government agency, the CRG hopes it will assist in the process of regulation and governance of new genetic technologies. Founded in 1983, the

Council for Responsible Genetics is a nonprofit, nongovernmental organization based in Cambridge, Massachusetts. CRG aims to "foster public debate about the social, ethical, and environmental implications of genetic technologies." This "bill of rights" was posted in Spring 2000 by CRG.

Preamble

1 Our life and health depend on an intricate web of relationships within the biological and social worlds. Protection of these relationships must inform all public policy.

2 Commercial, governmental, scientific and medical institutions promote manipulation of genes despite profound ignorance of how such changes may affect the web of life. Once they enter the environment, organisms with modified genes cannot be recalled and pose novel risks to humanity and the entire biosphere.

3 Manipulation of human genes creates new threats to the health of individuals and their offspring, and endangers human rights, privacy, and dignity.

4 Genes, other constituents of life, and genetically modified organisms themselves are rapidly being patented and turned into objects of commerce. This commercialization of life is veiled behind promises to cure disease and feed the hungry.

5 People everywhere have the right to participate in evaluating the social and biological implications of the genetic revolution and in democratically guiding its applications.

6 To protect our human rights and integrity and the biological integrity of the earth, we, therefore, propose this Genetic Bill of Rights.

The Genetic Bill of Rights

7 All people have the right to preservation of the earth's biological and genetic diversity.

8 All people have the right to a world in which living organisms cannot be patented, including human beings, animals, plants, microorganisms, and all their parts.

9 All people have the right to a food supply that has not been genetically engineered.

10 All indigenous peoples have the right to manage their own biological resources, to preserve their traditional knowledge, and to protect these from expropriation and biopiracy by scientific, corporate, or government interests.

11 All people have the right to protection from toxins, other contaminants, or actions that can harm their genetic makeup and that of their offspring.

12 All people have the right to protection against eugenic measures such as forced sterilization or mandatory screening aimed at aborting or manipulating selected embryos or fetuses.

13   All people have the right to genetic privacy including the right to prevent the taking or storing of bodily samples for genetic information without their voluntary informed consent.

14   All people have the right to be free from genetic discrimination.

15   All people have the right to DNA tests to defend themselves in criminal proceedings.

16   All people have the right to have been conceived, gestated, and born without genetic manipulation. ◆

CRITICAL THINKING

1. What is a "bill of rights"? Why was it written and what does it seek to protect? What motivated the creation of this document? In what ways does the document reflect current issues connected to human cloning and genetic enhancement and testing?

2. Is there such a thing as "genetic identity"? Should we have such a right? How could our genetic identity be violated? Write an essay exploring the concept of genetic identity and what it might mean for the future.

3. Draft your own genetic bill of rights. Referring to the CRG document as a prototype, list your articles, and any preamble you wish to preface it, expressing your own position on the issue of genetic enhancement and human cloning.

RESEARCH PROJECTS

4. Go to the Council For Responsible Genetics Web site at **www. gene-watch.org/programs/privacy.html** and review the resources and articles addressing the issue of genetic privacy. Write a letter to the Council expressing your own viewpoint on the issue of genetic privacy, referring to the Genetic Bill of Rights and its articles.

Additional essay topics, writing assignments, research guidelines, and readings for this chapter can be found online at **www.pearsoned.ca/goshgarian**.

7

Making
the Grade
Education Today

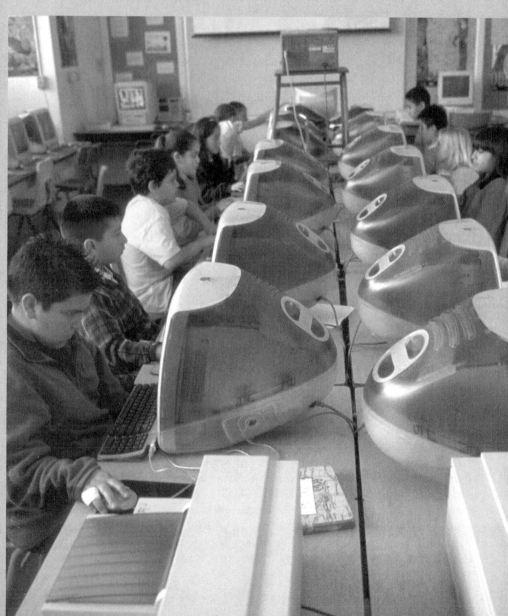

By the time you have reached college, you have spent over 20 000 hours in school between the ages of 5 to 18—not including the time used to complete homework or participate in extracurricular activities. Most people would agree that a good education is the key to success later in life, whether students pursue a professional career, enter a technical field, raise a family, pursue public service, or join the military. Basic tasks, from balancing a cheque book, filling out a job application, or reading a set of instructions, all depend on what we learned as children in school. So it isn't surprising that education has been the subject of much political, intellectual, and social debate. This chapter examines a few of the issues facing education today.

Thirty-year public school veteran Evan Keliher discusses the resurgence of school reform movements, arguing that such plans have failed to improve education, despite years of innovative teaching techniques and alternative classroom models. In "Forget the Fads—The Old Way Works Best," Keliher explains that the best way to improve education is to look to the past, when a room of eager students faced a teacher with a blackboard.

Then, in "The Vanishing Art of Domestic Sciences: They Don't Call It Home Ec. It's Life Sciences in 2002," Janice Kennedy writes about a course that is appearing on fewer and fewer school curricula across Canada. Home economics, now referred to as family studies, is disappearing for a variety of reasons, including rising costs and a traditionally dismal image. Kennedy argues that its disappearance could present problems for future generations.

The next article, "If Girls Can Succeed Only at the Expense of Boys, Maybe We Need Segregated Schools" by Link Byfield, is a defence of the growing movement for gender-segregated schools at a time when many fear that education systems are geared more for the learning style of girls.

The next piece moves to the college campus, where James Shapiro wonders what is happening to the great works of literature. In "When Brevity Rules the Syllabus, 'Ulysses' Is Lost," Shapiro explains that long novels are being cut in favour of shorter ones of less quality in an effort to accommodate students' busy lifestyles. Will such books disappear from the literary canon? And are college students getting the short end of the stick in addition to the shorter books?

Don Drummond explores the rising cost of post-secondary studies in Canada in "Wise Up on Education Spending." Who benefits from an educated society and who should foot the bill? Drummond argues that Canada needs a clear plan to address the upcoming crisis.

Our Viewpoints section addresses the issue of sex education. REAL Women of Canada (RWC), a conservative lobby group, argues in "Sex Education—An Expensive Failure" that teaching "safe sex" is essentially telling kids to go out and have sex. On the other side, in "Purely Illogical: Abstinence-based Sex Ed Is Just Asking for Trouble" *Calgary Sun* columnist Bill Kaufmann argues that abstinence-based sex education, such as that advocated by RWC, doesn't work and is, in fact, dangerous—young people won't know how to protect themselves against sexually transmitted diseases such as AIDS.

We close this chapter with Cheryl Petten's "Where Are All the Native Grads," an examination of the reasons Aboriginal students are graduating at a rate that is far below the Canadian national average.

Forget the Fads—The Old Way Works Best
Evan Keliher

School reform movements since the 1960s have sought the educational holy grail—a system that engages students, promotes learning, advances graduation rates, and prepares students to be responsible adults. If all the political hullabaloo is any indicator, so far, we haven't found the magic formula. But are we trying too hard? In this piece, Evan Keliher says he knows what will fix public education. It is as simple as a teacher, a blackboard, and a roomful of willing students. With 30 years of teaching under his belt, he ought to know.

Evan Keliher is a retired public school teacher and the author of several books, including *Guerrilla Warfare for Teachers: A Survival Guide* (1996), *Motor City Miracles* (2001), and *Triple Play* (2001). This editorial appeared in the September 30, 2002 "My Turn" column in *Newsweek*.

CRITICAL THINKING   Think about the classroom format and educational system(s) you experienced in your elementary and high schools. Did you have team teaching, open classrooms, traditional classrooms, peer-tutoring or group-mentoring styles? Did any format work better, or worse, than others?

1 I've never claimed to have psychic powers, but I did predict that the $500 million that philanthropist Walter Annenberg poured into various school systems around the country, beginning in 1993, would fail to make any difference in the quality of public education. Regrettably, I was right.

2 By April 1998, it was clear that the much-ballyhooed effort had collapsed on itself. A *Los Angeles Times* editorial said, "All hopes have diminished. The promised improvements have not been realized." The program had become so bogged down by politics and bureaucracy that it had failed to create any significant change. How did I know this would be the result of Annenberg's well-intentioned efforts? Easy. There has never been an innovation or reform that has helped children learn any better, faster or easier than they did prior to the 20th century. I believe a case could be made that real learning was better served then than now.

3 Let me quote Theodore Sizer, the former dean of the Harvard Graduate School of Education and the director of the Annenberg Institute for School Reform, which received some of the grant money. A few years ago a reporter asked him if he could

name a single reform in the last 15 years that had been successful. Sizer replied, "I don't think there is one."

4   I taught in the Detroit public-school system for 30 years. While I was there, I participated in team teaching, supervised peer-tutoring programs and tussled with block scheduling plans. None of it ever made a discernible difference in my students' performance. The biggest failure of all was the decentralization scheme introduced by a new superintendent in the early 1970s. His idea was to break our school system into eight smaller districts—each with its own board of education—so that parents would get more involved and educators would be more responsive to our students' needs. Though both of those things happened, by the time I retired in 1986 the number of students who graduated each year still hadn't risen to more than half the class. Two-thirds of those who did graduate failed the exit exam and received a lesser diploma. We had changed everything but the level of student performance.

5   What baffles me is not that educators implement new policies intended to help kids perform better, it's that they don't learn from others' mistakes. A few years ago I read about administrators at a middle school in San Diego, where I now live, who wanted a fresh teaching plan for their new charter school and chose the team teaching model. Meanwhile, a few miles away, another middle school was in the process of abandoning that same model because it hadn't had any effect on students' grades.

6   The plain truth is we need to return to the method that's most effective: a teacher in front of a chalkboard and a roomful of willing students. The old way is the best way. We have it from no less a figure than Euclid himself. When Ptolemy I, the king of Egypt, said he wanted to learn geometry, Euclid explained that he would have to study long hours and memorize the contents of a fat math book. The pharaoh complained that that would be unseemly and demanded a shortcut. Euclid replied, "There is no royal road to geometry."

7   There wasn't a shortcut to the learning process then and there still isn't. Reform movements like new math and whole language have left millions of damaged kids in their wake. We've wasted billions of taxpayer dollars and forced our teachers to spend countless hours in workshops learning to implement the latest fads. Every minute teachers have spent on misguided educational strategies (like building kids' self-esteem by acting as "facilitators" who oversee group projects) is time they could have been teaching academics.

8   The only way to truly foster confidence in our students is to give them real skills—in reading, writing and arithmetic—that they can be proud of. One model that incorporates this idea is direct instruction, a program that promotes rigorous, highly scripted interaction between teacher and students.

9   The physicist Stephen Hawking says we can be sure time travel is impossible because we never see any visitors from the future. We can apply that same logic to the subject of school reforms: we know they have not succeeded because we haven't seen positive results. But knowing that isn't enough. We should stop using students as lab rats and return to a more traditional method of teaching. If it was good enough for Euclid, it is good enough for us. ◆

FREEWRITING ASSIGNMENT

In your opinion, what is the best way for students to learn? If you could give the department of education advice based on your own educational experience, what would it be?

CRITICAL READING

1. Keliher states in his introduction that he knew that the Annenberg project in public educational reform would fail to make any difference in the quality of public education. Review the Annenberg Foundation's report on this effort at **www.annenbergfoundation.org/usr_doc/lessons_&reflections _report.pdf**. Would the foundation agree with Keliher that the project was unsuccessful? What is your opinion?
2. Keliher notes that he has taught in many different classroom models and educational formats, including team teaching. Team teaching was very popular in the late 1960s and 1970s, but many schools are abandoning this style because it has been judged ineffective. Research this classroom model online. What made it popular? Why did it fail?
3. What words reveal Keliher's opinion of "fad" teaching styles? Identify adjectives and phrases in his essay that reveal his position. How do these words influence his audience? Explain.
4. In paragraph 6, Keliher states that we must return to traditional teaching methods—"the old way is the best way." What is the "old way"? Can we truly go back to the old way? Or has technology made this an unlikely possibility?

CRITICAL WRITING

5. *Personal Narrative*: Write a personal narrative describing your memories of a favourite teacher. What made that teacher special? What teaching methods did he or she use? What could other teachers learn from this person? Explain.
6. *Research and Analysis*: What causes poor academic performance? Poor schools? Ineffective teachers? Inattentive or uninterested parents? Student apathy? Is it a combination of factors? Write an essay in which you discuss the factors that contribute to school performance, drawing from your own experience, and information you gather online.

GROUP PROJECT

7. In paragraph 8, Keliher states that the way to foster confidence in students is to give them "real skills—in reading, writing, and arithmetic." As a group, discuss the skills that a student should have upon graduation from high school. Are these skills as simple as reading, writing, and arithmetic?

Are others required to successfully live in today's world? Or do these basics provide the foundation everyone needs?

The Vanishing Art of Domestic Sciences: They Don't Call It Home Ec. It's Life Sciences in 2002
Janice Kennedy

Don't look for it in the course catalogue under *H* for Home Ec. Try *F* for Family Studies or *L* for Life Sciences. The name change reflects the enlarged scope of the field of study once associated with thimbles and cookie cutters. "Family studies" now addresses skills like money management and parenting, practical tools for people about to establish households of their own. And in the current population, these courses offer not only the chance for a multicultural buffet, but also an invaluable experience in socialization.

Despite its new relevance, however, there are problems with the delivery of this kind of program, including fighting a quaint reputation that's difficult to shake, and facing increased cutbacks in school budgets and a scarcity of qualified teachers. If those courses once known as Home Ec and now rechristened Family Studies and Life Sciences disappear, claims Janice Kennedy, then more than recipes will be lost.

Janice Kennedy writes on a variety of social and cultural issues. Her column appears every Sunday in *The Citizen's Weekly*. This article appeared in *The Ottawa Citizen*, November 2, 2002.

CRITICAL THINKING
How is the housework in your home delegated? Does one person do most of it? Where did he or she learn household maintenance? From a parent? At school? From books? Through trial and error?

1   Maybe you called it Domestic Science. Or Home Economics. Or, in the shorthand that makes educational worlds go round, simple Home Ec.

2   However it fixes itself in your memory, the name conjures up a host of images and instinctive responses. To some women of a certain age—say, those no longer in dread of turning 50—Home Ec is synonymous with bad cooking, loopy sewing, laughable knitting. And don't even mention crochet.

3   Home Ec is appalling white sauce made in Miss Martin's cooking class, pallid sludge staggeringly bland and pocked with lumps. It is a single coarsely knit sock, its stitches a riot of inconsistency reflecting various friends' help with turning the heel and getting the monstrosity finished. It is a formless half-sewn apron, thrust pleadingly at an exhausted mother late at night, mere hours before its completed incarnation is due in class.

4   If you're a woman who went to school 40 years ago, Home Ec was something the boys didn't have to take, because they got to do neat things with hammers, saws and wood instead. It was everything that was wrong with being a girl at a time when girls were expected to know their feminine, homemaking, subservient place in the world. To any self-respecting female of that era without a good teacher to soften the blow, Home Ec was nothing less than a bad joke.

5   And then, somewhere along the line, the universe changed. Home Ec expanded, got treated seriously, attracted classes with something approaching gender balance. Along with all the old associations, it even shed its name.

6   "We don't call it Home Economics any more," says Janice Beaumier, delicately. Beaumier taught Home Ec for 25 years, most of them at Ottawa's Rideau High School, and is currently head of both the school's student services and its Social Sciences and Humanities department—which includes the discipline formerly known as Home Ec.

7   "It's called Family Studies now. That changed when we tried to get away from the stitching and stewing aspect of the '40s, '50s and '60s. We branched out, and that's why we've got courses now like Independent Living and Parenting. Why we've got Food Science as opposed to just cooking, Fashion Design as opposed to just sewing. It's more all-encompassing now, with sociological aspects to it."

8   She's not kidding. A glance through Ontario's current high school curriculum reveals a rainbow range of options, 13 different courses, to prepare kids for nothing less than Life After School, in both workplace and home.

9   A grade 9/10 course called Food and Nutrition covers attitudes toward food, issues of body image, scientific approaches to nutrition, food preparation, examinations of Canadian food heritage, a look at industries and global food issues—a far cry from the days of lumpy white sauce. Grade 11's Managing Personal Resources gets students ready for the adult world with lessons on things such as budgeting, shopping and job-hunting. In Grade 12, The Fashion Industry explores the history of fashion and design, places the Canadian fashion industry in the world context, provides practical experience in garment design, production and care.

10   In the state-of-the-art kitchen at Rideau High School, Home Ec teacher Collette LeFrancois (who trained in Manitoba where the degree still carries the older designation) teaches students not only how to prepare dishes but how to observe the principles of hygiene and food safety while doing so. Her classroom—a bright, airy space with a tilted overhead mirror that allows students to see what she is chopping, folding in and stirring—is tidy and gleaming, everything in its place. And it's filled with . . . boys!

11   According to Rideau principal Pat Irving, a large number of male students these days take the food courses. In part, she acknowledges, it's to get some of the food itself; in part, it's because the subject is not academic, and there won't be heavy essay demands. As well, a number of them get entry-level jobs in the kitchens of busy area restaurants, and a few have even gone on to the chefs' program at Algonquin College.

12   Some area schools focusing on technical education also use the cafeteria as a training ground for their food service classes.

13   At Rideau, with the strong ethnic mix of its student population, Family Studies has also become a conduit for multicultural understanding. Cooking classes, says Beaumier, might take ground meat, for example, and examine how different cultures treat that product, what they do with it, what the addition of just one new spice or herb does to it. "Oftentimes kids learn respect for a culture based on the fact that 'Oh, this tastes good. Your food's good.'"

14   Family Studies, says Irving, can provide a platform for all kinds of life lessons. She likes to recount the experience of her colleague, principal of an elementary school with a largely disadvantaged population. Feeling that the kids would be broadened by the experience, the principal staged weekly tea parties, involving the students in preparing the fancy little events where the silver tea service was brought out and lessons in etiquette were learned. Just to make it special, a distinguished guest would always be invited.

15   And, says Irving, "she always tells the story of how one of her students actually told a school superintendent, 'Excuse me, please. Take your elbows off the table.'"

16   Such moments aside, Irving says that type of experience in socialization is very much the kind of thing good Family Studies courses encourage. "A cooking class can provide a venue for far more than information on nutrition."

17   Adds Beaumier, "A lot of our students live on their own or take care of things while mom and dad are at work. They need many of the skills that are gained through Family Studies kinds of courses"—courses, she says, that are really about self-esteem, value systems, goal-setting, communications and practical skills.

18   And that, in short, is the face of Family Studies. The new Home Ec is ambitious, wide-ranging, world-expanding, stimulating, practical, relevant, co-ed, multicultural. It is an educational situation that is clearly win-win.

19   Or at least it would be—if all those fabulous courses were really available to all those eager students.

20   "The school system," said one delegate to a recent national conference of food professionals, "is failing us."

21   The delegate, from Saskatchewan, observed that Home Ec was disappearing from his province's schools and that, consequently, kids are growing up without cooking skills. It has become a truism that many of today's parents—specifically mothers—no longer possess the domestic aptitude of their counterparts even a generation ago. Since they have little to pass on, if the schools don't fill in the gap, coming generations will lack the necessary home skills previous generations always took for granted.

22   The roomful of conference delegates, the majority from Ontario, applauded what the man had to say about the educational system.

23   Thirteen Ontario Family Studies options notwithstanding, the perception is indeed that schools are falling down on the job.

24   Browse through the current course-offerings booklet of the Ottawa-Carleton District School Board on a school-by-school basis. Over the five-year range (OAC is still part of the structure this year), you'll find that a small number of academic schools offer a total of six Family Studies courses, while a few offer five. Earl of

March Secondary School offers four, Nepean High School and Glebe Collegiate two, Colonel By and Hillcrest one, Lisgar none.

25   "When we were in school," says Irving of the 1960s, "you had to choose between secretarial or academic. It's too bad that they had to be mutually exclusive, but they were. Now it's happening all over again."

26   Irving worries that schools are segregating themselves, dividing themselves into specialized technical and academic areas. "Magnet schools are getting entire programs, and you're seeing them disappear from the community schools." As a result, some excellent academic students who would enjoy and benefit from Family Studies courses just can't take them.

27   That is one of several reasons today's Home Ec is an endangered species.

28   It's also difficult to fit into a student's schedule, says Beaumier. The Ministry of Education wants students to get through high school in four years, but it also insists they complete a large number of compulsory courses. When they add in their own university or college prerequisites, their elective choices are drastically reduced. Add to that the questions of prestige and unreasonable ambitions.

29   "In our case," says Irving of her school, "there are kids who really should be taking practical courses like this, but they have expectations that are way beyond the reality. They'll say, 'I don't want a course like that,' not recognizing their limitations or what would be good for them." Many kids who should be taking decision-making skills courses, learning how to cook and to budget, look down their noses at courses that aren't the traditionally serious ones.

30   That creates its own problem. "If you don't have a course with a profile," says Beaumier, "it just gets lost. You need to promote it and get a critical mass, a large critical mass, or it just doesn't run."

31   Says Irving, "What you offer is what the kids want." If only 10 students sign up for something, you can't offer it.

32   And that, in turn, leads to another roadblock on the Home Ec highway: qualified teachers. The fact that there are few Family Studies positions available at any one time creates its own scarcity. Trained Family Studies teachers get siphoned off into other areas, while a single class that might crop up at a school ends up being shuffled off to someone who needs to fill out her schedule, even if she has no training at all in the discipline.

33   And something else.

34   "In the foods courses and technical subjects," says Beaumier, "there's a cost involved in terms of equipment upkeep, food purchasing, materials. With the cuts to education, when they're looking at what they can offer, some of these courses have had to go by the wayside. We used to teach sewing here, but it became too costly. The kids had to pay for their materials, and the sewing machines—which are sitting upstairs, they haven't been used in years—had to be maintained."

35   Says Irving, "The board used to pay to service equipment centrally, but now it's up to the school. And if the school is not able to generate a lot of funds on its own, the program is going to reflect that." If they want sewing back, she says, they'd have to be assertively entrepreneurial."We'd have to find someone from Singer or God knows who else—some company—to partner with us to be able to offer these programs in the schools."

36   But, she shakes her head, "once you've lost it, you never get it back."

37   A generation ago, Home Ec had to fight its image and the criticism (not entirely unjustified) that it was a starched prison designed to maintain the convenient cycle of women-as-domestic-servants. Much-circulated on the Internet is a list of do's and don'ts for future wives, purportedly taken from a 1954 Home Ec text book—and clearly the work of feminists determined not to let their sisters forget recent history: "Have dinner ready on time," the admonitions begin. "This is a way of letting him know that you have been thinking about him . . . Prepare yourself: Take 15 minutes to rest so you will be refreshed when he arrives. Touch up your make-up, put a ribbon in your hair and be fresh looking . . . Prepare the children . . . Minimize the noise . . . Don't greet him with problems or complaints . . . Have a cool or warm drink ready for him . . . Listen to him . . . Let him talk first." The list itself may be apocryphal, but the tone is spot-on. Women of a Certain Age can recall similar texts in vivid, not to say horrified, detail.

38   A couple of generations before that—at the beginning of the 20th century when the American Home Economics Association was founded—feminists of the day railed against Home Ec as a distraction that kept women from pursuing more serious academic interests. Wrote Latin teacher Mary Leal Harkness in a 1911 edition of the *Atlantic Monthly*: "The idea that every woman needs practical instruction in house-keeping as part of her education is as absurd as would be the claim that every man needs to be taught in school to plant corn or milk a cow."

39   Today, Home Ec or Family Studies is waging uphill battles against negative images of a different type, against curricular gridlock, against administrative quag-mires, against budget cuts. The difference this time is that, if it loses the war, the casualties will cut across all academic, gender and class lines. And chances are, the impact will keep reverberating.

FREEWRITING ASSIGNMENT

Did you take a course that would have formerly been considered "Home Economics," such as food science, family studies, or independent living in high school? Do you feel that the course was beneficial? What do you think a course like this *should* teach?

CRITICAL READING

1. What does the author suggest might be the danger if family studies should disappear completely from school curricula? Do you agree with her claims?
2. What are the reasons for family studies courses disappearing from the current curricula of many Canadian school boards?
3. Who is Kennedy's audience? What tells you this?
4. According to Kennedy, why was the school subject once known as "Domestic Science" or "Home Economics" considered a "bad joke"? How has this subject evolved?
5. Why is the cost of running family studies courses so high?

CRITICAL WRITING

6. *Exploratory Writing:* Many students are rejecting practical courses like family studies in favour of the traditionally more "serious" courses. With fewer life skills being taught in the home, where do you think future generations will learn the basics about life after school?
7. *Explanatory Writing:* In paragraph 17, Janice Baumier says that family studies courses "are really about self-esteem, value systems, goal-setting, communications and practical skills." In a brief essay, explain how family studies courses as described in this article would help develop those aspects of a student's life. If you disagree with Baumier's statement, write your essay on how other courses could address this need.

GROUP PROJECTS

8. In paragraph 36, Kennedy refers to the following excerpt supposedly taken from a 1954 home economics textbook. After reading it, every member of your group should find at least four women, preferably of different ages, and share this reading with them. Note their reactions and comments. Do they remember how home economics was taught at their schools? Share this reading with a number of men. How do they react to it? Did they ever take a home economics course? Share your findings with the class.

Lesson Three from a 1950's Home Economics Text: *The Fascinating Womanhood Way to Welcome a Man When He Comes Home from Work* (Check those you already do):
GET YOUR WORK DONE: Plan your tasks with an eye on the clock. Finish or interrupt them an hour before he is expected. Your anguished cry, "Are you home already?" is not exactly a warm welcome.
HAVE DINNER READY: Plan ahead, even the night before, to have a delicious meal, on time. This is a way of letting him know that you have been thinking about him and are concerned about his needs. Most men are hungry when they come home and the prospects of a good meal is part of the warm welcome needed.
PREPARE YOURSELF: Take fifteen minutes to rest so you will be refreshed when he arrives. This will also make you happy to see him, instead of too tired to care. Turn off the worry and be glad to be alive and grateful for the man who is going to walk in. While you are resting you can be thinking about your Fascinating Womanhood assignment and all you can do to make him happy and give his spirits a lift. When you arise, take care of your appearance. Touch up your makeup, put a ribbon in your hair and be fresh looking. He has just been with a lot of work-weary people. Be a little gay and a little more interesting. His boring day may need a lift.
CLEAR AWAY THE CLUTTER: Make one last trip through the main part of the house just before your husband arrives gathering up schoolbooks, toys, paper etc. in a bucket or wastebasket and put them in the back bedroom for

sorting later. Then run a dust cloth over the tables. Your husband will feel he has reached a haven of rest and order and it will give you a lift too. Having the house in order is another way of letting him know that you care and have planned for his homecoming.

PREPARE THE CHILDREN: Take just a few minutes to wash the children's hands and faces (if they are small), comb their hair and if necessary change their clothes. They are his little treasures and he would like to see them look the part.

MINIMIZE ALL NOISE: Especially give heed to this if your husband has to join rush hour traffic. At the time of his arrival eliminate all noise of the washer, dryer, dishwasher or vacuum.Try to encourage the children to be quiet at the time of their father's arrival. Let them be a little noisy beforehand, to get it out of their system.

BE HAPPY TO SEE HIM: Greet him with a warm smile and act glad to see him. Tell him that it is good to have him home. This will make his day worthwhile. If there is any romance left in you, he needs it now.

SOME DON'TS: Don't greet him with problems or complaints. Solve the problems you can before he gets home and save those you must discuss with him until later in the evening. Also, don't complain if he is late for dinner. Count this as a minor problem when compared to what he may have gone through that day. Don't allow the children to rush at him with problems or requests. Allow them to briefly greet their father but save demands for later.

MAKE HIM COMFORTABLE: Have him lean back in a comfortable chair or suggest he lie down in the bedroom. Have a cool or warm drink ready for him. Arrange his pillow and offer to massage his neck and shoulders and take off his shoes. Don't insist on this however. Turn on music if it is one of his pleasures. Speak in a soft, soothing, pleasant voice. Allow him to relax—to unwind.

LISTEN TO HIM: You may have a dozen things to tell him, but the moment of his arrival is not the time. Let him talk first, then he will be more responsive later.

MAKE THE EVENING HIS: Never complain if he does not take you out to dinner or other places of entertainment. Instead, try to understand his world of strain and pressure, his need to be home and relax. If he is cross or irritable, never fight back. Again, try to understand his world of strain.

THE GOAL: Try to make your home a place of peace and order where your husband can renew himself in body and spirit. Then add to this the application of all the principles of Fascinating Womanhood and your husband will want to come home. He will then rather be with you than with anyone else in the world, and will spend whatever time he possibly can with you. Try living all these rules for his homecoming and see what happens. This is the way to bring a man home to your side, not by pressure, persuasion, or moral obligation.

If Girls Can Succeed Only at the Expense of Boys, Maybe We Need Segregated Schools
Link Byfield

Throughout the last half of the nineteenth century and the first half of the twentieth century, public education systems across North America separated the boys from the girls. Today many educators and families are arguing for a return to this mode of education. The traditional reasons, such as students not worrying about how they dress or whom they impress when the distraction of the opposite sex is removed, are being replaced by a new concern over the different learning styles of the genders. For instance, some argue that girls prefer a quieter, more intimate learning approach, whereas boys prefer an approach that is more energetic and fast-paced. In the following article, Link Byfield explores this issue and argues that modern composite high schools aren't working; therefore, sex-segregated schools for those students and parents who would prefer them should be an option in the public system.

Link Byfield published the newsmagazine *Alberta Report* for 18 years. He is now chairman of the Citizens Centre for Freedom and Democracy.

CRITICAL THINKING   What is the impact of gender-segregated schools? How might they be empowering for students and teachers? How might they be limiting?

1   Anyone who has been convinced these past 10 years that the school system favours boys will have been heartened by last week's news that it doesn't. Girls, it turns out, are now doing as well as boys in math and science, and have widened their long-standing lead in reading and writing. This comes from the national School Achievement Indicators Program (SAIP), conducted jointly by Statistics Canada and the Council of Ministers of Education. The happy part is that girls may be doing better. The bad news is that boys may be doing worse.

2   The gender comparisons in SAIP's massive report occupy only part of one chapter, consisting of measurements taken only four years apart. So, while the information is probably useful, it's far from conclusive. Besides, it's always hard to, know—especially in complex interprovincial data-crunching exercises like this—whether the results are really comparative over time, or even within each year.

3   All the same, some things do become clear. High school girls on average are matching boys in the technology-related subjects of math and sciences, and are far ahead in language skills. The number of boys graduating is declining. The number of girls graduating is rising, to the point where there are now more girls finishing than boys.

4   Which leads to an interesting question. Is this progress or regress? Must advances among girls come at the expense of boys? Or is there some way of turning this from a zero-sum game into a win-win, where both sexes come out ahead? And

now that we can turn off [the] feminist alarm, which for 10 years has been ringing down the hallways that girls are being cheated, is anyone going to worry about the flagging proficiency of boys?

5 Readers may remember the hue and cry in the 1990s that girls were being frustrated by a male-oriented instructional system. Boys are more competitive, risk-oriented and dominant, and teachers (even women teachers) were said to favour them. Girls were ignored. In addition, the courses themselves were written and presented in a straight linear and logical fashion, not in the more intuitive, co-operative and circuitous manner that supposedly suits the female mind. Appended to which was the usual litany of complaints about girls feeling threatened and harassed by the sexually robust high school atmosphere created by boys, who of course run everything.

6 If any of this is true, and for all I know some of it is, the only fair solution would be to divide schools, or at least classrooms, by sex. That was how I was schooled after Grade 5, and it seemed to work well enough. My wife started high school in segregated classes, she remembers, and when the boys and girls were mixed the following year almost every one's marks dropped. So why not divide them?

7 But that would offend the "socialization imperative" which in every public education debate turns out to be the bottom line. The fear is that unless we are endlessly and constantly mixing people—boys and girls, religious and non-religious; smart and less-smart, rich and poor; dark-skinned and pale, normal and handicapped—society will be riven by misunderstanding, ignorance, selfishness and distrust. This strange pessimism about human nature always becomes the sacrosanct absolute of government-funded education. "We will force them to meet each other and we will make them like each other." That is the attitude.

8 Well, if today's high schools are anything to go by I'd say it isn't working. For one thing, it's now girls who seem to run everything. In one high school I noticed, for instance, that the entire student council consisted of girls. The good girls (the ones who will probably become teachers themselves) run the council, and the bad girls—the ones who dress, act and talk like hookers (pardon the bluntness)—run the culture. The boys just tune out.

9 I'm sure there are schools much better than this—schools fighting hard for dress codes and some which emphasize boys' interests as much as girls'. But my impression, for what its worth, is that all too many high schools are moshpits of vulgarity where youth is free to run itself according to the values it has absorbed from MuchMusic and 12 years of automatic passing and parent-free sex instruction.

10 Whenever I enter a composite high school, I'm struck by how thoroughly unnatural the environment is. The large modern high school is unlike anything else in human experience except perhaps the large modern university. It's nothing like any workplace in the world, and certainly unlike any home. These institutions should be smaller. Students should show more respect for teachers and for each other. There should be a more studious, less anarchic atmosphere.

11 One way of breaking them up would be to develop sex-segregated schools for those students and parents who prefer them. A few already exist; more of them might be started. Maybe boys' performance is declining because the public system

is now geared consciously for girls. Let's allow both sexes to suit themselves. Not only might they learn better, it could improve their respect for each other.

FREEWRITING ASSIGNMENT

In paragraph 8, Byfield states that in high schools today, "it's now girls who seem to run everything . . . The good girls . . . run the council, and the bad ones...run the culture." Respond to this statement.

CRITICAL READING

1. Identify the author's thesis and evaluate each of his supporting elements. Does the author allow for alternative points of view? Does he try to see multiple sides of the issue? Explain.
2. What is "the socialization imperative" referred to in paragraph 7? Do you agree with the author that it represents a "strange pessimism about human nature"?
3. What evidence does Byfield use to demonstrate that gender-mixed schools aren't working?
4. In paragraph 10, the author states that composite or mixed-gender high schools have an "unnatural" environment. What does he mean by this? Based on your own experience, would you agree with this assertion?
5. Byfield sums up the attitude of government-funded education as follows: "We will force them to meet each other and we will make them like each other." Imagine that you are an administrator promoting mixed-gender schools. How might you rephrase this sentiment in a more positive way?

CRITICAL WRITING

6. *Exploratory Writing:* Byfield mentions the fears about a "male-oriented instructional system" (paragraph 5). Do you feel that your own high school was geared more for boys or for girls? Use specific examples in your response. How did this affect your secondary school experience?
7. *Exploratory Writing:* Think of examples of nonacademic situations in which the genders are segregated—prisons or athletic competitions, for example. What are the reasons for the segregation? Could any of these reasons be applied to an academic setting? Alternatively, in one or more of your chosen examples should the genders be integrated?

GROUP PROJECTS

8. In your group, debate the issue of sex-segregated schools. Divide your group into two and debate the usefulness of gender-segregated education. One of these smaller groups should speak in favour of the practice and the

other should argue against it. What might be some of the advantages and disadvantages of sex-segregated schools?

9. Contact local schools in your area that are practising sex-segregation. If possible, interview some teachers or administrators and write a group report evaluating the effectiveness of segregation. Share your findings with the class.

When Brevity Rules the Syllabus, 'Ulysses' Is Lost

James Shapiro

You may not realize it, but the great works of literature you read in college may be quite different from the ones the generations before you read. But this isn't because better books have been written—just shorter ones. James Shapiro explains that in an effort to preserve favourite authors, many English teachers are forced to abandon longer works in favour of shorter ones. He fears that students are being shortchanged. Even worse, great writers will be forgotten as literary selections become more uniform, and brevity dictates the curriculum.

James Shapiro is a professor of English and comparative literature at Columbia University and a regular contributor to the *Chronicle of Higher Education* in which this article was first published.

CRITICAL THINKING	Think about the great works of literature you have read in high school and in your college courses. What other works and authors that you haven't read come to mind?

1 If there's one thing that teachers of literature across the ideological spectrum would agree upon, it's that size matters. Given the way that books are taught in today's college classrooms, in courses that meet for an hour or so a few times a week for 15 weeks, it has become increasingly difficult to assign long and complex works of literature. No doubt, that is due in part to the extraordinary demands placed upon today's college students (a far higher percentage of whom now commute, hold down a job or two, and even raise children than did students a generation ago). But the explanations don't much change the inexorable logic of canon formation: In America today, if a book is not taught, it's unlikely to remain part of the literary canon for long.

2 And novels that are more than 350 pages long—even if they are by celebrated writers like Charles Dickens, James Joyce, George Eliot, and Henry James—are

regularly rejected by professors who have learned from experience that it's wiser to play it safe and substitute a shorter work, one that students will be more likely to finish. I learned my lesson after asking hard-pressed undergraduates to read Eliot's 900-page *Daniel Deronda* over a 10-day stretch; I won't try that again soon.

3   Those who teach the history of the novel tell me that classics like Henry Fielding's *Tom Jones* and Laurence Sterne's *Tristram Shandy* appear less and less frequently in courses. And you can forget about Samuel Richardson's influential *Clarissa*—it's hard to imagine a teacher with the nerve to assign its more than one million words. (I can imagine the revenge students would exact in their course evaluations, if anyone dared.) Who out there is still regularly assigning heavyweight books? And who will be teaching the next generation of readers the current crop of important long books, including Don DeLillo's *Underworld*, Thomas Pynchon's *Mason & Dixon*, Philip Roth's *American Pastoral*, and A.S. Byatt's *Possession?*

4   Long poems are already headed toward extinction. John Milton's *Paradise Lost* and *Paradise Regained* are taught far less frequently in their entirety than they once were, as are Edmund Spenser's *The Faerie Queene* and Alexander Pope's *Dunciad*. These epics have either been reduced to anthologized fragments or consigned to the limbo where the once-loved though no-longer-much-read long poems of Dryden, Byron, Tennyson, Longfellow, and Pound wander aimlessly in search of readers.

5   In this age of literary triage, teachers know that they have to abandon longer works if they are to rescue their favorite authors from oblivion. I informally polled a number of friends around the country who teach English, and they all offered versions of the same story. One scuttled his favorite Faulkner novel, *Absalom, Absalom!*, and assigned instead the shorter and less vexing *As I Lay Dying*. A Joyce scholar taught *Portrait of the Artist as a Young Man* rather than the all too formidable *Ulysses*. Triage means that Gertrude Stein's *The Autobiography of Alice B. Toklas* has displaced her brilliant but now nearly unread *Making of Americans*, despite Stein's efforts to trim the first edition of that book from 925 pages or so down to a more manageable 416. Friends who teach Henry James and love *The Golden Bowl* and *The Wings of the Dove* nonetheless ask their students to read *Daisy Miller* or *The Turn of the Screw*. Dickens seems to have suffered more than most; gone are *Bleak House, Dombey and Son*, and *Our Mutual Friend*, replaced more often than not by *Hard Times*. *Billy Budd* apparently gets far more readers these days in college classes than *Moby-Dick*. Conrad's *Heart of Darkness* has firmly displaced *Nostromo* and *Lord Jim*. Admirers of Pynchon's *Gravity's Rainbow* still end up teaching *The Crying of Lot 49*. One friend wondered how many people now know that Charlotte Bronte wrote *Villette*. The Bronte novel of choice, overwhelmingly, is the comparatively brief *Jane Eyre*. Writers lacking the foresight to have left behind a teachable short novel—their numbers include Proust, Cervantes, Rabelais, and Sir Walter Scott—have no one to blame but themselves.

6   Colleagues in comparative literature tell me that the same holds true for novels in French, Russian, and German, even in translation. For every student assigned Dostoevsky's *Idiot*, many more are asked to read the more manageable *Notes From the Underground*. Forget about *War and Peace*—*The Death of Ivan Ilyich* is fast becoming Tolstoy's representative work. Franz Kafka's brief *The Metamorphosis*

outpaces *The Castle*, arguably his greatest work. Several colleagues who teach German literature told me that not too long ago, students could be counted on to read Thomas Mann's *Doctor Faustus* and *The Magic Mountain*; today, what is read of Mann by American students has shrunk to *Death in Venice*. Again and again, it comes down to relative length; all other things being equal, the shortest novel almost always wins out.

7   Curious to see whether the views of my friends were representative, and armed with the recent Modern Library list of the top 100 English-language novels of the 20th century—an arbitrary list, but as useful for my purposes as any other—I headed off to Labyrinth Bookstore (perhaps the best scholarly bookstore in New York City, and the preferred bookstore for those who teach literature at Columbia and Barnard).

8   It turned out that 21 of the 100 novels on the list were ordered last semester at Labyrinth, for a wide range of undergraduate and graduate courses. Of those, only three were over the unspoken cutoff of 350 pages: Richard Wright's *Native Son* (398 pages), Ralph Ellison's *Invisible Man* (568 pages), and Theodore Dreiser's *An American Tragedy* (874 pages). Of the other 18 novels, seven were under 200 pages.

9   Clearly, only the longer novels have suffered neglect, and suffered badly. If the statistics are representative, such books will remain untaught and sooner or later will disappear from the canon.

10   Setting the Modern Library list aside, the most popular works of American, British, or Continental fiction ordered at Labyrinth were, again, quite short. Mary Shelley's *Frankenstein* (196 pages) was the most popular, ordered for seven classes. Three novels, each ordered for six classes, tied for second place: Joseph Conrad's *Heart of Darkness* (126 pages), Aphra Behn's *Oroonoko* (86 pages), and Daniel Defoe's *Robinson Crusoe* (252 pages). Right behind were two books assigned in five courses: Kafka's *The Metamorphosis* (127 pages) and Virginia Woolf's *Mrs. Dalloway* (296 pages). Once again, brevity seems to have been the common denominator.

11   The problem with today's choices is not their reputed ideological leanings, but the fact that they are increasingly cut off from the literary conversations that their authors took for granted: To read *Frankenstein* without having the familiarity with *Paradise Lost* that Mary Shelley would have assumed, or to come to *Heart of Darkness* without recognizing the ways in which Conrad invoked Dante, is to diminish the resonance of literary masterpieces. The current classroom practice (facilitated by the growing popularity of critical editions) of substituting snippets of cultural context—situating the work historically, biographically, and theoretically— only exacerbates the problem. I'm as guilty of assigning those supplementary readings as anyone, torn between a desire for my students to have some kind of historical and intellectual context for what they are reading and the desire just to have them read more (and longer) important literary works.

12   Until recently, anthologies included briefer works of fiction supplementing the longer novels that teachers ordered separately for their courses. Today's anthologies have rendered additional readings superfluous: They simply reproduce, in their entirety, the most popular short novels. Flip through the pages of the major antholo-

gies that are the basis for most students' exposure to English literature and you'll discover the exact same choices. The forthcoming edition of *The Norton Anthology of English Literature* and its newly released competitor, *The Longman Anthology of British Literature,* include the complete texts of—you guessed it—*Oroonoko, Frankenstein,* and *Heart of Darkness.*

13   Such anthologies take their own approach to triage. Rather than abandoning texts, they prefer to save nearly all of them, even if doing so requires performing radical surgery on long ones—amputating parts and leaving what's left frailer and lesser, if still alive. So, for example, the 6,000-page *Longman Anthology* makes room for 23 pages of Joyce's 783-page *Ulysses* and 11 pages of his 628-page *Finnegans Wake.* The editors' implicit argument is that, in exposing students to fragments, they will inspire them to read the full version in subsequent courses. But that works only if those courses actually assign the longer books. To offer just one ominous example, over the past quarter-century, classroom orders of Ulysses have fallen steadily. It's also hard to imagine students inspired to read long works after exposure to truncated versions. What the anthologies seem to be offering is a kind of validation: Students with 20 pages of *Ulysses* under their belts get the desired credential of having read Joyce.

14   The culture warriors are right about one thing: A canon embodies values. But they are mistaken in assuming that such values are necessarily defined along political lines. Not too long ago, many of the books that were passed down from one generation of teachers and students to the next took a while to read. We no longer have the time or patience for that. Today's literature classes increasingly reflect and perpetuate the values that our society holds most dear: expediency, brevity, uniformity. ◆

FREEWRITING ASSIGNMENT

Consider Shapiro's final sentence, "Today's literature classes increasingly reflect and perpetuate the values that our society holds most dear: expediency, brevity, uniformity." What is Shapiro saying here? Respond to this statement with your own opinion.

CRITICAL READING

1. Why are some books being cut from college literature courses? What are the reasons behind their removal? What could happen to the works that are cut over the long run? Explain.

2. What is the literary "canon"? What books are traditionally ascribed to the canon?

3. Have you read any of the works or authors Shapiro cites in his essay? Did you read the shorter pieces, or the longer ones? If you read a longer work, did you find it too lengthy for the course? If you haven't read any of the longer pieces, do you feel that you are missing out?

4. Should the factors Shapiro cites in his first paragraph that have contributed to the shift in reading assignments in college English classes be the concern of educators and college curricula? Why or why not?

5. What are the inherent problems with assigning short pieces, such as Mary Shelley's *Frankenstein,* at the expense of longer ones? How are educators addressing these problems?

6. How does Shapiro feel about the move many literature anthologies have made to include excerpts of longer works in their selections? Is an excerpt better than omission? Is it likely to encourage students to read the longer work? Why or why not?

CRITICAL WRITING

7. Respond to Shapiro's essay, writing from your own experience. Do you agree that your exposure to literature is suffering because shorter works are selected in favour of longer ones? Explain.

8. *Exploratory Writing*: Shapiro laments that many great works of literature are being replaced by shorter works of lesser quality. He fears that the great works of the canon will be lost. However, a list of best books is open to debate. What do you think should be the criteria for judging the best works? What makes a book one of the best? Should it be required reading regardless of its length? Why or why not?

GROUP PROJECTS

9. In paragraph 7, Shapiro mentions the Modern Library's list of the top 100 novels in the English language. Access the most recent Modern Library list at **www.randomhouse.com/modernlibrary/100bestnovels.html**. Do you agree with this list? What books would you recommend be on the Modern Library list that are not there, and why? Compare your list with those developed by other groups.

10. List all of the works that Shapiro cites in his essay. As a group, identify all of the ones members of your group have read. How many have you heard of, but have not read? How many are completely unknown to you? Based on your discussion, does Shapiro's argument that great works are likely to disappear and be forgotten hold weight? Explain.

Wise Up on Education Spending
Don Drummond

Canadians often express pride in our strong, publicly funded post-secondary education system, but as you are probably already aware, the system is expensive and no one can agree on who should be paying for it. Different provinces have different schemes, but colleges and universities are crying out that they are strapped for cash and students across the country are graduating with often crippling levels of debt. In this article, economist Don Drummond argues that the future standard of living of Canada as a whole may very well rest on the plan we develop now to fund post-secondary education.

Don Drummond is chief economist and senior vice-president of TD Bank Financial Group. This article first appeared in *The Globe and Mail* on March 18, 2004.

CRITICAL THINKING	Who benefits from an educated society? Should the cost be borne by the individual student and his or her parents, or by society as a whole?

1 The strong postsecondary education system Canada built a generation ago still serves us well, but years of underfunding have left it creaking. We must shore up the system now, because we are going to need it more than ever. Unfortunately, recent policy initiatives have been piecemeal and inefficient. Knowledge has become the prime determinant of the wealth of nations. It is key to reversing Canada's slide to eighth place in the Organization for Economic Co-operation and Development in income per capita. Moving further up the value-added economic chain is the only effective response to the competitive threat from emerging economies like China and India.

2 Public funding of postsecondary education in Canada has declined 30 per cent on a real, per-student basis since the early 1980s. On the same basis, public funding has increased 20 per cent in the United States. Higher tuition fees for Canadian students have offset some of the cuts, but the signs of stress are clear.

3 The portion of young Canadians attending university is near the OECD average, but well below that of its leaders. Enrolment in graduate programs has fallen far short of the U.S. rate. Student-to-faculty ratios have soared, as have admission requirements.

4 With enrolment expected to increase 30 per cent by 2011, the funding stresses will only intensify. The Association of Universities and Colleges of Canada estimates that as much as $6.2-billion more will be needed annually in operating revenue and $1.9-billion more in capital costs. Who should bear the cost? So far, students have been losing by default.

5 Ontario's new government has promised a two-year freeze in tuition, but if the institutions are not compensated for the funding shortfall, the quality of education

will take another blow. Quebec is considering lifting its freeze on tuition, but there is concern that this could lead to cutbacks in provincial grants.

6   The cost of postsecondary education has risen steeply, but it's still a good deal for students. Studies indicate that the higher future income stream resulting from the investment in a college or university education is equivalent to an average annual return of more than 12 per cent after inflation and taxes. Despite higher tuition fees, Statistics Canada reports that the gap in postsecondary education participation across income groups has not widened. But that only means nothing has changed: Children of lower-income families are still far less likely to attend.

7   The trouble is, Canada's student financial-assistance regime is a hodgepodge of loans, grants, redemptions, tax incentives and savings incentives, with each tuition hike eliciting another appendage. When Ottawa introduced the Canada millennium scholarship fund, it largely replicated provincial programs and prompted the provinces to withdraw some of their student support.

8   To encourage parents to save more, the government added the Canada education savings grant—a federal top-up to contributions to Registered Education Savings Plans. But higher-income families are four times more likely to use this than low-income families. Education tax credits aren't much help to students or parents with low incomes. And in most provinces, students are not able to borrow against their full education costs.

9   The recent Throne Speech hinted that the March 23 budget might contain further measures to assist students and encourage their parents to save. Good: We need to shift our thinking, so that saving for education gets as much attention as saving for retirement. If a parent is to cover the almost $90,000 (in today's dollars) cost that TD Economics projects for a four-year university education in 2020, roughly $2,900 would have to be put into a RESP each year starting now. But the huge unused savings room in lower-income Canadians' RRSPs suggests that income constraints make this enormously difficult. In the meantime, students are on the hook. For their sake, we must consider fundamentally reforming student financial assistance.

10   The United Kingdom is introducing a new system whereby students can borrow fully against university costs, and repayment after graduation is tied to income earned. They're also offering sizable grants for students from lower-income families.

11   Canada debated such an income-contingent repayable loan scheme in the 1990s, and we should look at it again.

12   The research side of postsecondary education is shaping up as a success story. Research conducted by universities rose from $3.8-billion in 1991 to $6.8-billion in 2001 and accounts for almost a third of all Canadian research, a much larger slice than in almost all other OECD nations; increased public funding was a major catalyst. And relative to most other countries, Canadian businesses also contract a larger portion of their research to universities and fund a larger portion of total university research budgets. That bodes well for improving Canada's weak record on commercialization.

13   But random acts of good intention aren't enough.

14   We need a comprehensive plan, formulated together by the federal and provincial governments, students, the private sector and the education institutions. Canadians' future standard of living depends on it.

FREEWRITING ASSIGNMENT

How are you funding your own studies? What, if any, financial assistance are you receiving?

CRITICAL READING

1. Drummond claims that knowledge "has become the prime determinant of the wealth of nations." What is meant by this?
2. Drummond asserts that "[e]ducation tax credits aren't much help to students or parents with low incomes." Why would this be true, if these credits are meant to offset the cost of education for everyone?
3. The author says that "the research side of postsecondary education is shaping up as a success story." What reasons does he give for this success?
4. What policy currently in effect in the United Kingdom does Drummond suggest we should look at here in Canada? Why?
5. What, according to Drummond, is the problem with "Canada's student financial-assistance regime"?
6. Why, given the high cost of post-secondary education, is it "still a good deal for students"?

CRITICAL WRITING

7. *Persuasive Writing:* Who should shoulder the cost of education? Is it a public responsibility, or is it up to the individual student who benefits? Write a well-reasoned persuasive essay defending your position.
8 *Research and Analysis:* What is the financial situation of Canadian university students graduating today? What is their debt load and how does this affect their quality of life? Begin your research with a recent Statistics Canada report on the subject at **www.statcan.ca/Daily/English/040426/ d040426a.htm**. Then check out some students' views at **www.canada studentdebt.ca/**.
9. *Research and Analysis:* Research the current federal and provincial policies on student loans. Who is eligible for a loan? What factors determine how much financial assistance an individual qualifies for? What are the terms of repayment?

GROUP PROJECTS

10. With your group, find out how many student loans fall into default through non-repayment each year. What measures are taken to ensure repayment? What is the effect on an individual's future ability to obtain credit when a student loan defaults? Try to find personal accounts of former students who have stopped repaying their loans, or who never started. What reasons do they give for this failure to honour their contract? What is the larger effect on the economy when student loans are not repaid? Present your findings to the class.

11. With your group, visit the Web sites of universities across Canada. Divide the country into regions and have each group member research the cost of attending university in that region for one year. Take into account the cost of tuition, housing, books, and living expenses for that period. Also investigate the financial aid available from each university, and the degree to which that might defray the total cost. Where, according to your research, is the least expensive area in Canada in which to attend university at this time?

VIEWPOINTS

▶ **Sex Education—An Expensive Failure**
   REAL Women of Canada

▶ **Purely Illogical: Abstinence-based Sex Ed Is Just Asking for Trouble**
   Bill Kaufmann

More than 42 000 young women aged 15 to 19 years become pregnant in Canada each year. The vast majority of them are unprepared for parenthood, emotionally or financially. Causal factors abound: poor impulse control, ignorance about contraceptives, myths about pregnancy and fertility, the ubiquitous peer pressure, and perhaps the youthful sense of invincibility that should, but doesn't, confer immunity from sexually transmitted diseases.

It would seem obvious that the best place to reach young people with important information is in the schools, but in the view of some Canadians, like REAL Women of Canada, the teaching of such material is tantamount to endorsing early sexual experimenting. REAL Women of Canada is a conservative group whose motto is "Women's rights, but not at the expense of human rights." A visit to their Web site will further clarify their position on a variety of social issues. Bill Kaufmann is a regular columnist for the *Calgary Sun*, where this article originally appeared on March 15, 2004.

CRITICAL THINKING Does teaching young people about safe sex encourage them to have sex? On the other hand, does teaching only abstinence work?

Sex Education—An Expensive Failure
REAL Women of Canada

1 Since its inception in Canada in 1972, Planned Parenthood has relentlessly lobbied for sex-education programs in our schools. It has argued that such programs would help prevent the escalating number of adolescent pregnancies. It is no accident that Planned Parenthood has been the recipient of huge grants from both the federal and provincial governments to assist it in foisting such programs on our children.

2 For example, according to its annual financial statement filed with Revenue Canada in 1994, Planned Parenthood Federation of Canada received $261,684 in federal and provincial grants that year. Significantly, it received only $15,000 from membership dues in that same year.

3 After so many years of being sustained by the taxpayer, it's time to make a careful assessment of what, if anything, has been accomplished by Planned Parenthood and its methods. The answer: very little indeed.

4 The teenage pregnancy rate in Canada has risen sharply in recent years, and an increasing number of these pregnancies are ending in abortion. Between 1987 and 1994, the number of teen pregnancies rose by 18%. Statistics Canada has also seen a major shift in the outcome of teenage pregnancies. In 1974, 26% of teenage pregnancies ended in abortion while in 1995, 45% ended in abortion. According to a report by Statistics Canada researchers, Surinder Wadhera, and Wayne Millar, "Teenagers have not only a high abortion rate, but also a high repeat abortion rate." The authors of the report concluded that teens apparently "have not fully benefitted" from sex education and the wide availability of contraceptives.

5 Is Planned Parenthood embarrassed by these results? Of course not; it wants even more taxpayers' money thrown at the problem. According to Bonnie Johnson, executive director of Planned Parenthood Federation of Canada, governments should introduce major initiatives to foster more open and positive discussions among teenagers about sex!

6 Society has managed to curb cigarette smoking and drunk driving by education—and by applying legal and social sanctions against such activities. This has greatly reduced the incidence of these unhealthy activities.

7 We obviously can't take legal sanctions against pregnant teenagers—but we can make teenage pregnancy less socially acceptable. Today, easy welfare or ready abortions provide the official "answers" to the problem. There is rarely any attempt to find the underlying cause of so many pregnancies in adolescents. Sex education programs tell the teenagers that it's okay to engage in pre-marital sex if they feel like it, and downplay the consequences if pregnancy does occur.

8 It's common sense, however, that increasing numbers of teenagers falling into the minefield of sexual promiscuity will result in more and more casualties, which is exactly what is taking place.

9   It's time to stop misleading teenagers and to start telling them the truth—namely that there is no such thing as "safe sex" and there are serious consequences to pre-marital sexual activity.

10   Instead of telling adolescents that "everyone" is sexually active and it's acceptable behaviour for them, we should start treating them with dignity and respect by telling them that they do have the will and ability to say "no" and to remain sexually abstinent. Further, we can tell them that society expects them to remain abstinent rather than sexually active. There will still be some casualties with this "novel" approach, of course, but such directness will certainly reduce the number of problems that have arisen with Planned Parenthood's outdated, naive approach—an approach which has turned out to be a colossal failure.)

 # Purely Illogical: Abstinence-based Sex Ed Is Just Asking for Trouble

Bill Kaufmann

1   Let's pretend really, really hard that ignorance is bliss.

2   It's becoming a harder trick to master all the time, given what we're learning about the track record of so-called abstinence-based sex education.

3   A new survey of 15,000 teens unveiled last week revealed 88% of those taking a pledge of abstinence until marriage as part of sex education programs failed to keep their vows.

4   And once they've predictably succumbed to the weakness of the flesh nature has inflicted on us, they were less likely to use a condom because they lacked the practical training that comes with safe sex education.

5   The rate of sexually-transmitted diseases among the products of abstinence-only education was just as high as the "less chaste" among them.

6   Such a pledge did reduce the number of carnal partners while also resulting in earlier marriage—the latter hardly a positive byproduct.

7   Then there's news out of the University of Alberta suggesting fully one-quarter of its students have some kind of sexually-transmitted disease.

8   In Calgary, the rate of chlamydia and genital herpes has shown a slow but steady increase among youth.

9   Imagine how much higher those numbers would be if our youth were shielded from the horrors of safer sex and instead taught refusal skills, told to just hold hands and think pure thoughts?

10   A central plank in the abstinence-only sex-ed curricula holds that condoms are immoral and largely ineffective.

11   Another part of their platform is that when teens do use birth control, they don't employ it properly.

12   So their answer is don't teach them. These deep thinkers should at least be given credit for their sense of irony.

13   Didn't you know that providing students with potentially life-saving information will encourage them to have sex?

14   Best not discuss homosexuality either—it might assist the vast conspiracy of perversion in their recruitment drive.

15   It's good to know basic human biology has nothing to do with it either. Denial's definitely the cosiest prophylactic.

16   In a world where rigid ideology and religious politics trumps sense, abstinence is called a foolproof approach in avoiding the pitfalls of sexual activity.

17   Too bad it's only effective if people stick to it—a notion that's been proven anything but foolproof. "There's a real myth sex education leads to sexual activity—if anything, it postpones it," says Shelly Philley, manager of sexual-reproductive health for the Calgary Health Region.

18   About 50% of teens between the ages of 15 and 19 in Canada are sexually active—a number that's held fairly constant over the last several years, she adds.

19   Under a mixed abstinence-safer sex curriculum, Alberta's teen pregnancy rate fell from 6.25% in 1992 to 4.68% in 2000.

20   There's yet to be any research showing any significant value to abstinence-only education.

21   In the U.S., an independent evaluation by the Department of Human Sciences recently came to the same conclusion.

22   Even so, we have George W. Bush proposing to double the money spent on abstinence "education" to $270 million—more than four times what he wants devoted to beefing up the ranks of math and science teachers.

23   Fortunately, even in right-wing Alberta, there's little evidence of pandering towards a political base by promoting ignorance in places of learning.

24   And so we shouldn't, since we're not headed towards granting equal time in biology class to creationist "science" either.

25   Only about 2% of parents in Alberta opt their children out of classes consisting of abstinence and safer sex instruction.

26   But it doesn't hurt to remain vigilant, particularly when teens in other jurisdictions are being deprived of information that could spare them an HIV life sentence.

27   Sixty-eight percent of those contracting STDs in 2002 were in the 15–24 age group, "which makes them the target group for this (safer sex) message," says Colleen Roy, a nurse at the Calgary Sexually Transmitted Disease Clinic.

28   "People are coming to us with questions."

29   They are questions lectures on abstinence and fanciful flirting with "secondary virginity" won't address.

30   Pining for the alleged innocence of the 1950s, when sex education was limited to racy *National Geographic* issues, and STDs were rare, is gauzy nostalgia at its most irrelevant.

31   Thinking we can stuff today's norms and moral standards back in the bottle is a social engineering bridge too far.

FREEWRITING ASSIGNMENT

Did you have a sex education program in high school? Was it useful? Did it encourage abstinence? Did it discuss "safe sex"? What was particularly effective? What would you have changed?

CRITICAL READING

1. Both of these pieces use statistics to make their points. In fact, some of these statistics seem to be contradictory. What are the possible reasons for this?
2. REAL Women of Canada (RWC) suggests making teenage pregnancy less socially acceptable. How do they propose to do this? Do you feel that teenage pregnancy is "socially acceptable" now?
3. How does Bill Kaufmann use irony to make his point?
4. What are the reasons that RWC attribute to sex education's "colossal failure"?
5. Do these articles contain prejudicial or emotionally loaded terms that affect the validity of their arguments? What are they, and what is their effect?

CRITICAL WRITING

6. *Research and Exploratory Writing:* REAL Women of Canada makes reference to Planned Parenthood. Visit the Planned Parenthood Federation of Canada Web site at **www.ppfc.ca/ppfc/content.asp?cn=false**. What is their philosophy? Their goal? How do you think they would respond to RWC's argument?
7. *Research and Persuasive Writing:* Online, find writers who support the idea of teaching abstinence in schools, and others who believe that sex education, including information on contraceptive methods, is better for students. Do any of these writers bring up points that did not appear in the two articles in this chapter? If so, what are they? After your extra reading on the topic, has your opinion changed? In a brief essay, take one side or the other and defend your position, using the most compelling supporting points you have found.

GROUP PROJECTS

8. While one piece argues for and the other against sex education, they both would seem to agree on one point: teens shouldn't be having sex. In your group discuss the proper age for people to engage in sex.
9. Visit the Web site of the Public Health Agency of Canada and view the Canadian Guidelines for Sexual Health Education at **www.phac-aspc.gc.ca/publicat/cgshe-1dnemss/cgshe_index.htm**. You may wish to browse this

very long document, but for this project it will suffice to read the Fact Sheet and Q's and A's (links at the left side of the page). What components of "sexual health education" are included in this site? Do any of them surprise you? Does the PHAC seem to have realistic expectations of how to teach practical, useful information on sexual health? Are there aspects of a comprehensive sexual education program that you think are missing here? What are they? How does the philosophy of sex education as presented on this site compare with courses on the subject that you have taken in the past? Compile your findings with those of other members of your group, and present them to the class.

 RESEARCH ISSUE

Where Are All the Native Grads?
Cheryl Petten

When comparing graduation rates across the country, we see that Canada's Aboriginal students are lagging behind the rest of the population. Canada's auditor general has said that it may take Aboriginal high school students up to 28 years to match non-Aboriginal graduation rates—and the gap is growing. The 2001 census reported that just over 40 percent of reserve residents had a high school diploma compared to almost 70 percent of the general population. For Aboriginal leaders, these figures are disturbing, to say the least. In this article, which first appeared in *Windspeaker* in April of 2003, Cheryl Petten talks to some leaders in this field and discusses a number of the reasons why Aboriginal students are dropping out and what can be done about it.

1   While the most recent statistics show the number of Aboriginal students completing their high school education is on the rise, the graduation rate still lags behind that of their non-Aboriginal classmates.

2   Deborah Jeffrey has been very active in the area of First Nations education for a number of years. Department head for First Nations Education Services with School District 52 in Prince Rupert, B.C., Jeffrey is also president of the First Nations Education Steering Committee in B.C., and has co-chaired the Minister's National Working Group on Education, which recently released its final report.

3   "I would say, in terms of the general population, First Nations students, Aboriginal students, lag behind considerably, and are certainly denied opportunity and access to post-secondary education by extension, greatly diminishing our nation-building capacity within our respective nations to build healthy and sustainable communities, "Jeffrey said.

4   "I think it is a huge problem that has been long ignored by the public school systems to date, and it's something that, certainly, that we're grappling with in varying degrees across the country.

5   She said British Columbia is starting to make some headway, with graduation rates hitting 42 per cent provincially.

6   "But there's still some significant factors, I think, that hinder the overall quality of education for our children."

7   One of those factors, Jeffrey explained is "probably the often ignored, denied oppression of First Nations people, the colonial legacy in which we're imbedded. And I still think for the most part that public schools, there's still a great deal of conformity and misguided notions of assimilation that are at play. It's systemic, and deeply rooted. And certainly they have to be challenged on all fronts."

8   Another factor, and one that has been evident in the public school systems for decades, is that some Aboriginal students don't do well in school because nobody expects them to do well, she explained.

9   "There is very low expectations of Aboriginal children, and I would say that's very much at play today, although it's something that isn't really acknowledged. But I would say that's evidenced in the high drop-out rate, the streaming of First Nations children that still goes on within the public school system, the overrepresentation of our children in special needs, the over-representation of our students in the alternate program.

10   Perry Bellegarde is chief of the Federation of Saskatchewan Indian Nations (FSIN) and chairs the Assembly of First Nations Chiefs' Committee on Education. He believes many of the problems experienced by today's students can be traced back to the experiences their parents and grandparents had in residential school.

11   "There's still a lot of social dysfunction amongst our people, in terms of the poverty. Because we're still feeling the impact of the residential schools, which of course, was a form of cultural genocide. So the people coming through those institutions aren't healthy parents, they're not healthy individuals. You know, after you faced that onslaught of being deprived of your whole language, your value system, your whole way of life, it's no good. So that's got an impact. And then you throw in the sexual abuse, physical abuse, all of that, you're not a healthy individual coming out of that system. So therefore, if you're not healthy as an individual, you're not going to be able to raise a healthy family. And so a lot of people turn to alcohol and drugs to escape that," he said. "A lot of these kids, our children that are going to high schools, are living in those homes."

12   Another problem faced by Aboriginal students is that they don't see themselves or their cultures reflected in what's being taught, Bellegarde explained. "The curriculum that's being taught has to be adapted so that our children can see all of the positive contributions that First Nations people have made to this country and this world. I'm talking about the medicines, our languages, names of the provinces, the vegetables—pumpkin, squash and beans—all those things come from First Nations contributions. And even the treaties being taught in the school system, and then having our languages being taught. So from our worldview, our perspective, there's not enough of that in the curriculum. So people, our students, can't identify with it, so there's really nothing to grapple or grasp on to, so they retract, they go away from it.

13   Other reasons Bellegarde sites for the lack of student success in high school is that there aren't enough positive Aboriginal role models for them to look up to and try to emulate, and support services provided to Aboriginal students are often inadequate, or non-existent.

14   While he pointed to some of the ways current education systems are failing Aboriginal students, Bellegarde said he is optimistic that in the future, the situation can change for the better. "There's hope, in the sense that we're getting healthier. Our people are getting healthier. And there's hope in the sense that Indian control of Indian education—it's life-long learning—that is starting to be accepted and adapted. Development of our own institutions is starting to happen. Developing more curriculum materials so they can be taught. So things are moving, but never quick enough," he said.

15   "Our children at all levels should be nurtured, supported. And the ones that do make it through that system, big congratulations and a pat on the back. Our Elders tell us we need two systems of education now as First Nations people. And by that they mean the kindergarten to Grade 12, your math, your sciences, all those good things. And now it's university as well, the technical/vocational skills we need. That's on one hand. Then on the other hand, we have to couple that and combine that with our languages, our customs, our ceremonies, and our traditions as First Nations people. You combine both, you're going to be strong, you're going to be in balance. Too much of one, you're out of sync. So we need two systems now.

16   "The old people always say, education for our youth is like the buffalo of old. The buffalo gave everything we needed, food, shelter, clothing and weapons. Now education becomes that buffalo for our children. It'll provide them a livelihood. That's the message we keep saying to our young people."

17   "The messages in First Nations education have always been consistent, from reports written decades ago, to reports written today," said Jeffrey. "Our aspirations and hopes for our communities and children haven't changed. But I am optimistic, because there seems to be signs of shifting attitudes amongst those in the public school system to be more inclusive. And in addition to that, there are a large number of very committed First Nations people working very hard on behalf of their children and communities to ensure that our children are getting a quality education. So that's very heartening."

CRITICAL THINKING

1. What is meant by "the colonial legacy in which we're imbedded" (paragraph 7) that Deborah Jeffrey blames for low Aboriginal graduation rates? Would you agree that it plays a factor in today's schools?
2. Deborah Jeffrey notes that there are "very low expectations of Aboriginal children" in schools. Why do you think this is so?
3. What are the two systems of education that Jeffrey feels are needed for today's Aboriginal students? What is the danger of relying on only one system?

RESEARCH PROJECTS

4. Research the history of residential schools in Canada. Search the Web for facts on the schools themselves, personal accounts of student residents, negotiations between former students and the federal government for compensation, and the response of school administrators to the charges of systemic abuse in these institutions. What social and historical factors might account for the establishment of these schools? How were residential schools a form of "cultural genocide" for First Nations people? How might they be responsible for the "social dysfunction" that Perry Bellegarde comments upon, especially regarding the ability of some to act as "healthy parents"? What do you think should have been done differently at the time when these schools were thought to have been a good idea? Read carefully the Statement of Reconciliation (**www.irsr-rqpi.gc.ca/english/reconciliation.html**). Do you feel the statement is satisfactory?

5. A lack of "positive Aboriginal role models" (paragraph 13) is cited as one of the reasons that Aboriginal students don't do well in high school. Research some possible positive First Nations role models. You might want to begin your search at the Role Models List at **www.saskschools.ca/~aboriginal_res/rmlist.htm**. Design a lesson plan to teach about your chosen role model(s) and present it to the class. Are there in fact Aboriginal people who excel in certain fields who might act as role models to Aboriginal students? Assign each member of your group a different field (visual arts, politics, cinema, music, sports, medicine, and others you will think of); find Aboriginals who have excelled in this field. How famous are these individuals, both within the Aboriginal community and in Canada generally? What are their specific accomplishments?

6. Deborah Jeffrey explains how First Nations people have had to overcome the colonial legacy. Explore how First Nations people were portrayed in print advertising before 1950 at PaperStuff.com (**www.paperstuff.com/**). Click on the catalogue labelled Indians. What do these images suggest? Have we overcome these stereotypes or are they still influencing our perceptions today? Can you think of contemporary images of First Nations people in film or advertising that contradict or perpetuate these notions?

Additional essay topics, writing assignments, research guidelines, and readings for this chapter can be found online at **www.pearsoned.ca/goshgarian**.

Gender

8

Perceptions

Has Anything Changed?

We have witnessed enormous changes in the social and professional lives of men and women over the past century. Traditional ways of defining others and ourselves along gender lines have been irrevocably altered. Only 100 years ago, the full financial responsibility of a family was squarely on the shoulders of men. Women could not vote and had limited legal resources at their disposal. Sex was something that happened within the confines of marriage. Women were expected to remain at home, relegated to housework and child-rearing. Men were expected to be the disciplinarians of family life, with limited involvement in the daily lives of their children. Now, women may pursue many different career options and lifestyles. Men are not expected to be the sole breadwinner, and men and women together often share financial responsibilities. Sexual mores have relaxed, and both men and women enjoy greater freedoms socially, professionally, and intellectually than they ever have before.

Most college-age men and women were born after the "sexual revolution" and the feminist movement of the 1970s. But it was largely these movements that have shaped the way men and women interact, view each other, evaluate opportunity, and envision the future. However, while much has changed and we have moved toward greater gender equality, vestiges of gender bias and sexism remain. The essays in this section examine how society has changed its expectations of gender, and how these changes have affected men and women as they continue to define themselves and their relationships with each other and society as a whole.

In "My Most Attractive Adversary," Madeleine Begun Kane, a former lawyer, describes how expressions of subtle sexism, such as physical compliments paid by men to women in professional settings, belittle women and reinforce dated notions about women in the workforce. Michael Abernethy questions the way men are portrayed by the popular media in "Male Bashing on TV." Why is it acceptable, he wonders, to make men look stupid on television?

In "Man Trouble," Andre Mayer continues this examination of men in contemporary society by looking at a number of the ways that some men are dealing with the new notions of manhood. He wonders how men today are adjusting to their new status in a post-feminist world.

From there, we examine the issue of housework—who does it and why?—in "Why Get Worked Up over Housework?" In Canada, women are still doing the lion's share of housework, but Anne Kingston, who has elaborated on this discussion in her recent book, *The Meaning of Wife* (2004), argues that, in fact, women want it that way whether they know it or not.

The Viewpoints section explores how feminism has—or hasn't—changed the way women perceive themselves. Why has feminism, a movement meant to improve the lives of women, and men, by gaining greater gender equality, suffered from so much negative press? Why are some young women, who are essentially feminist in their thinking, hesitant to identify themselves as such? Susan Faludi and Karen Lehrman go head to head about what it means to be a feminist and discuss the phenomenon known as "Revisionist Feminism."

The Viewpoints section is followed by an opinion piece addressing an issue facing women living in the most patriarchal societies—Muslim countries. Semeen Issa and Laila Al-Marayati explain in the Research Issue entitled "An Identity Reduced to a Burka" that this clothing does not represent all Muslim women, nor do all Muslim women feel oppressed by it. Such assumptions are stereotypical and demeaning, ignoring the rich diversity of Muslim women across the world.

My Most Attractive Adversary
Madeleine Begun Kane

In the next essay, Madeleine Begun Kane holds that subtle sexism maintains gender differences. Women may seem to have made tremendous progress professionally and academically, but they are held back by indirect sexist comments and attitudes. They are caught in a Catch-22: if they react against these seemingly small slights, they appear to be overreacting or too sensitive. But to let such comments pass may signal that they are somehow acceptable.
Madeleine Begun Kane is a New York writer and humour columnist. This article was first published in *Women's Village*.

CRITICAL THINKING Do we have certain ingrained gender expectations when it comes to job positions? For example, do we expect men to be mechanics or lawyers or firefighters, and women to be teachers or nurses or secretaries? Are these expectations changing, or are they still common assumptions?

1 "Our Portia has come up with an excellent solution." A trial judge said this about me several years ago in open court, when I was still a full-time litigator. I've never forgotten it. Not because it was a compliment to be compared to so formidable a lawyer as Shakespeare's Portia, although I think he meant it as a compliment. But what I really remember is my discomfort at being singled out as a woman in what, even today, remains a predominantly male world.

2 Despite our progress in the battle against workplace discrimination, the fact of being a female is almost always an issue. It may not be blatant, but it usually lurks just below the surface. We are not lawyers, executives and managers. We are *female* lawyers, *female* executives and *female* managers. Just when we are lulled into believing otherwise, something happens to remind us and those around us of our gender, in subtle yet unsettling ways.

3 Men often use physical compliments to call attention to the fact that we are different. References to "my lovely opponent" or "my most attractive adversary" remain remarkably common. It's a clever technique because any response, other than a gracious "thank you," seems like a petty over-reaction.

4   Consequently, unless the remark is obviously offensive, as in references to certain unmentionable body parts, a simple nod or "thank you" is usually the prudent response. Of course if you're feeling less cautious, you may want to return the compliment. Done with a slight note of irony, this can be an effective way to get your point across. But saying, "You look very handsome yourself, Your Honor," is probably not a good idea.

5   Concern for the tender female sensibility rivals compliments in the subtle sexism department. I've experienced this most often during business meetings—high-powered meetings where a lone female is surrounded by her peers and superiors. At some point during the meeting the inevitable will happen. One of the men will use an expletive—a minor one in all likelihood. The expedient course is to ignore it. She is a woman of the world. She has heard and possibly used such language—and even worse.

6   But is she allowed to ignore it? Of course not! That would be too easy. The curser inevitably turns to the lone female (who until this moment has somehow managed not to blush) and apologizes. This singles her out as a delicate female who doesn't quite belong and needs to be protected. This also reminds everyone that the rest of the group would be ever so much more comfortable, at ease and free to be themselves, if only a woman hadn't invaded their turf.

7   This has happened to me more times than I care to recall. And I still don't know the proper response. Should I ignore both the profanity and the apology? Is it best to graciously accept the apology, as if one were appropriate? Or should I say what I'm always tempted to say: "That's all right, I swear like a sailor too."

8   Most women, myself included, overlook these subtle forms of sexism. I'm troubled by this, and I worry that by being silent, I'm giving up an opportunity to educate. For while some men use these tactics deliberately, others don't even know they're being offensive. Nevertheless, I usually smile discreetly and give a gracious nod. And wonder if I'm doing the right thing, or if I'm mistaking cowardice for discretion. ◆

FREEWRITING ASSIGNMENT

What profession do you hope to pursue? Is your profession a male- or female-dominated one? Or is it balanced with both sexes? Do you think that gender will ever be an issue in your chosen profession?

CRITICAL READING

1. Kane opens her essay with a story about how she was called Portia by a judge. Who is Portia? Why is Kane uncomfortable with what she believes to be a compliment by the judge? Explain.
2. Kane objected to physical compliments made by male professionals, such as "my lovely opponent," and "my most attractive adversary." How do such compliments undermine her role as a lawyer and a professional? Do you think the men intended to slight her? Why or why not?

3. In paragraphs 5 and 6, Kane describes a situation in a business meeting in which men apologize to a woman for their offensive language. Why does she object to such apologies? What assumptions do the men make in making such an apology?

4. Kane observes that it is difficult for women to openly object to physical compliments because to do so could backfire on them. How could their objections work against them? Explain.

5. Why does Kane worry about remaining silent against subtle sexism? What could happen if she doesn't remain silent? What would you do?

CRITICAL WRITING

6. In her second paragraph, Kane states that women are not "lawyers, executives and managers." Instead, they are "*female* lawyers, *female* executives, and *female* managers." Interview a woman who holds a professional position in law, medicine, or business and ask her about this observation. Does she feel that the word *female* floats in front of her professional title, unspoken but still "lurking beneath the surface"? Summarize your interview and analyze the discussion.

7. *Personal Narrative*: Write about a time when you felt awkward because of your gender. Describe the situation, the experience, and why you felt uncomfortable. With a critical eye, analyze the situation and think about how social expectations of gender may have contributed to your feelings of discomfort.

GROUP PROJECTS

8. Kane argues that gender bias "lurks beneath the surface," reminding women that they are women in what were traditionally male professions. When does referencing gender cross a line into sexism? Is it sexist to refer to a woman as a "lady doctor" or a man as a "male nurse"? Are such references as common as Kane maintains? As a group, make a list of professions and their titles. Include old titles and their newer ones (for example, "mailman" to "postal carrier"). Has renaming the titles of these professions decreased sexism in the workplace?

9. In paragraph 7, Kane laments that she has experienced the apology-for-swearing scenario at many business meetings. As a group, consider her situation and develop a few comebacks she could use if she faced the situation again. Share your comebacks with the class.

Male Bashing on TV

Michael Abernethy

Because television reaches a broad and diverse audience, it can influence cultural and social opinion. For example, homosexuality was a taboo topic before programs such as *Ellen* and *Will and Grace* made the topic more acceptable television fare. Now, every major television network includes a program with at least one gay character. Before programs such as *The Mary Tyler Moore Show*, women were primarily depicted on television as subservient housewives. Television helped promote, and thereby make acceptable, the concept of women in the workforce with independent personalities. Such is the influence of television. But as a conduit for social persuasion, could television harm one group of people as much as it may help another? In the next essay, Michael Abernethy questions the depiction of men as lazy, incompetent, insensitive, or simply stupid on television programs and in commercials. While such depictions may seem funny, stereotypical "male bashing," argues Abernethy, hurts men, and society as a whole.

Michael Abernethy is an adjunct writing instructor at Indiana University Southeast. He is a film and television critic for the online magazine *PopMatters*, in which this essay was first published in January 2003.

CRITICAL THINKING	Think about the ways men and women are portrayed on television and in television commercials. Are there certain gender-based stereotypes that seem common? What makes a male character interesting and engaging? What makes a female character noteworthy and interesting? Is the criterion different?

1 Warning for our male readers: The following article contains big words and complex sentences. It might be a good idea to have a woman nearby to explain it to you.

2   It's been a hard day. Your assistant at work is out with the flu and there is another deadline fast approaching. Your wife is at a business conference, so you have to pick up your son at daycare, make dinner, clean the kitchen, do a load of laundry, and get Junior to bed before you can settle down on the sofa with those reports you still need to go over.

3   Perhaps a little comedy will make the work more bearable, you think, so you turn on CBS's Monday night comedies: *King of Queens, Yes, Dear, Everybody Loves Raymond,* and *Still Standing.* Over the next two hours, you see four male lead characters who are nothing like you. These men are selfish and lazy, inconsiderate husbands and poor parents.

4   And the commercials in between aren't any better. Among them: A feminine hygiene ad: Two women are traveling down a lovely country road, laughing and having a great time. But wait. One of them needs to check the freshness of her mini-pad, and, apparently, the next rest area is six states away. A women's voice-over interjects, "It's obvious that the interstate system was designed by men."

5   A digital camera ad: A young husband walks through a grocery store, trying to match photos in his hand with items on the shelves. Cut to his wife in the kitchen, snapping digital pictures of all the items in the pantry so that hubby won't screw up the shopping.

6   A family game ad: A dorky guy and beautiful women are playing Trivial Pursuit. He asks her, "How much does the average man's brain weigh?" Her answer: "Not much."

7   A wine ad: A group of women are sitting around the patio of a beach house, drinking a blush wine. Their boyfriends approach, but are denied refreshment until they have "earned" it by building a sand statue of David.

8   Welcome to the new comic image of men on TV: incompetence at its worst. Where television used to feature wise and wonderful fathers and husbands, today's comedies and ads often feature bumbling husbands and inept, uninvolved fathers. On *Still Standing*, Bill (Mark Addy) embarrasses his wife Judy (Jamie Gertz) so badly in front of her reading group, that she is dropped from the group. On *Everybody Loves Raymond*, Raymond (Ray Romano) must choose between bathing the twin boys or helping his daughter with her homework. He begrudgingly agrees to assist his daughter, for whom he is no help whatsoever.

9   CBS is not the only guilty party. ABC's *My Wife and Kids* and *According to Jim*, Fox's *The Bernie Mac Show, The Simpsons, Malcolm in the Middle,* and (the recently cancelled) *Titus*, and the WB's *Reba* also feature women who are better organized and possess better relational skills than their male counterparts. While most television dramas tend to avoid gender stereotypes, as these undermine "realism," comic portrayals of men have become increasingly negative. The trend is so noticeable that it has been criticized by men's rights groups and some television critics.

10   It has also been studied by academicians Dr. Katherine Young and Paul Nathanson in their book, *Spreading Misandry: The Teaching of Contempt for Men in Popular Culture.* Young and Nathanson argue that in addition to being portrayed as generally unintelligent, men are ridiculed, rejected, and physically abused in the media. Such behavior, they suggest, "would never be acceptable if directed at women." Evidence of this pattern is found in a 2001 survey of 1,000 adults conducted by the Advertising Standards Association in Great Britain, which found that 2/3 of respondents thought that women featured in advertisements were "intelligent, assertive, and caring," while the men were "pathetic and silly." The number of respondents who thought men were depicted as "intelligent" was a paltry 14%. (While these figures apply to the United Kingdom, comparable advertisements air in the U.S.)

11   Some feminists might argue that, for decades, women on TV looked mindless, and that turnabout is fair play. True, many women characters through the years have had little more to do than look after their families. From the prim housewife whose only means of control over her children was, "Wait till your father gets home!" to the dutiful housewife whose husband declares, "My wife: I think I'll keep her," women in the '50s and '60s were often subservient. (This generalization leaves out

the unusual someone like Donna Reed, who produced her own show, on which she was not subservient.)

12 Then, during the "sexual revolution," TV began to feature independent women who could take care of themselves (Mary and Rhoda on *The Mary Tyler Moore Show*, Julia; Alice and Flo on *Alice*; Louise and Florence on *The Jeffersons*). So now, 30 years later, you'd think that maybe we'd have come to some parity. Not even.

13 Granted, men still dominate television, from the newsroom to primetime. And men do plenty on their own to perpetuate the image of the immature male, from Comedy Central's *The Man Show* to the hordes of drunken college boys who show up every year on MTV's *Spring Break*. What's the problem with a few jokes about how dumb men can be? C'mon, can't we take a few jokes?

14 If only it was just a few. The jokes have become standard fare. Looking at a handful of sitcoms makes the situation seem relatively insignificant, but when those sitcoms are combined with dozens of negative ads which repeat frequently, then a poor image of men is created in the minds of viewers.

15 According to *Gender Issues in Advertising Language*, television portrayals that help create or reinforce negative stereotypes can lead to problems with self-image, self-concept, and personal aspirations. Young men learn that they are expected to screw up, that women will have the brains to their brawn, and that childcare is over their heads. And it isn't just men who suffer from this constant parade of dumb men on TV. *Children Now* reports a new study that found that 2/3 of children they surveyed describe men on TV as angry and only 1/3 report ever seeing a man on television performing domestic chores, such as cooking or cleaning. There are far too few positive role models for young boys on television.

16 Moreover, stereotypical male-bashing portrayals undermine the core belief of the feminist movement: equality. Just think. What if the butt of all the jokes took on another identity? Consider the following fictional exchanges:

"It is so hard to get decent employees."
"That's because you keep hiring blacks."

"I just don't understand this project at all."
"Well, a woman explained it to you, so what did you expect?"

"I can't believe he is going out again tonight."
"Oh please, all Hispanics care about is sex."

17 All of these statements are offensive, and would rightfully be objected to by advocates of fair representation in the media. However, put the word "man" or "men" in place of "blacks," "woman," and "Hispanics" in the above sentences and they're deemed humorous. Are men who ask to be treated civilly overly sensitive or are we as justified in our objections as members of NOW, the NAACP, GLAAD, and other groups which protest demeaning television portrayals, whether those portrayals are on sitcoms, dramas, advertisements, or moronic TV like *The Man Show*.

18   Most of the shows I'm talking about are popular. Maybe that means I am being too sensitive. Yet, many U.S. viewers didn't have a problem with *Amos and Andy* or *I Dream of Jeannie*, both famous for their offensive stereotypes. These shows enjoyed good ratings, but neither concept is likely to be revived anytime soon, as "society" has realized their inappropriateness.

19   All this is not to say buffoonery—male or female—isn't a comic staple. Barney on *The Andy Griffith Show*, Ted on *The Mary Tyler Moore Show*, and Kramer on *Seinfeld* were all vital characters, but the shows also featured intelligent males. And these clowns were amusing because they were eccentric personalities, not because they were men. The same could be said of many female characters on TV, like *Alice's* Flo, *Friends'* Phoebe, or Karen on *Will & Grace*. Good comedy stems from creative writing and imaginative characterizations, not from degrading stereotypes.

20   Fortunately, some people are working to change the way television portrays men. J. C. Penney recently ran an ad for a One Day sale, with a father at the breakfast table, with his infant crying and throwing things. The father asks the child when his mother will be home. Lana Whited of *The Roanoke Times*, Syndicated columnist Dirk Lammers, and the National Men's Resource Center were just a few who objected to this image of an apparently incompetent and uncaring father, one who would let his child cry without making any attempt to calm him. Penney's got the message; their recent holiday ad features a father, mother, and son all happily shopping together.

21   Few men I know want a return to the "good ole days." Those generalizations were as unrealistic as the idea that all men are big slobbering goofballs. Hope lies beyond such simplistic oppositions, in shows like *The Cosby Show or Mad About You*, which placed their protagonists on level playing fields. Paul Reiser and Cosby did, on occasion, do moronic things, but so did Helen Hunt and Phylicia Rashad. People—because they are people, not just gendered people—are prone to fall on their faces occasionally.

22   Undoubtedly, there are men out there who are clones of Ward Cleaver, just as there are men who resemble Al Bundy. But the majority is somewhere in between. We're trying to deal the best we can with the kids, the spouse, the job, the bills, the household chores, and the countless crises that pop up unexpectedly. After all that, when we do get the chance to sit down and relax, it would be nice to turn on the TV and not see ourselves reflected as idiots. ◆

FREEWRITING ASSIGNMENT

Consider the contrast between male sitcom characters and men in real life. Do male characters on television mirror men in the real world? Explain.

CRITICAL READING

1. Evaluate how the author supports the thesis of his essay. First, identify Abernethy's thesis. Then, analyze each supporting element he uses to

prove his point. Does the author allow for alternative points of view? Does he try to see multiple sides of the issue? Explain.

2. Dr. Katherine Young and Paul Nathanson observe (paragraph 10) that the portrayal of men as "generally unintelligent" would "never be acceptable if directed at women." Respond to this statement in your own words. Support your response with examples from the essay and your television viewing experience.

3. In paragraph 15, Abernethy notes that "television portrayals that help create or reinforce negative stereotypes can lead to problems with self-image, self-concept, and personal aspirations." In your opinion, what is the cultural influence of the programs Abernethy cites? Does he make a valid point? Explain.

4. Watch a television program Abernethy cites in his essay and write a short description of the male and female characters. Then reverse the gender of these characters.

5. Abernethy's essay identifies *Everybody Loves Raymond* in several places as a program that particularly portrays men as insensivitive and inept. Watch the program and evaluate it for yourself. How are other characters depicted in the program, such as Robert, Debra, and Ray's parents? Is Debra a role model? His parents? Robert? Explain.

6. Abernethy notes that "some feminists may argue" that the portrayal of men as mindless on television could be "fair play," and mere justice for the many years women were stereotyped. Is this a valid argument? Why or why not? Explain.

7. What does Abernethy want to happen as a result of his essay? For what is he advocating? What solutions does he offer?

8. Paragraph 16 outlines some fictitious exchanges in which the word *man* or *men* is replaced by another group. How do these examples demonstrate his point? Do they support his argument? Are they compelling? Respond to his examples with your own opinion of each.

CRITICAL WRITING

9. *Research and Analysis*: Abernethy observes in paragraph 8 that television programs used to present men as "wise and wonderful husbands and fathers." How were women portrayed on these programs? Make a list of programs before 1970 featuring husbands or fathers. How were the men portrayed? What about the women? Could the argument be made that women used to serve as the comic "foil," and now men have assumed this role? Is that fair? Acceptable? Write a short essay describing your results and conclusion.

10. Write a response to Abernethy in which you either agree or disagree, in whole or in part, with his argument. Cite specific areas in his essay with which you agree or disagree, and provide supporting evidence of your own to back up your point of view.

11. *Exploratory Writing*: Write about a male or female television character that you particularly enjoy watching. Explain why you chose this character and what made him or her so appealing to you. Do you see this character as a role model, or simply entertaining? Explain.

12. *Exploratory Writing*: Consider the ways Hollywood influences our cultural perspectives of gender and identity. Write an essay exploring the influence, however slight, film and television have had on your own perceptions of gender. If you wish, interview other students for their opinion on this issue, and address some of their points in your essay.

GROUP PROJECTS

13. Visit the network Web sites of the CBC, CTV, CBS, NBC, FOX, ABC, and the WB. Working as a group, identify the male lead characters in prime time programs (exclude dramas as Abernethy does), and try to categorize each character. Provide a brief explanation next to each, supporting your categorization of the character. Do any characters not fall into any category? If so, which ones and why? Share your list with the class. Did other groups categorize characters differently? Discuss.

14. Consider Abernethy's ideas in the context of our broader culture. Do you agree that producers present men as inept or stupid because that is what our society thinks is funny? Working as a group, prove or disprove this idea, using movies, television, and printed media, such as advertisements and popular music.

Man Trouble
Andre Mayer

In a post-feminist, post-capitalist world, what is the status of the millennial man? Has the pendulum swung so far from the patriarchal, repressive '50s that men in today's world feel diminished and disempowered? Are men now the objects of media caricature and the victims of judicial gender bias? Or are they simply having difficulty adjusting to the questioning and undermining of their once-privileged social status? In this article, Andre Mayer provides some glimpses into the lives of men who may or may not be victims of the new "misandry." The author's ambivalent tone accurately reflects the subjective nature of his material: victimhood may lie in the eyes of the beholder.

Andre Mayer is a freelance writer based in Toronto. He currently works as a Web producer at CBC Arts Online. The following article appeared in *This Magazine* in October 2004.

<table>
<tr><td>

CRITICAL THINKING

</td><td>

Has men's status in society diminished over the past several decades? Do you think that men are confused about the changing roles of the genders in current society? Are they less sure than they used to be about what is expected of them in the domestic sphere? In the business world or in their careers? In professional, personal, and romantic relationships?

</td></tr>
</table>

1 As a blissfully married and, I like to think, reasonably well-adjusted man, I must own up to a certain obliviousness to the so-called struggles of my gender. I appreciate that there are men who feel aggrieved. I sympathize, but I can't relate.

2   In fact, the only thing more astonishing than the notion of disgruntled masculinity is any discussion of gender at all. Maybe I'm living in a post-feminist utopia, but I don't know many people who identify themselves by their sex (except when looking for a public washroom).

3   Which is why it's so startling to open a book like *What Makes a Man: 22 Writers Imagine the Future*, a just-published collection of essays edited by American author and social activist Rebecca Walker. In it, she and other scribes explore the enormous and, in some cases, untenable expectations placed on modern men. In the leadoff piece, Walker recounts the day her 11-year-old son came home from school convinced that "girls will like me if I play sports." What I see as an innocent remark, Walker views with utter gravitas—momentous enough to inspire a book. She sees her son's realization as symptomatic of society's disposition. Men must repress their gentler impulses in order to take up arms against each other in an unrelenting fight for dominance, a cut-throat competition that begins with school athletics and begets the narcissistic quest for the best cheekbones, the best job and the most money, and reaches its apex on the geopolitical scale with the most fearsome military. "This war against what is considered feminine that is wounding our sons and brothers, fathers and uncles, is familiar to women," Walker writes, "but now we see that it is killing the other half of the planet, too. But instead of dying of heartache and botched abortions and breast cancer and sexual trauma and low self-esteem, this half is dying of radiation from modern weaponry, suicidal depression, and a soul-killing obsession with the material."

4   Walker is not alone in her anxiety. Her book is merely the latest chapter in a growing literature beset by the waning status of men. Author Susan Faludi may have galvanized the issue in 2000 with her fulsome bestseller *Stiffed: The Betrayal of the American Man*. She attributed the decline of men's self-worth to the shrinking military of the postwar era and the rampant downsizing in corporate America, as well as the rise of feminism. The fact that men feel diminished has led to proportionately higher secondary school dropout rates and lower university enrollment rates compared with women. These are relatively new developments, but San Diego-based author Warren Farrell believes the devaluation of men is more entrenched. He likes to remind readers that in the military, a man is more likely to die in war than his female counterpart, and that prostate cancer, one of the worst killers of men, gets much less funding than breast cancer, a predominantly female affliction.

5   Farrell is widely thought to have fathered the men's movement; his 1974 book *The Liberated Man* is the masculine corollary to *The Feminine Mystique*. A feminist during the rights movement of the 1960s, Farrell changed his ideological orientation in the '70s to examine the unspoken plight of men. In his 1993 book *The Myth of Male Power*, Farrell outlined the 25 worst professions based on a combination of salary, stress, work environment, outlook, security and physical demands. He called the results—which included cross-country truck driver, sheet-metal worker and construction worker—the "death professions." He found that of these 25 jobs, 24 of them were 95 to 100 percent male. Where feminists speak of a glass ceiling, Farrell talks of a glass cellar. "In the industrialized world, there has never been a time when men have been so unappreciated," says Farrell. "For about 30 years, it hasn't really been a battle of the sexes, but a war in which only one side has shown up. And women have been shooting the bullets and men have been putting their heads in the sand hoping the bullets will miss."

6   Farrell has an affinity for pat analogies, and not everyone buys his reasoning. "Men have and still hold the power—political, economic, cultural—in every way. They own the property, they control the businesses," says Kay Armatage, an associate professor of women's studies at the University of Toronto. "So the notion of discrimination against men is ridiculous, as far as I'm concerned. However, you can argue that they pay a certain price for their power, for their ownership, for their domination." Sending young males to war isn't discriminatory, Armatage contends; combat is an activity men have always initiated and engaged in.

7   Whatever the reasons, there is evidence of a deep dissatisfaction among men. It's generally accepted, for example, that men commit 80 percent of the suicides in Canada. The standard explanation is that men don't like to talk about their feelings; if pushed to the emotional brink, they would sooner die by their own hand than reach out for someone else's. (That said, a 1999 research study by Health Canada noted that "while men commit suicide more frequently, women attempt suicide more often but are more likely to fail in their attempts.") The notion of men and their inscrutable emotions is a favourite subject of female advice columnists, but as the stats demonstrate, the cliché holds more than a whisper of truth.

8   Alan Mirabelli, executive director of the Vanier Institute of the Family, feels that more and more men are opting to talk it out. "[They have] realized that to bottle it up and carry the stress leads to a direct line to Prozac or the psychiatrist's couch. And that's not the way they want to live their lives. They want to find a way to enjoy life, and if that means being vulnerable to some extent but not carrying that stress, so be it." It's not a perspective all men share. The model is still the strong dominant male. Although there are more "sensitive males," their liberalism is continually challenged by our culture—most often by advertisers, who ridicule men for weakness or indecision.

9   "Men get a conflicting message," Mirabelli says. "On the one hand, women want them to be gentle, but at the same time, they want them to be strong. Which is it? Or is there room for both?"

10   The reality is that both sexes grapple with conflicting cues. "Simone de Beauvoir said, 'Women are not born, they're made,'" Armatage submits. "In exactly

the same way, men aren't born, they're made. Obviously, those gender constructions for men and women are equally forceful, although in different directions." One
thing both sides agree on is that as a society, we default to outmoded stereotypes,
that women are gentle and nurturing but also self-doubting and needy, and men are
strong and protective but prone to infidelity and violence.

11   If you want to experience the frontier of male disaffection, spend a Tuesday
evening with the FACT group. The advocacy organization Fathers Are Capable,
Too agitates for equal shared parenting time, and each week it convenes a support
group in the basement of All Saints' Kingsway Anglican Church in Toronto's west
end. The room is garlanded with bunny paintings and alphabet charts; a Little Tikes
climbing apparatus sits at the front of the room. During the day, it's a childcare
facility; Tuesday nights, it becomes a soapbox for collective rancour toward the
family courts.

12   The dozen or so men—and one woman—assembled on this night sit facing
David Osterman and Gene Colosimo, the FACT directors who typically lead the
meetings. The faces are long and worn with misery; these are people whose existence is no longer defined by their career accomplishments or even their families.
The measure of these men is how long they've been in court. One man, Terry Lear,
has spent 17 years in litigation—so far.

13   The meeting begins when a newbie floats a candid question. "I need an honest
opinion on what chance I've got if I go to court," says the tall, gangly fellow, who
looks to be in his late 20s. Embittered chuckles ensue. The man is separated from his
wife, with whom he has an eight-month-old son. FACT's position on the justice system is firm: judges inexorably grant custody to women, and lawyers exist merely to
draw out the proceedings and pocket the exorbitant fees. The organization lobbies
various levels of government to rectify this perceived injustice but, for the most part,
all FACT members can do is console one another. FACT's message can be distilled
in two words: make do. Osterman encourages him to attempt a reconciliation with
his wife rather than proceed to litigation.

14   The young guy is skeptical. Right now, he gets to see his son for only two hours
a week, in his wife's apartment, under her supervision. "You will get as much
access as she allows you," quips Colosimo, who has no patience for platitudes.
"You're the hostage, she has a gun, and you're trying to work out a deal." Over the
course of the evening, Colosimo will dispense a litany of caustic refrains, many of
which are imbued with a subtle misogyny. "Love is grand, but divorce is
100 grand," he says, simpering. You can tell he's used that one before; it elicits
knowing laughter. His repertoire also includes "She got the goldmine, he got the
shaft" and "It's cheaper to keep her."

15   An outsider might find Colosimo insufferably mordant, but his cynicism is
earned. He separated from his wife in 1991, and the custody battle over their daughter cost him $80,000; his wife spent as much as $160,000. He kept up the child-sup-
port payments for a while, but his ex-spouse wouldn't allow him access to their
daughter. After two years, Colosimo stopped paying. In doing so, he became a deadbeat dad, but he felt he couldn't sustain the arrangement. He hasn't seen his daughter in 10 years, which is about as long as he's been out of work. The lawyer's fees

and support payments had reduced him to penury, and the mental strain had driven him to severe depression. Three therapists told him he was unfit to work; he quit his job in appliance repair in 1993.

16   Colosimo puts on a doughty bravado in the meetings, but his wounded humanity comes out in the poems he has written about his estrangement from his daughter, who is now in her teens. "Divorce was quite a revelation/Not just a split but devastation," he declaims in the church parking lot after the meeting. "They took my child, my joy, my soul/And left my life a gaping hole." As he recites these lines, his gaze is almost pleading. Of all the issues plaguing the male sex, the perceived discrimination in child-custody battles remains the most damaging. In 1988, mothers won sole custody of their children in 75 percent of divorce proceedings; this past May, the federal Department of Justice reported that, for the first time, less than 50 percent of custody cases went directly to women. Most judgments opted for joint custody. This would appear to be an improvement, but FACT director Brian Jenkins says it's misleading. The concept of joint custody is actually broken down into separate categories: "joint physical custody" and "joint custody with primary residency." The former is a total sharing of responsibility, the latter means that although the parents make major decisions together, the child spends most of his or her time living with one parent. According to Jenkins, the parent who provides primary residency tends to hold sway; in most cases, it's still the woman.

17   "Men who lose their connection to children lose their connection to society," Osterman notes. As Colosimo likes to remind FACT members, eight men commit suicide in Canada every day. The likelihood of suicide rises considerably among divorced men. According to 1995 Statistics Canada figures, the national suicide rate among divorced men was 42.5 per 100,000, four times the overall men's rate. The ideology of family courts can be debated endlessly, but the fact remains that a distressing number of men find divorce so financially and emotionally taxing that they consider death their only recourse.

18   The blinkered stereotypes that complicate child-custody battles are also perpetuated in mass culture. Look no further than Homer Simpson. Crude, insensitive, moronic and quite possibly the worst father in television history, he's the icon of male inadequacy.

19   Two Canadian researchers, Paul Nathanson and Katherine Young, found enough instances of misandry—a more refined word for male-bashing—in television, film, comic strips and books to write a fairly thick tome. Published in 2001, *Spreading Misandry: The Teaching of Contempt for Men in Popular Culture* delineates stereotyping throughout the 1990s. Nathanson and Young take aim at movies like *Sleeping with the Enemy, The Color Purple* and *The Hand That Rocks the Cradle* for portraying men as either violent reprobates, hopeless patsies or women in a male guise.

20   "The people who make these movies aren't necessarily trying to make that point, and the people who consume these products aren't necessarily conscious of it," says Nathanson. "You come out of a movie and you either like or you don't like it. But very few people think, 'Well, what does that say about me?' That takes a level of conscious reflection that a lot of people don't have. Some women have it,

because they've been trained for 30 years to look for misogynistic elements. But for men, at least in the 1990s, it was a little harder to do that."

21   One of their targets is the forgettable sitcom Home Improvement. In it, actor Tim Allen played Tim "The Tool Man" Taylor, a sheepish joe who wielded tools at work and simply acted like one at home. Alternately macho and dim-witted, Tim continually shot off his mouth, only to be summarily scolded by his wife, Jill (played by Patricia Richardson). The spate of daytime talk shows also reinforced our worst fears about men. Whether it was Oprah, Geraldo, Sally Jesse Raphael or Montel, topics like domestic violence and male perfidy were recurring themes.

22   According to Nathanson and Young, misandry was first promoted in political and academic circles to redress a history of female oppression. Eventually it radiated out into the wider culture. Nathanson says the cumulative effect of these stereotypes is that they warp men's sense of who they are. "If you don't provide boys with a positive identity, then they're going to embrace the negative one," he says.

23   Ironically, amid the flurry of unwitting male stereotypes, our culture began to reclaim many of them. If some men were feeling ill at ease about their collective image, the Maxim-ization of pop culture did them no favours. Thanks to the outbreak of lad mags, increasingly loutish pop stars (Oasis, Kid Rock, countless rappers), crass television series like Beavis and Butt-head, guy-oriented talk-radio stations (Toronto's MOJO) and even whole television networks dedicated to men's programming (Spike TV), it's become all right—downright amusing, in fact—to be boorish, hedonistic and blatantly sexist, all those qualities glibly associated with the male id.

24   David Shackleton produces a lad mag, of sorts—he's the editor and publisher of Everyman, a quarterly journal devoted to men's issues. What you won't find in its pages, however, are airbrushed pictures of bosomy supermodels, tips on building adamantine abs or how to uncouple a bra with one hand. With its low-budget paper stock, black-and-white appearance and humourless, didactic tone, Everyman is not for every man. It's a zine for disillusioned males, dealing with topics like divorce and family law. The periodical has a circulation of 500 copies, which Shackleton prints in his Ottawa home.

25   He became involved in the magazine in 1994—eventually taking it over from co-founder Andrew McDonald—after a shocking personal revelation. In 1987, Shackleton's first wife left him. He concedes that the split was upsetting but inevitable. It was her methodology, however, that truly rankled him. Instead of laying out the reasons in person, she left the house with their dog—under the pretence of seeing the veterinarian—and then called to tell him she wanted a divorce. When he asked her why she had chosen to break up in such an impersonal manner, she said she feared he might get violent.

26   Having never exhibited an aggressive tendency, Shackleton was stunned that his wife of seven years had so profoundly misunderstood him. The more disturbing inference, however, was that all men have a propensity for brutality.

27   "Up until then, I'd been kind of living out the cultural script of, you know, career success, et cetera. I started to look around at the stereotype that men are violent. And what I saw was that the whole gender story that was in play in society

was the story of female victimhood, and it didn't ring true to me," he says. "I felt that there was a whole piece missing." Shackleton believed that any discussion of how men were feeling was viewed as either anti-feminist or simply petty. "I got a sense why we were so caught up in women's experience about gender and why we're silent and unresponsive to men's stories. I found myself steering my life more and more into that work."

28   In 1993, Shackleton quit a well-paying engineering job at Nortel Networks to devote himself to the male cause. "I decided the world didn't need more technical products," he says. "What we needed was some more social insight." Shackleton, who has remarried twice, divides his time between publishing *Everyman*, hosting gender workshops and doing speaking engagements. (Male advocacy is not a lucrative field, so Shackleton supplements his income with desktop publishing and technical consulting of the sort he did at Nortel.) One of his recent speeches was at Stories of Healing, a two-day conference this past June organized by the Men's Network and Kitchener-Waterloo Counselling Services. Held in the auditorium of a Waterloo, Ontario, community centre, the annual assembly is a forum for abused and otherwise beleaguered males, as well as counsellors, to share tales of personal renewal.

29   On the morning of the second day, Shackleton stood before a still-somnolent crowd and narrated his story. A tall fellow with a close-cropped white beard, Shackleton has a muted intonation; although he's thoughtful and articulate, his voice will occasionally become tremulous. Outlining his points on an overhead projector, Shackleton explained that his investigation of gender roles has led him to one overriding theory. He doesn't deny that historically, women have been victims of male tyranny, but he says that men and women actually have a mutually oppressive relationship. Men subjugate women with physical, economic and political power; women, on the other hand, subjugate men with sexual, emotional and moral power. Shackleton's belief: for all of men's overbearing qualities, women have the power to shame. You could sense a collective tension in the room. People stiffened in their plastic chairs. Shackleton is quite used to offending people, and he took the acute silence in stride. Even so, when it came time for questions, he gazed around the room with nervous anticipation. One man stood up to the microphone and extolled Shackleton's wisdom and courage. The majority of participants, however, took issue with his essential point. Another male counsellor approached the microphone and said, "Among my friends in their 20s, 30s and 40s, I don't know anyone who thinks that way." Shackleton smiled uneasily and mumbled something about welcoming differing opinions. Event organizer Randy Scott ended the discussion on a cheerfully contrite note, thanking Shackleton for his time but offering nothing in the way of an endorsement.

30   I could appreciate the heartbreak that inspired Shackleton's rhetoric, but his conclusions seemed misguided. I found it difficult to liken shaming to physical abuse in terms of severity. Perhaps the most awkward thing about Shackleton's speech was that it dispensed fault at an event honouring personal triumph. "I was really hoping we'd moved past that sort of thinking," muttered one participant when I asked her about the presentation. "We don't need any more assigning of blame." I

have to concur. If men are feeling plagued by negative stereotypes, reacting with equally hoary female stereotypes seems, at the very least, counterproductive.

31   If you ask Warren Farrell, a battle-hardened women's and men's libber, he'll tell you the way forward is to take a more mature approach. "We've had a women's movement blaming men, when what we should have had is neither a women's movement blaming men nor a men's movement blaming women. We should have been having a gender transition movement moving from the old, rigid roles that were survival-based to new, more flexible roles." That ultimately means unlearning the gender myths, particularly the fiction that men can't articulate their feelings. For too long, they've been told, and dumbly accepted, that they're incapable of doing so. For men and women, the key to transcending this ridiculous drama is to play against type.

FREEWRITING ASSIGNMENT

In this essay, Alan Mirabelli claims that today men are getting a "conflicting message," that "women want them to be gentle, but at the same time, they want them to be strong." What are your feelings about this? If you're a woman, what are your expectations of men? If you're a man, do you experience the pressure of Mirabelli's conflicting message?

CRITICAL READING

1. What is the tone of the beginning of Mayer's article? How does this tone help the reader understand Mayer's relationship to the material he is discussing? Does he agree with the writers he refers to regarding men's victimization? Does he disagree? Or is he objective?
2. What is *misandry*? According to writers cited in this article, where did it begin, and how is it most often spread? What is the effect of this phenomenon on boys looking for role models?
3. What is the occupational phenomenon described by Warren Farrell as "the glass basement"? Contrast this with the more familiar "glass ceiling." Are the two comparable? Do you think that men can more easily rise out of the glass basement than women can penetrate the glass ceiling? Why or why not?
4. Writer Susan Faludi "attribute[s] the decline of men's self-worth to the shrinking military of the postwar era and the rampant downsizing in corporate America, as well as the rise of feminism." Do you agree that men's self-esteem is in fact lower than it once was, and if so, do you think this is due to the factors Faludi lists? How would each of these trends affect men's images of themselves?
5. How does the author present the members of FACT? Does he appear to feel that their position on divorce and custody issues is justified? What words or phrases specifically indicate his opinion?

CRITICAL WRITING

6. *Research and Exploratory Writing:* Search the Web for information on the men's movement. Is there a consistent set of principles or goals? If so, what are they? Does this movement appear to have formed spontaneously to meet the needs of men at this particular time in history, or was it created in reaction to the women's movement?

7. *Research and Analysis:* Mayer offers the "generally accepted" statistic that men commit 80% of suicides in Canada. Does this surprise you? Research this statistic yourself and see if your findings corroborate it. Does your research provide explanations for so many more men than women taking their own lives?

GROUP PROJECTS

8. Mayer says that advertisers "ridicule men for weakness or indecision." With other members of your group, observe several television commercials over the course of a week. How do these commercials present men? How do they compare with the way commercials present women? Does the portrayal of one gender appear more realistic than the other? If so, which one, and in what ways?

9. Kay Armatage of the University of Toronto says that "the notion of discrimination against men is ridiculous, as far as I'm concerned. However, you can argue that they pay a certain price for their power, for their ownership, for their domination." Discuss with your group whether or not Armatage is correct. What is "the price" that she is referring to?

Why Get Worked Up over Housework?
Anne Kingston

Someone, like it or not, has to do the housework, and surveys show that even though Canadian women are increasingly working outside of the home, they are still performing the lion's share of work within the home, spending about twice as much time as men on total unpaid housework. In this article, Toronto journalist Anne Kingston argues that there's nothing "shocking" in these statistics; if women are doing most of the housework, it must be because they want to. Kingston has explored this issue in detail in her latest book, *The Meaning of Wife* (2004)—an appraisal of the Western ambivalence toward the notion of "wifedom"—in which she asks the following questions: How does marriage affect a woman's sense of self? Is it possible to place a dollar value on a mother's work? And how has our idea of the wife been shaped over the decades?

Anne Kingston is an award-winning journalist who has written for numerous publications, including *The Globe and Mail, Toronto Life,* and *Saturday Night,* and is currently a columnist for the *National Post.* Her best-selling book *The Edible Man: Dave Nichol, President's Choice and the Making of Popular Taste* (1994) won the 1995 National Business Book Award.

CRITICAL THINKING   What is your own relationship with housework? In your household, who does most of the housework? How does that person feel about it? If you live alone, how do you feel about doing it?

Predictable hand-wringing accompanied last week's publication of 2001 census data that found women spend more than twice as much time as men on domestic responsibilities, or as Statistics Canada calls it, "unpaid housework."

2   Headlines were freighted with subjective generalizations and inadvertent housework put-downs. "Women still doing the 'grunt' work," proclaimed *The Kitchener-Waterloo Record.* "Housework still women's work," was the headline in *The Winnipeg Free Press.* "Women do lion's share at home," announced *The Globe and Mail.*

3   Shock was also registered that the numbers remained unchanged from the 1996 census, the first year information on domestic labour was collected.

4   But why? Why should we be shocked that 21% of Canadian women say they spent between 30 and 59 hours doing housework in the week before the census was taken in May 2001, while only 8% of men spent the same amount of time? Why should we be surprised that nothing has changed in five years?

5   More importantly, what can be drawn from this finding? Continuing female oppression? Women's secret addiction to fabric softener fumes? A level of Martha Stewart Living enslavement heretofore unknown?

6   Why not simply take this data with the same objective calm accorded our attitudes on other census findings? And that would be to presume, quite logically, that if women are doing more work than men within the home it's because it's the way they want it to be, even if they gripe like hell about it.

7   But no, sociologists were trotted out such as Muriel Mellow, a professor at Lethbridge University in Alberta, who was quoted in a number of newspapers decrying the situation, saying that, "there are extreme inequalities in terms of unpaid work."

8   Perhaps. But inequalities do not necessarily equal injustice. And what makes "unpaid housework" seem intrinsically unjust, ironically, is the fact it's described as "unpaid," which in fact it isn't. Whoever works "unpaid" in the home receives compensation via the shared household income. If both partners "work outside of the home," as we now carefully refer to it, then it is up to them to negotiate a fair exchange of labour within the relationship. But this is dicey, as it's become impolitic to suggest that the person who works more outside of the home should not be expected to work as much within.

9   Just as it also appears unfashionable, even in the 21st century, to suggest that men have a rightful place in the domestic realm unless they're pretending to be

Jamie Oliver. A piece on the census in the *Globe*, for instance, made the lame joke that the average Canadian man—the same guy who would be expected to know how to hook up a DVD player—"still has trouble finding the 'on' switch on the vacuum cleaner."

10   Such an indulgent attitude is more widely reflected in television commercials in which women heroically remove stains as if it'll win them the Nobel Peace Prize, while men are portrayed as utter household incompetents, lacking the basic cognitive skill required to separate whites from colours. Perhaps such ridiculous imagery is what justifies the fact that 13% of Canadian men say they do absolutely no housework at all, as opposed to 16% in 1996.

11   If women do twice as much household labour as men for no justifiable reason, it's either because they are utter fools or because they are receiving some psychological payoff—a power premium of sorts. And that would be a holdover from the Victorian era in which men dominated the so-called "public" sphere while women controlled the "private" realm, a notion that continues to be reflected in the outside-inside breakdown in which men handle exterior work—taking out the trash, raking the leaves, shoveling snow—while women handle the interior labour, otherwise known as "the lion's share."

12   Even as more than 76% of married women hold down jobs, maintaining that control in the private sphere remains important, as revealed in media commentary following the census. In a Canadian Press story, Sally Ritchie, a television producer who does most of the house cleaning but shares child-raising duties with her husband, referred to herself as "a freak" because she refuses to do "absolutely everything" around the house like most married women she knows.

13   Cynthia Pugh, a "mom" interviewed in the *Globe*, said her husband does 35% of the housework (whether she works outside the home or what percentage of work "outside of the home" he does were never specified).

14   Her comments made clear, however, that she had a role in perpetuating the unequal distribution of labour with her husband. "The odd thing is," she said, "the more he does to help, the harder I find it. The less I do around the house, the less I feel like Mom."

15   That would be her choice, abetted by centuries of cultural conditioning. But the statement is also telling of the complex remuneration scheme accorded "unpaid" domestic labour, one that cannot be quantified by traditional economic measures, and one that shouldn't only apply to women, as much as the census reveals they may want it to.

FREEWRITING ASSIGNMENT

Do you find it "shocking" that women spend more than twice as much time as men on domestic responsibilities? Why or why not?

CRITICAL READING

1. Anne Kingston claims "if women are doing more work than men within the home it's because it's the way they want it to be, even if they gripe like hell about it." Would you agree with this statement? Explain.
2. The author suggests that "unpaid housework" is an inaccurate term since "[w]hoever works 'unpaid' in the home receives compensation via the shared household income." How might a single parent respond to this statement?
3. According to Kingston, what is the psychological payoff, for women, of household labour?
4. Cynthia Pugh states that "[t]he less I do around the house, the less I feel like Mom." Is motherhood connected to housework? In other words, can women be exemplary mothers even if they do no housework? Explain.
5. What does the author mean by her claim that "unpaid housework" only *seems* unjust because it is in fact paid work? Do you agree with this claim?

CRITICAL WRITING

6. *Exploratory Writing:* In paragraph 10, the author suggests that television commercials portray the sexes in a conventionally clichéd manner. With your group, think of commercials that exemplify this claim. Can you think of commercials in which the opposite is true? Discuss the attitudes that these commercials might perpetuate. Who benefits from these depictions?
7. The Nova Scotia Advisory Council on the Status of Women has a Web site entitled, "Unpaid Work: Some Selected Statistics." Visit the site at **www.gov.ns.ca/staw/unpaidw.htm**, and read the chosen quotes and statistics. How do you respond to these? How might Anne Kingston respond? Write down your ideas in a brief essay.
8. *Research and Analysis:* Read a chapter of Anne Kingston's latest book, *The Meaning of Wife* (2004). In a brief essay, summarize the chapter and tell us whether or not you agree with her assertions.

GROUP PROJECTS

9. In your group, develop a questionnaire that each member will pose to a number of households. If possible, try to question different types of households, such as ones in which the members are from different generations or ones in which the members are roommates. Your questionnaire should inquire which member(s) of the household perform most of the housework, how many hours those members spend on housework, and what type of work they perform. Do you notice a split between inside labour and outside labour, as Kingston suggests? What conclusions can you draw from your findings? Share your results with the class.

► **Revisionist Feminism: A Dialogue**
Susan Faludi and Karen Lehrman

The next article is the beginning of a multiletter dialogue between feminist writers Susan Faludi and Karen Lehrman featured in *Slate MSN*, in which the two women discuss the meaning of "real feminism." Faludi objects to the "revisionist feminists," who seem to feel that feminism denies them their femininity. Lehrman responds by explaining that the leftist political agenda of conventional feminism has clouded the goals of the movement, and has alienated both men and women.

Susan Faludi is the author of the critically acclaimed books *Backlash: The Undeclared War Against American Women* (1991) and *Stiffed: The Betrayal of the American Man* (1998). Her articles have appeared in many journals and magazines, including *Newsweek* and *Esquire.* Karen Lehrman is the managing editor of *Consumer's Research* magazine and the author of *The Lipstick Proviso: Woman, Sex & Power in the Real World* (1997).

CRITICAL THINKING   Look up the word *feminism* in the dictionary. Does the definition surprise you? Does North American society seem to have a different understanding of what feminism means? Explain.

Dear Karen,

1   I enter into this conversation with you about feminism with some misgivings. Not because I don't want to talk to you. It's just that I suspect it will be like a phone conversation where the connection's so bad neither party can hear the other through the static. I say this because in my experience, there's no getting through to the group of "feminists" (and I use that word with heavy quotation marks and highly arched brows) who are your sister travelers. I mean the group that maintains that an "orthodoxy" of "reigning feminists" (your terms) torments the American female population with its highhanded fiats, its litmus tests of "proper" feminist behavior, its regulatory whip seeking to slap the femininity out of the American girl. Christina Hoff Sommers, Katie Roiphe, Laura Ingraham, Danielle Crittenden, and the rest of the inside-the-Beltway "revisionist feminists" (as the media would have it) condemn feminism for its "excesses" over and over on the *New York Times* and *Washington Post* op-ed pages and the major TV talk shows (while complaining they are viciously "silenced" by the "reigning" feminists, who hardly ever get an airing in the aforementioned forums).

2   And you, too, Karen. Your own book-length addition to this chorus repeats the argument that feminism has turned women off by denying them the right to display and revel in their feminine beauty and sexuality. You then adorn that old can of

"revisionist" contents with a fancy new label, The Lipstick Proviso, which you define as "women don't have to sacrifice their individuality, or even their femininity—whatever that means to each of them—in order to be equal."

3   For the longer version of my response to the "revisionists" and their charges against feminism. For the shorter version, to your book specifically, here 'tis:

4   Earth to Karen! Do you read me? . . . 'Cuz back on planet Earth, feminists don't "reign" and they certainly don't stop women at checkpoints to strip them of their "individuality" by impounding their lipstick (though what a pathetic "individuality" that must be if it depends on the application of Revlon to achieve it). Bulletin from the front: I wear lipstick, and I've spotted it on other feminists, too. I've watched, in fact, legions of "militant" feminists apply makeup brazenly in public ladies' rooms, and no femi-Nazi police swooped down and seized their compacts. And you know why? Because lipstick is not what feminism is about.

5   What's clear in your book is you feel gypped by feminism. You feel the feminists of the '60s and '70s made a promise to your generation of women that they didn't keep. Let us assume you are sincere, and I have no reason—in your case—to think otherwise. But why do you feel so betrayed? Maybe the answer lies in your definition of feminism. You write in your book that "as a young woman eager to escape the confines of a traditional household," you embraced feminism, which, you believed, "was going to turn all women into liberated women, into women who would unfailingly exhibit serene confidence, steely resolve, and steadfast courage. Unburdened by the behavioral and sartorial restrictions of traditional femininity, we would all want to trek alone through the wilds of Indonesia, head IBM, run for president." You then go on to lament, "Yet it doesn't seem as though the first generation of women to come of age with feminism . . . has metamorphosed en masse into briefcase-toting, world-wandering Mistresses of the Universe."

6   Now here's the problem: Your definition of feminism is gleaned not from '70s feminism but from '70s advertising. In that decade, Madison Avenue and Hollywood and the fashion industry and mass media all saw a marketing opportunity in "women's lib" and they ran with it. Feminism as reinterpreted through television commercials for pantyhose and marketing manuals for Dress for Success bow ties would do just what advertising is supposed to do: Inflame your hungers and your anxieties, then offer to mollify them with a product that makes ludicrously inflated promises. So just as Hanes tried to convince shoppers that slipping on a pair of pantyhose would turn them into raving beauties with a million suitors, so the faux-feminism of Consumer America tried to convince a younger generation of women that "liberation" led to Banana Republicesque treks in the Himalayas and starring roles in the executive penthouse suite. All young women had to do to get that liberation was smoke Virginia Slims. As Christopher Lasch (that raving liberal!) wrote prophetically in 1979 in *The Culture of Narcissism,* "The advertising industry thus encourages the pseudo-emancipation of women, flattering them with its insinuating reminder, 'You've come a long way, baby,' and disguising the freedom to consume as genuine autonomy."

7   Now you are trying to reclaim that promise, proclaiming in your book that women have the "right" to liberate themselves via the marketplace. You champion

women's right to express themselves through makeup, lingerie, cosmetic surgery, aerobics classes, and corsets. You even say that "entering a wet T-shirt contest" can be a "liberating" act for some women.

8   But, but, but . . . you are mad at the wrong folks. Feminists never promised you a rose garden in Lotusland; the consumer culture did. Feminism, unlike advertising, is not about gulling you into believing you could win the sweepstakes. Feminism is and always has been about women acting in the world as full-fledged citizens, as real participants in the world of ideas and policy and history. That doesn't have anything to do with wearing lipstick or not wearing lipstick or even about making obscene amounts of money. It's about insisting on the right of women to dignity, a living wage, meaningful work, and active engagement in the public arena. As for lipstick: For most women who work in the cruddy lower reaches of American employment, the problem isn't being denied the "right" to wear makeup and lingerie; it's about the right not to be forced to dress and act the way their male bosses demand. You may recall that flight attendants in the '60s fought one of the earliest battles of feminism's second wave so that male corporate bosses could no longer fire them over their weight, age, dress, or marital status. (Stewardesses were also, by the way, required to wear girdles—and didn't consider it liberating when their supervisors conducted company-mandated "touch checks.") Feminism, real feminism, is about freeing women to be genuine individuals—and recognizing that such individuality doesn't come in one size only or out of a bottle.

9   You propose that we cleanse feminism of political content and even "abolish" the term "women's movement." "This next wave" of feminism, you say, "needs to be primarily devoted to developing our emotional independence." Well, we certainly are in an "emotional" era. That's because we are steeped in a consumer culture where emotional manipulation is the name of the game and political analysis interferes with the Big Sell and so is discouraged. Now you are asking that feminism junk the politics and join in on the consumerizing of the American female public. Well, you can ask. You can cheerlead for that all you like, of course. And I'm sure a lot of powerful institutions will be only too glad to enable your cheerleading for their own selfish ends. But you can't call what you're asking for feminism, or progress. You can't say we've come a long way when you are still championing our "right" to stand on the stage in a wet T-shirt and be called baby.

10   . . . Am I getting through, or does this all sound like static on the line?

Sincerely,
Susan

Dear Susan,

11   Well, I think there would be much less static between us if you had read my book more carefully, did not take my words out of context, and did not lump me in with women with whom I clearly have little in common. I also think we'd have a much better connection if you'd drop the sneery, condescending tone you always seem to adopt when writing about women with whom you disagree. I respect you;

I'd probably even like you if we met under slightly less fraught circumstances. Yes, I disagree with some of your philosophical and political views. But those views don't make you any less of a feminist. As long as you believe that women should have the same rights, opportunities, and responsibilities as men, you can have whatever political agenda, lifestyle, or wardrobe you wish.

12   Unfortunately, you don't seem to feel the same way about me or millions of other women. You say that "feminism, real feminism, is about freeing women to be genuine individuals—and recognizing that such individuality doesn't come in one size only or out of a bottle." But much of what you've written on the subject—in your book, magazine articles, and already in this dialogue—would indicate that you don't really mean it. And the same, I'm afraid, is true about most of the other self-appointed spokeswomen for feminism.

13   You each appear to believe that, to be allowed to use the term feminist, a woman has to adhere to a well-defined leftist political agenda, consisting of, at the very least, affirmative action, nationally subsidized day care, and "pay equity" (formerly known as comparable worth). In your *Ms.* article, you call a handful of women who happen to disagree with you politically (myself included) "pod" or "pseudo" feminists. You say that we're right-wing misogynists or pawns of right-wing misogynists. Perhaps most curiously, you imply that we're also racist. In 1992, the National Organization for Women tried to start a "women's party," offering a distinctly leftist "women's agenda." During the last election, NOW president Patricia Ireland said women should vote only for "authentic" female candidates, Gloria Steinem called Texas Republican Sen. Kay Bailey Hutchinson a "female impersonator," and Naomi Wolf described the foreign-policy analysis of Jeane Kirkpatrick as being "uninflected by the experiences of the female body." The desire to enforce political conformity is even worse in academia. Many women's-studies professors regularly judge texts and opinions in terms of their agreement with the orthodox political agenda. (For an honest "insider" account, check out *Professing Feminism*, by Daphne Patai and Noretta Koertge.)

14   Fortunately, all women don't think alike, and as far as feminism is concerned they certainly don't have to. The only items on the real feminist agenda are equal rights and opportunities, a society capable of accepting the widest array of women's choices, and women strong and independent enough to make rational ones. This in no way means that feminists should "junk the politics." It means that feminism is a moral ideal; how women achieve it is a matter of political debate.

15   It's true that some of the women you mention above and in your *Ms.* article do oppose abortion rights, do deny that discrimination exists, and do believe that it is a woman's God-given duty to have children and stay home with them—all anti-feminist notions. Some have minimized the very real problems of sexual harassment and date rape, and seem far more interested in self-promotion than in the future of feminism. Yet the surveys suggest that the vast majority of women—and men—who have criticized the women's movement in recent years do believe in women's essential equality and are simply unhappy with the fact that feminism has turned into an orthodoxy, that it now means precisely the opposite of what it was intended to mean—namely, freedom.

16   Feminist theorists have gotten much better at not explicitly stating that women need to follow a certain lifestyle or dress code to be a feminist. But an implicit criticism of more traditional choices is still quite apparent. In *Backlash*, for instance, you blame the fact that women are still primarily clustered in the "pink ghetto" or low- to mid-level management positions entirely on discrimination. Some of it surely is discrimination, and some of it is due to the fact that women are still working their way up. But much of the explanation can be found in the choices of women themselves. The vast majority of women—even young women with college degrees who have grown up with nearly every option open to them—still prefer to give their families higher priority than their careers. According to the Women's Education and Research Institute (hardly a bastion of conservative thought), employed mothers are significantly more likely than fathers to want to stay at their current levels of responsibility and to trade job advancement to work part time, work at home, or have control over their work schedules. Four-fifths of mothers who work part-time do so by choice.

17   The larger problem is that most feminist theorists still refuse to acknowledge that there appear to be significant biological differences between the sexes. They still seem to believe that equality with men has to mean sameness to men, that until all aspects of traditional femininity are abolished, women will not be free. Thankfully, this is far from necessary. Women, on average, may always have a stronger need than men to nurture, a need that will at times eclipse their desire for power. Restructuring the corporate world to better accommodate two-career families may certainly help women to deal with these conflicting goals, but I don't think they will ever disappear. We may not like the choices many women continue to make, but not only are they really none of our business, there's precious little we could do about them if they were.

18   Biology also still seems to be turning up in courtship (the desire of the vast majority of women to want men to pursue them), sex (the ambivalence most women have toward casual sex), and beauty (the energy most women give toward making themselves attractive). As you well know, I do not say anywhere in the book that women have to wear lipstick to be feminist or even feminine. I use lipstick as a metaphor for all of the traditionally feminine behaviors that feminist theorists have at some point condemned as being degrading and exploitative—from being a mother to staying home full-time with one's children to wearing miniskirts and makeup. In *Backlash*, you implicitly argue that the desire of many women to buy feminine or sexy clothing and indulge in cosmetic products and services is wholly the result of manipulation by the beauty and fashion industries. You call women's desire for sexy lingerie "fashion regression," and argue that happy and confident women don't care about clothes. Actually, I think the desire of most women to not hide their sexuality is a sign of progress, evidence that many women now feel they no longer have to renounce a fundamental aspect of themselves in order to make a symbolic point.

19   I do not feel "gypped" by feminism. On the contrary, feminism has offered me the opportunity to live my life in a way that was considered reprehensible just 40 years ago. What I do feel is that the feminist revolution is not complete, and it's

incomplete in ways that differ from the orthodox feminist line. There's still more political work to be done, to be sure, especially involving the issues of rape and domestic violence. But there's also much personal work to be done. This is a major theme of my book, yet for some reason you have chosen to purposefully misread what I wrote about it. Where do I say anything about "the consumerizing of the American female public"?

20   Of course the advertising industry exploited feminism; that's their job. But that has nothing to do with what I'm talking about. I use the term emotional independence to refer to self-development, which was a prominent part of feminist theorizing and activism in the early days of the Second Wave. Actually, it's not that surprising that you chose to ignore what I was saying and turn the focus back on how society has victimized women. Feminists have unfortunately been doing that for the past 20 years, which may partly explain why women lag so far behind in their emotional development. While enormous attention has been paid to how the "patriarchy" mistreats women, little has been written about how women mistreat themselves. Even focusing on how women should take responsibility for their problems is often dismissed as naive, sexist, or "blaming the victim."

21   (By the way, you also took my point about "entering a wet T-shirt contest" completely out of context. As you well know, I was actually saying that just because women now have the freedom to do something doesn't mean it's the most rational thing to do. "Only each woman can decide if her actions are self-destructive and thus unfeminist," I wrote. "What is self-destructive for one woman—entering a wet T-shirt contest, for instance, or being a full-time housewife—may be liberating for another.")

22   It's true that the orthodoxy is breaking up, and other feminist voices are finally being heard. But that's no thanks to you, Susan. I think you have focused more energy on stifling dissent than perhaps any other feminist writer. In your book, you castigate Susan Brownmiller, Betty Friedan, and Erica Jong for having the gall to suggest that the women's movement's refusal to acknowledge biological differences between the sexes is hurtful to women. You can't blame the media for the fact that two-thirds of women still don't call themselves feminist. The media may very well highlight the extremes, but it has also given Gloria Steinem, Naomi Wolf, Patricia Ireland, and yourself plenty of space and air time to alienate the majority of women through your restrictive view of feminism.

23   Feminism—real feminism—deserves to be respected and honored. Every woman today should proudly call herself a feminist. But that is not going to happen until prominent feminist writers such as yourself admit to a couple of things. One, that a Republican housewife who annually has her face lifted and daily greets her husband at the door wearing only heels can be a feminist if she knows her mind, follows her desires, and believes that every woman has the right to do the same. Two, that the notion of sisterhood is false, outdated, and sexist. Women don't "owe" each other anything: They don't have to like each other, agree with each other, vote for each other, or hire each other for feminism to succeed.

24   Three, the notion of a "women's movement" has outlived its usefulness. Men must be just as aware and involved as women—on both a personal and political

level—for feminism to work. Four, women can act differently from men. Even if that means that Congress, corporate boards, and CEOs will never be 50 percent female, as long as women are making their choices freely, feminism will not be undermined. And finally, each woman is fundamentally unique. No assumptions can be made about her politics, values, goals, and beliefs.

25   Instead of fighting about whether or not feminism has turned into an orthodoxy, I think it would be far more useful if this dialogue—as well as the larger feminist debate—were focused on the complexities that women must deal with today. For instance, how does the corporate world learn to judge women strictly on their merits yet recognize the obvious differences—e.g., that women are the only ones who get pregnant? How do we help women deal with their ambivalence toward responsibility and power? How do we help women develop the strength and independence to demand boyfriends who don't abuse them, and raises that they deserve? These are tough questions, and I'd really like to know what you think about them.

Sincerely,
Karen

 FREEWRITING ASSIGNMENT

What does the word *feminism* mean to you? Explain.

CRITICAL READING

1. Why does Faludi express "misgivings" about entering into a conversation on feminism with Lehrman? What tone does she set for the dialogue? How does Lehrman respond to this tone?
2. Summarize Faludi's argument. What is her definition of "real feminism"? Why does she object to "revisionist feminism"? Explain.
3. Summarize Lehrman's argument. What is her definition of "real feminism"? Why does she object to Faludi, and other "self-appointed spokeswomen for feminism?" Explain.
4. In what ways has consumer culture clouded the goals of feminism? How has advertising exploited feminism? Explain.
5. On what points do Faludi and Lehrman agree? If you were the moderator of this dialogue, how would you use these points of agreement to help them reach a consensus?
6. Do Faludi and Lehrman enter this dialogue on feminism in order to reach an understanding or middle ground? What evidence is there, if any, on either side of their discussion to try to reach a consensus or at least understand the other's point of view?

CRITICAL WRITING

7. You have been asked to write an article about feminism at the beginning of the twenty-first century for inclusion in a time capsule to be opened at the beginning of the next century. Describe your own perception of feminism, and include examples from popular culture and your experience. How are women portrayed by the media? How are they perceived in North American culture? How do you think things will have changed in 100 years? Explain.

8. *Research and Analysis*: Is it harder to grow up male or female in North America today? Using information from the articles in this section, as well as outside resources, write an essay explaining which gender faces the greatest and most daunting challenges, and why. Will this situation get worse? Offer suggestions to help ease the gender-related challenges children face growing up in today's culture.

9. *Exploratory Writing*: Write an essay in which you consider your own sense of cultural conditioning. Do you feel your behaviour has been conditioned by sex-role expectations? In what ways? Is there a difference between the "real" you and the person you present to the world? If there is a difference, is it the result of cultural pressure? Explain.

GROUP PROJECT

10. Thirty years ago, men were expected to earn more than women. Do we still hold such beliefs? Poll students outside of class as well as other people on campus to find out their opinions regarding income status. Create some questions that will allow both men and women to discuss how they feel about this issue. Do males feel that they should earn more? Would they feel less masculine if their girlfriends or wives earned more then they did? Do females look for higher incomes when they consider a partner? Analyze your results and draw some conclusions from your survey.

 RESEARCH ISSUE **An Identity Reduced to a Burka**
Semeen Issa and Laila Al-Marayati

With much media attention focused on the Middle East, generalizations can become misconceptions. As these two Muslim women explain in the opinion section of the *Los Angeles Times* (January 20, 2002), the issues Middle Eastern women face are much more complex than the burkas they wear. Semeen Issa is president of the Muslim Women's League and a teacher in Arcadia. Laila Al-Marayati is a Los Angeles physician.

A few years ago, someone from the Feminist Majority Foundation called the Muslim Women's League to ask if she could "borrow a burka" for a photo shoot the organization was doing to draw attention to the plight of women in Afghanistan under the Taliban. When we told her that we didn't have one, and that none of our Afghan friends did either, she expressed surprise, as if she'd assumed that all Muslim women keep burkas in their closets in case a militant Islamist comes to dinner. She didn't seem to understand that her assumption was the equivalent of assuming that every Latino has a Mexican sombrero in their closet.

2   We don't mean to make light of the suffering of our sisters in Afghanistan, but the burka was—and is—not their major focus of concern. Their priorities are more basic, like feeding their children, becoming literate and living free from violence. Nevertheless, recent articles in the Western media suggest the burka means everything to Muslim women, because they routinely express bewilderment at the fact that all Afghan women didn't cast off their burkas when the Taliban was defeated. The Western press' obsession with the dress of Muslim women is not surprising, however, since the press tends to view Muslims, in general, simplistically. Headlines in the mainstream media have reduced Muslim female identity to an article of clothing—"the veil." One is hard-pressed to find an article, book or film about women in Islam that doesn't have "veil" in the title: "Behind the Veil," "Beyond the Veil," "At the Drop of a Veil" and more. The use of the term borders on the absurd: Perhaps next will come "What Color is Your Veil?" or "Rebel Without a Veil" or "Whose Veil is it, Anyway?"

3   The word "veil" does not even have a universal meaning. In some cultures, it refers to a face-covering known as niqab; in others, to a simple head scarf, known as hijab. Other manifestations of "the veil" include all-encompassing outer garments like the ankle-length abaya from the Persian Gulf states, the chador in Iran or the burka in Afghanistan.

4   Like the differences in our clothing from one region to another, Muslim women are diverse. Stereotypical assumptions about Muslim women are as inaccurate as the assumption that all American women are personified by the bikini-clad cast of "Baywatch." Anyone who has spent time interacting with Muslims knows that, despite numerous obstacles, Muslim women are active, assertive and engaged in society. In Qatar, women make up the majority of graduate-school students. The Iranian parliament has more women members than the U.S. Senate. Throughout the world, many Muslim women are educated and professionally trained; they participate in public debates, are often catalysts for reform and champions for their own rights. At the same time, there is no denying that in many Muslim countries, dress has been used as a tool to wield power over women.

5   What doesn't penetrate Western consciousness, however, is that forced uncovering is also a tool of oppression. During the reign of Shah Mohammad Reza Pahlavi in Iran, wearing the veil was prohibited. As an expression of their opposition to his repressive regime, women who supported the 1979 Islamic Revolution marched in the street clothed in chadors. Many of them did not expect to have this "dress code" institutionalized by those who led the revolution and then took power in the new government.

6   In Turkey, the secular regime considers the head scarf a symbol of extremist elements that want to overthrow the government. Accordingly, women who wear any type of head-covering are banned from public office, government jobs and academia, including graduate school. Turkish women who believe the head-covering is a religious obligation are unfairly forced to give up public life or opportunities for higher education and career advancement.

7   Dress should not bar Muslim women from exercising their Islam-guaranteed rights, like the right to be educated, to earn a living and to move about safely in society. Unfortunately, some governments impose a strict dress code along with other restrictions, like limiting education for women, to appear "authentically Islamic." Such laws, in fact, are inconsistent with Islam. Nevertheless, these associations lead to the general perception that "behind the veil" lurk other, more insidious examples of the repression of women, and that wearing the veil somehow causes the social ills that plague Muslim women around the world.

8   Many Muslim men and women alike are subjugated by despotic, dictatorial regimes. Their lot in life is worsened by extreme poverty and illiteracy, two conditions that are not caused by Islam but are sometimes exploited in the name of religion. Helping Muslim women overcome their misery is a major task. The reconstruction of Muslim Afghanistan will be a test case for the Afghan people and for the international community dedicated to making Afghan society work for everyone. To some, Islam is the root cause of the problems faced by women in Afghanistan. But what is truly at fault is a misguided, narrow interpretation of Islam designed to serve a rigid patriarchal system.

9   Traditional Muslim populations will be more receptive to change that is based on Islamic principles of justice, as expressed in the Koran, than they will be to change that abandons religion altogether or confines it to private life. Muslim scholars and leaders who emphasize Islamic principles that support women's rights to education, health care, marriage and divorce, equal pay for equal work and participation in public life could fill the vacuum now occupied by those who impose a vision of Islam that infringes on the rights of women.

10   Given the opportunity, Muslim women, like women everywhere, will become educated, pursue careers, strive to do what is best for their families and contribute positively according to their abilities. How they dress is irrelevant. It should be obvious that the critical element Muslim women need is freedom, especially the freedom to make choices that enable them to be independent agents of positive change. Choosing to dress modestly, including wearing a head-scarf, should be as respected as choosing not to cover. Accusations that modestly dressed Muslim women are caving in to male-dominated understandings of Islam neglect the reality that most Muslim women who cover by choice do so out of subservience to God, not to any human being.

11   The worth of a woman—any woman—should not be determined by the length of her skirt, but by the dedication, knowledge and skills she brings to the task at hand. ◆

CRITICAL THINKING

1. What is a burka? Why are they worn? What do they represent to most Westerners?
2. According to the authors, why are Westerners misguided by the concept of burkas, chadors, and hijabs? In what ways can banning these items be just as extremist as mandating their use?
3. Consider the authors' title for their essay. What does the title mean? How can identity be reduced to a burka? Could their title also be ironic? Explain.

RESEARCH PROJECTS

4. The authors of this essay point out that Muslim women are diverse. Depending on where they live, they can be highly educated and involved in political and economic arenas or oppressed to the point where they cannot leave their homes without a chaperone. Visit the Web site of the Muslim Women's League at **www.mw/usa.org/** and read more about Muslim women in North America. Write a short essay describing one of the issues North American Muslim women are dealing with today (racial profiling, civil rights, cultural misconceptions, etc.). Share your own opinion about the issue as well.
5. In paragraph 2, the authors note that most discussions about Muslim women concentrate on their wearing "the veil." Research the Muslim tradition of the veil and write a short history about it. A good resource to begin your research is About.com's guide at **womensissues.about.com/cs/abouttheveil**. Include in your report modern opinions about the veil, and if possible, interview a Muslim female student for her opinion about this article of clothing.

Additional essay topics, writing assignments, research guidelines, and readings for this chapter can be found online at **www.pearsoned.ca/goshgarian**.

Youth

and Crime

There are many misperceptions about youth and crime in Canada and the United States. Certainly, some Canadians believe that youth crime, especially violent crime, is on the rise. But statistics, often confusing, show that this isn't necessarily the case. In fact, the overall rate of youth crime in Canada has declined over the past decade. Violent crime peaked in 1995, declined for four years following that, and then peaked again in 2001. Some analysts attribute the apparent rise in some statistics to the fact that more people are reporting crimes to the police as schools adopt a zero-tolerance policy. This perceived increase in youth crime generates much discussion and disagreement: on the one hand, Canadians are concerned about young people who are troubled, but at the same time a segment of the population is unable to move beyond the prejudice that all young people are a threat to public security and personal safety. And although many argue about how to reduce the incidence of youth crime, almost everyone agrees that its roots are deeply embedded in society. In this chapter we examine those roots and look at some of the strategies that are being adopted to combat youth crime.

We begin with "A Bad Rap," an excerpt of an article by Rupert J. Taylor, that examines how the media portray youth crime in Canada and how this affects public perceptions of youth and even the implementation of stricter laws. We follow this with a discussion of children and crime in contemporary America. In "Children as the Enemy," Peter Elikann explores how society views juvenile offenders, how juvenile crime has changed, and how the American political atmosphere encourages tougher laws and more severe punishments.

The next article questions the media frenzy that seems to accompany each new act of school violence. The underlying tone of most of this coverage is one of overwhelming shock and outrage. We do not expect this behaviour from children, and certainly not in school. Historian David Greenberg, however, disagrees. In "Students Have Always Been Violent," he explains that students and school violence has a long and disturbing history. It is not that students have become more violent, says Greenberg; it is simply that they have access to more destructive weapons, and there is increased media coverage of their actions.

The next piece looks at the issue of guns and schools. In "Guns, Sex, and Education," Jamie O'Meara provocatively suggests that one way to demystify guns and strip them of their power is to write them into the school curriculum. He proposes teaching kids how to handle guns and even how to fire them as part of a supervised school activity, in much the same way as we teach them about safe sex.

Next is a student's perspective on youth violence. In "Violent Culture: The Media, the Internet, and Placing the Blame," Darren Beals explores the connection between the media, the Internet, and the rise in youth violence in America's schools. Written while Beals was a student at Northeastern University, the essay raises some interesting questions about our society and our desire to find a scapegoat to blame.

The Viewpoints section at the end of this chapter explores the issue of violence in video games. Video games, especially games that involve fighting or killing opponents as part of the action of play, have come under close scrutiny in the past few years. The concern has even reached commercial markets. In 1999, Disney pulled all the violent video games from the arcades in its theme parks. However, in "Games Don't Kill People—Do They?" Greg Costikyan, a game designer, cautions that before we rush to damn the video-game industry, we should consider the cathartic aspects of video gaming. Virtual reality designer Mark Pesce disagrees. In "The Trigger Principle," he explains that as he played one of the new violent video games, he experienced more nausea than catharsis.

Finally, the Research Issue looks at Canada's Youth Criminal Justice Act, which in 2003 replaced the old Youth Offenders Act. Lori Saunders discusses some of the changes in "Crime and Punishment: Toughening the Young Offenders Act."

A Bad Rap
Rupert J. Taylor

Are youth today more violent than they were in the past? Given the way that the media reports on youth and youth crime, the answer would appear to be a resounding yes. But the statistical data in Canada is confusing and even misleading at times. A small number of sensational cases tend to dominate the headlines, and these become the basis for society's perception of today's troubled youths. What types of youth crimes, if any, are actually on the rise, and who's committing those crimes? In this piece, Rupert J. Taylor explores these questions and the manner in which the media depicts youth crime in Canada.

Rupert J. Taylor writes for *Canada and the World Backgrounder*, where the complete version of this article appeared in December 2000.

CRITICAL THINKING Do you have the impression that youth crime is on the rise in Canada? On what do you base your opinion?

1 To judge by the media headlines, we're on the verge of installing metal detectors at the doorways to kindergartens and frisking the little tykes for weapons before they go into class. As is often the case, media headlines can be misleading.

2 Young people get a very bad press. Doesn't it seem as though the only time people under 24 make it into the media it's because they've done something wrong?

3 "Police Charge Second Youth After Vicious Beating"—Halifax, June 1999.

4 "Teens Assault Girl on Remote Beach"—Ucluelet, B.C., December 1999.

5 "Youth the Link in Weekend Shootings"—Toronto, April 2000.

6 "Youth Gang Rivalry Tough to Handle"—Montreal, July 2000.

7 There, the media's done it again; focussed on the negative. The truth is that most young people never get into trouble with the law; most study hard, most work hard, and most make successes of their lives. But, that doesn't make for very colourful front pages or evening newscasts. The real trouble is caused by a small minority and it's their antics that grab the media's attention. A schoolyard stabbing

is guaranteed more news coverage than the story of a kid who aces every exam, captains the volleyball team, goes to church on Sunday, and volunteers at the hospital.

8   Melissa Rosato understands what's going on. An 18-year-old student at Loyola Catholic Secondary School in Mississauga, Ontario in the spring of 2000, she told *The Toronto Star*: "I don't believe youth crime is on the rise. I think the media is choosing to report more incidents of it . . . the society we live in enjoys violence." Barbara Hall is a former youth worker and now Chair of the National Strategy on Community Safety and Crime Prevention. She faults the media for putting too much emphasis on youth crime because it "tends to demonize young people and to suggest that young people are themselves a problem, rather than saying that young people, like other groups, face certain problems."

9   Statistics from the federal Department of Justice say that youth crime declined by 23% between 1991 and 1997. It looks like an open-and-shut case; the public, reacting to media hype, is getting hysterical over a non-issue. And, some politicians reacting to public opinion are taking a hard line on youth crime.

10   But, hold on; Statistics Canada reports that violent youth crime increased by 77% between 1988 and 1998.

11   If this sounds confusing it is. What's going on is that the rates for some types of youth crime are going down while the rates for others are going up. Rosemarie Gartner, Director of the Centre of Criminology at the University of Toronto, explains: "The most reliable data on serious crimes [shows] there has been no increase over the past ten years. However, level one crimes, minor assaults, including threats, show a big increase over the past ten years."

12   And, many of those minor crimes are taking place on school property. But, is it the rate of crime that's going up or the reporting of crime that's increasing? We know that most schools have introduced zero-tolerance policies over the last decade. In the past, a corridor body-check, insult, or locker trashing might have been brushed off as "Kid stuff." Victims were told this sort of thing happens—"Deal with it."

13   That attitude has changed. Most schools now recognize that letting bullying and harassment continue unchecked was a bad move. If it isn't stopped at the beginning very much worse things are likely to happen to both the victims and the perpetrators. Frequently, the most violent acts are committed by the victims of bullying. After years of taunting they snap and lash out violently, sometimes at another student, sometimes at themselves. Attempting suicide is not an unusual way of dealing with the intolerable pain of being a target.

14   In April 2000, a Grade 10 student at Cairine-Wilson Secondary School near Ottawa stabbed four students and a staff member; he then slashed his own wrists and arms. Fortunately, none of the people involved suffered life-threatening injuries. The Grade 10 student who went on this rampage had been a victim of teasing. His severe acne was something other students ridiculed and his curly hairstyle got him the nickname "pubic head." One student admitted that "In Grade 9, I used to make fun of him a lot. I just went along with what everyone else said."

15   A similar scenario played itself out at the W.R. Myers High School in Taber, Alberta, only with grimmer consequences. In April 1999, a 14-year-old male,

described by many as an outcast, shot and killed one student and severely wounded another. While shocking in themselves these attacks were seen in the context of the sometimes-violent culture of young males and were therefore not all that surprising.

16 But, the crime that really shocked Canadians a couple of years earlier came as a huge surprise.

17 Reena Virk was not a popular girl. So, when a clique of girls asked Reena to meet them one night in November 1997 she couldn't resist. Perhaps, these girls wanted to be her friends. But no; they wanted to beat her up. There were about a dozen of them and they punched and kicked her severely. Reena managed to escape and headed across a small bridge. But, two of the gang followed her and beat her unconscious. These two dragged her to a shallow inlet and held her head under the water until her life of 14 years was ended. What shocked Canadians was that all but one of Reena Virk's attackers were female; 14- to 16-year-old girls are not supposed to be murderers. So, the psychologists (amateur and professional) have jumped in to try to explain.

18 Late in 1999, a conference in Toronto was told that aggression is just as common among girls as it is among boys. However, with boys it tends to be physical, while with girls it is more likely to be verbal. Mental health expert Kenneth Goldberg says that up to age three girls are still physically aggressive in getting something they want. At that age, though, they learn by example to become manipulative. As they grow older they refine their aggression so that by the time they reach their teen years they have developed techniques such as spreading false rumours, belittling people to their faces, and premeditated manipulation. Researchers have also noticed an increase in physical aggression among young women during the 1990s.

19 So, what's missing in the lives of these girls? York University psychology professor Debra Pepler is doing research on girlhood aggression. She says, "The critical factor is parenting." Girls who come from families that lack the resources to provide good parenting are most at risk, and this means families that are rich as well as poor. Excessive aggression is both treatable and preventable, but it first requires involved parents who can recognize symptoms and have the motivation and skill to seek out help.

20 Also, it pretty much goes without saying that a child raised in a home where violence, abuse, and victimization are a daily occurrence is more than likely to learn that those are the skills needed to resolve a conflict.

21 In New York, psychologist Ron Taffel has developed a theory around what he calls "the second family." He agrees that violent movies, games, and music lyrics play a part, but it's only a secondary role. He says that children are desperate to be seen and noticed, but often their parents are too busy and stressed out to do this. That's when youngsters turn to a violent culture to fill the void created by parents who don't spend time with them. This violent culture becomes their "second family." The world of Eminem, The World Wrestling Federation, Doom, and the Terminator would seem to be just about the worst role models you could pick as a substitute for one-on-one time with an involved parent.

22   The buzz-words are "quality time." But, this is not what child development experts are talking about. It's not about flying the family down to Disneyworld for March Break and then letting them look after themselves for the remaining 51 weeks. Jan Drucker of the Child Development Institute in New York talks about parents and kids "hanging out" together. It doesn't have to be some super expensive manufactured entertainment. It's more like watching a ball game on TV together, making preserves, reading to each other, playing cards or board games, and especially eating meals together as a family.

23   Most of the girls involved in the attack on Reena Virk were from broken homes. They shared a contempt for all authority figures: parents, teachers, youth workers, police. Most had already been in trouble with the law, frequently as a result of violence.

24   Just look at the background of one of the convicted girls. When she was six years old her father was murdered while she was in the house and her mother was charged with the crime. She was then left at another home where she was kept in the basement. She received counselling over her father's death but did not respond, often remaining silent throughout therapy sessions. Later caregivers were warned the girl would likely have trouble as a teen, particularly with violence.

25   Debra Pepler is clear about what needs to be done. "We must surround these [problem] children and their families with support," she wrote in a *Globe and Mail* article in March 2000, "to enable them to move off a negative and onto a positive developmental path. It's never too late to try to support the healthy development of troubled children. Comprehensive programs . . . have proved effective in enabling aggressive children and adolescents and their families to make a new start."

26   Dr. Pepler prescribes three levels of intervention. The first comes in our schools. Here, all young people are given the skills and attitudes that promote positive interactions and discourage aggression. Researchers have found that non-aggressive young people who do not intervene to stop a bullying incident are actually encouraging the bully. Of course, it takes a brave person to step forward and aid a victim. However, a universal program involves everyone in a school and creates a climate in which helping becomes the standard approach and standing by and doing nothing is a rarity.

27   The second level of intervention is early identification. Kindergarten and primary teachers are very good at spotting troubled children. This is where support, mostly in the form of counselling, for at-risk children and their families must be mobilized. The earlier the help is provided, the less intensive and expensive it needs to be.

28   If little or nothing is done at the earliest stages, then the third level of intervention is necessary. This is costly and less effective than the other two. It involves intensive support for the troubled young person in the family, at school, with friends, and in the community. Such intervention does give some violent teens a fresh start.

29   There are complaints that government money is too scarce to be used this way. However, the cost of doing nothing is higher. A stay in prison is the likely alternative, and this is hideously expensive in both financial and social costs.

FREEWRITING ASSIGNMENT

Was there an occasion in your youth when you felt that you or a friend were treated unfairly by people in a position of authority due to the public perception of youth violence?

CRITICAL READING

1. Rupert Taylor begins this piece with a series of headlines. Is this an effective strategy to communicate his message?
2. In this article, Melissa Rosato states that the media is reporting more incidents of youth crime because "the society we live in enjoys violence." Do you agree with this assertion?
3. Do you agree with the author that "young people get a very bad press"? Explain.
4. How does the author explain the seemingly contradictory statistics about youth crime? What does this suggest about the use of statistics in general?
5. The 1997 case of Reena Virk was particularly shocking because the perpetrators were girls. Are girls as aggressive as boys? According to this article, what is the difference in the way that boys and girls express their aggression?
6. What is "the second family" theory?
7. What is meant by "a bad rap," and who is getting one according to the author?

CRITICAL WRITING:

8. *Exploratory Writing:* If a youth commits a crime, who is ultimately responsible? At what age should we consider a person fully responsible for his or her actions? Should we admit that society has a role in the development of every youth and that when a youth commits a crime it is a failure of the system as a whole? Explore this idea in an essay.
9. *Exploratory Writing:* How do you feel about the idea that some people are simply bad, and no matter what, they are going to commit criminal acts? Do you believe that this is a possibility? If so, what can we do about such people? If not, what should the justice system be doing differently to increase the chances of rehabilitation?
10. How does Hollywood present young offenders? Watch a film that uses the "kids in trouble" motif, such as *The Basketball Diaries*, *The Outsiders*, or *The Good Son*. How does your chosen film portray youth and crime? In these films what motivates the young people to commit crimes, and how do society and "the system" treat these troubled youth? Present your observations in an essay.

GROUP PROJECTS

11. With your group, research Canadian news media for headlines on youth. Would you agree that it seems as though "the only time that people under 24 make it into the media it's because they've done something wrong?" Compare your findings with those of other groups.

Children as the Enemy
Peter Elikann

It seems that with alarming frequency we hear of another horrific criminal act committed by a young person—a boy shoots his classmate at recess, teenagers give birth and then abandon their babies in Dumpsters, angry youths mow down their peers in a school corridor, a disgruntled student kills his teacher for disciplining him. Are children today becoming more violent and immoral than in the past? Are we raising a generation of "superpredators"? Will prosecuting children as adults curtail this violent behaviour? Criminal defence attorney Peter Elikann argues that although children are not getting worse, our public perception is that they are dangers to society. This attitude, says Elikann, works counter to solving the real problems of youth violence, and will, in fact, make it even worse.

Peter Elikann is a Boston criminal defence lawyer, author, and a former professional journalist. His articles have appeared in the *Boston Sunday Herald*, *New Lawyer* magazine, and *Western New England Law Review*. He has published several books, including *The Tough-on-Crime Myth* (1996) and *Superpredators: The Demonization of Our Children by the Law* (1999), from which this essay was taken.

CRITICAL THINKING In this essay, Peter Elikann states that "no child is born evil." What does he mean by this statement? Consider a possible conclusion to this statement: if no child is inherently evil, he or she must therefore *learn* to be evil. What is your own viewpoint on these ideas?

1   When I was about eight years old, I lived with my family in a small village on the Saint Lawrence Seaway outside of Montreal, Canada, for two and a half years. My father's job had transferred him there and it was the only time we lived outside the United States. It was an almost magical time and place. We had a lot of friends and were very much entrenched in the community there.

2   One Saturday, a friend and I went door to door in a nearby neighborhood selling candy for a kids' group to which we belonged. In later years, I would have been too shy to do such a thing. I've never really had a salesman-type personality. But on

this day, it was a wonderful adventure. Everywhere we went, people seemed friendly and welcomed us. When the door to one home opened, we recognized a classmate. Her parents, whom we had never met, invited us hard workers in and made us each a sandwich. As the day wore on, our sales were high.

3   *Then it happened. At one house, a girl, not much older than us, answered the door and, although her parents weren't home, told us she wanted to buy the candy. Unfortunately, she didn't have the full 25 cents to pay us. She only had 23 cents.*

4   *But we were filled with a generosity of spirit and quite magnanimous. Sure, we'd give her the candy for 23 cents. We were no penny-pinching, miserly, green-eyeshade-type businessmen solely fixated on the bottom line.*

5   *As we walked away from her home, though, after having completed the sale, it suddenly dawned on us that we had our first business dilemma on our hands. Suddenly, we were operating at a deficit. We realized that when it would come time to hand in our money, we would be 2 cents short. We were now in the red. What to do?*

6   *But we were sharp, cunning businessmen, and like a bolt of lightning it suddenly hit us. We'd make up the difference by charging the next person an extra 2 cents.*

7   *Twenty-seven cents must have seemed like an oddly priced amount, but the elderly man who fell for our con job paid it readily. Once again, our books were balanced and we were in the black. Then our customer did a curious thing. He handed the candy back to us.*

8   *"No, you paid for it," I said. "It's yours."*

9   *"No, it's for you," he replied. "I don't really eat candy. But it seemed like you boys are out here working so hard selling this that you should be able to have some, too. I bought it for you."*

10   *It was a truly elegant gesture.*

11   *Yet, though we were only eight years old, we were two young men upon whom the irony was not lost. The one person that day who we had conned and cheated was the one person who, with great generosity of spirit—a total stranger, mind you— spent money to buy us a gift. We walked away from his door, awash in guilt. We were destroyed. We talked about it between us, and although we gave the candy away to some kid on the street who was even younger than us in an attempt to assuage our temporary self-loathing, we were moved by the concluding events of the day.*

12   The reason I bring up this story from the 1960s is because, ultimately, it raises a much larger question for me. As I began to hear reports in the late 1990s of a coming youth crime wave—of a new generation of increasingly violent young people without remorse or conscience—I wondered if it was really true. Are there any differences between my generation of young people and today's generation? To be sure, as my story indicates, we were eminently capable of behaving badly and doing the wrong thing, even participating in criminal behavior, minor though this 2-cent crime may be. But, on the plus side, we did have a conscience. We did know the difference between right and wrong. Upon reflection, we were able to acknowledge the wrongfulness of our conduct, feel badly about it and even be disappointed in ourselves. In other words, we certainly had the ability to mess up as much as the next

guy, but we weren't entirely lost causes because, at the very least, we were aware our behavior was bad. That's a starting point.

13   But what of this generation? Anecdotally, at least, reports of brazen cruelty by young people with seemingly few regrets appear increasingly across the radar screen of our public consciousness. The question invariably arises—are we raising a nation of increasingly sociopathic children without feeling, repentance or empathy?

14   An attorney I know who represents many juveniles accused of crimes told me:

> Let me give you my take on this thing. When I represent an adult accused of a crime, they'll usually do one of two things. They'll either admit that they did the crime or they'll deny it to me. But they'll never tell me that the crime itself wasn't a bad thing. I represent these young kids and many of them don't even get that what they did was wrong.

15   Only the week before, a young client, whom I had represented previously on a very minor offense, called to inform me that he had once again been arrested. This time a relative of his had been involved in an incident where someone had cut someone else off in their car and angry words had been exchanged. He told me that, after learning of the event, he had gone to the place of work of the person who had cut his relative off, bringing along some of his friends. He and his friends were arrested after being accused of threatening the person and coaxing him to fight.

16   Although he denied making the threats, he still asked me, "Is that really a crime? Can they arrest you for that?"

17   In an article appearing in the March 25, 1996, issue of *U.S. News and World Report* entitled "Crime Time Bomb," Florida psychotherapist and criminologist Kathleen Heide tells the story of a teenager who shot and paralyzed a jogger who wouldn't give up his gold chain. When asked what would have been a better outcome of the encounter, the teen shooter replied, "He could have given me his rope (chain). I asked him twice."[1]

18   Heide commented that many juvenile killers are "incapable of empathy."

19   Are we really entering a new world without a moral or ethical center? No.

20   I dispute the view of today's youth as an incorrigible ethical wasteland. Many of the young people I spoke with always had a solid core of morality. But I was also fascinated with stories told to me by children who had done very bad things in the past, yet were somehow able to be turned around through remorse and a sense of conscience and shame.

21   One 16-year-old I'll call Joe told me of an incident that happened three years earlier:

> I robbed somebody once. I couldn't do it any more. I needed cigarettes, marijuana, beer. So, at nighttime, I saw some lady walking. I just stuck a knife in her back and said, "Give me your purse." So, she gave it to me and left. After that, the next day, I was thinking about it and said to myself, "If I do that to people—old ladies and guys—how would they survive if they're not working?" Say if I put myself in their position, how would I feel? I imagine myself

in their position. I picture myself old and someone sticking a knife in my back.

Joe's horrible act was never repeated due to his sense of real empathy and he now works as a community youth organizer and still attends school.

22   Yet the wrongheaded perception that today's younger generation is more amoral and dangerous than ever is coupled with a widely held belief by a great number of criminologists that "you ain't seen nothin' yet." That's because it's long been generally acknowledged that the peak crime-committing years are ages 14 through 24 with some residual up until about the age of 40. Crime in this country went down beginning in 1992 at, coincidentally, the same time that the population-dense baby boomers started to age out of this crime-prone age. This was no surprise to criminologists, since historically, crime in the United States has gone up every time there's a large population of 14- through 24-year-olds. Conversely, it goes down every time that age group dwindles. So it is believed by many that this current respite may be short-lived. That's because the bulk of the children of the baby boomers—the baby boomerangs—already feared to be more dangerous and with less conscience, will soon be hitting those teen years. The logical, but erroneous, conclusion to this line of reasoning is that this will result in the long-feared coming youth crime wave.

23   Perhaps that's why one California police chief in the late 1990s quipped that he was not taking credit for the drop in crime because he did not want to be blamed for an increase if and when it comes.

24   Calling juvenile crime the "demographic crime bomb," John J. DiIulio, Jr. predicts that, by 2010, there could be three times the current number of juveniles incarcerated.[2]

25   Yet this increasing belief that today's young people are more immoral and dangerous and can't be reached on our ethical plane has now led to a profound and defective alignment in the way many politicians want to treat children headed on the wrong path. Harsh and severe punishments are now in vogue, including eliminating juvenile courts and many juvenile facilities in favor of trying children as adults before sentencing them to lengthy incarceration in adult facilities. The United States is already one of six countries in the world that sentence minors to the death penalty along with Iran, Pakistan, Nigeria, Saudi Arabia and Yemen. A centurylong tradition of treating youthful offenders differently from adults—of trying to turn their lives around through rehabilitation and education—is being abandoned.

26   Kent Scheidegger, legal director of the Criminal Justice Legal Foundation, echoed that opinion by saying, "You have a system that was designed for shoplifters, truants and joyriders that is now filled with rapists and murderers and people shooting each other with guns."[3]

27   When in 1997 the United States Congress passed a law requiring that juveniles aged 14 or older charged with federal crimes be tried as adults and incarcerated in adult prisons, they were following the lead of every state in the country.

28   But despite the tremendous popularity in lowering the age of adulthood by the criminal justice system, there's no evidence that it works to lower crime. In fact, ironically, the evidence shows the opposite.

29   Certainly there are juvenile psychopathic murderers from whom, if released, the public could never be assured of protection. But as nightmarish as are those headline cases of brutal murders by juveniles, they make up an infinitesimal fraction of serious youth crimes. Most juveniles who are tried in adult courts and sent to adult prisons are sent there for lesser crimes than homicide and will be released someday.

30   Every study available so far, as this book will reveal in greater detail, shows that those juveniles who are sent to adult prison have higher recidivism rates than those who remain in juvenile facilities. That means that juveniles sent to adult prison tend to endanger the public and get rearrested at much higher rates once they've been released.

31   The reason youths who have served time in adult prison are so much more dangerous when released than their counterparts who have served time in juvenile facilities is that, for those who are capable of having their lives turned around, they stand the best chance of picking up the life skills they need in juvenile facilities. For most—but not all—education and treatment in youth facilities that are set up to try to save kids really does work.

32   Certainly, rehabilitation doesn't have a 100 percent success rate, particularly in those rare instances when the youngster either is incapable of or not open to it. One teenager I spoke with whom I'll call Jesse had abandoned a fine family with seemingly caring working-class immigrant parents and successful siblings for an essentially homeless life of no school, fighting and crime. He couldn't articulate to me why he preferred his rootless life and in a rambling interview he continually answered with "I just don't know." He told me:

> Maybe I'm the black sheep. All my brothers and sisters are doing good in school. Me . . . I got kicked out of school. From the time I was five years old, I was stealing . . . food, candy. Fighting, too. The cops would take me to the station and then my parents would sit and have a talk with me. Sometimes they'd hit me and tell me I couldn't go outside and play. Didn't have any effect. I was fighting all the time. Because I was in a gang. I don't know why. . . . I've been surviving by myself for years now. I don't have a home. I bounce to friends' homes . . . sleep here or there. I got no job. Sometimes, I can't find a place to stay and stay up all night. Just try to stay up and walk around. Sometimes I stay on one corner or sit on someone's porch. I just can't stay out of trouble. I have no clue why. I go to a party and get into a fight. I want to stop. Can't. Right now I'm too lazy to do something. Too lazy to go out and get a job. I don't even have a dollar in my wallet. My parents didn't do anything. I'm the stupid one. I just go day by day.

33   Jesse's story is the rare one. In the following chapters are studies showing the phenomenal success rates of intervention programs and, in the case where someone is sent to a youth facility, remarkable statistics of youths having their lives turned around. In contrast, adult prisons today have largely abandoned trying to prepare young inmates for life on the outside world, once released.

34   It's not surprising that hanging out for years with older, more violent, hardened criminals while doing absolutely nothing to prepare yourself to cope better with the outside world once released, is a prescription for disaster.

35   An older prisoner with whom I have had a longtime correspondence and who spends much of his time counseling the young inmates who serve time with him, agrees on this point:

> I don't claim to know what the answer is, but I'll tell you what the answer is not—putting them side by side with hardened convicts whose sense of morality is long since gone. They become better thieves and harder thugs. They become repeat offenders.

Many police and corrections officials feel the same way.

36   "Sure, some kids are dangerous and should be locked up in secure juvenile facilities," said former San Jose police chief Joseph McNamara, a police officer for 35 years and now with the conservative Hoover Institution in a June 11, 1997 interview on MSNBC News. "But this doesn't make any sense to put them in with hardened adult criminals. We know that they'll be brutalized and we know that when they come out, they'll be worse than when they went in. They really will be violent people."[4]

37   But the alarmists are wrong. There will not be a coming youth crime wave.

38   In 1995, juvenile crime stunned most criminal justice experts by actually moving downward, although it was a dip in a high plateau. Overall violent crime arrests for youths dropped 2.9 percent. The following year confirmed it wasn't just a temporary aberration, with an even more significant drop of 9.2 percent. "This drop, I think, is real now," said Attorney General Janet Reno in 1997. "I don't think we can talk about it as a blip."[5] Then, for the third year in a row, in 1997, it dropped again, this time by 4 percent. That's more than 16 percent in three years. Minority arrests had fueled much of this rise in great disproportion to their actual numbers for reasons this book explores.

39   In fact, despite the hysteria over the highly publicized school shootings that took place over the 1997–98 school year, the number of violent school deaths has actually declined since 1992. While even one school death is too many, school is still the safest place for a young person to be since more than 99 percent of all violent youth deaths take place outside of school.[6]

40   Besides, even during its worst period between the mid-80s and mid-90s, it was very geographically concentrated, with a third of the nation's killings by youth taking place in just 10 counties. It rarely happened anywhere else, so perhaps the concept of an overall American youth crime wave was misleading.[7]

41   So, the explanation for the turning around of the rising youth crime rate beginning in 1995 appears to be that serious efforts were made to attack youth crime in just a handful of cities. For example, when the youth crime rate was significantly lowered in just one city, New York, that was enough to help send downward what were once rising youth crime statistics for the entire nation.

42   Contributing to the lowering of the youth crime rate were a diminished access to guns, less childhood poverty due to an improving economy, the beginning of a turnaround in the vanishing American family, and community policing. Still, the

fact that youth crime may actually be declining is no excuse for us to rest on our lau-
rels. It is down from an almost unprecedented level and is still way too high.

43   But the point which needs the most serious debate is whether individual young
people commit a much greater number of acts of violence than ever before, or their
violence is just more lethal. The often cited example is that the old schoolyard shov-
ing match or fist fight of yesteryear has given way to just shooting a classmate, as
kids are entering school buildings with handguns in absolutely unprecedented numbers. I will argue in detail that today's child isn't a great deal more violent; he's just
better armed.

44   This is borne out by statistics. The walloping increase in homicides by youth
from the mid-80s to the mid-90s was solely the result of guns. The fact that murders
by juveniles tripled during that period is interesting when you realize that gun murders quadrupled during that period while juvenile murders by all other weapons did
not increase one iota.[8] If America's youth were more predisposed to kill than ever
before during that period, we would have seen a rise in every kind of murder, not
just gun murders.

45   Youth crime rates for nonviolent crimes didn't go up either. It's guns, guns,
guns. . . . Guns are the sole area of youth crime that has shown a marked and significant increase.

46   "Academics and politicians . . . need to go to the president, congress, the media
and say, 'It's the guns, stupid!,'" echoed Vincent Schiraldi, director of the Justice
Policy Institute in Washington, D.C., and attorney Mark Kappelhoff.[9]

47   But rather than intervene and attack the problem of youth crime at an early
stage—keeping in mind that no child is born evil (though there may be an almost
microscopic number who are born with congenital mental health problems)—politicians, for the most part, seem to have come up with only a short-sighted two-part
approach: (1) adult trials and adult prison, and (2) a wholesale disinvestment in
youth. Year by year, they've chipped away at after school programs, education,
mentoring and recreation, decrying them as "pork," "big spending," "coddling,"
"pampering," and the deadly conversation-stopper "liberal." Deep funding cuts in
areas that could be used to prevent crime in the first place by bolstering up and supporting families are abandoned in favor of doing nothing and just waiting for
tragedies to occur. Then a greater amount of money is spent, after the fact, to process
and warehouse people in prison, where they learn to be better criminals from the
older, more violent ones.

48   There is a real and reprehensible beat-up-on-children mood pouring across the
political landscape. Children are the scapegoats of this generation. To be a child
today is to be suspect. There does appear to be a sad combination of both abandoning them and then meting out severe and Draconian punishments once they falter.
Several people have suggested that since we no longer have the specter of
Communism hanging over our heads as our main threat and nemesis in the world,
we've replaced Communists with children. Children are now, for our intents and
purposes, the new Communists. "What we are really frightened about is guns, but
instead of launching a war against guns, we are launching a war against kids," says
Barry Krisberg, head of the National Council on Crime and Delinquency.[10]

49   Even the way we speak about children makes it easier for us to go after them. The now popular term "superpredator" is the ultimate example. You wouldn't want to squash and brutalize a "child" would you? But squashing and brutalizing a "superpredator" wouldn't generate too much sympathy, would it? These terms help distance us from children. After all, you're attacking a "thing" or a "beast," not a person.

50   When Representative Bill McCollum introduced the 1997 federal bill to try to incarcerate more children as adults, he cynically first named it the "Violent Youth Predator Act." It was as if he was preparing us for a social Jurassic Park. Eventually, he was forced to change it to the "Juvenile Crime Control Act."

51   Rebecca Young, director of Citizens for Juvenile Justice, says:

> Well, we don't even talk about adult offenders as superpredators. I personally think part of what's scary about using that kind of language is that the sort of thinking that goes behind that language is the sort of thinking that led to the Holocaust. It's this sense that these people, well, they aren't people. And you'll hear people say that. You'll hear people say that about people who have committed certain offenses. They'll say, "He's not a human being. He's an animal. He should be in a cage."
>
> As soon as you start drawing that kind of a line, you say, "Based on this act you committed, you're not human anymore." Well, as soon as you're not human anymore, boy, we can do anything to you, and we can feel like we're morally superior. And that's pretty frightening. Now I'm not saying that the people who coined that term and the people who continue to use it are thinking, are actually aware of thinking, "I'm trying to dehumanize this group of people," but I personally think that's, in fact, what's going on.

52   Young is correct when she points out the hypocrisy that we don't even refer to adults as superpredators. This, in light of the fact that 90 percent of all children under 12 and 75 percent between the ages of 12 and 17 who are homicide victims are killed by adults.[11]

53   It is so very popular for so many politicians to join in on the war against kids, in spite of the fact that a survey of police chiefs across the country conducted by Northeastern University found that charging youthful offenders as adults was their least favorite option. The police said that intervening in young people's lives at an early age with crime prevention programs is the best way to reduce crime.[12]

54   But perhaps, as David Broder, the dean of American political journalists, wrote in his syndicated column, "It is a fascinating paradox of current politics that the further removed an official is from the front lines of the war on crime, the tougher he is likely to talk. That is particularly the case when it comes to violence by juveniles."[13]

55   Robert G. Schwartz, the executive director of the Juvenile Law Center, says the reason politicians don't hesitate to vilify youth is "a no-brainer. . . . Kids don't vote."[14] . . . Even if you start incarcerating children in numbers like we've never even dreamed of before, there'll always be an endless, limitless new crop of children coming over the horizon and approaching those peek crime-committing years. This is because the greatest myth of all which politicians campaign on is that if you give

out enough severe, Draconian punishments to children, you'll "send a message" to the other youths that this is what will happen if you commit bad acts.

56   Typical of politicians is Los Angeles District Attorney Gil Garcetti who, on the May 9, 1997, *NBC Nightly News,* declared, "The point is that juveniles do know what the law is and if they know they're going to be treated as an adult with adult sanctions, there, indeed, will be some deterrent effect."[15]

57   This is dead wrong. Most crimes of violence, particularly those committed by young people, are acts of impulse. They don't sit down and rationally and logically do a cost/benefit analysis on the pros and cons of what will happen if they get caught. They don't even think about it and, if they do, they don't assume they'll get caught. They don't ludicrously say to themselves, "I'm going to do this crime. I know I'll get caught, but I'll do it anyway because I'll only have to spend a few years incarcerated in a youth facility. If I was going to have to go to an adult facility, then I'd change my mind and I wouldn't do it." Of course, it would be ridiculous to think that any of these sometimes heartless, impulsive, violent people are doing some logical information processing before they commit their acts.

58   The proof that simply "sending a message" doesn't work is found merely by looking at the now quarter-century-long war on drugs where today more people are in for drugs and for longer sentences than ever, and it still hasn't made a dent. Today in the United States, drugs are more available, cheaper and purer than at any time. A whopping 70 percent of all people entering federal prison today are going in for drug offenses, and about 35 percent of all people entering state prisons and jails.[16] It hasn't made a dent, and yet still politicians stand in front of the scene of a major drug arrest and say things like, "This will send a message to drug dealers." It's just so much hype. Drugs and crime are such serious problems that they need to be dealt with less cynically.

59   The young person we'll call Jimmy who enters his classroom with a gun and starts shooting and killing the people inside, already knows his life will now be grievously ruined and damned forever if he has any ability to think at all, and yet he still does it. So, threatening him with a longer sentence or one in another type of facility won't stop him. Sure, you may have to lock Jimmy up forever to protect people in the future from him. But if you want to prevent other younger people from doing such acts, don't count on the younger kids' learning of Jimmy's fate and then calmly and rationally reevaluating and reconsidering the act they might have done.

60   If we want to protect the future of the public's safety, we've got to intervene in young people's lives before they get into trouble. We can't just hope and count on all the trouble-bound children hearing about the penalties and immediately straightening out their behavior on their own.

61   Former Republican U.S. Attorney General Elliot Richardson, who earlier had served as a state and federal prosecutor, called on politicians in 1996 to "skip the soundbites and slogans and focus on serious solutions. . . . Locking up serious criminals is a necessary defense, but you can never win a war if you're only fighting defense. When we take the offensive by investing in early-childhood and youth development, we can win the war against crime, and make our communities safe for our families."[17]

62   It's very little solace to victims and their families to just spend money to punish after the fact. Sure, we may need to do it. But better to avoid the whole thing by intervening in the lives of children at very young ages. We can do this the first-best way—shoring up disintegrating American families—or reluctantly, the still effective, albeit second-best way—providing role models and mentors in the lives of young people in order to save them. The best way of fighting juvenile crime is to interfere with, intervene, bother and love children before they get into trouble. This will be cheaper and make us safer than spending money on courts and jails and victim compensation after the child has committed a crime and a tragedy has occurred.

Bibliography

1. Ted Gest with Victoria Pope, "Crime Time Bomb," *U.S. News and World Report* (March 25, 1996), p. 30.
2. Anna J. Bray, "Who Are the Victims of Crime?," *Investor's Business Daily* (December 12, 1994), p. A-1.
3. Lisa Stansky, "Age of Innocence," *ABA Journal* (November, 1996), p. 66.
4. John Siegenthaler, "Interview with Joseph McNamara," MSNBC News (June 11, 1997).
5. Michael J. Sniffen, "Arrest Rate for Juveniles Dropped in '95," Associated Press (August 9, 1996); Gary Fields, "Youth Violent Crime Falls 9.2%", *USA Today* (October 3, 1997); Michael J. Sniffen, "Youth Crime Fell in '97, Reno Says," Associated Press (November 20, 1998).
6. "Despite String of Shootings, U.S. Says School Crime is Down," Associated Press (October 15, 1998); Elizabeth Donohue, Vincent Schiraldi, and Jason Ziedenberg, "School House Hype: School Shootings and the Real Risks Kids Face in America," *Justice Policy Institute Policy Report* (Washington, D.C.: Justice Policy Institute, July, 1998), pp. 4–5.
7. Gary Fields, "Youth Violent Crime Falls 9.2%," *USA Today* (October 3, 1997), p. 1A; Vincent Schiraldi and Mark Kappelhoff, "As Crime Drops Experts Backpedal—Where Have the 'Super Predators' Gone?" *JINN* (May 2, 1997); Steven A. Holmes, "It's Awful! It's Terrible! It's . . . Never Mind," *New York Times* (July 6, 1997), p. 3; Eric Lotke and Vincent Schiraldi, *An Analysis of Juvenile Homicides: Where They Occur and the Effectiveness of Adult Court Intervention* (Washington, D.C.: National Center on Institutions and Alternatives and Center on Criminal and Juvenile Justice, 1996).
8. Beth Carter, "Federal Juvenile Proposals in Perspective," *Crime & Politics in the 1990's* (Washington, D.C.: Campaign for an Effective Crime Policy, May, 1997), p. 3; Lori Montgomery, "A Divide on What's Fueling Youth Crime: Teens Raised for Violence or Just Well Armed," *Philadelphia Inquirer* (July 28, 1996), p. 1.
9. Vincent Schiraldi and Mark Kappelhoff, "As Crime Drops Experts Backpedal—Where Have the 'Super Predators' Gone?" *JINN* (May 2, 1997), p. 3.
10. Fox Butterfield, "States Revamping Youth Crime Laws," *New York Times* (May 12, 1996), p. 1.
11. Howard N. Snyder, Melissa Sickmund and Eileen Poe-Yamagata, *Juvenile Offenders and Victims: 1996 Update on Violence* (Washington, D. C.: Office of Juvenile Justice and Delinquency Prevention, June, 1997).
12. David Broder, "Funding Prevention Still Fights Crime Best," syndicated column (July 28, 1996).

13. *Ibid.*
14. Lisa Stansky, "Age of Innocence," *ABA Journal* (November, 1996), p. 62.
15. Gil Garcetti, "In Their Own Words," *NBC Nightly News* (May 9, 1997).
16. Editorial Board, "A System Sentencing Itself to Despair," *Los Angeles Times* (April 25, 1993), p. M4.
17. "New Poll of Police Chiefs Shows Overwhelming Agreement," press release (Washington, D.C.: Fight Crime: Invest in Kids, July 26, 1996). ◆

FREEWRITING ASSIGNMENT

In his concluding paragraph, Elikann states that "the best way of fighting juvenile crime is to interfere with, intervene, bother and love children before they get into trouble." Evaluate and respond to his "solution."

CRITICAL READING

1. Evaluate Elikann's use of a personal narrative as the introduction to his essay. How does this technique engage the audience? What were your impressions of his narrative? Could you relate to his experience? Why or why not? How did his narrative connect to the rest of his essay overall? Explain.
2. Elikann provides many examples of actual juvenile offenders and their interactions with both the law and their own impressions and feelings. Compare the examples of the juveniles described in paragraphs 15 and 17 with that of Joe in paragraph 21. How do these examples support the points he makes in his essay? Make a list of the juvenile offenders he features in his essay and record your impressions of each.
3. What is the "demographic time bomb"? On what logic is it based, and why does Elikann disagree with its premises?
4. Why, according to Elikann, is incarcerating juveniles as adults a bad idea? Do you agree or disagree with him, and why?
5. Elikann notes calling juvenile offenders names such as "superpredators" enables us to brutalize them and treat them with indifference and scorn. Analyze this use of "predator" as a metaphor for juvenile offenders. What ideas are associated with predators?
6. Analyze Elikann's use of pronouns in this essay. When he says "we" to whom is he referring? How does he identify groups or individuals that are not part of "we"? How does his use of pronouns position him in relation to his argument?

CRITICAL WRITING

7. *Personal Narrative:* In his introduction, Peter Elikann shares with his readers a personal experience from his childhood in which he became acutely aware of the difference between right and wrong. With the clear hindsight

of adulthood, he is able to analyze his experience and the impression it made on him both as a child and as an adult. Write your own personal account of a childhood experience in which you felt guilty for deceiving, stealing, or hurting someone else. Describe the experience itself, how you felt about it when it happened, how it may have affected your life, and what you think about the experience now that you are an adult.

8. *Exploratory Writing:* Elikann comments that one reason politicians seem to have little concern for the long-term welfare and rehabilitation of juvenile offenders is because these individuals cannot vote. Explore this idea in an essay. Is it fair that people who cannot vote for the politicians who make the laws be subjected to them? If the voting age is set at 18 because it is deemed the age of reason and maturity, is it ethical to apply adult penal codes to individuals under 18, who presumably lack the ability to maturely judge their actions? Explain.

GROUP PROJECTS

9. With your group, make a list of crimes that you think teenagers committed 30 years ago. What is the nature and severity of the crimes? Can you come up with a profile of a "bad kid" from that time period? Then try to profile the types of crimes committed by teenagers today. Is there any difference? What does today's "bad" teenager do? Does teen crime just seem worse because we have more data and the media exposes it more, or is it really worse than a generation ago? Share your two "profiles" with the rest of the class. What similarities and differences exist between different groups' profiles?

10. Elikann disagrees with the idea that "draconian punishments" send a message to children not to commit "bad acts." Rather, he argues, teens commit violent acts on impulse, and without considering the ramifications of their actions. Conduct a survey of teenagers with your group. Develop questions around the issue of punishment as a deterrent for youth crime, and the motivation behind violent acts. For example, you could ask teens if they are aware of punishments meted out for particular crimes. Or you could ask them what would deter them from crime and what would not. Do they think violent acts by teens are the result of impulse or premeditated decisions? Survey at least 15–20 teenagers under the age of 18 and apply their responses to Elikann's argument.

Students Have Always Been Violent

David Greenberg

With each new and highly publicized account of school violence, many people ask why students have now become so violent. It seems as if no one is safe anymore—our schools are battlefields and children and teachers are the innocent victims. But is this simply a matter of perception or of reality? In the next piece, writer David Greenberg explains that historically, students have always been violent, they are just better armed today.

David Greenberg is a history columnist for *Slate* at MSN. He is a graduate fellow of the Institute for Social and Economic Theory and Research at Columbia University. In addition to publishing many articles, Greenberg is the author of *Nixon's Shadow: The History of an Image* (2003). He wrote this column for the May 6, 1999 issue of *Slate*.

CRITICAL THINKING   Think about your experiences in elementary and high school. How much violence did you witness? What was the student reaction when someone shouted "fight"?

1   Judging by the histrionic Columbine massacre coverage you'd think that children are by nature innocent, free of violent or sexual thoughts until corrupted by our culture. That schools have traditionally been safe. That the recent spate of killings is unprecedented.

2   History says otherwise. In every era, American schoolchildren—especially teen-agers—have been unruly and destructive. As late as the 17th century, those "children" we now call teen-agers were considered adults. And preteens swore, drank, had sex, even dueled with guns. If school violence wasn't a problem back then, it's only because few children went to school.

3   In colonial America, most young children were taught at home. Those who attended school were just as prone to be disorderly as today's youths. Teachers kept problem children in line with corporal punishments that seem positively barbaric today: They tied children to whipping posts and beat them or branded students for their crimes—a "T" for thievery, a "B" for blasphemy. Occasionally children were put to death.

4   Branding fell from favor in the 18th century, but students were still flogged or tied to chairs.

5   In the early 19th century, school reformer Horace Mann reported that he saw 328 floggings in one school during the course of a week. As the principles of humanitarianism spread and the era of mass schooling arrived, Mann and others replaced or supplemented the elite academies with taxpayer-supported "common schools," which admitted young students from all walks of life. (Later, attendance

become compulsory.) In the Gilded Age, as immigrants and migrants flooded the cities, public elementary schools proliferated. Finally, the Progressives championed the view of adolescence as a stage of childhood, and high schools (the first of which opened in the 1820s) multiplied as well.

6   It appears that more students meant more violence. In 1837, Mann noted that almost 400 schools across Massachusetts had to be shut down because of disciplinary problems. In most institutions, keeping order took precedence over teaching. One observer in 1851 likened the typical American school to "the despotic government of a military camp." In the colleges, where the teen-age students were bigger and less docile, violence was even worse. Princeton University, to take just one example, witnessed six major riots between 1800 and 1830, including the burning of the library in 1802 and a rash of campus explosions in 1823 that caused half of one class to be expelled.

7   School violence persisted into the 20th century, taking different forms according to the climate of the day. In politically charged times, students became violent in the name of political causes. In 1917, for example, when New York City introduced a "platoon" system to deal with an influx of pupils, students rebelled—literally. Between 1,000 and 3,000 schoolchildren picketed and stoned P.S. 171 on Madison Avenue and attacked nonstriking classmates. Similar riots erupted across the city, resulting in furious battles between student mobs and the police. Likewise, the civil rights movement and anti-Vietnam War protests brought different forms of "political" violence to places ranging from Little Rock Central High in Arkansas to Kent State University in Ohio.

8   More politically sedate times didn't translate into student acquiescence, however. In the post–World War II years, urban strife and suburban anomie gave rise to school violence of the sorts broadly rendered by Hollywood in the 1955 films *Rebel Without a Cause* and *Blackboard Jungle*. The nation waxed hysterical over "juvenile delinquency," as the vogue phrase had it—alienated adolescents unaccountably sullen in the bountiful Eisenhower years. Though history had recorded public concern over bands of violent teen-agers ever since the beginning of the republic, the fear of "gangs" (a term coined in the 1930s) caught the nation's fancy. *Time* magazine headlined a story, "Teen-agers on the Rampage," which detailed a weeklong outbreak of violence in high schools from Maine to California. Congress held hearings on the delinquency epidemic, calling comic-book artists to testify about whether their drawings inspired children to violence.

9   Youth rebelliousness surged in the 1960s. While crime grew overall, juvenile crime grew faster. Sociologists, social workers, and policy wonks turned their attention en masse to offenses ranging from vandalism to gang-related crime, from drug use to student-upon-student assaults. Schools implemented safety plans, bringing in adult hall monitors and setting up bodies for hearing student grievances. Urban schools hired professional security agents—and later adopted the surveillance cameras, metal detectors, locker searches, and other measures more commonly seen in prisons. But a major study conducted in 1978 confirmed what experience had been teaching. Teen-agers were more likely to be victims of crime at school than anywhere else.

10   If student violence has now been a major concern for decades now, what seems to distinguish '90s violence is the suburban- or rural-school massacre. West Paducah, Ky.; Jonesboro, Ark.; Pearl, Miss.; Moses Lake, Wash.; Springfield, Ore.; and now Littleton, Colo.—in each case, young students, armed with guns, committed multiple murders in or near the school itself. To be sure, similar atrocities have occurred in the past. In 1927, a 55-year-old school-board official detonated three bombs in the Bath, Mich., schoolhouse, killing 45 people. And to be sure, the string of recent killings in fact reveals nothing, statistically speaking, about our society. Yet they remind us that the number of children killed by guns skyrocketed in the '80s and while tailing off in the '90s remains far higher than in decades past. According to one recent study, the growing trend of violent altercations ending in death is attributable "almost entirely" to the proliferation of guns among children.

11   The study, by James A. Mercy and Mark L. Rosenberg, tracked data between 1973 and 1991. They point out that "A surprisingly large proportion of adolescents report that they routinely carry guns and bring them to school"—14 percent of boys, according to one study, and 7.9 percent of students overall.

12   History makes it clear that children and teen-agers are no strangers to violent impulses. There have always been, and always will be, maladjusted or deranged students who unleash those impulses. That they do so is inevitable. How they do so may be within our control. ◆

FREEWRITING ASSIGNMENT

During the 1950s, the phrase *juvenile delinquency* was coined. What is a juvenile delinquent? What does the term imply?

CRITICAL READING

1. Greenberg presents a historical overview of violence in schools to support his argument that students of the past were just as violent as students today, and perhaps even more so. How persuasive is his information? Does he seem credible? Did his information change your perception of violence in schools? Explain.

2. In paragraph 2, Greenberg comments that if school violence wasn't a problem in the seventeenth century, it is "only because few children went to school." Evaluate the effectiveness of this argument.

3. Evaluate Greenberg's statement that "the string of recent killings in fact reveals nothing, statistically speaking, about our society" (paragraph 10). What does he mean by this statement?

4. What assumptions does Greenberg make about his audience? Cite some examples from the text that reveal those assumptions.

5. What connections does Greenberg make between student violence and the overall culture of the time? Does culture shape behaviour? Explain.

CRITICAL WRITING

6. *Persuasive Writing:* Are schoolchildren inherently innocent, or naturally violent, as Greenberg implies? Write an essay in which you explore this idea. Refer to information from Greenberg's essay, as well as your personal experience.

7. *Research and Analysis:* Arrange to interview seasoned educators from several school levels (early elementary, middle, late elementary, or secondary) to develop a profile of students today and students from past decades of their teaching experience. Have student behaviours and attitudes changed since, say, the 1970s? If so, in what ways? What might account for the perceived change? If not, ask them to discuss the perception that kids today have changed. Detail their answers and develop conclusions of your own based on their responses.

8. *Personal Narrative:* Were you a "good" or "bad" kid in school? Did you get into trouble, serve frequent detentions, or even get suspended? Discuss your behavioural role in school and the motivation behind it. Why did you behave the way you did? Was it out of boredom, peer pressure, fear of parental reprimand, physical punishment, or simple anger? Explain.

GROUP PROJECTS

9. Greenberg points out that in the seventeenth century, those we call teenagers were considered adults. Discuss with your group the concept of childhood and adolescence in our society. In light of the fact that many U.S. states are pushing for legislation to allow courts to try those teenagers as adults who commit serious crimes, are our constructions of the separation between "child" and "adult" outmoded? Write down your group's key discussion points and share them with the class.

Guns, Sex, and Education
Jamie O'Meara

Guns and schools—put these two nouns together and immediately you conjure up tragedies such as Columbine High School in the U.S. or Myers High School in Taber, Alberta. Naturally, most people would concur that firearms have no place in our schools. But in this article from *Saturday Night*, Jamie O'Meara argues that in order to counter children's natural curiosity, gun education should, in fact, be part of our schools' curricula. Gun education, he argues, including handling and even firing guns, is the only way to remove the mystique of firearms and the only way to get kids to think about guns in a responsible manner.

Jamie O'Meara is the editor-in-chief of *Hour*, an alternative weekly newspaper in Montreal. This article first appeared in *Saturday Night* on May 20, 2000.

Do you feel that guns have a place in our schools under controlled circumstances? What might be the benefits of introducing firearms into the current curricula of our high schools?

1 The first thing I noticed was its weight. It wasn't just cold, it was heavy, like the rock you pick up when you're six years old, with visions of windowpanes dancing in your head. By itself, it's just a rock. In your hand, it has power. That's how the gun felt.

2 It was a 9-mm military-issue Browning semi-automatic, I think, obtained from a friend who had joined the army cadets. Because of its weight, I had a hard time levelling it at the car battery we'd put halfway up the slope of the abandoned gravel pit at the back of our rural Ontario farm. This was where my brother and I spent a good part of our summers, with our .22-calibre rifles and .177 pellet guns, keeping the pop-bottle population under control. This gun, though, felt different than the ones we'd been shooting since we were kids. Fascinatingly so.

3 Borrowing my stance from every cop show ever made, I lined up my plastic prey and squeezed the trigger five times in quick succession. The first shot hit the battery and the next four thumped into the earth about twenty feet in front of me. A box of fifty rounds later, I was no closer to hitting my target with any regularity and, frankly, my hand was beginning to hurt. I packed the gun away and returned it to my buddy. (He, after exhausting its cachet among our friends, tossed it in a local river.)

4 All in all: boring.

5 And that may be a hard concept to grasp if, like most North Americans, you were raised on a steady diet of *Rambo*, *The Terminator*, and *Mad Max*: they showed that guns are fun, the implements of adventure. If you're holding one, people do what you want them to do. All of that's pretty attractive to young people, for whom power and control often seem in scarce supply. So why would a kid voluntarily give up the chance to play with a handgun?

6 Certainly not because of parental warnings. Lock the booze cabinet with double-plated armour and that's not going to save your Smirnoff. Threaten blindness and the wrath of all saints and that's not going to stop adolescents from masturbating. And tell children that guns are dangerous and that's not going to stop them from wanting to use one if it's accessible—in the gun cabinet, from a store, or in the schoolyard. All you can hope to do is teach them to act responsibly if the occasion arises.

7 Which is why guns belong in our schools.

8 Any parent knows that the best way to defuse the curiosity of a child is to address it head on, to transform the mysterious into the mundane. If memory serves, there is no place more mundane than school. Adding a firearm component to the current curricula in regions where guns are prevalent would achieve two things: it would satisfy the inherent inquisitiveness that children have about guns; and it would allow educators to monitor the reactions children have to the weapons— something that might have been of inestimable value to the faculty at Columbine High School in Colorado.

9   In Canada, it may be argued that guns aren't prevalent enough—in homes or on the streets—to warrant a proactive approach to gun education. Tragedies such as the one last year in Taber, Alberta, and the recent spate of youth shootings in Toronto indicate otherwise.

10   Put a kid on a firing range under strict controls, oblige him to fire hundreds of rounds at a circular target over lengthy periods of time, and what happens? Dirty Harry becomes a junior biathlete, without the skis. The kids who maintain an interest can be funnelled into gun clubs, where they can work through their attraction under the watchful eyes of trainers adept at spotting potential problems.

11   As long as guns have a mystique, they'll seem powerful. As long as kids feel there's power in guns, they'll be tempted to get their hands on them. And sooner or later someone who possesses a gun is going to want to use it. The solution is to address this desire early on and supply children with the rules of conduct. It's the same principle that lies behind sex education.

12   Think about it: sex education is taught so that kids will have a better understanding of how their bodies work, why they feel sexual desires, and how to act (or not) on those desires. Basically, we equip our kids with sexual knowledge so that they'll have the confidence to act responsibly. The same argument holds true for gun education: that, armed with knowledge and familiarity, kids will be better equipped to think about guns in a responsible manner. (In fact, the classic argument against sex education—that by providing kids with dangerous information they can't handle, we're encouraging them to run out and recklessly try it for themselves—is exactly the objection you're likely to hear raised against gun instruction.)

13   We accept the natural sexual curiosity of children and teenagers, and have legislated protection for them in the form of education, rather than pretending that the curiosity doesn't exist. Children are also curious about guns. We should give them the same protection. We don't want our kids shooting first and asking questions later.

FREEWRITING ASSIGNMENT ————————————

Where do children form their ideas about guns if not in school? How do you think O'Meara would respond to this question?

CRITICAL READING

1. In paragraph 12, O'Meara compares sex education to gun education and argues that as with sex, "armed with knowledge and familiarity, kids will be better equipped to think about guns in a responsible manner." Do you feel this is a fair comparison? Compare it to the arguments put forth in the Viewpoints section of this book's chapter on Education.

2. O'Meara opens his essay with a personal narrative of his first experience with a gun as a child. What point is he trying to make with this example? Is this an effective way to reach his audience?

3. O'Meara argues that guns will seem powerful to young people as long as they have a "mystique." Can you think of other issues or examples in society that could benefit from being demystified through the education system? Explain.

4. According to the author, why might a firearm component on the school curriculum of Columbine High School have been of "inestimable value"?

CRITICAL WRITING

5. *Personal Narrative:* This essay begins with a personal narrative about O'Meara's first experience with a handgun. Recall your own first experience with something forbidden, and write a personal narrative describing how you handled it. What was your attitude toward the subject prior to your experience? Did the experience defuse your curiosity or "demystify" your attitude?

6. *Research and Analysis:* Investigate the connection between aggression and children playing with toy guns. Recent studies have suggested that there is no connection, and that in fact, banning toy guns can lead to even more violence. Research this issue and summarize your findings in an essay.

7. *Persuasive Writing:* Write a brief essay from a viewpoint opposite to O'Meara's—that is, persuade your reader that gun education has no place in the academic curriculum. Be sure to respond to all of his points, and include other support for your position.

GROUP PROJECTS

8. O'Meara claims that films like *Rambo, The Terminator,* and *Mad Max* show that "guns are fun, the implements of adventure." Select three characters from a film or television show you would associate with guns. Describe the way that the character relates to guns. What is the prevalent attitude? Discuss with your group the message that each show sends out about guns. What conclusions might you draw from your findings? Does what you've discovered affect your attitude toward O'Meara's conclusions?

9. Despite the relative rarity of guns in Canada, O'Meara argues, tragedies such as Taber, Alberta in 1999 and recent youth shootings in Toronto indicate that our attitudes toward guns deserve attention. Canada prides itself on being much less a gun culture than the United States, and books and films, such as Michael Moore's *Bowling for Columbine,* help to promote this perception. How are the personal ownership and use of firearms perceived in Canada? How does this contrast with the way they are perceived in the U.S.? Research these questions with your group, summarize your findings, and present your conclusions to the class.

10. With your group, explore a number of gun catalogues online. How do these sites present firearms? How do different companies try to make their products stand out? What kind of language do they use to describe their products? Share your findings with the class.

Violent Culture: The Media, the Internet, and Placing the Blame
Darren Beals

In the next essay, expository writing student Darren Beals responds to the media coverage of Kipland Kinkel, the student convicted of murdering his parents and several of his classmates on May 21, 1998. While watching the extensive coverage, he noticed that many broadcasts frequently mentioned the role the Internet played in Kinkel's actions—how it helped him learn about bomb construction, how it fed his anger, and how it may have provoked him to act out that anger. In addition to examining this scapegoating of the Internet, Beals conducts an experiment in which he finds out firsthand how easy it is to obtain violent information online.

CRITICAL THINKING   Do you think that extensive media coverage of extreme acts of violence by juveniles—such as school shootings of classmates and teachers—encourages other troubled teens to commit "copycat" acts? Why or why not?

1   On May 21, 1998, a 15-year-old boy walked into his high school cafeteria and began shooting his classmates. Later, the public learned that he had already killed his parents, and had also placed explosive devices around the house, perhaps with the intention of taking out a few police officers who would later investigate the scene (*Associated Press* to *Boston Globe*).

2   As I watched the media coverage on every channel, I was struck by how many different television programs presented their side of Kip Kinkel's shooting spree. Tabloid-type programs revealed the "shocking" warning signals that were "ignored." News programs reported the gruesome details and updated us on Kinkel's status. Kinkel was featured on shows from *Face the Nation* and *Dateline* to *Inside Edition* and *Extra*. Everyone, it seemed, had something to say about Kip Kinkel. And the big question everyone was asking was "why?"

3   "Yes, why?" asked my viewer-self. And as television has always been there with a ready answer, it did not fail me now. Was it his parents who failed to see the warning signs? Was it the police who did not lock him up when they found the first

gun the day before? Was it the media exposure of similar high-profile school killings in West Paducah, Kentucky, and Jonesboro, Arkansas (Bragg)? No, said television. It was the Internet.

4   Although the details reported from program to program focused on different aspects of Kinkel and his horrible actions, few broadcasts failed to mention, however briefly, his connection to the Internet. The Internet showed him how to build bombs. The Internet allowed him to discuss explosives with other sickos. The Internet exposed him to violence. The Internet supplied the tools he needed. The Internet told him about guns and ammo. The Internet, one might assume from the reports, drove this 15-year-old to kill.

5   As a critical television viewer, I began to wonder about the Internet's role in this tragedy. Was it really to blame? Or was television pointing its finger to shift the blame away from itself? After all, wasn't all this media attention simply encouraging other psycho-teens to seize their own ten minutes of fame? At least they know what gets our attention. It may even seem logical that copy-cat killings are more frequent. Kill your classmates and get your face on TV.

6   TV, on the other hand, would naturally want to redirect the blame. The new kid on the block, the Internet, is the natural scapegoat. And don't forget, you can't be watching television if you are online, can you? Knock a rival and shift the blame at the same time. Seems pretty convenient. But what if television is right? What if the Internet really did play a role in all this tragedy? Is the Internet responsible in some way, or is it simply another component of our inherent culture of violence?

7   I decided to investigate the issue myself. If I was 15 years old, how much information could I tap into on the Internet? How would I find out how to build a bomb, buy a gun or ask questions on explosives? How much information is really out there? And how easy is it to get? I then embarked on a weekend exploration of Internet violence. I found out that there are definitely more Kip Kinkels out there, and plenty of people willing to teach them.

8   But who is Kip Kinkel? Before examining how he may have used the Internet to feed his twisted mind, it may be useful to try to profile him. Was Kip really that different from the average suburban kid? To answer this question, we need to find out exactly what is the average high school student. The answer would surprise most people. A quiz posted online by *Dateline NBC* the week of May 25, 1998 reports that "out of every 100 students . . . an estimated 71 [of them] have carried a weapon to school. Typically boys carry weapons four times more often than girls. Weapons include guns, razors, knives, and clubs" *(Dateline NBC).* This same quiz reports a more frightening statistic. Twenty out of every 100 suburban high schools boys are likely to own a gun. "A Justice Department report found that one in five own a gun and 45 percent of suburban high school boys have been threatened with a gun or shot at on the way to or from school" *(Dateline NBC).* Thus, the fact that Kinkel even had a gun isn't that unusual according to these statistics.

9   Other critics cite the National Rifle Association and its recent media campaign aimed at kids. Kristen Rand, the director of federal policy for the Violence Policy Center attacks the NRA's recent advertising campaign featuring movie star Charlton Heston in which he is surrounded by a group of children with the caption "are gun

rights lost on our kids?" Says Rand, "the motivation for the NRA and firearms industry to create a generation of pro-gun kids is two-fold—to future customers for the industry and political foot soldiers for the NRA" (Violence Policy Center).

10   Despite some odd behavior such as stuffing firecrackers down gopher holes, shooting at squirrels in the woods and tossing rocks at cars from overpasses, many neighbors and friends felt that Kip was a regular kid. A *Boston Globe* reporter relates that his strange antics were attributed to "phases" and typical male adolescent behavior (Jacoby). In a culture where violent movies and television are the norm, who can blame a kid for boasting about his firearm skills? After all, we admire such skills in Schwarzenegger, Stallone, Willis and Segal.

11   But there is a big difference between boasting and acting, and Kinkel acted. Many people point to the media as the reason. Extensive coverage of other school shootings may encourage other students to do the same thing. Even President Clinton believes there may be a connection—on the same day as Kinkel's shooting spree, he ordered the Department of Justice to examine school shootings and determine whether there may be a "copycat" phenomenon at work.

12   So assuming that Kinkel was not that different from many kids his age, what separates him from his peers? Was it his access to the Internet and the information he gathered there? If Kinkel was born 20 years earlier before the Internet would he have acted the way he did on May 21st? If we are to believe the television coverage, the Internet helped make Kip Kinkel a killer. The question is, how?

13   Let's say you are a 15-year-old boy with an interest in guns. Just an interest— you're curious to find out what kind of guns there are, how they kill, and maybe how you might buy one. A quick Altavista word search yields 121,470 matches to the word query "gun types." The query "killing with guns" returns 462,390 matches. Scanning the matches quickly reveals relevant pages such as a site called "The Killing House" located in England where you can "test your shooting skills." Another site provides information on handguns and how to use them (Ultimate Weapons Systems, Handguns).

14   Instead of being satisfied, your interest is now raised—there is so much information out there. From guns and bullets you move to bombs. You haven't given up on guns, you are merely increasing your "arsenal" of information. You want to know more about explosive devices. How do you make one? How can you share information with other people who know what they're talking about? You go to a newsgroup and start reading. After trying simple words like "bomb" you discover that many professions use the word—so you become more specific. You use the word "explosives" which yields successful results. After reading the postings there, your vocabulary has enlarged greatly, allowing you even more detailed access to specific groups often linked to the topic, such as "anarchy." You note the e-mail names of some of the people posting on these sites, and you get in touch with them.

15   E-mail, like IRC, allows personal one-on-one correspondence. You can go to a chat room to discuss pyrotechnics. You can spill your guts to other crazies who hate the world on an IRC. If you don't mind waiting a bit, e-mail allows you to send messages to groups of people at a time, doubling your responses and information. There

are many, many angry people out there, and they are happy to tell you how to get even. They may even live out their violent fantasies through a 15-year-old boy who "has the guts" to do what they only talk about.

16   After spending a great deal of time online, I began to formulate some conclusions. The first was that there are a lot of sickos out there. Information is easy to find on just about everything. And there are many people who don't hesitate to share their "knowledge" with anyone—child or adult—who will listen. The second thing I noticed was that there really is no regulation on the Internet. With the exception of controlled servers, anyone can post anything they want.

17   So where were Kip Kinkel's parents when he was gathering all his Internet information? Can a parent really not know what their child is up to? My guess is that they did have some idea, but it is easy to deceive. Set a bookmark to the Disney homepage and with a click of a button it is on the screen before Mom and Dad enter the room. Clever parents will hit the "back" button to see where their children were before. And the bottom line about Internet use is indeed parental control. Some people may argue that some parents don't even know how to use a computer, let alone monitor their child's activities on the Internet. My answer to this claim is if you don't know how to use a computer, learn. It is a parental responsibility when you purchase a machine for your home to know how to operate it. If you won't learn, don't provide online access. Or better yet, if your children are under 12, get "net nanny" software such as Patrol, Cybersitter, Cybersnoop or X-Stop (Monro).

18   Am I blaming Kinkel's parents? No. Likewise, I don't hold the Internet responsible, or television, or other media. We can keep pointing fingers, while avoiding the real issue—our national culture of violence. While the Internet (or a library, for that matter) can supply the details, we must remember that Kinkel had to first have an interest in violence. We would be hard pressed to prove that the Internet actually incited his interest in guns and bombs. It more likely provided information to his already hungry and violent brain. Our culture is more responsible for the evil seeds in his head. So who really is to blame? Why do we even ask "why?" Do we really want to know?

Works Cited

Associated Press. "Troubling Image of Troubled Youth." *Boston Globe.* (22 May 1998.)

Bragg, Rick. "Past Victims Relive Pain As Tragedy Is Repeated." *New York Times.* 25 May 1998, natl.ed. (27 May 1998.)

Dateline NBC. With Stone Phillips and Jane Pauley. NBC. May 1998. Online. Internet. (26 May 1998.)

Jacoby, Jeff. "The Classroom Culture That Spawned Kip Kinkel." *Boston Globe.* (28 May 1998.)

Johassen, Robert. *rjohnss@aol.com.* "Using Semi-automatic weapons." Online posting. *Newsgroupalt.firearms.semiautomatic.Usenet.* (25 May 1998.)

"The Killing House." Online. Internet. (24 May 1998.)

(Alias name: kinderbomb). *kinder@mail.com.* E-mail to alias kinderbomb. (28 May 1998.)

Monro, Kathryn. "Parental Filtering Utilities: Net Nanny." *PC Magazine* Online. March 1998. Online. Internet. (27 May 1998.)

Ultimate Weapons Systems. "Tactical Weapons and Firearms Accessories for Law Enforcement Personal Protection—Security—Military—Defense." 1996. Online. Internet. (27 May 1998.)

Violence Policy Center. "Arkansas School Shooting Focuses New Attention on Youth Gun Culture." March 1998. Online. Internet. (27 May 1998.) ◆

FREEWRITING ASSIGNMENT

In this essay, Beals explores the "big question everyone keeps asking"— Why?—that follows an act of violence such as Kipland Kinkel's tragic shooting spree. Record your own impressions of this question. You can choose to explore your own answers to the question, or discuss the public reaction to the question in your response.

CRITICAL READING

1. Beals asks many questions in this essay. How does he attempt to answer these questions? How effective are his responses? Explain, referring to specific examples from the text.
2. What writing techniques does Beals use to engage his readers? For example, evaluate Beals's tone in this essay. Does his tone help him connect with his audience? Why or why not? What points is he trying to make in this article? How well does he support these points? Explain.
3. Beals comments that television scapegoats the Internet because the Web is a primary competitor for viewers' attention (paragraphs 5 and 6). Do you agree or disagree with his logic? Explain.
4. Evaluate the organization of this essay. If you were writing this essay, would you organize it differently? If so, explain how you would reorganize it to make it more effective. If not, explain why it is effective as it now appears.

CRITICAL WRITING

5. *Persuasive Writing:* Beals comments that all the media attention surrounding acts of extreme violence by juveniles encourages other teens to "get their face on TV." Write an essay in which you explore this idea. Does media coverage of such crimes, in fact, promote copycat acts? Why or why not?
6. *Research and Analysis:* Beals conducts an experiment in which he researches how difficult (or easy) it is to find information on firearms, bomb making, and acts of anarchy on the Internet. Conduct your own Internet research project. Using several different search engines, try to duplicate Beals's experiment. Record your findings, and your impressions of both the process and end results of the project.

GROUP PROJECTS

7. In this essay, Beals notes that many people blame television for the rise in youth violence and that television, in turn, takes every opportunity to

blame the Internet. Discuss this issue with your group. Which, in the opinion of your group, is more to "blame" for youth violence? Are there other sources of influence on youth violence? Refer to television, newspapers, movies, the Internet, and any other sources your group identifies as you formulate your response. Present your group consensus to the class for discussion and debate.

8. With your group, go over the media coverage for several high-profile juvenile crimes from the past two years. For this exercise, your group should make a list of the crimes you intend to research, and then determine when these crimes occurred. Using your library's archived periodicals and Internet resources, evaluate the media coverage of these events. Consider the covers of magazines, any books that were written about the crime, and newspaper coverage immediately following the crime. What is the public reaction to the crimes and the coverage? Do crimes committed earlier affect coverage of crimes that occur later?

VIEWPOINTS

▶ **Games Don't Kill People—Do They?**
Greg Costikyan

▶ **The Trigger Principle**
Mark Pesce

Do video games contribute to the culture of violence and encourage children to be more violent themselves? Video games have radically changed over the past 10 years, now featuring realistic three-dimensional video, stunning graphics, and authentic sounds. And more games than ever embrace violent themes in which players must kill—monsters, animals, human characters, and even each other—to win. A 1999 *Time*/CNN poll reported that 75 percent of teens aged 13 to 17 years believe the Internet is partly responsible for school shootings such as Littleton, and 56 percent of them blame video game violence. The next two essays explore the issue of violence in video games, particularly as it relates to interactive "adventure games." Greg Costikyan reasons that these games allow us to vent frustrations and anger in a safe way. He further explains that the truly gory games that fail to challenge players are quickly pulled from the market due to lack of interest. Virtual reality computer guru Mark Pesce presents an alternative view. If these games did not numb us to violence and the act of killing, reasons Pesce, why are the armed forces so interested in using this technology to train soldiers?

Greg Costikyan is an award-winning author of many popular science fiction and fantasy role-playing games. He is also the author of several novels, including *By the Sword* (1994) and *First Contract* (2000). This article first appeared in Salon.com. An online version remains in the Salon archives. Mark Pesce is chair of the Interactive Media Program at the University of South Carolina's School of Cinema-Television. He is the co-inventor of virtual reality modeling language (VRML), which helped bring virtual reality to the Web. His most recent book is *The Playful World: Interactive Toys and the Future of the Imagination* (2000).

Games Don't Kill People—Do They?

Greg Costikyan

1   About 10 years ago, I had drinks with Frank Chadwick, then president of a game publisher called Game Designers Workshop. At the time, the Game Manufacturers Association was trying to reposition hobby games as "adventure games"—which we both thought risible. Chadwick said, "You know, a better name for our industry would be 'violence gaming.'"

2   I flinched, of course. But Chadwick had a point: hobby games then consisted mainly of war games—war is certainly violent—and role-playing games, whose players spend much of their time in combat against fantastic monsters or comic-book supervillains and such.

3   Violence is intrinsic to many, many games. Even as abstract a game as chess can be seen as a form of military conflict.

4   When I was a kid, "gaming" meant the mass-market boardgame industry and a small hobby-game appendage that together grossed perhaps a few hundred million dollars at retail. Today, it includes computer, console and arcade gaming and is a $7 billion industry in the U.S. alone—the second largest entertainment industry in the world, after film and television.

5   As McLuhan would have it, every medium has a message. If violence is intrinsic to gaming, and if gaming is an increasingly predominant form of entertainment, is the likely consequence to our society an increase in violence?

6   Are the critics who attack gaming in the wake of the Littleton massacre correct on the fundamentals? Should Congress ask the surgeon general to prepare a report on how video games spur youth violence, as it is considering? Do games stoke our violent instincts—or sublimate them? Is there such a thing as "good violence" and "bad violence" in games?

7   Let's step back a moment. What *is* a game?

8   A game is an interactive structure that requires players to struggle toward a goal. If there's no interaction, it isn't a game; it's a puzzle. If there's no goal, then the players have no reason to choose one option over another, to undertake one task instead of something else; there's no structure. If achieving the goal isn't a struggle, if winning is easy, the game is dull; winning's no thrill.

9   Struggle implies conflict. Just as conflict is at the core of every story, conflict is at the core of every game. That doesn't mean all conflict must be violent; in a story,

the central conflict can be the protagonist's own feelings of inadequacy, or the obduracy of her in-laws, or the inequities of society. But violent conflict has its uses; otherwise, we wouldn't have horror stories and mysteries and thrillers. Not to mention *Hamlet* and *Henry V*.

10 There are as many ways to create conflict in a game as in a story. Adventure games like *Myst* use puzzles. Games like *Diplomacy* require negotiation. Builder games like *Civilization* require you to overcome economic and technological obstacles.

11 But there's no way to avoid conflict entirely. No conflict, no struggle. No struggle, no obstacles. No obstacles, no work. No work, no fun.

12 Where does violence come into the picture? Violence is an easy out. It's the simplest, most obvious way to make a game a struggle. If achieving your goal requires you to get through a horde of ravenous, flesh-eating monsters, the conflict is clear—and the way to win is equally clear. You kill them.

13 Obstacles-of-violence, to coin a term, are compelling; the kill-or-be-killed instinct is wired into our hind-brain, part of our vertebrate heritage. Games like *Quake II* trigger a visceral, edge-of-the-seat response. Precisely because you can be killed at any moment by strange and nasty creatures, because only quick reactions can defeat them, *Quake* is a compelling experience.

14 *Quake* uses violence well. By that, I mean that it achieves precisely the effect its designers wished to achieve, and succeeds in delivering a compelling, stimulating, entertaining, intense experience to the player. It is a fine game.

15 But still: Violence is not the *only* way to achieve struggle in games. It is merely the easiest, the simplest, the most obvious tool in the game designer's armamentarium.

16 So—are games fundamentally violent and therefore bad? No. Chadwick was wrong; games are not *about* violence. Games are about struggle. Because violence is the easiest way to create struggle, many games are violent—but far from all.

17 But perhaps a more sophisticated argument still holds water? Perhaps game designers have insouciantly awoken the beast, cavalierly creating entertainment so violently compelling that it teaches violence, desensitizes us, spurs increased violence in our society?

18 There *is* a lot of violence in computer gaming. Some of it is very ugly. The two most popular categories in computer games at present are the first-person shooter (*Quake, Unreal, Half-Life*) and the real-time strategy game (*StarCraft, Myth, Total Annihilation*). Both categories are "games of violence," if you will.

19 Developers play the same games, they see the same movies, they fraternize with people like themselves and they develop some pretty weird mind-sets. Violence is perceived as cool—no, not real violence, but violence in games.

20 Consider *Postal*, published two years ago. It's a shooter in which you play a deranged, psychotic loser. You wander around shooting completely innocent people at random.

21 It's hard to imagine why anyone thought this was a good idea. For one thing, innocent people do not make good obstacles: They're unlikely to shoot back. They're not particularly threatening. Never mind the moral considerations; this makes for a dull game.

22   And the moral considerations should certainly have made *Postal's* developers (a company called Running With Scissors) think twice. No doubt, they assumed that the "edgy" nature of the project would get them a lot of press and boost its sales. They did get a lot of press, almost all of it negative, and no doubt that did spur some sales to the kind of people who actually think *Beavis & Butthead* is funny.

23   But you know what? *Postal* failed. It didn't achieve anywhere near expected sales. The reviews were almost uniformly negative. It failed because it was a bad game.

24   In March, an advertisement for an online games retailer appeared in the computer gaming press (for instance, *Computer Gaming World,* March 99, page 89). Its dominant image is that of the naked torso of a woman, lying on an operating table, the rest of her body outside the frame. In the foreground are surgically-gloved hands, holding a scalpel. In the woman's bare flesh are incised the lines of a tic-tac-toe game.

25   I buy a lot of computer games. I generally buy them online. But the image of someone cutting a woman's flesh in order to play the most patently brain-dead game imaginable did not make me want to patronize this company's services. God only knows why they thought it would motivate anyone else.

26   Certainly, it is an arresting image. Arresting enough to make the gorge rise. Only the computer gaming culture could possibly view any of this as effective, appropriate or funny. So perhaps the critics are correct, at least to this degree: The coolness of violence, as portrayed in computer games, has persuaded computer game developers, if no one else, that nauseating depictions of violence, whether or not effective, are cool.

27   Every year, Brian Moriarty gives a speech at the Game Developers Conference, one of the industry's main trade shows. Every year, it is the best-received speech at the conference. Moriarty is a brilliant speaker, but more than that, he is one of the industry's *eminences grises*—one of the original Infocom crew, creator of *Loom* and *Beyond Zork,* now in charge of development at MPlayer (one of the biggest of the online-game communities).

28   Last year, Moriarty's speech was on the subject of violence in games. As he spoke, two short clips appeared on a screen behind him, repeating hypnotically. One was a clip from *The Great Train Robbery,* a silent film historians call the first real movie hit, showing a mustachioed Westerner shooting a gun directly toward the camera; the other, a short sequence from *Quake,* showed a guard being shot.

29   Compelling images both—and compelling in that both show that violence has been an important part of two very different media, virtually from their inceptions.

30   The speech itself was a meditation on two issues: first, the nature of violence in gaming; and second, the idea of "rhythm of play." Moriarty says that, if you observe people playing a game—observe them, not the game itself—you find that they engage in repeated cycles of activity. And this repetition, the rhythm created, is one of the strongest draws for people to interactive entertainment. It's hypnotic. It's involving.

31   Violence, he says, creates dissonance. It breaks the rhythm. Dissonance is not bad in itself; dissonance, consciously and creatively used, can be an extremely effective technique, in gaming as in music.

32   "If you want to include violence in your games," says Moriarty, "do it, and put your heart and soul into it, do it with awareness—not because violence is easy, or because it shocks, but because you need dissonance, and you know how and why it strengthens your game."

33   To paraphrase: Violence used artistically is effective; violence used crudely is vile. It's a lesson most computer-game developers have yet to learn—and if one of the upshots of Littleton is that they begin to think more clearly about the issue, that will be to the good.

34   First-person shooters are violent games. Yet they are not depictions of endless, orgasmic mayhem; in their solo-play mode, they are mainly about exploration and puzzle-solving, with opposition provided in the form of monsters you shoot. Though violence, and the edge-of-the-seat tension it builds, is a key part of the game's aesthetic, impressive 3D technology and art and clever "level design" (where exploration and puzzle-solving come in) are at least as important.

35   The "violence" is against monsters, defined as such, who are clearly attempting to kill you; the back story, such as it is, presents them as some kind of horrible, *Lovecraftian* intrusion into the real world. Hence they are, in a sense, totally depersonalized opponents. But the notion that this kind of thing therefore "desensitizes" people to violence and makes them more willing to commit it seems dubious. Shooters are really about the "booga-booga" fright instinct: A scary monster appears out of nowhere and roars at you; you have to turn quickly and blow it away.

36   And of course, you die frequently yourself. The feeling engendered is not "I'm an immortal Rambo, I'm so cool I can kill anything"—rather, it's more like, "God, that was a hard level, those spider things with the cannon launchers are really tough, I'm glad I finally got through it."

37   Interestingly, the multiplayer online version is very different. You shoot not monsters but other players, who are running around trying to kill you. And they aren't depersonalized; they look just like you, you can chat with them (but rarely do because the game is too fast-paced), and so forth. This has been portrayed as something new and frightening—but frankly, it's no different from paintball and not much different from tag.

38   The development of shooting games over time has not been toward more and more megaviolence; rather, it's been toward prettier and more-impressive 3D rendering (Unreal) and toward more compelling story-lines, interwoven more effectively with the game (Half-Life).

39   Yes, these are violent games—but as is usually the case when the media latches onto something, they have been caricatured. Violence is only a part of their appeal. The idea that film or television or books make people violent has been debunked again and again. (For one thing, if it were true, Japan would, judging by its popular culture, surely be filled with violent pederasts instead of the civilized world's most peaceful and orderly population.) But perhaps com-

puter games are different—so uniquely compelling that violence in games does breed violent behavior?

40   Violence, and the attraction of violence, is a fundamental part of human nature. It is particularly appealing to young adolescent males, for it is a clean break with the rules-bound environment in which they have lived, a rejection of parental order. In every society, violence is most common among young men.

41   It is foolish to try to change human nature; it is immutable, or mutable only through the slow process of evolution. What can be changed is society. Society can develop institutions and mechanisms to channel antisocial impulses to pro-social purposes. That's one reason for armies, of course; they institutionalize violence in a mechanism designed to protect rather than damage society.

42   And games of violence? They allow players to *be* violent, to act out their violent impulses, to hunt and shoot and kill—in a way that harms no one. Violent computer games don't spur violence; violent computer games channel antisocial impulses in societally acceptable ways.

43   If *you* are concerned about violence in gaming, I have one piece of advice: Go buy a copy of *Quake II*. Install it on your machine. Download a walkthrough, so you won't fear humiliation when you play. And give it a try.

44   I think you'll find that it's not so frightening. You may even have a good time. You might even find yourself—like me—shopping for a home networking kit and running cable, so you can play games with your kids.

 The Trigger Principle
Mark Pesce

1   A few days after the millennium began, I came across a newly uncrated bin of the video game everybody loves to hate (yet secretly plays)—*Quake 3 Arena*. I don't game much—perhaps an occasional whiff of N2O on my Playstation 2 but, as an aficionado of the virtual world, *Quake* has always fascinated me. So beautiful, so fast, so violent. I popped the CD into my Sony VAIO, installed the program, and then, muttering, "C'mon, honey, show me what you've got," under my breath, I launched the app.

2   And nearly puked.

3   *Quake 3 Arena* looks like what we think the virtual world should be: sinister, a bit dirty, and just a little Gigeresque. It now handles "curved" shapes—something that had previously been beyond even the prodigious programming abilities of John Carmack, id Software's twentysomething programming prodigy. I had expected the high-octane realism of the visuals, but when my nineteen-inch monitor (running at sixty frames per second—double the speed of your television) displayed a torso blasting into a gelatinous ball of viscera, raining torrents of blood, and studded with the impacts of various limbs, one horribly predictable thought ran through my mind: Columbine.

4   That probably sounds like a bleeding-heart, anti-NRA, knee-jerk reaction from someone crying, "but what about the children?" for all the wrong reasons. Let's face it: the relationship between virtual violence and real-world acts is far more complicated, far more than those holier-than-thou voices in the U.S. Congress—seeking to infantilize adolescents—would admit. Even the defenders of these games have a hard time saying there's no relationship between the violence portrayed on screen and violent acts. We live in a bell-curve culture, and someone, somewhere just might see *Quake* as the practice ground for a sociopathic melee. But for most of us, the unremitting violence in *Quake* becomes comedy: a natural reaction to an overwhelming situation.

5   id's earlier games—*Wolfenstein 3D* and *DOOM*—had their fair share of enemies perishing under a hail of gunfire, but those characters looked so primitive it felt like a shooting gallery filled with G.I. Joe dolls. *Quake* treats violence as if it were as boundless as cyberspace itself: there are few limits and no consequences; you can blast apart as easily as you regenerate. It's not the gore, then, that troubles, but the specific way *Quake* detaches that violence from the usual moral universe that surrounds it—an ironic trait for a product that so prides itself on verisimilitude. And the question I kept asking myself was, How much of that violence was somehow imbedded in the original technologies behind virtual reality, and how much has been foisted on it by subsequent explorations? It's easy to dismiss *Quake* as a corruption of VR's otherwise innocent roots, but what if the seedlings of Carmack's carnage had been there all along?

6   In the early nineties, games like *Spectre*—a multiplayer Macintosh version of the venerable Atari 3D tank game, *Battlezone*—became common. Fast and dirty software-rendering engines—which took the power of the graphics supercomputer and brought it to the PC—became core components in a new generation of video games, allowing nearly anyone to create a virtual world for any reason at all. Most games followed the lead of *Wolfenstein 3D*, with a deceptively simple mission: search and destroy. Using the arrow keys and the space bar, you could blast away at Nazis or evil space aliens or ravaging wolves all day long—with a fair degree of realism. These games showed you the world from a "first-person" point of view, as if the monitor had become your own eyes.

7   It shouldn't surprise anyone that the trigger finger shows up so often as the major component of computer games. It's the extension of keyboard, the repetitive click, click, click that very easily becomes bang, bang, bang. If id programmer John Carmack had been offered something else by way of interface, *Quake 3 Arena* would be quite different. It's as simple as that. But because we are constrained by our interfaces, we build games that reflect our actual, physical relationship with computers. Give someone a trigger, and they'll build a gun.

8   My own academy, the University of Southern California, recently inked a $45-million deal with the U.S. Army to create the Institute for Creative Technology. The goal: To use the very best in VR technology to make a better soldier. The Army believes that creating "realistic" virtual environments can help train soldiers for the kinds of twenty-first century tasks they're expecting to handle in a post–Cold War world—such as peacekeeping in hostile foreign environments. The Army's dream is

to harness the power of Hollywood—that factory of the imagination? by using its creative talent to fuel simulation design, so they've set up shop at the "local" university, hoping that the best writers will come to work in their little "studio."

9   They're also looking for VR talent, so they came to me. I was assured that this wasn't going to be a project to make a better killer (and with things like *Quake 3 Arena* around, I doubt we'd need it) but I couldn't shake the feeling that they were really up to something else—let's call it brainwashing. How might this work? Witness the following gedanken experiment:

10   Plop a squadron of recruits into a virtual world, just before they're deployed to some far away location within an alien (and potentially hostile) culture. This virtual world contains a realistic simulation of that culture, in the physical look of the place, but also in the types of emotional engagement these soldiers will likely encounter: gun-waving warlords, screaming mothers, and young punks. The platoon grows comfortable in the environment; they learn to work as a team to handle the unpredictable tasks that accompany peacekeeping. Now ship those kids to their destination in the real world, and they'll react on the basis of their synthetic experience.

11   It's tempting to react negatively to any military appropriation of VR, but it's at least conceivable that such a system might be explicitly designed to minimize casualties in the real world, by teaching trainees composure under situations of severe stress. Would it save lives? Possibly, if it could accurately model the dizzyingly complex worlds of Somalia or Bosnia. Is that accuracy feasible? Maybe not. Emotional "verisimilitude" is an elusive quality in most virtual environments because the designers themselves (mostly young white male engineers) are, more often than not, out of touch with their own feelings.

12   Eliminating the threat of physical harm—or of death itself—from the experience of violent confrontations amounts to more than just a rounding error in the simulation. Any military simulation—peacekeeping or otherwise—will necessarily suffer from this lack of consequences. Soldiers trained in a world where physical force is little more than a metaphor will be just as disoriented in the field as a team trained in zero gravity. Then again, perhaps our video games have raised the threshold, making any conceivable abomination just another "game over." From a distance, that pathology seems at least a part of the rampage of Klebold and Harris. Who knows how many others are similarly numbed to the consequences of extreme violence?

13   When Hollywood got on the patriotic bandwagon and produced *Why We Fight* for the armed forces of the Second World War, it found that the graphic depiction of enemy atrocities actually drove enrollments down. This time, it appears that Hollywood has little interest in helping the Army, either because of its vast liberal conspiracy, or because it feels a little uncomfortable with the arrangement. Most of the creatives I've spoken with have their sights set on their next movie deal, not on some long-term project with patriotic intent and questionable ethics. As for myself, I don't want to see my program at USC funded by the Army even though the offer has been made; I'd much rather do business with Fox or MTV, because at least I know they're playing with the minds of consumers, not killers, and I can sleep at night

knowing that. But I wonder if John Carmack ever ponders the power of his own creations, or if he ever dreams himself in *Quake's* arenas, fleeing implacable, emotionless peacekeepers. ◆

FREEWRITING ASSIGNMENT ───────────────

Greg Costikyan analyzes the elements of game play. Answer his question for yourself, "what is a game?"

CRITICAL READING

1. How do the two authors of these essays frame their arguments? On what points do they seem to agree? On what points do they disagree?
2. Is there such a thing as "good violence" and "bad violence" in games? How does Costikyan feel about different "types" of violence? How do you think Pesce would respond to this question?
3. Costikyan argues that violent games that rely on blood and gory graphics without offering players a challenge are quickly dropped from the market. How does this statement support his argument? What about violent games that *do* challenge the player?
4. Compare Costikyan's concluding statements to Pesce's introductory ones. How do their comments contribute to their individual arguments?
5. Evaluate Costikyan's statement that there is little difference between video games in which players shoot other players and a game of old fashioned tag (paragraph 37).
6. Pesce describes how the U.S. Army applies video game technology to train soldiers. How does this fact support Pesce's point? What might it suggest about violent video games designed for the teenage market?

CRITICAL WRITING

7. *Exploratory Writing:* In an exploratory essay, evaluate game developer Brian Moriarty's conclusion about violence in video games: "Violence used artistically is effective; violence used crudely is vile." What is your viewpoint on this comment? Support your response with facts gathered from the articles in this chapter as well as your own experience.
8. *Research and Analysis:* Does repetitive violence numb children and teenagers to the ramifications of actual violence? To explore this question, search for resources on the Internet and interview some young people who play video games. Write an essay answering this question using information gathered from your research.

GROUP PROJECTS

9. With your group, research the different types of popular video games (for ages over 12) on the market today (such as *Quake*) and evaluate their level of violence. Do certain games seem to appeal to or target certain age groups? In the opinion of your group, do these games apply the principles of "good" or "bad" violence?

10. Costikyan wonders if Congress should ask the Surgeon General to prepare a report on how video games spur youth violence (paragraph 6). Your group has been appointed by Congress to prepare this report. As part of your research, interview several teens for their opinion on whether video games stimulate young people to be more violent. For additional information on violent video games and teenagers, research resources on the Internet. Present your report to the class for discussion.

RESEARCH ISSUE

Crime and Punishment: Toughening the Young Offenders Act
Lori Saunders

In Canada, the Young Offenders Act (YOA) has been much criticized since it replaced the Juvenile Delinquents Act in 1984. Many view the YOA as ineffective and soft in its emphasis on youth accountability, rehabilitation, and detention alternatives for less serious crimes. For this reason, the Canadian government introduced the Youth Criminal Justice Act in 2003. In this piece, Lori Saunders simplifies some of the key elements of this legislation. This article first appeared in the summer 2000 issue of *Faze Magazine*.

1 Early last year, Anne McLellan, Minister of Justice and Attorney General of Canada, introduced the new Youth Criminal Justice Act, which replaces the Young Offenders Act (YOA) as part of the Government of Canada's Youth Justice Strategy.

2 It's probably not a bad idea to know what our lawmakers are talking about: especially when it affects you. Lately, the hot topic of discussion at Parliament Hill has been Teen Crime and Punishment.

3 According to McLellan, our government decided to overhaul the youth justice system in response to what Canadians were telling them, "Most had lost confidence in the Young Offenders Act. The system didn't seem to be working very well, with increasing numbers of young people in jail for relatively minor offences."

4 The federal justice minister spoke at a youth justice conference as her proposed young offenders legislation was under scrutiny in the House of Commons in Ottawa. She says that calls for tougher sentences for young offenders are a simplistic answer

to a complex problem. Throwing children or teenagers who break the law into prisons designed for adults makes no sense, she says.

5   The proposed legislation drew criticism from the opposition Reform party for being too easy on youth who get in trouble with the law. The Reform party wants the age of offenders covered by the law to be lowered to 10 from 12 and says youth older than 15 should be automatically transferred to adult court. McLellan isn't buying it.

6   "Putting kids in jail, though sometimes necessary, is not an effective response to youth crime," McLellan says. "Once you talk to Canadians, they're the ones who tell us putting more young people in jail for longer will not make this a safer society," she says. The legislation also proposed lowering the age of those who could get adult sentences to 14 from 16 and imposing supervision on all young offenders who have done time in jail. She feels, "We need to acknowledge that when serious things happen, there need to be meaningful consequences." The Reform party says youth get caught in a cycle of crime because they know there are no serious consequences.

7   Perhaps they're right. *Faze Teen* spoke with 'John Doe' who at the age of 15 was charged with Grand Theft Auto and Possession Over $1000. When asked why he did it, he responded, "I did it for something to do—it was all for fun." John went on to say, "I knew the law. I knew the worst thing that could happen was serving some community hours because I was a young offender and it would be my first offence."

8   However, when we asked John if he would have still committed the crime if he knew the consequences would be severe, he answered, "I thought I would get away with it so it didn't matter what the penalties were."

9   According to the Canadian Criminal Justice Association, lawyers who are familiar with young offenders are unanimous in stating that, "These youths, at the time of their offence, gave no consideration to the consequences of their actions and that they would in no way be deterred from committing offences if they knew that their name would be published in the paper; no more than they would be if they knew that they would be subjected to more severe sanctions."

10   *Faze* spoke with another young offender, 'Shaniqua Doe.' When asked what was going through her head as she attacked a young girl with a knife, she answered, "She had provoked me for months, so at the time, I was mad—and she was just making me madder!" At 14, Jane was charged with Aggravated Assault with a Weapon. She recalls, "There were four teachers, two principals and several students watching, so I knew I'd be caught but didn't care at that time."

11   Would severe consequences have deterred her from the assault? She says, "I probably still would have done it since I wasn't thinking about the punishment anyway."

12   Needless to say, this new legislation will not please everyone.

13   Justice Minister McLellan says that the legislation is part of a wider strategy dealing with youth crime that doesn't always involve judges and jails, but community-based efforts to prevent kids from becoming criminals.

14   Based on government statistics, of the approximately 110,000 cases heard in Canadian youth courts in 1996–97:

24% involved 17-year-olds
24% involved 16-year-olds
22% were 15-year-olds
15% were 14-year-olds
8% were 13-year-olds
3% were 12-year-olds

The Youth Criminal Justice Act Simplified

15 Key elements of the new legislation includes provisions that:
- Allow an adult sentence for any youth 14 years old or more who is convicted of an offence punishable by more than two years in jail, if the Crown applies and the court finds it appropriate in the circumstances.
- Expand offences for which a youth is "presumed" to receive an adult sentence from murder, attempted murder, manslaughter and aggravated sexual assault to include a new category for repeat serious violent offences.
- Lower the age for youth who are presumed to receive an adult sentence to include 14- and 15-year-olds.
- Permit the publication of names of: (i) all youth who receive an adult sentence; (ii) 14- to 17-year-olds given a youth sentence for murder, attempted murder, manslaughter, aggravated sexual assault or repeat serious violent offences, unless a judge decides to maintain publication ban based on rehabilitation and public interest considerations; and (iii) youth at-large considered by a judge to be dangerous.
- Maintain youth sentences for murder at a maximum of 10 years for first degree murder and a maximum of 7 years for second degree murder.
- Promote a constructive role for victims and communities to be involved in the youth justice system, including victim impact statements in court.
- Give the courts more discretion to receive as evidence voluntary statements by youth to police.
- Create a special sentence for serious violent offenders who suffer from mental illness, psychological disorder or emotional disturbance to include an individualized plan for custodial treatment and intensive control and supervision.
- Require all custody be followed by a period of controlled supervision in the community equal to half the period of custody subject to mandatory conditions like keeping the peace, reporting to authorities and not possessing weapons. Optional conditions may be imposed to establish structure in the youth's life, such as attending school, maintaining employment, obeying a curfew, abstaining from drugs and alcohol, attending counselling; preparing a reintegration plan; or staying away from gangs. A youth may be returned to custody if these conditions are not met.
- Permit tougher penalties for adults who willfully fail to comply with the court to properly supervise the youth who has been denied bail and placed in their care.

- Permit the provinces to have young people or their parents pay for their legal counsel in cases where they are capable of paying.
- Encourage community-based sentences and alternatives for youth who commit non-violent offences, such as compensation or restitution to the victim; community service or probation; police warnings or police cautions; referral to community programs or a "family group conference" that may involve the young person, victim, parents, community agencies or professionals.
- Require police to consider informal alternatives before laying charges; and allow provinces-territories to require the Crown counsel to screen charges before they are laid against a youth.
- Give provinces-territories more flexibility in moving youth who reach adult age. A maximum of 20 would be established as the limit for the youth justice system, but the legislation would permit provincial authorities to retain an offender in the youth system beyond this age, if appropriate.

CRITICAL THINKING

1. When asked if he would have committed his crimes if he had known the consequences would be severe (paragraph 7), "John Doe" responds that he thought he was going to get away with his crimes, and therefore the penalties were irrelevant. How do you feel about the argument that tougher sentences don't work because most criminals don't expect to get caught?
2. Despite the public perception, Canada is actually tough on young offenders. Every year, about 25 000 young Canadians are sentenced to some form of custody and about 4000 are detained on any given day. Canada's incarceration rate for young offenders is actually higher than that of the United States, although Americans tend to receive longer sentences. What do you think is the cause of this gap between reality and perception?
3. Lori Saunders is writing for *Faze Magazine*, which describes itself as "an exciting magazine published for young Canadians" and "a refreshing break from the standard dumbed-down teen magazines that only serve up regurgitated American pop culture and prom diet tips." Explore their site at **www.fazeteen.com/main.htm**. What issues does this magazine cover that an American counterpart might not? Do you think the Young Offenders Act is an appropriate subject for a magazine like this? Would it interest teens? Why or why not?

RESEARCH PROJECTS

4. In April 2003, the Young Offenders Act was replaced by the Youth Criminal Justice Act (YCJA). Begin your research of the YCJA at **www.mapleleafweb.com/features/crime/youth-act/youth-criminal-justice-act.html**, and write an essay in which you argue for or against these new changes.

5. Explore some of the alternatives to putting young people in jail. Begin by examining the Peacemakers Trust site at **www.peacemakers.ca**. Summarize some of the views you find, and come up with your own idea about the best way to deal with youth crime in Canada.

6. Read what Amnesty International has to say about juveniles and justice at **www.amnesty.ca/child/juvenile.php**. Go over their 10 basic principles for how the law should treat young people under the age of 18. Does Canada's YCJA satisfy these principles? Present your findings to the class.

Additional essay topics, writing assignments, research guidelines, and readings for this chapter can be found online at **www.pearsoned.ca/goshgarian**.

Credits

Image Credits

Page 39, ALTOIDS ® is a registered trademark of KF Holdings and is used with permission; **page 81**, Evan Agostini/Getty Images; **page 45**, CP Photo/Tom Hansen; **page 95**, reprinted with permission, National Eating Disorders Association; **page 123**, CP Photo/Steve White; **page 148**, top left, NIKE and the Swoosh Design logo are trademarks of Nike, Inc. and its affiliates, used by permission; **page 148**, top right, courtesy of Coach; **page 148**, middle, courtesy of Lexus; **page 148**, bottom left, courtesy of Ripcurl; **page 148**, bottom right, courtesy of Cingular Wireless; **page 152**, courtesy of American Honda Motor Co., Inc.; **page 154**, courtesy of the Phoenix Companies, Inc.; **page 156**, courtesy the Michael J. Fox Foundation for Parkinson's Research; **page 195**, Stephanie Rausser/Taxi/Getty Images; **page 234**, Vince Bucci/Getty Images; **page 237**, The Image Bank/Getty Images; **page 273**, Michael Shay/Taxi/Getty Images; **page 319**, David Young-Wolff/PhotoEdit Inc.; **page 351**, Lise Metzger/Stone/Getty Images; **page 385**, © David Young-Wolff/PhotoEdit, Inc.; **colour plate 1**, © General Motors Corporation 2004, photography by John Kenny; **colour plate 2**, courtesy of Vans; **colour plate 3**, image courtesy of Apple Computer, Inc., photography by Doug Rosa; **colour plate 4**, courtesy of Nokia; **colour plate 5**, courtesy of Hitachi, Ltd.; **colour plate 6**, courtesy of bp, photography by Sasha Bezzubov; **colour plate 8**, image courtesy of www.adbusters.org.

Text Credits

Michael Abernethy, "Male Bashing on TV" from *PopMatters*, January 2003.

American Academy of Pediatrics, "AAP Discourages Television for Very Young Children." Reprinted by permission.

Margaret Atwood, "Letter to America," from the *Globe and Mail*, Friday, March 28, 2003, p. A17. Reprinted by permission of Margaret Atwood. Originally published in *The Nation*. Copyright © 2003 by O.W. Toad.

Patricia A. Baird M.D., "Should Human Cloning Be Permitted?" from the *Annals RCPSC*, June 2000. Reprinted by permission of the author.

Rosalind C. Barnett and Caryl Rivers, "The New Nostalgia," from *She Works He Works* by Rosalind C. Barnett and Caryl Rivers. Copyright © 1996 by Rosalind C. Barnett and Caryl Rivers. Reprinted by permission of the authors.

Darren Beals, "Violent Culture: The Media, the Internet, and Placing Blame." © Darren Beals. Reprinted with permission of the author.

Link Byfield, "If Girls Can Succeed Only At The Expense Of Boys," from *Alberta Report*, March 13, 2000, volume 26, issue 49, p. 4. Reprinted with permission, United Western Communications.

Index
of Authors and Title

Authors

Titles